MENNONITES IN THE RUSSIAN EMPIRE AND THE SOVIET UNION

Mennonites in the Russian Empire and the Soviet Union is the first history of Mennonite life from its origins in the Dutch Reformation of the sixteenth century, through migration to Poland and Prussia, and on to more than two centuries of settlement in the Russian Empire and the Soviet Union.

Leonard G. Friesen sheds light on religious, economic, social, and political changes within Mennonite communities as they confronted the many faces of modernity. He shows how the Mennonite minority remained engaged with the wider empire that surrounded them, and how they reconstructed and reconfigured their identity after the Bolsheviks seized power and formed a Soviet regime committed to atheism.

Integrating Mennonite history into developments in the Russian Empire and the USSR, Friesen provides a history of an ethno-religious people that illuminates the larger canvas of Imperial Russian, Ukrainian, and Soviet history.

(Tsarist and Soviet Mennonite Studies)

LEONARD G. FRIESEN is a professor of history at Wilfrid Laurier University.

Mennonites in the Russian Empire and the Soviet Union

Through Much Tribulation

LEONARD G. FRIESEN

UNIVERSITY OF TORONTO PRESS
Toronto Buffalo London

© University of Toronto Press 2022
Toronto Buffalo London
utorontopress.com

ISBN 978-1-4875-0551-6 (cloth)   ISBN 978-1-4875-0568-4 (EPUB)
ISBN 978-1-4875-2465-4 (paper)   ISBN 978-1-4875-0567-7 (PDF)

Tsarist and Soviet Mennonite Studies

___

Library and Archives Canada Cataloguing in Publication

Title: Mennonites in the Russian empire and the Soviet Union through much tribulation / Leonard G. Friesen.
Names: Friesen, Leonard G., author.
Series: Tsarist and Soviet Mennonite studies.
Description: Series statement: Tsarist and Soviet Mennonite studies | Includes bibliographical references and index.
Identifiers: Canadiana (print) 20220166382 | Canadiana (ebook) 20220166455 | ISBN 9781487505516 (cloth) | ISBN 9781487524654 (paper) | ISBN 9781487505684 (EPUB) | ISBN 9781487505677 (PDF)
Subjects: LCSH: Mennonites – Russia – History. | LCSH: Mennonites – Soviet Union – History.
Classification: LCC BX8119.R8 F75 2022 | DDC 289.7/47 – dc23

___

We wish to acknowledge the land on which the University of Toronto Press operates. This land is the traditional territory of the Wendat, the Anishnaabeg, the Haudenosaunee, the Métis, and the Mississaugas of the Credit First Nation.

University of Toronto Press acknowledges the financial support of the Government of Canada, the Canada Council for the Arts, and the Ontario Arts Council, an agency of the Government of Ontario, for its publishing activities.

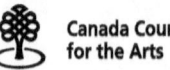

To James Urry

Through much tribulation you must enter the kingdom of God.
                                                          Menno Simons, 1539

We wander, we wander
From one place to another
And barely do we stop and stay
Fate drives us and our loves away.
                                                          Anna Baerg, 1921

Contents

Maps and Illustrations ix

Acknowledgments xi

Abbreviations xv

A Note on Transliteration and Nomenclature xvii

Introduction 3

Part I: Mennonite Origins

1 Foundations: An Ancient Faith, a Swiss Reformation, and Anabaptist Renewal 17
2 Melchoir, Münster, and Menno: From Early Dutch (Melchiorite) Anabaptists to Mennonites 32
3 A Faith Community on the Move: Mennonites, Poland, and Prussia, 1536–1800 49

Part II: Mennonites in Imperial Russia

4 A New Homeland in New Russia: Mennonite Settlement in the Russian Empire, 1789–1830 69
5 Pietistic Progressivism: Johann Cornies and the Transformation of Russian Mennonitism, 1800–1848 86
6 A Community in Crisis: A Divided Faith, the Revolt of the Landless, and Threatened Military Service, 1860–1874 105
7 From Crisis to Consolidation: The Flourishing of Russian Mennonitism, 1865–1883 123

8 Glory Days: The Apogee of Russian
   Mennonitism, 1883–1904   142
9 Confession or Sect? German or German-Speaking?
   Mennonite Identity Politics on the Edge of
   the Abyss, 1881–1917   161

Part III: Mennonites in the Soviet Era

10 After Eichenfeld: Soviet-Era Mennonites between
    Reconstruction and Emigration, 1917–1927   183
11 When God Leads You into the Wilderness: Mennonites
    in the Stalinist Crucible, 1927–1934   205
12 The Road to Rochegda: Soviet Terror, Nazi Occupation,
    and Stalinist Repatriation, 1934–1953   228
13 Detour to Dzhetisai: The Soviet Mennonite Renaissance
    in Stalin's Shadow, 1953–1991   251
14 Coda: Zaporozhe 1989. One Story Ends and Another
    Begins   274

Notes   289

Bibliography   355

Index   397

Maps and Illustrations

Maps

1 The Vistula Delta. 53
2 Mennonite settlements in European Russia. 146
3 Mennonite and other German congregations in the Soviet Union, 1980. 253

Illustrations

1 Jan Luyken, "Pieter Pietersz. Bekjen." 35
2 Henry Pauls, "Bernhard and Helene Pauls Farmstead, Island of Chortitza," 1975. 70
3 Portrait of Johann Cornies. 89
4 Agricultural work south of the village of Altonau in the Molotschna settlement, circa 1900. 115
5 "Gruss aus Chortitz" postcard. 125
6 *Friedenstimme. Ein christliches Volks-und Familienblatt*, 22 April 1906. 171
7 A mass grave seventy-seven feet long with fifty-eight bodies in Tiege, Sagradowka Colony, following a raid by bandits. 184
8 Mennonite members of a collective farm (kolkhoz), 1939. 207
9 Parade of ethnic German youth in front of Heinrich Himmler in Halbstadt/Molotschna, 31 October 1942. 243
10 The Great Trek. 246

11 Thanksgiving celebration in a church, Dzhambul,
    Kazakhstan. 258
12 A baptism service held on the Dnieper River at Zaporozhe (old
    Chortitza), Soviet Ukraine. 280

Acknowledgments

I never intended to write this book. In fact, I had completed more than a third of it before I accepted that I would stay the course and finish it. More than that, and to my astonishment, the drama of the Mennonite experience told in these pages captivated me from the outset. Before long, I concluded that this project was a perfect fit at this stage of my career, the culmination of decades spent working all around its edges. Thus, the unlikeliest of projects for me became the most obvious one to undertake, and immensely satisfying upon completion.

I am indebted to many for their assistance in making this happen.

Thanks to Audrey Voth Petkau for the opportunity she has given me through TourMagination to lead tours to the former Mennonite homelands of Ukraine and to the incomparable cities of Moscow and St. Petersburg in Russia. I see them all as interwoven into the same story. I have benefited from the questions and observations that participants have raised over the years, and from numerous chance conversations along the way with Russians and Ukrainians, often while sitting on village park benches under shade trees or at farmsteads spread out along dusty roads. On most of these trips I have been joined by Olga Shmakina, local guide extraordinaire, whom I first met back in 1989 when we were both still learning the ropes. It has been a good run. At a time when the West continues to rely on negative stereotypes of all things Russian, and is barely better informed about Ukraine, I've come to see these tours as an important part of cross-cultural bridge building.

I thank Harvey and Anne (Konrad) Dyck, for decades of encouragement and support, for visits to Purple Valley and Sherwood Avenue, and for their unwavering confidence that I could write this book. I have previously written about Harvey's impact on my life and will not replicate those comments here.[1]

David G. Rempel and Walter Sawatsky both demonstrated at the start of my career that one could combine a passion for Imperial Russian and Soviet history with a strong engagement in Mennonite history. I am indebted to David for his steadfast support at a time when I was just finding my way and when early employment challenges arose. Visits and long conversations at his home in Menlo Park stand out. I like to think he would be pleased to see me finally deliver on his hopes and expectations. Walter Sawatsky has kindly and thoughtfully engaged my chapters on the Soviet era especially and shared many insights from his own rich experiences in that world. I am delighted that both David and Walter became part of the story told in these pages, actors in the drama itself.

It was in Menlo Park that I first became acquainted with James Urry, as it was there that David encouraged me to read through their voluminous correspondence. Over time I participated in that correspondence but confess that I could never keep up with either of them. Then distance set in. David died in 1992, and for more than two decades I lost contact with James.

That changed when I began to write this history. Early on I contacted James and asked if he would be willing to comment on my draft chapters. He was enthusiastic from the start and unstintingly helpful. Long after I had completed the entire manuscript James was still sending me thoughtful challenges, commentaries, and additional sources to consider. More than that, a brief consideration of my bibliography makes plain that he has had a generational impact on this field. It is a pleasure for me to dedicate this work to James as modest thanks for his remarkable career of scholarship in Mennonite studies and for his generous assistance to me as I worked on this volume.

Others who have shaped this project along the way include Alexander Beznosov, Oksana Beznosova, Svetlana Bobyleva, Irina Cherkazianova, Johannes Dyck, Waldemar Janzen, Lawrence Klippenstein, Peter Letkemann, Colin Neufeldt, Troy Osborne, Henry Pauls, Andrei Savin, Anna Schmidt, George Schmidt, John Staples, John Toews, and Nataly Venger. I thank them all.

Special thanks to Laureen Harder-Gissing of Conrad Grebel University College for unfettered library access in an age of COVID-19, and to Mandy Macfie and Ruth Steinmann for their assistance in getting me the valuable resources I needed. This project would have been indefinitely delayed without their kindness and expertise. How long before we forget what it was like to wear face masks everywhere, including in near-empty research libraries?

Stephen Schapiro has been wonderful as acquisitions editor on this project for UTP. He encouraged me from the start, responded promptly to e-mails sent to him, offered sound advice, and generally made the overall process as smooth as I could have hoped. In addition, I thank the three anonymous reviewers chosen by the Press for the thoughtful manner with which they engaged my manuscript, as well as for their overall endorsement of it. I am honoured that it will be published by the University of Toronto Press and as part of its series on Tsarist and Soviet Mennonite Studies. I thank the Research Program in Tsarist and Soviet Mennonite Studies at the Munk School of Global Affairs, University of Toronto, for much-needed financial assistance.

The History Department at Wilfrid Laurier University has been a most congenial place for me to teach, do research, and write. It remains as such, even though I miss my dear friends and colleagues: George and Michael.

As always, thank God, there is Mary, who has tolerated my passion for most things Slavic over more than four decades of marriage. Even better have been the occasions when Mary has joined me in those lands, of which time spent in Leningrad/St. Petersburg stands out. I owe her much more than what a few words in this section can even hint at, especially for the rich life we have shared with our children and grandchildren. I've written this book partly with them in mind; my attempt to tease out one of the threads which make up the rich fabric of their lives. Beyond them, I've written it for all who have heard of these Mennonites, or are from these Mennonites, and want to know how their story fits together and fits in, start to finish. I will be grateful indeed if this accounting helps in that process.

Norman St.
Waterloo, ON
January 2022

Abbreviations

AHR	*American Historical Review*
AQ	Aquila
ARA	American Relief Administration
ARMAA	All-Russian Mennonite Agricultural Association
AUCECB	All-Union Council of Evangelical Christians-Baptists
CCECB	Council of Churches of Evangelical Christians-Baptists
CM	Canadian Mennonite
CPSU	Communist Party of the Soviet Union
CGR	*Conrad Grebel Review*
DB	*Der Bote*
Direction	*Direction: A Mennonite Brethren Forum*
GAMEO	Global Anabaptist Mennonite Encyclopedia Online
GULAG	Chief Administration of Corrective Labour Camps
JMH	*Journal of Modern History*
JMS	*Journal of Mennonite Studies*
KG	Kleine Gemeinde
KM	Kirchliche Mennoniten
MB	Mennonite Brethren
ME	Mennonite Encyclopedia
MF	*Mission Focus*
MH	*Mennonite Historian*
MJ	Mennonitisches Jahrbuch
ML	*Mennonite Life*
MLex	Mennonitisches Lexicon
MQR	*Mennonite Quarterly Review*
MR	Mennonitisches Rundschau
MWR	*Mennonite Weekly Review*
NEP	New Economic Policy
NKVD	People's Commissariat of Internal Affairs

RH   Russian History
RR   *Russian Review*
USSR   Union of Soviet Socialist Republics
Verband   Union of the Citizens of Dutch Lineage in Soviet Ukraine
Vestnik   Vestnik Volgogradskogo Gosudarstvennogo Universiteta

A Note on Transliteration and Nomenclature

This work relies heavily on Russian, German, and English language sources, even though much of the drama takes place in a region of modern Ukraine known variously over time as the borderland, the Black Sea steppe, New Russia, and southern Ukraine. That immediately raises questions of nomenclature that defy easy resolution, and I ask the reader's forbearance as I sort them out in this study. Add to that the challenge of transliteration from Russian where even historians cited do not always agree for themselves on whether I should transliterate a first name as Aleksandr or Alexander, Petr or Peter, or a family name as Toews or Tőws.

The following will inform this publication.

In general, place names will be in Russian forms within the Russian empire and Soviet Union, both because Russian forms had greatest geopolitical currency throughout the period of this study and because that is how Mennonites themselves named them. Thus, Mennonites first settled in the Russian empire along the Dnieper River, not the Dnipro.

I have not chosen to identify the first two Mennonite settlements in the Russian empire as "Khortitsa" and "Molochna" but as "Chortitza" and "Molotschna." This is a break from my recent practice and goes against current practice among scholars, but I have done so because I now believe the Germanic forms are the most appropriate. Mennonites did learn Russian, and even Ukrainian, over time. But they came to the empire with a variety of Dutch, Plautdietsch, and Germanic dialects. For them it was almost always Chortitza and Molotschna. I am concerned that my imposition of a Russian transliteration might suggest something about both Imperial Russian governance and Mennonite acculturation that distorts the reality.

Coming up with consistent nomenclature for Mennonite church leaders proved particularly challenging, as terms changed all the time, as have standards of translation. As a colleague wrote to me, "I think whatever you choose is problematic, so why not choose what you feel the most comfortable with!" Upon reflection I have decided to go with Ältester (for elders, or bishops), ministers (for Lehrer), and deacons. Together they comprised the ministry council (for Lehrdienst) for much of the period under discussion here.

It is almost anachronistic to state it, and certainly historiographically unfashionable, but I am sympathetic to von Ranke's famous challenge that historical inquiry document "the way it essentially was" ("wie es eigentlich gewesen"). That is what I have tried to do here, in every instance, and in all its lexical and transliterative messiness. Then again, that very messiness bears witness to the lexical and transliterative richness of the Mennonite world portrayed here, in all its triumph and tragedy.

MENNONITES IN THE RUSSIAN EMPIRE
AND THE SOVIET UNION

Introduction

This book charts the history of Mennonites who first emerged as part of a larger Anabaptist movement in southern, central, and northern Europe in the sixteenth century. It concentrates on those Mennonites from northern Europe who resettled in Imperial Russia from the late eighteenth century onward. I follow their history into the Soviet era and end with the collapse of the Soviet Union, which marks the start of a new Mennonite history in those same lands. As such, this study subsumes the history of Mennonites in modern-day Ukraine, Russia, and Central Asia against a backdrop that encompasses nothing less than the unfolding of the modern age.

To date, no such comprehensive history of Mennonites in Imperial Russia and the Soviet Union exists. There are earlier general accounts that incorporate part of the story I wish to tell, though many of these are dated, including an impressive collection of essays edited by John J. Friesen and published in 1989.[1] This is not to suggest that Mennonite historians have not been busy, as I have benefited greatly from three distinct swaths of literature for this study. First, a rich historiography dates to at least Alexander Klaus's *Nashi Kolonii* (Our Colonies) in 1867, which contained substantial information on Mennonites, and David H. Epp's centenary history of the first Mennonite settlement in the Russian empire, published in 1889. More studies followed, both by Mennonites and non-Mennonites. Recent scholarly contributions by Oksana Beznosova, Petr Epp, Viktor Fast, Aileen Friesen, Peter Letkemann, Colin Neufeldt, Andrei Savin, Walter Sawatsky, John Staples, John B. Toews, James Urry, and Nataly Venger have dramatically increased our understanding of the Mennonite story covered here. Of these, Urry's *None but Saints* remains the benchmark study on Imperial Mennonite history, and Walter Sawatsky has similarly carried the banner for Soviet Mennonites, most especially in the post-Stalinist era.[2]

Second, primary source materials have long been available to historians. These date from Franz Isaak's *Die Molotschnaer Mennoniten*, published in 1908, which contained a treasure trove of documents from the mid-nineteenth century, and Peter M. Friesen's massive tome from 1911, which documented the formation of the Mennonite Brethren. Friesen's work is also available in English.[3] In addition, Mennonites became prolific diarists, journalists, and investigators in the nineteenth century already and carried it on into the twentieth century. Scholars, including Harvey Dyck, Petr Epp, Viktor Fast, Olga Shmakina, John B. Toews, and Paul Toews, have either translated or published key materials in the past several decades and thereby increased their accessibility. Historians have also gathered significant collections of source materials since at least David G. Rempel's explorations in the Leningrad archive in 1962, though an even earlier pride of place resides with Peter Braun, who began to gather materials for posterity as the Russian empire collapsed around him in 1914. Harvey L. Dyck and George K. Epp almost simultaneously uncovered the so-called Peter Braun archive during the Gorbachev years. More recently, other historians have continued to make archival records available, including Petr Epp, Andrei Savin, and members of the so-called Dnepropetrovsk (Dnipro) school.[4] The émigré community based in Steinhagen, Germany, has been particularly active in the recent publication of Soviet Mennonite materials covering Soviet Russia and Central Asia, as has the University of Toronto Press – thanks to the collaboration of Harvey L. Dyck, John Staples, and Ingrid Epp – which has published from the voluminous Johann Cornies materials. Aileen Friesen has gained access to rich materials on the Mennonite experience of the Stalinist revolution in the 1930s in Soviet Ukraine.[5]

The larger historiography represents a third valuable source base for this study. Russian historians have re-evaluated almost every aspect of Imperial Russian and Soviet history since the collapse of the USSR in 1991. To give but one example, historians now largely reject the image of the "Hungry Village" in the late imperial countryside, and they most certainly reject the previous teleological arguments that suggested the inevitability or centrality of the Russian Revolution of 1917. That being the case, it behoves Mennonite historians to rethink previous truisms, including the suggestion that Mennonites somehow got what they deserved in the 1917 Revolution due to their disregard of peasant poverty all around them.[6] Historians who previously focused on Mennonite victimization during the worst years of the Stalinist revolution now confront a larger historiography by Lynne Viola and others who have stressed agency on the part of the vulnerable, even in the midst of calamity. The sudden collapse of the Soviet Union under Gorbachev challenges totalitarian assumptions of a tightly controlled Soviet police state. It calls on scholars to reconsider the role that they previously assigned to state repression in the post-Stalinist state, as opposed to post-Stalinist Soviet acculturation.[7]

This study attempts to rethink this Mennonite history in light of such a transformed world, but I also intend "transformed world" to refer to a much larger transformation than simply Imperial to Soviet, or Soviet to post-Soviet. No Mennonite historian to date has systematically engaged the question of Mennonite transformations in the modern age as it manifested itself in the Russian empire and Soviet Union. The work of historical anthropologist James Urry comes closest, though he shifts his investigation to Mennonite society in Canada at the end of the 1920s.[8] By modern age, I refer to the way by which Europe's Secular Age – in Charles Taylor's telling – appeared to supplant an earlier medieval vision.[9] Our historical understanding of the modern age developed slowly over several centuries and included such diverse subjects as industrialization, the rise of the nation state, the end of a Catholic Christendom, the separation of church and state with a corresponding secularization of politics, the rise of individual subjectivity, and the privatization of religion. Commonly associated in the West with such terms as the Renaissance and the Enlightenment, the modern age included stunning scientific advancement in Europe, along with urbanization and dramatic technological advances. According to Immanuel Wallerstein, Europe's entry into the modern age coincided with its conquest of the rest of the world, starting in the sixteenth century, and the establishment of a single global capitalist economy, all ruthlessly applied in distant lands through conquest, subjugation, and colonization.[10] Such world-focused capitalist economies originated in England and the Netherlands, of which the latter features prominently in this study.

Over the past five hundred years Europe underwent a remarkable series of changes which informed every aspect of this history of European Mennonites. Taylor highlights three distinct characteristics of how Western society understood the world in 1500: first, God acted directly in the natural world, from great storms and plagues to famine or bountiful harvests, such that the divine and the physical world were inseparable; second, God also made social collectives intelligible, including everything from the extended family to the village to the church to the kingdom. No one could explain any aspect of human organization without reference to the divine. And third, people lived in an "enchanted" world, a term that harkens to Max Weber, who concluded that the advent of the modern world coincided with the triumph of science and the corresponding diminution of religion's public role in society.[11]

Taylor sees that entire medieval world view under siege in the modern age. In its place, and consistent with Weber's conclusions, we have the emergence of the secular over the religious, the individual over the community, and profane or flat time over higher (God's) or transcendent time. Hannah Arendt argued that mundane work takes on an elevated meaning in our time, as does the worker. *Homo Faber* wins out over *Vita Contemplativa* in Arendt's succinct depiction; a world of instrumentality over a life of thought-filled contemplation.[12]

Konrad Jarausch identifies three political forms this modern age took in the twentieth century: communist, national socialist (fascist), and liberal (commonly associated with capitalism). Jarausch deems liberalism the best possible option, and it was liberalism's triumph at the end of the Cold War which allowed Europe, finally, to pull itself "Out of Ashes." But what if Jarausch's optimism is misplaced and liberalism itself is a deeply flawed ideology? What if there are aspects to its development and unfolding that are destructive, starting with its rampant consumerism, environmental degradation, and widespread existential angst? Scholars have pointed to these flaws and champion instead those who resist the modernity associated with our age. To cite but a few examples, Talal Asad has identified this modernity as hierarchical and institutionally violent, by which the categorization of religion and the secular into discrete categories negates the lived experience of countless other societies which have not recognized that distinction. In Brad Gregory's turn of phrase, the West erred when it no longer viewed "Religion as More-than-Religion." Marshall Sahlins rejects the uniform triumph of the West's impositional world system associated with modernism and does not believe that resistance to this oppressive uniformity is dead. It survives across the globe in places where the "local," a broad term which does not recognize "religion" as a category distinct from the "secular," survives through a complex pattern of accommodation and resistance. Stephen Smith and Joseph Ratzinger have both suggested that a disenchanted and secular public square restricts the very sort of lively debate our planet needs to survive. For that to happen both suggest – from very different starting points – that we need to rekindle a truly public square, one that allows the religious to have their say, especially as they have never really disappeared. And Kathleen Davis suggests that the very categories of medieval and modern impose homogeneities which occlude minority histories of the oppressed.[13]

I offer this study on Mennonites as one of those minority histories that Kathleen Davis wants to make space for amid a larger hegemonic culture linked to modernity. This turns us once again to Mennonites themselves. By way of context, in 2015 Mennonites worldwide numbered an estimated 2.12 million members. Of those 2.12 million Mennonites, the largest growth in members over the past generation has been in the Global South. In 2015 more than 730,000 Mennonites lived in Africa; another 430,000 in Asia, Pacific, and Australia; and 200,000 in South America. An impressive 539,000 lived in the United States and more than 143,000 in Canada, though absolute numbers there began to decline in the late twentieth century.[14]

Of course, all of this raises an important question: what is a Mennonite? Even a working definition of the term lands the investigator in historiographical controversy. A recent study suggests that Mennonites and Mennonitism are peculiarly difficult to define given their "decentered nature," which has rendered their communities "vulnerable to rupture," such that "often it is difficult to know who counted as a Mennonite at all ... Even the name 'Mennonite' is little more than a misnomer." Another argues that the term itself "lacks historical provenance. Generally speaking it is a catchall term indicating a set of attributes that twentieth-century Mennonite intellectuals bundled together to articulate the confession's essential religious, cultural, and sometimes even racial, character."[15]

I see it otherwise and intend to have this study speak for itself when it comes to Mennonite identity. As a working definition at the outset, authorities in the Netherlands first applied the term Mennonite to followers of a renegade priest, Menno Simons, who broke with the Roman Catholic Church in 1536. Over time both Mennonites and non-Mennonites agreed on who a Mennonite was, even if moments of contestation did arise. But I briefly want to address the suggestion that this larger indeterminacy is unique to Mennonites. A comparative approach suggests otherwise. Opponents initially named Lutherans after their leading figure and intended it as a negative attribution; the same was true of Calvinists and John Calvin. Eventually those thus named appropriated the title, as with Mennonites. Other scholars view many modern identities as inherently ambiguous and subject to division. For example, Brad Gregory argues in "The Unintended Reformation" that ecclesial divisiveness characterized the entirety of the Reformation, and not any one sect within it, with effects that rippled out for centuries thereafter. Similarly, Zygmunt Bauman maintains that all identities are fluid and ever shifting in an age of "Liquid Modernity." In yet another reflection on collective identities, Immanuel Wallerstein asks if it would "not make more sense to try to understand peoplehood for what it is – in no sense a primordial stable social reality, but a complex, clay-like historical product of the capitalist world-economy through which the antagonistic forces struggle with each other." This study adopts this larger perspective, which resonates with Walter Sawatsky's and Johannes Reimer's suggestion that Mennonite identities have been, and continue to be, organically determined over time and space. That works for me as I set out to examine the history of these particular Mennonites.[16]

I want to add something apropos of Wallerstein's reference to the history of the emergent capitalist world economy and Bauman's reference to Liquid Modernity, and for that I need to return to the 2.12 million Mennonites worldwide as of 2015. Though impressive, their numbers paled in comparison to the registered 2.38 billion Christians in a planet of over 7 billion people. Of those registered Christians, Roman Catholicism claimed 1.2 billion and all Protestant faiths together registered 426 million, of which Anglicans, Lutherans, Reformed, and Methodists each claim more than 60 million.[17] All of this is as far away from Menno's intention as could be imagined as he, like many other reformers, believed in the ability of his message to be universal in its final outcome.

At one point in his 1539 signature work on theology for a renewed Christianity, Menno pondered the explosion of religious movements that had happened in an era we now identify as the Reformation. He acknowledged the "various congregations, churches, and sects" of his time, all of which presumed to speak in Christ's name. In particular, he named "Roman Catholics or papists, Lutherans and Zwinglians and the Christians who are revilingly called Anabaptists." Save for the last grouping of re-baptizers, all the rest claimed to follow Christ but, instead, "they revile and slander and are basically at variance with it." Later he will link them to the devil.[18] Yet all was not in despair, Menno wrote, as the gospel of Christ remained the true gospel and was certain to triumph in the end, even if it was a faithful remnant awaiting Christ's return. This, he claimed, was the new Christianity that had suddenly become possible across Europe, already manifest in the movement driven by re-baptizing Anabaptists.

That movement of Anabaptists preceded Menno in the Netherlands by several years, though his ability to unify its scattered adherents soon prompted authorities to name this movement's followers after him. In his various writings Menno rejected the sacramental nature of the Catholic Church and stressed instead the need for a pure church, united in discipline and a disciplined life, committed to non-violence and adult baptism, among other tenets. In our first chapter we consider the late medieval Roman Catholic Church so as better to understand trends already at work which later irrupted in the Reformation. We shift to

Menno Simons and the emergence of Dutch Anabaptism in the second chapter, though we will be particularly interested in the relationship of this new movement to the birth of the modern age underway in the Netherlands.

Many of Menno's earliest followers, a potpourri of Dutch, Flemish, and north German adherents, sought an escape from the persecution visited upon them after the debacle at Münster from 1532 to 1535 (to be discussed in chapter two). In almost all cases, they found haven eastward in the imperial city of Danzig and in Kingdom Poland, which became the centre of this movement for some two hundred years. Danzig developed a close connection with Amsterdam in the sixteenth and seventeenth centuries, which once again placed Mennonites at the centre of Europe's mercantilist ascendance. Mennonites negotiated their space and faith in this new setting, one that forbade proselytizing. Some new converts managed to join the Mennonite fold in Danzig and Kingdom Poland, though they remained the exception. In some areas and professions Mennonites managed to achieve a degree of economic independence and cultural accommodation at the expense of Menno's vision of a renewed Christianity that resided as a faithful remnant at arm's length from the world. We will examine the way in which Mennonites negotiated this new space, including how they secured military exemptions and worshipped surreptitiously until such time that authorities permitted them to construct meeting houses (churches). In some rural areas they worshipped with Lutherans, hence the adoption of Lutheran hymns before immigration to Imperial Russia. These first three chapters can be deemed "Mennonite origins" for the purposes of this study, and together they form Part I.

Chapters four through nine comprise Part II and shift our geographic focus once again, this time to the Russian empire. It is here that this study diverges from most histories of the modern age, which focus overwhelmingly on Western Europe and North America. By contrast, we will follow Mennonites eastward to a modernizing Russian empire.[19] Mennonites repeatedly re-negotiated their space in the empire as its officials worked through several overlapping modernizing strategies between 1789 and its dramatic collapse in 1917. It is particularly significant that authorities initially required Mennonites to govern themselves at the local level within a larger empire-wide system controlled by imperial officials. This local governance led, paradoxically, both to greater integration and separation from the larger modernizing empire, as we shall see. Additionally, it created unprecedented challenges when it came to defining Mennonites, who now took on seemingly incongruous secular and religious identities. As a condition of settlement, Mennonites also became a discrete legal designation by Russian officials, one that separated them out from German Lutherans, German Catholics, Bulgarians, and so on, all of whom also governed themselves within the empire's larger rubric. Such discrete legal categories should not surprise in an empire which lacked an all-embracing notion of citizenship before 1900. It did mean that a Mennonite remained a Mennonite, even if that person ceased to attend religious services.

Mennonites flourished in the Russian empire across the nineteenth century. Russian officials understood Mennonite success as directly connected to their role in the empire's modernization, most clearly manifested in Johann Cornies during the first half of the nineteenth century, a leading Mennonite and imperial servitor of his time. I devote an entire chapter to him and his efforts to modernize Mennonites. Their empire-wide fame by the mid-nineteenth century was such that the Russian emperor Alexander II visited their villages twice during his reign, including a memorable occasion when he visited Cornies himself at his estate in the Molotschna settlement. By the early twentieth century their success was such that it prompted historian David G. Rempel later to speak of their flourishing world as a distinct Mennonite Commonwealth.[20] As part of it, Mennonites financed and constructed well-appointed secondary schools, hospitals, municipal buildings, and churches in their settlements. They established large-scale, empire-leading modern industries where they manufactured agricultural implements and similarly scaled flour mills. Wealthy Mennonites established massive estates and industrialists also established themselves as part of Russia's landed elite; they immersed themselves in regional and empire-wide politics.[21] At their peak, children of the Mennonite elite formed almost a world unto themselves, as their offspring studied in Germany as well as the best schools of the empire.

In short, Mennonites experienced great success and considerable renown in the imperial era, though they also confronted a series of community-threatening crises at mid-century. In one, most Mennonite households had become landless and disenfranchised by the 1850s, all to the gain of the landed elite, who refused to address the situation. In another, a new internal religious movement threatened to destroy what ecclesial unity existed across the Mennonite settlements. In both crises the Mennonite powerless appealed to St. Petersburg itself when all other options failed, and in both instances imperial authorities intervened to force a solution on the powerful. Did all this suggest that the most corrosive elements of modernization had reduced contemporary Mennonites to a shell of Menno's vision for a new Christianity? We will investigate, especially considering the other challenges faced by

Mennonites across the empire up to and including the catastrophe known as the First World War (1914–18). This might be a good place to point out that the subtitle of this book, "Through Much Tribulation," comes from that same foundational work written by Menno Simons in 1539. The faithful Christian, he wrote, entered the Kingdom of God through tribulation. I mention it here to indicate that some of the tribulation experienced by Mennonites over the years was self-inflicted, as was largely the case with the crises of the mid-nineteenth century.[22]

We examine imperial collapse, Austro-German Occupation, and the era of the independent peasant armies across the south in chapter ten, as well as the diverse strategies Mennonites adopted in response. Thereafter a very different regime came to power as Lenin and the Bolsheviks seized the moment and ostensible Communism took shape in what soon became the Soviet Union. This chapter also signals the start of Part III of our study: Mennonites and the Soviet Era. Igal Halfin and Nina Tumarkin have suggested the degree to which the new regime embodied a full secularization of Christian theological and apocalyptic teaching. Other studies have followed Stephen Kotkin's conclusion that the Soviet project was very much a modernizing project with broad engagement, despite its chaotic implementation.[23] The Soviet era presented Mennonites and tens of millions of others with unprecedented challenges, celebrated socialist successes and piercing moments of horror. Once again, Mennonites developed a wide range of strategies as they confronted a regime that often took a stridently atheistic position. It did not help that Soviet officials also regarded Mennonites as bourgeois and German, for which they soon paid a stiff price. In the past Mennonite historiography focused on those Mennonites who emigrated when able to do so in the 1920s or escaped with the retreating Nazi forces in the Second World War. Fortunately, historians have more recently turned their attention to those whom authorities initially exiled to the far north, Siberia, and Central Asia and thereafter found their place as Soviet Mennonites. We will pay particular attention to their story.

Though the historiography of this period remains a work in progress, most historians now accept that the Soviet regime was less systematically totalitarian than it was episodically brutal and at least somewhat popular. One can make a case that 1929–56 marked the single most devastating period for Mennonites in the entire five-hundred-year history under examination here. Yet amid immense devastation, Mennonites remained actively engaged, including many who worked within the bureaucratic machinery of the Soviet state itself. As police rounded up Mennonites and others in the hundreds of thousands, banned their religious practices and destroyed their churches, even then countless

Mennonites remained actively engaged in the determination of their fate and identity. There is good reason to argue that the dominant Soviet Mennonite paradigm shifted under Stalin from Homo Faber back to Arendt's *Vita Contemplativa*, although Mennonites never entirely abandoned the former. Events in the twentieth century also make plain that Mennonite women played a crucial role in safeguarding what spiritual vitality existed within devastated Mennonite settlements. We consider Mennonites and the Soviet regime in chapters ten to thirteen and conclude with a chapter that takes us to the end of the Soviet regime and the dawn of a new millennium for Mennonites in the suddenly former Soviet Union.

I believe this particular Mennonite engagement with the modernity confirms Brad Gregory's genealogical reading of the past, by which he rejects a supersessionist approach. The latter originates in the belief that the birth of Christ in the New Testament ushered in an entirely new story, one that fully supplanted the Jews as God's Chosen People. Gregory suggests that we have too easily accepted a supersessionist view of history to argue that the modern supplanted the medieval, the secular supplanted the religious, and so on. No turning back. He concludes that such a view distorts our understanding of the present, which is far more complex than many scholars let on. He also points out how religious traditions have an unaccounted-for resilience which a supersessionist view of history cannot explain. By contrast, he proposes a genealogical approach, one that recognizes that traits found in the past continue to influence the present, largely because they endure. By this approach the past is never really passed.

Gregory has contemporary Roman Catholicism in mind, but his argument is equally applicable to the way in which the Mennonite past continued to inform the Mennonite present over the course of this history, and especially during the worst decades of the Soviet era.[24] Even then, enfamished young Mennonite mothers, often widowed or with husbands lost in the depths of the Gulag, still sang their children to sleep with Christian lullabies that spoke of God's final victory over sin and the Stalinist terrors of their present predicament. Not all of them did so, of course, but enough to make a difference to the whole. Soviet sociologist V.F. Krest'ianinov, a vocal critic of Mennonites, observed in the late 1960s that the Mennonite identity persisted within Soviet society, and Mennonites continued to play a leading role as prized Soviet workers, even though large numbers of them had seemingly vanished into Baptist and Evangelical congregations or had secularized outright. Soviet citizens should know that there was something about Mennonite identity that persisted, he warned, and would not disappear any time soon. A decade later Soviet sociologist A.I. Ipatov reached the same conclusion and issued a similar warning.[25]

Walter Sawatsky captures this genealogical telling of the Mennonite story when he asks a question of the last Soviet generation of Mennonites, the most Sovietized one: "What were the elements of their Radical Reformation heritage that these Russian Mennonites emphasized with many contextual adaptations along the way, then also lost along the way, and regained again, in very limited fashion or in places more fully?" His answer takes the reader back to Menno Simons' foundational treatise of 1539 as Sawatsky links this enduring Mennonite identity directly to the "Lordship of Jesus Christ and the authority of Scripture."[26] I concur and so intend to end this history where it begins, with followers of Menno struggling to live out their lives in a newly reimagined Christianity in the midst of a world seemingly headed in a very different direction. Mennonites in between the start and finish lived out their beliefs and embraced their collective identity in a thousand different ways, yet almost always as Mennonites actively engaged in the world around them. We need to cover a lot of ground to make any sense of it, so it is best to get started.

PART I

Mennonite Origins

Chapter One

Foundations: An Ancient Faith, a Swiss Reformation, and Anabaptist Renewal

Peter M. Friesen, the renowned Imperial Russian Mennonite educator, released his *magnum opus* in 1911 when he published *Die Alt-Evangelische Mennonitische Brüderschaft in Russland*.[1] Though raised in the Molotschna Mennonite village of Sparau, Friesen had been educated in elite schools farther afield, including in Switzerland, Odessa, and Moscow. Fluent in several languages, Friesen devoted over twenty-five years to recording the history of Mennonites in "Russia," which is how he identified the lands north of the Black Sea. But what stands out is the way in which he identified the earliest Mennonites as one of several persecuted peoples who had struggled for centuries against the Roman Catholic Church. Friesen declared that Mennonites, and the Swiss Anabaptists of 1525 who preceded them, were the spiritual descendants of the twelfth-century Waldensians, a sect Rome had long deemed heretical. It was from this true and centuries-old persecuted church that the sixteenth-century Swiss Anabaptists were born, and from whose shadow the Dutch Mennonites soon emerged.

By this means Friesen laid out a lineage of counter-cultural protest as a persecuted minority for his fellow nineteenth-century Mennonites within the Russian empire, which is all the more remarkable given that there is no evidence of any linkage between the twelfth-century Waldensians and sixteenth-century Anabaptist-Mennonite beginnings. Contrary to the way in which Friesen and countless others have told this story, the Anabaptist movement that gave birth to the Mennonites after 1535 was part of a much larger reform movement over several centuries that historians now refer to as the "long reformation." This contradicts a previous generation of primarily Protestant scholars who argued that the Reformation irrupted in the early sixteenth century when Protestant reformers broke dramatically with a corrupt and monolithic Catholic church.[2]

Scholars more recently have argued that key aspects of Protestantism emerged almost seamlessly from a vibrant debate underway within the Catholic Church over several centuries. For example, Charles Taylor argues that the Lateran Council of 1215, which made individual confession universal among believers, reinforced the view that each person individually faced the judgment of Christ at the point of death. It reinforced larger trends of rapid urbanization already underway in the Italian peninsula. Here peasants abandoned their villages for the relative anonymity of Florence, Venice, and Milan, among others, and here they encountered the newly emergent Mendicant Orders of the Dominicans and Franciscans, who brought the call of faithfulness to all who lived in these new arenas. This is also the context in which P.M. Friesen's Waldensians began, though in their case the universal (Catholic) church declared them to be heretical. Jan Hus, founder of the Moravian Reformation, emerged out of a Catholic church which had turned increasingly eschatological and reformist in the late fourteenth century, even as loyal priests railed against the church's corruption. As late as the mid-sixteenth century the Catholic hierarchy admitted that much of the spark that led to the formation of the *Unitas Fratrum*, perhaps the oldest Protestant movement in Europe, had emerged out of an orthodox Catholicism.[3] R.N. Swanson has pointed to significant continuities between the medieval church and the Protestant irruption in Western Europe. In particular Swanson has declared that the medieval church's profession of itself as "one, holy, Catholic and apostolic" reflected a commonality of faith rooted in the ancient creeds and under the "organizational headship" of the pope.[4] But below that seemingly monolithic surface, the Church comprised a remarkably diverse universe by 1500; one that included English Carthusians, Italian Benedictines, and Dutch Augustinians, among others. Many of these orders were not limited to monastic endeavours but included a means by which, in the Franciscan case, lay followers could embrace spiritual disciplines within their daily lives. In addition, national movements increasingly had an impact on church polity by 1500 as the unity of the Holy Roman Empire began to give way to localized secular rulers.

Swanson argues that these rulers sought control of three key aspects of the Catholic Church, including: churchly appointments within their respective realms; churchly finance, both in acquisition and distribution; and overarching civil matters, in particular within jurisprudence.[5] Lastly, the Catholic Church may have been what Swanson calls "an international institution," but it functioned across Europe in a plethora of relatively autonomous entities, whether at the provincial, diocesan, or parish level.[6] The steady rise in the European population after the demographic devastation of the Black Death (1346–53) meant the church needed more parish priests in a relatively short period of time. Demand exceeded supply, and evidence suggests that the continuous growth of local parishes across the fifteenth century increased the need for lay involvement in the church and made greater local autonomy possible.[7]

Not only was the late medieval Roman Catholic Church organizationally complex and institutionally varied, it was also subject to corruption. That was certainly the case by the late fifteenth century, when many argued that the church needed significant internal reform. Catholic scholar John Vidmar has pointed to the "absenteeism, concubinage, luxury, a lack of clerical training, [and] the lax spiritual life of the clergy."[8] Jonathan Israel concludes that there were harsh critics of the Catholic Church everywhere across the Netherlands by the early sixteenth century, though nowhere was this more evident than in the paintings of Hieronymus Bosch (1450–1516).[9] For example, in his painting *Ship of Fools* (c. 1490–1500), Bosch literally depicted a ship of fools engaged in all manner of sinful machinations: these fellow travellers eat and drink to excess, leer lustfully at each other, play music that is clearly secular, and all the while the captain pays no heed to a ship that is headed for destruction. First and foremost, in the ship's cast of woeful characters are a monk and a nun who occupy the immediate foreground. The nun is playing a lute, which symbolizes sexual desire, and there are other indications that their relationship is hardly chaste. It appears that all of them have turned their backs on Christ's teachings. All have lost their way and are adrift at sea.[10]

Scholars believe Erasmus of Rotterdam (c. 1460–1536), the staunch Catholic and lettered Dutch humanist, was particularly fond of *Ship of Fools* and its critique of the contemporary church. As Erasmus would provide a vital link to the religious movement from which Mennonites emerged, it behoves us to consider his development and theology more closely. The son of a priest and his illegitimate wife, historians believe Erasmus was born in Rotterdam, though we are certain he received his education in Deventer, where Thomas à Kempis had studied almost a century earlier. Thomas had been at the heart of the *Devotio Moderna* movement, which had eschewed churchly hierarchies in favour of a theology that stressed the spiritual development of the individual, the primacy of Christ, the study of the Bible and the centrality of the early church to determine the shape of the contemporary church.[11] Thomas would later write *The Imitation of Christ*, which enjoyed a broad and devoted readership across the Netherlands and beyond in the fifteenth and sixteenth centuries. The work is singlehandedly said to have popularized piety among the laity. He began with a stirring proclamation:

> "'He who follows Me, walks not in darkness,' says the Lord (John 8:12). By these words of Christ we are advised to imitate His life and habits, if we wish to be truly enlightened and free from all blindness of heart. Let our chief effort, therefore, be to study the life of Jesus Christ. The teaching of Christ is more excellent than all the advice of the saints, and he who has His spirit will find in it a hidden manna. Now, there are many who hear the Gospel often but care little for it because they have not the spirit of Christ. Yet whoever wishes to understand fully the words of Christ must try to pattern his whole life on that of Christ."[12]

Two points leap out from this section: first, à Kempis single-mindedly focused on Christ, though more on Christ as exemplar of the virtuous life for all than on Christ's role as the sacrificial lamb who made salvation possible. In powerful exhortations à Kempis urged his readers to study and copy Christ's life and to pattern their own lives directly upon it. Moreover, those who wanted to follow Christ had to live out the Good News as his faithful disciples had done and not merely proclaim it. À Kempis also warned that the followers of Christ would likely be a minority voice within society, as many who heard the gospel would refuse to repent their ways and be conformed to their Lord. In contrast to churchly tradition, nowhere did à Kempis identify a sacramental shortcut by which believers could earn God's favour by partaking in the Eucharist in their dying days after a life poorly lived. Both themes – the focus on Christ's life and teachings and the emphasis on a small, redeemed community of the saved – will be pronounced in the writings of Menno Simons, whose followers would eventually be known as Mennonites.

Historian Jonathan Israel concludes that à Kempis's *Devotio Moderna* revolutionized the way in which readers could comprehend the acquisition of Christian faith, even though it did not include an explicit challenge to the institutions or polity of the Catholic Church. What à Kempis did challenge was the view that Christians needed the church's institutional mediation to understand Christian faith. On the contrary, he maintained that those who truly sought after Christ could realize their faith individually if they but diligently searched the Scriptures.[13] Indolent and insincere priests need not be a barrier as they could be sidestepped, as could the vast sacramental regime the churchly elites – and those same indolent priests – oversaw. Henceforth individuals could follow the path to salvation via the humble study of the Bible and not the purportedly sacred waters of baptism or the sacrament of Confession, let alone the Mass itself.[14]

Unwittingly *The Imitation of Christ* was foundational for a revolutionary movement known as Dutch humanism. Italian scholars had previously birthed the humanist movement in the fourteenth century when they turned with sudden passion to "the sources," most particularly to the ancient Roman and Greek civilizations. At its heart humanists rejected the power of the sacramentally based and hierarchically structured Catholic Church, as they celebrated the innate ability of all critically to engage the world. By looking back to the ideals of ancient civilizations it was possible to chart a new course for European society that could bypass the power long held by the magisterium and traditions of the Catholic Church. Rudolph Agricola bridged the gap between the Dutch north and humanist beginnings in the Italian south. Born in 1443 as the illegitimate son of a cleric from the Dutch province of Groningen, Agricola travelled to Italy as a young man in pursuit of the educational opportunities that had unfolded there. He later brought this newly acquired learning to the north, where he was credited by Erasmus as the source and origin of humanism in the Netherlands. Eventually the followers of Agricola transformed the curriculum at Deventer when they introduced Greek and Latin as well as philosophical inquiry rooted in the classical texts. No wonder the Dutch humanist movement, henceforth centred in Deventer, easily blended the central precepts of the Catholic faith with the newfound emphasis on Greek civilization. Greek refugees who flooded westward across Europe following the collapse of Constantinople in 1453 intensified these trends.[15]

As part of that pan-European movement, Dutch humanists opened the door for Christians to humbly ground their faith directly in Christ, live peaceably in his presence, and prepare themselves for the imminent divine judgment of the world, all without excessive reliance on church hierarchies or sacraments. Of crucial importance, everyone could enjoy the unmediated, interior, reflective life, "The Joy of a Good Conscience," as one heading in *The Imitation of Christ* put it. Christ alone, and not priestly or churchly interventions, assured that the believer would live joyfully and faithfully even amid adversity. The invention of the printing press, with its moveable type, in the mid-fifteenth century popularized the spiritual direction offered by à Kempis and the *Devotio Moderna* across Northern Europe. Though printers focused on large volumes for the first generation of production – as in the Bible or biblical commentaries – they shifted to smaller formats by the latter decades of the fifteenth century. Thereafter they produced news pamphlets, smaller devotional studies, and argumentative works, often in the vernacular. These works had other advantages. They were easily concealed and highly transportable and suggested that publishers by 1500 realized they would find vast markets for their wares if they shifted from scholarly treatises to works of a more accessible and recreational nature.[16] Frédéric Barbier has argued that this new technology was almost innately subversive, as it offered readers the opportunity to read for themselves. Even worse from the vantage point of established authorities, it made it possible for individual readers to think for themselves and to reach their own conclusions when it came to faith and life.[17]

However, not all who embraced the printing revolution conjoined with Dutch humanism sought to undermine the established church. Erasmus of Rotterdam is the clearest example of a Dutch humanist who remained loyal to Rome, even if many who followed in his footsteps did not. Born in 1466, Erasmus studied at Deventer at a time when the humanist winds stirred by Agricola were blowing through its classrooms. Deventer's ecclesial importance had increased when Geert Groote founded the first community of the *Brethren of the Common Life* here in the fourteenth century. These lay communities, initially opposed by the church, were devoted to the teachings of the *Devotio Moderna*. They consisted of lay Christians, often from a variety of artisanal trades, who "wore, plain clothes, kept their eyes to the ground, uncomplainingly helped their neighbors, and occasionally uttered short prayers."[18] The communities themselves – men and women lived in separate buildings – were active in some of the first educational initiatives in the north of Europe, and their vigorous publication of devotional works by 1500 made them extremely influential. Even Martin Luther studied in one such community in Magdeburg before he commenced university studies in Erfurt.

These communities would have had an incalculable impact on Erasmus, as they inhabited several buildings across Deventer and lead directly to Anabaptist – and later Mennonite – understandings of the faithful community. Moreover, Deventer had acquired a printing press as early as 1477, which made it a leading centre for the publication of devotional material.[19] Not surprisingly, from his earliest days in Deventer Erasmus sought to reform the Catholic faith along the lines of the devotional communities he encountered there, even as he remained unwavering loyal to it. True to his era, Erasmus advocated for a reform rooted in ancient wisdom as found in the teachings of the Church Fathers. All else, including the more recent traditions of the church, were extraneous at best, and obfuscatious at worst. In the end, all that mattered for him was the urgent need for all to seek Christ directly, even if the community of faith in like pursuit would necessarily be small.

The devastating pandemic known as the Plague fundamentally transformed Erasmus's own life when it struck the Netherlands in 1483. His parents both died from it, and the suddenly orphaned Erasmus was compelled to enter an Augustinian monastery. Though his stay there was not a long one, his devotion to the church remained steadfast as he left the monastery to become a priest at the age of twenty-five (in 1492). Even then he received a permanent papal dispensation not to serve as a parish priest but instead devoted himself to the study and explication of theology. He published his first works in the 1490s and contemporaries soon deemed him to be among the greatest of contemporary Christian humanists. Erasmus mastered Greek as many other emerging humanists had done, but he disagreed with those who argued that the new insights had superseded Christian faith. Quite the contrary, he consistently maintained that the new knowledge was meaningless if it was not rooted in devotion to Christ and the church. We get a sense of his theology in these excerpts from his famed *Enchiridion*, written in 1501: "A man compelled toward virtue alone is turning toward Christ; a man serving his own vices is surrendering to Satan. Let your eye be clear, therefore, and your whole being will be full of light. Look at Christ alone as the absolute Good, so that you may love nothing, marvel at nothing, want nothing but Christ or because of Christ."[20] And how should followers of Christ react to those who made other choices? Here the counsel given by this early sixteenth-century writer was unequivocal. The rule stated that "the mind of a man eager for Christ should part company as sharply as possible both with the actions and the opinions of the general run of people, and not look for an example of virtue from any quarter other than Christ alone."[21] Erasmus believed Christ had served as an antidote to an Old Testament theology that was rooted in the law. Actions, it seemed, spoke louder than words. In the same way as an individual's holiness was entirely dependent on an inner, spiritual transformation made possible by Christ, so did Erasmus reject any suggestion that the external rites, sacraments, or priestly orders of the Catholic Church could vicariously achieve the same result.[22]

Rather than abandon the Catholic Church, however, he called for its restoration and rebuilding, to which end a fresh consideration of the Christian New Testament was essential. Thus, Erasmus began in 1500 to study Greek, and only one year later was at work on a commentary on the Pauline letters based on original texts and the Vulgate. Though that study was never finished, he did complete for publication his first edition of the Vulgate – then the translation of the New Testament that Rome recognized – in 1516 alongside the original Greek and accompanied by his own extensive annotations.[23] The work was an immediate success, such that he released a second edition in 1519. Subsequent editions appeared in 1522, 1527, and 1535.[24] He followed this massive initiative when he published an edition of the Psalms alongside his own extensive annotations, which he released from 1515 to 1533.

Historian Abraham Friesen has ably demonstrated how influential Erasmus was to Menno Simons.[25] It is a foundational theme to which we will return in the following chapter. But that direct path from Erasmus to Menno does not account for the emergence of the Dutch Anabaptist movement of the 1530s, which preceded Menno's own conversion from Catholic priest to fugitive sectarian leader. To account for the beginnings of Dutch Anabaptism we will need to account first for the dawn of Swiss Anabaptism, where Erasmus was no less influential. Key here was the leadership and conversion of the greatest of Swiss reformers, Ulrich Zwingli, alongside the city council of Zurich.

Zwingli was a young village priest in the Swiss rural town of Glarus when he first visited Erasmus in Basel, some eighty miles away, just as the latter's influence was at its peak. We know that Zwingli had become enamoured by the renowned Dutch humanist somewhere between August 1514 and May 1516. Zwingli's reading of Erasmus's "The Complaint of Jesus" had affirmed the young priest's own belief that Christians should cease all prayer to the saints, or veneration of the Virgin. Zwingli agreed with Erasmus's views that both practices were unbiblical, nor had the early church practised either of them. Moreover Zwingli now declared that prayers to the saints or the Virgin steered believers away from the exclusively Christocentric world view which alone could save them.[26] Such destabilizing views on contemporary Catholic practices placed Zwingli on a collision course with his rural parish, and so in 1516 he transferred to another setting, this time the town of Einsiedeln, where his preaching offended those who venerated the miracle-working depiction of the Black Virgin housed in the town's Benedictine monastery. Yet he would not be silenced, as he now condemned the very idea that Christian pilgrimage – foremost to Einsiedeln's icon – could grant forgiveness of sins and the assurance of salvation. Only God the Father could save, Zwingli declared, and He could only be reached through his Son, Jesus. By now Zwingli's mastery of the Greek language was complete as he followed Erasmus in calling the church back to the sources and to expunge the residue left by churchly traditions. Even the Bishop of Constance dared to support this upstart priest, and he urged Zwingli to seek a position in Zurich's most prestigious church, the Grossmünster. He applied, was offered the post,[27] and preached his first sermon there on New Year's Day 1519. It was immediately apparent that Zwingli had brought with him the ideas he had developed in more rural settings, all of which would appear front and centre in the earliest Mennonite theological developments.

Zurich at the time was hardly one of the great cities of Europe, though it was Switzerland's most powerful city, built on an ancient Christian foundation that featured, in Zwingli's time, Dominican, Franciscan, and Augustinian orders along with two female cloisters and a number of churches. By one estimate Catholic clergy comprised a striking 15 per cent of the city's entire population in 1500,[28] though true authority lay in other hands. By the time Zwingli arrived Zurich had been an independent city republic for three hundred years, with a wide range of artisanal guilds which dominated an autonomous political system of councils. Nor was this influence merely political, for although Zurich's ecclesial structures remained nominally subservient to Rome via the bishop of Constance, the Zurich council increasingly asserted its control over churchly polities within its borders.

Zwingli initially flourished in this new setting as his preaching electrified his parishioners. He continued to condemn all aspects of the Catholic Church that he deemed inconsistent with the New Testament church. By now he had added the practice of fasting and the doctrine of purgatory to his list. He was not alone in Europe, of course, as in 1517 another former Catholic priest, Martin Luther, had challenged the notion that priests could serve a sacerdotal function, that they alone had the ability to communicate directly with God. Luther also rejected the contemporary Catholic practice by which the purchase of indulgences could provide Christians with the assurance that their souls would be saved. Quite the contrary, Luther's careful reading of the Scriptures led him to conclude that only God could save Christians from fiery damnation. That unmerited divine gift was grace, and it was available directly to every believer. We get the clearest exposition of this in 1537 when Luther composed a Confession of Faith. He began with a declaration of standard Christian (and therefore also Catholic) doctrine:

> I. That Father, Son, and Holy Ghost, three distinct persons in one divine essence and nature, are one God, who has created heaven and earth. II. That the Father is begotten of no one; the Son of the Father; the Holy Ghost proceeds from Father and Son. III. That not the Father nor the Holy Ghost but the Son became man. IV. That the Son became man in this manner, that He was conceived, without the cooperation of man, by the Holy Ghost, and was born of the pure, holy [and always] Virgin Mary. Afterwards He suffered, died, was buried, descended to hell, rose from the dead, ascended to heaven, sits at the right hand of God, will come to judge the

quick and the dead, etc., as the Creed of the Apostles, as well as that of St. Athanasius, and the Catechism in common use for children, teach.

Of this there was no dispute, so Luther held the teachings of the Catholic Church to be truthful in this regard and consistent with the Christian Bible. The controversy erupted in what followed immediately:

1] That Jesus Christ, our God and Lord, died for our sins, and was raised again for our justification, Rom. 4:25.

2] And He alone is the Lamb of God which taketh away the sins of the world, John 1:29; and God has laid upon Him the iniquities of us all, Is. 53:6.

3] Likewise: All have sinned and are justified without merit [freely, and without their own works or merits] by His grace, through the redemption that is in Christ Jesus, in His blood, Rom. 3:23f

4] Now, since it is necessary to believe this, and it cannot be otherwise acquired or apprehended by any work, law, or merit, it is clear and certain that this faith alone justifies us as St. Paul says, Rom. 3:28: For we conclude that a man is justified by faith, without the deeds of the Law. Likewise 3:26: That He might be just, and the Justifier of him which believeth in Christ.

5] Of this article nothing can be yielded or surrendered [nor can anything be granted or permitted contrary to the same], even though heaven and earth, and whatever will not abide, should sink to ruin. For there is none other name under heaven, given among men whereby we must be saved, says Peter, Acts 4:12. And with His stripes we are healed, Is. 53:5. And upon this article all things depend which we teach and practice in opposition to the Pope, the devil, and the [whole] world. Therefore, we must be sure concerning this doctrine, and not doubt; for otherwise all is lost, and the Pope and devil and all things gain the victory and suit over us.

Thus, Luther claimed the church was powerless in its claims of sacerdotal intervention as it implied that salvation was the result of something other than grace. It suggested that salvation could be earned, as when believers participated in Catholic Mass to find their salvation in the priestly intervention and in bread and wine purportedly transformed into the body and blood of Christ. But in Luther's words: "the Mass in the Papacy must be the greatest and most horrible abomination, as it directly and powerfully conflicts with this chief article, and yet above and before all other popish idolatries it has been the chief and most specious." Of course, in many ways Luther was cut from the same cloth as Erasmus, whose criticisms of the priesthood and whose stress on the primacy of a personal faith and salvation within a larger faith community were no less pronounced. Nor does it surprise that their relationship was a collegial one initially. However, matters between them deteriorated sharply by the mid-1520s as Erasmus remained within the Roman Church that excommunicated Luther in 1520.[29]

Nor was this doctrinal dispute undertaken exclusively in closed quarters as Martin Luther became Europe's first great publishing superstar. His ideas were disseminated everywhere in print and passionately engaged, including the Netherlands, where Luther's earlier writings especially influenced Menno Simons. Luther's sudden popularity benefited from technological changes that made his writings widely available. Thus, by the end of 1522 Luther had composed more than 160 writings which had already appeared in a staggering 828 German-language editions. German publishers, for whom Luther was a boon, published an additional 1,245 editions before 1530. Most publishers prior to Luther had relied on large books written in Latin and directed at the scholarly and priestly community. But not so with Luther, who used the popular medium to even greater effect than Erasmus.

Yet it is too simple to suggest that Zwingli was merely a closet Lutheran. Put simply, Zwingli refused to travel through the door Luther had opened when the latter had claimed that nothing mattered more than faith in a God who saved his followers through an act of unmerited grace. Zwingli countered that religion was about much more than merely seeking God's forgiveness through unwarranted grace, by which the whole world might be saved. Instead, and following more closely alongside Erasmus than Luther ever would, Zwingli maintained that true faithfulness required not only correct worship but also correct living. Whereas Luther had built his edifice on a foundation which repeatedly declared that no one could truly please God, Zwingli insisted that a Christian's grace-filled faithfulness was null and void if not accompanied by Christian action.[30] In perhaps his most impressive work, published in 1525, "Commentary on True and False Religion," Zwingli declared: "Faithfulness, and piety, demands, first, that we learn from God in what way we can please Him, in what manner we can serve Him. Next it demands that we shall add nothing to what we have learned from Him, and take away nothing."[31]

In 1522 Zwingli abandoned his priestly benefice and declared himself to be entirely under the leadership of Zurich's civil authorities. Within a year he had denounced the Roman Catholic Church's position on a host of additional issues, including the Mass, though he never broke completely with Rome, nor did the Church categorically cast him aside.[32]

Zwingli also established a study circle (sodality) by at least 1520 for young Christian humanists drawn to his cause and who wanted to assist in the work of churchly reform.[33] These included Conrad Grebel, the son of a prominent merchant, and Felix Manz, a canon's son from the very Grossmünster where Zwingli served. Two trajectories were soon on a collision course: first, it became clear to the young humanists that Zwingli, their much-vaunted leader, was reluctant to challenge the expressed positions of city magistrates in Zurich; and second, his younger followers became increasingly suspicious that Zwingli had surrendered the determination of biblical truths to those same civil authorities. But surely only the church could wield authority on biblical matters. Something had to give, and when it did, the Anabaptist movement was born, from whence would come the followers of Menno within a short tumultuous decade.

Two controversies were present at the Anabaptist onset. The first controversy pertained to tithes, which the church collected for the maintenance of local parishes. Over time many of these, often acquired from the most vulnerable, had been diverted and used by the church to support its monasteries, convents, and superstructure, such that the lower clergy were often bereft of adequate funds. Initially Zwingli had spoken out against the payment of tithes, though by June of 1523 he declared that such tithes were lawful and that all Christians must pay them.[34] The position of the Zurich radicals took on added political significance in June of 1523 when peasants in nearby villages refused to pay their tithes. State authorities who claimed the right to oversee the dispersal of these funds were understandably alarmed, especially as the protestors' voices challenged all authorities. The revolt of a few villages gained steam across the German lands in the fall of 1524 and exploded into a full-fledged peasant war in 1525. Peasant representatives who met in March of 1525 in Memmingen drafted a twelve-part declaration known as "The Twelve Articles."[35] In it they demanded the right to govern their settlements autonomously, the abolition of the tithe, and denied the right of anyone henceforth to treat them as their property. In the final article the delegates promised to withdraw any article that was not deemed consistent with the Word of God (the Bible), the clearest indication that they saw no distinction between the profane and the ecclesial.

Local authorities crushed this peasant revolt by the end of 1525, though not before entire towns had succumbed to peasant forces that numbered in the thousands. No wonder its lingering effects endured for generations. Princes and other local authorities declared that henceforth they would only tolerate religious reformers who accepted the overarching authority of the state. Historian James Stayer quotes Peter

Bickle: "Now the princes had to take over the Reformation. Only if they could bring it under political control could revolt be eliminated root and branch. They had to shear the Reformation of its revolutionary components, which they did by denying the communal principle as a mode of Christian life both in theory and practice."[36] In short, reformers such as Zwingli and Luther, who recognized the emergent secular power of the princes over their jurisdictions would fare better than Zwingli's more radical cohort, who appeared to sympathize with peasant rebels in their challenge to civil authorities. In Arnold Snyder's interpretation, Zwingli recognized that city officials would not determine divine truth. They would, however, as a "divinely instituted authority," determine the "pace of institutional reform."[37]

This brings us to the second place of disagreement between Zwingli and his increasingly disillusioned young followers in Zurich: baptism. It seems as if Zwingli and his circle had all agreed as late as 1523 that "children should not be baptized before they were of age" and had received instruction in faith. This would have directly challenged the contemporary Catholic position of infant baptism. But Zwingli reversed his position somewhere between 1523 and 1525. Moreover Zwingli, according to his own account of these momentous events, persuaded municipal officials that the young radicals were not only anti-church in their call for believers' baptism, they were also a threat (again) to contemporary political authorities. Though Snyder questions the validity of this claim, it is clear in the context of the mounting peasants' war that the allegation stuck. Henceforth adult baptism was associated with civil disobedience. The issue was joined in the summer of 1524 when the Zurich magistrate became aware that several families in local parishes had refused to have their newborn infants baptized.[38] The council identified Wilhelm Reublin as instigator, and his known involvement in the withholding of tithes reinforced official concerns. Authorities arrested Reublin and notified the families involved that their children must be baptized. Meanwhile in Zurich the issue of infant baptism became a lightning rod for discontent in the fall of 1524. The city council responded in January of 1525 when it decreed that it would banish all those who did not baptize their children. It named two of Zwingli's inner circle as under suspicion: Conrad Grebel and Felix Manz.[39]

Grebel, Manz, and Georg Blaurock, a Catholic priest from Zurich's environs met with others on the night of 21 January 1525 in an event recorded by the Hutterite Chronicle as the founding event of the Anabaptist movement, out of which so-called Mennonites soon emerged. Extant sources suggest that after some discussion and prayer Blaurock asked Grebel to baptize him. When he had done so, Blaurock in kind baptized Grebel and Manz. The movement, begun in such a simple yet revolutionary manner, spread quickly as all three became active baptizers; that is, until authorities captured, tortured, and killed Blaurock and Manz. Police agents captured Manz in 1526 and drowned him in the Limat River in the centre of Zurich in January 1527, making him the first of the Anabaptist martyrs. They burned Blaurock at the stake in 1529; yet even with widespread persecution the movement spread rapidly.

Those at the heart of this new re-baptizer movement did not structure their worship services around the Catholic Mass, nor does that surprise given the theological and ecclesial legacy that these new sectarians inherited from Erasmus via Zwingli. Instead the earliest converts worshipped in barns, houses, caves, and other secluded settings where leaders read from the Scriptures and discussed what they had read, praying beforehand that God would lead them to the truth. A prayer from the minister followed, who then presided over a celebration of the Lord's Supper, which participants no longer deemed the actual body and blood of Christ. Instead they concluded that the communion realized in the Lord's Supper symbolized a communion they had already achieved in Christ. Neither did the early Anabaptist leaders believe that anything transformative happened during the act of baptism. Across the board sacraments gave way to symbolic acts suggestive of a prior transformation of faith, with no power in themselves.[40] All told, this movement of religious disenchantment and ecclesial division had gained a solid foothold across southern Germany and Switzerland. Could the north of Europe be far behind?

Conclusion

Mennonites may have emerged in the 1530s as followers of the renegade Catholic priest Menno Simons, but many of their foundational identity markers were in place beforehand. They were part of a movement which dated back to the Mendicant Orders of the twelfth century, had flowered into the Catholic *Devotio Moderna* movement of the fifteenth century, and been refined by Erasmus thereafter, then Zwingli. In some ways the Anabaptist reformation sparked by Grebel, Manz, and Blaurock signalled continuity as much as change when they baptized each other in the home of Felix Manz on the banks of the Limmat in 1525.

Yet their abrupt challenge to this very tradition was equally undeniable. Almost from the start followers of this broad reform movement stressed the primacy and authority of the biblical sources over churchly traditions. They were convinced that those very traditions were harmful to a life of faith as they denied someone an unmediated access to

Christ, who was immediately available to those who sought him with their whole heart. No need for saints by this new reckoning. No need for the intercession of the Virgin. No need for a host of purported sacraments that simply could not deliver what they promised, nor for the payment of special tithes or indulgences whereby priests could magically forgive sins. No need, also, for special communities of the faithful in secluded monasteries. No need for the magisterium of the church when all believers, and not the pope and his cardinals, had access to the truth of the gospels. In fact, all these practices and beliefs were condemnatory as they all suggested that laypeople could somehow pass on the demands, and rewards, of Christian faith. Yet nothing could be further from the truth for these early modern reformers.

Nor was this merely a matter of belief because reformers within and – increasingly – beyond the Roman Catholic purview in the early sixteenth century maintained that the fruits of a faith rooted in Christ should be evident for all to see in a life of faithful discipleship lived in His name. One had to believe, and the truest mark of that belief was in a life well lived. In their acceptance of this deeply held conviction the first Swiss Anabaptists walked through a theological doorway that Ulrich Zwingli had already utilized, as had Erasmus of Rotterdam before him. This was a great challenge to contemporary Catholic faith and practice, of course, but it threatened no less Martin Luther's emphasis on abundant grace over costly discipleship. Many questions remained as to the exact ecclesial shape this reformed faith would take going forward, and tensions abounded.

"The blood of the martyrs is the seed of the church," or so declared Tertullian less than two hundred years after the church was born in Pentecostal fire. The same applied to the Anabaptist movement sixteen centuries later, whose first followers were relentlessly hunted down by all sides, Protestant and Catholic. Yet the movement spread quickly, in large part thanks to the likes of Melchior Hoffman, who would join this fledgling movement in Strasbourg. The beginnings of Dutch Anabaptism, and the Mennonite faith, were at hand.

Chapter Two

Melchoir, Münster, and Menno: From Early Dutch (Melchiorite) Anabaptists to Mennonites

Mennonites emerged in Holland as followers of Menno Simons, a renegade Catholic priest who converted to an Anabaptist movement that had originated in Zurich in 1525. The movement itself had spread to northern Europe prior to Menno's conversion in 1536 thanks to the tireless efforts of Melchior Hoffman. It is for good reason that the first converts were identified as Melchiorites. Born in or about 1495 in Schwäbish Hall, a city in the south German state of Baden-Württemberg, Hoffman was initially a devotee of Martin Luther, so much so that he visited Luther in Wittenberg in June 1525. Though a furrier by trade, Hoffman modelled himself after the apostle Paul, famed for his far-flung New Testament missionary journeys. This latter-day apostle travelled northward into the north German states after 1523 and into Livonia (including Dorpat and Riga), Sweden, and Denmark (Schleswig-Holstein). Everywhere he went Hoffman quickly established his renown as a vigorous and captivating preacher.

Hoffman had not converted to Anabaptism by the time he arrived in Strasbourg in June 1529, but he most certainly had by the time he left that city less than a year later.[1] Sectarian movements flourished in this great imperial city in the 1520s and included a strong Swiss and south German Anabaptist presence from as early as March 1526 when Wilhelm Reublin, recently arrived from Zurich, served as one of Strasbourg's earliest Anabaptist leaders. Within months an Anabaptist community had formed, rooted in the very biblicism that had marked its beginnings in Zurich.[2] More Anabaptist preachers arrived in the autumn of 1526, all of whom opposed infant baptism and denounced Luther's steadfast support of it as unbiblical. Strasbourgian Anabaptism also took on a decidedly more apocalyptic tone than had been evident earlier in Zurich thanks to the prophetic work and apocalyptic visions of transplanted peasants Ursula and Lienhard Jost. Ursula's first visions began in 1524, then dried up shortly thereafter only to reappear in 1529, the very year of Hoffman's arrival in Strasbourg. Hoffman had no prophetic gifts of his own but was quickly drawn to the Josts' apocalyptic fervour. In 1530 he published an edition of Ursula's visions, whom he merely identified as "a lover of God" (Gottesliebhaberin). Though hardly systematic in approach, her visions stressed the sovereignty of God, the coming judgment against oppressors of the faithful, and the need for the redeemed to live lives worthy of the salvation they had secured. Hoffman made certain that his volume of Ursula's visions received a broad readership during his travels in the Netherlands as it reinforced both his present authority and future expectation. By the former, it helped that Hoffman put both Ursula and Lienhard on par with the biblical prophets of the Old Testament and they, in turn, deemed Hoffman to be the reappearance of the biblical prophet Elijah and considered themselves his earthly followers. It is from the Josts that Hoffman concluded that Strasbourg would be the "spiritual Jerusalem" when Christ returned in glory; a return that was imminent.[3]

Melchior Hoffman stayed in this great Rhenish city for two years during which time he drew near to the Anabaptist movement. He was baptized into it in 1530 amid intensified state persecution of Anabaptists as imperial authorities had reacted violently to the Peasant War of 1525 and its association with Anabaptist beginnings. They now executed Anabaptists across the south, such that Strasbourg became a refuge of sorts, especially as a series of rural famines and the inflation in food prices transformed Swiss and German peasants into landless refugees, many of whom flooded into Strasbourg. The influx was such that civil magistrates became increasingly uneasy as conditions worsened and as the number of Anabaptists in Strasbourg increased from some 250 in 1528 to almost 2,000 by 1530; by which point they may have accounted for 10 per cent of the city's population.

In a move that marked his final break with Luther, an apocalyptically driven Hoffman soon abandoned infant in favour of adult baptism. But baptismal predilections marked just one aspect of his theology, and it is worth the time to identify other aspects of his theology given the enormous influence Hoffman would soon have on Menno Simons and the early Dutch Anabaptists. Hoffman believed in a classically Christian and triune God, though not in a classical manner. He did believe that an omnipotent heavenly Father had created the world and all humankind, only to see humans slip into sin. To break sin's hold on the world, God had entered the world in Jesus Christ to free it from sin, as only God could do. But in Strasbourg Hoffman diverged from almost all orthodox understandings of Christ as fully human and fully divine when Hoffman became persuaded by Casper Schwenkfeld's argument that, even on earth, Christ was only fully divine. In other words, Hoffman now concluded that the Catholic Church wrongly maintained that Mary, the mother of Jesus, had granted her physical nature to her son. Had she done so, how could Christ have been free from sin, which was the inescapably human condition? Once persuaded, Hoffman henceforth declared that all who wished to be saved from the eternal judgment to come had first to declare their faith in this monophysite Christ and thereafter be baptized accordingly. In a theological departure that would mark early Mennonite theology, Hoffman rejected the Catholic solution that Mary could have passed on her human nature to Christ because she had been sinless due to her own Immaculate Conception. Once that had been rejected, there seemed no out save for a Christ who was fully divine, a Christ who had been carried by Mary in her womb for nine months but had never taken on her flesh. We will return to the significance of this position for the earliest Mennonites when we look directly at Menno Simons.

It was in Strasbourg that Hoffman first declared that adult baptism was an essential indication of a believer's commitment to Christ. But he refused to deem it a sacrament, from which it follows that it played no sacerdotal role. Nor was the Eucharist a sacrament, as Hoffman declared it to be a symbol of a community that had been transformed in Christ, nothing more. Once baptized as adults, it was incumbent upon the redeemed to live lives worthy of the salvation they had received, one they could as easily lose should they turn again to the Prince of Darkness. Hence the community of the redeemed, the new church, had to live as those who were already the elect of Christ, and the need to do so was all the more urgent given Hoffman's firm conviction that the end of the world was at hand. This was so, he maintained, because the Roman church had been exposed as Satanic by the newly emergent church.

Hoffman had long been attracted to the Old Testament's prophetic book of Daniel with its end-times imagery as well as the New Testament Apocalypse, or book of Revelation, and by his time in Strasbourg he had narrowed his historical timeline enough to suggest that the world would end soon with Christ's return in 1533 or 1534. Now a newly minted Anabaptist, Hoffman allowed for the fact that those who were faithful might be called by Christ to establish an outpost in the form of an earthly theocracy as they awaited His imminent return. Much would soon come from this allowance.

Thus equipped with a missional calling, a radical theology, and a profound sense of urgency, Hoffman left Strasbourg in the spring of

Figure 1. Jan Luyken, "Pieter Pietersz. Bekjen." From C. Commelin, *Beschryvinge van Amsterdam* (Amsterdam, 1693). Photography courtesy of the Rijksmuseum (Object No. RP-P-AO-28-18-1).

1530 and returned north to East Frisia. Why there, and what did he encounter upon his return? It may be that Hoffman imagined he had reached the centre of the world as he travelled north, a region in the midst of its own futuristic apocalypse, even as he continued to believe Strasbourg retained its pride of place as the epicentre of the new age to come.

East Frisia was only one small part of a region in the midst of a remarkable transformation in the early sixteenth century as the seaside cities of the European north began to outpace the erstwhile powerbases of Flanders and Brabant. Cities such as Bruges, Brussels, and Ghent remained dominant into the fifteenth century, but all lacked the dynamism of the mercantile cities to the north by 1500. The south was also more firmly under the control of Philip V (1500–88), which strengthened the Catholic Church's ability to quell Protestant unrest. The province of Holland had emerged as a strong pillar in the Low Countries by the time of Philip's reign, and although Amsterdam had long been no match for the cities further to the south, the overall pace of urban growth in the north after 1450 was without precedent across Europe. For example, 45 per cent of the population of Holland was deemed urban in 1477 and another 48 per cent in Overijssel, compared with approximately a third of the population in Flanders.

What had changed? For one, the expansion of Baltic trade in the late fifteenth and early sixteenth centuries favoured maritime trade, and that favoured the north. Hollanders were among the first to develop new technologies of transport when they perfected full-rigged seagoing ships.[4] This allowed their sailors to be major players in the exploitation of the North Sea's herring fisheries and for the transshipment of Baltic grains and timber from Poland and beyond, all of which were needed for the increasingly urbanized population in Holland and adjoining provinces. Holland's merchant fleet by the mid-sixteenth century had far surpassed that of any other European country, and dwarfed the volume that the previous powerhouse, Venice, had reached a century earlier.[5] With increased rural depopulation in the Dutch north, the inhabitants turned increasingly to a wide range of artisanal trades as shipbuilders, rope makers, traders, barrel makers, weavers, and brewers (especially of beer) took centre stage. Here was the demographic seedbed of Melchiorite, and later Mennonite Anabaptism. This movement of the population to various urban centres in the north was facilitated by the fact that the region had a relatively weak seigniorial class. Guilds also developed more quickly in the north, and institutions of civic life more generally.

This had two implications for the emergence of Anabaptism in the north: first, the economic emergence and political integration of the Dutch north coincided with a relative decline in power by Charles V, still the purported Holy Roman Emperor of the region.[6] But Charles was unable to quash the emergence of political statecraft in the north, especially given the relatively modest role nobles played in the Dutch lands (no part of rural society was represented in the political assemblies of Zeeland, for example). In place of such erstwhile restraints, local officials often viewed both religious protest movements and the increased politicization and civic engagement by an increasingly urbanized population as parallel attempts to overcome imperial power. Thus, magistrates across the north tended to sympathize with these new religious movements initially and blocked attempts by Charles to impose his imperial will in their jurisdictions.

Second, and corresponding to the lack of centralized state power, the power of the Roman Catholic Church was similarly circumscribed in Holland and the northern Dutch provinces. Bishoprics across the Spanish Netherlands were ungovernably large in 1500, as there were only five for a population of three million, two of which covered the entirety of the Dutch-speaking provinces. It did not help that priests had a lowly reputation across Europe (recall the paintings of Hieronymous Bosch). Up to a fifth may have maintained concubines and, not surprisingly, the number of priests and nuns in holy orders had declined. Nor was this merely a quantifiable matter, as Erasmus warned as late as 1525 that there was a popular antipathy towards Catholic monks across Flanders, Holland, and Zeeland. Under the circumstances, Erasmus penned his polemics as much to awaken the church hierarchy as to appeal to the personal piety among the lay. Those most loyal to the Catholic Church – including Erasmus – had reason to conclude that the church had brought the Protestant curse upon itself. The papal nuncio, cardinal Campeggio, declared in 1524 at the Diet of Nuremberg: "One need only live by the church's original teachings and all grievances would vanish ... Later generations have often been astonished at how candidly the most ardent defenders of the church conceded the presence of corruption in the clerical ranks. As though anyone could still deny the terrible vices in the face of the (massive) evidence and the attentively (listening) Lutherans."[7]

The rise of an urban and artisanal population in the Dutch Netherlands was not without its challenges, however, as was particularly the case after 1530 when economic conditions worsened year by year. Several factors accounted for this: Amsterdam's meteoric rise came at the expense of other cities in the north and compelled many artisans to relocate to the capital of Holland; increased competition from England directly challenged Dutch hegemony in maritime trade, especially in the manufacture of domestic textiles; and, lastly, an ongoing conflict between emperor Charles V and Denmark after 1531 threatened to curtail all Dutch shipping and fishing fleets in the north. Danish aggression also restricted the entry of ships carrying Polish grains into Dutch markets at the very time those markets had become reliant on Polish produce. Famine and disease were on the rise across the north, and the movement of artisans *en masse* to Amsterdam led to increased rates of unemployment across the urban sector. Wages were depressed as prices shot up. No wonder officials described this as a time of famine across the north.

Many of the artisans who suffered believed their present economic hardships were part of a global crisis that portended the end of the world. Nor were they alone, as the Black Death that struck most of Europe in 1348 caused severe demographic contraction for a century and was widely understood as divine judgment. The recurrence of famine in every generation thereafter – including one that almost killed Zwingli in 1519 – reinforced those who warned of an imminent apocalypse. Nor was this merely a physical phenomenon, as contemporary Catholic theologians viewed Luther, Zwingli, John Calvin, Jan Hus from the previous century, and other Protestant leaders as the devil's spawn. Many saw this sinister portrayal confirmed when authorities apprehended large numbers of religious sectarians in nighttime forest gatherings which the Catholic Church had condemned. Surely the devil and his minions were everywhere, and the end of the world near, after which God's judgment would follow. Add to this the fall of (Christian) Constantinople to the (pagan, Muslim) Ottoman Empire in 1453 and the siege of Christian Vienna by those same Muslims in 1529, and one can easily see how all of Europe was ripe for apocalyptic thinking, the Dutch Netherlands included.

No one preached the coming apocalypse more effectively in 1530 than Melchior Hoffman. He initially intended to seek asylum in East Frisia after Strasbourg's City Council had ordered his arrest on 23 April 1530. In truth, Hoffman's recent conversion to Anabaptism and his subsequent rejection of infant baptism gave him a ready audience in the north, where some parents even prior to his arrival had refused to have their children baptized. The Duke of East Frisia, Enno II, understood such refusals to be acts of protest against his authority as much as against the Church, though he initially had little power to intervene. Still others had begun in the 1520s to stay away from the obligatory Easter Mass. Hoffman initiated the first mass protest in May 1530 as he had soon rebaptized about three hundred adults. His message was as simple as it was direct. People were living in the final age. The judgment of God was at hand. Only the elect would be saved from destruction, and they would only be known to Christ if they had previously surrendered to him as adults in the covenant of baptism.

Those who were rebaptized often had been active in the Catholic conventicles, formed by those who had walked in the footsteps of the *Devotio Moderna* that devotees had established in the 1520s and earlier. By the 1530s that very Catholic movement had taken on a distinctly sectarian bent. Hoffman referred to this new movement of the rebaptized as the true church, one that stood in the direct lineage of the New Testament church in Corinth (recall that Hoffman saw himself as an apostle in the footsteps of the apostle Paul). Those who gathered in these latter days were nothing less than the Bride of the Lord, the people of the

New Covenant. They were already victorious in that they would be spared the final judgment, having already been put to death with Christ in baptism. Even the threat of martyrdom appeared to energize them.

No wonder Hoffman's new Anabaptist movement flourished, even though Hoffman fled Emden in June 1530 as the count's forces moved to arrest him. He would never return to the north. However, before his departure Hoffman appointed leaders in his stead, among them Jan Volkeerts Trijpmaker (a cobbler by trade) and Sikke Snijder (of whom little is known), both rebaptized as adults during Hoffman's brief stay in East Friesland. In short, the Anabaptist movement in the Dutch north that would soon give birth to the Mennonites was underway by the spring of 1530, though this was only the beginning.[8] Three distinct phases followed in short order. It was the third of these which resulted in the formation of the Mennonites.

The first phase can be dated from 1530 to 1533 and was one of evangelical fervour and apocalyptic urgency, driven by Hoffman's prophecy that Christ's return was imminent. Nor were members of this movement easily identified by their adult baptism after authorities executed Hoffman's designated leader, Jan Volkeerts, on 5 December 1531. Even earlier Sikke Freerks became the first Anabaptist martyr in the Netherlands when authorities in Leeuwarden executed him on 20 March 1531. A shaken Hoffman, already absent, ordered a two-year moratorium on such baptisms, which made the subsequent growth of the movement difficult to determine. On the other hand, the intensely decentralized nature of Dutch Anabaptism within a larger Dutch Protestantism in those early days resulted in a large number of prophetic anti-Catholic voices between 1532 and 1535.[9] Volkeerts' own appointment as sectarian leader suggests the vital role artisans played in Dutch Anabaptist beginnings, though the same must be said about converted midwives who moved freely about the Dutch countryside without notice from suspicious authorities. As to the former, historian Gary Waite has shown that a stunning 240 of the 242 Anabaptists (known initially as Melchiorites) brought to the attention of the courts in The Hague and Amsterdam were artisans. Almost forty of these were women. This points both to the lack of theological training or sophistication in the earliest Melchiorites as well the degree to which the social and economic turmoil mentioned above, alongside the fast-paced urbanization of the Netherlands, contributed to the growth of this movement.[10] Even though the movement was spawned across the towns and villages of the Dutch north, most converts soon migrated to the port city of Amsterdam, where magistrates were surprisingly tolerant in the early 1530s (Volkeerts had been executed in The Hague).

But what drew Dutch artisans to this broadly based Melchiorite and Anabaptist movement beyond mere protest? One doubts that many would have understood, much less been motivated by, Hoffman's monophysite Christology. Rather, Alistair Hamilton argues that two aspects of Hoffman's theology found purchase: first, the belief that the imminent end of the world and Christ's return would be signalled by the "destruction of the godless" and, second, that the elect, Christ's true followers, would play a leading role as they would literally prepare the way for His fiery, vengeance-filled return in glory.[11] By this means dispirited Dutch artisans found consolation in the assurance that their hardships would soon be overcome and the evildoers destroyed in the coming apocalyptic steamroller, nor would they be mere bystanders as it all unfolded. Under the circumstances, who would not want to join, even if initially many who followed Hoffman's edict of 1531 declined to be rebaptized? Not only had Hoffman identified an imminent end to the world with Christ's return, he had also identified the very place where Christ's New Jerusalem would be situated: Strasbourg. It is for that reason alone that Hoffman willingly returned to that Alsatian city and the certain imprisonment that awaited him. Surely, he reasoned, Christ himself would shortly free him from his confinement.

Hoffman's apocalyptic discourse reached its zenith in the Münster rebellion of 1534 and marked the second phase of Anabaptist beginnings in the north. This incident began when the Protestant reformer and evangelical cleric in that city, Bernard Rothmann, accepted the Anabaptist practice of adult baptism in 1533. This had two immediate consequences: first, it placed Rothmann at odds with the German emperor, who had previously declared adult baptism a capital offence, and second, Rothmann transformed Münster into a magnet for Anabaptist reformers in the north. Jan Matthijs was one such who came. A self-declared prophet and erstwhile baker from Amsterdam, Matthijs immediately overturned Hoffman's moratorium on adult baptisms. Even more, he declared that Münster, not Hoffman's Strasbourg, was the epicentre where Christ would soon return and establish his New Jerusalem. Moreover, he prophesied that all this would happen on Easter Sunday, 1534. Upon that foundation Matthijs inaugurated the end times in a city that by then was under siege by imperial forces. They killed Matthijs that Easter when he moved beyond the walls of the city to proclaim Christ's final victory, and his death paved the way for the Anabaptist Jan van Leiden to seize control of this rebellious north German city.

Van Leiden, who was Dutch and formerly a tailor by trade, now declared himself king and successor to Matthijs. Reports suggest that he instituted polygamy for the hundreds of Anabaptist followers who were ensconced in Münster after 1534. In addition, van Leiden abolished private property within the city and ordered the forcible expulsion of all adults who refused to be rebaptized. Food was to be shared and eaten in public squares, and he ordered that all books other than the Bible be burned. He further decreed that church steeples be demolished and their interiors ransacked to rid them of artefacts previously deemed sacred. Such violent acts were necessary, van Leiden decreed, because "if we are sons of God and have been baptized in Christ, then all evil must disappear from our midst ... If, however, you do evil, then beware! The [Anabaptist] authorities wield the sword not in vain; they are God's servants, his avengers to punish the evildoer."[12]

In the end, the siege of van Leiden's Münsterite kingdom, overseen by the city's deposed bishop, continued for sixteen months before the bishop's forces overwhelmed the city in June 1535. The three key Anabaptist leaders, including "King" van Leiden, were summarily captured, tortured, and executed; their bodies thence displayed in cages suspended from St. Lambert's (Catholic) Church, where they hang to this day. The Münster rebellion and its collapse immediately changed the course of Dutch Anabaptist history in two distinct ways, both of which profoundly shaped the larger Mennonite story.[13] By the first, a new generation of Anabaptist leaders emerged after Münster's devastation, foremost among them initially David Joris, though Menno Simons became paramount by the early 1840s.[14] By the second, the threat posed by Anabaptist Münster's civil defiance resulted in a period of intense persecution of this newly emergent sect in the Netherlands, such that many followers of Menno would seek refuge further east. Taken together Menno's emergence amid a period of intense persecution comprised the third and final phase of Dutch Anabaptism as it pertains to our story.

Menno Simons and the Emergence of "Mennonite" Anabaptists

In 1535 a Catholic priest wrote his first known work in opposition to the Münster rebellion. In it he roundly condemned how Jan van Leiden had usurped the authority of Christ Himself. And to what end? In the place of eternal truths van Leiden had trafficked in "shameful deceit and blasphemy."[15] In particular, the writer rejected the very idea that Christ, having ordered Peter to sheath his sword in the Garden of Gethsemane, would somehow permit his followers to resort to violence in Münster. Such earthly punishment of the godless could only proceed after Christ had returned, and not merely in anticipation thereof. In the interim, those who followed Christ had to forsake the sword. Instead they needed to walk the way of suffering even as Christ had, though believers would do so in the certain knowledge that the Lord would strengthen the souls of all who faithfully awaited his return. The writer buttressed his missive with a host of citations from the Bible. For example, the following verses are used as justification for the tract's first two sentences: 1 Peter 2:9; Colossians 1:13; Hebrews 11:15, Deuteronomy 29:18; and 1 Corinthians 1:18.

The priest's name was Menno Simons, and his impassioned outburst against the Münsterite rebellion may have been motivated by the sad reality that authorities had captured and executed his younger brother, Pieter, after Anabaptists had briefly overrun the Cistercian Bloemkamp Abbey in Friesland in March 1535.[16] But there is no evidence to suggest that the older Menno had already joined this radical religious movement by then. That said, he was surely well on his way. This future leader of a movement that would bear his name was born in 1496 to what were likely prosperous peasants, near Witmarsum in Friesland. His family moved shortly thereafter to Pingjum, which is where Menno grew up, though details of his education and upbringing are rather opaque. He appears to have been oblivious to Luther's reformation exploding all around him, which has led Abraham Friesen to conclude that Menno likely did not attend institutions of higher learning, where Luther's ideas proliferated.

Despite the lightest of theological preparations, Menno was ordained as Catholic priest to the Pingjum parish of Friesland – his hometown – in 1524. He would later confess that, at the time, he had yet to read the Bible in whole or in part. Nor would that have been exceptional as he would have joined countless priests, and the holy Church itself, in his manifold reliance on the sacraments. Yet in time he began to doubt the utility of the Mass, and most especially the church's doctrine of transubstantiation. Somewhere in 1525 he appears to have read Martin Luther's *Babylonian Captivity*, with its full-throttled attack on the Mass as the heart of Catholic worship.[17] Though he would soon dramatically part company with Luther's theology, it was not before the German reformer had opened the door for Menno to read the Bible for himself. He did so in the second year of his priesthood, 1526, and thereafter rethought every aspect of Catholic worship. By his own account, Menno first encountered Anabaptism in March 1531 when he learned that officials in nearby Leeuwarden had beheaded Sikke Snijder for the crime of rebaptism. It prompted him earnestly to investigate the Scriptures, and to his dismay he found nothing in them which legitimized infant baptism.[18] More investigations followed, and over the next decade Menno Simons gradually shifted from Catholic priest to fugitive Anabaptist leader. In the words of historian Sjouke Voolstra concerning Menno, "it was no sudden conversion, but rather a process lasting more than ten years and consisting of several phases – ignorance, rumors, of reform, growing doubts and uncertainty, Bible study self-criticism, criticism of Christianity, cautious internal church reforms, Anabaptist influences, resistance and then surrender to these, break with the traditional church, call to leadership."[19] We are not even certain when he was (re)baptized, though most likely within a few months of 12 January 1536, when he suddenly abandoned his position as parish priest of Pingjum. Menno would later refer to this act of abandonment as taking on "the cross of Christ," the time when he finally left Babylon and entered Jerusalem.[20]

From that point Menno Simons' star rose quickly within Anabaptist and Melchiorite circles such that he was the only one of their leaders named in an edict issued by the Holy Roman Emperor Charles V in 1542. Two years later Menno represented at least a portion of the Dutch Anabaptists who engaged in discussions with the emerging Dutch Reformed Church, a certain sign that his leadership was already recognized both within and beyond the movement. Why the dramatic rise? It was in part, as we shall see shortly, because of the fierce and devastating persecution authorities directed against Anabaptists after the Münster debacle, and partly because other key leaders, such as Obbe Philips (who almost certainly baptized Menno), fell away; though none of this detracts from the important role Menno played as publicist for the faith. Beginning in 1536 he wrote and released what amounted to significant, reasoned apologias for the Anabaptist faith.[21] Many of his works would enjoy a wide readership among Mennonites who settled in the Russian empire, and as late as 1897 a leading Mennonite living in Chortitza proudly proclaimed that Menno Simons was someone who "contributed immeasurably to the strengthening and enlargement of our churches and who has become to us all an example of faithful discipleship."[22]

Menno's greatest influence was undoubtedly felt in the immediate aftermath of Münster's failed rebellion when Melchiorite Anabaptists were in disarray. In concert with other Anabaptist leaders, including Dirk Phillips (brother of Obbe) and Lenaert Bouwens, Menno's writings provided an anchor from the mid-1530s to the late 1550s, by which time a faith community in disarray had found its moorings. Three key components can be identified in Menno's theology: the role of the believer, the role of the church, and the role of the state. Each will be considered briefly in turn with particular attention to Menno's "Foundation and Plain Instruction of the Saving Doctrine of Our Lord Jesus Christ."

Known simply as his *Foundation of Christian Doctrine*, Menno first published this book in Dutch in 1539, though it would subsequently be repeatedly republished in Dutch and in German translation. Deemed to be his most important work, it would later serve as a key catechistical work for Mennonites who settled in the Russian empire after 1789. Menno addressed his tract to "the God-fearing reader," the community of such readers known as the church, and "the magistrates," and all readers generally.[23]

As to the God-fearing reader, Menno begins with an urgent call to discipleship for all who claim Jesus as Lord. He writes with urgency both because he anticipates Christ's imminent return and because of the proliferation of false teachers in these last days. But for him the true gospel and call is clearly stated in the Scriptures: humans, made in God's image, had allowed themselves to be seduced by the devil into a life of sin, so much so that they could not free themselves of it. Yet God the Father, in his mercy, sent his Son to both model what a life free from sin might look like and as expiation for sins. This very expiation – played out in the events of Good Friday and Easter Sunday – resulted in a grace-filled demand on every believer. Henceforth the redeemed needed to respond with contrite hearts, to accept Christ's salvific role in their lives, and thereafter to live lives of moral purity and penitential devotion in Christ's name. Baptism was the only acceptable sign of such a transformed life, and it was sign not sacrament.

Those who had repented of their ways for Christ's sake and committed themselves to a new life in his name were commanded to form congregations of the saved. Such congregations would always find themselves at odds with a society that remained rooted in sin, yet for that reason alone the faithful had to separate themselves out from the lost. Put succinctly: "We also teach and admonish from the Word of God that all genuine children of God, born again of the incorruptible living seed of the divine Word, who have according to the Scriptures separated themselves from this idolatrous generation, who have in obedience assumed the yoke and cross of Christ, and who are able to judge between true and false doctrines, between Christ and Antichrist, that these must according to the scriptures shun all seducing and idolatrous preachers in regard to doctrines, sacraments and worship."[24] In Sjouke Voolstra's words, they were to be a "colony of heaven," a community marked by a purified Christianity, one in which the Lord's Supper was a sign of their purity, with no sacramental utility of its own.[25]

Menno Simons devotes particular attention in his *Foundation of Christian Doctrine* to the role of preachers. In sharp contrast to what he had himself lived and observed as an erstwhile Catholic priest, Menno now called forth preachers who had themselves repented of their sins and turned fully to Christ in word and deed. "It is not enough that in appearance a man speaks much of the Word of the Lord. It must also be verified by devout and unblameable conduct, as the Scriptures teach."[26] Preachers are to fear God more than humankind and more than any earthly institution. They are to love the Scriptures and study them earnestly so as to know the unblemished Word of God, which is Christ above all. And they must serve their flocks, must preside over them, with the voice of the Good Shepherd constantly in their hearts and minds, even if it will leave them permanently at odds with the world.

Menno Simons appeals directly to the magistrates in his *Foundation of Christian Doctrine*. In opposition to radical reformers who deemed the state and its servitors as necessarily evil, Menno initially accepts the fact that earthly "lords and princes" will themselves seek to follow "Christ, Gospel, redemption and kingdom."[27] This is good, for their "task is to do justice between a man and his neighbor [and] to deliver the oppressed out of the hand of the oppressor."[28] Remarkably, he affirms the need for magistrates to restrain all who deceive, regardless of whether they are "priests, monks, preachers, baptized or unbaptized," though he denies their right to do so by "tyranny."[29] Yet Menno firmly maintains that those same authorities have nothing to fear from the Anabaptists, and for two reasons: first, because Anabaptists have, in fact, found the very Truth of Christ that the magistrates themselves long for, and second, because in contrast to those at Münster who had clearly been led astray, the true followers of Christ have no "weapons" save for "patience, hope, silence and God's Word."[30] Nor should the true followers of Christ necessarily fear all magistrates, for even they were not beyond reach of the perfection of Christ, even as Menno acknowledges their God-given authority over temporal affairs, including the obligation to yield the sword.[31] But such acknowledgment is coupled with Menno's warning that the sinful use of that same sword by the magistrates will lead to God's eternal judgment.

Menno knew of what he wrote in that warning about the sinful application of state force because he emerged as the leading voice of Dutch Anabaptists at a time when they were intensely persecuted. Münster was the primary, though not sole, justification for state persecution, as Dutch Anabaptists armed with swords had also run through Amsterdam in March 1534 as they called on the godless to repent. Still other Anabaptists had been apprehended by officials as they made their way from across the Netherlands, bound for Münster in anticipation of Christ's return. Less than a year later a band of rebaptized men and women ran naked through the streets of Amsterdam, where they proclaimed (again!) the imminent end of the world, and it was in March 1534 that disturbances by yet another group at the Bloemkamp Abbey in Bolsward, Friesland, led to the apprehension and execution of Menno's brother Pieter, mentioned above. Is it any wonder authorities reacted with malice aforethought?

The persecution of religious dissidents reached its apex across Europe between 1524 and 1540, and it was into this maelstrom that Menno published his *Foundation of Christian Doctrine* in 1539. His mark was such that Pieter Visser has concluded that the writings of Menno outsold all other first-generation reformers in the Low Countries. No wonder that, of all religious dissidents from this time, historian Gary Waite estimates that fully two-thirds – perhaps two thousand or so – were Anabaptists.[32]

Conclusion

Anna von Oldenburg-Delmenhorst was regent of East Friesland when she received a demand in 1543 from the Holy Roman Emperor Charles V for information on fugitive sectarians. He accused Anna of harbouring Anabaptists on her lands because she prized their economic prowess to such an extent that she had disregarded their heretical views and subversive associations, let alone the imperial edict that they be expelled. The emperor identified various Anabaptist splinter groups that concerned him, including those led by David Joris. When Anna did not respond, the sister of the emperor – herself the regent of the entire Netherlands – wrote to her again the following year, and it was in this 1544 missive that "Mennists" were first identified as those Anabaptists who were followers of the renegade priest Menno Simons.[33]

Renegade indeed. Married in 1536 to Geertruydt Jansdochter, he spent most of the next two decades living the life of a fugitive with a price on his head. Those who harboured him were executed if caught, such that in 1544 Menno wrote that his "poor wife and our little children" could not find even a cabin or hut for more than a passing night.[34] Thus we cannot say with certainty where he stayed during that time, though contemporary evidence suggests he moved back and forth from the Netherlands to the German provinces and eastward as far as Poland on at least one occasion, rarely staying in the same place for more than a few nights. Even so, he was dogged by controversy from even those identified as Mennonites, most especially as concerned the application of the ban, as we will see in the following chapter. Historian Abraham Friesen believes that controversy and poor health epitomized the former priest's final years. His wife having preceded him in death, Menno Simons died on 31 January 1561 in the village of Wüstenfelde in Schleswig Holstein. He was buried in the garden behind his home.

Menno's earthly end may have come in the mid-sixteenth century, but his name would live on for centuries among his followers, and for good reason. Menno Simons' conversion to the Anabaptist movement and his swift shift into a leadership role coincided with the onset of one of the darkest periods of the Reformation as the Münster rebellion appeared to justify the worst fears of civil and churchly leaders alike. As many commentators have observed, Menno managed to undergird the Anabaptist movement in a distinctly pacifistic direction. He steered a path between the Scylla of Münsterite violence proclaimed after 1535 by Jan van Batenberg and the Charybdis of David Joris's apocalyptic spiritualism.[35] He repeatedly condemned the violence directed against this fledgling movement, but he did so in a manner – at least initially – that also undergirded the state's God-given mandate to rule. But, he later wrote, it had to rule justly. And as one execution surmounted another, Menno used even that to build up the faithful. What else could Christians expect, he wrote, if those who had chosen to follow Christ in these last days picked up the heavy cross of suffering that was theirs alone to carry?[36]

Though the cross of suffering was central to the Christian life for Menno, it was essential that the faithful remnant live sinless lives and for the congregation to safeguard itself as a pure corporate body of Christ. It was a tall order, especially given that the church could not rely on saints or sacraments to make it happen. Instead, believers would need to reach this goal through individual discipline, contrition, and repentance. For that to happen preachers had first and foremost to live the life of Christian faithfulness. And he insisted that they fearlessly proclaim the pure Word of God, which was Christ and the Gospels above all.

At first glance much of this harkens back to the Roman Catholic Church of Menno's upbringing, and for good reason. Abraham Friesen his pointed out that Menno's condemnation of the contemporary Catholic Church was little more than a retelling of similar attacks on the church made by the Dutch Catholic humanist Erasmus of Rotterdam. Nor does this surprise, as Menno was highly familiar with Erasmus's writings.[37] For example, Friesen concluded that Erasmus's own explication of the New Testament Scriptures led Simons to renounce infant baptism. Menno used Erasmus's translation of the Bible (and notably not Martin Luther's) for his 1539 epistle on Christian baptism. In that same epistle he appeals to a contemporary's assessment of Erasmus as "very wise and learned ... a man who has read and understood all the worth-while writers of the world." More than a decade later Menno explicitly commended Erasmus's New Testament annotations to the fugitive leader's non-Catholic readers.[38] In short, Menno Simons may have left the Catholic Church in 1536, but he remained theologically tied to at least the *Devotio Moderna* movement and the theological positions taken by Erasmus. Menno's embrace of a "practical-experiential piety" founded in the "solitary and suffering Christ" and his devaluation of the priestly role in the assurance of individual salvation came naturally to him from developments within the Catholic Church that anticipated the Protestant Reformation.[39]

Yet, if there are continuities, Menno Simons also represented a significant rupture from Rome as he opened a door that has long been associated with the birth of *The Secular Age*. In Charles Taylor's telling of it, the premodern European world circa 1500 was defined by a belief that the natural world had a God-given role to play within the cosmos; that "God was implicated in the very existence of society"; and, finally, that the world was itself "enchanted," a world of "spirits, demons, and moral forces."[40]

Taylor suggests that the modern world shifted dramatically away from each of these assumptions. What of Mennonites, or at least, what of Menno Simons and his theology? The question is highly relevant in a study such as this one, as identity markers will be of particular interest to me, and particularly given that many have long ascribed the role of modernists to Mennonites. If that ascription is true, was the seedbed for that already prepared by Melchior, Menno, and the rest of the early Anabaptists? Though Menno clearly and steadfastly professed the first two of Taylor's identity markers, he was less categorical when it came to the third. After all, for Menno, the supposed sacrament of the Last Supper was merely symbolic, as was baptism. As has been discussed at various points throughout this study, neither played a salvific role as such. Nor could believers rely on the prayers of the saints to intercede for them, and even Christ (for Melchior and Menno) was deemed fully divine but not fully human. No wonder that some commentators have concluded that Menno promoted a rationalistic faith, one that disregarded the traditions of the larger church.[41] Did all this represent a first step by Menno and his followers into Taylor's Secular Age? Perhaps, though it was still too early to tell in the Netherlands of the mid-sixteenth century. However, from here we shift away from Anabaptist beginnings to the Mennonites of northern Europe, and Poland, *en route* to the Russian empire.

Chapter Three

A Faith Community on the Move: Mennonites, Poland, and Prussia, 1536–1800

Dutch Mennonites who settled in the Russian empire after 1789 joined countless other immigrants through time and space when they named their new villages after those they left behind, including – in their case – the villages of Ladekopp, Einlage, Schönhorst, Fishau, Fürstenwerder, and Lichtenau.[1] That will not surprise, though it may to realize that the erstwhile homeland they thereby commemorated was not the Dutch Republic. Instead, those first Mennonites who settled the Black Sea steppe carried with them the memory of village life in Royal Prussia, Kingdom Poland, most especially Danzig and environs where they and their forebears had lived for almost two hundred years. Indeed, it is one of the ironies of their history that a people who would later identify themselves as Russian Mennonites or Russian Germans had lived much longer in Polish lands than in the land of tsars and Soviets.

This chapter considers the two dynamic processes by which Dutch Anabaptists became Polish/Prussian Mennonites. By the first, we pick up the story that began in the previous chapter when Dutch Anabaptists endured intense persecution across the Spanish Netherlands in the 1530s. It then spread from the north to the southern Netherlands, where it continued off and on until the end of the century. During that time many Anabaptists – of whom the majority were soon identified as Mennonites – sought haven in Poland. We will also consider those factors that made the port city of Danzig and its environs such an attractive destination for Mennonites in particular.

Second, this chapter considers the dynamic way by which Mennonites transformed their identities given the relative tolerance they experienced in Poland, northern Germany, and the Netherlands after 1600. Under these changed circumstances Mennonites could hardly regard themselves as a persecuted people by the dawn of the seventeenth century, even as they themselves worked to enshrine the earlier Anabaptist martyrdom into their foundation myth. Mennonites became necessarily political in this period, even if full political involvement eluded them. To safeguard their place within Polish – and later Prussian – society Mennonites relied on negotiated Privilegia with local and state authorities. These Privilegia are of particular interest because it is by this very method that Mennonites in 1789 established their first colony in the Russian empire.

Political stability and economic prosperity led to significant changes within Mennonite communities in Royal Prussia, as we shall see. To give but one example, Mennonites became increasingly orthodox theologically and structurally as they sought to demonstrate their similarities with other Christian faiths to safeguard their position within society. That said, they continued to struggle with what it meant to be separate from a fallen world given the speed with which they acculturated to it. This struggle partly resulted in a Frisian/Flemish division that threatened any coherent Mennonite identity both in Poland and later in the Russian empire, even as other divisions disappeared.

Persecution eased first in the northern Netherlands and only much later in the south, where they had been effectively expunged from the southern Netherlands by 1600, either through martyrdom or flight. However, the northern Netherlands by that point had become a sanctuary of toleration for Anabaptists, Jews, and others, such that Anabaptist congregations remain there to the present day. The internal dynamism in the Polish lands of Royal Prussia were fundamentally different. There were no Mennonite martyrs in Royal Prussia, as Dutch Anabaptists were tolerated from the start, even though they had to pay, literally, for their exemption from military service. In addition, Mennonites were denied a formal role in politics, although that did not stop them from being actively engaged in economic and cultural aspects of society. So it was that Mennonites prospered in Poland for more than two hundred years.

The First Shift: Mennonite Migration from the Low Countries to Poland

Many Dutch and Flemish Mennonites migrated to Poland over the sixteenth century as they sought to evade persecution in their homelands. Available data will not allow us to tease Mennonites out from other Anabaptists in the Low Countries, especially as thousands of Anabaptists who stayed in the Netherlands never explicitly identified themselves as followers of Menno. However, all Anabaptists were subject to capital punishment when the Holy Roman Emperor issued a series of edicts following the Münster debacle of 1534–5, and at a time when local sympathy for this fledgling movement had evaporated.[2] Magistrates executed the greatest number of Anabaptists in the 1530s – reaching upwards of two hundred in Amsterdam alone – though the pattern of their subsequent persecution differed from north to south.

Authorities responded with malice aforethought in the Dutch north after many chose to be rebaptized in the provinces of Holland, Friesland, and Groningen. Even after the high-water mark for persecution had been reached in the 1530s, magistrates continued to drown, decapitate, or burn Anabaptists at the stake for decades. For example, Hippolytus Persijn, president of the Court of Friesland, issued dire warnings into the 1550s about the increase in religious heretics whom he alleged had rejected the sacraments, engaged in brazen acts of thievery, and plotted to exterminate all Christians. It did not help that Mennonites and other Anabaptists worshipped primarily at night for reasons of personal safety and were therefore vulnerable to accusations that they were possessed by demons.[3] Unwittingly, Reytse Ayssesz became the last Mennonite martyr in the Dutch north when she was drowned on 23 April 1574 in Leeuwarden, the provincial capital of Friesland. Within a decade of her death the United Provinces of northern Netherlands declared their independence from Spanish rule, and with it ushered in an era of significant religious toleration.[4] By then, however, a host of Dutch Anabaptist followers of Menno had fled eastward, even as others had remained, and would soon be an integral part of a self-described Dutch Golden Age.

The story unfolded somewhat differently in the southern Netherlands, where the Spanish grip was unrelentingly harsh for the entire sixteenth century, even as Anabaptist Mennonitism always seemed to find new converts. A.L.E. Verheyden has concluded that Melchiorite teaching had penetrated the Flemish cities of Bruges and Ghent by the early 1530s thanks to the peripatetic movement of Anabaptist merchants and artisans across the Netherlands.[5] Though some were tempted by the Münsterite example to seize earthly power in the south after 1534, even more desisted, such that Menno's appeal for a peaceful Anabaptism found a ready audience there from the mid-1530s onward. As with the Netherlands, the first Anabaptist converts in the south were a mixture of artisans, merchants, and those formerly in religious orders. Hundreds were attracted to this movement, as we know from the fact that publishers in Antwerp had released six hundred copies of Menno Simons' writings in 1544 alone for distribution, at the very time when Calvinist preachers also began to make inroads.

With such impressive sectarian growth, the empire could be counted on to strike back, especially as its hold on the largely Catholic south was much greater than the Dutch north. Successive Habsburg emperors Charles V and Philip II worked determinedly to exterminate the Protestant scourge throughout the Netherlands, though they were much more successful in the south, where their power was largely unassailable. Gary Waite has shown that Anabaptists comprised a preponderance of all Protestants who were tried and executed, including 58 per cent of all martyrs in Ghent, 67 per cent in Bruges, and 60 per cent in Brussels. Even in jurisdictions where Anabaptists were a minority among those tried in the sixteenth century, as was the case in Brabant (they comprised only 26.8 per cent, as Calvinists and Lutherans also suffered), Mennonites still comprised a staggering 87 per cent of those executed.[6] Local officials in the south who relented from such violent acts, as happened briefly when regent Margaret of Parma urged tolerance in the mid-1560s, incited the empire to ever fiercer responses. In this instance, the Duke of Alva initiated a particularly bloody attack on Anabaptists when he was appointed governor of the Netherlands under Philip II in 1567. Those victimized by his brutal inquisition into the Protestant disturbances of the previous year referred to it as the "Court of Blood" for the executions he ordered. Jan van Paris, Pieter van Cleves, Hendrick Maelshalck, and Lauwerens Pieters were typical in this regard. All four were captured in the Flemish city of Ghent in January 1568, even though they were Anabaptist novices who had yet to be baptized. They were taken to the count's castle, where all professed their newfound faith to the Spanish provost. All were subsequently sentenced to death during Passion Week of that year. They were strangled and burned by Spanish soldiers who had been brought into Flanders for this very purpose.[7] It was under the Duke of Alva's watch that the northern Netherlands withdrew from the Holy Roman Empire, an event which coincided with the final Anabaptist execution in the newly formed Dutch Republic in 1574. By contrast, the final execution of an Anabaptist in the south occurred a generation later, in 1598, by which time most of the Flemish Anabaptists had fled to the Dutch north or beyond.[8]

There were other differences between the north and south. Unlike their experience in the Dutch north, Anabaptist converts in the Flemish south explicitly identified with Menno Simons from the middle of the sixteenth century onward, including during times of the new sect's greatest growth. Southern publishers actively reproduced Menno's writings and widely distributed them by at least 1544. Surprisingly, Flemish Mennonite Anabaptism appears to have flourished in the 1550s as persecution intensified and as preachers such as Joachim Vermeeren

A Faith Community on the Move 53

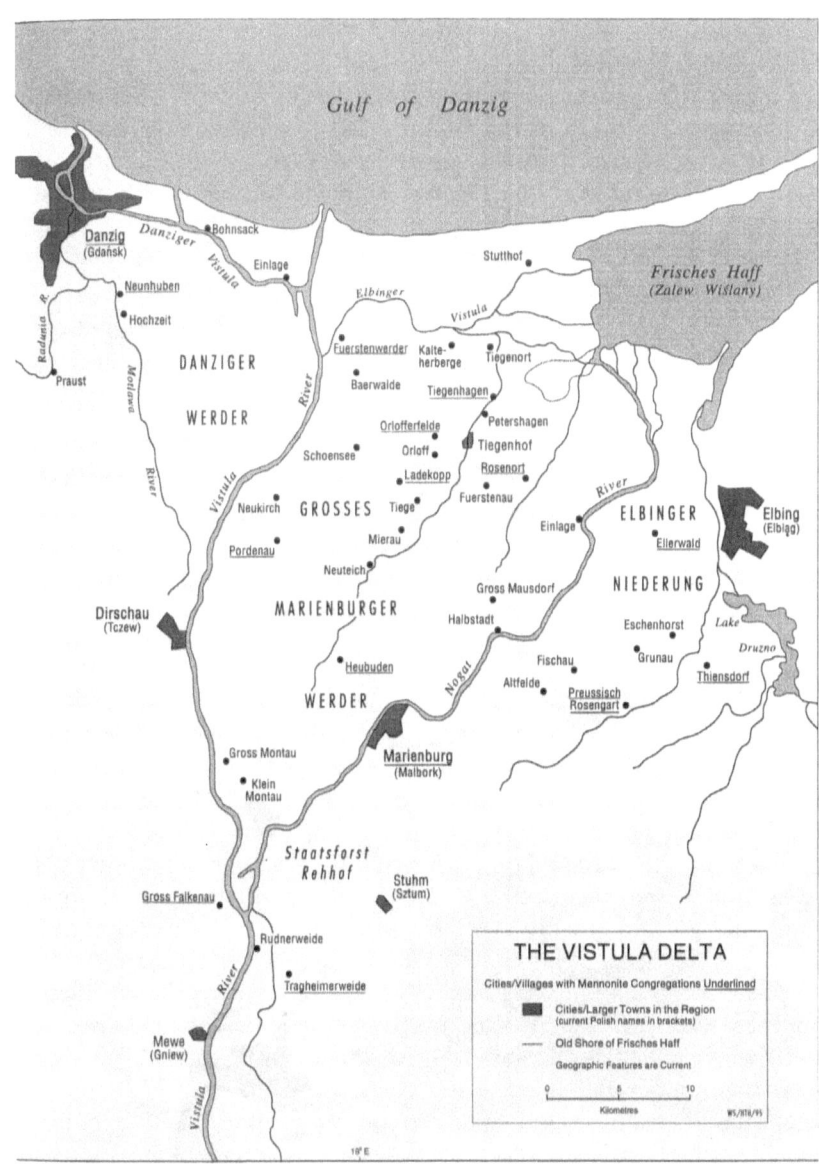

Map 1. The Vistula Delta. From William Schroeder and Helmut T. Huebert, *Mennonite Historical Atlas*, Second Edition. Used by permission of Augusta Schroeder and Dorothy Hubert.

actively propagated Menno's teachings. No wonder Brad Gregory concludes that "martyrological self-awareness" catalysed many Anabaptist separatists.[9] Those who escaped execution in the south soon joined their northern co-religionists as they found sanctuary elsewhere. Already in 1550 preachers in southern Netherlands, such as Jan van Sol, reported that Mennonite congregations were openly taking shape far to the Baltic east in the port city of Danzig. But why Danzig?

Several reasons present themselves. For one, Poland was eager to settle the entire Vistula delta after it had defeated the Teutonic Order of Knights in 1466. The subsequent Treaty of Thorn recognized the Polish crown's suzerainty over the delta and environs, which included the port city of Danzig. Significantly, Prussian estate owners in the environs of Danzig had allied themselves with the Poles against the Teutonic knights, as did Prussian merchants and urban inhabitants in Danzig itself, along with neighbouring Elbing. It helped that the Polish crown had promised Prussians a considerable measure of political autonomy in exchange for their support against the knights. With that, the semi-autonomous territory of Royal Prussia was formed within Poland after 1466. It continued to enjoy relative autonomy until 1772.[10]

Although Danzig had been an important port city on the Baltic since well before the Polish victory of 1466, its commercial significance grew exponentially thereafter as an unprecedented urbanization in Europe's Low Countries – the birthplace of the Mennonites – and England fuelled the demand for Polish grain across Northern Europe. All that Polish grain reached European markets by way of Danzig, which was one more reason why Prussian merchants were so eager to strike a condominium with the Polish crown in 1466; it gave them unrivalled access both to the Polish hinterland and Dutch markets. Dutch shipping companies moved quickly to seize control of the transshipment of Polish grains, timber, and hemp to Amsterdam, and salt, spices, almonds, and other products back to Poland. It helped that many Dutch citizens migrated eastward at this time and cemented relations between the two major port cities. Though only 11 Dutch ships reached Danzig in 1460, the number ballooned to 160 by 1475 and 235 by 1530. A century later more than a thousand ships arrived per annum at Danzig as from 84,000 to 100,000 tons of grain moved eastward each year.[11] It is for good reason that Baltic merchants viewed the Dutch economy as the "*moedercommercie* (mother of all commerce)."[12]

Thus, Flemish and Dutch Mennonites who were eager to flee their homelands in the sixteenth century wisely made their way to Danzig and its environs. Rumours even circulated among Swiss Anabaptists in the late 1520s that an end to persecution awaited them in the Vistula delta, though most Anabaptist refugees arrived from the Netherlands after 1530,[13] much to the chagrin of those who opposed the resettlement of Mennonites to Poland. Officials were deeply suspicious of any sect associated with the Münster rebellion of 1534, especially after a group of Anabaptist Melchiorites known as the Batenburgers kept the Melchiorite spirit of open rebellion alive after Münster. Known also as the *Zwaardgeesten* (sword-minded), these followers of Jan van Batenburg engaged in acts of arson, robbery, and murder across the Dutch lands for decades until finally suppressed. What guarantee was there that the newly arrived followers of Menno would not travel down the same path as these *Zwaardgeesten*?

For their part, Mennonites refused to be associated with the Batenburgers and denounced the latter's support of the Münster rebellion. Nevertheless, Mennonites' steadfast refusal to swear oaths of allegiance to the state, or to serve in the military, meant they were not welcomed everywhere. Despite initial uncertainties, then, conditions were right in Poland for new Mennonite beginnings.

The Second Shift: From Martyrdom to Accommodation within Poland

Mennonites experienced more than a geographic shift when they migrated to Poland from the Spanish Netherlands, as their identities were profoundly reshaped in their new homeland. Three aspects of this transformation are worth our attention, all of which point to the broader integration of Mennonites into the larger society around them.

Mennonites as Economic Actors

Dutch immigrants, including Mennonites, were initially welcomed in Kingdom Poland because of their ability to secure the productivity of marsh and river delta lands immediately adjacent to the growing port cities of Danzig and Elbing. Though Danzig had been constructed as the seaport of a complex for seven navigable rivers that flowed into the Vistula River, the Vistula delta itself was low lying. Ironically, Danzig's merchants by the early sixteenth century had successfully managed to transport grains to market from the Carpathians a thousand kilometres away but were unable to profit from lands immediately adjacent to their city.[14] Farmers had unsuccessfully attempted to secure those delta lands (known as *werder*) through a network of dykes and dams for centuries, but with no lasting success. They left behind abandoned homesteads and underutilized werder. A contemporary noted: "Anno

1540 on February 22 the Vistula dike broke ... Many cattle drowned and the waters flowed all the way into Danzig, all the way to the fish market ... One could go by boat from the storage granaries to the werder."[15] Historian Peter Klassen records how in 1547 the city of Danzig sent its representative Philip Edzema to the Netherlands in the hopes that he would find settlers able to restore the city's floodplains and werders to full productivity. Mennonites, at that time in the throes of Hapsburg persecution, were among those who accepted the invitation to resettle, and the success of their endeavour was soon apparent. Within a decade the city council reported the following in response to those who complained that sectarian Mennonites had begun to settle in large numbers in their midst:

> Villages [in the Danzig werder] that used to have 15, 16 or 20 farmers before the flooding now have few or none at all. One can imagine the financial loss to Your Majesty's city of Danzig as the income declined. When the administrators of this area urged the remaining farmers to take better care of dikes and drainage channels, they encountered resistance, as well as refusal to carry out the necessary maintenance ... When we saw our efforts were fruitless, some people from the Netherlands as though guided by fate came to us and offered their help. To these persons we offered the deserted lands of the low-lying village of Landau and asked them to restore it at no cost to us. For this, we offered them four years with no payment to us ... These Netherlanders, gracious king, in short time have created wonderful drained land, so that instead of the desolate acres we now have 27 rent-paying farms. The new settlers have increased our annual income from 39 marks to 108 marks. We have recognized the outstanding industry and skilled planning ... of these Netherlanders and have taken them into the ranks of regular farmers.[16]

Mennonites also quickly established themselves within the burgeoning cities of Danzig and Elbing, which should not surprise given the close link between Anabaptist beginnings and Dutch and Flemish artisanal trades. Mennonites may have initially been denied residency within Danzig itself, but Catholic ecclesiastics soon and enthusiastically invited them onto their lands for the income they generated. Mennonites excelled as bakers, tailors, metal workers, distillers, weavers, and cobblers, so much so that the most persistent opposition to their activity came from the various guilds that saw their monopolies threatened. Beyond work undertaken in the Vistula delta, Mennonites also connected to a vast network of co-religionists in the seventeenth century who stretched back to the Dutch cities of Zaandam, Amsterdam, and

Haarlingen, as well as the German city of Hamburg, where Mennonites controlled most of the herring and whaling industries, along with several shipyards.[17]

Though demographic accuracy remains elusive, Edmund Kizik has concluded that Mennonites remained a small and predominantly rural minority within the Vistula delta. He maintains that there were fewer than 13,000 Mennonites at their peak in the 1770s, or about 3 per cent of the entire region. Of these, a few hundred may have lived in Danzig and Elbing, respectively. Mennonites did comprise almost a fifth of all inhabitants of Marienwerder, and closer to 10 per cent in the area adjacent to Elbing, and it was here that so many Mennonites lived in villages that their descendants would eventually replicate as they migrated to the Russian empire. Occasionally Mennonites occupied entire villages, though there are also numerous instances, as with Montauerweide in Marienwerder, for example, where Mennonite households lived in a mixed settlement with Lutheran households.[18] However small their numbers were in absolute demographic terms, Mennonites punched above their weight as their economic prowess grew over the centuries. Nor was this merely of economic significance, as it signalled a second great shift in Mennonite identity formation; one no less dramatic than the shift from the Netherlands to Poland's Vistula delta.

Mennonites as Political Actors

Mennonites found themselves in an enviable position by the mid-sixteenth century as the years of intense persecution faded into the distant past. By then both the Dutch Republic and Poland had granted them a qualified freedom to worship, along with an exemption from military service, through a series of legal contracts or privilegia which Mennonites had negotiated with local authorities. It is worth spending some time on these agreements given the significant role they play in Russian Mennonite historiography and the manner in which Mennonites came to rethink their place within the larger world as they negotiated their place within society. James Urry, historian of Russian Mennonites, has demonstrated how important privilegia were to Mennonites from the sixteenth century on, and at a time when ecclesiastical law was giving way to secular state-driven law.

Times were changing. The Treaty of Westphalia in 1648 that brought an end to the bitter Thirty Years' War across much of Europe gave political rulers the exclusive right to determine the state religion in their lands. A representative constitutional text from 1603 declared: "Because unity in religion is also the true bond of freedom and trust in political affairs; therefore, in this city and its associated churches and congregations the true, pure religion ... will be held to firmly and, by the grace of Almighty God, will be propagated for posterity."[19] Though this worked well for Catholics in France or Poland, Calvinists in the Dutch Republic, and Lutherans in many of the north German states, it offered little to Mennonites, Jews, and other minorities, let alone for Calvinists in Poland or Catholics in Prussia. Minority rights within the emerging European statecraft had to be established and negotiated with individual rulers, and rights granted "in perpetuity" had to be renegotiated when rulers died and their successors came to the throne.[20]

Even negotiated privilegia rarely afforded Mennonites equal treatment with others at the political level. For example, almost all jurisdictions denied them the right to hold political office though their economic prowess was such that several Mennonites headed the Danzig Chamber of Commerce in the seventeenth century. Authorities in the Polish city of Elbing first granted Mennonites citizenship rights and then revoked them as late as 1684.[21] This is why privilegia mattered; they allowed non-citizens – like Mennonites in seventeenth-century Holland and Poland – to secure rights which their non-sectarian counterparts had received as a matter of course. For example, Michael Driedger describes the privilegium of 1601, which granted François Noë, brothers Cornelius and Hans Simons, and brothers Walrave and Hilger Hilgers the right to trade in luxury goods in Altona, a Danish holding north of the city of Hamburg, even as it denied them the right to worship publicly. Most privilegia also denied Mennonites the right to proselytize, something that would have been difficult in any event in Poland given the persistence of the Dutch language among Mennonite settlers.

Military exemptions came at a cost, as Mennonites commonly paid an extra tax in order to be exempt from both military service and the obligation to quarter troops, and they paid even more in times of war, as when the city of Elbing in Royal Prussia was occupied by the Swedes and Poles in succession during the Great Northern War (1700–21). Lastly, Mennonites occasionally objected to conditions imposed on them, as when Mennonite business leaders in Danzig appealed to the city council that they be freed from paying Lutheran church dues at a time when Mennonites were denied their own places of worship. Though unsuccessful, the appeal process itself made plain the emerging Mennonite identify of self-representation and political engagement within the limits proscribed by the state.[22]

Mennonites benefited economically and politically by the highly fractious political landscape in the Vistula river delta. Any unified opposition to Mennonite immigration required the unlikely alliance of the Polish crown, various ecclesiastical authorities, guilds, large estate owners, and relatively independent city councils, especially in Elbing[23] and Danzig. Mennonite economic success in any one jurisdiction soon drew the attention of neighbouring jurisdictions, and even those initially opposed soon saw the advantages that these sectarians could bring them. Second, the landscape was also fragmented religiously as Catholic Poland and the largely Lutheran urban populations lived in relatively close quarters, along with the coincidental immigration of Dutch Calvinists, all of whom made a unified religious opposition to Mennonite immigration difficult. Jews also experienced a greater leniency within the diverse religious and political jurisdictions of the Vistula river delta.

Mennonites actively negotiated such privilegia with all manner of ecclesiastical and secular authorities, and if the political path to full citizenship remained closed to them, the economic one had largely opened by 1600. This is where Mennonites thrived, though their mark in Danzig also carried a robustly artistic signature thanks to Willem van den Blocke and his sons. In some ways Willem encapsulates the migrational movement of this chapter. Born in 1550 in the southern (Spanish) Netherlands and of Flemish nationality, Willem and his family fled northward to the Dutch Republic to escape persecution. The son of a sculptor, Willem entered his father's profession, first in Königsberg (East Prussia) where they initially settled, and on to Danzig in 1584. Along the way, the Mennonite Willem had numerous commissions, though none more impressive than when he constructed the Prussian city's so-called High Gate. Completed in 1588, and ornamented in the style of the Italian Renaissance, it remains a landmark within the city. Of his three sons, all of whom carried on their father's creative work, the most noteworthy was Isaak, also a Mennonite, who in 1608 painted the high ceiling of Danzig's city hall. Composed of twenty-five distinct paintings, each on a separate oak panel, he called his crowning jewel the Apotheosis of Danzig. It featured a rainbow which united the Vistula River with Danzig, over which the hand of God reached down in blessing. By this means Isaak celebrated Danzig as the successful marriage of the secular and sacred. Isaak van den Blocke's decision to paint the ceiling in the *au courant* Northern Mannerist style suggests the degree to which he followed the cultural trends of his day. As one of Danzig's leading painters, city officials later commissioned Isaak to complete an additional four-painting cycle of Old Testament themes for the Treasury Department of the City Hall building.[24] Gone it seemed, was a Melchiorite and Mennonite separation between the church and the world. Could it be any different for his Mennonite co-religionists by the start of the seventeenth century?

"Obedient Heretics": Mennonites and the Faith in Royal Prussia

Michael Driedger applies the felicitous term "Obedient Heretics" to Mennonites in Hamburg and environs in the seventeenth century. The term allows Driedger to tease out two strands of north German Mennonite identity: that they were "religious non-conformists" in that they parted ways with Roman Catholics and Lutherans alike, and that they believed it was possible to live in obedience both to Christ and to their political overlords. Driedger thereby refutes an earlier historiography which stressed Mennonite non-conformism and non-engagement with the larger society. Instead he suggests that Mennonites were only selectively religious nonconformists as they quickly became political conformists. Even on matters theological and ecclesial Mennonites moved towards a greater theological orthodoxy as time progressed.[25] Though Driedger is primarily concerned with Hamburg and environs, the high degree of overlap in the sixteenth and seventeenth centuries among the Dutch, German, and Royal Prussian (Polish) Mennonite communities means we can grasp a fuller picture of Mennonites and their faith in Royal Prussia through a consideration of the region as a whole.[26]

Mennonite theological and confessional understandings were dramatically transformed during this era of increased religious toleration across the Baltic. In some ways, this happened naturally as the cessation of persecution and socio-economic acculturation challenged Menno's original declaration that his followers were a persecuted minority, an isolated outpost of heaven, all of which stressed the incompatibilities between Mennonites and the world around them. Writing in 1997, James Stayer argued that the so-called Radical Reformation which gave birth to the Mennonites quickly became moderate in many of its positions. Among its earliest leaders, Stayer argued that Menno Simons was someone who was able to extend "gestures of adaptation and accommodation to the surrounding world."[27]

Confessions of Faith were a key element of Mennonite "adaptation and accommodation," even after Menno.[28] One of the first Confessions of Faith was written by the Dutch "Waterlander" Church (recall that Anabaptists in the Netherlands did not identify themselves explicitly with Menno) in 1577, though various other confessions soon followed. In many instances, Mennonites across northern Europe adopted these Confessions, some of which were subsequently brought to the Russian empire. These Confessions sent powerful signals about Mennonite identity for adherents and detractors alike. For one, they stressed that Mennonites were essentially orthodox Christians, a vital signal to send at a time when the emerging state structures demanded uniformity of belief, a trend buttressed by the formation of Catholic, Lutheran, and Reformed state churches across Europe.[29] Under this circumstance, Mennonites who hoped to avoid persecution had no choice but to demonstrate their orthodoxy to these state churches and their political patrons. This was especially important given that Menno Simons himself had denied – following Hoffman – that Christ had been both fully human and fully divine, a denial that opened his followers up to the charge of heresy. No wonder that most Mennonite confessions, in ironic contrast to their progenitor, began by stressing their Christian orthodoxy, especially as it pertained to the two-fold nature of Christ. Mennonites grounded their Confessions in the ancient creeds of the church, especially the Apostolic, which also suggested larger ties across Christendom. Mennonite hymnody reflected this change. Whereas the first Anabaptist hymns had been composed by their earliest followers, Mennonites in Poland increasingly adopted Reformed and Lutheran hymns for their worship services. The message was clear: their Anabaptist forbears may have claimed during the initial phase that they alone were the One True Church, but Mennonites by the seventeenth century had begun to abandon such claims in favour of pan-Christian identities.[30]

Secondly, Confessions of Faith also allowed Mennonites to entrench their loyalty to the states in which they resided. They consistently proclaimed the legitimacy of state authority and the importance of Mennonite subservience to those magistrates except in rare instances where they conflicted with "the Word of God." In their own words, Mennonites desired "to live in quiet and peace and to be obedient to the authorities in all matters which are not against God and our consciences."[31] Though Mennonites normally rooted this perspective in theological language and biblical verses, Troy Osborne has concluded that Mennonites by the late sixteenth century based their argument for toleration on their long history of obedient and meritorious behaviour to the state, as well as to the orthodoxy of their beliefs.[32]

But Mennonites wanted to accomplish much more with their Confessions than affirm their Christian orthodoxy. At the same time, these Confessions had to justify Mennonite exceptionalism, a challenge that was all the greater because of the plethora of Anabaptist and Mennonite movements that emerged in the first half of the sixteenth century. Mennonites at this time varied endlessly on matters of faith and practice, most especially the latter given their conviction that the redeemed of

Christ should be expected to live sinless lives. It followed that those who fell short needed to be removed from the church if their failings were deemed sufficiently egregious. But deemed by whom, for what sin(s), and to what degree? Should a wife be expected to shun a husband who had been placed under the ban by the church? These matters were endlessly and passionately debated by early Mennonites at a time when they had hoped to achieve a greater confessional unity. And although such overall unity remained elusive, newly formed Confessions allowed Mennonites to form vibrant congregations, even at a time (in Poland, but generally across North Europe) when Mennonites were still denied the right to build their own church buildings. In Urry's words, Mennonite believers and congregations utilized their newly formed Confessions to both unite and separate.[33]

By way of internal religious divisions, the most noteworthy for our study occurred when Mennonites across northern Europe formed Flemish and Frisian congregations. Though initially this division reflected an ethnic division between the Dutch north and the Flemish south, it had lost its ethnic character by the time of resettlement to Kingdom Poland. Nor was this division rooted in dogmatic differences. Instead, Flemish and Frisians differed most vehemently on the use of the ban and some "external customs," though even here it is difficult to be specific.[34] Take this attempt to identify the Flemish/Frisian divide by historian Edward Kizik: "Contemporary reports regard the Frisians as the more conservative of the two groups, in that their dress was modest and their homes frugally appointed, although this did not prevent them from hoarding luxuries." Mennonite Frisians and Mennonite Flemish established separate churches across northern Europe and into the Russian empire, though Mennonites in Kingdom Poland occasionally shared the same visiting preachers from the Netherlands regardless of the Frisian–Flemish distinction.[35]

As importantly, Flemish and Frisian Mennonites came together at crucial points, even after they formally separated in 1566. They negotiated with one voice for their various privilegia in Kingdom Poland and beyond, even if periodic attempts to unify their congregations failed. They also widely shared Mennonite congregational structures and worship practices. They quickly formed congregations of between 500 and 1,500 souls upon settlement in Kingdom Poland, and often decades before authorities allowed them to construct actual churches. In fact, Mennonites in Danzig met in homes for more than a century before they were permitted to construct their first Frisian and Flemish churches (in 1638 and 1648, respectively). Mennonites outside of Danzig fared better, as authorities permitted Mennonites in the village of Muntau to erect a church building in 1586, four years before one was permitted in the port city of Elbing.[36] Mennonites in Royal Prussia adopted worship practices similar to what they had experienced in the Netherlands, a pattern reinforced when authorities did not permit them to print religious materials in Danzig. Most chose to print materials in the Netherlands instead, which underpinned their use of Dutch as the language of worship. Ministers read from the Bible and exhorted the flock in often lengthy sermons. Congregations encouraged singing unless authorities had banned worship services as a whole, though they set aside plain musical forms of the sixteenth century by the late seventeenth century as Mennonites introduced organs into their newly established churches.

Other changes were also evident. In particular, the last Dutch hymnal used by "Polish" Mennonites was printed in the Netherlands in 1752, and expressly for the churches in Danzig and its hinterland, though Mennonites by then had also begun to utilize German-language materials. They subsequently printed many of their worship materials in Danzig and Elbing, which marked a significant step into the largely Germanic culture of Polish Royal Prussia. Mennonites appointed ministers from among their midst as well as deacons who were charged with mutual aid in the event of fire or flood, or for the widowed and otherwise destitute in their midst. Also, from the outset Mennonites elected Ältester from the previously elected ministers. Ältester, variously translated as "elder" or "bishop" comprised the highest ministerial authority and oversaw the ministers who together formed the ministry council (Lehrdienst). Ältester preached, ordained ministers – who assisted in the preaching – served communion, and baptized new believers.[37]

Future church growth depended on immigration from the Netherlands and, even more so, the baptism of Mennonite youth. Parents expected their children to seek baptism in their early twenties, though it was not unusual for those over thirty to request it. Thus, "believers' baptism" was voluntary but expected. Churches baptized the youth in specially designated services held once or twice a year, and as such signified one of the distinct markers which separated Mennonites out from other Christians. The other was the Mennonite foundational commitment to pacifism and their refusal to serve in any army. Although Mennonites successfully negotiated for an exemption from military service in their various privilegia in Kingdom Poland, it did come at a cost. In a single seven-year span between 1665 and 1672 Mennonites in the Netherlands paid over a million guilders to free themselves from military duty, while those in Royal Prussia faced similar demands.[38] In other instances Mennonites in the Polish lands only secured the right to worship in their own homes once they had paid their state-enforced church dues, regardless of whether they were destined for Catholic or Lutheran coffers. Part of the Mennonite politicization of space came as they protested those very dues, the payment for which they blamed on the various guilds they competed with at an economic level.

There was one additional price Mennonites in Royal Prussia were ready to pay, and it had to do with proselytization. Briefly put, authorities forbade it and Mennonites largely acquiesced, which is one of the reasons why even the publication of Mennonite worship materials was long banned in Danzig. Some Poles did convert to the Mennonite faith, as is evident from the addition of a string of "Slavic" names into the Mennonite fold, including Sawatsky, Rogalsky, and Shapansky. Such conversions normally happened when Mennonites lived in villages that were not exclusively theirs, and even then congregations normally sent Catholic converts to the Netherlands, where they were baptized into the new faith before returning to Kingdom Poland, often for marriage to a Mennonite. Some villages in Prussia were particularly noted for their converts to the Mennonite faith, including Ladekopp and Tiegenhagen.[39] In other instances it was Mennonites who converted to the dominant faith, but the net effect was the same. Mennonite reluctance to proselytize did more than satisfy the demands of the state, and the state church not to steal away its members. It also allowed Mennonite ministers to maintain notions of moral purity and boundary maintenance at a time of increased acculturation and socio-economic integration.

The Martyrs' Mirror amid Prosperity and Acculturation

Mennonites across Europe enjoyed vastly different lives by the seventeenth and early eighteenth centuries than had their earliest namesakes, or the Anabaptists who preceded them. From persecution to prosperity they had entered the mainstream of society even if full political rights still eluded them.[40] They largely secured a place within Dutch, German, and Royal Prussian society thanks to their economic prowess and civil subservience on all but a handful of non-negotiable issues. Even then, they happily paid the state handsomely for the right of military exemption, itself not an issue in this time prior to universal military conscription. Ironically, they objected to the payment of church dues to Lutherans and Catholics but not to the upkeep of navies and armies. In so many ways the Mennonites fit well in a Golden Age that may have been primarily identified with Holland but which, in truth, spread across the north to the gateway city of Danzig. But the more they fit in, the more it raised questions about Mennonite identity. Who were they in this state of increased accommodation beyond their Flemish and Frisian ancestry with a sprinkling of Poles thrown in? No wonder historian Gary Waite initially concludes that Mennonites, after the debacle of Münster, "gave up their charismatic past and moved toward a more rationalistic, Protestant form of piety."[41]

It is into this place of an identity seemingly adrift that Mennonite leaders and publicists responded with a new identity marker: Mennonites as martyrs of the One True Church. As noted earlier, Anabaptists had begun to collect martyrologies in the mid-sixteenth century, when persecution was at its height. Anonymously released pamphlets were already in circulation by 1539 and told the stories of individual persecutions. Then in 1563 a compilation of the Dutch Anabaptist martyr stories was released with the evocative title *Het offer des Heeren* (The Sacrifice of the Lord). Further editions soon followed, and all proved extremely popular, especially after the time of persecution had ended.[42] Almost a century later the Dutch Anabaptist Thieleman Janszoon van Braght published the masterwork, entitled *The Bloody Theater or Martyrs Mirror of the Defenseless Christians who baptized only upon confession of faith, and who suffered and died for the testimony of Jesus, their Saviour, from the time of Christ to the year A.D. 1660*. Van Braght's work brought three key features together, all of which say a great deal about evolving Mennonite identity in the mid-seventeenth century: first, his work began with Confessional statements which pointed to both Mennonite Trinitarian orthodoxy and Mennonite exceptionalism; second, he directly tied Anabaptist martyrs to Stephen and the martyrs of the early church, thereby suggesting that Mennonites were the true continuation of the apostolic church and that Rome was not; and third, he made it plain that Mennonites were born in martyrdom and still owed their faith to those who suffered and died. It was clear that prosperous and increasingly acculturated Mennonites living in the Dutch Republic, the German lands, and Royal Prussia would have much to ponder when it came to the roots of their faith. As it happened, they would soon need to address the increasingly fine line that separated their coincidental positions of accommodation and resistance, this time from within a Kingdom of Poland that was about to undergo its own hour of tribulation.

PART II

Mennonites in Imperial Russia

Chapter Four

A New Homeland in New Russia: Mennonite Settlement in the Russian Empire, 1789–1830

Mennonites who attended a packed Saturday morning event convened by the Russian Consul to Danzig on 19 January 1788 must have found it too good to be true. They came to hear firsthand that the Russian empress Catherine II had invited them to migrate to the Russian empire and settle on recently conquered lands north of the Black Sea. Their anticipation had been building for months, ever since their co-religionists Jakob Höppner and Johann Bartsch had returned to Danzig in the fall of 1787 after a year of travel in search of a new Mennonite homeland in the Russian empire. Initial returns looked promising as Catherine had even granted the two an audience in Kremenchug as she travelled southward to inspect the region, which officials formally named New Russia, a clear indication of the promise it held for her empire. Höppner and Bartsch accepted Catherine's spontaneous invitation to travel with her retinue to Crimea. Along the way they explored possible lands for large-scale Mennonite settlement. After much deliberation, the two scouts selected a site on the lower Dnieper River near the Black Sea coast and just upstream from the emerging port city of Kherson. Here they envisioned a substantial Mennonite colony, one that would replicate the world of Danzig and environs that had been their homeland for more than two hundred years. In their efforts, the two Mennonite representatives were escorted by Georg Trappe, the Russian official tasked with wooing Mennonites and Germans alike to settle in New Russia.[1]

Mighty oaks from tiny acorns grow, and within a year more than a thousand Mennonites were on their way from Danzig to the Russian empire. In barely more than a century Mennonites in the empire had grown to over one hundred thousand, by which time they were dispersed far and wide across the south, from the Dnieper to the Volga and well into Siberia. This chapter tells the story of Mennonite beginnings in the Russian empire, and most especially how these Dutch sectarians

Figure 2. Henry Pauls, "Bernhard and Helene Pauls Farmstead, Island of Chortitza," 1975. Conrad Grebel University College. Photograph by Mary C. Friesen.

from a Polish kingdom taken over by a Prussian monarch founded the massive "Mother Colonies" of Chortitza (Khortitsa) in 1789 and Molotschna (Molochna) in 1804. But we begin with the push and pull factors that drove them away from the Baltic coastline around Danzig to the Black Sea coastline of New Russia.

Push: The End of Kingdom Poland

Mennonites in 1788 may have wanted to live for generations more in Kingdom Poland, but they were not given that option as Poland itself was on the edge of obliteration. The balance of power had shifted in the Baltic over the course of the eighteenth century, even as commerce in the region continued to grow exponentially. Great Britain's rise as the world's dominant merchant marine coincided with the Dutch

Republic's demise, though events to the east were equally significant after Peter I of Muscovy secured his foothold on the Baltic in 1703. He quickly founded St. Petersburg, declared it to the capital of the new state in 1718, and in 1721 the Russian Senate formally named Peter as emperor (Imperator) of a newly minted Russian empire. "Russia" had clearly arrived on the world stage, and Peter's was a clarion call for his Ottoman, Swedish, and Polish neighbours to pay heed. All saw their fortunes significantly diminished in the decades that followed. Poland quickly felt the economic sting as the rise of St. Petersburg coincided with the collapse of Danzig, which had already suffered from Amsterdam's decline as Western Europe's preeminent entrepôt. More losses were in store for Poland as the Russian empire steadily curtailed the political autonomy of its neighbour. Some Russian voices even called for its total annexation, though St. Petersburg eventually took a more cautious approach as it worked in concert with Vienna (the Hapsburg Empire) and Berlin (Prussia) to secure Poland's demise. In the first partition of Poland, undertaken in 1772, Prussia gained control over previously Polish Royal Prussia, save for Danzig itself. The port city's relative autonomy ended two decades later in 1793 when Prussian forces stormed and seized control of Danzig during the second partition of Poland, though Berlin had severely weakened the port city's autonomy prior to the actual seizure.[2]

An estimated 12,000 Mennonites found themselves under Prussian control after the first partition of 1772, and that made all the difference for them as Berlin ended the relative political autonomy they had enjoyed under Poland. Prussian officials now imposed their political will on the entire region and challenged those who sought exemptions from the needs of a modern, centralized state. Mennonites were front and centre here as they refused to serve in the military. Officials initially imposed a tax of 5,000 talers on Mennonites who wished to avoid military service (they had previously imposed one on Mennonites living in Danzig itself).[3] Though costly, Mennonites accepted it as a workable compromise. They were much more concerned when their Prussian overlords indicated that they intended to restrict Mennonite land acquisition in their newly acquired region. The problem was two-fold from the state's perspective: first, a decline in soldiers associated with any military exemption directly threatened Prussia at a time when it deemed its military prowess as central to its statecraft; and second, any increase in Mennonite landowners potentially reduced the coffers of the Lutheran (state) church and threatened unnecessary conflict between church and state. Already in 1774 Kaiser Frederick cautioned officials not to readily grant Mennonites permission to purchase land from non-Mennonites, while the Chambers in Marienwerder denied Mennonites the right to take on new artisanal trades. Even though Mennonites secured a Prussian Charter of Privileges in 1780 which purported to secure their permanent exemption from military service, Mennonites remained uneasy. Mark Jantzen suggests that this marked the first occasion when Mennonites had to confront a state which demanded political homogeneity even as it allowed for a level of religious diversity.[4] Despite the increased tensions, however, Mennonites were able to live with relative freedom in Prussia for the remainder of Frederick's reign.

His death in 1786 ushered in a new era as Frederick Wilhelm II succeeded the late Kaiser. The new monarch made clear at the outset that he opposed Mennonite exceptionalism. He insisted that any future land purchases within Prussia could not weaken the military obligations associated with them. In a formal document released in 1789 and entitled "Edict for the Future Regulation of Mennonite Affairs" Frederick Wilhelm II declared that Mennonites had a right to a pacifist position, though it could not trump the state's right to deny such pacifists any future land acquisitions.[5] Even lands that Mennonites had acquired since the first Polish partition of 1772 were subject to reclamation after 1789. No wonder previously Polish and now Prussian Mennonites were restless by the mid-1780s and showed up in force to hear of the Russian empress's invitation on that Saturday morning in January 1788. But that was only half the story.

Pull: New Russia and a Door Opens

Initially Peter the Great did not want to establish a window on the west in what became the imperial jewel of St. Petersburg on the shores of the Gulf of Finland. Instead, he first set his sights on the south, and in a war with the Ottoman Empire, Russian troops briefly acquired and then surrendered a foothold on the Black Sea in 1696. Only thereafter did Peter turn to the Baltic, though he never abandoned his hopes of an expanded southern frontier along the shores of the Black and Azov seas. Nor did his heirs, as all understood that an enlarged southern border would bring with it the prospect of increased European trade via the Bosporus and the Dardanelles, the gateway to the Mediterranean. A Russian empire with maritime borders also promised to remove the challenges associated with an irksome and ill-defined southern frontier zone. Lastly, Russian officials knew that seizure of the south would increase their social control of the empire, as the vast unregulated southern prairie zone north of the Black Sea had long served as a magnet for fugitive serfs, drawn to the Cossack communities that had taken shape there over centuries. Cossacks dwelled within the large river valleys that flowed southward to the Black and Azov seas.[6] Here they found both a satisfactory distance from Muscovy's servile conditions and a measure of protection from the nomadic Nogai Tatars who occupied the vast steppe that engulfed the rivers. Of these Cossack communities, the most significant for our story were the Zaporozhian Cossacks, who had long established their headquarters (*Sech*) below the series of rapids that crossed the lower Dnieper River valley. Their name suggested their location, as "Zaporozhia" translates as "beyond the rapids." The one exception to this picture of deep-cut river valleys and steppe in the south was Crimea, where sedentary Tatars predominated on an arid peninsula that stretched into the Black Sea, a landscape that was only broken by the mountain range at its southern edge.

These Black Sea steppe lands had long been a significant buffer zone between the Polish, Russian, and Ottoman empires, of which the last retained political control during Peter's reign and after. This changed dramatically when the Russian empire, under Peter's niece Anna, overwhelmed Turkish forces in the war of 1735–9, though that was mere prelude to the Russo–Turkish war that began in 1768. Fought under the leadership of a young Russian empress, Catherine II, the Ottoman Porte sued for peace in 1774, at which time St. Petersburg seized control of the entire Black Sea littoral. The one exception to this massive land grab, the Crimean Peninsula, was still nominally independent, though Catherine formally annexed it in 1783, making Russia's hold on this entire region complete.[7] With that victory the "New Russian" era had begun, as evidenced by Catherine's order of 8 August 1775 to dissolve the Zaporozhian Cossack *Sech*. This destruction of the *Sech* was mere subtraction by subsequent addition as St. Petersburg intended to replace the quasi-independent Cossacks and nomadic Nogai Tatars in the region with a flood of true subjects of the empire, regardless of origin.

Catherine II demonstrated the centrality of New Russia to her vision of the empire when she appointed the powerful Prince Grigory Potemkin as the region's first viceroy in 1774. He was charged with overseeing its rapid settlement, a task deemed essential for both security reasons and because so-called populationist and physiocratic (agriculturalist) policies were in vogue across much of Europe in the late eighteenth century. By then, experts tied the strength of empire directly to the robustness of its rural population. Here the examples of Great Britain and Holland led the way, and other European states followed.[8] St. Petersburg needed immigrants for this to work, and it sought them from all directions.

St. Petersburg proceeded with a multifaceted approach to the settlement of New Russia. Administratively it formally divided the newly acquired lands into three provinces (*guberniia*) in 1802: Ekaterinoslav, Tavrida, and Kherson, and it further divided each into districts (*uezds*) and even smaller subunits (*volosts*). As a measure of New Russia's overall coherence in imperial thinking, officials named Odessa the regional super-capital in 1805. Catherine had only founded the port city by imperial decree in 1794, an indication of how quickly it rose in imperial prominence. Strategies were quickly implemented to attract both foreign and domestic settlers. By way of the latter, Catherine granted the empire's nobility vast tracts of land for the establishment of private estates in New Russia, though these tended to be in its northern reaches, where safety was more assured. Unfortunately, the size of these estates overwhelmed the serfs available to maintain them. To help make these newly allotted estates viable, the empire opened the floodgates to fugitive peasants from the north as they spontaneously relocated to New Russia. Little attempt was made to return them to their rightful owners. The movement of fugitive serfs and state peasants (those who had no noble overlord but lived instead on state-owned lands) was such that the state allocated vast tracts to state peasant villages, especially in the more southerly reaches. Whereas the average noble estate owner rarely had more than fifty serfs to work his land, state peasant villages of more than a thousand households were not uncommon in New Russia by the nineteenth century, especially towards the south. St. Petersburg even initially welcomed religious sectarians, including Dukhobors, to settle on the coastal zones of the Sea of Azov.[9]

Foreign colonists were equally welcome, such that officials established a special Bureau for the Guardianship of Foreigners (hereafter the Guardians Committee)[10] in 1763. The task was not an easy one, as potential colonists had to be identified and then wooed away from states that had their own populationist and physiocratic policies in place and were reluctant to lose anyone to an emerging great power. Nevertheless Catherine II issued a manifesto on 14 October 1762 to prospective European colonists in which she promised a wide range of inducements for them to settle in the empire's borderlands.[11] All subsequent agreements between the Russian state and foreign colonists were premised on that manifesto, which included promised assistance with travel, relocation, and building materials; irrevocable exemption from military and civil service; the right to govern themselves; the freedom to worship as long as they did not proselytize the empire's Orthodox peasants; and generous land allotments at no cost with a temporary exemption from the payment of taxes.[12]

Catherine's manifesto could accomplish nothing without representatives of the Russian state to champion it, so she – or, more accurately, Potemkin – appointed agents and directly tied their compensation to their success at wooing immigrants. Russian diplomats had failed in an earlier attempt to accomplish this task. This new strategy was successful as German Catholics, Lutherans, Greeks, and Danes all resettled to New Russia in the quarter-century before 1800. Yet none of these established the reputation of Mennonites who settled in New Russia after 1788, thanks to the efforts of Georg Trappe, whom Potemkin appointed as his personal emissary in 1786. Trappe was awarded the right to secure colonists in and around Danzig, then in turmoil due to the first partition of Poland in 1772. Potemkin awarded this region to Trappe because of the latter's claim that he was personally familiar with Mennonites to the extent that he even spoke their Plautdietsch, a German dialect distinct to the region closest to the Netherlands.[13] Trappe moved quickly after he was appointed in early 1786. He had arrived in Danzig by July. By August he had already contacted Peter Epp, an elder in the largest Mennonite congregation in Danzig. Epp was interested in the New Russian option from the start, and with Trappe's arrival in Danzig the *push* of the First Partition of Poland had been joined to a possible *pull* made possible by the Russian conquest of New Russia.

The Chortitza Colony: Hopes Dashed and Accommodation Made

Catherine's 1763 manifesto was initially read in all Mennonite churches in Danzig and environs, and those who heard it responded enthusiastically. Prussian officials were not amused. They summoned Mennonite leaders and ordered them to ignore any Russian invitations to resettle.[14] Thereafter the Danzig Mennonite communities continued to pursue the Russian option, but they did so surreptitiously. After some deliberation church leaders agreed to send a delegation to New Russia to scout out prospects. We were already introduced at the start of this chapter to Jakob Höppner and Johann Bartsch as they returned from a yearlong investigation of New Russia. It remains to be said that Höppner was a Flemish Mennonite and Johann Bartsch a Frisian, thus they were able to give some assurance that they represented the entire Mennonite community in Danzig. Höppner and Bartsch promised up to three hundred families in the initial wave, with more to follow. No wonder Russian officials enthusiastically agreed to fund their exploratory trip. It was upon their return to Danzig in late 1787, with a privilegium in hand and a settlement site selected, that the first delegation of Mennonites prepared themselves for departure from Prussia. They needed to move quickly, as Prussian authorities early in 1788 banned Trappe from Danzig and ordered his immediate removal.[15]

Though exact numbers elude us, some 220 families comprised the first wave of Prussian Mennonites to immigrate to the Russian empire,[16] fewer than Höppner and Bartsch had promised. It did not help that the Prussian state – which already treated Danzig as its possession – denied passports to all but the poorest Mennonites. Those with means had to emigrate covertly and by indirect routes. Most who now left made their way by ship eastward on the Baltic in 1788, though those with even modest means travelled by horse-drawn cart. Ninety Lutheran families, also from Danzig, accompanied them to the port city of Riga, formally a Russian possession after Sweden surrendered it in the Treaty of Nystad in 1721. There they wintered.

Höppner departed from Riga with an advance party in March 1789. He intended to go ahead to the site he and Bartsch had previously selected on the lower Dnieper adjacent Berislav and near the newly established port city of Kherson. Höppner stopped first at Potemkin's headquarters in Chernigov, where the imperial viceroy abruptly informed him that Mennonites would not be permitted to settle near Berislav as previously agreed due to ongoing hostilities in the area. Instead they were ordered to make their way to the erstwhile Zaporozhian Cossack headquarters of Khortitsa, where they were to establish their new colony on one of Potemkin's personal estates. Historians have long debated whether this was a mere ruse by Potemkin to compel Mennonites to settle on one of his lands and thereby link their vaunted agricultural prowess to himself. Mennonites at the time viewed this switch in the most negative light given the inferior location of the Khortitsa Island and environs. Many blamed Höppner and Bartsch directly, alleging that these two profited personally from this change. Both were eventually accused of profiteering and excommunicated from the Mennonite church. It would take generations for them to get the recognition they deserved.

As the above suggests, Khortitsa was less an ideal setting for the first Mennonite colony in New Russia. The land was marked by deep-cut river valleys, numerous ravines, rock outcroppings, and barren plains. There were few woodlots for the construction of shelters, and officials were slow to supply any building materials that had been promised as a condition of settlement. Though there was a fortress nearby in Alexandrovsk it was, at most, a modest market town, and offered few possibilities for Mennonite artisans or agriculturalists. Beyond Alexandrovsk the private estates of the nobility that surrounded their prospective colony remained sparsely settled for years. On top of that, Höppner's advance party determined that the soils in Khortitsa were far inferior to those he and Bartsch had scouted out near Berislav. Even where good soils were found the settlers would have to choose: they could either found their villages with ready access to water – typically in the deep-cut stream-fed ravines or river valleys – or place them in close proximity to the fields on the high arid plains, but distant from sources of fresh water. The contrast with Danzig and the Vistula river delta could not have been starker.

No wonder the recriminations against Höppner and Bartsch surfaced immediately upon arrival. Nevertheless, officials compelled those first Mennonites to make their new homes in what became known as the Chortitza colony. The settlement itself was massive as the state granted the colonists over 20,000 *desiatinas* of land, though woodland comprised a mere 240 desiatinas, much less than they had been promised. Another 13,000 desiatinas were deemed unproductive. Mennonites had hoped to establish discrete farmsteads in their new colony, but the dangers caused by marauding bands compelled them to settle in villages for protection. They founded eight in 1789: Chortitza, Rosental, Einlage, Neuenburg, Schönhorst, Neuendorf, Alt Kronsweide, and Insel Chortitza.[17] All were located on the right bank Dnieper except for Insel Choritza, which was located on the island of Khortitsa. At over 12 kilometres in length it was the largest island on the entire river and situated at the lower end of a series of rapids that impeded the easy transshipment of goods. On average some twenty-five to thirty households were set up in each village. They allotted 65 desiatinas of non-partible land to each household, and villages were charged with the fair allocation of land based on soil quality and access to meadows, sources of water, and woodlots. One and a half desiatinas were allotted also for the individual homesteads, gardens, sheds, and barns, and these were normally situated on both sides of a single main avenue that intersected the village lands.

The early years were difficult for the Chortitza colony, and it might have continued to flounder had an additional 118 families not arrived when they did in 1793–6. This second wave emigrated shortly after the second partition of Poland by which Prussia formally seized control of Danzig itself. The new settlers were more prosperous than the first ones as they arrived with livestock in the hundreds, both horses and cattle. They were also Frisians, whereas the first cohort was predominantly Flemish. Some families from this second wave integrated into the existing villages, though they also formed two new ones: Schönweise, on the right bank of the Dnieper where it adjoined the fortress town of Alexandrovsk; and Kronsgarten, which was well to the north of the Chortitza colony and closer to the provincial capital of Ekaterinoslav.

Mennonites continued to trickle into the region from Prussia after 1796, which prompted the state to purchase additional lands adjoining the original Chortitza colony. They founded two new villages on those lands: Nieder Chortitza and Burwalde, both in 1803. Thereafter, officials deemed the Chortitza colony to be essentially filled, though they did eventually permit the establishment of four additional villages on surplus lands within the colony. However, after 1803 the focus of Mennonite settlement shifted eastward of the Chortitza settlement and well east of the Dnieper.

The Molotschna Settlement: Founding and Early History

The Russian state realized by 1800 that Mennonites needed better lands than they had received in Khortitsa if they were to succeed as anticipated. State councilor Samuel Contenius reported to the Guardians Committee in 1799 that the region where Mennonites had first settled was poorly suited to agriculture: "In spite of their industry, however, those at Khortitsa will hardly ever achieve a prosperous condition. It is a predominantly rolling country on which, due to the dryness of the soil and the lack of rain, the grasses usually burn out and the grains grow poorly. Thus the plowman often tills and plants his field in vain. And few are those who harvest enough to provide for themselves for the entire year."[18]

He recommended that the state give any future Mennonite arrivals land in a very different setting, one where they would be able to exercise their vaunted agricultural prowess. Back in Prussia, Mennonites received an added incentive to emigrate after Emperor Paul I, who succeeded his mother Catherine II upon her death in 1796, issued a new privilegium in September 1800.[19] In it Paul confirmed all rights and privileges granted to Mennonites during his mother's reign. In addition, he now permitted them to establish factories, both on their lands and in the empire's emerging cities. In one other major concession the new privilegium permitted them to brew beer and spirits on their lands for domestic use and for sale, but only within their villages.[20]

Regardless, few Mennonites immigrated under Paul I, who sought an alliance with Prussia and did not want to aggravate its relations with Russia through mass immigration schemes. All of this changed after 1801 when Alexander I ascended to the throne. The largest of the Mennonite immigrations into the empire was about to begin, facilitated by the decision of the Prussian government in that same year to issue its most restrictive measures yet against Mennonites. Henceforth Kaiser Frederick Wilhelm II banned all land sales to Mennonites unless they purchased land from co-religionists, and even then, they risked the loss of their military exemption. Mennonites repeatedly petitioned Berlin against this legislation but to no avail, even as the Prussian state continued to discourage emigration.

By 1803 hundreds of Mennonite families indicated their intent to quit Prussia for the Russian empire, again by way of Riga on the Baltic. St. Petersburg needed to move quickly to allocate lands for this massive influx of settlers and make it of sufficient quality to allow them to prosper. Eventually the state settled on land found in Tavrida province to the south-east of Chortitza and along the relatively modest Molochnaia stream. Almost nothing about this new landmass resembled the one previously offered to those who had settled Chortitza. Though both colonies were situated far from market towns, and the new colony may have been even more devoid of fresh water sources, it was at least flat, not hilly, and the rich black soil was superior to that found in the original colony. Mennonites named the new colony Molotschna after the local stream. At approximately 120,000 desiatinas it was gigantic compared to Chortitza. Molotschna's "neighbourhood" was also starkly different from the first Mennonite colony. Whereas massive private estates surrounded Chortitza Mennonites, there were none around Molotschna. Instead the state itself owned all surrounding lands, which made the land grants easier for St. Petersburg to accomplish. The state allotted lands adjacent to the Molotschna settlement to a vibrant hodgepodge of Orthodox state peasants in massive villages; previously nomadic Nogai Tatars, whom the state intended either to exile or settle into permanent villages, and Dukhobor and Molokan Orthodox sectarians who similarly resided in very large villages.[21] Of these only the Nogai predated the arrival of the first Mennonite settlers in 1804.

Mennonite immigrants settled the new Molotschna colony apace. According to historian David G. Rempel the first contingent of 162 families departed Prussia in November 1803. Most left from Danzig with limited means, which is why they were able to obtain passports as quickly as they did. As with the Chortitza settlers, the Russian state promised loans to most of the Molotschna settlers for their travel, provisions en route, and for the rudiments needed to build their new homes upon arrival, all of which had to be repaid within ten years.[22] Of course the Russian state at the time made promises more easily than it fulfilled them, a harsh lesson Mennonites learned early on. Russian officials themselves concluded in 1798 that more than 80,000 of 114,000 rubles promised to Mennonites as inducements to immigrate remained unpaid.[23]

All those bound for Molotschna stopped first at the Chortitza colony, where they learned of local conditions, received advice on working with the often-cumbersome Russian bureaucracy, and wintered over several months if the weather proved inclement. Some even stayed on permanently in Chortitza, though most moved on when weather permitted. Another 166 Mennonite families left Prussia the following summer, their departure delayed by Prussian officials. This was a much wealthier contingent, as it arrived with cattle, horses, cash, and household items. One reason for this shifting profile of immigrants is that the Russian government after 1804 no longer promised the subsidies it had previously, as the rapid pace of settlement in New Russia allowed it to be more selective and less generous.[24]

In sum more than 350 Mennonite families immigrated to New Russia between 1803 and 1806, and the vast majority of these settled in the newly formed Molotschna colony. A brief hiatus followed as the Napoleonic wars made immigration almost impossible. But it picked up quickly thereafter. More than 250 families arrived between 1815 and 1820. In fact, approximately 1,200 families and 6,000 Mennonites settled in Molotschna before the state finally closed immigration to that colony in 1835. By that time Mennonites had founded some thirty-five villages, with an average of approximately thirty-five households per village. Most of the villages in Molotschna were founded along two great pathways that had been used for generations by carters (*chumaki*) as they made their way along the vast Eurasian plain. Many of these same villages had been named after ones they had left behind in what had been Kingdom Poland, a world that had by now vanished.

Mennonite Life and Identity in New Russia: The Founding Years

Worship

Mennonites continued to be rooted in Christian worship during their settlement years in New Russia, even though the exact shape of corporate worship was contested from the outset. Prussian and Dutch Mennonite leaders repeatedly expressed the hope that the new Mennonite colonies would not be marred by a Flemish–Frisian churchly division. To give but one example, Mennonite leaders in Groningen and Friesland exhorted all immigrants to the Russian empire to permit intermarriage between the Flemish and Frisians. The issue arose when Georg Trappe observed the oddity of this hard and fast division. In response, the Prussian church leaders wrote to the faithful of both communities: "We wish to make it clear that the practice of not allowing the (inter) marriages should cease. Mr. Trappe is working with councilors and learned men in order to find a way to abolish this practice ... Dear Friends and Brothers this business is so serious and the request made by Mr. Trappe so just that we venture to take this opportunity to make our feelings known to you."[25]

It is perhaps with this in mind that the Prussian churches did not initially select leaders for the new colonies of Chortitza and Molotschna, such that the first settlers were compelled to make do as they wintered in Dubrovna. Eventually ministers and deacons were elected in a rather convoluted process when church leaders in Prussia confirmed those elected by the immigrant community, a source of initial dissension. Yet despite pleas for unity, both Flemish and Frisian congregations had built their own meeting houses by 1791 in the Chortitza colony (in the villages of Chortitza and Kronsweide, respectively). A similar pattern unfolded in Molotschna a decade later, when separate Flemish and Frisian congregations constructed separate church buildings in Ohrloff (1809) and Petershagen (1810), respectively. To add to the ecclesial divisions, a third Mennonite congregational entity was formed in 1812, when Mennonites in the Molotschna colony formed the *Kleine Gemeinde* (Small Congregation). Led by Klaas Reimer of Petershagen, the *Kleine Gemeinde* opposed what it deemed to be the worldliness of both Flemish and Frisian Mennonites in their new homeland. Its members also opposed the broad Mennonite determination to support the Russian state through voluntary financial offerings during the Napoleonic wars. Whereas the Flemish and Frisians worshipped in church buildings, the *Kleine Gemeinde* preferred to worship in homes.[26]

Thus, Mennonites in New Russia failed at the outset to achieve the religious unity many in Prussia desired for them, and instead maintained the plethora of ecclesial structures they had established in Kingdom Poland. There were other legacies. Though Mennonites first worshipped in homes and sheds, both the Flemish and Frisian congregations soon established church buildings modelled after the unobtrusive buildings authorities in Poland had eventually permitted them to build. Their "Prayer Houses" – or *Betshäuser*, as Mennonites commonly referred to their churches in this earlier period – resembled slightly larger houses, with similar windows and entrances. Architectural historian Rudy Friesen has observed that there was little to distinguish the exterior of these new churches from surrounding dwellings, in part because Mennonites valued simplicity. The rectangular interiors also lacked ornamentation, as no images, icons, or crosses adorned the walls. Male and female parishioners sat separately in a U-shaped pattern around a slightly elevated dais, where the ministers presided.

Mennonite households themselves paid for the churchly structures which they first constructed out of wood and later with brick or stone. Russian officials banned the proselytization of peasants but encouraged religious practices among all colonists, as long as those religious institutions demonstrated fealty to the Russian state.[27] They themselves contributed to costs which, for example, allowed Mennonites to construct the Petershagen prayer house with stone from the outset.[28]

Language and Culture

Most Mennonites at point of settlement in New Russia spoke a version of Low German called Plautdietsch, an amalgam of languages spoken in the Dutch and north-east German lands. Mennonites had adopted it as their *lingua franca* when they first settled in Kingdom Poland, in part because Plautdietsch was able to absorb the various Frisian, Franconian, and Low Saxonian dialects and vocabularies which Mennonites had initially spoken. By contrast, Dutch had been the language of instruction and the churchly language in Kingdom Poland.[29] Ministers and Ältesters in New Russia initially delivered all sermons in the Dutch language, a tendency reinforced by the fact that many simply read their sermons from collections made available from Prussian and Dutch Mennonite ministers and Ältesters. But Plautdietsch ruled the daily discourse and would do so for generations. David G. Rempel observed that Russian officials first transliterated Mennonite names into Russian from the Plautdietsch and not German, as evidenced by references to the widows "Sarra Giesbrechtsche, Katrina Pennersche, Helene Wiebsche, Katrina Klassensche and so on,"[30] instead of the widows Giesbrecht, Penner, Wiebe, and Klassen in their Germanic forms. Ironically, Mennonites began to shift away from Plautdietsch and Dutch after 1796 when the regime of Paul I insisted that all Mennonite correspondence conducted with Russian officials be undertaken in German. It also helped that Mennonites who settled in Molotschna villages after 1800 tended to be more acculturated into German and all matters Prussian than had the earliest immigrants to Chortitza.

But what did the term "Mennonite" signify at the point of settlement? Three distinct aspects soon emerged. First, as suggested above, Mennonites were most immediately a religious entity for which the word *Gemeinde* best applied with its connotations of a Christian congregationally based collective. They constructed their prayer houses in such a way as to emphasize interpersonal contact through the U-shaped design. They could not help but look each other in the eye in that setting, and the greatest sanction imposed on disobedient members was exclusion from that very Gemeinde and the Lord's Supper as its non-sacramental symbol of unity. To be a Mennonite initially was to be connected to a particular Gemeinde and to see oneself as heir to a tradition that reached back to the New Testament church, the very one reignited by Menno Simons in Friesland. It was a Gemeinde with past and present commingled, and with an assured future as members of Christ's elect in this world and the next. Nor does any of this surprise given developments already observed in Kingdom Poland.

Second, the Russian ban on proselytization, which mirrored restrictions imposed by officials in Kingdom Poland, reinforced endogenous trends within the Mennonite Gemeinden. It did not take long for an emergent Mennonitism to include distinct cultural components as exemplified by contemporary linguistic practices.[31] The Russian state both reinforced and shaped Mennonitism as an ethno-cultural phenomenon when they classified Mennonites as "Mennonites" regardless of their religious affiliation, and even as there were always those who did not affiliate with Frisian, Flemish, or Kleine Gemeinde congregations. Officials before the reforms of the 1870s also maintained a sharp distinction between German Lutherans, German Catholics, and Mennonites, as they never explicitly identified Mennonites as "German." Thus, from the outset individuals could live within the Chortitza and Molotschna colonies, maintain no active religious affiliation, and still be identified as "Mennonite." The Russian state gave them literally no alternative.

The Russian state also reinforced a third signifier of the Mennonite identity in New Russia, and it was Mennonites as political actors. That may not have been entirely new, as Mennonites had long engaged politically with the state in Kingdom Poland in defence of their rights and privileges. Now Mennonite political involvement took on an entirely different shape in New Russia, where the empire lacked the infrastructure needed to govern effectively.[32] As a result, it required incoming colonists to govern themselves, subject to the authority of the state by way of the Guardians Committee. St. Petersburg appointed directors to oversee the governance of Chortitza colony until 1801 when an imperial edict established a system of self-government among all colonists. Henceforth all villages in the Chortitza and Molotschna colonies were instructed to establish their own village assemblies, comprising all male farm-holders. Those assemblies, in turn, elected their own mayors (*Schulz*) and two assistants (*Beisitzer*), as well as a clerk, all for two-year terms and all by majority vote. Lastly, both colonies (that is, Chortitza and Molotschna as a whole) elected a district head, or *Ober-Schulz*, who worked out of the district office (*Geblietsamt*). These assemblies exercised enormous power within the villages once established, though even then the state could directly intervene where it willed, as the following chapter will make plain.[33]

The administrative structures introduced by the Russian state highly politicized Mennonite society at the point of immigration. By contrast, Swiss Mennonites who settled at this very time in the United States of America and Upper Canada (Canada today) entered lands where others performed the political functions of state.[34] Thus Swiss Mennonites eschewed active involvements in politics in the "New World," but their Dutch/Polish/Prussian and now Russian Mennonite counterparts in "New Russia" could not. Moreover, Urry has ably demonstrated that tensions inherent between ecclesial and political structures profoundly shaped the Mennonite experience in the Russian empire and transformed both their colonies and their churches. These tensions will become immediately apparent in the following chapter.

Postscript: *Am Trakt* and *Alt Samara*

In some ways, the founding of the Chortitza and Molotschna colonies put an end to the initial settlement process in the Russian empire. Both were deemed the Mother Colonies, and although both functioned cooperatively in times of crisis, it can also be said that their relationship was often highly competitive and occasionally fractious.

The Russian state established two more Mennonite colonies after it formally closed immigration into the Molotschna in 1840. By then, however, the frontier had shifted from New Russia to the trans-Volga. The need for additional colonies arose when Prussian Mennonites applied to immigrate to the Russian empire after 1850 when Berlin refused any further exemptions from universal military conscription for religious reasons. After some deliberation they were welcomed by St. Petersburg, and they again received land grants, though they were only exempted from military service for a twenty-year period. With that the Mennonite Am Trakt (Trek) colony was formed in 1853 on almost 20,000 desiatinas of land in Samara province on the mid-Volga. The name itself paid homage to the prairie roadway (the Trek) adjacent to the colony, by which caravans had travelled for centuries from Siberia and beyond into the Russian interior. Mennonites formed ten villages here, from Hahnsau in 1854 to Medemtal in 1872.[35]

Mennonite immigrants established their final colony in the Russian empire in 1859, when the Alt-Samara, or Alexandertal, colony was formed, though by then land was no longer granted by the Russian state. Mennonites had to buy it outright, which they did with the purchase of over 10,000 desiatinas on a parcel located on the left bank of the

Volga, some 150 kilometres from the Samara itself. Mennonites founded eight villages here between 1859 and 1870. Once again, almost all settlers came directly from Prussia.[36] Most were prosperous and quickly established themselves, as had those who settled in the Am Trakt colony. There were other changes, as Mennonites in both colonies only spoke German upon arrival, an indication of how the Plautdietsch of earlier generations had been left behind.

So it was that the period of Mennonite immigration to the Russian empire had come to an end. But life itself in this new land, including a series of later internal migrations from the original Mother Colonies to new settlements elsewhere in the region and empire, had just begun.

Chapter Five

Pietistic Progressivism: Johann Cornies and the Transformation of Russian Mennonitism, 1800–1848

On 5 August 1826 a Mennonite named Johann Cornies from the Molotschna colony began his letter to Daniel Schlatter with the following:

> Our all-knowing God will accompany you on your long journey and keep your ship from sinking. May He remain in your sight and may you know that His noble intentions, which He himself has laid upon your soul, must guide your every breath and step. And should the sea claim your body, your soul would still reach the same haven as if you had stood on solid ground. My joy rests in the hope that there will be no parting for us in His realm and that, embraced by the love we share for our Lord and Master, we will experience His abundance in eternal, unchanging companionship.[1]

Cornies proceeded to highlight several concerns with Schlatter, a Swiss pietist and non-Mennonite who had begun missionary work among New Russia's Nogai Tatars four years earlier and whom Cornies had befriended. Among them, Cornies reported on fellow Mennonites who had slandered him and his reputation, as well as on a Russian official who had urged Cornies to travel to Saxony in search of better sheep breeding stock for New Russian agriculturalists. This same combination of the spiritual and material is found in other correspondences between them, such as in Cornies' letter of 6 November 1826, in which he describes his new sheep barn, changes in leadership within the Molotschna colony, his own hopes regarding the development of Nogai culture, and the grasshopper infestations that had devastated New Russia. Clearly his interests are vast, yet he claims in this November letter that the Christian faith alone motivates him: "Through the grace of Jesus, we endeavor to preach with our hands and otherwise to keep silent, which is better than the opposite."[2]

Cornies undertook his correspondence with Schlatter during a time when Mennonites in the Mother Colonies of Chortitza and Molotschna utterly transformed their worlds in a process Cornies himself largely oversaw. By 1850 almost all these colonists had replaced their first dwellings – often thatch-roofed huts built right into the earth (*zemliachka*s) – with uniform clay brick homes they had constructed at uniform distances along uniform village streets which they had lined with uniformly spaced trees. They had topped their homes with uniformly tiled roofs, and they had connected their homes to barns, which they similarly constructed from brick and tile. There were other changes. Mennonites had maintained schools from the outset, but the structures went from cramped and primitive *zemliachkas* in 1800 to roomy, light-filled brick buildings by 1850. Mennonites may have initially existed at a subsistence level in New Russia, but by mid-century their large herds, burgeoning wheat fields, and impressive implement inventories bespoke of a people well integrated into larger market systems.

Others noticed. Observers from within and beyond the empire routinely visited Mennonites by mid-century as they travelled through the region, and almost always praised them as model agriculturalists for the whole empire. Mennonites by then had built and maintained strong ties to the Russian state, in part because they had from the outset smoothly enmeshed their own administrative structures with the state's own. Nor did this transformation take place in a vacuum, as Mennonite success contributed to and benefited from the rapid development of Russian port cities on the Black and Azov sea coasts, all of which linked Mennonite agriculturalists to markets and competitors as far flung as Australia, England, Prussia, Argentina, and America.

This chapter charts out the path Mennonites took from their first earthen *zemliachkas* in 1800 to the tree-lined brick-faced model villages of a half-century later. At first glance this might be deemed an economic transformation, but it was always much more than that. This takes us back to Cornies' exchange with Schlatter, where observations on sheep, grasshoppers, and Nogai Tatars intermingle with seemingly heartfelt reflections on their shared Christian faith. John Staples has recently argued that Johann Cornies desired a socio-economic revolution within and beyond the Mennonite world of New Russia because of his commitment to the "aesthetics of civilization," to use Staples' evocative turn of phrase. But it was an aesthetics rooted in the language of Christian pietism, and this appears to put Staples at odds with Urry, who decades earlier boldly identified Cornies as the Mennonite "Prophet of Progress."[3] For Urry, Cornies unwittingly secularized the Mennonite world during his lifetime when he shifted the locus of authority within the Mother Colonies from Mennonite ministers to Mennonites whose authority came from Russian officials and not from the church. This recent debate between Staples and Urry points to a much larger historiographic dispute that has marked Cornies' legacy from the beginning. Already before his death in 1848 many within the Mennonite colonies had villainized Cornies, even as Russian officials and later Mennonites lionized him.[4] With his legacy in such dispute how might one make sense of the whole? I will attempt in this chapter to steer a course between Staples and Urry as I argue that both are, in fact, correct: as Staples has shown, Cornies rooted his radical transformation of Russian Mennonitism before 1850 in his deeply held pietistic convictions. However, Urry is no less correct when he concludes that it was Cornies' very pietism which opened the door to the secularization of authority within the Mennonite world, and here Charles Taylor's broader explication is particularly helpful.[5] We begin with the pietist winds that blew through the Mennonite colonies in the early nineteenth century and consider their impact on Johann Cornies in particular.

Pietism and the Transformation of the Mennonite Faith

Johann Cornies, whose correspondence began this chapter, was born in the Prussian village of Bärwalde, near Danzig, in June 1789 and migrated to the Russian empire with his siblings and parents in 1804. Bärwalde was a mixed village, which meant Cornies grew up with Lutheran and Catholic neighbours even as his family attended a Flemish Mennonite congregation noted for its conservatism.[6] But the influence of Lutheran pietism would have been everywhere around him. Upon immigration to the Russian empire his family lived in the Chortitza colony for two years before they settled in Ohrloff, a village Mennonites had founded in the Molotschna colony the previous year. There his father took possession of a full (65 desiatina) farmstead. The younger Johann likely encountered a vast and diverse world in Ohrloff, as Nogai Tatars, Orthodox sectarian Dukhobors and Molokans, and even Greeks regularly visited his father, known as a skilled herbalist and healer. As a young man Cornies tried his hand at various trades and even for a while carted goods to the emerging Crimean cities of Simferopol, Feodosia, and Sevastopol. Cornies had to cross the barren steppe to reach those markets, and he later referred to the steppe landscape as a place of "great darkness."[7] He must have demonstrated considerable business acumen, as in 1811 he purchased his own full farm in Ohrloff. Financially he never looked back.

Figure 3. Portrait of Johann Cornies. Source: Bethel College archives, 1909.
https://mla.bethelks.edu/archives/numbered-photos/pholist2.php?num=2005-0101

The pietistic theology Cornies first encountered in childhood Prussia, and which emanates from his correspondence, had emerged in the Dutch and German lands in the late seventeenth century, most especially in Utrecht, Frankfurt, Leipzig, and Halle. Its links to the British Isles made it truly a continental movement. Once rooted it spread quickly, from Scandinavia in the north to distant North America across the Atlantic. Though difficult to categorize, the earliest pietists stressed personal, heartfelt Christian renewal and new spiritual birth rather than creedal formulations and theological treatises. Its proponents wanted to separate the religious from the ecclesial in the hopes that it might create a larger pan-Christian unity.[8] Cornies clearly embraced pietism of this sort by the 1820s, as is evident in the selections that began this chapter. There are countless other examples, as in his letter of 10 September 1826 to Wilhelm Frank, also a non-Mennonite, where Cornies suddenly exclaims: "Dear God, how good you are that even now as in times of old, you scatter your blessings like salt over meat, in order that they not spoil and be destroyed." His prose is heartfelt, personal, and well removed from the creeds, whether Nicaean or Apostolic.

Pietism's close association with the Lutheran church, and its acceptance by Cornies and other Mennonites, necessitated the abandonment of previously exclusive Anabaptist understandings of faith in favour of a more broadly based religious renewal.[9] Pietists could find spiritual brothers and sisters outside of their own narrow confession as exemplified by Cornies in his correspondence to his non-Mennonite spiritual brothers. Pietists stressed the spiritual nature of faith, though a founding father of the movement, August Franke, had also urged fellow believers to remain actively engaged with the world. Franke set the standard when he founded an orphanage in Halle in 1695. Thus, social reform and evangelical missions intermingled easily for Lutheran pietists who sought to realize God's kingdom in all the earth, the evidence for which would be both redeemed lives and transformed communities. Once again, as had previously been the case with Anabaptist beginnings, the absence of a sacramental theology necessitated the evidence of transformed lives here and now. No wonder Cornies stressed faith, work, and labour as inseparable in his correspondence with the Mennonite pietist and preacher David Epp. In a letter to Epp of 14 August 1826 Cornies even describes God as the One who works to accomplish "His exalted purpose." Our challenge, Cornies continues, is to work and pray to God and "His judgement."[10]

Cornies encountered pietism in his Prussian childhood but also in adult friendships, which ranged from Moscow merchants (including the pietist Traugott Blueher) to Swiss missionaries in the south (Daniel Schlatter). He encountered them even though he permanently resided in either the Molotschna village of Ohrloff or a nearby estate for the remainder of his life. But how did the region's Mennonites as a whole encounter this new pietistic take on an old and Anabaptist faith? Here the influences were equally manifold. Lutheran pietist ministers and missionaries routinely made their way from the German lands to their coreligionists in New Russia in the nineteenth century, let alone to the neighbouring Nogai Tatars, as with Schlatter. Once in the region they added the Mennonite colonies to their circuit, where they occasionally preached in Mennonite churches and taught in their schools.

Most Mennonites, such as Cornies, who immigrated into the region after 1800 had already absorbed pietist elements while in Prussia, as none had lived in isolation from their non-Mennonite neighbours. Their acculturation was such that in 1808 the Prussian Flemish and Frisian congregations had unified, well ahead of any such unification in Russia. Those newly unified Mennonites who arrived thereafter and founded the twenty new Molotschna villages, from Margenau in 1819 to Wernersdorf in 1824, were culturally more Germanic and religiously more pietistic and Lutheran than the first Mennonite settlers to New Russia. Not surprisingly pietistic hymns soon made their way into Mennonite worship services, including those which later descendants would identify, ironically, as authentic Mennonite hymns. The first and last stanzas of the hymn *"Ich bete an die Macht der Liebe,"* composed by the Rhenish pietist Gerhard Tersteegen in 1750 are emblematic:

I pray to the power of love,
which reveals itself in Jesus;
I give myself up to the free-flowing stream
whereby I, a worm, was loved;
I want, instead of thinking about myself,
To immerse myself in the sea of love.

In this precious name of Jesus
the Father's heart opens;
a fountain of love, peace and joy
wells up in me so gently
My God, if only the sinner knew –
His heart would surely have to love you.[11]

Nor were Mennonites the only ones in the empire attracted to pietism. Most remarkably the Russian emperor and conqueror of Napoleon, Alexander I, played an important role in this drama. The autocrat became so interested in mystical Christianity that he attended Quaker services during an official visit to London in 1814. Impressed by what he saw, Alexander invited Quakers to visit the Russian empire. One of their members, William Allen, visited both the Chortitza and Molotschna colonies on his subsequent tour of New Russia. He met with Mennonite ministers who even permitted him to speak at services in both the Chortitza and Petershagen village churches. Firm contacts between the Mennonite colonies and the larger world of pietism soon developed, especially when the British & Foreign Bible Society helped found a Russian Bible Society in 1812. By 1820 this society had formed strong ties with Mennonites in New Russia and reinforced a pietistic vision of a pan-Christian spiritual fellowship.[12] Nor was this the last mark left by the Russian emperor because Alexander personally visited the Mennonite colonies twice, first in 1818 and, more poignantly and secondly, within weeks of his unexpected death. On the final occasion he entered the home of Johann Cornies on 22 October 1825, where the emperor of all the Russias and the Molotschna Mennonite visited over tea.[13]

Lutheran pietism represented both continuity and change for Mennonites. Akin to their Anabaptist forebears, pietists stressed the importance of biblical literacy and steadfast adherence to the Christian faith. Pietists also stressed a non-sacramental path to salvation manifested in transformed lives, a transformation that had much in common with Weber's later reflections on the Protestant work ethic.[14]

Pietists introduced significant change to Mennonite theology. Mennonites had emerged from within an Anabaptist movement that had seen itself as neither Catholic nor Protestant, both of which they deemed perversions of the faith.[15] Only Anabaptists preserved the One True Church; all others had damned themselves. Only those who practised believer's baptism, eschewed all forms of violence, and refused to swear oaths could claim to be "right thinking Christians." Other forms of worship, pietistic or otherwise, were irrelevant at best and demonic diversions at worst.[16] Though this confirms Urry's understanding of Mennonites as a closed society, as opposed to the open which Cornies helped initiate, it must be said that all Christian faiths, from Catholic to Lutheran, were equally closed in the late sixteenth century. None envisioned an all-embracing salvation. None viewed themselves as a mere denomination. Thus, Mennonites were a closed society at point of entry into the Russian empire, but so were all other expressions of the Christian faith. It might be more accurate to see them all in the mid-eighteenth century and earlier as pre-modern societies. Congregations were at the focal point of these societies, such that only members in good standing could participate in Communion services (the Eucharist). There was no other authority within the Mennonite world greater than the Mennonite church, and that applied to all aspects of Mennonite life. Nor did this suggest that Dutch/Prussian and thereafter Russian Mennonites ever saw themselves as somehow the Quiet in the Land. They never did.

Within this context, Cornies and others directly challenged Mennonite ecclesial and theological understandings when they adopted aspects of Lutheran pietism. Nor did it necessarily stop with the substitution of one expression of Christian faith for another. Charles Taylor argues persuasively that pietism was no bulwark against secularism. Instead, it served as a midwife for secularism when it emerged across the Protestant world in the eighteenth and nineteenth centuries, which placed the life and times of Cornies at the chronological heart of this innovation.[17] Of particular relevance, pietists eroded congregational and Mennonite ministerial authority when they stressed pan-Christian movements. They undermined congregational authority when they formed authoritative non-ecclesial institutions and associations, such as Bible societies, school boards, and agricultural associations, all of which occurred under Cornies' leadership in the Mennonite colonies. Lastly, pietists such as Cornies stressed individualism over congregational polities when they affirmed the centrality of personal, emotive, religious experience over creedal and confessional conformity.[18] The fact that Cornies remained a loyal member of the Flemish Mennonite congregation throughout his life does not negate the various ways in which his pietism undermined the erstwhile basis and scope of Flemish pre-modern congregational authority.

It also will not surprise that those opposed to Cornies' various reform efforts within the Mennonite colonies often expressed that opposition ecclesially. Most dramatically, in 1822 the Altonau (Molotschna) Mennonite minister Jakob Warkentin formed the autonomous Large Flemish congregation that comprised three-quarters of the original Flemish adherents in the colonies. The reason? They disapproved of the growing pan-Christian movements underway in the colonies, as well as intrusions from the Russian Bible Association along with those church leaders who had permitted these non-Mennonite pietists to preach and take Communion in Mennonite churches.[19] Cornies would work with the state successfully to dismantle this congregationally based Flemish opposition over the succeeding decades, by which time he had eclipsed the absolute power of Mennonite ministry councils and congregations. But it is equally important to see all aspects of Mennonite life during the first half of the nineteenth century, from education to governance to the introduction of massive forestation projects, as equally contested spaces within the transformation of Mennonitism that Cornies and others initiated. We consider the key transformations in the sections that follow.

Education

Tobias Voth was on the forefront of revolutionary change in Mennonite polity. Voth was born in 1791 into an isolated Flemish Mennonite congregation in Prussia, which left him heavily influenced by the much larger non-Mennonite communities around him. He even married a Lutheran. Voth studied in both Leipzig and Berlin, where he obtained his teacher's certificate, and in 1820 accepted a position in New Russia as instructor of a newly established Mennonite secondary school in the Molotschna village of Ohrloff.[20] Voth brought with him the latest pedagogical and pietistic trends from Central Europe, both of which had taken on a radically different shape following Napoleon's defeat of

Prussia in 1806. That crushing defeat prompted both Lutheran theologians and state officials to rethink the relationship of church and state. On the one hand, Prussian theologians now argued that pietistic Christians should leave the affairs of state to the state and limit their own attention to circumscribed spiritual matters. On the other hand, Prussian officials after 1806 argued that Prussia's future as an enlightened state required the political centre to seize control of the mechanisms of state and citizen formation, of which education was front and centre.[21] It was simply too important to remain under ecclesial control.

True to his time, Voth began his new position in Ohrloff firmly committed to both pietism and the necessity of state tutelage over education. He also began at a time when Russian officials had increased their influence over Mennonite education practices. In their earliest phase of settlement, Mennonites and other colonists had maintained a large degree of pedagogical autonomy. Indeed, the chronically understaffed Russian bureaucracy necessitated it, even as the relatively few Orthodox, servile, and state schools scattered across the empire enjoyed a similar autonomy from St. Petersburg.[22] Modest inroads towards the creation of a single educational system only began during the reign of Alexander I, and most especially for our purposes in 1817, when the Tsar created a centralized Ministry of Religious Affairs with direct ties to the previously moribund Ministry of Education.[23]

Conservative Mennonites feared this new organization would increase state intervention and undermine the firm control their congregational councils had heretofore exercised over educational matters. The sole purpose of education, they maintained, was to assist the church in the development of Christian men and women. Truth was only worthy of instruction if it drew sinners back to Christ and His faithful and exclusively Mennonite church. Hence the earliest Russian Mennonite pedagogies focused on the acquisition of a rudimentary literacy, whereas older children received intensive Bible study. Conservatives warned against even advanced Bible study if it was divorced from the local congregation and not directed by the ministry council. They warned of the dangers that lurked if Mennonites abandoned their fidelity to the faith of their forebears in favour of pietistic and pan-Protestant platitudes.

Events that unfolded after 1817 confirmed the fears of conservatives as state officials increasingly bypassed church leaders in favour of unelected Mennonite leaders within the colonies. Foremost among these was Johann Cornies, who enjoyed unassailable control over Mennonite schools and schooling by the 1840s as the role of Mennonite ministry councils correspondingly diminished. We have already encountered

Cornies the pietist Christian, but that only opened the door for him as the efficient servant of the Russian empire in transition.

A Revolution in Governance

Cornies catapulted to administrative prominence in 1817, when the empire's Guardians Committee appointed him to oversee the settlement of two hundred Mennonite families from Prussia, themselves steeped in pietism and contemporary Prussian pedagogical thinking. His successful undertaking of this assignment prompted officials in 1820 to appoint Cornies to oversee the settlement near the Molotschna colony of German immigrants from Württemberg. Four years later the Guardians Committee tasked Cornies with the improvement of sheep herds and wool production in the Mennonite colonies. At the same time, the Ministry of Internal Affairs appointed Cornies to inspect colonists, peasants, and Tatars in New Russia to determine what agricultural improvements, if any, had been undertaken. In January 1825 Andrei Fadeev of the Guardians Committee appointed Cornies to investigate the Russian Orthodox sectarians who lived in New Russia to ascertain the difference between Molokans and Dukhobors. One year later Samuel Contenius of the Guardians Committee directly instructed the elected Mennonite officials of the District Office in Halbstadt village of Molotschna colony to pay heed to Cornies, whom Contenius identified as "the authorized representative" of Molotschna Mennonites.[24] The Guardians Committee created at least two more committees in the Mennonite colonies: the Forestry Committee in 1830, responsible for the cultivation and distribution of afforestation projects throughout Molotschna, and the omnibus Agricultural Union, created in 1836 and which superseded all previous associations. In every instance the Guardians Committee consulted closely with Cornies before formally appointing him as chair for life. Thereafter the committee formed a similar organization in Chortitza colony and again appointed Cornies as its chair for life. Nor were these committees narrowly agricultural in focus. As indication thereof, the Guardians Committee gave Cornies free reign over all economic aspects within the Mennonite colonies. Finally, in 1843 Evgenii Hahn, senior deputy within the Guardians Committee, ceded all power over education in the Mennonite Mother Colonies to the Agricultural Union and its chair, Johann Cornies. No wonder Cornies enjoyed virtually unassailable power within the New Russian Mennonite heartland throughout the 1840s. What was going on?

Several factors combined to make Cornies the most powerful Mennonite of his or any time in the Russian empire. First, Mennonite life in the early nineteenth century unfolded within an empire that had engaged in state institution building since the reforms of Peter the Great in the early eighteenth century. As part of it, Peter's refusal to permit the Orthodox church to name a new patriarch in 1703 and the subsequent formation of an administrative Holy Synod in 1721 transformed church–state relations. Russian officials henceforth welcomed the church to attend to spiritual matters, though the state reserved the right to oversee everything else. Nor was this division of authority limited to the Orthodox. Paul Werth has shown how St. Petersburg's desire to manage non-Orthodox faiths increased dramatically during the reign of Catherine the Great, when vast numbers of Catholics and Protestants entered the empire through either conquest (as with Poland) or immigration (as with Mennonites, German Catholics, German Lutherans, and so on). In all cases, churches did not draw the ire of officialdom if they maintained order within their ranks, professed loyalty to the state, and left what the state deemed non-spiritual matters to others to sort out.[25]

Catherine further strengthened the role of the state during her reign when she insisted on a state-centred governance model based on the rule of law, or *Polizeistaat*. Of course, such a model required state servitors, and their ranks increased at an unprecedented rate during her reign and after. Even though numbers still paled in comparison to their West European counterparts, the empire's bureaucracy had begun to take shape by the mid-nineteenth century.[26] Members of the Guardians Committee stood front and centre within this centralized and so-called enlightened officialdom. The written record of Cornies' correspondence makes plain that such officials increasingly directed Mennonite economic activity and that their first choice was to direct it through him. They did so because they believed European colonists had a vital role to play in the agricultural development of the entire region, and Mennonites most preeminently.[27] As we shall see, the Guardians Committee by the 1840s warned that the Mennonites' very privileges obtained in their treasured Privilegium at point of settlement depended on their ongoing lead role within New Russian society. By one recent reading, Johann Cornies accepted that reading of the Privilegium and insisted that Mennonites keep up their side of the bargain to survive. It helped that his pietism was sufficiently strong to accept contemporary readings of religion as primarily a spiritual matter, even if pietistic concerns embraced the whole of society.[28]

But why did Russian officials at key points disregard the elected Mennonite officers who sat in the Molotschna Administrative Office and instead work with Cornies, who had never won an elected office? Two reasons present themselves, both of which made the Cornies era possible. First, the paucity of officials meant the state had little choice but to enlist representatives from religious minorities, including Mennonites; and second, as J. Arch Getty has recently demonstrated, the Russian state had long relied on patrimonial systems of governance whereby elites preferred clients and dependent servitors rather than autonomous bureaucratic systems or the vagaries of an electoral process.[29] Cornies worked well within this system, though almost all Mennonites in conflict with him likewise appealed directly to the state, a key indicator of patrimonialism. Ironically, by the end of Cornies' life one can conclude that almost all Mennonites had adopted and accepted a patrimonial relationship with the Russian state, even if the process by which that happened was tension filled.

We have already identified one such incident: the Warkentin affair of 1822, when the vast majority of Molotschna Mennonites formed a separate Large Flemish congregation led by Ältester Jakob Warkentin from the village of Altonau. Though not a direct protest against Cornies, it nevertheless pitted conservatives against the new Mennonite pietists, which included Cornies.

The next significant conflict followed on its heels. It began innocently enough in April 1826 when individuals throughout the Molotschna alleged that Cornies had stolen horses that he had retrieved from the adjacent Nogai settlements. Though unfounded, Cornies felt aggrieved and accused the *Gebietsamt* of being complicit in these rumours when it did little to squelch them. In time the Guardians Committee became involved, sided with Cornies, and pressured the Gebietsamt to identify and punish the culprits. It did so in a letter to all village offices of Molotschna on 15 May 1826, but not before Cornies had resigned from his formal duties and responsibilities. From then on, he relied entirely for his authority within Molotschna on his ties to Russian officials, which were many and formidable.[30]

Other conflicts irrupted, as in 1829 when Cornies removed the German pietist Tobias Voth from his teaching position at the new-era Orloff village school.[31] He replaced Voth with the Lutheran pietist Heinrich Heese, and he undertook this even though his *de jure* oversight over all Molotschna Mennonite schools did not commence for another decade. Even this was mere prelude to yet another conflict that exploded in June 1846 when a Mennonite farmer in the village of Blumenort struck his labourer, a purported Hutterite. It escalated when members of the Large Flemish Mennonite congregation refused to execute corporal punishment against the labourer when ordered to do so. Cornies became involved, and in short order he, the Gebietsamt, and the Large Congregation had all made representations to the Guardians Committee. The issue was eventually resolved, but not before the Guardians Committee intervened directly in this matter and pronounced sentence. Nor did it end there, as the committee subsequently intervened in the Gebietsamt elections, reaffirmed Cornies' authority, ordered the dissolution of the Large Flemish church into three smaller (and more malleable) entities, and permanently exiled several of the key players and preachers involved in this drama from the Russian empire.[32] It was a stunning moment, and an unqualified victory for Cornies.

Governance within the Mennonite colonies shifted dramatically in the first half of the nineteenth century. Scholars have variously described the Cornies' era as "the waning of congregational authority" and "the breaking of the *Aeltesten* [churchly leaders]." Both of those appellations fit, though Cornies' triumph was not simply a blow to ecclesial authority. It also challenged participatory and civil decision-making models within Molotschna, and gradually also in Chortitza. For his was no less a victory for imperial Russian patrimonial bureaucratization. In time Mennonite conservatives and liberals, as well as secular and ecclesial bodies within the colonies, would all appeal directly to the Russian state to settle intra-Mennonite conflicts. Every such appeal further bound Mennonites to their empire.

Agriculture

In 1843 the peripatetic Hanoverian agricultural scientist August von Haxthausen wrote the following after his epic journey to the Russian empire: "The strict Mennonites regard agriculture as a religious duty, from which no one is exempted, unless by absolute necessity, according to the words of Scripture, 'In the sweat of thy face shalt though eat bread.'"[33] More than 150 years later the famed German sociologist Max Weber observed that there was a striking correspondence between Protestants intent on a strict pietistic regimen and their corresponding commitment to economic flourishing. Of the religious sectarians, he noted that Mennonites separated themselves from the state when it came to military service, but he saw no such separation when it came to their role as "social carriers of industry."[34]

Mennonites clearly established and maintained that link between a pietistic expression of faith and a strong economic engagement as they played a major role in the profound transformation of New Russia in the first half of the nineteenth century. The region grew dramatically at this time as its population more than doubled between 1825 and 1860 alone, even as it remained relatively sparsely settled. Nor was this merely a rural and peasantist increase, as the empire's determination to secure a series of regional and international markets proved successful. Odessa, the regional powerhouse and New Russian capital continued to grow apace before 1850, as did the Black Sea port cities of Kherson and Nikolaev. No less important for Mennonites was the founding of Berdiansk on the northern shores of the Sea of Azov in 1835. With it Molotschna Mennonites went from a remote agricultural backwater to within 100 kilometres of immediate sea access to burgeoning European and North American ports. By 1860 Moscow and St. Petersburg remained the most urbanized Russian provinces, though, strikingly, Kherson (home to Odessa, Nikolaev, and the city of Kherson) and Tavrida (home to Berdiansk) provinces now occupied the next two positions. By midcentury only St. Petersburg outpaced Odessa when it came to the empire's export trade, and the gap was closing.[35]

Mennonites mirrored market trends and opportunities across New Russia when they concentrated on sheep breeding until 1840 and then shifted to grain. Several reasons presented themselves. British markets had an almost insatiable appetite for wool at the end of the eighteenth century given the rapid expansion of their woolen textile industry, and Russian officials were keen to put their empire's producers at the forefront. Already in 1797 V.P. Kochubei, the former minister of internal affairs, petitioned for the introduction of fine-fleeced sheep in New Russia. The region's peasants had large herds of their own but had long preferred to breed smaller, coarse-wooled sheep, which were less vulnerable to disease, better able to withstand the periodic droughts that wracked the region, and also able to provide highly valued sources of food and fat (the latter could be used for lamp fuel as well as cooking). State officials, more focused on international markets, encouraged estate owners and colonists to shift to fine-fleeced merino breeding stock, which they first introduced into the region in 1804, the founding date of the Molotschna colony.[36] Though there were some initial gains, New Russian fine-fleeced stock took a step back following the unusually harsh winter of 1812–13 when thousands died. It took years to recover.

Eventually the Guardians Committee engaged the services of Cornies to improve the breeding stock of merino fine-fleeced sheep in the region. In early 1824 A.M. Fadeev of the Guardians Committee instructed Cornies to travel to St. Petersburg to obtain merino breeding stock from the empire's experimental farm in Tsarskoe Selo. He returned to the colonies in August of that year, whereupon he distributed the merinos across the Molotschna and Chortitza colonies. Less than a year later authorities commissioned Cornies to travel to Saxony to purchase robust merino breeding stock, even as he acknowledged that harsh winter conditions made it difficult for the region's breeders to obtain sufficient fodder.[37] As evidence of such, Molotschna Mennonites alone lost over 10,000 sheep during the severe winter of 1824–5. Cornies reported that many had lost their entire herds, though the losses also suggest how dramatically Mennonites had embraced fine-fleeced sheep breeding.[38]

Mennonite sheep herds continued to grow rapidly as Mennonites pastured their herds on reserve lands within Molotschna and Chortitza that had been set aside for future growth in the colonies. By 1825 Cornies had also started to sharecrop his own sheep herds in neighbouring Nogai villages, though this was only the tip of the iceberg when it came to his personal holdings.[39] From modest beginnings, Cornies had over 14,000 merinos on his own lands by 1845 and sharecropped another 8,000 on Nogai lands. He earned a staggering 454,000 rubles from the sale of wool alone between 1825 and 1845, by which time he was one of the largest sheep breeders in New Russia. At peak production in 1838 Mennonites pastured more than 170,000 sheep, well beyond almost all producers in the empire. Though some, like Cornies and Wilhelm Martens, had particularly large herds, Mennonites averaged 125 sheep per household by 1838, up from 46 in 1830. Mennonite wool producers sent their wool to foreign textile producers by way of annual markets in Ekaterinoslav, Kharkov, Elisavetgrad, and Kremenchug from which they primarily exported their products via the port cities of Odessa and Berdiansk.[40]

Although New Russian sheep breeders, Mennonites among them, experienced considerable success in the first third of the nineteenth century, their fortunes collapsed rapidly in the late 1830s. By that time many breeders had exhausted their pastures by over-grazing. Resulting epidemics decimated entire districts. In addition, Australian sheep producers had begun to flood world markets after 1830, just as changes in British manufacturing techniques and consumer tastes mitigated against New Russian breeds and breeding. Lastly, the rapid population growth of the Black Sea steppe lands squeezed out previously vacant lands and brought a close to the era of virtually limitless pasture lands. In its place New Russian agriculturalists, including Mennonites, turned to grain cultivation. Once again Mennonites quickly became regional leaders thanks to Cornies' increasingly draconian supervision of this dramatic shift. This was, after all, the time when Cornies, the state-appointed president for life of the Mennonite Agricultural Society, had unassailable power within the colonies. He was determined to make good use of it as he compelled Mennonites to adopt the latest practices in grain cultivation.

To that end Cornies read broadly in diverse fields, from viniculture to sericulture to the latest practices in grain cultivation. He observed new techniques from St. Petersburg to the German lands and ordered their implementation by Mennonites. During his tenure with the Agricultural Society initially for Molotschna and, later, over Chortitza he imposed new regulations on crop-rotation systems on all farm holders. By this means Mennonites steadily increased the widespread production of wheat, though they also cultivated rye, oats, and barley in rotation. Cornies also insisted that Mennonites keep a quarter of their arable lands fallow to ensure natural regeneration. He experimented with the use of manure as a natural fertilizer, though even that did not compare to his impact in afforestation projects. Here he was encouraged to act by Samuel Contenius of the Guardians Committee, who had experimented with tree plantations on his own experimental farm in Ekaterinoslav. Cornies quickly saw the value of afforestation projects and imposed his will on what had been the treeless landscape of the Molotschna colony. By 1825 Mennonites had planted over 200,000 trees across the colony, for a wide range of purposes. Trees planted as hedgerows protected the colonists from the harsh continental winds and raised water tables on this semi-arid steppe. Fruit trees, from apple to pear to cherry to apricot, contributed directly to Mennonite diets and produced a surplus to sell at regional markets. Nor did it stop there. David G. Rempel has calculated that Mennonites had planted more than six million trees in the Molotschna colony by 1855, and more than a million in Chortitza. No wonder visitors, from Germans to Russian officials to the tsar himself, repeatedly valorized this Mennonite oasis in the broad steppe lands of New Russia.

Thus, Cornies worked under the leadership of the Guardians Committee successfully to transform Mennonite agricultural practices at a time when sheep breeding had ceased to be viable. Mennonites experienced robust increases in grain yields in the first half of the nineteenth century. They cultivated more land more effectively. Whereas Mennonites had yielded a five-fold return from seed in 1809–14, their yields ballooned almost fifteen-fold by 1844–8.[41] Nor did any of this happen by chance, especially under Cornies' watch, as he regularly inspected the lands within his jurisdiction, set regulations that he expected to be enforced, and ordered that those who failed to comply be fined or otherwise punished. He flooded the Mennonite colonies with rules and regulations. For example, he did not simply nor indeterminately order Mennonites to plant trees on their lands. Instead, he ordered that these trees be planted in "a straight line, at a distance no greater than one faden [six feet] from one another." Mennonites were ordered to weed their fields and plantations, and he told them when and how to do it properly. He ordered them to trim the newly planted trees "back to three or four buds in the year in which they are planted." He ordered Mennonites to prevent too much sap from rising to the crown of the trees, and so on. Cornies deemed no regulatory matter too small, and he brooked no opposition, especially when the state, the mighty Russian empire, arguably the most powerful landed stated in the world by 1830, itself supported him. No wonder opposition arose against Cornies when it did and that his legacy was, at best, a mixed one.

Conclusion

Johann Cornies oversaw a profound transformation of Mennonite life in the second quarter of the nineteenth century. Mennonite agriculturalists diversified and intensified their farming operations, at least in part because of innovations that he mandated. Despite the opposition Cornies encountered, Mennonite sheep herds and crop yields increased, and Mennonites strengthened their tie to markets at the very time New Russia's entrepôts emerged as empire and European powerhouses. Mennonites by the 1840s lived in sturdy homes within their villages, made so in part because of instructions from Cornies which stipulated the size of home, material and shape of construction, the use of firewalls, the minimum thicknesses of exterior walls, the exact dimensions of roof overhangs, windows, and the swing of their doors. Building distances between households were equally regulated under Cornies' watch, as were the trees that surrounded Mennonite yards and the brick fence lines which lined their villages' broad avenues.[42]

Nor was his influence limited to Mennonites, as the Guardians Committee repeatedly charged Cornies to lend his services to a wide range of agriculturalists in New Russia, whether Jewish agriculturalists, Dukhobors, Molokan sectarians, or Hutterites. Cornies played a particular active role in the state's efforts to settle the region's long-nomadic Nogai Tatars in permanent villages.[43] St. Petersburg's decision to bring all the colonists, Tatars, and state peasants together in 1836 in the powerful new Ministry of State Domains was pivotal here, as it began to create a level playing field across diverse peoples, Mennonites among them. This meant Cornies could rely on immediate imperial backing at the height of his powers.

Historian David G. Rempel has observed that Cornies never accepted any payment for a lifetime of state service. Though true, it must be said that Cornies became a fabulously wealthy Mennonite during his time of greatest influence. He developed and maintained massive sheep herds, became similarly engaged in grain cultivation, and founded his own experimental farm on Yushanlee, near Orloff. Cornies repeatedly sought full title to the rented Yushanlee estate, even though no private estates were permitted in Molotschna. Yet in 1836 the emperor Nicholas I finally relented and awarded these lands to Cornies as his own private domain. After a period of lease arrangements that dated back to 1812, he could finally claim title outright to almost 4,000 desiatinas of land within Molotschna (recall that a full allotment holder received 65 desiatinas). Cornies purchased an additional 6,000 desiatinas outside of Molotschna, which, along with his distilling licence and other involvements, made him among the wealthiest of Mennonites by the time of his death. Urry has estimated Cornies' annual income by the late 1830s to be an astonishing 60,000 rubles.[44]

There is no doubt that he played his role well as Russian servitor, in Harvey Dyck's apt formulation. But was he ever a Mennonite hero?[45] He certainly was not originally, when even those reputed to be his friends, such as the Chortitza Mennonite preacher David Epp, described Cornies as "more despotical than Christian." Only eight of forty-four surviving Molotschna Mennonite village histories published in 1848 paid tribute to Cornies, even though he died that very year, an indication of how negatively Mennonites viewed him at the time of his death. As Dyck has made plain, it would take a half-century before Mennonites would begin to use hagiographic language about Cornies, evidenced with P.M. Friesen's astonishing claim, published in 1911, that only Menno Simons was his peer within all of Mennonite history.[46]

Some Mennonites clearly opposed Cornies because of the occasionally draconian manner with which he initiated reform. However, an even more principled opposition arose from Mennonite preachers who opposed Cornies' pietistic progressivism. Thus Cornies' time was less about the stark opposition between faith and secularism, as it is often depicted, and more about what kind of faith would be held, and what would be the limitations thereof, in any. Cornies' pietistic expression of faith broke away from erstwhile Mennonite understandings even as it stimulated a broader religious revival, and everything changed as a result. To give but one example, he sided with state officials in his determination to remove ministerial oversight of Mennonite education, one of many ways in which he weakened the power of Mennonite ministry councils. The very designation of jurisdictions that were the purview of ministers and Ältesters, as opposed to those that were not, was itself a pietistic development that was hitherto unprecedented in the Mennonite world. Nor was this the final time that pietistic thought impacted the Mennonite colonies of New Russia. We shall turn to the pietistic influence again in the next chapter when it precipitated a threefold crisis in the middle of the nineteenth century, one that shook the Mennonite world to its core and utterly transformed it in its resolution.

Chapter Six

A Community in Crisis: A Divided Faith, the Revolt of the Landless, and Threatened Military Service, 1860–1874

In dramatic fashion the Russian emperor Alexander II warned the Moscow nobility in March 1856 that the empire would soon abolish serfdom: "the existing condition of owning souls cannot remain unchanged. It is better to abolish serfdom from above than to await the time when it will begin to abolish itself from below." His was a clarion call, and the so-called Tsar Liberator emancipated the empire's serfs less than five years later, assisted every step of the way by an enlightened bureaucracy which had come of age in the first half of the nineteenth century. Other reforms followed as the empire created and empowered provincial and district councils (*zemstvos*) in 1864, the same year in which St. Petersburg enacted the first of several sweeping judicial reforms. As a bookend to the servile emancipation of 1861 Alexander II emancipated state peasants in 1866 and introduced urban and municipal reforms in 1870. In 1871 he approved legislation which brought the empire's colonists into juridical conformity with former serfs and state peasants as the empire literally took the law out of the colonists' hands.[1] Finally, in 1874 St. Petersburg completely overhauled the imperial military. No wonder historians have referred to the 1860s as the era of the Great Reforms, as even this listing only identifies the most outstanding reforms introduced by Alexander as he overhauled the empire after its humiliating defeat in the Crimean War (1853–6).[2] The pace and promise of change was such that even the regime's sharpest critics, such as Alexander Herzen, optimistically proclaimed that Alexander II had brought new life to the empire.

By contrast the Mennonite communities of New Russia experienced a tumultuous and fraught period after the Crimean War as they confronted three distinct crises between 1860 and 1874. By the first, a new Mennonite religious movement decades' long in pietist formation exploded onto the scene in 1860; one that threatened the confessional integrity and cultural identity of the Molotschna and Chortitza settlements, risked direct engagement of imperial authorities in Mennonite domestic matters, and pitted family against family. Three years later a second crisis irrupted when 153 landless Mennonites appealed for assistance from the empire in their struggle against more powerful Mennonites in their midst. When they did, a crisis that had its origins in the earliest settlement period suddenly burst into the open. Landless Mennonites were powerless at a time when only male landholders had the franchise. No wonder the landless, who comprised the majority of Mennonites in New Russia by mid-century, appealed to the Guardians Committee in Odessa in 1863 as they sought access to land and the right to vote.

There are several striking similarities in these two crises. In both Mennonites proved unable or unwilling to resolve the crisis internally as the aggrieved parties sought assistance from the multilayered Russian state. The Crimean War played a significant role in the instigation of both crises, and both resulted from long-term trends that had developed within and beyond the increasingly porous boundaries of the Chortitza and Molotschna settlements. Finally, and in a manner that mystified imperial bureaucrats, both pointed to the lack of a civil and ecclesial coherence within the settlements themselves. The latter point may be particularly surprising, as Johann Cornies enjoyed almost unassailable authority across the Russian Mennonite world at the time of his unexpected death in 1848. However, Cornies failed to secure that authority institutionally, and almost immediately Mennonite civil and ecclesial leaders sought to reclaim the authority he had denied them in a struggle that dated back to the very settlement of Chortitza. There was a certain correspondence between church and state leaders within the Mennonite settlements, as Mennonite ministers often aligned themselves with those (landed) Mennonites who had voted them into office, and with the village and settlement councils which the landholders oversaw. Often there were also strong familial connections between ministers and mayors. Yet such civil and ecclesial alliances within Chortitza and Molotschna proved incapable of avoiding the crises that irrupted after 1860. On the one hand, the emergence of a new Mennonite pietist/separatist movement undermined what limited ecclesial unity had existed in the Mennonite settlements by mid-century while also spurring on sectarian movements among Orthodox peasants in the region.[3] On the other, even when most Mennonite ministers formed a united front alongside most Mennonite village and district councils they were powerless to stop those disgruntled and disenfranchised landless who chose to appeal directly to the empire's vast bureaucracy.

The third crisis irrupted after 1870 when St. Petersburg initiated a comprehensive military reform across the empire based upon universal conscription. Mennonites quickly realized that this signalled the end of their "permanent" exemption from military service. For many it also signalled that Mennonites would soon be compelled to emigrate from the Russian empire in search of a homeland which would honour their longstanding refusal to abandon their pacifist position.

We investigate all three crises in this chapter.

A Crisis of Faith: The Founding of the Mennonite Brethren

Eighteen Mennonites pulled no punches on 6 January 1860 when they addressed a letter to "the total body of church elders of our Molotschna Mennonite Church."[4] In their very first sentence they denounced "the decadent condition of the Mennonite brotherhood," most of whom lived "satanic lives." The signatories, none of whom served as ministers or Ältesters, feared the Russian state would not tolerate such immoral behaviour much longer, at which time it would rescind all rights and privileges granted to Mennonites at point of settlement. Their abhorrence was such that the eighteen immediately disassociated themselves from the entire Mennonite fellowship, itself a de facto act of mass excommunication. As their most dramatic act, they henceforth refused to participate in Communion services with "the many covetous, drunkards and blasphemers" of Molotschna. They would have nothing more to do with those who "walk in the flesh."

How, then, did the eighteen propose that God's future judgment might be averted and right relations restored within the Molotschna colony? Their declaration offered a road map forward. For starters, Mennonites needed to return to the teachings of their faith's founder, Menno Simons, and they needed to be "born again," as Christ had once asked of Nicodemus in the Gospel of John. Mennonites needed to claim a true baptism of faith, not merely one learned by rote or adopted by convention. Finally, the eighteen urged Mennonites to confess their sins and to lead new lives of repentance. The signatories alone, it seemed, were the true church and Menno's spiritual progeny.

Mennonites in Imperial Russia produced no document more extraordinary than this one. Were the eighteen correct when they depicted their fellow Mennonites as uniformly debased in matters of faith and practice? Were Mennonites uniformly anything in the mid-nineteenth century? At the outset there appears to be good reason to believe that such ecclesial unity existed, especially after New Russia's Mennonite congregations formed a unified church structure in 1850 when almost all congregational Ältesters and ministers came together in a *Kirchenkonvent* (Church Council). Both Flemish and Frisian congregations agreed to cooperate within this new structure as only the minority Kleine Gemeinde refused to participate.[5] Mennonites had only unified in 1850, however, after the state had insisted upon it as officials had grown weary of the multiple voices coming from the Mennonite settlements, none of whom appeared to have authority over the whole. It was a problem they rarely encountered elsewhere, from Orthodox to Catholic to Lutheran settlements.

Mennonite leaders based the *Kirchenkonvent* of 1850 on earlier ecclesial coalitions which congregations had formed in New Russia, and Prussia before that, as they unified periodically in the face of shared challenges. The Guardians Committee reinforced this tendency as early as the 1820s when it addressed its circulars to the then non-existent Mennonites' "spiritual council." However, in the end the *Kirchenkonvent* of 1850 produced little more than the chimera of cooperation, nor did it have any authority to intervene in individual congregations unless the congregations themselves requested it. Instead, strong, and varied congregations existed well into mid-century, something belied by the unilateral depictions of the 1860 missive.

For example, Cornies' death prompted many to turn against both Cornies' Agricultural Union and his Ohrloff congregation. Both the Flemish congregation in Alexanderwohl and the Frisian congregation in Rudnerweide quickly reasserted their autonomy after 1848, even though their leaders dutifully signed the *Kirchenkonvent*. If that was not enough, a rival for Ohrloff as a progressive Mennonite voice in Molotschna had appeared in 1833 when forty families immigrated to New Russia to found the village and congregation of Gnadenfeld. Led by minister Wilhelm Lange, himself a reformed Lutheran, the new village represented a significant sea-change within Molotschna. Even the succession crisis that followed Lange's death in 1840 did not subvert Gnadenfeld's influence in the religious tumult of the 1850s and 1860s. As a measure of their Germanic acculturation the Gnadenfelders preferred High German over the peasantist Mennonite Plautdietsch in everyday discourse, and they wore contemporary German clothes, all of which set them apart from their Mennonite coreligionists, who derisively referred to the recent arrivals as Lutherans and Moravians. Even though this new congregation ostensibly shared the Old Flemish Mennonite faith of the first Mennonites to settle in New Russia, its expression was profoundly different. Thus, ironically, Mennonite leaders signed the 1850 *Kirchenkonvent* at the very time when centrifugal forces were pulling them apart, ecclesially speaking.

In addition, missionaries for a new and more assertive pietism had begun to enter New Russia by mid-century. Unlike their pietistic forebears, whom we examined in the previous chapter, this younger generation preached a fiery message. They were no longer content to influence those who remained in churches that clung to the old ways. Instead, they condemned those churches as spiritually corrupt and ethically bankrupt, such that further compromise with the unfaithful was unthinkable. The greatest proponents of this new movement hailed from Württemberg and combined pietist separation with the proclamation of Christ's imminent return in judgment. As one might expect, the established Lutheran church moved to silence these new pietists or send them to the furthest reaches of German European settlement. Church authorities sent one of these proponents, Eduard Wüst (1818–59), to New Russia in 1845, where he pastored a colony of Swabian separatists who had settled after 1835 in four villages between Molotschna and the port city of Berdiansk, having wintered en route in the Mennonite settlements.[6]

Unlike almost all Mennonite ministers, who normally preached sermons from published collections passed down by congregations for decades, Wüst preached extemporaneously. In some ways Wüst proclaimed a personal faith that mirrored what pietists of the previous generation had done, and as we considered in the previous chapter. But in a radical departure, Wüst combined this call for radical love with the demand that the new believers separate themselves out from the established – and therefore fallen – church. He declared that those wanting to join his movement needed to do so through an explicit and often highly emotional conversion. He deemed the earlier Mennonite baptism to be insufficient, as ministers had performed it within spiritually bankrupt congregations. Wüst also declared in impassioned sermons that God's manifestation in the lives of His true followers would necessarily be emotional. Alexander K. Brune, a state investigator of the new religious movement initiated by Wüst, noted in his report of 30 September 1864 that converts to this new form of worship "sing, jump, rejoice, dance and kiss everyone (without distinction of sex). They explain these outrageous outbursts of joy as experiencing the unction of the Holy Spirit, adding that they are being especially blessed and are living with the foretaste of eternity. They consider themselves to be the community of saints."[7] This itinerant preacher's impact on the movement of religious renewal across New Russia was such that historian P.M. Friesen, writing a half-century later, declared that only the faith's founder, Menno Simons, was Wüst's peer in terms of evangelical import. It was an astonishing claim but indicated how dramatically Wüst transformed the Mennonite communities of New Russia, for better or worse.[8]

However significant Wüst's influence may have been on Mennonites, it was not alone as many Mennonites had aligned themselves to pietist-separatists for decades. Those who settled in the Molotschna village of Gnadenfeld in 1835 had previously been in the Mennonite (Old Flemish) Brenkenhofswalde-Franztal congregations in Brandenburg, Prussia, where the Moravian Brethren had mentored them since at least 1812. Not surprisingly, the Gnadenfelders sought to build on their pietist legacy when they established the so-called Brethren Mennonite School in 1857 dedicated to pietistic-separatist pedagogy. This connection was such that Moravian Brethren of Württemberg contributed 400 rubles to the construction of the school and a Moravian brother from Moscow named Maibom donated a piano. Unlike the traditional Mennonite school in Molotschna, the Gnadenfeld congregation designed the new school after similar Moravian institutions and mission schools. School instructors taught their pupils "enthusiastic" (*froehliches*) worship until a series of challenges forced the school's closure in 1863.[9]

Pietist-separatists maintained other arenas to exert their influence, including in the village of Alexanderwohl, founded in 1821, where the congregation taught a theology of German pietism. As part of it, Ältester Peter Wedel challenged classically Mennonite teachings from the start. He refused to declare that Mennonites alone practised the true faith. He accepted the legitimacy of pietist faiths which practised infant baptism, supported the use of force, and proclaimed an open communion. Mennonite acquisition of High German corresponded with this theological shift. Previously foundational leaders – including Menno Simons and Dirk Philips – had solely written in Dutch, but that language and culture now gave way. Even works in translation, such as van Braght's *Martyrs' Mirror*, waned in appeal as many Mennonites turned to German-language pietistic literature, from Jung-Stilling's popular novel *Heimweh* to the printed sermon collections of non-Mennonite German pietist preachers.[10]

The Crimean War (1853–6) dramatically increased Mennonite engagement with the world beyond their villages, including with the world of pietist-separatism. Mennonites actively participated in the hostilities even if they did not serve as combatants. Their men travelled to and from the front in the thousands as part of their required service to the empire. They hauled grain to feed the armies and hauled away and cared for the wounded, with up to five thousand of the latter treated in Molotschna, where Mennonites established a special hospital in Gnadenfeld for that purpose.[11] Officials particularly prized

Mennonites for cartage because of the relative superiority of their wagons. Any sense Mennonites may have had about their community's isolation faded away as they watched troops march through their villages and their own Mennonite men cart the wounded back, or as they themselves passed through non-Mennonite village after village as they hauled grains to the front lines. These treks allowed Mennonites direct access to the German pietist-separatists who had settled across New Russia in anticipation of the apocalyptic reign of Christ. Many renewed acquaintances with those pietist-separatists who had wintered with Mennonites as they immigrated into the region. Elsewhere Mennonite merchants who had recently settled in Berdiansk – where Wüst had visited them – sought refuge in German pietist-separatist villages when belligerents threatened to attack the port cities on the Sea of Azov. Even without the Berdiansk Mennonites, a disproportionate number of Mennonite merchants embraced the individualized message proclaimed by Wüst and other pietistic separatists, nor should this surprise as these merchants had long traversed the broad New Russian steppe as part of their vocation. They had long ago stretched the horizons of their world beyond the confines of Chortitza and Molotschna.

Thus, Mennonites were ripe for conversion once Wüst began to engage them in his periodic regional mission festivals. Though not situated in Molotschna he held them in adjacent German colonist villages that were close enough for Mennonites to attend and participate. They responded positively when Wüst challenged them to abstain from alcohol consumption, an omnipresent scourge in the Mennonite colonies by mid-century, especially at the annual regional markets. They listened to Wüst's fervent sermons, took in the Bible studies that followed, sang the emotion-laden hymns, stood up and danced to the free movement of the Spirit, embraced and kissed each other regardless of gender or marital status, pledged themselves to purity, and increasingly felt alienated from the existing churches of Molotschna and Chortitza.[12] Only the Gnadenfeld congregation appeared receptive to this new movement, such that pietistically inclined Mennonites across Molotschna gravitated to it by the mid-1850s. Even here adherents tended to meet surreptitiously, often in village homes, where they sang hymns, danced, jumped, kissed, prayed, and studied the Bible, all with ecstatic physical engagement. They read pietist-separatist materials which travellers had brought into New Russia from Wurttemberg, informally referred to each other as Wüst's Brethren, and denigrated the established Mennonite congregations and their ministry councils.

James Urry has suggested the degree to which those initially drawn to this movement were unusual within the larger Mennonite world.

They tended to be better educated and have professional backgrounds as merchants or entrepreneurs which connected them to the world beyond Molotschna's borders. The individualized nature of pietist faith appealed directly to them. Others were prosperous landholders who felt overly constrained by village limitations on holdings. Some had pietist roots that stretched back to Tobias Voth's days in the 1820s when pietists first flexed their spiritual muscles in Cornies' Molotschna. Still others, such as the Gnadenfelders, who comprised the majority of the first Wüst Brethren, had previously immersed in pietist-separatist discourse. Almost all were young, rarely over forty.[13]

Mennonite pietist-separatists also emerged in the Chortitza settlement in the 1850s thanks to early followers who circulated the sermons of German evangelist and pietist Ludwig Hofacker (1798–1828). Mennonite pastors read his sermons from the pulpit well into mid-century despite their implicit challenge to Mennonite ecclesiology. Up to fifty Mennonites in the Chortitza villages of Einlage and Kronsweide had converted to this new movement by 1853, which suggests that this new message appealed to both Flemish (Einlage) and Frisian (Kronsweide) Mennonites.[14] A contemporary, Abraham Unger, later recounted the physical manifestations of these conversions: "They were almost always corporeal [Unger's expression]; for example, when an individual was moved, the person began to bemoan and lament his agony of sin; some to wrestle with God and to cry for mercy, and so on until, after some hours or days, they found grace, forgiveness and peace. These people were full of joy and praised God and assembled as often as possible and had a fervent love for one another." However, the Baptists played a much greater role in Chortitza thanks to the renowned preacher Johann Oncken (1800–84). Known as the "Father of the Continental Baptists," Oncken first encountered Mennonites in Prussia in 1833. His influence was considerable in Chortitza in the late 1850s thanks to an ongoing correspondence with Unger. This may also account for why the Baptist stress on the conversion experience may have been stronger among Chortitza Mennonites than in Molotschna.[15]

Thus, Mennonite pietist-separatists emerged in both Chortitza and Molotschna by the late 1850s, without the support of elected Mennonite ministers. With ever-increasing fervor, they maintained that the existing Mennonite congregations offered no solution for the increasingly degenerate actions of Mennonites themselves. An 1856 survey of Molotschna settlement reinforced this perspective when the schoolteachers surveyed decried the state of Mennonite morality. Similarly, Mennonite ministers had for decades expressed their dismay that Mennonites had committed a host of sins, including drunkenness, a refusal to accept church discipline, marital infidelity, bestiality, theft, a disavowal of Christ's lordship, and financial impropriety.[16] Unfortunately it is not possible to determine if such violations of church discipline were true and if so, if they were something new or something disproportionately worrisome in that moment. Nevertheless, to those wishing to receive confirmation of their salvation through a conversion experience it appeared that signs of moral failure were everywhere.

Regardless, Mennonite pietist-separatists concluded that the situation had worsened such that their co-religionists across the district needed to repent. They called for a radical new beginning akin to what Menno Simons had brought to the Reformation, and to that end they requested in 1859 that Ältester Lenzmann of the Gnadenfeld Congregation preside over a separate communion service for the Wüst Brethren. Lenzmann's abrupt refusal prompted the Wüst's Brethren to gather privately in late November in the home of Cornelius Wiens of Elisabethtal, whereupon the assembled men and women "broke bread." Mennonite church leaders soon found out about this clandestine gathering and threatened the Brethren with excommunication.[17] Tensions were at the boiling point, and it is in this context that the infamous eighteen composed and sent their declaration of 6 January 1860. Matters did not stop there as the Brethren instituted a new form of baptism in March 1862 when Gerhard Wieler (re)baptized Abraham Unger and Heinrich Neufeld by immersion in the Tokmak Stream. It signalled both the Brethren's alignment with the Baptists on such a significant faith marker and their rejection of established Mennonite baptismal practices that involved sprinkling and pouring, but not immersion. Within two years Brethren leaders in both Chortitza and Molotschna settlements mandated the new form of baptism for its adherents as the movement quickly took shape across the Mennonite villages.

The Mennonite leadership of New Russia responded vociferously to the fledgling Brethren movement. In short order the *Kirchenkonvent* angrily turned the matter over to Mennonite civil councils, who denounced the Brethren. More ominously Mennonite district authorities from the outset in 1860 appealed to the State's Guardians Committee to ban the movement and exile all who persisted within this new sectarian movement. Mennonite authorities demanded that the Brethren no longer assemble either publicly or privately. Mennonite civil leaders pointed out that the new Brethren had begun to proselytize Orthodox peasants across New Russia, an illegal act. Imperial Russia strictly forbade such conversions, and by 10 July 1863 the governor of Tavrida province identified certain Molotschna Mennonites as particularly egregious in their actions.[18] Clearly the stakes were high for Mennonite ministers in the *Kirchenkonvent* and for Mennonite civil authorities. Meanwhile one of the new Brethren leaders, the merchant Johannes Claassen, disobeyed local Mennonite authorities and travelled to St. Petersburg, where he received support from the city's Baptist leaders. Most importantly, Claassen in May 1862 directly petitioned the tsar himself to intervene on the Brethren's behalf, an indication of how powerful some of the earliest Mennonite pietist-separatists had become. It helped that Claassen had previously worked with Eduard von Hahn during the latter's time as head of the Guardians Committee. Hahn's transfer to St. Petersburg in 1849 placed him near the administrative pinnacle of the unfolding controversy. Claassen's efforts bore fruit in February 1864 when the Ministry of Justice informed the Ministry of Internal Affairs that it had ordered Alexander Brune to investigate the newly emergent Mennonite sect. Coming as it did on the aftermath of the Polish uprising of that year it was clear the empire would be vigilant in its assessment of any potential disturbance on the New Russian frontier.[19] Clearly this was a crisis of immense proportion for Molotschna and Chortitza Mennonites.

The Mennonite Landless Crisis

The tumultuous emergence of the Brethren movement in the 1850s shook the Mennonite settlements of New Russia to the core. However, an equally grave crisis irrupted in 1863 when 150 landless Mennonites petitioned the Guardians Committee to intervene on their behalf in their dispute with Mennonite civil and ecclesial authorities in Molotschna. They asked the Committee to extend the franchise among Mennonites to include landless males and to distribute all remaining lands within Molotschna to the landless to fulfil the expressed purpose of these lands at point of settlement. With this petition, and one they had submitted earlier, the Mennonite landless exposed a sore that had festered for generations within Molotschna.[20] To understand more requires a consideration of initial settlement conditions and terms, all of which David G. Rempel laid out in his 1933 doctoral dissertation.

The Russian government chose hereditary over repartitional landholding tenure for all foreigners when it formed New Russia in 1764 and passed a Land Decree which welcomed European colonists to settle it. In doing so the empire systematized practices for the wide range of European settlers anticipated. Rempel argued that Catherine wanted to avoid the problems which had already arisen with servile peasants who periodically divided up existing holdings into ever smaller portions, always at the expense of agricultural viability. By contrast colonist

Figure 4. Agricultural work south of the village of Altonau in the Molotschna settlement, circa 1900. Collection of Nikolai and Alla Krylov, Melitopol University.

landholdings would be indivisible such that only one child would inherit the familial farmstead. The state also introduced several provisions to offset the problem of future landlessness that would increase exponentially with each new generation. For one, a sixth of all lands in any given colony were to be set aside as *surplus lands* for future distribution to the landless. *Reserve lands* were also to be set aside in all colonies so that future generations of landless could establish new villages of their own and obtain the land they needed. Lastly, the state declared that all colonist settlers should make provision in their villages for male householders who preferred artisanal to agricultural pursuits and for whom a small household plot would suffice.[21]

Mennonite settlers in Chortitza and Molotschna largely followed the 1764 statutes, even in places where the legislation, and bureaucratic inefficiency, allowed for variations. Nor did the special agreements reached in 1787 and the famed Charter of 1800 revise these provisions, even though they did alter other terms of settlement. For example, at 65 desiatinas Mennonites received substantially larger farmsteads than most other European colonists, an indication of the exemplary role assigned to them.

This system of inheritance worked well initially as individual Mennonite villages maintained communal oversight of the reserve and surplus lands, both of which seemed to be in abundance at a time when land was plentiful and sheep breeding predominant. And the system worked to a degree even after point of settlement. Molotschna's vastness allowed Mennonites to form new villages on these reserve lands into mid-century, including Konteniusfeld, Gnadenfeld and Waldheim in the 1830s, Hierschau in the following decade, and Nikolaidorf, Paulsheim, Kleefeld, Alexanderkrone, Mariawohl, Friedensruh and Steinfeld in the 1850s.[22] Of these, Waldheim (founded in 1836) was the final village formed from immigration abroad to Molotschna as forty Prussian Mennonite families had settled there by 1840. By contrast, Hierschau became the new model of Molotschna village expansion when thirty landless Mennonites from the villages of Pragenau, Waldheim, Portenau, and Gnadenheim settled there in 1848. No wonder observers maintained that the system established in the eighteenth century worked well. Trouble, however, brewed steadily below the surface.

Although Mennonites established a string of villages to alleviate landlessness within Molotschna after 1848, most landless in the district found the financial bar unreachably high to secure new homesteads. By mid-century a household required up to an astronomical 2,000 rubles to acquire a 65 desiatina farmstead. As a rule, wealthier farmsteads could launch the next generation on such farmsteads; poorer farmsteads and those already landless could not. By this means some 50,000 out of 123,000 desiatinas of land in Molotschna remained as reserve and surplus in 1840, most of which Mennonite civil authorities had lent by long-term arrangement to select Mennonites. For example, a cloth manufacturer named Klassen began to lease 3,000 desiatinas of Molotschna land in 1824 for wool production. Two other Mennonites, a Cornies and a Schmidt, leased over 8,000 desiatinas for sheep breeding, and all this added to the 3,595 desiatina estate awarded to Cornies and his descendants at Yushanlee as well as a similarly scaled estate at Steinbach. Another 16,000 desiatinas were set aside for two ancient, massive east–west carting trails that passed through the entirety of the settlement.[23] Meanwhile the number of Mennonite landless continued to grow, such that 1,700 of 2,733 families were landless in Molotschna by 1841. More than 60 per cent of Mennonites in Molotschna were without land less than twenty years later, as were half of all Mennonites in Chortitza.

Before we proceed, one caveat is in order: not all landless Mennonites were necessarily impoverished by mid-century. Many Mennonites who had immigrated to New Russia worked as artisans. In fact, only 60 per cent of household heads in Molotschna listed their occupation in 1808 as agriculturalist. Others actively worked in the cloth trade or as carpenters, weavers, blacksmiths, millers, tailors, and at least one clock maker. As landlessness persisted into the nineteenth century more Mennonites either developed their own trades or worked as labourers for farms or enterprises. Often identified as the first Mennonite industrialist, Peter H. Lepp was born in Einlage village of Chortitza on 29 December 1817. His father, a cabinet maker, sent Peter back to Prussia, where he learned the art of clock making and precision machinery. He returned to Chortitza village, where he established a shop directly across from the main church. Soon he was manufacturing clocks, candles, spoons, grain wagons, scales, and other goods, which he sold to Mennonites as well as adjacent Russian estate owners. By 1840 he had invented a mechanical reel which allowed for continuous spinning from cocoons. As a result, Mennonite silk producers quickly entered the market, where they thrived until American and English producers outpaced them. When Australian sheep breeding and American cotton largely wiped out Mennonite wool production Lepp was well placed to lead the transition in manufacturing to support New Russia's burgeoning grain production. His interest in clock making waned as his energies shifted to wagon, threshing machine, and mechanical reaper production. In all this Lepp was "landless," though hardly impoverished.[24]

So not all landless Mennonites were destitute by mid-century, but those who were had their circumstances worsen considerably during and immediately after the Crimean War. Several factors account for this. As noted above, Mennonites avoided direct participation in the hostilities but were nevertheless obligated to haul foodstuffs to, and the wounded from, the front. All Mennonites were required to participate in this task, often repeatedly, which particularly hit those who had limited means such that they needed to rent a wagon and team to meet their obligations. Others paid a surcharge in rubles or labour-equivalent to their wealthier co-religionists for the privilege of having someone else take their place. Meanwhile Mennonite wagon manufacturers profited greatly from the war given the technological superiority of their products, as did Mennonite grain producers who sold vast amounts to the army as inflationary pressures drove prices higher. The sharp rise in prices during the war meant that Mennonite landless who purchased grains now also paid more just to survive. Many more were compelled to hire themselves out as labourers for the very Mennonites – often relations – whose stock rose accordingly.

Russian officials dealt an unexpected blow to the Mennonite landless immediately after the war when fifty thousand Nogai Tatars who had previously settled just to the south of Molotschna abruptly quit

New Russia in 1860–2 for the Ottoman Empire. The landless, many of whom had rented these lands for years in lieu of lands in Molotschna, had hoped the state would now simply grant the vacated land to them. When the empire decided to settle Bulgarians there instead it drove the landless back to their own villages, though they were now determined to revolutionize landed relations within Molotschna.[25]

There had been those before who had worked to address the problem of mounting Mennonite landlessness, including Johann Cornies. David G. Rempel argues that Cornies had sought to reduce the rubles that landless Mennonites needed to obtain a farmstead. Cornies had also wondered if the full-household indivisible 65 desiatina allotments might be reduced to 35 or 40 desiatinas to create more farmsteads in each village, and he envisioned a settlement adjacent to Halbstadt for industrial and artisanal activity.[26] Thus Cornies founded the new village of Neu-Halbstadt in 1842, which became the hub of industrial activity within Molotschna. Though the Mennonite industrial centre would soon shift to Peter Lepp's locale in Chortitza, Neu-Halbstadt did respond to a need for both increased industry and livelihood. But it was insufficient to meet the mounting needs by the early 1860s, and landowners soon snuffed it out as they prioritized cheap labour from their landless co-religionists over the latter's right to an equitable livelihood. To that end they obviated alternate forms of employment at a time when grain cultivation required even more labourers than had been the case with sheep breeding.[27]

For years the landless had sought an internal resolution to their deepening crisis, or at least internal support from Mennonite civil and ecclesial authorities, but to no avail. Unfortunately, they had little ability to influence anyone because, as landless Mennonites, they could not vote on matters civil or ecclesial, and this resulted in the cruelest of ironies for them. On the one hand, the Russian empire continued to rely heavily on the male poll tax to meet its budgetary needs, which applied equally to landed and landless Mennonites. On the other, the lack of franchise within Molotschna and Chortitza meant that those same landless had all the obligations but few of the benefits of the current system. It did not help that Mennonite landholders elected ministers who largely supported their positions, in part because ministers were often landholders themselves and normally related to other landholders in the community. Thus, the Molotschna Mennonite landless confronted a nexus of landholders, village and district councils, and ministers, all Mennonite, who were unsympathetic to their plight.

Though tensions also surfaced in Chortitza at this time, scholars agree that its civil leaders and state officials acted earlier to alleviate the plight of the landless. The Russian state had come to the assistance of the Chortitza landless when it allowed them to settle on a 9,540 desiatina tract of land in Mariupol District of Ekaterinoslav Province in 1833. Landless Mennonites established five new villages from 1836 to 1852 in what became known as the Bergthal settlement. Chortitza landless also benefited from their involvement in the so-called Judenplan, which the Russian state established in 1847. Situated 120 kilometres west of Chortitza, some fifty Mennonite families relocated there in the 1850s, where they settled among Jewish villagers whom they intended to shape into model agriculturalists.[28]

Molotschna had not similarly alleviated its own landless crisis, which is why it irrupted so dramatically and openly in the early 1860s. Indeed, the stage had been set some years earlier when David Friesen (1807–93), the highest civil Mennonite official in Molotschna district, taunted the landless for their failure to manage well the half desiatina parcels that many had acquired. By what logic, he wondered, should they now be eligible to receive even more land? The still powerful Mennonite Agricultural Commission also initially rejected the appeals of the landless.[29] With almost all the Molotschna elites opposed to them, it seemed doubtful that any good could come from the landless after they appealed to the Russian state. As with the religious crisis of the pietist-separatist Brethren it appeared as if mid-century Mennonites had again rent their world asunder, exposed their internal animosities to imperial scrutiny, and created a problem that defied easy resolution.

Military Reform and the End of "Permanent" Exemption Status

To their "shock and dismay" Chortitza Mennonites in 1871 read accounts from St. Petersburg newspapers that the empire planned to introduce university military conscription. As a pacifist religious faith Mennonites had long relied on their 1800 privilegium to secure their "permanent" military exemption. Now, with radical change afoot all around them since 1855, it seemed certain that the permanent assurance had become merely provisional and would soon be terminated.[30]

The tribulations endured by New Russia's Mennonites appeared largely self-inflicted when it came to pietism and land, but the empire's threatened removal of their military exemption in 1871 was a different matter altogether. Two interconnected trajectories came together after the Crimean War to bring about this momentous shift in imperial policy and Mennonite polity. Major-General D.A. Miliutin initiated the first, though the longest to bring to fruition, when he called for a radical overall of the Russian military even before the Crimean War had ended. Historian John Keep has argued that the failed war effort cost the empire dearly in materiel and human and financial capital. Imperial servant Miliutin and others now urged the empire to undertake sweeping military reforms. As newly appointed minister of war, he advised the emperor on 15 January 1862 to abandon the empire's reliance on a massive standing army, which experts now deemed expensive and inefficient. Instead Miliutin favoured a small standing army with a massive, trained reserve. Even with Alexander II's support bureaucrats stumbled to implement it because such armies, as per the Napoleonic model, required universal conscription founded on an empire of fully fledged, literate citizens.[31] Where would such citizens come from in an empire as stratified as Russia's?

By the second trajectory, historians have written on the Russian empire's attempt in the nineteenth century to create such a modern citizenry. Both Elise Kimerling Wirschafter and Paul Werth have described initiatives in the 1860s which sought to create juridical equality across the empire; one where all would be granted freedom of conscience.[32] Yet reformers intent on the creation of a pan-Russian citizenry ran into the resilience of Imperial Russia's governing model through social estates (*soslovie*), traditionally understood to demarcate peasants, nobles, clergy, and townspeople. Gregory Freeze has argued that these social estates continued to dominate well into the nineteenth century, such that all reformers in the 1860s reckoned with their role in the maintenance of social stability. Lastly, Alison K. Smith has demonstrated that the very content of these social estates continued to evolve across the nineteenth century as the state steadfastly worked to transform the peasant *soslovie* into a single category. For example, it subsumed "free agriculturalists," a previously freed serf category, into the peasant *soslovie* in 1823.[33] It subsumed a variety of peasants into the state peasant category in 1838, including peasants in military settlements, and in 1861 and 1866 it merged both the former serfs and former state peasants into a single category. Thus, the peasant *soslovie* grew dramatically in the era of the Great Reforms, even as reformers wrestled with how to introduce an overarching notion of fully fledged citizens into the Russian body politic.

This dynamic development and expansion of the peasant *soslovie* had a profound impact on Mennonites when, in 1871, Emperor Alexander II signed a decree which abolished the heretofore discrete category of colonist within the empire.[34] The state now transferred those previously categorized as such, including Mennonites, into the new omnibus peasant *soslovie* category, the very one that had subsumed former state peasants in 1866. Henceforth Mennonites might be wealthy. They might be poor. But all were legally peasants, and when the state introduced universal military conscription in 1874 there was nothing to keep them out of the imperial armed forces.[35]

The new legislation, which officials floated late in 1870 in the state publication *Praviltel'stvennyi Vestnik* (Government Messenger) called for all conscripts to serve six years in active duty and thereafter to enter the army reserves for an additional nine years. It was news from this publication that so alarmed Chortitza Mennonites as word spread quickly across the colonies. With the imminent loss of their treasured military exemption Mennonites had reason to believe that the state had pulled the rug out from under them. How could they continue to live in the Russian empire and still consider themselves Mennonite and faithful to the gospel? Only time would tell.

Conclusion

"Love here is in a very bad way." So wrote preacher Jacob Epp in his diary on 23 May 1865 as he reflected on the animus which Ältester Gerhard Dyck directed at the new sect of brethren in his congregation. Epp noted with dismay how the Chortitza Mennonite District Office had written to the Guardians Committee in Odessa and asked it to banish the new brethren from Chortitza. Jacob Pätkau, Epp's own brother-in-law, had even dared to suggest to the Ältester that such exclusionary actions were "not in keeping with God's Word."[36]

A cursory glance at the disparate crises of the 1860s makes plain that Mennonite society across the board was truly "in a very bad way." In less than half a century the dream of a Mennonite commonwealth had given way to a dystopian nightmare as powerful landed and ecclesial voices refused to accommodate voices of reform and supplication in their midst. More than that, the powerful had turned to outside authorities either to quell or expunge those calling for change in their midst, and when the powerless made their own appeal to the state the issue was joined. It was a pivotal moment in Mennonite history during the imperial era, and circumstances appeared to worsen when St. Petersburg served notice in 1871 that it intended to abolish universal conscription as part of a larger integration into the empire.

What did it all mean? On the one hand, it is possible to look at these three crises as discrete entities, with two of them completely in house and the third only coincidentally connected. On the other, such a depiction ignores the profound sea-change underway across New Russia in the second half of the nineteenth century as the once-frontier steppe land had transformed into an increasingly integrated borderland.[37]

Population expansion was such that those who wanted new land had to cast their eyes to the Volga and beyond as the shift from sheep breeding to grain cultivation had put a premium on lands at the very time that land available for rent from the Nogai Tatars had disappeared from the market. If that was not enough, the empire's humiliating defeat in the Crimean War removed any doubts about how vulnerable the region was to invasion. No wonder Mennonites, German Lutherans, Russian- and Ukrainian-speaking peasants, and countless others suddenly warmed to a message of apocalyptic pietism.[38] No wonder those in positions of power lived and ruled as though that very power base was fleeting in a world of flux. None of this assumes that Mennonites had somehow become less religious or pious by mid-century compared to the end of the eighteenth century, or that Epp was correct in his lament that love was particularly and relatively weak by the 1860s. But it does suggest that Mennonites by the 1860s encountered crises that appeared to be well beyond an easy resolution. Little did they know that the golden era of Mennonite life in New Russia was about to dawn.

Chapter Seven

From Crisis to Consolidation: The Flourishing of Russian Mennonitism, 1865–1883

Mennonite minister Jacob Epp participated in a revolutionary act on 1 November 1871 when he travelled down to the Chortitza District Office from his home in the Judenplan. The Mother Colony of Chortitza had recently purchased the 3,700 desiatina Baratov estate for 121,800 rubles, some 100 kilometres to the west, and now wanted to distribute it among those who would eventually pay for it. Epp hoped to be one of the initial seventy-four landless Mennonites to receive a full farmstead.[1] In the event, the Chortitza office cast lots and awarded Epp with a homestead in the planned Village Number One. He promptly paid a deposit of 50 rubles for the land and then voted to elect a mayor for the newly formed village. After farmsteaders elected Jacob Wiebe to that office, they then elected Diedrich Epp, Jacob Redekopp, and Jacob Epp himself to supervise Peter Regier, the appointed surveyor, as he situated the new village on the massive former estate.

Epp drove to Baratov twice over the next several days to oversee this process until its completion on 6 November 1871, when villagers gathered again to draw lots, this time to allot the thirty-five newly demarcated farmsteads. Epp recorded in his diary that he drew lot number 18 that day, his brother Diedrich drew number 17, and his brother-in-law drew number 7. Within a week Epp returned, by which time the newly elected mayor Wiebe had determined fair grazing rights for all farmsteads on the village's shared pasture. They had much work ahead of them, but three years later Epp, then fifty-four years old, relocated to the erstwhile Village Number One, which settlers had renamed Gnadenthal (Valley of Grace) in the Baratov colony. By then the new villagers had already built a village school and several windmills. A store followed soon thereafter.[2]

By this means of personal resettlement Jacob Epp participated in a robust expansion of the Mennonite footprint in New Russia when he relocated to Baratov from the Judenplan. Harvey Dyck has determined that Mennonites founded approximately six new villages every year from 1865 to 1914, with most of these founded in New Russia.[3] That by itself is remarkable, but this dramatic expansion was one of only three such remarkable transformations that occurred after 1861 as Mennonites resolved the trio of crises which some had feared would destroy the best fruits of Mennonitism within the empire. And although fully a third of Mennonites emigrated for North America in the 1870s, the overall record suggests that those who remained had by 1880 largely resolved the crises that so bedevilled them only a few years earlier. Thanks in large part to the active oversight of imperial servitors, the empire's Mennonites went from chronic crisis to dynamic growth and consolidation, such that Mennonites could justly claim by the late nineteenth century that they were on the cusp of a golden age. This chapter considers the strategies by which Mennonites successfully responded after 1860 to the ominous crises of ecclesial disunity, inequitable land distribution, and threatened military conscription.

Ecclesial (Dis)Unity Institutionalized

Historians generally deem the public denunciation signed by eighteen disgruntled Molotschna Mennonites under the influence of Baptist-pietist-separatist preachers to be the birth of the Mennonite Brethren Church. For example, a popular online survey history concludes: "On 6 January 1860, a number of the Brethren met in the village of Elisabeththal, Molotschna, and took steps to form a separate church."[4] Scholars have made similar claims.[5]

By contrast James Urry has argued persuasively that the Mennonite Brethren movement emerged more gradually after 1860. He identifies three phases: first, a rather diffuse set of religious splinter movements from at least 1860 to June 1865, in which Molotschna pietists took the lead; a second phase after 1865 when the new movement was primarily led by Chortitza pietists who favoured closer ties with Baptists and at a remove from other Mennonites; and a third phase after 1870 when Mennonite pietists rejected a possible alliance with Baptist congregations as they returned to a primarily Mennonite identity. Each phase requires some comment.

By the first, historians broadly agree that the new pietistic movement was remarkably diffuse in the 1860s, even if the 6 January 1860 missive suggests otherwise. Several reasons present themselves. For one, this separatist movement was initially covert and correspondingly decentralized given how aggressively the established Mennonite churches

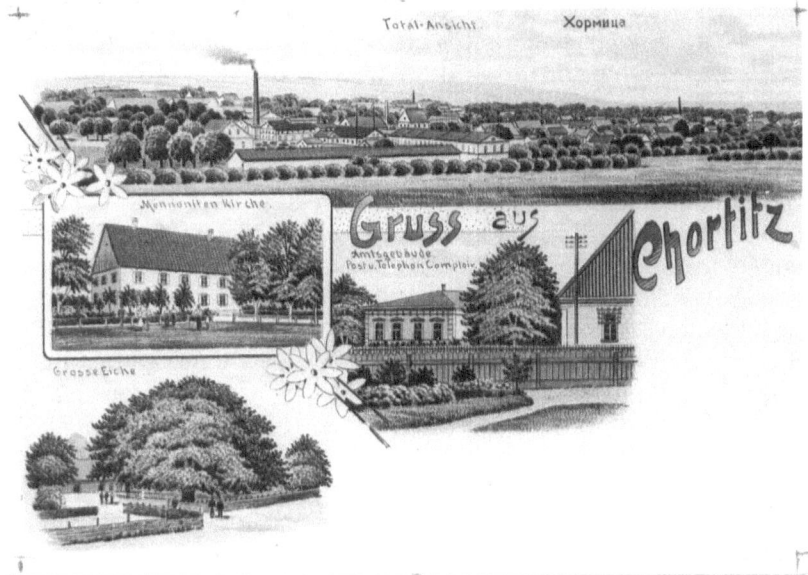

Figure 5. "Gruss aus Chortitz" postcard. Gerhard Lohrenz Photo Collection, Mennonite Heritage Archives.

and civil authorities reacted to it. They threated to excommunicate the new adherents and urged imperial authorities to exile adherents of this "secret society" to a Siberian wasteland. Mennonite authorities arrested those who stayed in their midst, including Jakob Wall of the village of Pastwa in Molotschna. There were allegations of torture. Those who did not return to their congregations, including Isaak Matthies of Rudnerweide, faced economic ruination as Mennonites boycotted their businesses and stores (recall that many of the earliest pietist-separatists were prosperous merchants). Mennonite councils banned adherents of this new pietism from any public worship and levied strict penalties if caught.[6]

The supporters of this new movement responded in several ways to this onslaught. A few returned to the fold. Others met in secret conventicles under cover of darkness, either outdoors or in people's homes, all of which reinforced the diffuse and seemingly subversive nature of this new movement. The new movement also suffered from a crisis of leadership, as many of the earliest signatories pledged not to lead the movement until such time as the government granted it legal status, which they hoped would happen soon. Yet years passed, and so the new movement elected its first leaders from a second tier of candidates. With a weaker leadership and more diffuse worship practices necessitated by their clandestine nature, the new movement also lacked any liturgical discipline or civil order, even as most within the new movement soon adopted baptism by immersion as its principal marker. But this earliest phase was the one characterized by the greatest excesses in worship, whether through dance, the use of instruments, or the holy kiss across genders and regardless of marital status. Emerging congregations added new members willy-nilly, with little uniformity of practice across the settlements. Those who joined and subsequently challenged the movement's leadership and practices were quickly excommunicated by leaders who deemed themselves to be Christ's direct apostles. At one point the self-proclaimed "Apostle" Gerhard Wieler of the Einlage (Chortitza) Brethren had excommunicated more members than were left in the movement, including Wieler's own brother and father. Soon Benjamin Bekker of the Molotschna radicals also declared himself to be an apostle and banned all who sought moderation or conciliation from within this emerging movement. Clearly this first phase left its earliest followers longing for stability and sustainability.

That is exactly what this movement got in 1865, thanks to Johannes Claassen's return to Molotschna after he had visited a new settlement farther to the east. His return marked the onset of its second phase of identity formation. Claassen's longstanding ties outside of the settlements proved particularly useful as they made him a known entity in St. Petersburg. It is thanks to his repeated interventions that the state eventually granted official recognition to these ecclesial reformers, and that made all the difference. He first needed, however, to bring internal coherence to the movement itself. After a wide range of consultations Claassen initiated a conclave of pietist-separatist Mennonite brethren in June 1865 in the Molotschna village of Gnadenfeld, out of which came the aptly named June Protocols.[7] Briefly put, the protocols diminished the power of the previously self-proclaimed apostles in favour of congregational authority. The protocols also restricted the instances where congregational leaders could excommunicate new members, they reinstated many whom the former apostles had excommunicated during the period of excess from 1860 to 1865, and banned the exuberant extremism of the dance, the drum, and the not-so-holy kiss. The increased order that Claassen brought to the new movement did a great deal to assuage the worst fears of both the existing Mennonite churches and the Russian state, even as he sought to steer this movement in an entirely new direction.

Claassen realized that the new movement needed to have both institutional order and a larger accountability for it to survive. To that end he and other adherents sought increased ecclesial ties with German Baptists. The emerging Einlage congregation in Chortitza took the lead in this second phase, and most especially under the leadership of Abraham Unger. From their earliest days most of the followers of this diffuse movement had referred to each other as the Brethren, though some in Molotschna identified themselves as the Wüst Brethren. Those in the original Mennonite congregations derisively referred to them as separatists (*Ausgetretenen*).[8] Now, thanks to Unger's increasingly close ties to the Baptists, the movement sought the tutelage of the renowned Baptist preacher Johann Oncken.[9] The Einlage Brethren first consulted with Oncken in 1861 and then with increasing frequency after 1863 as moderates sought to curb the movement's worst excesses. Urry suggests that by 1869 Unger had managed to shape the Einlage congregation into a "proto-Baptist congregation." In that year Oncken himself travelled from Hamburg to New Russia. He first met with the Baptist congregations in the Alt and Neu Danzig settlements near Chortitza before travelling on to Einlage.[10] There he baptized new members in the emerging Brethren congregation and ordained new congregational leaders, suggesting the degree to which the Einlage Brethren identified themselves as Baptists. One year later Aron Lepp (1827–1913), the Ältester of the Einlage congregation, again petitioned the German Baptists to send someone to assist them in their organizational efforts. In the end Baptist preacher August Liebig arrived in June 1871 and stayed among the Chortitza Brethren for a full year, even as he personally resided in the nearby village of Andreasfeld with his wife and child. Prior to his departure in 1872 Liebig arranged for the first annual Conferences in Andreasfeld, which brought together Brethren from Chortitza, Molotschna, and beyond.[11] Had these efforts continued, the emerging Brethren movement may well have entered the Baptist fold. Some believed they already had.

Yet by 1876 the very same Aron Lepp moved to terminate the Baptist connection in favour of a distinctly *Mennonite* Brethren Fellowship. This is where Urry correctly suggests that the threatened end to military exemptions compelled the earliest followers of this Brethren movement to reassert their Mennonite identity in the hopes that they could maintain their military exemption. The issue was joined in 1873 when, with a new military law in the offing, imperial bureaucrats asked Mennonites in New Russia to clarify if the new Brethren movement was Baptist or Mennonite. The issue was pivotal, as Baptist theology did not endorse a pacifist theology, whereas Mennonites did. The Brethren now realized that they would only receive some sort of exemption from military service if the imperial state deemed them Mennonites, not Baptists. This was a particularly delicate issue at a time when most may have considered the Molotschna Brethren to be theologically Mennonite but not so with the Chortitza Brethren, who had openly courted Baptist tutelage for years.

It is in this context that the Einlage (Chortitza) Brethren Congregation issued a statement in 1876 entitled "Differences Between the United Mennonite Brethren Churches, the Baptist Churches and Old Mennonite Churches."[12] The statement sought to maintain a delicate balance. On the one hand, it declared that the Baptists were a "genuine church" and a "fellowship of true children of God who were born again." On the other hand, the Einlage – and now firmly *Mennonite* – Brethren congregation identified three significant points of departure from the Baptists: pacifism, the swearing of oaths, and foot washing. Although the Einlage Brethren continued to maintain that the "Old" (existing) Mennonite congregations were spiritually dead, they nevertheless had one thing in common with the Einlage Brethren. All were Mennonites, and by 1880 the powerful Ministry of the Interior agreed as it recognized the new Brethren as Mennonites, distinct from the region's Baptists.[13] Thus a movement that had begun as a rather diffuse Brethren movement in 1860 had taken shape as a Baptist movement after the Protocols of 1865, only to claim to be a distinctly Mennonite Brethren movement by 1876 and recognized as such by 1880.[14]

The Kuban Settlement

Johannes Claassen (1820–1876) was undoubtedly one of the most remarkable leaders of the early Mennonite Brethren.[15] It was Claassen, mentioned above, who had risked arrest when he travelled to St. Petersburg to appeal directly that the state recognize and protect the new movement after the eighteen pietist-separatists had signed the January 1860 missive. In his petition to Russian emperor Alexander II on 21 May 1862 Claassen added one other request: that the empire grant crown land to the fledging brotherhood movement for their own settlement far away from the controversy that had irrupted in Molotschna. Though Claassen hoped for a land grant in Crimea, officials directed him instead to Stavropol in the foothills of the Caucasus, where lands had recently come available with the exodus of Nogai Tatars after the Crimean War.[16]

Claassen travelled to the Caucasus in May 1863, the first of several trips over the succeeding years. He inspected the 6,500 desiatina tract of land the state had offered and negotiated terms of settlement with the region's governor. Finally, in the fall of 1863, the state formally granted the land parcel, which was deemed sufficient to permit one hundred Brethren families from Chortitza and Molotschna settlements to establish 65 desiatina farmsteads.[17]

The first party of new settlers began the arduous two-week, 300 kilometre journey from New Russia to Kuban that fall. Men came first, along with their livestock, to clear the land and build temporary shelters; women and children followed the following spring. Though both settlements struggled in the initial years such that some families returned to the Mother Colonies in New Russia, the sixty-seven who remained eventually established two prosperous villages: Wohldemfürst and Alexanderfeld.[18] Some two thousand Mennonites lived there by 1900. It was from the Kuban that Claassen returned to Molotschna back in 1865 to establish the June Protocols and bring stability to the fledgling movement. However modest it was in size and number, the Kuban settlement opened a vital new chapter in Mennonite history as it marked the first of many so-called daughter colonies that Mennonites established in the 1860s, and one of the first such established outside of New Russia.[19]

The General Conference of Mennonites, 1883

Thus, contemporary Mennonite Brethren may legitimately claim that their church's foundational document was the January missive of 1860, though it took an explicitly Mennonite shape only in the early 1870s, even as members of that movement settled in the Caucasus. Nor was the course clearly set by the mid-1870s as the Brethren continued to find their way between their Mennonite and Baptist identities in the years that followed. For example, the Mennonite Brethren introduced Sunday Schools, a Baptist innovation, to their weekly worship services in the 1870s as they did extemporaneous preaching. They continued to utilize Baptist theological materials in the decades that followed. Baptist speakers routinely spoke at annual mission festivals and conferences of the Mennonite Brethren in New Russia, and the emerging Brethren movement modelled its earliest Confessions of Faith on Baptist Confessions. No wonder Russian bureaucrats remained confused by the distinction between Mennonite and German Baptist.[20]

Yet the Brethren stayed steadfast to their Mennonite identity after the discussions of the early 1870s. Ironically, the existing Mennonite churches in New Russia also adopted many of the innovations first introduced by the Baptists, even if the transition was not always smooth. For example, Jacob Epp reported in January 1860 that a disturbance had taken place at the recent Epiphany Sunday worship service of the Novozhitomir (Mennonite) church in the Judenplan west of the Chortitza settlement. According to a trusted source, the service's precentor, Heinrich Olfert, had upset many in the congregation when he announced that congregants would sing the final hymn in cipher, a contemporary form of four-part singing that had never been utilized before in that church. Isaac Klassen, the presiding minister, disapproved and deliberately disrupted proceedings when he stood during the singing and loudly pronounced the benediction. Chaos ensued as some immediately walked out while others stayed to sing the remainder of the hymn. When subsequently challenged, Olfert declared that cipher singing in Mennonite churches was surely acceptable if Mennonite children sang in cipher in Mennonite schools.

On another occasion, Epp and his wife attended a day-long service held at the Kronsgarten (Mennonite) church in September 1864, where both observed Ältester Peter Wedel and ministers Schröder and Riedger preach. Amazingly, in Epp's words, "all three preached by heart," and although Epp concluded that Riedger's sentences often "did not hang together," the other two preached well.[21]

The esteemed preacher Bernhard Harder was emblematic of this shift within the existing congregations. Born in the Molotschna village of Halbstadt in 1832, Harder received baptism into the Mennonite faith as a young man, by which time his beliefs had already been profoundly shaped by evangelists Eduard Wüst (spiritual father of the Molotschna Brethren) and the published sermons of Ludwig Hofacker (spiritual father of the Chortitza Brethren at Einlage). Yet P.M. Friesen, historian, and himself a leader in the Mennonite Brethren Church, declared that Harder never forsook his first baptism to be rebaptized by immersion. He always remained at arm's length from the new movement.[22]

Harder initially worked in the local Mennonite District Office (Gebietsamt) and taught at a variety of Mennonite schools before he successfully put his name forward in 1860 for election to serve as minister of the Ohrloff Mennonite Church. It was here that he worked steadfastly to revitalize the church. He had a "burning love for Christ and sinners," in Friesen's words. He desired to unite them "for all eternity" in what Friesen deemed a genuine call to conversion.[23] In direct contrast to his church's established practice, Harder began to preach extemporaneously in the very style Jacob Epp commented on. He encouraged other innovations in music and spiritual education as Epp also observed.[24] Harder was a leading voice in the formation of the first General Conference of Mennonite Congregations in the Russian empire in 1883. As distinct from the long-established Kleine Gemeinde and the more recently founded Mennonite Brethren Church, the General Conference was by far the largest of the Mennonite organizations in the empire as it comprised more than three-quarters of the Mennonites in the empire.

Thus, Mennonites had consolidated their ecclesial world by 1883, even as they had created one more institutional fragment in the Mennonite Brethren. Events of the coming years made it plain that Mennonites could form a reasonably united front when it mattered most, and of these, no front seemed greater than the one needed to confront the crisis over land.

Daughter Colonies and Estates: Landlessness Addressed

Molotschna Mennonites overcame the landed crisis that irrupted in the early 1860s through a wide-ranging strategy; one that required first a radical revision of civil polity within Molotschna itself and, thereafter, a robust and multifaceted program of land acquisition beyond its borders. We consider both aspects and the dramatic way in which a state-imposed solution to an internal landed crisis profoundly reshaped the Mennonite footprint within the Russian empire.

Internal Crisis Resolution: Molotschna First, Then Chortitza

If the Mennonite landless understood anything by 1860, it was that they needed more than moral suasion to win the day against the overlapping Mennonite ecclesial, civil, or landed elites. They needed to have their voices heard, and for that the landless needed the political power that would come with the right to vote and elect officials, especially at a time when they represented a majority within the settlement. No wonder the political franchise became the cornerstone of their demands, even as they realized that no such dramatic transformation of Mennonite civil polity could happen if the powerful within Molotschna remained absolutely and categorically opposed.

Under the circumstances the landless needed a break. They got it the form of two champions connected to Johann Cornies' home village of Ohrloff; both of whom began to side with the landless in their plight. Franz Isaak (1816–99) was first. A full-household farmer whom the Ohrloff congregation elected as minister in 1850, Isaak added his name to the November 1863 appeal sent to the Guardians Committee. Thereafter he continuously wrote on behalf of the landless and eventually published a major documentary collection on this and other crises.[25] The second individual, Philipp Wiebe (1816–70), had much greater gravitas within and beyond the Mennonite world. As son-in-law of the late

Johann Cornies, Wiebe inherited Cornies' famed private Molotschna estate of Yushanlee. He also continued many of Cornies' initiatives, including as president of the Agricultural Commission after Cornies' sudden death in 1848. Wiebe did not come immediately onside with the landless, but his connections proved invaluable once he did, especially to the powerful Ministry of State Domains (who reported directly to the Russian emperor) and to Evgenii von Hahn, a Russian member of Senate and former head of the Guardians Committee.[26]

Though the details need not concern us, the Molotschna landless and their opponents waged a pitched battle in the 1860s as each sought to persuade Russian officials to side with them. The landless and their advocates focused initially on the Guardians Committee in Odessa. It intervened on their behalf in December 1863 and ordered David Friesen, the Molotschna district Oberschultze, to resolve the crisis fairly. Friesen proffered a resolution, but largely one which stymied the Mennonite landless such that they changed tack by the second half of 1864 as they began to appeal to officials beyond the Odessa-based Guardians Committee. They now utilized the influence and connections of Philipp Wiebe, who wrote two letters on their behalf directly to the Ministry of State Domains in St. Petersburg. The ministry, caught up in the massive reforms underway with state peasants, sent state councilor Vladimir Islavin, former head of the Guardians Committee, to investigate in August 1865. Islavin soon sided with the landless. In landmark decisions that followed, the ministry ordered the removal of Friesen as district head of Molotschna and accepted many of the recommendations that an ad-hoc Commission of the Mennonite landless had made. Even thereafter, the Mennonite landed elites dragged their heels for several more rancorous years, until St. Petersburg issued an imperial edict and imposed a final settlement.

Among its key provisions, the imperial edict granted all Mennonite male homesteaders the franchise, regardless of their landholding, and thus deprived the full 65 desiatina farmsteaders their monopoly of power. It further ordered Molotschna's Gebietsamt to make 16,000 desiatinas of surplus lands in Molotschna available to the landless immediately, which included lands obtained when Mennonites narrowed the two ancient and broad ox-cart (*chumak*) paths on which they had first established their villages.

Thus, the Molotschna landless won the day thanks to the support of champions within, and the full weight of imperial authority from without. Both Chortitza and Molotschna also began to levy a new poll tax of all lands at this time. The settlements added this capital to a common pool of funds made available from the ongoing lease of all remaining surplus lands, which created large-scale opportunities for landless Mennonites that had hitherto been unavailable to them.

Daughter Colonies

As problems mounted, we need to mention one more, the dramatic demographic increase in New Russia's Mennonites throughout the nineteenth century. James Urry has calculated that Mennonite births outpaced deaths across the century by a factor of two to one. Add to that the ongoing immigration from Prussia and one can understand why Molotschna and Chortitza were demographic time bombs by the 1860s. Molotschna doubled its population from 1826 (6,538) to 1846 (14,750), and up to a staggering 24,768 by 1866. Chortitza, by contrast, increased from 4,134 in 1826 to over 10,000 by 1866.[27]

It is within this context that one can appreciate why Mennonites founded Bergthal as their first so-called daughter colony in 1836, made possible when the Russian state allocated a 10,000 desiatina tract of land to the Chortitza settlement in 1833.[28] The Russian state also made two other tracts of land available to a fresh influx of Mennonites after Prussia instituted universal military conscription in 1850.[29] With no more space available in either of the two original settlements, or in New Russia more broadly, St. Petersburg offered Mennonites two parcels of land on the lower Volga. Here, as mentioned in chapter four, 109 Prussian Mennonites in 1854 founded the Am Trakt Colony on approximately 14,000 desiatinas south of the administrative capital of Samara. Four years later the empire granted incoming Prussian Mennonites another 10,000 desiatina block, also near Samara. Known as Alexandertal, Prussian Mennonites formed ten villages here by 1870, making it the last of the original Mennonite settlements.[30] When state officials offered the emerging Mennonite Brethren land in the early 1860s, they did so with a parcel that was even farther afield in Kuban, the foothills of the Caucasus. At approximately the same time, Mennonites declined the offer of land in the distant Amur region of Siberia as St. Petersburg sought to settle lands it had only seized control of in 1857. Thus many concluded by 1860 that New Russia had no more land available, such that any future Mennonite settlement would need to be on lands situated progressively eastward, up to and including the lands that approached the Pacific Ocean almost 9,000 kilometres away.

None of the above explains why Chortitza and Molotschna Mennonites after 1861 suddenly had an almost limitless supply of lands available to them in New Russia for long-term lease or outright purchase. What had happened in so short a time? The answer, briefly stated, is that the servile emancipation of 1861 had a profound impact on Mennonite landholding practices in New Russia. At first glance one could assume that such an impact would have been minimal, as serfs comprised only a third of New Russia's peasant population in 1861, compared to peasants on state lands who comprised 60 per cent of the total.[31] Serfs, however, were located on generally massive estates owned by nobles who unloaded their estates at a feverish pace after 1861. In fact, New Russian nobles sold almost 100,000 desiatinas of estate land per year between 1863 and 1892, and they leased out countless thousands more, often by informal arrangements.[32] This meant that Mennonites had available to them a vast pool of former estate lands which nobles placed on the market at the very time the Molotschna landed crisis burst into the open. It was an offer that was too good for Mennonites to refuse, even before an impatient state imposed a solution on the Molotschna landless crisis in 1869.

Initially selected groups of Mennonites rather than entire settlements acquired new lands, as exemplified when Mennonites purchased or leased new lands in Crimea, a land mass that many had encountered during the recently completed war of 1853–6. Individual landless Mennonites, primarily from Molotschna, founded the Crimean villages of Annenfeld in 1860 and Karassan five years later. They established both private farms and villages in the coming years, and though most came for the land, still others who were members of the Kleine Gemeinde wanted to distance themselves from Chortitza and Molotschna, where the main Mennonite churches predominated. Kleine Gemeinde members founded the settlement of Markusland in 1863 and two years later founded the Borozenko colony on over 6,000 desiatinas of land, once again named after the former Russian estate owner.

By contrast the whole of Chortitza took responsibility for the purchase of Fürstenland (translated as "the Prince's land"), which they jointly established on land leased from a brother to emperor Alexander II in 1864. Molotschna Mennonites, who moved at a slower pace than Chortitza, only founded their first daughter colony in 1872, when they jointly purchased Count Lev Kochubey's 21,000 desiatina estate. They named the new settlement Zagradovka, and almost five hundred primarily landless Mennonite families settled there in sixteen villages by 1880. In virtually all cases the new daughter colonies modelled themselves after the Mother Colonies, even to where they included reserve lands set aside for the purchase of new settlements once the need arose. Farmsteads in the daughter colonies averaged 50 desiatinas, making them highly viable.[33]

By this means Mennonites purchased over 60,000 desiatinas of land in New Russia by the time prices forced them to look farther afield after 1890, and even then they continued to acquire new lands.[34] In total they had formed six daughter colonies and forty-three villages by the close of the New Russian land markets. By itself this was an astonishing increase in land holdings by Mennonites over a single generation. Yet in terms of their landholding in New Russia, this was only the half of it.

Mennonite Estates

In 1862 Abram Bergmann, a thirty-nine-year-old recent Mennonite immigrant from Prussia, purchased a massive 4,436 desiatina estate located between Chortitza and the provincial capital of Ekaterinoslav.[35] In doing so Bergmann unwittingly found himself at the dawn of a golden era in Mennonite estate acquisition. Even earlier Klaas Wiens may have been the first Mennonite estate owner when the state awarded him land for service rendered as settlement *oberschultze* during the settlement of Molotschna. He established the Steinbach estate on the southern edge of Molotschna in 1812, and officials eventually awarded Johann Cornies his prize estate of Jushanlee, but Mennonite estate owning did not become a widespread phenomenon until the land boom after 1861 as the state had forbidden it earlier. With restrictions abruptly lifted, Mennonites purchased estates in New Russia and well beyond in the following decades, though the so-called Schönfeld Colony had a pride of place.

Select Molotschna and recently arrived Prussian Mennonites founded Schönfeld when they purchased the 4,873 desiatina estate north-east of Chortitza from Russian officer Dmitrii Brazol in 1868. A year later another cohort purchased the adjoining Chonuk estate, which the new owners subsumed into Schönfeld. In short order Mennonites had established hundreds of private estates of varying sizes on the Schönfeld settlement, crisscrossed by the Gorkaya and Tersa rivers and interspersed by peasant and German holdings. Other Mennonites arrived and formed the villages of Schönfeld and Rosenhof, which became the artisanal core of the colony. In time Mennonites built fourteen elementary schools for their children and one at the secondary level in this enormous estate settlement, along with three church buildings,[36] and they had immediate access to three railway stations on the empire's burgeoning rail network. Whereas Russian officials integrated almost all Mennonite daughter colonies and estates into existing municipal structures, they recognized that Schönfeld was comprehensive enough to warrant its own political entity. The many peasant, German (Catholic and Lutheran), and even Bulgarian villages found within its boundaries were often administratively excluded, even though all were intermingled with Mennonite estates. In other instances, Mennonites persuaded officials to include peasants in their newly formed administrative units to have immediately available a pliant labour force.[37]

The Schönfeld estate owners were part of an emerging layer of New Russian Mennonite society, one that Urry has identified as "Mennonite magnates."[38] Though many maintained connections to Molotschna especially, they generally functioned as distinct entities. Mennonite magnates married within their immediate circles and rarely "down" to Mennonite villagers. Culturally they were as comfortable in Russian as they were in Menno-speak, and many maintained even broader cultural connections with Europe. Estate owners initially constructed their homesteads with simple wood designs, though they soon replaced these with elaborately finished brick exteriors and metal roofs. They constructed their yards with sturdy outbuildings and enclosed the whole with majestic gateways that live on in many a photo collection.[39] They were a world unto themselves, or so it appeared.

Thus, Mennonites responded to the landed crisis of the mid-nineteenth century with a comprehensive strategy that centred on the purchase or long-term lease of so-called daughter colonies and the widespread establishment of private landed estates. There was one other significant outlet for landlessness, but to understand it we need first to revisit the military crisis of 1870.

Mennonites and Universal Conscription: Emigration and the Foresteidienst

Mennonites mobilized quickly when informed in late 1870 that Imperial Russia intended to revoke their long-cherished and "permanent" exemption from military service. In some ways, the threat solidified even momentarily a pan-Mennonite identity within the Russian empire. We have already seen how the new Mennonite Brethren movement had by 1873 explicitly distanced itself from Russian and German Baptists, most especially when it came to the new movement's commitment to pacifism. The Brethren managed to persuade the Russian bureaucrats of their "Mennoniteness," and that made all the difference. Although Mennonites suddenly found themselves within an increasingly bureaucratized state, they responded, as had long been the case, through direct individual appeals. Molotschna Mennonites sent their first delegation to St. Petersburg in 1871, where they joined forces with a similar delegation which arrived from Chortitza in February of that year.[40] Together they now appealed directly to high-ranking officials up to and including O.L. Hayden, the president of the Imperial Commission, which had drafted the new legislation. Hayden assured Mennonites that the empire would not negotiate an exemption to universal conscription, though he did promise them that Mennonites would never need to carry weapons. Instead, Mennonites would serve in a variety of non-combative roles when conscripted.

For some Mennonites this was already too great a compromise, coming as it did on the heels of new legislation which had ordered the mandatory instruction of the Russian language in all schools, Mennonite included.[41] Others were prepared to live with compromise, though fearing increased acculturation, Mennonite leaders insisted that Mennonite youth only serve where they would be isolated from Russians and other colonists.[42] At least two more Mennonite delegations travelled from Chortitza and Molotschna to St. Petersburg, though the state refused each time to budge from this initial position. More than that, officials chided Mennonites for their failure to communicate adequately in Russian, though this reflected more on the linguistic limitations of senior Mennonite clergy than the younger Russian-speaking Mennonite merchants who accompanied them. Officials pointed out that Mennonites had already engaged in a host of measures in support of the Russian empire that dated back to the Napoleonic wars and, more recently, significant Mennonite activity during the Crimean War. They questioned how sincerely Mennonites held to pacifism given the previous decade's acrimonious debates among Mennonites over religious identities and landlessness.[43]

In the end, Imperial Russia promulgated the new law on universal military conscription in January 1874, though it made provision within it for Mennonites as follows: "The Mennonites are exempted from bearing arms. On the basis of special regulations, their service is performed in the work-places of the marine department, the fire brigades and in the special mobile detachments of the forestry department."[44] The law further clarified that this exemption only applied to Mennonites who lived in the empire as of 1 January 1875. Thus, it seems as if Mennonites had won in their longstanding dispute with the state. Yet the mass emigration fever that irrupted coincidentally across the Mennonite settlements of New Russia suggested otherwise.

Up to one-third of the empire's Mennonites, a number estimated to be as high as 15,000–18,000, immigrated to North America between 1874 and the end of the decade. Thereafter only a trickle of Mennonites emigrated before the 1920s.[45] Though the reasons for doing so varied greatly, it is safe to say that those who left generally believed that prospects in North America were better than in the Russian empire. Cornelius Janzen, a Mennonite, played a pivotal role in making this happen.[46] Born in Prussia in 1822, Janzen worked as a grain broker. He immigrated to the Russian empire around 1850, where he worked as a grain merchant in the port city of Berdiansk. He returned to Prussia for several years and then returned to Berdiansk as Prussian consul in 1856. Janzen maintained strong ties with British merchants, and even the British consul James Zohrab, through his burgeoning grain trade. As the crisis of the early 1870s developed Janzen became a vital conduit of information on the emerging markets and landholding possibilities in North America. Both the British (who continued to oversee Canadian foreign policy after Confederation in 1867) and American consuls became involved as they plied Mennonites in New Russia with promises of military exemptions and an abundance of inexpensive lands. Eventually, the Russian state exiled Janzen from the empire, but not before he had brought the promise of a fresh start in North America to thousands of Mennonite households. In 1873 the Mennonites of New Russia sent a delegation to North America, where they met with government officials in both Canada and the United States, as well as with their Swiss co-religionists: approximately twenty thousand Mennonites who had settled in Pennsylvania and the US Midwest and another ten thousand in Ontario, having immigrated from the Swiss lands and South Germany in the late eighteenth and early nineteenth centuries.[47]

From Pennsylvania and Ontario, the delegates made their way westward, first to the American Midwest, then north to Manitoba, where they arrived on 4 June 1873 and proceeded to scout out the lands available for settlement. The delegates then shifted to Ottawa, where they negotiated terms and conditions prior to their return to the Russian empire. They arrived back in New Russia in August of that year overjoyed by what they had seen and been promised. Hundreds of Mennonite families now readied for departure despite the challenges before them, starting with the empire's refusal to grant them exit visas. Those intending to leave auctioned off their goods and properties while they waited for essential exit documents. They made final visits to friends and families and attended emotional congregational meetings where participants passionately debated whether to emigrate. In almost all instances Mennonites who stayed behind profited as they generally offered well below market rates for goods on sale.

Alarmed by the potential mass exodus of these model agriculturalists, the Ministry of State Domains in September 1874 dispatched an emissary to visit the Mennonite heartland in New Russia and hopefully persuade the colonists to stay. They chose a hero of the recently completed Crimean War for the task, General Totleben (a fabulous name, in translation, as General Dead-life). Totleben, a Lutheran, knew of the Mennonites and admired their prowess on several fronts. His arrival in the settlements caused its own sensation given his fame, though he quickly realized he was too late to ease the emigration fever. A significant minority plead for the freedom to leave, while others indicated they would consider likewise unless the state immediately granted Mennonites the right to maintain their own form of separate and alternate military service. Totleben agreed to press their case on both counts, and successfully did so.

Thus, the state issued exit visas to those Mennonites intent on emigration. The first Mennonite emigrants departed in May 1874, followed by another large party the following month. In the end, up to ten thousand Mennonites settled in the US Midwest (primarily Kansas and Nebraska) by the end of the decade, and up to eight thousand in Manitoba. Historians have generally concluded that the more conservative settled in Manitoba, where the new Dominion allowed them to replicate their block settlement pattern to the south and east of Winnipeg, and where Mennonites also received stronger assurances of exemption from military service.

Back in the empire, however, the Russian state's promise in 1874 to devise a made-for-Mennonites form of alternate service took some time. Though Totleben had initially proposed several alternative forms of service there was only one that interested Mennonites: they wanted the isolation that would come if their young men worked and lived in separate forestry camps. These were a natural fit for Mennonites, whose forestation projects dated back to Johann Cornies and coincided with a longstanding state wish to encourage similar developments across the region. In April 1875 St. Petersburg approved a supplement to its conscription legislation which guaranteed Mennonites an alternate for of service.[48] Several years of negotiation followed and resulted in a final agreement issued on 1 January 1880. Mennonites now agreed to participate in the new program and cover most of its costs through a new property tax. Starting with Velikii Anadol and Azov, Mennonites established six such camps in short order, all in the vicinity of either Chortitza or Molotschna. They established subsequent camps in Siberia to coincide with Mennonite settlement there before 1914. In addition, they also established a phylloxera camp in Crimea so Mennonites could assist with the campaign against a root disease which had struck viniculturalists on the peninsula.

Within two years Mennonites placed up to 347 men in these camps, each for a four-year term. Up to seven thousand men, chosen randomly by lot, served in these camps up to the start of the First World War. In those years they planted and maintained forests, distributed nursery stock free of charge to the region's peasants, and oversaw model orchards from which peasants obtained nursery stock at no cost. A Mennonite elder (*starshii* in Russian) in each camp dealt directly with the Forestry Division of the Ministry of State Domains, which oversaw the camps and which ordered that military discipline be maintained therein.[49] Young men wore uniforms as a sign of their state responsibilities, and Mennonites also assigned an elder in each camp, known informally as the camp's *papa*, who functioned as a spiritual guide. All in all, the Foresteidienst proved enough of a working compromise for two-thirds of the empire's Mennonites in 1874 to stay put.

Conclusion

So it was that Mennonites overcame a series of tribulations after 1860, some of which were self-inflicted. All had demonstrated the degree to which they had embedded themselves into the civil fabric of a rapidly changing Russian empire. That could hold both promise and peril going forward, but the earliest returns were positive. For example, the institutionalization of the Mennonite Brethren movement had led to an increased structural coherence within the older Mennonite congregations, which formed their own General Conference in 1883. And despite the bitter divisions between them, the crisis over military exemption had demonstrated the degree to which all Mennonites could make common cause when circumstances necessitated.[50]

Imperial officials largely stayed clear of this church crisis in the 1860s apart from their offer of the Kuban Settlement to the Mennonite Brethren as an escape valve.[51] That was not the case with the landless dispute, however, where Russian officials eventually imposed a settlement on the overlapping Mennonite landed, civil, and ecclesial elites. Yet once implemented it resulted in a dramatic expansion of Mennonite landholding across New Russia and beyond. Add Mennonite private estate purchases to the mix – the emergence of the "Mennonite magnates" – and it is clear how far Mennonites in 1880 had moved from the days of Chortitza and Molotschna alone. Some historians maintain that this landed settlement resulted in a new era of civil peace for Mennonites. True, they never again had the same sort of civil disruption as was evident in the 1860s, but it is almost certainly the case that the gap between Mennonite wealth and poverty only increased in time. Though some of the landless found their problems solved in new daughter colonies, others found their plight merely institutionalized.

We see the same tension at work in the way the state resolved the crisis over universal military exemption. That one-third of Mennonites who emigrated did not randomly choose to do so. Quite the contrary, the most conservative and – for want of a better term – "traditional" of Mennonite voices tended to be the ones who left at this time, with the entire Kleine Gemeinde chief among them.[52] When the latter left they did so with their congregations intact. Their voice would be wanting in the years to come given the empire's explicit intent to integrate Mennonites and all "colonists" into the new categories of citizenship being formed. Even the solution of the Forsteidienst came with challenges. In his memoir of life in "Russia," the respected Mennonite Ältester Jacob H. Janzen describes his childhood where he grew up in one of those camps in which his father served as a chaplain for several years. Janzen identified the conduct of most Mennonite men in these camps as highly deleterious to Christian faith formation. In graphic images, he relays a saying that Mennonite youth tended to leave their consciences hanging on the poplars just outside of the actual camp so that they could pick them up again when they left.[53] Of course this was not everyone's experience, but the memory of it remained significant enough for Janzen to mention it decades later.

Thus, the forty thousand or so Mennonites who remained in the Russian empire after 1874 believed with good reason that the worst was behind them and that a new Golden Age was upon them. Only time would tell if they were correct.

Chapter Eight

Glory Days: The Apogee of Russian Mennonitism, 1883–1904

David G. Rempel was born on 17 November 1899 in the village of Nieder Chortitza on the banks of the Dnieper River. Decades later Rempel still recalled precise details of his childhood and youth. For instance, he remembered how his parents hired an "ageless peasant woman" from nearby Razumovka named Marika to assist his mother when David's father was away on business. More than a helper, Marika became part of the family, such that she even picked up a rudimentary proficiency in Plautdietsch. David recalled how his mother, who spoke Ukrainian, baked a steady supply of foods, including small buns (*Tweeback*) from her own past and tall Russian loaves called *bulki*, which Mennonites called *Bultje* in Plautdietsch. On Saturdays his mom made *Plautz*, a fruit-topped coffee cake and *Pirozhki*, or Russian pastries.

David also recalled fondly how he accompanied his father Gerhard on trips throughout the region. Gerhard, a grain merchant and small store owner, purchased wheat and barley from Mennonites and non-Mennonites alike, whereupon his teamsters, or Gerhard himself, hauled the grains from the farms to the district town of Alexandrovsk or its adjoining Mennonite village of Schönwiese, both situated across the Dnieper River. Mennonite millers in either location ground some of the harvest for sale as flour within the empire, though Rempel also sold the grains to Jewish traders, who controlled much of the export trade. Stevedores loaded crops destined for export onto covered flat-bottomed barges, which sailed down the Dnieper to the Black Sea ports of Odessa and Kherson, and from there to lucrative European markets via Constantinople, where they competed with Canadian, American, and Argentinian goods.[1] Needless to say, Gerhard spoke a variety of languages as required, including Russian, Ukrainian, Yiddish, High German, and Plautdietsch.

David G. Rempel began to record his childhood memoirs in the 1970s when the recently retired history professor, living in Menlo Park, California, also wrote an overview history of what he termed the "Mennonite Commonwealth in Russia."[2] In his overview, Rempel concluded that "Russian" Mennonites achieved a level of success that outpaced other Mennonite societies worldwide in the half-century before 1914. Rempel highlighted their stellar record in agriculture, industry, and milling. Mennonites realized such wide-ranging and generally recognized success because they had formed a commonwealth in Russia, by which they built and maintained their own hospitals; educational institutions; specialized institutions to care for the elderly, the orphaned, mentally infirm; and so on. Rempel concluded that Mennonites themselves believed they had created a "state within a state" in Russia.[3]

This chapter follows Rempel's lead as it investigates how Mennonites created what many in hindsight deemed a Golden Age in Imperial Russia. We first consider their robust demographic and geographic expansion within the empire. We then investigate key economic aspects of this remarkable half-century as Mennonites realized strong agricultural gains as well as a robust expansion of Mennonite manufactures and milling. Changes were everywhere in the half-century before 1910, all of which have presented historians with a conundrum. On the one hand, evidence suggests that the gap between Mennonite elites and the dispossessed by 1900 had never been greater, nor had they ever been more economically diverse or geographically scattered. On the other, countless Mennonite memoirs as well as historical investigations suggest that, despite that immense diversity, a coherent Russian Mennonitism had formed, sufficiently strong to label this as a Golden Age. Is it possible to bring these contradictions together? Here we consider the unifying role played by Mennonite church conferences, educational institutions, broadly conceived cultural advances, and a host of pan-Mennonite institutions, from hospitals to orphanages. Even the newly launched daughter colonies played a vital role in this process of greater coherence amid increased geographic diffusion, as did the external pressures on their faith and identity, which we examine in the following chapter.

Of course, talk of a coherent Russian Mennonitism raises the issue of the Mennonite commonwealth. Did it exist? Sociologist E.K. Francis first identified it in 1947 when he argued that the Mennonites who had immigrated to Manitoba from Imperial Russia in the 1870s constituted one such commonwealth. For Francis the term captured the reality that Mennonites by the 1870s had formed themselves into a homogenous group akin to an ethnos and distinct from the larger society. Rempel and James Urry have both picked up the language of commonwealth in their investigation of the Mennonite world in the Russian empire and broadened its applicability. Both have argued that the Mennonite commonwealth observed by Francis in the 1870s had strengthened considerably in the decades before 1914. By contrast John Staples has recently derided the term, arguing that any suggestion of a coherent Mennonitism distorts both the complex reality of who Mennonites were and of how intensely they lived intertwined lives with others in the empire.[4] Thus some discussion of this term and its applicability is unavoidable as it ultimately answers how one can best come to terms with Mennonitism at the end of the Imperial Era.

I argue here that a distinctive Mennonite commonwealth had taken shape in the empire since the settlement of 1789 but as a means of imperial integration, not separation, and at the expressed direction of state servitors. Rather than isolate Mennonites or create a monolithic Mennonitism, this commonwealth was dynamic enough to allow Rempel's mother to incorporate previously "Russian" foods into her household economy; for his father to learn Yiddish, Russian, and Ukrainian; and even for Russian Old Believer merchants to set up shops in many Mennonite villages.[5] In short, a Mennonite commonwealth did take shape before 1900, one that remained dynamically engaged with the larger world, and in spite of its occasional internal incoherence.

Demographic and Geographic Overview

Mennonites more than doubled in number between 1860 and 1914, from approximately 40,000 to over 100,000, and at a time when almost none immigrated from the German lands. Extant data suggests that Mennonite birth rates exceeded most other groups in the empire, with an annual increase listed variously between 2.54 and 3.18 per cent. More anecdotally, Rempel is representative of many when he records families that had between seven and thirteen children over several generations. He calculated that the population easily would have doubled every twenty years or sooner if only half of the children born survived to adulthood.[6]

Such impressive fecundity outpaced the Russian empire, which still grew from approximately 74 million in 1860 to over 125 million subjects by 1900. Under the circumstances, the empire needed a release valve for its growing population, and it found one, at least in part, in its increasingly aggressive desire to secure Siberia and safeguard its eastern borderland from Great Power interference. As a signal of Siberia's strategic importance, Alexander III announced in 1890 that the empire would build a railroad across Siberia to Vladivostok.[7] Officials also encouraged prospective settlers to move past the borders of the traditional Russian heartland, symbolized by the Volga River, and populate the vast stretches that lay before them to the east. As an integral part of the empire Mennonites participated in this first wave of settlement when they founded the daughter colonies of Neu Samara (1891), Orenburg (1893), and Terek (1901). From modest beginnings, all three settlements grew steadily, such that Neu Samara comprised over 35,000 desiatinas by 1914 as 3,500 Mennonites lived in its 14 villages and 9 large estates.[8] It helped that land prices east of the Volga remained well below those in New Russia. For example, a desiatina of land in Ufa – where Mennonites founded a daughter colony along the Trans-Siberian railroad in 1894 – cost barely 9 rubles per desiatina in 1887, whereas the cost jumped to over 55 rubles per desiatina in Ekaterinslav guberniia, home of Chortitza.[9] As a rule these daughter colonies experienced the same hardships in their founding years as had been the case in Chortitza after 1789. They often suffered from a weak infrastructure, poor soils, harsh weather conditions that brought drought, and hostile relations with their new neighbours. But they persevered, such that many of these same daughter colonies flourished by 1900.

Mennonites expanded in one other and very different direction before 1900, when they relocated to the empire's cities in increasing numbers.[10] This by itself was not surprising, as many had immigrated to New Russia from Prussian cities or their suburbs where they had worked as artisans and merchants with little to no experience in farming. Many came to New Russia wanting to replicate that urban way of life. The problem, initially, is that cities had not emerged in New Russia at the time of Mennonite settlement, and when they did, the empire's passport system made it difficult for Mennonites to leave their home villages to live and work in urban areas. Even so, Mennonites often travelled to the emerging cities of Ekaterinoslav, Odessa, and Kherson to market their goods. An informal Mennonite community at the heart of the early Mennonite Brethren movement existed in the Azov port city of Berdiansk since its founding in the 1830s.

A new era began for Mennonites in 1857, when the empire passed legislation which permitted all colonists to acquire the "social estate" designation of "merchant." Suddenly they could live and work in cities without fear of reprisal or the need to seek community approval first. In short order Mennonites in significant numbers relocated to several cities, including Ekaterinoslav, Odessa, Orekhov, Alexandrovsk, Berdiansk, Kharkov, Moscow, and St. Petersburg. Some went to work, others to study. Mennonites also integrated quickly into Siberian cities after

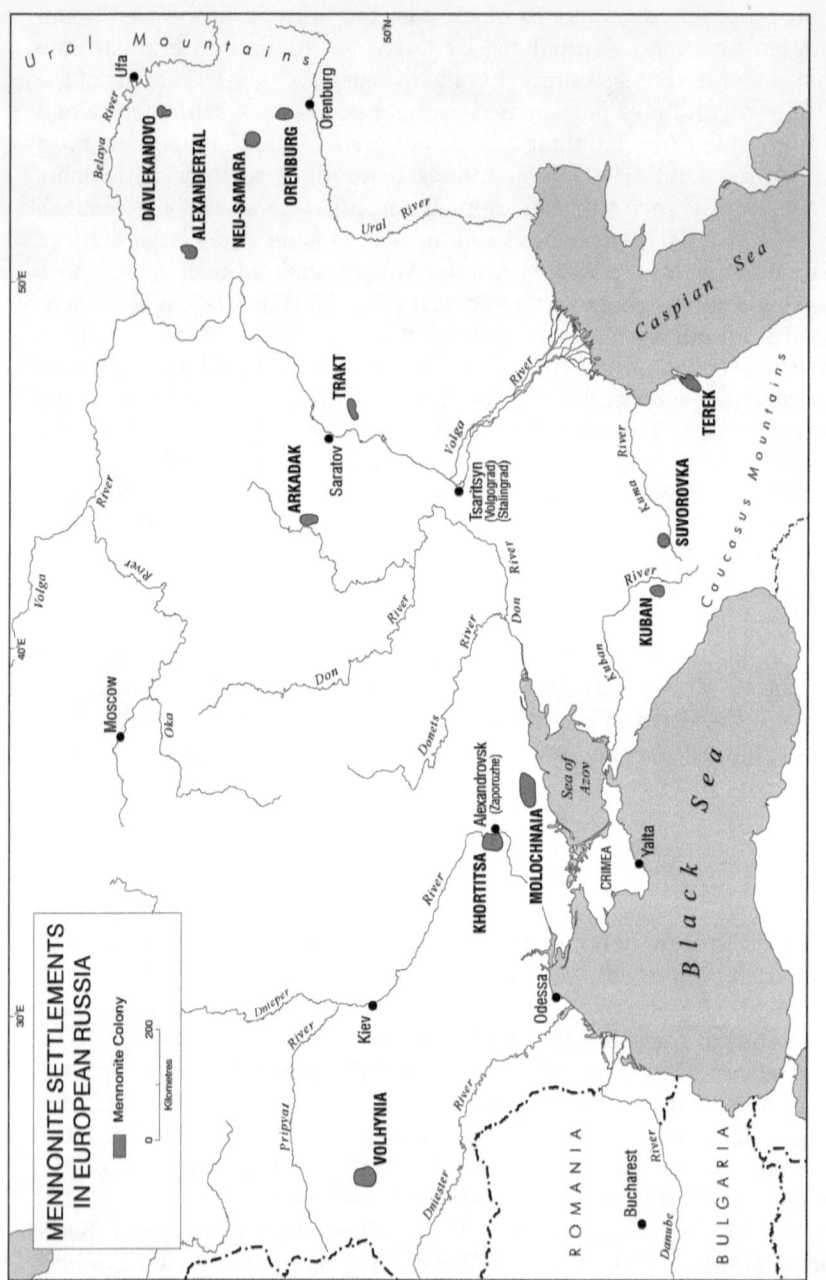

Map 2. Mennonite settlements in European Russia. From David G. Rempel with Cornelia Rempel Carlson, *A Mennonite Family in Tsarist Russia and the Soviet Union, 1789–1923*. Used by permission of Cornelia Rempel Carlson.

1890, including the regional centre of Omsk, where, for example, Peter J. Wiens established a commercial establishment in 1897 to sell agricultural machinery manufactured by Mennonites. At the same time, select Mennonite villages urbanized as milling and manufacturing predominated. In particular, the Chortitza village of Schönwiese, adjacent to Alexandrovsk and the only Chortitza settlement village on the left bank of the Dnieper, became such a strong manufacturing hub that the district capital annexed the Mennonite village outright in 1911.

In short, the Mennonite footprint had spread far beyond Chortitza and Molotschna by 1900. As a measure of this shift, only 37.7 per cent of all Mennonites still lived in the two Mother Colonies by 1914, down from 92.2 per cent in 1860. Though the absolute number of Mennonites in Chortitza and Molotschna had barely shifted in that period – up to 40,000 from 35,000[11] – the fact that over 100,000 Mennonites lived in the empire by 1914 spoke volumes about how they had spread far and wide. In terms of landholding alone, Adolf Ehrt estimates that Mennonites owned 750,000 desiatinas of land in the empire by 1914, of which estate owners possessed 328,000, the Mother Colonies 170,000 desiatinas, and an additional 175,000 in new settlements.[12] In some stretches, such as the one along the Dnieper bend between Chortitza and the provincial capital of Ekaterinoslav 80 kilometres to the north, non-Mennonite landowners had almost become the exception. Mennonites owned no less than 10 per cent of all lands in Ekaterinoslav and Tavrida guberniias, home to Chortitza and Molotschna colonies, respectively.[13]

Agriculture

Mennonites may have been scattered geographically by 1900, but they remained as united as ever when it came to agriculture. Even industrialists, as we shall see shortly, overwhelmingly linked their activities to grain cultivation, which had predominated over livestock breeding since the days of Johann Cornies. Mennonite agriculturalists steadily intensified their economics as they worked more land by 1900, and they worked it more efficiently in response to both demographic pressures and increased demand from imperial and international markets. Market potential abounded after the mid-nineteenth century as European industrial strategies relied on the importation of grains to feed the rapidly expanding cities. At the same time the steady urban growth within the empire assured that Russian grain producers, Mennonites among them, had ample market access. They responded accordingly.

A.A. Klaus estimates that Molotschna Mennonites tilled approximately 21.5 of their 65 desiatina farmsteads in 1851, as neither the markets nor the extant technologies allowed for more. Yet Mennonites in both of the Mother Colonies cultivated up to 25 desiatinas of their farmsteads by the 1870s, and almost double that by the late 1880s.[14] It represented a dramatic increase, made possible by new technologies and intensive use of readily available hired labour. Mennonites devoted almost all their arable land expansion to market crops, especially wheat, rye, and oats, and they did so with increased efficiency. Beyond grains, Mennonites maintained herds of cattle and horses, the latter especially for transport and cultivation. Mennonites also cultivated extensive vegetable and flower gardens and orchards around their yards, and they adopted the practice of large melon fields, known as *bashtani*, from the first settlers, where they grew *arbuze* (watermelons, *arbuz* in singular). The words, of Turkish origin but incorporated into Menno-speak along with the Russian *piroshky* and *bulki*, suggests the degree to which agriculturalists in this ethnically diverse region learned from each other. Mennonites commonly employed night sentries to guard their *bashtani*, especially when the melon fields expanded to several desiatinas and more in size.[15]

Increased cultivation by itself would have failed had St. Petersburg not moved aggressively to strengthen the infrastructure which connected producers to markets; and respond they did. There were barely any railroads in the empire at mid-century, with the first constructed in New Russia in 1863. Yet by 1914 the region had become a leader in rail construction, as only Moscow gubernia exceeded Ekaterinoslav in rail lines per square kilometre.[16] Rail lines played a vital role as they allowed agriculturalists, Mennonites among them, to get their goods to market at a time when fall weather conditions made dirt roads impassable. They also increased settlement densities across New Russia and helped make it one of the most urbanized regions in the Russian empire by 1914. This further increased market opportunities for Mennonites and others, as it did in Siberia with the onward construction eastward of the Trans-Siberian railroad. It helped that Chortitza Mennonites benefited from ready access to one of the key crossing points over the Dnieper at nearby Alexandrovsk.

Provincial and district parliaments (*zemstvos*), created in 1864, encouraged further improvements in agricultural practice when they established experimental farms, created and funded the work of regional agronomists, advised Mennonites and others on soil conditions and crops, and promoted improvements to crops sown and breeding stock for cattle and horses. All in all, Mennonites found themselves at the centre of a region, and empire, on the move, and they were keen to take full advantage.

Mennonite agricultural practices and geographic expansion before 1900 dramatically increased their contact with peasants near and far. Intensive grain cultivation required more labourers. Fortunately for Mennonites, along with estate owners, thousands of workers annually made their way south from the Ukrainian and Russian heartland in search of work, where they competed with local peasants for the prized positions. Once hired, seasonal labourers often returned to the same Mennonite farmsteads year after year. There are accounts of peasant children following in their parents' footsteps to work for Mennonites, even though many older Mennonites knew only a few words of Ukrainian or Russian. Though some sources stress Mennonite condescension to their labourers, others speak of almost familial relations, especially for the many Ukrainian women and adolescent girls who worked as nannies in Mennonite homes as David G. Rempel experienced it. In rare exceptions, peasants eventually purchased their own farms with monies earned as labourers for Mennonites.[17] We do know that peasants who lived adjacent to the Mother Colonies benefited from that proximity as they purchased old-generation implements from Mennonites who constantly sought to improve their inventories. By contrast, peasants who lived adjacent to private estates and daughter colonies purchased by Mennonites after the 1860s saw their lots worsen as Mennonites ended the long-term lease arrangements by which nobles had long made plentiful land available at inexpensive rates to local peasants.[18]

Mennonite Industry

The Mennonite artisanal impulse, which dated back to their origins in the sixteenth century, had intensified in New Russia, where inheritance practices guaranteed that the landless quickly outnumbered the landed. We have already considered the resultant beginnings of Mennonite manufacturing in the empire. However, the achievements of those early days were no match for Mennonite industrial activity after 1860 when the empire moved aggressively to jumpstart this sector, all to the benefit of those who lived in the Chortitza villages. For once, the settlement's geography proved advantageous over Molotschna, as the former's Dnieper bend location placed it at midpoint between the empire's richest iron ore deposits in Krivoi Rog and the coal-rich Donets basin (the Donbas). As a first step, the Welshman John Hughes began steel production in the Donbas in 1872, assisted by 100 miners and steel workers whom he brought with him from his homeland. His plants soon employed tens of thousands of workers, many of whom lived in the town of IUzovka ("Юзовка" in Russian, or "Hughes-ovka") that sprang up around his factories. IUzovka quickly numbered in the thousands.

A spur line to the main Donbas-Krivoi Rog railroad completed one year later connected Alexandrovsk to the emergent industrial powerhouse. It had once been a sleepy district town outpaced in development by the adjacent Mennonite manufacturing village of Schönwiese. That now changed as Alexandrovsk gained the upper hand. Its location immediately south of the Dnieper rapids made it a valuable collection point with direct access to the Black Sea ports and beyond. Countless settlers flooded into Alexandrovsk in search of employment, as did Mennonite merchants, millers, and manufacturers seeking to capitalize on the growth. By 1900 Alexandrovsk had grown to 35,000 inhabitants, up from barely 4,000 in 1850. By the later date Alexandrovsk claimed to be the region's undisputed entrepôt, as more than five hundred ships moved in one twelve-month period from its riverside wharves to the sea. In that year the Donbas accounted for 68 per cent of all coal mined in the Russian empire, as Mennonite industrialists in the Chortitza and Schönwiese villages positioned themselves at the epicentre of New Russia's industrial revolution.[19]

The top 567 Mennonite firms in the Russian empire had a declared value of almost 5.5 million rubles by 1908, though James Urry suggests that their actual wealth was larger given the Mennonite inclination to diminish their fiscal obligations as they under-reported their actual wealth, in part to reduce taxes owed to support the Foresteidienst.[20] Mennonites controlled a large section of the milling industry across the southern empire by the dawn of the twentieth century. They erected both wind and steam mills to take advantage of the burgeoning grain trade. Of these, Niebuhr milling concern based in Schönwiese predominated, as its eleven mills secured an annual income of 3 million rubles by 1907.[21] As impressive as the Mennonite hold on flour milling was, it paled in comparison to agricultural implement manufacturing, where Mennonites controlled an estimated 10 per cent of the empire's production by 1908, when officials appraised its value at over 36 million rubles. Once again, a few key families and enterprises controlled the entire market, among them A.J. Koop with plants in Schönwiese, Chortitza, and Kichkas. The firm of Lepp & Wallman employed seven hundred workers by 1911 in two massive factories located in Schönwiese and Chortitza, though by then it had established plants well beyond the Mennonite heartland, including the Azov port cities of Berdiansk and Taganrog. As one might expect, Mennonites concentrated on machinery which suited their purposes and satisfied exploding market demand, including the production of *bukkers*, drills, mechanical sowers, steam-threshers, and *lobogreikas*.[22] Mennonite village artisans developed secondary industries to repair these implements, and peasants learned the craft and eventually set up sales and repair shops in their own villages. Mennonites also developed a strong reputation for their other technologies dating back to services rendered during the Crimean War. Their wagons were larger and stronger, equipped with steel axels and wheels. Wagon manufacturers worked in both Chortitza village as well as in the Molotschna village of Halbstadt. Lastly, and most unusually, Kröger Clockworks of Rosental in Chortitza settlement produced a wall-clock modelled after a Prussian design which developed a large market among estate owners as well as German and Mennonite colonists. Many claimed that no decent Mennonite home in the empire would be without one and it therefore became an essential wedding present.[23]

Of course, Mennonite industrialists did not flourish in a vacuum as they greatly benefited from Russian protectionist legislation and international technological developments. By the former, Imperial Russia passed a new customs law in 1891 which protected domestic industry from international competition when it applied new tariffs to all imports. By the latter, Imperial Russia never joined the International Patent Union, which allowed Russian entrepreneurs to copy imported technologies without international restraint. This mattered particularly prior to 1891 when American and British industrialists flooded the Imperial Russian market with agricultural implements. David G. Rempel relates how his great uncle Kornelius eagerly investigated any such acquisition in his region: "According to Grandmother, whenever Kornelius heard someone had purchased a new (and imported) piece of equipment, he hurried to examine it. Invariably, he returned home with his suit covered in grease, mud, and dust, for his habit was to crawl over, under, and into pieces of machinery to find out how they were made and worked." From such investigations Mennonites and others in the empire managed to produce equipment better suited to regional conditions and better priced after 1891 especially, thanks to new Russian tariffs. Immense wealth came to select Mennonites from such innovations.[24]

Mennonites and Class Division: Myth or Reality?

Given the immense wealth enjoyed by relatively few Mennonite estate owners and industrialists, is it even possible to talk about a coherent Mennonitism by 1900? The question is not easily answered. We know that the empire's Mennonites coalesced into two discrete wealth-owning layers over time: first, the Mennonite magnates of estate owners and industrialists comprised perhaps 3 per cent of the population but possessed 34 per cent of Mennonite capital, followed by a second layer, the great mass of Mennonite village-based farmstead owners. These were scattered across the empire by 1900 where they owned almost all the remaining Mennonite wealth, roughly proximate to their 71.2 per cent of the population. But, as Urry points out, this leaves us with the uncomfortable conclusion that up to a quarter of all Mennonites were, at best, the working poor.[25]

Taken in turn, the Mennonite magnates have received considerable attention in the literature. We know they managed their estates rather than leased out their lands to neighbouring peasants as the nobility had done. We know they constructed their own flour mills, blacksmith shops, schools, and factories on their lands, and numerous photographic almanacs point to their increasingly ostentatious displays of wealth as they were among the earliest in the region to introduce indoor plumbing, electric lighting, and even chauffeur-driven automobiles. Mennonite estate owners and industrial elites simply lived different lives than most Mennonites. By 1900 they had typically built up their properties around a central yard dominated by the multistorey, brick manor house. They commonly constructed barracks for the scores of seasonal workers they employed annually, as did Mennonite industrialists.

Mennonite estate owners and industrialists integrated much more smoothly into Russian elite society, participated in local *zemstvo* and city councils, and travelled to Europe or the spas along the Black Sea, where they encountered other elites. As such they became the public face of Mennonitism in the empire, even as they remained, ironically, the most anomalous. Magnates rarely married outside of their ranks as they reinforced their wealth through what Nataliya Venger has called the "clan system" safeguarded by "inter-clan marriage."[26] These were vital as they allowed industrialists to avoid internal competition through the creation of joint stock companies. We also know that many reports stress the frugality of estate owners; their close relations with their labourers, whom they often laboured alongside; and their philanthropic generosity to community welfare projects. Schönwiese industrialists even provided basic health insurance and established factory hospitals to care for their workers. The picture, in short, is mixed, though their share of the wealth is beyond dispute.[27]

In a sense, the summary provided in this chapter deals almost exclusively with the majority who comprised that second layer, the

Mennonite village farmsteaders. Where scholars have disagreed, however, is on the existence of the Mennonite poor after 1860. For instance, Harvey Dyck concludes that Mennonites resolved the landless crisis of the mid-nineteenth century in such a way that left their society less polarized in the years that followed.[28] By contrast, David Rempel argued that the daughter colonies did resolve significant aspects of landlessness, but not enough to eliminate the plight of all landless Mennonites. Many of these drifted into the region's cities or clung to clusters of smaller household plots at the edge of Mennonite villages. In his village of Nieder Chortitza the Mennonite poor, primarily unskilled, lived apart in a stretch of poor sandy soil along the Dnieper River. Others referred to them derogatorily as "those stuck by the Dnieper," or the *Nippaenja* in Plautdietsch. Rempel estimated that they comprised approximately 30 per cent of the village. Such a ratio is consistent with Ehrt's finding for all Mennonites, which makes it more difficult to see Nieder Chortitza as an outlier. Many villages still had enclaves of the Mennonite working poor by 1900 and after, including the Molotschna village of Margenau, where villagers derogatorily referred to the poorer stretch of Mennonite householders on the edge of settlement as "Schönwiese." The name referred to the Mennonite industrial village adjacent to Alexandrovsk and suggests that at least some of the Mennonite labourers who worked for Mennonite industrialists also comprised part of this social underbelly.[29]

Regardless of their level of powerlessness and poverty, then, there is reason to conclude that Mennonites in Imperial Russia by 1900 were geographically scattered, economically diffuse, and socially complex. That being the case, what, if anything, still brought them together? Can one still speak of an all-embracing Mennonitism by 1900?

Culture: The Ties That Bound

There are several reasons why Mennonites later reflected positively on this late imperial era in their history. It helps, given the diversity highlighted above, that some 75 per cent of Mennonites identified themselves as farmsteaders, though even the working poor benefited from the occasional largesse of the magnates, many of whom were distant relations. This gets at the success story Harvey Dyck describes after the crises of mid-century. An examination of the Mennonite "thick culture," the rich complex of social and cultural interactions that continued to bind them together despite several powerful centrifugal forces, reveals that internally religion lay at its heart.[30]

Religion

At first glance it seems implausible that religion could have been a unifying agent in the formation of a common Mennonite identify by 1900. After all, both sides appear to have burned all bridges when the Mennonite Brethren broke away from the original Mennonite churches after 1860. What is more, the new movement instituted a form of baptism which excluded all other Mennonites from full fellowship and then refused to permit its adherents to marry across confessional lines. Communion, the Eucharist, was similarly exclusive. Both conferences developed their own missionary organizations thereafter and they separately sent missionaries overseas. The Mennonite Brethren never completely separated themselves from the German Baptists,[31] and the Kirchengemeinde long complained that the Brethren wanted to woo away its members to join the new sect.

Other movements arose that pointed to ongoing ecclesial division, including the *Tempelgesellschaft*,[32] though the most extraordinary was that initiated by Claas Epp in 1880 when he led six hundred Mennonites into the Central Asian wilds of Turkmenistan to wait for Christ's imminent return in the East. Eventually disappointed, many stayed in the region, where they became the most distant Mennonite outpost in the empire and included those who settled in the walled settlement of Ak Mechet, near the city of Khiva in Russian Turkestan. Some became actively engaged in missionary activity across Central Asia, including Johannes Bartsch, who worked as a colporteur for the British and Foreign Bible Society, and Hermann Janzen, who had first studied the Koran and developed fluency in the local Uzbek-Turkish dialect. It seemed as if the Mennonite footprint had expanded beyond any recognizable measure over just a single generation.[33]

All of that aside, one can still argue that the church may have played a greater unifying role among Imperial Russian Mennonites in 1900 than at any previous time. In some ways it was the last all-embracing institution standing. Since the point of settlement in 1789 Mennonite ministers had wrestled with Mennonite civil authorities in the Gebietsamts of Chortitza and Molotschna over who would be the final authority in their emerging society. Often the church lost thanks to the roles assigned to the Gebietsamt by the Guardians Office, though inter-congregational division and the larger-than-life figure of Johann Cornies also played important roles. So why did those centrifugal trends not continue in the second half of the century, especially given the acrimony which marked the birth of the Mennonite Brethren movement?[34]

Several reasons present themselves. For one, with limited exception all of Russian Mennonitism belonged to one of two churchly conferences after the Kleine Gemeinde emigrated in the 1870s: the Mennonite Brethren, with some 4,900 members in 1908, and the Kirchengemeinde, with 26,500.[35] In particular Mennonites in 1900 no longer divided along the Flemish–Frisian fault line as had been the case since the sixteenth century. Although the two remaining conferences continued to differ, as outlined above, they also cooperated on a host of levels by 1900, foremost in the Foresteidienst, which involved all Mennonites. Mennonite ministers assigned to the camps assumed spiritual oversight of all men stationed there, regardless of affiliation. They downplayed differences accordingly and stressed a common Mennonite spiritual orthodoxy.

Ironically, the daughter colonies, formed at the point of the Brethren-Kirchengemeinde division, played a surprising role in support of Mennonite unification. Mennonites often settled in those new settlements in advance of any formal congregational formation, which compelled newly appointed itinerant ministers of either conference to preside over services for both. Thus, the lines between Brethren and Kirchengemeinde blurred from the start as the two conferences cooperated in village schools and occasionally hosted joint annual Bible study gatherings and other faith-based conferences in the daughter colonies.

Both conferences worked together to safeguard Mennonites from the increased threat posed to all Mennonites by Russian nationalists in the late nineteenth century. In fact, the level of cooperation was such that voices in both conferences began to call in the 1880s for a joint seminary to train ministers. In 1906 the Kirchengemeinde began to invite Brethren observers to its annual conferences. Other Mennonite leaders sought a full unification of these two conferences, as appeared to happen when disgruntled members of the Mennonite Brethren movement in Molotschna formed the Evangelical Mennonite Church Movement – also known as the Allianz movement – in 1905.[36]

Even the most seemingly aloof sector in Mennonite society, the grand estate owners, often maintained their churchly connections from afar, a feat made easier by the fact that Mennonite churches only held Communion services twice annually in 1900. This limited the occasions when adherents needed to return. Lastly, Mennonite ministers and Ältesters spoke with increased authority over all Mennonites in the empire by 1900 because more of them had the benefit of a strong educational background; something previous generations of leaders had lacked.

Education and Intellectual Life

Jacob H. Janzen, introduced in the previous chapter, began his education in 1885 when he enrolled in a Mennonite village school in the Molotschna settlement. He did well, such that he moved directly to the Gnadenfeld secondary school where he completed the two-year program in one year. In September 1894 Janzen passed his teachers' examinations in the district city of Melitopol, in Russian of course, after which he began a long teaching career at several Mennonite institutions. A few years later Janzen passed another government examination in Kharkov, and he later studied at institutions in the German cities in Jena and Griefswald. Ordained as a minister in the Gnadenfeld congregation in 1906, Janzen taught at the newly opened girl's secondary school in Ohrloff from 1908 until 1921. Along the way he introduced German Lutheran Bible stories to his students, wrote his own short stories and plays, and coached his students as they performed excerpts from Glinka's *Life of the Tsar*. Janzen read the German *Odessaer Zeitung* and critically engaged the philosophers of Russian nihilism. Janzen's world, in short, flowed easily from the Mennonite village to the Ukrainian regional city to the German university, and from German to Russian and back again, let alone his native Plautdietsch. Yet in all of this, he lived, taught, and preached in a world grounded in what he referred to as "Mennonite culture."[37]

Mennonites clearly prized education as a key component of this somewhat amorphous "Mennonite culture," and they did so even after the state transferred control of all Mennonite schools to the Ministry of Education in May 1881. Thereafter Mennonites shifted to Russian-language instruction to satisfy new requirements, though religious instruction continued in the schools in German. Indeed, Mennonite acceptance of Russian placed them at odds with a host of other minorities in the empire who resisted the shift to Russian as the principal language of instruction.[38] In a sense Mennonite education existed on two planes by 1900: on the first, the primary and secondary levels, Mennonites enjoyed levels of literacy for boys and girls that far outpaced others in the empire and matched those found in Western Europe. As a rule, Mennonites had constructed brick-faced one-room primary schools with water heating in almost every village in the empire. As the daughter colonies grew Mennonites also constructed a tier of secondary schools, though initially only in Chortitza and Molotschna settlements. These further galvanized Janzen's "Mennonite culture" across the Brethren and Kirchengemeinde divide, even as these institutions also attracted German Lutheran and Catholic students from throughout the empire. Mennonite ministers exercised the most influence at this primary and secondary level, both through religious instruction and through their membership on local school boards. Mennonites also introduced their own texts into these schools after 1881, which included catechisms and histories. One new text identified the Mennonite world as a "Little Motherland," but one firmly at home within the Russian empire. That Mennonite self-representation of a Little Motherland, but unfailingly loyal to the empire, mirrors what Faith Hillis has recently said about "Little Russians" in Right Bank of Ukraine who also deemed themselves as integral to the empire at this time. And as a measure of Mennonite pedagogical success, the predominately Mennonite primary school division of Berdiansk uezd in Tavrida guberniia (which included Molotschna) won the Grand Prize at the 1900 Paris World Fair.[39]

Mennonites in a second but growing tier by 1900 continued with their education at a wide range of post-secondary institutions. Significant numbers of Mennonites studied in Odessa, Ekaterinoslav, Berdiansk, Kiev, Moscow, St. Petersburg, and Kharkov within the empire, and Berlin, Leipzig, Basel, and Hamburg beyond. As a rule, those who sought theological training did so at Baptist institutions in the German and Swiss lands. Those who studied generally returned to work in a constantly expanding set of professions, including as engineers, architects, medical practitioners, teachers, lawyers, publishers, factory managers, artists, writers, and other occupations. They founded German-language periodicals and compiled almanacs. Equally striking, Mennonites tended to feel most engaged with other Mennonites when away, and somewhat removed from the larger culture. Johann Klassen, a Mennonite who studied in Switzerland, observed that the Prussians (by which he meant the Germans) could not fully understand the "Russians" by which the Germans referred to Klassen and the other Mennonites.[40]

Mennonite Benevolence and Mutual Aid

The wealth that permitted Mennonite schools to be entirely self-financed also transferred to a wide range of benevolent activities, some of which dated back to the earliest years of settlement. In a detailed study for 1913 James Urry has demonstrated the breadth of the Molotschna settlements' involvement in mutual aid and benevolence. By that year it had annual expenditures of over 600,000 rubles, divided into the Gnadenfeld and Halbstadt volosts. Of this amount Mennonites set aside 130,000 rubles for a landless fund, 40,000 rubles to support the Foresteidienst, and 43,000 rubles for fire insurance.[41] To the latter, Mennonites had long had collective insurance for all structures in their settlements against fire. Property owners received full compensation in the event of fire, unless investigators determined that owners had committed arson. Many villages also provided insurance against cattle and horse theft and damage to grains caused by hail or locusts.

The Orphans' Bureau (Waisanamt) may, however, have been the most remarkable Mennonite achievement, and certainly one of the oldest. As with the others identified here, all Mennonites participated, as this bureau assisted widows and minor orphans with their farmstead economies or investments from any inheritance they had received. David G. Rempel concludes that the Orphans' Bureau acted as a banking institution for all Mennonites, and good that it did as in 1902, for instance, it carried holdings of almost 2 million rubles, from which it paid out almost 300,000 rubles to orphans in that year alone.[42]

Lastly, Mennonite institutions broadened their reach even further before 1900 as they established other special institutions to assist the Mennonite disadvantaged. Pride of place went to the Maria School for the Deaf, named in honour of the emperor's wife. Founded in 1881 in the Molotschna village of Tiege, the school offered room and board at reasonable rates and schooling over nine years. Mennonites constructed a new and architecturally stunning two-story building in 1890 able to house forty students and their teachers. At a cost of 40,000 rubles, individual donors contributed greatly to this project, as they did for the Bethsaida Mental Health Institute when it opened in 1910. Situated between Einlage and Alt-Kronsweide in Chortitza settlement, the building served the needs of those who struggled with "mental illness, epilepsy and nerve disorders."[43] One could also highlight the Mennonite hospitals constructed entirely by Mennonite funds, or a special school for deaconesses, but in every instance we get a sense of Mennonite engagement in the whole of their society.

The Mennonite Commonwealth as Imperial Integration, Not Isolation

We return to the language of Mennonite commonwealth, for it is no wonder why Urry and Rempel both deemed it to be an apt description of Russian Mennonitism in the late imperial era. Those who critique it stress the presumption of isolation that comes with it, a presumption that later popular histories reinforce. For example, one Mennonite memoirist living in Canada, P. Riediger, later framed the "Russian" Mennonite experience as follows:

> Through their many migrations forced by persecution and want, our Mennonite people found it necessary to unite closely and help one another in

every isolation. Our people in Russia had a unique character, they lived and breathed the same atmosphere and spoke with their own, distinct voice. Because it was a homogenous group of people who had matured under pressure, much like an individual person, they subconsciously created a distinct culture. A unique opportunity to do this was afforded them by their isolation on the empty steppes of Russia. Here, undisturbed, they could develop, guided by their deep faith, and their peculiar character, into an independent community. Here they were allowed to build closed settlements and establish congregations, create churches and schools, and exercise self-government.[44]

Riediger presents us with the key theme of oblivious isolation that has been at the heart of the "Mennonite commonwealth" critique. Yet proponents of the commonwealth thesis offer no such perspective, and for good reason, as Mennonites engaged with their larger society from the very moment of settlement. The empire itself had required a measure of autonomous governance of all colonists after settlement, even as it did in the Polish lands after conquest and the Tatar lands long before that in the days of Ivan the Terrible. Indeed, the eminent Ukrainian historian Serhii Plokhii argues that such rich diversity made southern Ukraine (New Russia) unique within a nascent Ukraine and, by extension, the empire. Dilaram Inoyatova makes the same case for Mennonites in Central Asia by 1900 where they lived in dynamic engagement with their Ukrainian, Russian, and Muslim neighbours. She quotes the district head of Aulie-Ata in Turkestan, who wrote to the military governor of Syr-Darya province on 15 November 1904: "The belief that Mennonites do not share or, better to say, hide from others their improved economic system, is beneath all criticism."[45]

In other words, Mennonites along with all other settlers integrated into this multi-faith and under-governed empire through multi-commonwealth formation.[46] There is little evidence to suggest that they wilfully created a state within a state, which does not seem to capture their principal dynamic. In addition, Mennonites integrated smoothly into a new governance model when the larger empire introduced the Great Reforms after the Crimean War. They only objected vociferously when the introduction of universal military conscription directly challenged a core plank of Mennonite faith: pacifism. A third of the empire's Mennonites deemed that demand already a bridge too far and emigrated. But those who stayed accepted the compromise of the Foresteidienst and thereby opened the door to the full flowering of Russian Mennonitism, even as their integration into the larger empire continued apace.

In a sense, this chapter has suggested that Mennonites increasingly integrated into the larger empire by 1900, even as their own peculiar Mennonitism thrived. Perhaps Kornelius Braun, the uncle of David G. Rempel, can serve as exemplar of this complex shift. Braun taught in the village of Rosental in the heartland of the "original" Chortitza settlement. Decades later Rempel recalled his uncle's wit and humour; how he regaled Mennonite audiences with readings from his personal library, including Plautdietsch works by Fritz Reuter, Shevchenko's Ukrainian writings, and Gogol's Russian tales.[47] Plautdietsch, Russian, and Ukrainian. This was the Mennonite mix, increasingly, at a time of the full flowering of the Mennonite commonwealth in the Russian empire.

Sadly, for them, this world was about to end as much tribulation awaited, some of it already evident in the rise of Russian nationalism. But to say more is to anticipate the next chapter.

Chapter Nine

Confession or Sect? German or German-Speaking? Mennonite Identity Politics on the Edge of the Abyss, 1881–1917

On 6 August 1907 Tsar Nicholas II confirmed his father's Russianist approach to autocratic rule when he presided over the sanctification of a new cathedral to mark his grandfather's assassination in the heart of the empire's capital, St. Petersburg. The tsar's late father, Alexander III, had ordered builders to construct the Cathedral of the Saviour on Spilled Blood on the very place where terrorists had assassinated his father Alexander II, on 1 March 1881. The new structure immediately stood out as peculiarly "Russian" in an otherwise "European" cityscape, and for good reason, as Alexander III insisted that architects model the new cathedral after ancient Russian cathedrals in Yaroslavl and Moscow. By contrast, Russian emperors from Peter the Great onward had developed this "Venice of the North" entirely along contemporary West European architectural lines with Romanesque columns and Italian Baroque facades. In that spirit, Peter had also banned the Russified title of "tsar" for Russian rulers as he insisted that subjects address him with the westernized form of "emperor" (*imperator*).

The very Russian-looking Cathedral of the Saviour on Spilled Blood dedicated in 1907 could not have been a more ironical memorial to Alexander II, as the assassinated monarch had worked harder than most emperors to westernize Imperial Russian statecraft through the so-called Great Reforms of the 1860s. St. Isaac's Cathedral in St. Petersburg, copied after the European domed cathedrals of St. Peter's in Rome and St. Paul's in London, embodied much of his vision for the empire when it opened in 1858. Alexander II was also the last Romanov to prefer the term "emperor" as his son, Alexander III, reinstituted the pre-Petrine title of "tsar." According to historian Richard Wortman, the shift was part of a grand strategy by Alexander III whereby he sought to abandon his father's stance of distance from the Russian people. Alexander II came to the throne with what Wortman calls a "scenario of love," but it was love for all nationalities of the realm, all equally bound in love for their monarch. Alexander II's coronation, for example, featured ceremonial roles played by Bashkirs; Armenians; Tatars; Cherkassy, a variety of Russian and Ukrainian Cossacks; and even one Mennonite, the district mayor of the Molotschna settlement.[1] All needed to work together with the empire's enlightened and westernized bureaucrats to overcome Russia's humiliation in the Crimean War.

By contrast, Alexander III sought Imperial Russia's future in a Russianized version of the empire's past. He abandoned the reform initiatives of his father and aborted any informal alliance with the bureaucrats, who now worked surreptitiously to continue the westernization of Russian state governance practices. Heavily influenced by conservative and Slavophilic ideologue Konstantin Pobedonostsev, Alexander III sought a pre-Petrine alliance with the true Russian people – the peasants – along with the Russian Orthodox Church. On a more superficial level, both Alexander III and his son Nicholas II wore beards, the very facial hair which Peter banned Russian elites from wearing because of its peasantist and priestly Orthodox associations. And Nicholas II, the last tsar of all the Russias, named his son and heir to the throne Alexei, itself a repudiation of the westernizing Peter the Great given the name's two-fold association. Alexei, the father of Peter, had been the last of the Muscovite tsars. Alexei, the son of Peter, had been executed on Peter's orders for his open opposition to the Petrine reforms. Nicholas II's decision to name his son, born on 12 August 1904, Alexei clearly signalled the tsar's core conviction that Russia's future lay in Muscovy's past.

Talk of cathedral design in St. Petersburg and the shift from the westernizing Emperor Alexander II to the Russifying Tsar Alexander III suggest the degree to which the Russian empire struggled to find its own identity in the late nineteenth and early twentieth centuries. Such a struggle carried weight in an empire where less than half of the 125 million subjects identified as native Russian speakers in the 1897 census. Petr Stolypin, perhaps Imperial Russia's most remarkable statesman, argued well after 1900 that the empire's future dynamism depended upon its ability to create a level playing field where nationality and religion mattered less and citizenship mattered more. Countless minorities, Mennonites among them, shared much of that vision and adapted to it even as they safeguarded their own collective identities. However, those same minorities found themselves on the outside looking in by 1900 as Russian nationalists demanded pride of place for those who identified themselves as ethnic Russian, Russian speaking, and Russian Orthodox. Such a newly conceived and Russo-centric empire threatened Mennonites, whom Russian nationalists increasingly identified as

German, at a time when Russian animosity towards the German empire rose abruptly. In the end, this Russian nationalist voice carried the day over Alexander II's all-embracing "scenario of love," and that made all the difference.

This chapter ends with the tsar's abdication in February 1917, though we first consider the rise of Russian nationalism in the late nineteenth century and its impact on the empire's Mennonites. We then consider the disruption caused by the Revolution of 1905 and how identity politics played out between 1907 and 1913. By 1913, despite the turmoil of recent years, there was reason to believe the empire had stabilized after recent crises and that better days lay ahead. Of course, time did not stand still, and the onset of the First World War in 1914 proved fatal for several empires, the Russian included. These war years marked a troubling chapter for Mennonites as they sought to demonstrate their loyalty to the empire in the face of mounting attacks from Russian nationalists who dismissed them as Germans whose loyalty lay with Berlin, not St. Petersburg. No wonder many Mennonites greeted the tsar's abdication in March 1917 as more promise than peril.

Mennonites and the Emergence of Russian Nationalism

Mennonites and other non-Russians had little reason to be concerned in 1833 when Emperor Nicholas I grounded his reign in the Official Nationality of Orthodoxy, Autocracy and Nationality."[2] After all, they readily declared their support for autocracy and understood that "Orthodoxy" was simply the counterpart to their own officially recognized faiths. And nationality? In 1833 "nationality" referred primarily to one's devotion to the autocrat. Indeed, E.F. Kankrin, Russian minister of finance under Nicholas I, declared that the proper "nationality" for members of the empire was not "Russian" but "Petrovian," as everyone owed everything to great Peter.[3] By this estimation Mennonites were unquestionably loyal Petrovians.

In such a world there was no singular Russian. Instead, the empire divided people first by faith; that is, by Orthodox or Roman Catholic and so on, as officials consistently distinguished between Mennonites, German Catholics, and German Protestants as discrete legal categories. Officials did classify them all as peoples who undertook local administration in the German language, but even that only happened after Mennonites acquired sufficient High German fluency in the first half of the nineteenth century, in part because the Russian empire required Mennonites to undertake all communication with the state in that language.[4] Officials similarly made legal distinctions among Orthodox

Christians according to their social estate (*sosloivia*). It did not matter if some of the "Russian" Orthodox nobles barely spoke the Russian language by mid-century as they aped West European culture in general and the French language in particular. All, as loyal subjects of the autocrat, were Petrovians.

Of course, this was the age of Romanticism as scholars in Napoleon's wake began to identify the collective particular amid the universal singular. Russian scholars did likewise. As a measure of this dramatic sea change, in 1819 Prince Viazemskii introduced *narodnost* as a Russian word, borrowed from the Polish who had attempted to translate the French word *nationalité*. By this means scholars across the empire sought to identify the organic "national" characteristic of suddenly "their" people. No wonder the 1820s and 1830s marked the onset of ethnographic investigations, as with Petr Kireevski, who compiled traditional Russian folk tales. At the same time, Petr's brother Ivan theorized about the essence of this newly discovered Russian nationality, as the Slavophile school of thought took shape. Of course, the converse also applied, for the 1830s marked the onset of Ukrainian theorizing about a distinct Ukrainian identity, even as German ethnographers streamed into the Russian empire in search of folkish identities among their own, as though they had always been that. Not surprisingly, this also marked the foundation of a distinctly Mennonite commonwealth which took shape under Johann Cornies, who was himself "discovered" by the famed German ethnographer August von Haxthausen. Even so, these newly emerging peoples and identities remained secure within the empire as long as they remained Petrovians who carried out the government's expressed purposes for them.[5]

Those bureaucrats who administered the Great Reforms after 1861 continued to have an expansive view of the Russian nationality, and they continued to distinguish between Russians and foreigners based on religious faith. That is not to say, however, that nothing changed, for they also introduced important changes consistent with evolving European developments in jurisprudence, foremost the end of special arrangements made previously with all foreigners. Henceforth one category of citizenship applied, and we have already considered how Mennonites realized a single exception to this empire-wide uniformity when they successfully obtained an exemption from military conscription in 1874. Even so, more ominous voices made themselves heard in the 1860s, many of them close to the halls of power in St. Petersburg, and all of whom challenged the notion of a Petrovian nationality. If communities like the Mennonites worried that emerging statist notions of the citizen after 1860 threatened their particular identities, the increasingly strident Russian nationalists retained that sense of multiple localized and collectivized identities within the empire, but they now clothed them in sinister garments.[6]

For example, conservative Mikhael Katkov, editor of the influential *Moskovskie Vedomosti* newspaper, threatened the empire's long-established practice of classifying populations by religion, and after 1860 ostensibly as individuals. According to Paul Werth, Katkov joined other voices in the reform era who warned the Russian state not to assume that all populations necessarily grounded their identity in religion. On the contrary, religious affiliations often pointed to political loyalties, which meant that, for example, seemingly harmless Polish Catholics could threaten the empire itself with their barely concealed support of Polish nationalism, as happened during the Polish rebellion of January 1863. In fact, Russian nationalists like Katkov stood the traditionally religious conception of foreigners on its head when they politicized non-Russian identities and deemed all to be potential threats to the integrity of the empire.[7]

Such rhetoric of identities based on ethnicity rather than religion posed an immediate question for Mennonites in the empire: As a mixture of Dutch, Flemish, and Polish extraction who had acquired a mixture of High and Dutch-infused Low German, even as many had by now begun to acquire Russian fluency, how long would commentators and bureaucrats acknowledge their unique status as Mennonites? The answer appeared in short order as the so-called German problem exploded onto the scene in Imperial Russia in the 1880s, with Mennonites and Baltic Germans at the centre of it. Nataly Venger has analysed the complex factors which gave birth to this phenomenon, starting with the very formation of the German empire in 1871.[8] The new Germany transformed the geopolitical map of Europe. Bismarck secured German unification when he formed the *Dreikaiserbund* in 1873, by which Vienna, Berlin, and St. Petersburg formed a conservative alliance. However, that alliance shattered in 1878 when Germany sided with Austria-Hungary and wiped away gains made by Russia during the Russo-Turkish War of 1875–8. The three monarchies managed to form a second *Dreikaiserbund* in 1881 only to have it collapse in 1887, whereupon Russia and Germany formed its own alliance. However, the new Kaiser Wilhelm's failure to renew that alliance in 1890 signalled Berlin's determination to support Vienna in every dispute with St. Petersburg over control of the Balkans as the Ottoman Empire unravelled.

Mennonites remained unfailingly loyal to the Russian empire throughout this period, and amid these shifting alliances and conflicts. However, the continued tensions with Central Europe's two Germanic states on its western borders inevitably turned Russian nationalists to the potential threat posed by the empire's own Germans, especially as they framed the Balkan conflict in national terms between the region's Slavic and Turkic peoples. Thus, Mennonites unwittingly found themselves deemed to be increasingly "German" at a time when that very nationality had become a thorn in the Russian side. This would have been a good time for Mennonites to fly under the Russian radar, but that did not happen. As the previous chapter made plain, Mennonites appeared to be everywhere by the 1880s as they purchased estates and daughter colonies throughout New Russia, Central Asia, and into Siberia. Mennonite industrialists cornered a large share of the manufacturing market across the south, and Mennonite millers dominated their trade.

Russian nationalists took note and soon linked Mennonite expansion within the empire to Germanic aggression beyond. Most ominously, A.A. Paltov, a Russian nationalist, toured New Russia in 1889 to report on what he called the German conquest of the Russian empire. The conservative Russian newspaper *Russkii Vestnik* first published his findings under the pseudonym of A.A. Velitsyn in a series of articles, and as a single monograph in 1893.[9] Paltov/Velitsyn claimed that Mennonites and other Germans unfailingly supported Germany, to the extent that they sought to conquer southern Russia for Berlin. He claimed that Mennonite homes routinely displayed portraits of the German Kaiser and chancellor Bismarck, that Mennonites steadfastly refused to assimilate into Russian society or even learn the Russian language, and that Mennonite expansion in his time depended entirely on privileges granted them at point of settlement, all of which officials had denied the first Russian settlers. Mennonites unjustly acquired their wealth, he concluded, at the expense of the region's Slavic population, and although other German colonists identified more robustly with the German Reich, Mennonites unquestionably had Germanic blood and still posed a real threat. Lastly, Paltov pointed to Mennonite Brethren attempts to proselytize Orthodox peasants and form an alliance with other renegade Orthodox sectarians in the south, including Shtundists and Dukhobors.[10]

Paltov's attack represented an exclusionary nationalism which bore no relation to the earlier "Official Nationality" of Nicholas I. Unfortunately, the Russian tsar after 1881, the very Russianist Alexander III, accepted much of the nationalist discourse, and thereby compelled Mennonites to counter the arguments made. Venger stresses the Mennonite resolve in the late nineteenth century to acquire the Russian language and to support the Russian empire's various military campaigns of the late nineteenth century to the extent that their faith permitted. David H. Epp bathed his history of Chortitza, published on the occasion of the settlement's centenary in 1889, in the language of monarchic devotion, from Catherine II to the "most gracious Emperor and Lord," Alexander III, who oversaw the benevolent governance which Mennonites enjoyed in his time.[11] Epp had more to say. In 1896 he added an extensive commentary to the catechism used by the Kirchengemeinde across the Russian empire which reinforced Mennonite loyalty to the Russian emperor: "as the emperor is 'the anointed of the Lord' a true Christian and sincere member of the [Mennonite] congregation will be a loyal, obedient and honest subject who will never support the instigators of, or make common cause with, any who attempt to overthrow the God-ordained civil order installed for our welfare…. Every true Christian feels himself tightly bound to his earthly fatherland and to the hereditary imperial (Romanov) family."[12] In that spirit Mennonites by 1900 regularly prayed for the emperor, his family, and the fatherland.

Mennonites worked hard to demonstrate their unwavering loyalty to the Russian emperor and his realm in the face of mounting nationalist accusations that they were a fifth column for the German Reich. Others also spoke in defence of Mennonites and other German-speaking subjects of the empire. In 1902 the Russian-language magazine *Mir Bozhii* (The World of God) included an article in support of the German colonists in New Russia: "Instead of raising our own spiritual and economic standard, we try in every way possible to lower this standard among the colonists."[13] Other publicists composed pamphlets in support of them, and the governor of Ekaterinoslav guberniia refused to criticize them in his reports to St. Petersburg. Still the rumours continued, such that the factory inspector of Ekaterinoslav launched an investigation in 1900 after informants repeatedly claimed that German and Mennonite industrialists mistreated their Russian workers. He concluded that the industrialists indeed hated and scorned their workers, as did German estate owners. No wonder collective popular demonstrations against German and Mennonite overseers had risen dramatically.[14]

Hence, Mennonites and Germans faced an increasing barrage of hostile allegations as the twentieth century dawned. But was there truth to those allegations? Some Mennonites and Germans undoubtedly mistreated their Ukrainian and Russian workers, and it seems clear that many Mennonites and Germans joined Russian estate owners and bureaucrats in having a generally negative view of peasants. However, Venger has observed that a careful examination of the Dnepropetrovsk and Zaporozhye archives has provided almost no specific examples to substantiate the negative conclusions reached by the Ekaterinoslav inspector. Moreover, the Factory Inspector for Kherson guberniia could only confirm isolated instances of abuse in his jurisdiction.[15]

We also have the evidence produced by the so-called Revolution of 1905.

The Revolution of 1905–7

The Russian empire became unglued in 1905 as a disastrous war against Japan stimulated a broadly based opposition movement against the tsar, spurred on by the massacre of innocents by tsarist troops on 9 January 1905, an event known as Bloody Sunday. Soldiers and sailors began to mutiny by summer. Peasant and worker disturbances increased throughout that year in quantity and aspirational demands until the fall, when peasants seized large numbers of estates outright. Meanwhile, workers and illegal socialist parties formed Soviets (labour councils) in factories. Astonishingly, it seemed as if the Romanov dynasty might collapse, especially in the summer of 1905, when large numbers within elite imperial society added their voices to those who called for regime change.

Where did southern Ukraine fit into the events of this tumultuous year, and to what degree were Mennonites a focal point of revolutionary unrest? First, New Russia experienced significant unrest in 1905, especially Ekaterinoslav guberniia, which registered the sixth-highest tallies in the empire.[16] That said, disturbances are difficult to measure as they ranged from woodlot thefts to mass village uprisings, and from the discovery of revolutionary pamphlets to all-out factory strikes. We can identify three areas where unrests appear to have been widespread.[17] First, workers in industrial centres across the region engaged in strike activity, including above all Odessa, Alexandrovsk, the Donbas, and Ekaterinoslav. Second, the first peasants to challenge local estate owners resided in the densely populated northern districts, especially Elisavetgrad and Alexandriia, where few Mennonites lived. Third, peasants increased their agitation along the capital-intensive estates of the Dnieper bend, where Mennonites were plentiful by 1900, though occasionally it involved local peasants who attempted to drive away the thousands of migratory labourers making their way south to compete with them for employment.

There is no evidence of widespread agitation directed at Mennonites or German colonists, though some Mennonites did find themselves under siege. For instance, hundreds of peasants congregated in lands purchased by German and Mennonite colonists in Dneprovsk district to stop surveyors and to otherwise resist expulsion as new owners took control. In almost all cases it had been peasants who had previously worked the land, even if the actual ownership had resided with large estate owners. Those peasant agriculturalists had good reason to conclude that their livelihoods would suffer if Mennonites purchased those same lands and worked them for their own profit. Helena Friesen, the daughter of a Mennonite estate owner, recalled later the panic many estate owners felt in the face of mass peasant disturbances as they fled to local train stations: "No one except the estate manager ... knew of our departure. When we arrived at the station, I remember the large crowd of people consulting to see which trains would be allowed to cross the border. There was an atmosphere of anxiety among the passengers on the train. It was a relief when, after a long period of uncertainty, the train began to move."[18] Not all fled, however. Mennonite Herman Bergmann, who had links to the governor of Ekaterinoslav guberniia and owned a massive estate, enlisted 180 Cossack troops with two cannons to bombard the adjoining village of Solenoe in December 1905 when its peasants threatened his estate. Elsewhere, workers struck for higher wages at Mennonite-owned factories in Chortitza and Schönwiese, where a strike began on 10 February 1905 and lasted for several weeks until workers won their pay increases. In another incident an unknown assailant shot and wounded a police officer who attempted to intervene at a strike in the Mennonite factory village of Osterwick. Masked revolutionaries attacked the Reimer estate known as Felsental, where they killed the Ukrainian sentry, bombed the entrance way, and demanded a large ransom to leave. Some Mennonites themselves became involved in revolutionary agitation, as illegal political pamphlets circulated broadly and came into Mennonite possession. Others reported of bandits who hid in the deep-cut river valleys near Chortitza where they robbed passing travellers. Mennonites also observed as revolutionaries stormed prisons to free convicts in the Crimean city of Simferopol.[19] Thus Mennonites, for the most part, viewed the revolutionary disturbances with horror, as those who had much to lose, even though there is little evidence to suggest that agitators targeted them for socio-ethnic reasons as was the case, for instance, with the region's Jews.[20]

Imperial Russia bent but did not break during the Revolution of 1905. In fact, it had largely reasserted control over the empire by the time peasant disturbances peaked at the end of the year. In particular, the Treaty of Portsmouth, signed in September 1905, brought the enormously unpopular war with Japan to a close and allowed St. Petersburg to increase its control over its armed forces. One month later Nicholas II issued the October Manifesto, which promised a national parliament (Duma). This largely satisfied the demands of the elites who returned to the imperial fold over the next half-year, confident they could influence the tsar to their own purposes. That was the safe option given the nobility's fear of mass revolt. Lastly, Nicholas appointed Petr Stolypin as prime minister in 1906. His ruthless oversight of all disturbances soon shut down the outstanding peasant and worker hotspots, including those in Central Asia, which directly threatened Mennonite settlements[21] and signalled the start of the Duma period in Russian history. It was not clear how Mennonites would respond, having stared the empire's dissolution in the face and occasionally experienced it firsthand.

Mennonites and the Duma Period, 1906–13

Mennonite anxieties about their place in Imperial Russia's future continued during the short-lived Duma period. More than ever they now relied on their own press to keep them informed of the latest developments, and the new press freedoms promised in the October Manifesto gave them wide latitude to observe and comment. By 1906 the principal Mennonite media consisted of two annual almanacs, *Christlicher Familienkalendar* (Christian Family Almanac) and *Mennonitisches Jahrbuch* (Mennonite Yearbook), as well as two newspapers, the twice-weekly *Der Botschafter* (The Messenger) and the weekly *Die Friedensstimme* (The Voice of Peace.) Though these publications formally divided into either Mennonite Brethren or Kirchengemeinde camps, the readership tended to blur ecclesial lines and included many German colonists across the south, even as Mennonites had long subscribed to German-language publications in the empire, especially the *Odessaer Zeitung*. Chortitza Mennonites, who numbered approximately 1,500 in 1905, read 85 different periodicals through a total of 1,211 subscriptions, whereas 25,000 Molotschna Mennonites received 2,367 subscriptions. Though difficult to calculate, the number of readers increased substantially if one considers that extended families often shared print materials and that some subscriptions went to village school libraries, with some of the larger Mennonite villages having libraries in the hundreds of volumes. Mennonite publishers thrived after 1905, of which the largest, Raduga Publishing in Halbstadt, Molotschna, had become one of the largest publishers of evangelical material in the empire.[22]

A brief survey of the Mennonite media makes plain that they devoted considerable attention to political developments within the empire. Both *Der Botschafter* and *Friedensstimme* routinely reported on the latest developments in St. Petersburg. Regular columns included those entitled "Political Weekly Review," usually on the first page, along with "A Chronicle of Town and Country" and "Of the Fatherland."

Figure 6. *Friedenstimme. Ein christliches Volks-und Familienblatt,* 22 April 1906. Photograph courtesy of Conrad Grebel University College.

Der Botschafter regularly translated articles from a wide range of Russian newspapers on issues of empire-wide importance. Duma reports appeared in almost every issue, as did other developments, including empire-wide harvest predictions, political assassinations, and the formation of new political parties.[23]

Mennonites had good reason to follow these developments closely as two of the dominant ideologies of the day presented dramatically different scenarios for the Russian empire's future. On the one hand, Tsar Nicholas II after 1905 fervently sought to reshape the empire into a pre-Petrine dynasty, as noted at the chapter's outset. A Russia of the future would be Orthodox and feature Russian peasants in communion with the Russian tsar. On the other hand, Stolypin wanted to create a modern European state, one in which individual identities trumped corporate ones, including the social-estate model on which the empire had been founded. Those Mennonites who paid attention to these developments – and not all did – tended to frown on either scenario, as did Tatars, Bashkirs, and many other emergent nationalities in the empire.[24] Should Nicholas II's vision win out, Mennonites believed his dynastic and nationalistic model would leave them forever on the outside as barely tolerated non-Russian, non-Orthodox subjects. By contrast, the Stolypin model threatened to drown a distinct Mennonite identity in a sea of Russian peasant subjects, one in which their hope for a permanent group military exemption was certain to wither.

Faced with two poor options going forward, Mennonites struggled to know where their political loyalties should lie, though few questioned that Mennonite political engagement was essential. St. Petersburg implemented voting procedures which grouped most Mennonites, including those who lived in the original Chortitza and Molotschna settlements, in the peasant category as they all technically owned their lands in a communal manner. Thus, Mennonite estate owners were most likely to have an impact with their vote. Most tended to vote initially for the relatively conservative Octobrist Party, which had adopted a centrist platform in support of religious freedom for non-Orthodox subjects. Unfortunately, the promises made by a desperate Nicholas II in the October Manifesto of 1905 crumbled away after troops restored order in 1906. In time most Mennonites shifted from the Octobrist Party as it adopted a strident pro-Russian conservatism by 1910, one that left Mennonites and other minorities out.[25] Mennonites tried a variety of strategies to have their voice heard thereafter, and even periodically sent delegations directly to St. Petersburg to lobby officials.

Mennonites in the First Duma had been unprepared for the elections and so had allied with German colonists, though it soon became clear that their interests differed on key points. Mennonite estate owners formed a new political faction with a single German estate owner on the eve of the equally short-lived second Duma to have their own political voice heard. Identifying themselves as "German-speaking Russian state citizens," they sought an alliance at the centre of the political spectrum with either the Octobrists or the Constitutional Democrats (the Kadets).[26] Though unsuccessful, they persevered, such that Hermann Bergmann, the aforementioned wealthy Mennonite estate owner, entered the third Duma as a full member of the Octobrist Party. Bergmann played a vital role as he regularly reported on matters of direct relevance to Mennonites during the third (1907–12) and fourth (1912–17) Dumas. Mennonites even formed their own political parties, of which the most curious was easily P.M. Friesen's verbosely named "Union of Freedom, Truth and Peace: Foes of all Violence, Proponents of Unceasing Civil, Economic and Moral Spiritual Progress." Known informally as the Friesen Party, it quickly disbanded as Mennonites relied on one or more of the empire-wide parties to address their concerns.

What were those concerns? Initially Mennonites embraced the October Manifesto and its promise of full freedom of conscience. They sent a message of thanks to the tsar and established two student stipends in his honour to mark the manifesto's release. The promised freedom of conscience legislation inspired Mennonite Brethren to move aggressively and openly to proselytize Orthodox peasants in Kharkov, Samara, and Saratov. Mennonites also reasserted control over their educational system as they formed an independent Teachers' Association and opened five new secondary schools, from Siberia to Crimea, all with increased instruction in German.[27] Regardless of the gains realized and the optimism engendered, it soon became apparent that the Romanov reassertion of imperial control coupled with the advent of Stolypin's prime ministerial reign spelled trouble for Mennonites on four distinct fronts.

First, Mennonites feared after 1907 that Stolypin's desire to create a Russian citizen at the expense of erstwhile divisions based on social estate would directly challenge their own special arrangement of the Foresteidienst in lieu of military service. *Der Botschafter* had already warned readers in December 1905 that any movement to broaden civil rights for all would necessarily entail the loss of negotiated special privileges for some, including Mennonites. Only full political engagement could forestall the loss of the beloved Foresteidienst, for how would Mennonites maintain their unique identity without it?[28]

Second, Mennonites feared new legislation contemplated by officials as early as April 1906 as it threatened to identify Mennonites as a sect, not a confession.[29] The change was significant as the famed privilegium granted to them at point of settlement had recognized Mennonites as a legitimate faith with corresponding privileges, and Nicholas II appeared to legitimize all faiths within the empire in the October Manifesto. But less than half a year later he signalled an end to such broad freedoms. Why? Paul Werth has argued that the Orthodox Church objected to the threatened removal of its primacy, especially as early returns showed large conversions from Orthodoxy to Catholicism and to the Baptists in the western borderlands. Such warnings of Orthodox collapse took hold across the empire, especially after 1907 when new voting rules transformed the third Duma into a much more Russian and Orthodox body than the first two had been. Aileen Friesen concludes that officials by 1910 warned that Siberia, the final frontier, risked becoming a haven for Russia's subversive sectarians, Mennonites among them.[30] There was merit in these concerns as Mennonites had a long association with Stundists and other Orthodox sectarians who had settled in villages that adjoined the Molotschna settlement, and the Mennonite Brethren had moved energetically after the issuance of the October Manifesto to proselytize Orthodox peasants. Of greater alarm, even Stolypin adopted this pro-Orthodox position by 1910, as had the Octobrist Party, which shifted to the political right in the Third Duma, ironically just as Hermann Bergmann joined its ranks.

A third area of concern among Mennonites flowed from the second, and it was the degree to which an increasingly Russianized Duma accepted the view that German-speaking Mennonites were, in fact, German by nationality and a direct threat to the Russian empire. Foreign policy considerations were at the heart of this shift as St. Petersburg moved increasingly into a de facto alliance with France and Great Britain after the Anglo-Russian Convention of 1907 resolved the longstanding rivalry between those two great powers in Central Asia. Barely one year later, Germany humiliated the Russian empire when it fully backed Austria-Hungary's unilateral annexation of Bosnia-Herzegovina. St. Petersburg might have gone to war against the German powers then had it not been for Stolypin's restraining influence, though he had adopted a stridently anti-German position by 1910.[31] Even so, his ability to hold Nicholas back from military conflict ended when Dimitrii Bogrov assassinated the prime minister in the Kiev Opera House in September 1911, with the tsar himself present.

Fourth, Stolypin implemented a series of legislative initiatives between 1906 and 1910 known as the Stolypin land reforms, which threatened landed Mennonites who had long relied on inexpensive state lands to supplement their incomes. David G. Rempel recalls how such lands existed not far from his home village of Nieder Chortitza and that Mennonite farmers from his village had long rented them out at inexpensive rates. Suddenly the new legislation removed those parcels from the market and dramatically raised rental rates on others as neighbouring peasants successfully petitioned the state to settle there on newly formed farmsteads. Rempel's father petitioned the state to permit a portion of the Mennonite landless in his own village to receive the same right of settlement on these newly opened lands. He was particularly concerned for Mennonite landless teamsters whom he employed but who lived marginal lives at best. Few even attended church, which they deemed the domain of the wealthy and landed. Rempel recalled the bitter discussions that took place in 1907–8 at village assemblies in Nieder Chortitza as Mennonite full-farmers sparred with their landless co-religionists. In the end the state sided with Rempel's father and the Mennonite landless and awarded them a share of the state lands. In response, the landed Mennonites boycotted his father's village general store and refused his services to haul their grains to market. The family business never recovered.[32]

Mennonites found themselves intertwined in all these developments, as St. Petersburg blocked all social and cultural ties between the empire's Germans, restricted the ability of Germans to purchase additional lands on the western borderlands, and threatened to expand those restrictions across the empire. Russian surveillance of all Germans in the empire increased after 1908. The state sharply curtailed the use of German in publications, education, and worship, and in every such instance authorities no longer distinguished between Imperial Russia's Germans and Imperial Russia's German-speaking Mennonites, all the more ironic as James Urry maintains that Mennonites remained suspicious of German Lutherans and Catholics whose "background, dialect and customs" set them apart.[33] It did not help that Mennonite industrialists in Chortitza village refused to display state flags in 1910 in honour of the tsar's birthday celebrations. Their pleas that such displays violated their religious convictions fell on deaf ears, as did their expressions of absolute loyalty to the tsar and the empire. Ominously, the local police reported that such calculated actions had demoralized the local populace.[34]

Historians have argued that most Mennonites across the empire may have maintained localized and insular identities well into the twentieth century and therefore been oblivious to larger developments. Even so, informed Mennonites had good reason to be alarmed by 1910, even though they enjoyed immense economic success during these years, and even as they continued to spread eastward across Siberia. In short order they confronted attacks for not being sufficiently Orthodox in faith, sufficiently civil minded to set aside their military exemption, and sufficiently Russian to displace their suspected loyalty to all things German. Faced with such an assault, Mennonites did what they had always done: they sent delegation after delegation to St. Petersburg to press their case. They also published a series of works, including David H. Epp's study of Johann Cornies (published in 1909) and Peter M. Friesen's massive tome on the Mennonite Brotherhood in Russia (1911). Both works stressed Mennonite steadfast loyalty to the tsar and their many positive contributions to the empire. Other works, published by Mennonites in Russian, picked up the same themes. Some argued that the Mennonite faith had its origins in the New Testament church, not the Protestant Reformation. In the political arena the editors of both *Friedensstimme* and *Der Botschafter* called for a reassessment of the major political parties on the eve of the Duma election of 1912. Both concluded that the Octobrist Party had failed to protect Mennonite faith and culture. They urged Mennonites henceforth to vote for the centre-left Kadet Party or, at most, the left Octobrist factions, as these promised the most of any party. With regret, they declared that Mennonites could not in good conscience support any of the right-leaning monarchist parties. If there was anything positive to come out of this, it may have been the All-Mennonite Conference of 26–7 October 1910, held in the Molotschna village of Schönsee, which may have been the closest Mennonite Brethren and Kirchengemeinde ever came to speaking with a single voice.[35]

Mennonites and the First World War

The Russian empire's decision to begin mobilization of its enormous army on 30 July 1914 in support of Serbia transformed a Balkan conflict over Bosnia-Herzegovina into a pan-European crisis. Berlin declared war on St. Petersburg two days later, as did Vienna on 6 August 1914, which placed Russia alongside France and Great Britain, and pitted against the Germanic powers. In an instant Mennonites across the Russian empire realized their situation had become perilous. Spontaneous rioters in Moscow, fuelled by the empire's most conservative newspapers, had already destroyed establishments deemed German in May of that year. In fact, Eric Lohr suggests it was such spontaneous acts of violence across the empire which prompted the state to take a harder line against Germans and other combatant nationals.[36]

Mennonites moved swiftly that fateful August to demonstrate their loyalty to the empire. Churches, which routinely prayed for the tsar and his family, now did so with greater fervency. They donated tens of thousands of rubles to the war effort. All Mennonite periodicals stressed that Mennonites should support the empire to the limit. In the words of David H. Epp, the editor of *Der Botschafter*:

> We Russian Germans have a dual obligation: together with our Russian brethren we need to stand for the freedom and honour of Russia. With our means we must support the families who have gone to war. Also, we must make it clear that we have been suspect without reason of having secret relationships with Germany. We need to show that we have kept the promise of faithfulness made by our forefathers ... our confession forbids us as Mennonites to spill blood, but binding wounds we hold to be our sacred duty. Medical service is open to us. We are certain this means that doctors and nurses to form a Mennonite medical corps will become available.[37]

Mennonite ministers encouraged their young men to answer the call as the draft extended to include all males from age nineteen to forty-two. Mennonite men laboured on medical trains across the empire and up to the front; men and women cared for the wounded in hospitals, including Mennonite hospitals in their settlements and on Red Cross trains; they built roads in the Caucasus and Crimea to facilitate troop movement; and they provided horses and grains when requisitioned. At its height Mennonites opened an administrate office in Moscow to coordinate these empire-wide initiatives. Perhaps most surprisingly, Mennonite industrialists retooled and shifted from agricultural implement production to the manufacture of military materiel. In 1916 alone A.J. Koop's factory produced military goods valued at almost 150,000 rubles, though a new consortium of the Lepp and Wallman factories in Chortitza dwarfed that sum the following year when it produced more than 1.5 million rubles of military ware for St. Petersburg's Main Artillery Administration.[38]

Initially St. Petersburg promised to maintain the rights of all Austrians and Germans so long as they lived peaceably within the empire. However, the empire soon abandoned that approach, as did Great Britain and almost every state involved in the quickly worsening conflict. By the end of 1914 the Russian state denied civil rights, including the right of judicial appeal, to anyone deemed an enemy subject, whom it penalized accordingly. Mennonites and Germans within the empire noticed the effects of this legislation almost immediately. The state banned the use of the German language in all public discourse and made it illegal for clergy to preach extemporaneously in German. It ordered all German-language publications to cease and that local authorities give

German-named villages new Russian names. All of this had a direct impact on Mennonites across the empire.[39] In a more curious twist, officials confiscated 1,992 weapons from Mennonite households in Molotschna in 1914, lest they form a fifth column for the Germans. Of these, six hundred were handguns. Though hunters utilized rifles to go after game, the handguns might suggest a growing concern for personal safety, especially after the revolution of 1905.[40]

There was more to come. On 2 February 1915 the state decreed the liquidation of land ownership and land tenure for all "Russian subjects of Austrian, Hungarian, or German Emigration."[41] Though they focused initially on those within the western borderlands, it soon became clear that local officials expropriated lands and drove any subjects deemed to be of German descent into the interior from the borderlands at a pace not legally permitted. Moreover, new legislation in the succeeding months expanded the geographic scope of such draconian measures to include the whole of the empire and came after a decade of dramatic expansion by Mennonite estate owners and villages in Siberia.[42] The stakes were high.

Of course, much depended on whether state officials deemed Mennonites to be of German descent. Not surprisingly, Mennonites repeatedly argued before state officials that they were Germanic by language but Dutch by nationality. Already in 1914, an anonymous Mennonite writer thought to be the Molotschna teacher Peter J. Braun made the case that Mennonites were Dutch, not German. Written in Russian and entitled "*Kto takie Mennonity*" (Who are those Mennonites?) the work came out in a second edition the following year and spoke directly against the expropriation of Mennonite lands. We do know that Braun diligently gathered Mennonite documents as the war began, to be able to preserve the Mennonite historical record in New Russia and demonstrate that they were anything but ethnically German.[43]

Mennonites persistently made the case that they had Dutch origins and had fled Prussia after it seized control of the Polish lands in the late eighteenth century. For example, a memo sent to the Ministry of Internal Affairs on 16 May 1916 began: "When our forefathers, who had come from Holland to Poland in the 16th and 17th centuries, came under Prussian rule in the second half of the 18th century and began to experience oppression with respect to the free exercise of their religion and especially because of their rejection of military service, Catherine's Manifesto of 22 May, 1763 was circulated amongst them."[44]

Already in 1915 the state sent a commission to the Mennonite settlements to determine if they were Dutch or German, and although it ruled affirmatively for the latter the following year, there is little indication that officials moved aggressively against Mennonite landholding. One wonders why. It may have been because Mennonite production of military weaponry and grains made them too essential to the war effort to expropriate. Even as it now stood, Mennonites produced less grain each year from 1914 to 1916 as their horses were commandeered, labourers went missing, and as Mennonites themselves sold off working livestock and lands rather than risk their confiscation by the state. Finally, J.H. Janzen, the respected Molotschna teacher and minister, pointed to open speculation that Mennonites bribed their way to a permanent exemption with financial gifts to officials at the regional and empire-wide level.[45]

Even so, the decline in Mennonite agricultural productivity pointed to a larger malaise that gripped their society as the war dragged on, even as it brought the empire to its knees. Few could claim by the end of 1916 that Mennonites remained the most faithful of monarchists. Quite the contrary, David G. Rempel asserts that Mennonites viewed the murder of Rasputin in December 1916 positively, as they hoped it would improve the culture that surrounded the tsar and his inner circle.[46] Meanwhile the Russian army continued to suffer unbelievable losses, and the tsar's decision to take over supreme command of the armed forced did nothing to reverse the tide. If anything, it removed Nicholas II from Petrograd (formerly St. Petersburg) in early January 1917 as all sectors of Russian society turned against him. Hundreds of thousands had taken to the streets of the capital as soldiers no longer enforced imperial order in the face of rampant inflation, mounting food shortages, and widespread dissatisfaction.

One morning in early March 1917 Jacob H. Brucks went for a walk in Moscow. Brucks, a young man from the Neu-Samara daughter colony east of the Volga, served in the Moscow Mennonite medical corps in lieu of military service. He was one of 22,000 Mennonites involved in some form of alternative service during the war, all supported by congregations increasingly unable to pay the bills. Inflation was rampant in Moscow, as were rumours of corruption at the highest levels. Thousands of troops had already deserted the frontlines of a failed, protracted, and devastating war effort. Their return to the villages signalled an increase in unrest there and mounting concerns among Mennonites for peace and security of person and possession. Chaos in the cities. Chaos in the countryside. Then, one morning in early March 1917, Brucks stepped out to discover a Moscow that had turned unusually quiet. No traffic. Few pedestrians moved about on the streets. The silence puzzled him. It broke when someone approached him and asked: "Have you heard the news? The Czar has abdicated his throne, now we shall have peace."[47]

PART III

Mennonites in the Soviet Era

Chapter Ten

After Eichenfeld: Soviet-Era Mennonites between Reconstruction and Emigration, 1917–1927

Thousands of peasant foot soldiers moved through the Mennonite village of Eichenfeld on the morning of 8 November 1919.[1] As part of Nestor Makhno's infantry, the White Army had routed them when it recaptured the important regional city of Alexandrovsk, just across the Dnieper River. While still in control of that city, Makhno on 4 November 1919 had blamed his imminent defeat on traitorous bourgeoisie elements and their minions in the region. He called for their immediate capture and execution. The categories were admittedly vague, but they seemed to apply to Mennonites, and Makhnovist counter-intelligence forces had already identified Eichenfeld as a hotbed of bourgeois pro-monarchist and anti-peasant activity. Moreover, local peasants claimed that the Eichenfeld Mennonites had a particularly aggressive Selbstschutz (self-protection unit), with links to the White Army as well as the hated Austro-German occupation army of 1918.

Though some have maintained that the events of that day had less to do with Makhno and more to do with localized grievances, there is no dispute about what unfolded in Eichenfeld on that Saturday. As harbinger of things to come, peasant forces that morning captured and executed Heinrich Kornelius Heinrichs, the father of the village's Selbstschutz leader. Then a lull, after which carnage unfolded as the sun began to set. Makhnovists sealed off the village and stationed troops at each home, whereupon they proceeded to slaughter all Mennonite males over the age of fifteen. Though not targeted for execution, attackers sexually assaulted all females, many of whom subsequently contracted venereal disease.[2] Eventually the survivors fled over the wintry fields, barefoot and barely clothed, to the neighbouring Mennonite village of Adelsheim, which peasant forces had largely spared. Days later they returned with men from Adelsheim to bury their beloved dead in four mass graves, though not before peasants from the neighbouring

Figure 7. A mass grave seventy-seven feet long with fifty-eight bodies in Tiege, Sagradowka Colony, following a raid by bandits. NP145-6-12, Centre for Mennonite Brethren Studies, Winnipeg, Mennonite Archival Information Database.

Ukrainian villages had scavenged through the Eichenfeld homes and taken everything of value.[3] In total, eighty-two residents of Eichenfeld had died in a single day, of whom all but six were men.

Now more than a century later, Eichenfeld remains a litmus test for how historians and popularizers assess the destruction experienced by thousands of Mennonites in the years of revolution and civil war, from 1917 to roughly 1922. Was the Eichenfeld massacre symbolic of how ruthless peasant anarchists and Bolshevik sympathizers unjustly targeted innocent Mennonites for death and devastation, or was the massacre the inevitable outcome of Mennonite mistreatment of their peasant neighbours in the past? In other words, however tragic, did the destructive actions of a few Mennonites contribute to the suffering of the entire community? Or is the entire discussion off base? Is it possible to see the destruction of the Mennonite commonwealth after 1917 as collateral damage in a larger struggle between massive opposing armies as they struggled for regional hegemony after the collapse of the tsarist regime? By this reading, Mennonites simply lived in the wrong place at the wrong time. Lastly, was the Soviet regime somehow responsible for this massacre even though formal assertion of Soviet power in the region was still years away? All these positions have had their advocates over time. Given the complexity of the questions involved, it also should not surprise that the erection of a memorial in the village of Eichenfeld in 2001 to mark the 1919 massacre brought these conflicting perspectives to the fore.[4]

This chapter attempts to address these larger questions as it considers three distinct episodes by which the Imperial Russian Mennonite experience abruptly ended and the Soviet era began. First, we consider the tumultuous transitions of revolution, civil war, and the onset of Soviet power, up to the famine of 1921–2. Second we highlight the multiple ways in which Mennonites adjusted to life in the Soviet Union, and on their own terms, so as to preserve their unique faith-based identity; and third we consider the emigration of roughly one-fifth of the Soviet Union's Mennonites to Canada between 1924 and 1927.

Part One: Descent into Chaos, 1917–22

February to October 1917

Though it is difficult to be categorical about 100,000 Mennonites spread across the vast Russian empire, many doubtless greeted the tsar's abdication on 2 March 1917 (15 March n.s.) with relief. The Provisional Government which assumed power almost immediately set aside the draconian land expropriation laws previously introduced by tsarist officials and directed against all those of Germanic origin. Mennonite landholdings seemed secure. Moreover, Mennonites along with millions across the empire applauded the Provisional Government's determination to bring the Great War to a speedy conclusion. Mennonite Brethren evangelists hoped that the new government's refusal to recognize the Orthodox Church as Russia's state church opened the door to Mennonite evangelization among peasants. Siberian Mennonites near Omsk called for a return to universal, cost-free education in the German language. Suddenly the future looked bright for Mennonites, whose sown lands had diminished by 20 per cent since the start of the war in 1914.[5]

Of course, not all welcomed the tsar's abdication. Anna Baerg turned twenty in 1917. Writing in her diary from the David Dŭk estate on the southern edge of the Molotschna settlement Anna recoiled at the "monstrous events" that had compelled the tsar to abdicate.[6] Still others feared the new regime would abolish social estates and introduce radical land reforms along with the universal franchise which would leave Mennonites at the mercy of 100 million Russian peasants. Gerhard Lohrenz, who lived in the vast Molotschna daughter colony of Zagradovka, 100 kilometres north-east of Kherson, recalled the instability of this time as deserted and armed soldiers and radical socialists flooded the countryside. One such band led by a Jewish medical doctor set up a workers' council (Soviet) in the Mennonite village of Alexanderwohl. Three Mennonites named Kroeker, Neufeld, and Wiebe, respectively, joined this new Soviet and demanded that local Mennonites supply them with clothing, food, horses, and other goods.[7] To the east, ongoing strike activity in the regional centre of Alexandrovsk threatened the peace in adjacent Chortitza, as did ongoing disturbances among Russian, Ukrainian, and Mennonite labourers in the Molotschna settlement and the adjacent regional centre of Tokmak. Even further eastward, Tatars and Kumeks exploited the collapse of imperial order in March 1917 as they raided Mennonite villagers in the Terek settlement in the eastern Caucasus. They stole horses and occasionally killed Mennonites who tried to stop them.[8]

It was no surprise, then, when most Mennonites sided with stability, the restoration of civil order on imperial terms. They longed for the promise of peace offered by the Provisional Government over the chaos already evident in widespread peasant and worker strikes and labour disruptions, Tatar depredations, mass desertions, trains that no longer ran on time, and police forces that had evaporated. As a sign of their support Chortitza leaders sent a telegram to Provincial Government leaders Prince Lvov and Mikhail Rodzianko in which they pledged their full support as the empire righted itself.[9]

Mennonites did not need to look beyond their settlements for social instability in 1917 as a new generation emerged within at this time, one that called for its own version of revolutionary change. The war had transformed Mennonite youth, thanks to their service as sanitation workers in field hospitals and other facilities across the empire. Mennonite youth had observed firsthand the empire and its budding revolution from a variety of vantage points, including Moscow, Petrograd, Ekaterinoslav, Odessa, Omsk, and the front lines of battle. They participated in public demonstrations and sampled the first fruits of change amid newfound freedom. Fluent in Russian and Russophiles at heart, many came back to the Mennonite heartland eager to lead more than follow as they demanded generational change and a share of the power. It helped that the Provisional Government issued a decree in May 1917 which discharged all teachers from active duty so they could prepare for fall classes. Many of the more educated and politically informed Mennonite youth returned home as a result, including Gerhard Schroeder, a resident of Schönfeld but stationed in Odessa, as well as Johann G. Rempel of Nieder Chortitza, stationed at the Red Cross Headquarters in Moscow.[10] As Schroeder later recalled, Mennonite youth learned freedom's call as they watched the masses congregate on the streets, where music and jubilation filled the air.[11] Mennonites hosted three conferences over the summer of 1917, all based in Molotschna, as they sought to create a central administrative body to respond to rapidly shifting realities. Additional sub-committees met in Moscow, among other locations, as the younger generation made its voice heard for the first time. Johann G. Rempel likened the generational shift at work akin to Turgenev's *Fathers and Sons*, a clear indication of the younger generation's familiarity with Russian culture. Many of the discussions covered a range of perspectives, especially at the final session, held in Halbstadt in August 1917, and on issues as sensitive and timely as land reform in Russia, freedom of the press, evangelization, the war itself, and assorted pedagogical matters. Both sides did agree to establish a General Conference of all Mennonites in Russia, to which they elected a five-member executive committee (Mennozentrum) of B.H. Unruh, Dr. Peter Dück, Heinrich Schröder, Heinrich Janz, and Heinrich Epp. The new organization remained committed to the independence of all congregations and conferences, though it stressed the importance of working together on matters of pan-Mennonite concern.[12]

Unbeknownst to all attendees, their plans would soon come to naught as the end was near for the Provisional regime by the time of the Halbstadt gathering that August.

The October Revolution and Soviet Power, November 1917 to March 1918

The October Revolution, or Bolshevik Revolution, brought Lenin's Bolsheviks to power on 26 October 1917 (7 November n.s.) and dramatically altered all power relations within the former Russian empire. Mennonite historians have described the onset of Soviet power in the Mennonite villages and estates as having occurred immediately after Bolsheviks stormed the Winter Palace in Petrograd and overthrew the Provisional Government. Of course, the situation on the ground was much more complicated. Though industrial centres in the Russian heartland shifted quickly to Bolshevik and Soviet power, most locales further afield experienced a slow and bloody transition. Even Petrograd did not fully conform to the Bolshevik model until closer to 1920 as Lenin only had a tenuous hold initially on power over the city's unions and Red Guard units. Thus, the presumably immediate Bolshevik Soviet takeover took years, especially given the fact that few in the lower Dnieper,

Central Asian, or Siberian steppe lands formally supported the Bolsheviks in the fall of 1917. Few had even heard of the Bolsheviks, much less could distinguish them from other radical parties, and even fewer deemed themselves as subservient to the Petrograd leadership. Political fragmentation seemed inevitable. For example, dominant voices in Omsk after November called for an autonomous Siberian polity within a renewed Russian state. What followed the Bolshevik Revolution, then, was much more chaotic than a coordinated Bolshevik takeover, and that made it much more deadly for Mennonites and others.[13]

Although a handful of Mennonites experienced the onset of Soviet power as their time to flourish, the vast majority experienced it as deprivation. As those who dwelt in a borderland, Mennonites in the south and in Central Asia faced the breakdown of social order as spontaneously formed Soviets and mutinous soldiers, sailors, and workers descended on their settlements in ever increasing numbers. Only unlike previous occasions, Mennonites now had literally nowhere to turn for order. In the most spectacular instance, a self-proclaimed Soviet of mutinous sailors from the Black Sea fleet based in Sevastopol commandeered the Molotschna Mennonite settlement on 5 February 1918. Over the next several weeks they robbed Mennonite villagers; sexually assaulted others; demanded ransom from the wealthiest; seized food stuffs, horses, and wagons; and publicly executed at least six Mennonite leaders in Halbstadt as the local Soviet declared war on the settlement. Similar assaults happened elsewhere across the south, though equally dispiriting must have been the actions of peasants adjacent to daughter colonies and estates who seized lands and possessions from Mennonites.[14] Eichenfeld was one such village affected, though it was hardly unique, as the class war unleashed by Bolsheviks and others made its way across the south. No wonder Anna Baerg wrote fervently in January 1918 of the need to trust in God and the Lord Jesus for protection, as Mennonites abandoned their estates and fled to the protection of the larger settlements.[15]

Mennonites in the Terek settlement in the foothills of the Caucasus also prayed for protection as social order disintegrated. They held prayer meetings in the winter of 1917 as neighbouring peoples began to attack their villages in large numbers without fear of reprisal. Descendants of the Black Sea Nogai Tatars declared that Mennonites should never have settled in the region in 1901 on that 23,000 desiatina parcel of land. As murders increased Terek Mennonites abandoned their settlement on 8 February 1918. They formed a five-kilometer caravan that sought haven at another Mennonite settlement in the Kuban, only to find it also under siege.[16]

Austro-German Occupation and the Selbstschutz: Spring–Fall 1918

As if the breakdown of imperial order on the Black Sea steppe lands did not present a sufficient challenge for tens of thousands of Mennonites, they also had to face four competing efforts by forces to impose their will on these lands after the October Revolution; Ukrainian nationalists based in western Ukraine and the Dnieper city of Kiev sought an independent Ukrainian state; Bolsheviks under Lenin's lead and Trotsky's direction sought to incorporate all the Black Sea lands into a Soviet state as it waited for the world communist revolution; local peasants sought a world that would not be subject to either Russian or Ukrainian overlords; and White forces sought a return to a tsarist state governed by tsarist rules. Before any of these could impose their will, however, the German and Austrian armies managed to occupy all the predominantly Ukrainian provinces, thanks to the Ukrainian nationalists who signed the Treaty of Brest Litovsk with the Axis powers in February 1918.[17] In doing so, they sought to keep the Ukrainian lands out of Soviet control, as Lenin himself accepted the terms of Brest Litovsk on 3 March 1918. Even that Ukrainian gambit failed on 28 April 1918 when the Axis powers deposed the existing Ukrainian government and declared Pavlo Skoropadsky as nominal hetman of a nominally independent Ukraine run by Austro-German forces. As a result, Mennonite settlements on the Black Sea steppe entered under Axis control in the spring of 1918.

Almost all Mennonites enthusiastically welcomed the German and Austrian troops when they arrived. Chortitza Mennonites fed and housed the troops, and Molotschna Mennonites greeted the first troops who arrived at the Mennonite-owned Lichtenau train station on April 19 with hymns of praise and a full banquet feast.[18] Many expected that these liberators would soon transport them to a new beginning in Germany, though in that they were mistaken. The Axis powers wanted two things from Mennonites and Germans in the region. First, they immediately began to ship grains from the occupied lands back to domestic markets in Germany and Austria-Hungary, which had become desperately short of food due to the allied blockade. Second, they sought to minimize their own troop deployment in the occupied lands through the formation of militarized units from among the local German and Mennonite populations.

But would Mennonites abandon their ostensibly non-resistant position, one of the last clear identification markers of their faith? The answer was fiercely debated when 283 Mennonite delegates gathered for a general conference in Lichtenau from 30 June to 2 July 1918. Three days of often stormy debate later, the closing session passed a resolution which affirmed the historic non-resistant position. In an attempt to avoid broad divisions within the Mennonite body, however, the conference passed a second resolution which recognized the freedom of individuals and individual congregations to adopt contrary positions if they deemed it a matter of conscience to do so.[19]

By July 1918 many Mennonites had already formed so-called self-defence (Selbstschutz) units. In part the German and Austrian troops initiated this, though evidence suggests that some Mennonites formed these units in 1917 as the social order around them disintegrated.[20] Former Mennonite estate owners played a particularly aggressive role in the formation of these units, and there are numerous examples where Mennonite villages drafted all males between the ages of eighteen and thirty-five to serve in newly established brigades. Lawrence Klippenstein concludes that almost every village in Molotschna organized such units, as did many in Chortitza and the daughter colonies, including Gerhard Lohrenz's Zagradovka.[21] These units patrolled the villages to protect the inhabitants and their property, though there are also numerous accounts of Mennonite units which aggressively entered neighbouring peasant villages during the Austro-German occupation to forcibly reclaim possessions which peasants had seized after the November Revolution. Units occasionally executed peasants in those villages when Mennonites deemed them ringleaders of past uprisings or potential leaders in future ones. These aggressive interventions did not end well for Mennonites.

Mennonites between Whites, Greens, and Reds, Late 1918 to Late 1920

Mennonite fortunes worsened dramatically when German and Austrian troops withdrew from Ukrainian lands following the end of the First World War in November 1918. By the late fall of 1920 the Red Army secured control over almost all Mennonite lands in the former Russian empire. That left a transition period of one to two years – depending on the region – during which time Mennonites and their neighbours endured a succession of occupation forces. The White Army launched several major campaigns, especially from the end of the German occupation to the spring of 1919, and again in the late spring of 1920 when monarchist forces tried one final time to seize control of the south. The Bolsheviks enjoyed fleeting success in late 1918 and 1919, as did other bands of socialists who claimed to be Mensheviks. Representatives of a Ukrainian nationalist state under the lead of the newly appointed president of the Ukrainian People's Republic, Syman Petliura, made inroads in the south, though these proved unpopular and unsustainable given the considerable diversity of Jews, Russians, Greeks, Germans, Mennonites, and Balkan settlers across the south.[22]

As challenging as this revolving door of invading armies was, it paled in comparison to the mass peasant armies that ravaged Mennonite settlements, including the most devastating one led by Nestor Makhno. Born on 26 October 1888 in the former state peasant village of Guliai Pole, Makhno came to head the largest peasant army in the former Russian empire. Estimates vary wildly from 40,000 to 100,000 troops at its peak, and their popularity reflected a mass peasant rejection of the Ukrainian, Soviet, and White statist options. Makhno himself had worked for several years from the age of twelve on a Mennonite estate owned by a Janzen in Schönfeld. He drove a team of oxen and later recalled how the bailiff's assistant beat him one day when he forgot to give them water.[23] He recorded other beatings of other workers and eventually concluded that peasants needed to overthrow all authority in their midst, including that of the state as well as of wealthy landowners like Mennonites. Though prominently identified with the nineteenth-century philosophy of anarchism, such peasant movements often had deeper roots in longstanding peasant attitudes to wealth and power in their midst. No wonder peasants referred to Makhno by the endearing peasantist term "bat'ko," or "father."

By 1917 Makhno could boast bona fide credentials as a battle-scarred leader when he returned to Guliai Pole after his release from the notorious Butyrka prison in Moscow, where he had been set to serve a life sentence for terrorist-related offences. He assembled a massive peasant army, which included many peasant deserters with experience in the Imperial Army. It soon made its mark conducting terrorist acts during the Austro-German occupation. Makhno's success owed a great deal to his ability to form his army in the south, where former state peasants dominated. Many of their villages had over a thousand households, including Guliai Pole. That said, there is evidence that local peasant units within the larger army played leading roles in many of the massacres, including that of Eichenfeld in November 1919. There are also many sources which suggest that Makhno's troops reacted most violently against those recently established daughter settlements, like Eichenfeld and Lohrenz's Zagradovka settlement, with active Selbstschutz units.[24] In the end, Makhno's troops, alongside a host of other independent and more localized peasant warlords, killed thousands of Mennonite men, whom, as with Eichenfeld, they either shot or hacked to death in front of their wives, many of whom they then sexually assaulted. Countless women later died of untreated venereal disease, still mourning the deaths of their sons, their fathers, and their husbands. By the time Makhno himself fled to Romania in August 1921 he left behind a failed anarchist experiment and a Mennonite landscape marred by mass graves, destroyed villages, and impoverished, disease-riddled survivors.

Red Victory and Mennonite Devastation, 1920–2

Siberian Mennonites escaped Makhno's fury but found themselves in the middle of a prolonged struggle between Red and White forces after 1917, which generally played out along the Trans-Siberian railroad, exactly where Mennonites had settled. At one point, Mennonites actively participated in an attempt by the Whites to construct an anti-Bolshevik "All-Siberian Union of Citizens of German Nationality." It is no wonder that Bolsheviks nationalized all Mennonite landed estates as they gained full control and viewed their owners as enemies of the people.[25]

Back on the Black Sea steppe, the White Army made one final push up from the Crimean Peninsula late in 1920, but its defeat, along with Makhno's escape the following April, marked the end of large-scale opposition to Bolshevik rule across the former Russian empire. Only Poland, Finland, and the three Baltic states managed to secure their independence in the civil war period. In most instances Mennonites experienced a degree of relief once it became clear that Bolsheviks had won as it ended peasant-initiated acts of violence against them. However, the actual transition to full Soviet rule took years, as local order remained chaotic long after the Red Army claimed victory. Small wonder that the army stayed in the Black Sea steppe region for three years, by which time civil authorities no longer required their support to maintain order. Tens of thousands of refugees roamed the streets and villages from Leningrad to the Pacific. They included a veritable ocean of orphaned and abandoned children, Mennonite and otherwise, victims of a state of perpetual war, disease, and starvation which dated back to August 1914.[26] As summarized by Anna Baerg in her diary entry of 3 January 1922: "There is a lot of stealing going on in some of the villages, particularly in those where there is no military occupation. And how many beggars have come by asking for a piece of bread which we can't always give them! Yes, the future looks very dismal if God doesn't help us soon."[27]

Anna Baerg had good reason to deem the future to be bleak by 1922 as the Bolshevik victory coincided with the appearance of a two-headed monster which ravaged the Black Sea steppe lands after 1920: typhus and famine. Neither should have surprised authorities given the losses endured. At first glance, the Chortitza settlement had held firm, with 11,000 Mennonites in 1910 and 13,600 in 1920, and Molotschna fared similarly. However, that figure disguises the fact that both settlements expanded considerably by the latter date as Mennonites fled the daughter colonies and private estates for relative safety in numbers in the mother settlements. Refugees even flooded into the distant Kuban settlement located in the Caucasus, where "thousands camped on the farmyards, in the gardens, on the streets, and wandered daily from house to house, to beg for a morsel of bread."[28]

More telling are the losses of sown area and livestock. For example, some four hundred households in Chortitza had more than five horses in 1914, though that had fallen to a single household by 1920. Of the 2,360 homesteads, 1,430 had no horses, and all that survived were emaciated. In the once prosperous village of Chortitza, the first Mennonite settlement in the empire, only a single wagon and horse remained by 1920. Farmers utilized what they had to cultivate the fields, including dairy cows. By the later date Mennonites across the empire could no longer sow even the portion of their fields allotted them, and the drop had been considerable. For example, Molotschna Mennonites only worked 11,325 desiatinas in 1921, down from almost 30,000 desiatinas in 1916. There was no food left in Nieder Chortitza by 1921 after a disastrous harvest on top of all other obstacles.[29] That drop in horsepower, human labour, and arable land left Mennonites vulnerable on all fronts.

Typhus struck the Mennonites alongside the arrival of the Makhnovite troops in December 1919. Infestations that spread from body lice and utterly unsanitary conditions, fuelled by dead bodies left to decompose *in situ*, resulted in an epidemic which spread like wildfire. At the epidemic's height David G. Rempel recalled that the dying and dead were everywhere, heaped high in Mennonite homes and in makeshift hospitals, in railway stations and churches, and in abandoned railway cars. He vividly recalled that Mennonites Petia Thiessen and others were among the Makhnovite dead, as were the first Mennonite physicians and nurses who attended them. Rempel assisted with the medical care until he himself contracted the disease, which left him too ill to attend the funerals of his father first, then his brother Heinrich, and finally his mother, all from typhus.[30]

Typhus contributed to the famine, and it did so in Ukraine and Siberia despite the fact that the Bolsheviks relented on their policy of War Communism in the midst of the tragedy when they introduced their more moderate New Economic Policy in March 1921. However, even before that shift could take hold the years of grain requisitioning had devastated the seed grain available to farmers, as did the refugee crisis which saw tens of thousands move through the Black Sea steppe lands in 1920 alone. By then peasants, Mennonites, and others were living off chaff, bark, and clay as an arid stretch from the fall of 1920 onward left little moisture for crops. Reports of cannibalism soared. In spring the heat scorched what little seed had germinated, and millions died of starvation. Once again people died as entire households, which left no one to bury their remains; others dug graves for their family members and themselves as they feared that loved ones would soon not have the strength to do so. No medical personnel survived among the Mennonites of Omsk oblast to assist the sick; all had themselves died by the summer of that year. In all an estimated five million died in the Volga and Ural regions and up to seven million in Soviet Ukraine, with countless Mennonites among them.[31]

Study Commission and American Mennonite Relief, 1919–22

Mennonite delegates met in the Molotschna settlement village of Rűckenau in late 1919. They hastily convened in the local Mennonite Brethren Church at a desperate time as Makhno's destructive forays had barely ended even as the first signs of typhus and widespread hunger appeared. Moreover, Bolsheviks continued to requisition almost all goods, nationalize all property, and close all churches from Siberia to the Black Sea steppe. Those who gathered decided to elect a Study Commission (*Studienkommission*), which they charged with two tasks: to travel abroad to appeal directly for essential aid from Mennonites who lived in Europe and North America and to investigate possible locations abroad where Russia's Mennonites might find refuge through immigration. Delegates elected A.A. Friesen to chair the Commission, B.H. Unruh to serve as principal secretary, and C.H. Warkentin as the final member.[32] The trio left almost immediately for Europe as they accompanied the retreating White Army to the Crimea and on to Constantinople along with those Mennonite young men who had fought alongside the Whites. Bereft of sufficient funds to proceed, they finally received financial assistance from Dutch Mennonites for the journey to North America. They landed in New York on 13 June 1920 and travelled throughout the Mennonite communities of the United States and Canada before Unruh returned to Germany on 1 November 1920.[33] Friesen and Warkentin carried on in North America, where they struggled to come to terms with wildly diverse Mennonites eager to assist but too unorganized and decentralized to do so.

The 90,000 Mennonites in the United States roughly equalled numbers in the former Russian empire at the time, where approximately 65,000 Mennonites on the Black Sea steppe and another 45,000 in the Trans-Volga region and Siberia. Mennonites in Canada numbered a little less than 60,000.[34] In both Canada and the United States Mennonites comprised those who had come from the Swiss and South German lands from the seventeenth to the nineteenth centuries, as well as those, a distinct minority, who had immigrated from the Russian empire in the 1870s. That which separated Mennonites from each other seemed to outweigh similarities at every turn. North American Mennonites divided by country of origin; whether they drove cars or horses; which churchly conference they belonged to; educational levels; language; whether, like the Amish, they even regarded themselves as Mennonite; and so on. In frustration A.A. Friesen wrote his fiancée Maria Goossen that he had encountered sixteen distinct Mennonite groups in the United States, none of which had previously cooperated with each other.[35]

Even before the Study Commission's arrival, many Mennonites in North America had become aware of the plight of their co-religionists in the former Russian empire. The latter had written letters to relations who had emigrated in the 1870s, they had published pleas in widely distributed Mennonite publications like the *Mennonitisches Rundschau*, and they had encouraged North American Mennonites to travel to the Russian lands and see for themselves. Already the Siberian Mennonites had successfully persuaded M.B. Fast and W.P. Neufeld of Reedley California to spearhead a relief effort which brought $40,000 in supplies to Omsk by way of the Pacific port of Vladivostok.[36] But the Commission wanted something all-embracing and so began to call for the various Mennonite groupings to gather together and make common cause for a much larger international project. From this, American leaders organized a series of meetings which culminated in a gathering of thirteen different Mennonite relief agencies in Chicago, Illinois, on 27 July 1920. Known as the Mennonite Central Committee (MCC), it almost immediately sent three young Mennonites – Orie Miller, Clayton Kratz, and Arthur Slagel – to the Black Sea steppe lands to investigate conditions and determine the best way for North American Mennonites to provide assistance. Over the next two years, the MCC engaged in complex negotiations with Moscow (capital of what would be named the Soviet Union in 1922) and Khar'kov (capital of the newly formed Soviet Republic of Ukraine) to permit the formation of food kitchens across the south. The dangers and uncertainties were great at the start as Clayton Kratz disappeared en route to Molotschna and was likely killed in the ongoing civil war. He was never heard from again. Yet MCC persisted and soon placed itself under the auspices of the American Relief Administration (ARA) directed by future US president Herbert Hoover. MCC's work also benefited greatly from the efforts of Peter F. Froese and C.F. Klassen, whom Trans-Volgan and Siberian Mennonites had appointed in July 1920 to represent their interests in Moscow. There they joined Alvin J. Miller, an American Amish Mennonite who had initially volunteered for relief and reconstruction in war-torn France under the auspices of the American Society of Friends (Quakers), itself seconded to the American Red Cross. By 1921 Miller had shifted to the newly formed MCC as he led the agency's relief and redevelopment efforts from its Moscow office from 1921 to 1926, even though the ARA itself ceased operations in 1924.[37]

Miller's arrival coincided with the onset of two long years of devastating famine in the Mennonite heartland from Soviet Ukraine to the Volga and on into Siberia. Millions died, even as the Soviets blocked Mennonite offers of direct assistance. Eventually, the American Mennonite pledge to feed all in their kitchens, regardless of Confession, won the day. The first Mennonite relief kitchen opened at the former Jakob Dűk lumber yard in Chortitza village on 16 March 1922. Within five months the MCC kitchens were feeding 40,000 people daily, and at its height MCC operated 140 field kitchens across the south. Mennonites in the Trans-Volga region travelled up to 80 kilometres in caravans to ARA depots for life-saving supplies, often with horses emaciated by famine and with threats of robbery en route ever present. No less importantly, MCC also delivered fifty tractors from the States along with two hundred horses purchased in the Soviet Union itself, all of which played a vital role in the reconstruction efforts among Mennonites.[38]

Reconstruction in Soviet Times, 1920–7

In a seminal article published in 1995 James Urry challenged the prevailing historiography on Mennonites and the 1920s, which focused on Mennonite attempts to leave the Soviet Union, a story told mainly by those who did just that. Urry urged scholars to consider the whole picture, including the many ways in which Mennonites sought to work with Soviet authorities and within the Soviet system in the 1920s.[39]

That fuller picture has become clearer as we now see the many ways in which Mennonites worked on reconstruction efforts in the 1920s. To that end, hundreds entered the political and administrative system at the lower level in order to transform it to their own purposes, and in a way that mirrored Tracy McDonald's findings for Riazan peasants and their village Soviets in the 1920s.[40] For example, Mennonite Gerhard

Schroeder, who had fled from Schönfeld to Chortitza-Rosental during the civil war, entered the Soviet Commissariat in 1920. He rose quickly through its ranks as he benefited from the relatively high educational levels and Russian fluency achieved among Mennonite youth, which contrasted sharply with many of the earliest Bolshevik party members at the local level. He began simply to receive "telephonograms" from the central regional office in Ekaterinoslav and communicate them in the newly established office in Chortitza-Rosental. From modest beginnings he rose to head secretary. As a further sign of their cooperation with Soviet officials, Mennonites hosted the funeral of the local Bolshevik commissar in the Chortitza Mennonite Church after anarchists murdered him.[41] Gerhard Lohrenz and Johann G. Rempel similarly engaged in state service.[42] The Red Army drafted Lohrenz in 1921, and his unit transferred to the regional centre of Nikolaev, where the commanding officer ordered Lohrenz to work in the office of the military unit. His skills shone, such that the commanding office soon appointed Lohrenz as office manager. In that role he managed to secure a position for his cousin Peter Warkentin. By 1923, Lohrenz's village elected him to serve as chair of the Village Soviet.

What is particularly striking about both Lohrenz and Schroeder is that their service to the Soviet state coincided with significant churchly involvement. Lohrenz undertook catechetical instruction in 1920, and on 21 June 1921 Âltester Jakob Rempel baptized him at the Nikolaifeld Mennonite Church in the former Zagradovka daughter colony. On 1 June 1920 the re-established Rosental Evangelical Mennonite Church elected Gerhard Schroeder, the Soviet bureaucrat, as preacher.[43]

Beyond these two individuals there is widespread evidence of a religious revival among all Christians in the 1920s, especially Protestants, who benefited when the Soviets passed legislation in January 1918 which separated church and state. Even Orthodox Christians developed strategies to engage the state and sustain parish life.[44] Mennonite ecclesial faith rebounded during the NEP years, when the horrors associated with War Communism and the civil war had ended and when the state, in Gregory Freeze's words, "limited its antireligious campaign to propaganda and agitation and avoided coercion" among at least lay believers.[45] Mennonites responded energetically as they resumed regular worship services and again practised open Christian funerals and baptisms. The latter proved particularly essential for Mennonite Brethren, who continued to practise immersion in rivers and streams. Mennonites resumed their church choirs and re-established churchly festivals and regular prayer meetings, which both often focused on Mennonite youth to compensate for increased state control of the education process and the requirement that atheism be taught in all schools. Historian John B. Toews goes so far as to talk about a "Molotschna Renewal Movement" in the early 1920s.⁴⁶

Much to their chagrin, Communist Party officials within the Soviet Republic of Ukraine and western Siberia confirmed the strengthening of religious belief in the 1920s. They identified a plague of Protestant "sects" that included Baptists, Evangelicals, Seventh Day Adventists, and, of course, Mennonites. They pointed to strong church leaders who informed state officials directly that Mennonites reserved the right to pass on the faith to their youth. Ministers controlled purportedly secular Mennonite organizations as they insisted that all members and officers be active believers. They utilized hardships within the Mennonite settlements to their own religious ends as lessons from God. Many ministers also taught school, which exacerbated the problem for Soviet authorities. No wonder Mennonite youth remained strongly committed to religious organizations in the 1920s as Mennonites continued to worship in buildings that Bolsheviks had nationalized along with factories, mills, and almost all non-residential structures. Correspondingly, Mennonite involvement in the new Soviet youth organizations remained low. Officials warned that Mennonites who served in the Soviet Red Army had weakened the morale in their regiments. At one point officials even deemed Mennonites fanatical in their continued allegiance to their faith. Few Mennonites bothered to join the Communist Party, even though many of their youth especially worked within the Soviet system. For example, only one of the 478 residents registered in the Chortitza settlement village of Burwalde in 1923 had joined the Communist Party.⁴⁷

The Mennonite attempt to secure the free exercise of worship and religious instruction culminated in the All-Mennonite Congress, held in Moscow in January 1925. Representatives gathered there from Soviet Ukraine, Trans-Volga, Central Asia, and Siberia after Soviet officials had further restricted civil freedoms. Rather than respond timidly, Mennonites concluded their assembly with a direct eight-point declaration to the Communist Party in which they insisted on the right to hold religious gatherings at home and in church buildings, to build new ones, and the right to instruct their youth on matters of faith. They claimed the right to import Bibles and other religious literature, as well as the right to operate a seminary within the Soviet Union. Lastly, they called for a permanent Mennonite exemption from military service in favour of a form of alternate service, and they did so even as they realized that Mennonites had tarnished their reputation as pacifists through the Selbstschutz and on those occasions when they had supported the

White and Austro-German occupation armies. In these ways Mennonite leaders made plain that faith was central to their identity in Soviet times. As the memorandum from the 1925 Moscow Conference made plain, Mennonites actively and directly engaged the Soviet state, much to the alarm of the Soviet state security establishment.[48]

Earlier, C.F. Klassen and P.F. Froese had represented the concerns of Siberian Mennonites in Moscow alongside Alvin J. Miller of MCC, even as they facilitated the efforts of Mennonites in Soviet Ukraine to engage central party officials. Most strikingly, Mennonite representatives met with Lev Kamenev as early as 1921 to secure American Mennonite famine relief in the south and into Siberia. Kamenev's leading role in the Politburo suggests that Lenin himself may have known about these relief efforts, thanks in large part to Mennonite determination and skill to make their voices heard. What accounts for this success?

Terry Martin has identified the multilayered challenge that Mennonites faced with the new Soviet regime, for good reason. It assessed them negatively as Germanic, faith-based, socio-economically bourgeois and kulak, and as people with a terrible track record from when they supported both the Whites and the Austro-German occupation troops during the recently completed civil war.[49] Yet Soviets also coveted Mennonite economic success and their access to potentially lucrative foreign capital and support, particularly at the start of the New Economic Policy, when the fate of the Soviet state itself hung in the balance. Such a strategy carried a risk, as some who aided in reconstruction efforts – Mennonites among them – believed the crisis would compel Moscow to abandon communism and adopt capitalism instead. For their part, in Urry's assessment, "some Mennonites threw themselves enthusiastically into the work of economic reconstruction, many were attracted by the promise of a new social order, and some were also influenced by the rhetoric of the time which promised a utopian future." According to Tatiana Nazarova, the Mennonite Central Committee allocated more than 600,000 (US) dollars to Soviet famine relief and reconstruction from 1921 to 1928.[50]

Mennonites also had a generation of occasionally tense negotiations with the tsarist state behind them and had learned the value of strong organizational approaches and unified initiatives. To that end they created two organizations: the Union of the Citizens of Dutch Lineage in Soviet Ukraine (known as the Verband), founded in 1922 with an office in the capital city of Kharkov, and the All-Russian Mennonite Agricultural Association (ARMAA), founded one year later for all Mennonites in the Russian Republic. The latter had its office in Moscow, in a house purchased by Mennonites at Taganskaia Ulitsa 8.[51] Both associations actively engaged in a wide range of activities, of which economic reconstruction was foremost. In particular, the Verband, led by B.B. Janz, oversaw American Mennonite relief operations, lobbied the Soviet state on behalf of Mennonite landowners and the Mennonite landless, arranged for cooperative fire insurance, encouraged new livestock breeds and crops to create more intensive economies, lent money to farmers, sought permission to found a Mennonite agricultural school, and increased support for Mennonite efforts to gain an exemption from military service.[52] Every Mennonite settlement had a representative in the Verband, and both the Russian and the Ukrainian assemblies of Mennonites cooperated on the many matters of joint concern.

None of this suggests that Mennonites had an easy transition in the Soviet era. The state had seized their private estates and many of their larger business and buildings. It had requisitioned goods at unsustainable levels prior to the introduction of NEP. All that aside, the concerted efforts by Mennonite leaders did yield positive results despite the almost complete lack of working livestock or implements at the start of the 1920s. Although the state reduced their farm holdings, at an average of 30 desiatinas Mennonites still exceeded many peasant farmers in the region. In sum, the activity of the Verband and the ARMAA made plain the Mennonite determination to negotiate new agreements at the highest political levels in Moscow.

Mennonites also obtained an exemption from active military service despite their sordid reputation in the self-defence units of the civil war, and they realized a significant resurgence in religious formation and confessional belief, as outlined above.[53] They accomplished all this because they adapted to Soviet rules of engagement, already evident in their creation of the Verband and the ARMAA, both designed ostensibly to put economics first. And although they realized significant gains, it often came at a price. For example, they achieved an exemption from active military service, though the Soviet state refused to recognize it as a collective exemption that applied to all Mennonite youth. Exemptions could only be achieved on a case-by-case basis, and only with youth who had not served in anti-Bolshevik units during the civil war. Still, it was better than no exemption at all. Mennonites made other compromises as well, such as when the Verband met for its annual conference in Donetsk province in the first days of March 1924. The meeting began not with prayer nor a Christian hymn, as would surely have happened before 1917. But these were Soviet times, and so it began with a moment of silence when B.B. Janz asked the assembly to honour the memory of Soviet leader V. Lenin, recently deceased. It was a loss, he declared, for the Russian and world proletariat especially. Only thereafter did the business of the Verband's annual Congress proceed.⁵⁴

Mennonite Emigration

David G. Rempel recalled the importance of 22 July 1923 to the end of his days, almost seventy years later.⁵⁵ That was the day he and his brother Jacob arrived in Rosthern, Saskatchewan, on the vast Canadian prairie after an arduous journey from his homeland on the banks of the Dnieper River. A native of Nieder Chortitza, Rempel's recollections have informed much of this chapter, as have his later historical investigations. But on that day the twenty-four-year-old Rempel arrived at the Canadian Pacific Railway station in Rosthern, where he and other former members of the Chortitza mother settlement found refuge and a new home among Mennonites from the 1870s emigration. As befits a fundamentally Christian movement, the peoples of these two Mennonite emigrations marked the occasion in song and worship. At one point, the incoming "Russlaenders" began to softly sing *"Lobe den Herrn den mächtigen Kőnig der Ehren"* (Praise to the Lord, the mighty King of honour). Soon the welcoming "Kanadier" Mennonites joined in. Observers that day listened in amazement as men removed their hats in homage. Many wept as they sang.⁵⁶

Rempel's arrival at the Rosthern station that day placed him at the forefront of a movement which saw almost 20,000 Mennonites emigrate from the Soviet Union to Canada between 1923 and 1927, one-fifth of their numbers. That it happened at all was remarkable, as many Mennonites in the former Russian empire had prayed seemingly in vain for a new domicile through the horrors of civil war, typhus, and famine after 1917. Over time they considered locations as scattered as New Zealand, the Netherlands, Germany, and Paraguay, though it quickly become apparent that North America had pride of place in their hearts. No wonder members of the Study Commission of 1919 focused on the United States and Canada as a possible refuge for their co-religionists even as they worked to send famine relief back. They faced an uphill battle at the outset, as neither country welcomed them. Canada's Order in Council from 1919 expressly forbade Mennonite immigration, and a new immigration quota system introduced by the Americans in 1921 did likewise. Uncertain of how to proceed, A.A. Friesen and C.H. Warkentin travelled to Mexico over the winter months of 1920–1 to explore immigration possibilities there. Ultimately, they believed Mexico lacked a sufficiently strong polity to provide the assurances of safety their people desperately needed.⁵⁷

At some point the Commission fixed its hopes on Canada, which coincided with the delegation's arrival in the western provinces in the summer of 1921. By the following spring, A.A. Friesen had assisted local Mennonite leaders as they formed the Canadian Mennonite Board of Colonization (CMBC). Ostensibly a counterpart to the US-based MCC, which diverse Mennonite conferences had formed to provide aid to starving Mennonites abroad, the CMBC soon became the focal point of Canadian Mennonite colonization efforts. A.A. Friesen served as its first secretary and principal link to the Soviet-era Mennonites by way of B.H. Unruh in Germany, though David Toews of Saskatchewan – affectionately known as the Mennonite Bishop of Canada – served as its president. The CMBC worked tirelessly to have the Canadian government overturn the Order-in-Council and to arrange with Canadian National and Canadian Pacific railways to cover transportation costs up front. They pledged to pay back this loan, or *Reiseschuld*, which eliminated a major objection from the Canadian government. Even so Friesen twice joined delegations of the CMBC as it appealed directly to politicians in Ottawa before Cabinet repealed the exclusionary Order-in-Council on 2 June 1922. With its removal the door opened for Mennonite immigration to Canada.[58]

B.B. Janz, as chair of the Verband, took the lead on the emigration among Soviet-era Mennonites, though he worked closely with P.F. Froese and C.F. Klassen in the Moscow office of ARMAA.[59] Already in 1922 Janz had stressed the Verband's commitment to secure Mennonite emigration as equal to its reconstruction efforts. Over the next four years Janz worked energetically to receive permission for Mennonites across the Soviet Union to emigrate and at one point accepted Paraguay as a destination even though he knew nothing about it. Soon, however, he also focused on Canada, which allowed him to work closely with A.A. Friesen and the CMBC. Janz made repeated trips to the Ukrainian capital in Kharkov (Kiev only became the capital of Soviet Ukraine in 1934) and Moscow. He worked patiently with a revolving door of Soviet bureaucrats and negotiated the complexity of Kharkov's relationship to Moscow as he juggled the Verband's twin aims of Mennonite reconstruction and emigration. Janz enjoyed initial success when he obtained permission in 1922 for the poorest Mennonites to emigrate on his argument that they offered little to Soviet reconstruction efforts. It was under these painstakingly negotiated conditions that David G. Rempel joined the first wave of Mennonite emigration in 1923.[60]

Janz worked closely with Froese and Klassen over the next three years as they sought to move as many Mennonites as possible and as Soviet officials became increasingly wary of such a mass exodus. Meanwhile, other complications arose on the Canadian front as Mennonite debt for the *Reiseschuld* mounted beyond reasonable limits and as Canadian officials refused to accept many whom they deemed of poor health.[61] Yet despite all these obstacles almost twenty thousand, or one-fifth of all Soviet Mennonites immigrated to Canada between 1923 and 1928, where they soon settled in cities and on farmsteads from Ontario to British Columbia.[62] Janz himself immigrated to Coaldale, Alberta, Canada, in 1926, and C.F. Klassen, from the Moscow office of the Siberian Mennonites, emigrated two years later.

Conclusion

"The situation back home is incredibly difficult. Have you ever stood by a blast furnace and watched through the small window as everything seethes, hisses and roars?"[63] With these words B.B. Janz attempted to capture the state of Mennonite life in the Soviet Union early in 1922, though he might just as well have used them to describe the bewilderment of his own life. Born in the well-established village of Tiege, Molotschna, in 1877, and already an ordained minister and teacher by 1910, his world crumbled after the onset of the First World War in September 1914. Seven long years of chaos and devastation followed before one could speak of an end to devastation in 1922. Those Mennonites who had survived these tumultuous years – and thousands did not – entered a new Soviet era with families, communities, and economies torn asunder. Under the circumstances, Janz's metaphor of a "blast furnace" seemed apt.

From out of the blast furnace, Janz and other Mennonites sought to engage the new Soviet reality on their own terms, through their own newly formed organizations. On the one hand, Mennonites worked to reconstruct their lives as they re-established economies around cooperative models, formed new worship communities in a state that proclaimed atheism, and found new ways to inculcate their youth in Mennonite faith and identity.[64] In some ways, "Mennonite" once again became a marker of Christian faith and community as the new state abolished the identities and ranks that had so defined Imperial Russian society, including Mennonitism itself.

The record makes plain that Mennonites had begun to emerge from the economic blast furnace by 1927, even as inventories and yields on Mennonite farms remained well below pre-war levels.[65] Nataly Venger has pointed to the proliferation of Mennonite artisanal activity in the 1920s, from blacksmithing to linseed oil extraction. Mennonites continued to produce and repair agricultural equipment as they expanded into other sectors, especially within their relatively young Siberian communities which moved more quickly than Chortitza and Molotschna to embrace cooperatives and Soviet forms of ownership and distribution. Despite sharp losses endured during the years of revolution and civil war, economic reconstruction in the Omsk district allowed Mennonites there still to cultivate more than 80 per cent of their arable land, as opposed to a district-wide average of less than 20 per cent. Thanks to the joint efforts of MCC and the ARMAA, Mennonites again experienced striking gains in cattle breeding and crop yields per hectare. These new forms came in all shapes and sizes, as when the Schroeder family formed the Primernoe cooperative on 22 February 1922 in the Omsk district of Siberia. It united twelve households to improve agricultural productivity generally, and in particular to gain better access to improved seed quality so as to minimize weed infestations.[66] Adolf Ehrt concludes that by 1927 fully 40 per cent of Mennonites in the Russian Republic worked from 25 to 50 desiatinas of land, and another 10 per cent cultivated over 50 desiatinas. Taken together, Mennonites had unquestionably begun to re-establish themselves economically; the worst seemed behind them. Nor were they alone, as Olga Red'kina concludes that Protestants and Orthodox sectarians – including Old Believers – generally played a significant role in the development of Soviet cooperatives in the 1920s.[67]

At the same time, Mennonite churches partially rejuvenated under the New Economic Policy as Mennonites published religious literature again and as they boldly baptized in public along the Dnieper banks, as well as a host of Siberian rivers and ponds. Moreover, the Soviet decision to renounce Russianization in 1924 and to implement a policy of "indigenization" (*korenizatsiia*) allowed Mennonites to reclaim their Germanic culture and, by extension, their identity. Though non-Mennonites did settle in their villages and cultivate land that previously belonged to their co-religionists, the number of non-Mennonites remained relatively small. It helped that in many instances Mennonites themselves served as local Soviet officials to implement Soviet policies, even if they did so for a wide range of reasons.[68] It is, of course, a mugs game to ponder what might have happened had the policies of the New Economic Policy and "indigenization" been allowed to continue as policy. They did not, and when Soviet leaders abruptly terminated them at the end of the 1920s it once again threw Mennonites into a very different, albeit very Soviet, blast furnace.

Chapter Eleven

When God Leads You into the Wilderness: Mennonites in the Stalinist Crucible, 1927–1934

Anna Ivanovna Schmidt was born on the first day of 1929, the year of Stalin's Great Turn (*perelom*).[1] Her own Molotschna Mennonite village of Margenau formed a collective farm (*kolkhoz*) in 1932, though the village's poorer households, also Mennonite, had already organized a rural association a year earlier. At some point the local Soviet, based in Gnadental, branded the more prosperous Margenau villagers as kulaks. It banished them to the far north, where many subsequently died. The 1932 harvest fell far short of the level demanded by the local Soviet to meet its quota. As a result, security police apprehended the entire kolkhoz executive, including Johann Schmidt, the kolkhoz's first chair (*predsidatel'*) and Anna Ivanovna's father. He died in August 1933 after he ate rotten fish along a riverbed in a labour camp near Vladivostok in the country's far east, to which the court had sentenced him. Fortunately, Anna's mother learned of her husband's death soon thereafter, not decades later, as often happened among Mennonite women in Stalin's time.

Johann Schmidt's arrest coincided with the onset of a terrible famine across Soviet Ukraine from which many villagers died, including Anna's paternal grandfather and her uncle Franz. But Anna, her mother, and brother survived, thanks in part to their ability to know which weeds in the surrounding fields were edible and nutritional and which ones caused harm. Authorities did not banish Anna's remaining family from the kolkhoz, as happened to countless others in a similar situation, but permitted them to live in a converted stable near the centre of the village. During the winter months Anna's *Tante Marichen* (Aunt Mary) and her three young children also shared the two-room, dirt-floored home. They took one room, and Anna and her brother moved into the other room with their mother. Such a combined household epitomized the degree to which Anna came of age in a woman's world. In fact, her mother taught her to be wary of any men who remained in the village by the end of the 1930s. After all, might they have agreed to become informers to survive capture and exile? The question contained the answer. Only one of Anna's thirteen childhood friends still had a father who lived at home by that time.

As a young girl Anna regularly accompanied her mother Katharina, who served as postmistress for Margenau. They walked daily across the fields to the village of Friedensdorf, and later Gnadental, where Katharina picked up the daily post for distribution. Anna also recalled how her mother told her and Georg Bible stories late at night after she had drawn the blinds in their neatly kept home. Church no longer existed by the mid-thirties, though Georg recalled the church funeral of their younger sister Irma, who died shortly after her birth in 1931. Local officials closed the Margenau church building shortly thereafter and demolished it, having already banished the last two ministers, Aron Dück and Petr Regehr, along with their families, in 1931 and 1933, respectively.[2]

In one way Anna Schmidt's story contains details so particular that they can only apply to her. However, any reader of Soviet history will instantly recognize features that applied to approximately 140 million peasants during the great Stalinist upheaval of the late 1920s and early 1930s. As one small part of that larger story, we will use Anna's experience to introduce the discombobulation of the Mennonite world from the end of NEP in 1928 to the onset of dekulakization and collectivization.

The End of NEP, 1926–8

Key Bolsheviks grew increasingly impatient with the pace of change in the 1920s as the goal of a Soviet socialist utopia appeared to recede into the distant future. Socialist initiatives lagged far behind capitalist and bourgeois formation under the Communist Party's watch, and that could not continue. Terry Martin has demonstrated how *korenizatsiia* had strengthened nationalist identities, not weakened them.[3] As a case in point, Bolshevik assessments of Mennonite society over the NEP years makes these trends plain, something possible given the strong work undertaken by historians in party archives since the collapse of the Soviet Union. We now know that Soviet officials from Moscow's political elite to those at work in the rural hinterland paid keen and disproportionate attention to Mennonite activity. To give but one example, the powerful Secretariat of the CPSU Central Committee in Moscow debated Mennonite matters six times between November 1925 and June 1928. By contrast, the Secretariat never discussed the Germans who lived outside the Volga German republic even though their numbers

Figure 8. Mennonite members of a collective farm (kolkhoz), 1939. Gerhard Lohrenz Photo Collection, Mennonite Heritage Archives.

exceeded Mennonites by a factor of four.[4] As regards the latter, party officials did not like what they saw.

By the mid-1920s officials routinely criticized the persistence of class divisions within Mennonite villages as well as Mennonite resistance to Soviet governance and socialist acculturation. At the local level a report of the Khortitsa Raion Party Committee on 10 July 1925 observed that the Mennonite Verband in Ukraine hindered the Sovietization of the countryside. The Verband's robust engagement with Mennonites in every village across the region weakened trade union and party work and provided a shield for Mennonite intellectuals, former landowners, and former factory owners to preserve their hold on the Mennonite masses. These former elites also corrupted newly formed Soviet-sponsored co-operatives when they entered and quickly dominated their executive branches. Such highly critical reports worked their way up to senior administrators. On 26 June 1926 the head of the CPSU's Agitation and Propaganda Department informed the Secretariat of the Central Committee in Moscow that the Mennonite Verband in Ukraine enriched individual Mennonite kulaks at the expense of the whole community. More than that, the very existence of a Verband had weakened the authority of local Soviets as Mennonites simply disregarded them. Thus, local officials had clearly warned their senior counterparts by 1926 that the Verband had set back socialist development among Mennonites and peasants alike and had even engaged in economic espionage to undermine the Bolshevik party.[5]

Soviet officials deemed the Mennonite emigration movement of the mid-1920s as a particularly corrupting element in the countryside. They expressed concern that Mennonites had merely paid lip service to the Verband's officially declared raison d'être of pan-Mennonite and regional economic reconstruction within the Soviet state. Instead Mennonite associations fostered anti-Soviet activity when they supplied false narratives of Soviet oppression and destitution to international agencies. Where they did engage in economic reconstruction it had often been to the benefit of Mennonites alone, as when they received land allotments in 1921 well above peasant norms. Officials in Omsk observed that Siberian Mennonites dominated the co-operative movement in the region, which gave them a disproportionate influence over access to credit, weed-free seed, better cattle-breeding stock, and dairy production. The results spoke for themselves, as Mennonite economies in Omsk *uezd* were two to four times more productive than the statistical uezd average. In Petr Vibe's summary, even though they had suffered great losses during the revolution and civil war the evidence suggested that Mennonites retained their entrepreneurial spirit and bourgeois practices and had obtained results to prove it.⁶

As noted in the previous chapter, Soviet officials by the mid-1920s consistently reported on the persistence of Christian belief among Mennonites, and they linked that persistence directly to anti-Soviet behaviour. Few Mennonites attended Soviet reading rooms, few joined the Komsomols (Communist Youth League) or atheist associations, and fewer still established communist clubs in their villages. In fact, already in 1925, the Central Bureau of the German Section of the Ukrainian Communist Party had urged officials to see the link between the German language and the persistence of Christian faith among Mennonites. German communications also hindered attempts by Soviet officials to integrate peasants into Mennonite settlements, especially as Mennonite ministers manipulated Mennonite economic associations and co-operatives to maintain their grip on believers. By this means ministers successfully organized boycotts through the Verband, which weakened the work of the Committees of Poor Peasants, the Lenin Young Communist League, and Soviet voluntary co-operatives. In sum, Mennonites tended to maintain a "narrow religious-national outlook," one that resulted in a "passive attitude of people toward Soviet social life."⁷

The Stalinist Revolution: An Introduction

Soviet frustrations with Mennonites in the 1920s epitomized the widespread disillusionment loyal Bolsheviks felt by 1926, the year that Soviet industrial strength returned to pre-1914 levels. Such a restoration could hardly be deemed exceptional given the overwhelmingly peasantist nature of the Russian economy at the dawn of the twentieth century. As worrisome was the fact that peasants, not workers, provided the main pool of candidate members to the CPSU, an ideologically unacceptable development. Religious belief persisted despite an aggressive campaign to promote atheism, and korenizatsiia had strengthened discrete national identities to the detriment of the socialist whole.

Then, amid growing disillusionment among the Bolshevik faithful, two crises appeared in 1927 which opened the door for a radical new departure in the Soviet policy. First, Soviet officials began to warn that Western powers, led by a British government which had recently cut diplomatic ties with Moscow, planned to invade the Soviet Union. Almost immediately authorities began to hunt for foreign spies and flush out anti-Soviet conspiracies. This culminated in the spring of 1928, when police arrested more than fifty engineers and managers in the Caucasus mining centre of Shakhty and charged them with foreign espionage. A public trial and executions followed, all of which confirmed the ominous truth that the Soviet Union faced commingled internal and external threats at a time when its reconstruction efforts had only yielded modest results, and even those largely to the benefit of capitalists and kulaks.

The second crisis irrupted in the spring of 1927, when Soviet grain stockpiles reached dangerously low levels despite a string of relatively strong harvests in the mid-1920s. What was going on? Peasants had been free since the onset of NEP to market their own grains, which they usually did through private entrepreneurs.[8] All agriculturalists worked the market to optimize their situation. They withheld grains when the state lowered prices, and by 1927 they had also begun to shift grains to more lucrative markets such as dairy production, just as urban consumers began to hoard all available grains as they responded to the war scare. To top it off, a lower harvest that year compelled the state to re-introduce grain rationing in cities, the very measure which had led to the collapse of the tsarist regime a decade earlier.

Under the circumstances, Stalin, and other key figures within the CPSU turned against the grain-procurement strategies employed during NEP. They rejected the claim that the reduced stockpiles reflected the normal give and take of grain producers and urban consumers. Instead, Stalin blamed the (essentially non-existent) class structure of the peasant village when he argued that *kulaks* (wealthy peasant exploiters) had gained too much power over the rest of the peasants. During NEP these odious kulaks had first re-established, then strengthened, their capitalist economies at the expense of poorer peasants and the state itself. Stalin, in alliance with the most radicalized workers of the CPSU, now moved to obliterate NEP through an aggressive strategy of socialist revolution. Initially the party endorsed a strategy developed in Siberia and known as the Ural-Siberian Method, which mandated poor peasant committees (*kombedy*) in all villages to turn the screws on kulaks with the imposition of harsh grain quotas. Stalin even travelled to Siberia in early 1928 as he demanded more aggressive measures against the kulaks, coupled with sharply increased taxes and grain quotas. Flying in the face of ideological expectations, peasants reacted violently to state attempts in Siberia to introduce these so-called extraordinary measures, a situation exacerbated by a generally low harvest in 1928, the second disappointing year in a row.[9] Meanwhile cities continued to suffer from increased shortages as the drive to industrialize languished. Something had to give.

This was the context in which Stalin unleashed what Beatrice Rosenthal has called "the primal energies of destructiveness (the Dionysian impulse) to demolish the old world and build the new." Similarly, Valerie Kivelson and Ronald Suny call the end of NEP "both a revolution and a counter-revolution, both a heroic and a tragic period for the Soviet people."[10] The Stalinist revolution comprised three coincidental and overlapping phenomena: the Bolshevization of Soviet society and culture, the rapid industrialization of the Soviet Union spurred on by a process of dekulakization, and the collectivization of agriculture. Every aspect of this revolution profoundly transformed Mennonite life as it did the lives of hundreds of millions of Soviet citizens.

The Stalinist Revolution (I): Culture, Faith, and Mennonite Identity

Thanks to Sheila Fitzpatrick we now understood more fully how much the Stalinist revolution was, first and foremost, a cultural revolution, one that sought a complete restructuring of society along narrowly ideological lines. To that end the Bolsheviks jettisoned old cultural elites in favour of a new cohort whose class origins placed them and their loyalty to the Soviet state above reproach. It was new wineskins for the new wine.[11] In a sharp reversal of korenizatsiia under NEP, influential party leaders now sought socialist acculturation of minorities and the elimination of religious belief. As to the latter, a Politburo resolution of January 1929 alarmingly declared that religious belief had grown through the 1920s, such that religious organizations were at the forefront of counter-revolutionary forces in the USSR.[12]

Such an all-embracing Stalinist cultural revolution directly challenged Mennonites as it undermined three markers which had defined and safeguarded their identity for generations. First, Moscow began already in the mid-1920s to eliminate all pan-Mennonite institutions and previously negotiated exemptions. For example, on 18 September 1925 the Presidium of the Central Committee made military service compulsory, thus ending a faith-based exemption that Mennonites, Tolstoyans, Evangelicals, and others had negotiated with the Communist state after 1917. A few months later, the Mennonite Verband met in the Ukrainian republic for the final time on 17–19 February 1926 as local officials denounced it for being anti-Soviet and at the mercy of Mennonite capitalist elites. Thereafter politically engaged Mennonites in Soviet Ukraine had few alternatives for broader civic engagement beyond Soviets and collective farms. Officials initially deemed the ARMAA in the Russian republic to be less aggressive and subversive in its tactics than the Verband, which allowed it to survive until May 1928.[13] Even so, a memorandum issued by the People's Commissariat of the Russian republic late in 1927 concluded that the ARMAA exclusively represented the prosperous elements of Mennonite society, including former factory owners, estate owners, and capitalist traders. In addition, it had established close ties with fascist organizations in Berlin, encouraged emigration against the best interests of the Soviet state, and undermined the social development of the most vulnerable Mennonites. With such a judgment the state terminated the union in 1927, though the executive continued to function until the summer of 1928.[14] In that year officials also terminated the last two pan-Mennonite publications in the country: *Unser Blatt* and *Der Praktische Landwirt*.[15] Thus, by mid-1928 Mennonites found themselves without a collective body or publication, which has prompted some historians to identify May 1928 as the endpoint of the Mennonite commonwealth. Nor were Mennonites alone on this, as countless other ethnicities suffered the same fate towards the end of NEP when Stalin adopted a program that was both militant and utopian against perceived non-Soviet cultures.

New legislative measures also sought to eliminate a second cultural pillar for Mennonites: the role of the church within their communities, and in particular the influence of Mennonite ministers and Ältesters. We have already shown that religious faith flourished during NEP despite Bolshevik hostility to all forms of religious practice.[16] But the Stalinist cultural revolution ended whatever Bolshevik religious tolerance remained by the end of NEP, as a series of draconian laws passed in 1928 and 1929 disenfranchised a wide range of Soviet citizens, including all clerics, Mennonite among them. They ordered the instruction of atheist pedagogies in schools and the removal of all religious expression from public life. Officials now linked collectivization and the cultural Sovietization of the countryside with the removal of religious organizations and their leaders. A final decree issued in December 1929 marked the onset of all-out secularization as it brought together four interwoven threads: a war on religious belief; a war on the materiality of religious faith, its churches, relics, hymnaries, and Bibles; a war on religious adherents; and a war on religious personnel.[17]

As to the last of these, ministers now faced an avalanche of penalties and punishing taxes unless they renounced their faith and position. Officials seized their homes and offered them to the landless, many of whom themselves were Mennonites. As declared enemies of the state, officials moved quickly to arrest ministers, executed many after hastily convened trials, and sentenced the rest to hard labour in the Soviet prison system (*Gulag*). Mennonites were hardly alone in this, as the state sentenced over five thousand Christian clerics to the Gulag in 1930 alone. Proportionally, however, Terry Martin concludes that Mennonite ministers were relatively hard hit, indicative of the state's mounting frustration with perceived anti-Soviet behaviour among all Mennonites.[18]

Additional legislation severely restricted the right of Mennonite congregations to operate and banned all children from attending. Police banned religious observances outright by the early 1930s. Andrei Savin argues that the CPSU intensified its anti-religious struggle in Siberia against Mennonites because it viewed even non-preachers as religious zealots who blunted communist inculcation. Party officials deemed Mennonite organizational skills as superior, which made their perceived threat more formidable and intolerable. It viewed Mennonite ministers and Ältesters as closely bound to Mennonite kulaks and Mennonite intellectuals, and as a key hindrance in the Soviet socialization of Mennonite youth.[19]

Examples abound of how the regime devastated Mennonite ecclesial leaders. In a representative instance, the Chortitza Mennonite Church ordained Heinrich Winter as Ältester on 4 November 1923. Heinrich Lemke, who had somehow managed to escape the Eichenfeld massacre of 1919, served as Winter's deacon. In 1929 authorities dispossessed both the Lemke and the Winter families of their homes and modest landholdings. Both families, by law, could not join the new collective farms that had formed, and as "non-persons" both household heads lost their civil rights, including access to a legal defence. Initially another family in the village of Neuenburg agreed to house Heinrich Winter's family in their summer kitchen, though such accommodations were dangerous. Officials repeatedly interrogated Heinrich Winter over the following months and at one point ordered Winter and his family to vacate from their host home within forty-eight hours. Thereafter an elderly couple in Kronsweide gave the Heinrich Winter family temporary shelter. Congregants supplied them with what foodstuffs they could, that is, until Good Friday in 1935, when NKVD officials arrested Winter for the final time. His trial and internal exile followed.[20]

Few ministers escaped arrest and exile between 1929 and 1935. Historian Colin Neufeldt has concluded that only ten ministers still lived in all the Chortitza villages in 1933, of the forty who had served in the late 1920s. Of seventy-two ministers who served in Molotschna in the late twenties, fewer than ten remained by August 1933.[21] At the same time, local Soviets closed church buildings and banned religious gatherings. They converted some structures for community use as clubs, theatres, or grain storage. They dismantled others, including Anna Schmidt's in Margenau, as officials repurposed materials to construct barns for the new kolkhoz. Much depended, it seemed, on individual Soviets. The Schönweise Soviet adjacent to Alexandrovsk forbade religious instruction as early as 1921, whereas churches in the Don Basin only began to close in 1929. At the other end of the spectrum, Osterwick closed its church building in 1934 and Molotschna's School for the Deaf and Dumb offered religious instruction until 1937. Nor did this happen in isolation, as Soviets also moved aggressively after 1928 to promote atheism through the dismissal of all teachers who did not denounce Christianity, the mandatory instruction in atheism in all schools, and the establishment of local chapters of the Komsomol in many Mennonite villages.[22]

The family was the third pillar undermined by the Stalinist cultural revolution. Soviet officials focused on the removal of men from the home, whether as clerics or kulaks. As we shall see, by the end of the 1930s many households had become fatherless, brotherless, and matriarchal by necessity, as Marlene Epp has captured most vividly in her study of Mennonite refugees entitled *Women without Men*. In a typical diary entry from 1931 a Mariechen Peters of Danilovka wrote of the arrest of her brother Isaak, which left his wife Sara alone to raise their six children. Police then arrested David Thiessen's sons in neighbouring Friedensdorf.[23]

Susan Toews of Ohrloff village in Molotschna captured this loss most poignantly when she wrote to her brother Gerhard on 1 January 1931. Gerhard, by then a resident in Canada, had asked about family life in Ohrloff, to which Susan responded: "First, our former neighbours: the entire family is torn apart. He and two of his sons, the eldest and the third, are in the far north; the second son is wandering about somewhere in the world seeking to earn what he can. His wife lives in Memrik with the youngest four children ... Now the latest news from here: all the young men have been drafted again. They had to leave December 15."[24]

The Stalinist Revolution (II): Dekulakization and Internal Exile

Peter Rahn recorded worrisome news in his letter of 31 March 1930 from his home in the Molotschna village of Conteniusfeld. For the first time he observed that authorities had banished someone identified as "EJW" from the village and had inventoried several other families. They had also inventoried five families in the adjoining village of Sparrau. In a letter written less than a month later Rahn noted that authorities had removed another four families ("W.B., J.D., F.F., and K.S.") and concluded "what all is going to transpire, we do not know."[25] Rahn could not know what happened to those whom police had forcibly evicted from Conteniusfeld, but the Jasch (Jakob) and Maria Regehr family of

Altonau village in the former Zagradovka Mennonite daughter colony did. Police arrested Jasch on 30 October 1930. Identified as a kulak, he immediately lost possession of his home and property. By June 1931 authorities loaded him and his whole family onto a cattle car along with others similarly incarcerated and then locked the door. They travelled for the next seven days and nights until they reached a barracks settlement in the northern Urals, all surrounded by marsh and forest. Nor did their nightmare end upon arrival. There is no food, she lamented to relations in Canada at the time, and "if help does not come soon, many, many will find their grave here."[26]

The events observed by Peter Rahn and experienced by the Regehr family were part of a mass movement known as dekulakization. It originated in 1927 as Stalin argued that the countryside needed to collectivize rapidly to develop a socialist foundation for the Soviet Union's urgently needed industrialization drive. Urban cadres imbued with Marxism needed to assist poor peasants with this transformation because wealthy kulaks held a stranglehold over the village. To assist in the revolutionary process Stalin launched a campaign in November 1929 which called for 25,000 impassioned Party loyalists and urban workers to implement the collectivization of Soviet agriculture by any means. One month later Stalin called for the liquidation of the kulaks as a class, by which the party declared war on an estimated 3–5 per cent of all peasant households in the Soviet Union.[27]

Colin Neufeldt has shown the multiple ways by which local officials identified kulaks within their jurisdictions and the way many of these criteria pointed directly at Mennonites.[28] As we have shown, they worked more land on average than neighbouring peasants in the 1920s, and with better implements. Many utilized hired labour under NEP, a certain indication of kulak status. Officials recalled that many Mennonites had owned vast estates and factories before 1917. They had supported occupation forces during the civil war that followed, even if it meant a rejection of their vaunted commitment to pacifism. Mennonites in the 1920s had fostered multiple linkages to foreign agencies and governments, as demonstrated in the emigration movement across the 1920s, all of which sealed their fate in the dekulakization campaign that followed. Though numbers are necessarily approximate, officials exiled an estimated 20–5 per cent of Mennonite households in Soviet Ukraine before 1933, and there is no reason to believe that Mennonites in the Russian republic suffered less. We do know that officials banished 18.2 per cent of all Mennonites in the Slavgorod (Barnaul) daughter colony of western Siberia. Officials exiled former estate owners, entrepreneurs, those who had prospered economically during NEP, and any officials who had served in the ARMAA in Soviet Russia and the Verband in Soviet Ukraine. Peter Letkemann has determined that officials dekulakized Mennonites in the Volga-Ural region at a ratio that was five times greater than neighbouring peasants. Even this masks the aggressive activity of selected local officials. For example, police forcibly removed fully one-third of all Mennonites in the Alt-Samara daughter colony: 55 families and 331 individuals in total.[29]

The mass deportation of Mennonites profoundly transformed the Mennonite footprint in the Soviet Union as it drove thousands far into the Gulag. We now know much more about the haphazard and contingent way the Gulag operated, which explains why Mennonites joined hundreds of thousands of prisoners exiled in minimally converted cattle cars to distant destinations where local officials were unprepared to host them. No wonder the fatality rates in transit and in the initial period of settlement were so high. One trainload of Mennonites, for example, had no access to food or water for their entire six-day journey to Arkhangelsk on the polar White Sea.[30] Once on site Mennonites struggled to find adequate shelter and food amid deadly working conditions that took them into the mines, factories, and forests of a rapidly emerging economy, often in the dead of winter. Karaganda in the Kazakhstan republic played an important and indicative role. This coal-rich area had been underdeveloped until 1931, when it suddenly became a focal point in the first Five Year Plan. Moscow created a massive complex in that year, as thousands arrived on the newly established rail line, Mennonites among them. They came from all parts of the Soviet Union, including Soviet Ukraine, the Alt and Neu Samara colonies on the Volga, and western Siberia. The state exiled many Mennonite ministers and Ältesters there, along with Baptists and assorted other evangelical clergy. More than 118,000 citizens lived in Karaganda by 1933, including those who comprised the newly established and massive Karlag (Karaganda Corrective Labour) camp, up from only 2,000 inhabitants in 1931.[31]

The regime of the camps played a profound and paradoxical role in Mennonite polity. On the one hand, it compelled Mennonites to engage openly and freely with non-Mennonites in the struggle to survive. By this means the Gulag became a Soviet school of socialization for thousands. On the other hand, places like Karaganda served as magnets for a new form of Mennonite polity. Mennonites found each other in the Gulag; they sought each other out, even as they formed fraternal bonds with Baptists, Evangelicals, Seventh Day Adventists, Orthodox, and other Christians similarly imprisoned. As representative, Aron Warkentin recalled the relief when Mennonites from the Suvorovka

Mennonite daughter colony in the Caucasus foothills re-congregated under confinement, in this case a Moscow detention centre: "Once more we Suvorovkavites [sic] were reunited. There was brother Gerhard Fast and B. Boldt from Fuerstental Johann Epp from Arival, Nickel from Blumental, Heinrich Wiebe from Suvorovka, Heinrich Friesen from Kuban and myself from Nikolaifeld."[32] Such reunions were not uncommon, especially as Mennonites formed communities in exile with co-religionists from across the vast area of their Soviet settlements.

The Stalinist Revolution (III): Collectivization and Famine

David Shearer has aptly characterized the Soviet collectivization drive as one that was "harsh, often brutal, and evoked strong peasant resistance." Similarly, Colin Neufeldt concludes that the collectivization of the Mennonite colonies of Chortitza and Molotschna was "chaotic, violent, and destructive, but ultimately successful."[33] Whereas only a few Mennonites had formed voluntary rural associations by 1928, almost all land in Chortitza had been collectivized by 1930, and barely less than that in Molotschna. In most cases individual villages formed a single kolkhoz, though there were exceptions. Chortitza and Rosental villages, for example, formed three kolkhozes between them: The Third Internationale; In the name of Engels; and The Red Flag. Of these, the Third Internationale Collective specialized in dairy operations which concentrated on sales to the burgeoning Dnepostroi Dam construction site adjacent to it.[34]

The rapid rate at which Mennonites collectivized reflected the degree to which dekulakization devastated Mennonite villages as police arrested and exiled key leaders, including the most enterprising families of the 1920s, former estate owners, entrepreneurs, virtually all ministers, Ältesters, and those teachers who refused to renounce their faith. Any opposition that remained by 1932 understood that it could not confront the state directly, especially after members of the revolutionary 25,000ers entered the Mennonite heartland, as Jacob A. Neufeld observed in his village of Gnadenfeld (Molotschna), now transformed into the Karl Marx kolkhoz.[35] Mennonites themselves played key roles in the collectivization drive as hundreds worked within the local Soviet bureaucracy at the end of the 1920s, a byproduct of korenizatsiia. They served on the Committees of the Poor (in part because a significant minority remained poor by the end of NEP), on Village Soviets, and on Workers and Peasants Inspection Committees. Many, including Anna Schmidt's father on the newly formed Red Star collective farm in Margenau, served as kolkhoz chairmen or in other executive capacities. At least two Mennonites, Heinrich G. Rempel and Johann P. Quiring, joined the Communist Party as members of the powerful regional (*raion*) executive committees. Such involvement may have helped to normalize the collectivization process, especially at a time when many of these same individuals eliminated opposition voices as they oversaw the removal of ministers and other Mennonite community leaders.[36]

There may have been other reasons why Mennonites collectivized when they did, including the hope that prosperous families might be able to avoid dekulakization if they freely gave their holdings to the kolkhoz and quietly merged into the collective. State officials raised taxes in 1930 to an exorbitant level for the recalcitrant, both in goods and in rubles, such that survival depended upon their willingness to join. Mennonites also took advantage of a Stalinist concession to allow individual kolkhoz members to maintain their own yards where they grew vegetables and raised a few chickens, pigs, and even a cow or two, which dramatically increased the chances of survival, especially in the early 1930s when life itself hung in the balance.[37]

Even so, collectivization led to a massive famine in 1932–3 across the grain-producing regions of the Soviet Union, most especially in Soviet Ukraine, Kazakhstan, and the Trans-Volga; all areas where Mennonites lived. Several factors combined to bring this calamity about, above all the devastatingly high grain quotas seized by the state from all producers. Weather turned particularly harsh in the early 1930s, with scorching heat in the summer and minimal precipitation. Also, immense stockpiles of seized grain rotted alongside railway stations in 1932, the victim of Soviet inefficiency, as officials waited for trains to haul goods away for export or to feed urban consumers. Still other farmers destroyed their working livestock rather than surrender it to the newly formed collective farms. Local officials warned Moscow by the fall of 1932 that the countryside faced imminent disaster, yet Stalin blamed kulaks and weak-kneed Communist officials for all shortfalls. The first reports of famine arose in Kazakhstan in 1931 and Soviet Ukraine in December 1932, yet the party only redoubled its efforts to destroy alleged saboteurs.[38] How did it effect Mennonites in the Soviet Union?

In a tragic sense, Mennonites did not always notice the famine given that correspondents wrote of persistent hunger throughout the first half of the 1930s. In letter after letter they sadly informed relations abroad that they starved for food all year long. Even when they realized modest yields from their own produce the state claimed them as quotas increased to the point where officials even seized seed grain and feed intended for working livestock. If anything, conditions worsened in the

Gulag, where prisoners were often responsible for their own foods. This was the world in which Anna Ivanovna Schmidt of Margenau learned to eat weeds to stay alive. Preserved family photos of this period attest to the emaciated physiques and gaunt faces.[39]

Even so relatively few Mennonites in Soviet Ukraine died of famine in 1932–3. By one recent estimate, 2–7 per cent of Mennonites in the Republic perished in those years, whereas the percentage is from 15 to 30 per cent for Ukrainian nationals and even higher in Kazakhstan. Peter Letkemann puts the figure closer to 1 per cent of Mennonite famine deaths. Several factors present themselves for why this is so, including the fact that the Ukrainian lands most hit by famine were further north, near Kiev and Kharkov.[40]

Mennonites sentenced to the "Special Settlements" of the Gulag undoubtedly experienced the worst brunt of the famine, and most especially in Kazakhstan, where fully one-third of the population perished from 1931 to 1933. Often those deported ended up in places where local officials were ill equipped to house and feed them. Many starved from neglect, not design. Mennonites in a camp near Tomsk reported up to five exiles died each day of starvation as early as 1930. Another reported that up to twelve children per day died in their camp, and high rates were also recorded at a camp near Tiazhin. Still others struggled to cope as "famine refugees" flooded the cities, including Karaganda, where they searched for food. Security police in January 1933 at the height of famine in the region reported on hordes of begging children who congregated in cities. The starving coalesced into small groups which attacked local shoppers and bakery shops. People died in the streets from starvation; others fought with what strength they had for scraps of food that had been tossed out. Observers saw buildings where the dead had been stacked like firewood. Once again conditions worsened as one entered the camps, including Karlag near Karaganda. Lack of food and inadequate sanitation in 1932–3 especially resulted in high rates of mortality from "typhus, scurvy, grippe, tuberculosis, dysentery, scarlet fever and pneumonia."[41]

The famine provided officials with one more opportunity to focus on Mennonite ministers, many of whom they now accused of inciting anti-Soviet behaviour. For example, the Siberian court located in Omsk on 31 October 1934 sentenced two Mennonite ministers, Jakob Boldt (Yakov Bol'dt) and Dietrich Koop (Ditrikh Koop) to be executed. Court documents describe Boldt (34) and Koop (44) as literate, not CPSU members, and individuals who had previously been deprived of their civil rights because of their role as ministers in a religious cult. Their crime? Both had fomented counter-revolutionary agitation under the cloak of religious observance among the Mennonite Brethren in their community.[42]

For Mennonites from Chortitza to Karaganda, then, it is perhaps more appropriate to describe the years from 1929 to 1935 as years of great hunger for all and devastation for many.[43] There is no doubt that Mennonites benefited when they successfully appealed in their plight to foreign agencies for food aid, most especially from Weimar Germany. Amazingly enough, German relief agencies sprang into action and provided much-needed assistance to Mennonites and Germans in the Soviet Union until at least 1935. In the process, however, German assistance proved deadly for Mennonites and Germans, especially after 1933. It did not help that Soviet authorities rejected the very language of famine and faulted Mennonites for having placed anti-Soviet agitators from among their numbers into leadership positions of the newly formed kolkhozes. A Soviet reckoning would not be long in coming.[44]

Mennonite Agency in a Time of Peril

The vast majority of Mennonites experienced the Stalinist revolution as deprivation and tragedy. Thousands died and thousands more saw their churches closed, their farmsteads obliterated, their ministers exiled, and their families torn apart. Nor were they alone on this Bolshevik assault on the countryside. At the same time Russian historians have challenged the portrayal of peasants solely as victims, not actors, amid crisis. The same applies to Mennonites, as we can see several key strategies by which they claimed agency amid the horrors unleashed at the end of NEP.[45] We briefly consider three of these here: faith, flight, and accommodation.

Faith

In a letter written on 10 May 1934 to relatives in Canada Maria Regehr struggled to explain the deeper meaning of why she and her family had ended up in the Soviet Gulag: "Thank God that he has led his dear child into the wilderness, for here in this deep, sincere silence He is alone with you, and His Word and His nearness will be everything to you." She also takes comfort in a poem she recently received from Canadian relations, which reminded her of Christ's own assurance that His full blessing would come once she had passed through this tribulation. Later, in the same letter, Maria expressed regret that her Gulag labour denied her the opportunity to attend an Ascension Day service, though perhaps that opportunity still lay in the future. After all, "All things are possible with God, even if things loom so dismally before us."[46]

Lynne Viola has observed that peasant expressions of protest turned Christian and apocalyptic as they struggled against the Stalinist state during collectivization. Such discourse restored their agency and allowed them to profess that their final victory was certain.[47] Many Mennonite clearly held to similar beliefs, which is why countless mothers and grandparents worked tirelessly to inculcate their children in the Christian faith, even after the state had outlawed such activity. Maria Regehr's correspondence repeatedly stressed God's omnipotence, itself an essentialist rebuke of the Stalinist regime. Her reference to Ascension Day rooted her faith clearly in the Lordship of Christ. It grounded her in the conviction that Christians had nothing to fear, as even the tragedies of this time only happened because God had ordained them. In the fullness of time He would set matters right.

Across the Soviet Union and in the former Molotschna settlement, Peter Rahn made similar declarations at the very same time. In a letter dated 23 December 1933 Rahn assured his readers that he and his family remained secure in God's hands, as not a hair on their heads would be disturbed unless God himself willed it. Rahn thanks God for his good health. God protects. God alone holds the future in His hands. Jesus will save those who put their faith in Him. On many occasions Rahn simply inserts a Bible verse without comment, confident that his readers would know its import.[48]

In a deeply personal article written on the anniversary of his father's arrest, Harry Loewen suggests that Mennonite faith went from corporate to individual under Stalinism, as ministers and church life disappeared and the state implemented the seven-day work week.[49] There is some truth to that, of course, as Mennonites joined all Soviet Christians in this assault on their corporate beliefs. Yet, at the same time, available evidence suggests that the corporate body of faith did not disappear altogether among Mennonites. Even as the Soviet state shuttered village churches, most Mennonites during the Stalinist years took solace – and received material aid – from a growing worldwide communion of co-religionists that stretched across Asia and Europe to North and South America. Equally striking, countless Mennonites who lived across the globe responded with words of comfort, gifts of hard currency, and food packets even as they themselves struggled through a worldwide depression.

Those who read their Bibles, considered prized possessions in the Gulag, also understood their lives connected to an even larger communion, one that stretched back to the children of Israel in Old Testament times. We see this as they repeatedly claimed the Davidic psalms of lament and assurance as words intended for them, and as they took comfort in the exilic writings of Isaiah, which prophesied God's imminent restoration of the faithful remnant from devastation. As with Anna Ivanovna's childhood experiences in Margenau, mothers risked their own lives when they told their children Bible stories at night instead of fairy tales.

Many Mennonites also clung to their corporate ecclesial faith. Even as the state began to arrest Mennonite ministers after 1928, others stepped forward to take their place, as happened with Wladimir Janzen. Born in the Molotschna village of Tiege in 1900, the Ohrloff-Lichtenau Congregation elected Janzen as minister in 1929 despite the threat of imminent danger. He soon disappeared into the Gulag. Minister David H. Epp baptized one hundred candidates in Chortitza on 8 June 1930, well into the Stalinist chronological danger zone. The few Mennonite ministers who remained in Soviet Ukraine after 1930 continued to press authorities for conscientious objector status and a corresponding non-military role for their parishioners, even after the state had outlawed such exemptions and exiled their advocates. When police locked church buildings Mennonites sought out empty granaries for worship, as happened in Kleefeld of Molotschna.[50]

Even as authorities snuffed out congregational life in the existing Mennonite villages it reappeared in the Gulag where exiled Mennonite ministers met, if only initially for shared prayer under the open sky, though gradually they formed provisional worshipping communities. They formed these in communion with their Baptist and Evangelical counterparts, though it did not take long for many Mennonites at least to worship on their own. By 1931 Mennonites in the Karaganda region had already formed a choir and begun to worship together, much to the chagrin of authorities who sent spies to infiltrate these gatherings. Exiled preachers I. Penner, J. Bergman, and A. Tövs (Toews) provided initial leadership, as small groups met in Bergman's and other lodgings in the Karaganda suburb of Maiuduk for Bible reading, prayer, and exhortation, that is, until secret police arrested them in 1934.[51]

The Flight to Moscow, 1928–9

Mennonites in the 1920s viewed emigration as a legitimate and providential response to their mounting challenges, though no moment captured this more dramatically than the rush to Moscow in 1929. Secret police based in Siberia reported on 10 August 1929 that emigration fever had gripped the tens of thousands of German colonists in the vicinity of

Omsk and Slavgorod. Mennonite sectarians comprised the great majority of those identified. The report noted that such a worrisome development reflected the leadership role played by ministers and kulak elements in their midst, as well as the failure of Soviet institutions to establish a secure foothold in their far-flung communities. Many of these Mennonites had applied for passports to emigrate to Canada and the United States, fuelled by the rumoured support of foreign agencies, the new American president Herbert Hoover, and the persistent activity of banned Mennonite agencies in Siberia itself. Still other Mennonites had relocated to the Soviet Union's Pacific region, where they hoped to cross over to China and thereafter proceed to North America. The report concluded that the Japanese government and fugitives of the White Army living abroad assisted these sectarians, who had become a beachhead for counter-revolutionary forces who sought a foothold in the USSR.[52]

There was some truth in that report, certainly when it came to the emigration fever among Siberian Mennonites in 1929. This fever began the previous year when Mennonites in that vast region reacted to the onset of the draconian Ural-Siberian method of forced grain collection. As peasant protest irrupted, some seventy Mennonite families fled in November 1928 to Moscow after local authorities had denied them exit visas. In desperation they sold their possessions and hid out in Moscow's outlying districts, where they daily begged officials for permission to emigrate. Over six months they spent their last rubles on what food was available, worked at odd jobs, and slept under the open sky or in apartments as they steadfastly sought exit visas. Soviet authorities eventually granted all seventy permission to emigrate.

The news spread like wildfire among the Mennonite settlements in the spring of 1929, such that by the end of the year approximately 13,000 had flocked to Moscow in search of their own exit visas, of whom an estimated 10,000 were Mennonites. They travelled from almost fifty-nine settlements in Siberia but also from the Caucasus, Kuban, Memrik, Crimea, and Alt Samara, and they settled in the burgeoning settlements and suburbs which surrounded Moscow.[53] Much to the embarrassment of Soviet authorities, state representatives from Canada and Weimar Germany soon entered the fray. Mennonites also made successive representations to elite political agencies and actors, including Lenin's widow Krupskaia, the writer Maxim Gorky, and the Politburo. The later body finally acted on 18 October 1929 when it objected to any further Mennonite emigration. Stalin himself signed the order, though by then Canada had withdrawn its invitation to take more as the Great Depression took hold.

In the end, Soviet officials relented yet again as they granted three thousand Mennonites exit visas and permitted them to accept the offer of a new home in Paraguay, where they settled on the state's frontier, the Chaco. But by November 1929 the Politburo served notice that it would issue no more exit visas, as it ordered the remaining eight thousand Mennonites to return to their home settlements or directly into internal exile. Officials now rounded them up in the thousands, deposited them onto cattle cars for forced relocation east, often well beyond their home settlements. Even so, Mennonites continued to lobby for the right to emigrate well into the 1930s, even after most doors in the west had closed. Soviet secret police continued to report on this emigration fever. As late as 4 January 1931 the Soviet Secret Police in western Siberia reported on the activities of I.I. Tevs (Toews) and Ia.I. Teikhrib (Teichrob), two Mennonites who continued to agitate among Mennonites for the right to emigrate to America. The report noted again that anti-Soviet elements led by Mennonite kulaks and ministers had orchestrated these illegal activities.[54] The emigration fever of the late 1920s and early 1930s reinforced Bolshevik perceptions that Mennonites had largely failed to transform into good Soviet citizens. Of course, that was not the case in all instances.

Accommodation: "Speaking Bolshevik"

In a groundbreaking study that urged a rethinking of the Stalinist revolution, Stephen Kotkin introduced the notion of "speaking Bolshevik," by which workers in Magnitogorsk learned how to speak the "proper words," even with "some degree of internalization" as they performed tasks which suggested loyalty to the regime. In the process they shaped Bolshevism on the ground, as much as it shaped them. Did they believe in the Stalinist cause when they "spoke Bolshevik," or was it all a ruse? Could it be both at once? Kotkin appears to leave us with some uncertainty, as he suggests that the workers themselves could not always be sure. In Sheila Fitzpatrick's terms, perhaps most citizens who spoke Bolshevik only gave the impression of loyalty as they concealed their true feelings through the use of performative masks. Elsewhere Fitzpatrick suggests that peasants became involved in collectivization for two different reasons: they either sought to maintain their traditional ways by only appearing to accept the new system, or they attempted to use collectivization to their advantage, either by becoming its champions or when they abandoned all initiative as they morphed from successful agriculturalists into "welfare-state recipients."[55]

Likewise, Mennonites learned how to speak Bolshevik in the Stalinist era and for a complex set of reasons. Anna Schmidt and countless others recalled how Mennonite *kolkhozniks* (collective farm workers) were everywhere in the 1930s. They milked cows on the new kolkhozes, oversaw seeding operations, drove and maintained implements and tractors, and gathered the harvests. Even in Karlag, the gigantic Karaganda labour camp, Mennonite Abram Berg played a key role in the cattle-breeding division so essential to the food chain of the region's burgeoning coal industry. Colin Neufeldt has written about the hundreds of Mennonites who worked within the state bureaucracy which made collectivization and dekulakization happen.[56]

Mennonites spoke Bolshevik when they denounced German efforts to supply Soviet citizens with material aid during the famine years, especially after Hitler's rise to power in 1933. Soviet officials deemed any reports of famine to be treasonous and they were particularly sensitive to the role Germans and Mennonites might play in destabilizing the Soviet state. Archival records suggest that many Mennonites made a public demonstration of their rejection of (German) aid as they insisted that reports of famine had been overblown. In a typical instance, Mennonites from the village of Miroliubovka of Isil'kulsk district of Siberia publicly informed the German consul that they "categorically rejected any assistance from Fascist Germany." As prosperous collective farmers they simply had no need of it. Moreover, they claimed, Germany had robbed its own workers to make those funds available for Soviet citizens. Those funds should now be directed to the working poor of Germany and Austria and not sent to the Soviet Union for trumped up reasons.[57]

The decision to construct the Dnepostroi dam across the Dnieper River adjacent to the Chortitza Mennonite settlement in Soviet Ukraine profoundly transformed Mennonite life. The construction was the industrial centrepiece of the First Five Year plan, though work had begun by 1927 already. Hundreds of Mennonites laboured on the massive construction project as engineers, artisans, and labourers, including scores of young men who undertook non-military service there thanks to the interventions of the few remaining Mennonite ministers. The new dam transformed the regional centre of Alexandrovsk into an industrial powerhouse with a new name, Zaporozhe. It figuratively swallowed up the former Mennonite village of Schönwiese and literally swallowed up the former Mennonite village of Einlage when engineers raised the water levels on the Dnieper above the dam once it was completed.[58] The completed Dnepostroi dam was the largest dam in Europe upon completion and one of the largest in the world. Soviet citizens took great pride in it, including Mennonite children like Anna Schmidt's brother Georg, whose school class travelled to see the new engineering marvel.

A construction project so close to Chortitza further integrated Mennonites into the larger Soviet society even without having left their villages. Officials awarded Peter Dyck, Gerhard Hamm, and Kornelius Pauls the prestigious Order of Lenin after they developed a state-of-the-art assembly line for the mass production of agricultural combines in Zaporozhe. Ivan (Hans) Werner devised a more efficient system for maximum proficiency in Soviet tractors, for which officials presented him with an award that included a trip to Moscow and coupons for the purchase there of highly prized consumer goods. The arrival of thousands of workers, including American engineers and Soviet experts, coincided with a dekulakization drive which left many homes empty. Russians and Ukrainians filled the void as they settled in villages that had long been exclusively Mennonite. There are numerous accounts of close relations between Mennonites and the new residents, to the point where Russians and Ukrainians decades later still recalled having learned Plaudietsch as they interacted with their new neighbours.[59]

What sense can we make of Mennonites "speaking Bolshevik"? Did Mennonites do little more than wear masks as they feigned Soviet engagement, or did many convert to a progressive, atheistic, and Bolshevik world view as captured by Jochen Hellbeck.[60] Though unknown numbers undoubtedly wore masks of deception, there are nevertheless two ways by which Mennonites converted to a new world view. By the first, some Mennonites did become apostles for the Bolshevik cause, whether as engineers, labourers, kolkhoz chairmen, and so on. Many of these may well have abandoned religious belief as they acculturated. We know from Susan Toews's diary entries that increasing numbers of Mennonite youth suffered from a lack of religious instruction. In her words, "if they are to locate the Gospel of Luke many search in the Old Testament and do not find it." Historians have demonstrated the degree to which Mennonite actors made the Stalinist revolution possible in the Mennonite heartland. For example, Nikolai Boldt joined the Communist Party in 1918 and after stints of service in the Red Army ended up as chair of the Hierschau (Molotschna) kolkhoz, where he oversaw dekulakization and collectivization. David Johann Reimer, originally of Chortitza, abandoned his Mennonite faith shortly after the revolution. He continued his studies and around 1930 published several works under the pseudonym Reinmarus in which he denounced Mennonites for the unfair advantages they had long enjoyed from imperial to early Soviet times.[61] Nor was he alone, as David Schellenberg and Gerhard

Sawatsky also left their faith behind after 1917 as they threw their lot in with the Soviet state.

There are hints in the extant literature which suggest that Mennonites integrated into Soviet society in a second and very different way from what Moscow intended. It is best captured by Moshe Lewin's evocative suggestion that Soviet society became a "quicksand society" in the 1930s. Officials maybe got what they wanted when the countryside collectivized, but not in a manner which yielded the New Soviet Man as they had expected. Instead, Socialist society bogged down as Soviet inefficiencies and indifference proliferated. In the Mennonite context, this may have been the decade where countless Mennonites jettisoned Weber's Protestant work ethic in favour of Soviet lethargy.[62]

We get a sense of this shift in Susan Toews's correspondence from Ohrloff village in the 1930s. She reports on 3 May 1929 that Mennonites have not taken well to collectivization: "the interest and enthusiasm for work is lacking here. One fulfils one's obligations but that is about all." Later she laments that people seem overwhelmed by chaos, and rather than subdue it they prefer to work enough just to survive. She observes that people are broken when they realize that "all struggle and opposition" is of no avail. Instead they begin to work mechanically. "You go as far as they push you, not further." No wonder, she laments, that theft is commonplace, piles of grains rot in storage, and weeds overwhelm once prosperous orchards. People have lost their will.[63]

In his reflection on Mennonite involvement in the Soviet system Colin Neufeldt offers several additional reasons for why Mennonites became active within the Soviet system. Some sought employment so they could survive through a measure of job security. Others hoped state employment would conceal their kulak roots and keep them out of the Gulag. Still others understood that their only means of safeguarding the larger Mennonite community – one that had been so devastated from 1917 to 1922 – was through state service in state institutions, especially at a time when the state owned literally everything.[64]

In sum Mennonite society had experienced a tidal wave of change by 1934 as the NEP years gave way to a three-pronged Stalinist revolution. Thousands did not survive, and thousands more managed to emigrate at the eleventh hour. Even so, and coincidental with this widespread devastation, Mennonites proved to be more than victims as they adjusted to a new world and as they sought to make of it what they could. Though no one would have believed it, an even greater tribulation lay ahead.

Chapter Twelve

The Road to Rochegda: Soviet Terror, Nazi Occupation, and Stalinist Repatriation, 1934–1953

Georgii Ivanovich Schmidt – known as Georg to his family – reached the end of the road on 8 October 1945 when he arrived in Rochegda, a Gulag labour camp situated in Arkhangelsk oblast in the far north of European Russia. On the last leg of his journey the "road" was actually the Northern Dvina River, as Georg's party of approximately four hundred repatriated prisoners travelled down its freezing waters on a side-wheeled steamboat.[1]

If the road to Rochegda ended for Georg in October 1945, when and where did it begin? Such a question is difficult to answer. On the one hand, it began on 28 January 1945 in the village of Schrimm (Śrem in Polish) midway between Warsaw and Berlin, where Georg, his mother Katharina, and his sister Anna had stopped for food and water along with thousands of other desperate refugees. Suddenly German soldiers sounded the alarm for all to flee the village as Soviet troops had appeared on its outskirts. Panic ensued. German troops ordered one person from each party to stay behind with the horse-drawn wagons while the rest fled on foot westward out of the city. So it was that Georg, the oldest male of this fatherless family, stayed behind, and in that moment lost all contact with his mother and sister, who disappeared into a vast sea of humanity.

Georg continued to travel west for several days as he searched in vain for the rest of his family. He even managed to cross the Oder River, reach Berlin itself, and travel more than 100 kilometres beyond it, but soon thereafter the Soviet army overran and detained him and his party of fellow-Mennonite *Flüchtlinge*. His hope of a reunion with his mother and sister dashed, Georg next hoped that Soviet authorities would send him and the others back to the Molotschna settlement and his home village of Margenau. But soldiers of the Red Army soon rid him of that notion. Instead, authorities shipped Georg and the other detainees by truck, train, and side-wheeled steamboat until they reached the end of the road, Rochegda.

There is another way to answer when exactly Georg Schmidt started out on the road to Rochegda. By this routing, the road began in December 1934, when Georg's teacher somberly informed his Grade One class in the Ukrainian Soviet Republic that someone had assassinated Sergei Kirov, First Secretary of the Communist Party, in Leningrad. Much followed from that one death. This chapter takes this second approach as it considers the Mennonite experience through three distinct periods between 1934 and 1953. First we consider the rebranding of Mennonites that coincided with Hitler's rise to power in 1933 and the murder of Kirov in 1934, one that culminated in the Great Terror of 1936–8 when the Soviet state decimated Mennonite settlements as part of a massive operation which saw hundreds of thousands of Soviet citizens banished into the Gulag and up to 1.2 million executed. Second, we consider Nazi Germany's invasion of the Soviet Union in June 1941 and its multifaceted impact on the Soviet Mennonite population. In this section we address the role played by Mennonites in the widespread attempt to exterminate all Jews during the Nazi occupation of southern Ukraine. Third we consider what happened to Mennonites in Soviet Ukraine after a rejuvenated and ferocious Soviet army ended the Nazi occupation and followed the retreating fascist forces to Berlin and beyond; far enough, in fact, to overtake Georg and hundreds of thousands of Germans and others fleeing its advance in January 1945.

From Terror to the Great Terror, 1934–8

Sergei Kirov's assassination on 1 December 1934 set off a tidal wave of arrests in the Soviet Union as Stalin personally oversaw the investigation into the death of arguably the second most powerful person in the USSR. Stalin demanded swift retribution for those whose wilfulness or negligence contributed to Kirov's death. He appointed Nikolai Yezhov to oversee the criminal investigation and issued a series of draconian laws which streamlined the judicial process. Within weeks the state had executed its first wave of convicted co-conspirators allegedly tied to the actual assassin, Nikolai Nikolaev.[2] Many more arrests followed. Within a year Yezhov had overseen the trials and imprisonment of previously elite Bolsheviks, including Lenin's comrades Grigory Zinoviev and Lev Kamenev. All confessed to their roles in the plot to assassinate Kirov and destabilize the Soviet Union. All confessions were undoubtedly bogus.

All of this might have been of little consequence to Soviet Mennonites had it not been for one event that occurred in another country almost two years before an embittered loner named Nikolaev shot and killed Kirov as he walked to his office in the Smolny Institute, his bodyguard mysteriously absent. That earlier event unfolded in Germany on 30 January 1933 when the aging German president Paul Hindenburg appointed Adolf Hitler as chancellor. By March Hitler had assumed near dictatorial powers as he sidelined the Reichstag through a series of so-called temporary measures. From the outset Hitler made no secret of his desire to establish a greater German Reich – a *Lebensraum* essential for its survival – by means of a rapid eastward expansion into Poland and the Soviet Union. He coupled his ideological disdain for communism with an animus towards all Slavs and Jews who peopled the lands of his envisioned "thousand-year Reich." By his reckoning, Nazis would need to clear the newly conquered lands of such scum except for a well-managed slave labour sector drawn from the ranks of the conquered and placed under Germany's complete control. But one way or another, Nazi Germany's future lay in the east.

Almost immediately Stalin responded in two complementary ways to Hitler's rise to power. By the first, he sought an international alliance against Nazi aggression, symbolized by the Soviet decision to enter the League of Nations on 18 September 1934, eleven months after Nazi Germany had unilaterally quit the League. He worked diligently to establish defensive pacts with a variety of European states, all intended to blunt Hitler's plans. Stalin adopted a second anti-Nazi strategy when he began to search for a fifth column of Nazi sympathizers within the Soviet Union itself. For the most part, he believed all Soviet Germans posed such a threat and, not surprisingly, his subordinates agreed as they began to hunt out and eradicate those Germans who allegedly sought to undermine the USSR from within. On 4 November 1934 Stalin sent a memo to Party leaders in all regions with German concentrations. It stated:[3]

> The Central Committee of the Communist Party has received information that in the regions, settled by Germans, in recent times, anti-Soviet elements have become more active and are openly carrying out counter-revolutionary work. Moreover, local Party organs and the organs of the NKVD [that is, the secret police] are reacting to these activities extremely weakly, in reality therefore aiding them, completely mistakenly thinking that our foreign policy requires such concessions to the Germans or other nationalities living in the USSR who are violating the principle of elementary loyalty to Soviet power.

... The Central Committee considers such behavior on the part of the Party and local organs and the NKVD completely incorrect and suggests that they immediately take repressive measures against the most active counter-revolutionary and anti-Soviet elements, carry out arrests, deportations and for notorious leaders, sentence to execution ... explain to the population [of these regions] that even the smallest attempt at anti-Soviet activity will not be tolerated ... the local organs should demand from the population a complete end to all ties with foreign bourgeois fascist organizations, the receipt of money or packages.

It is enormously significant to this history that security police and Soviet officials identified Mennonites as Germans from the outset as they hunted for anti-Soviet elements, a designation that took on even more weight given the disproportionate role Mennonites previously played as class-based kulaks and merchant-capitalists. All accepted that "Mennonite" could be determined by a person's last name, as would most Mennonite historians who followed in their wake. This is of immense significance when we come to Mennonites as agents of the Soviet state or the Nazi occupation as we may, in fact, be dealing with individuals who had denounced their particular Mennonite history or heritage, let alone their faith.

So that proviso aside, documents gathered by Andrei Savin make plain that officials identified Siberian Mennonites already as anti-Soviet in 1934 and 1935, and for several reasons. They argued that Mennonites continued to accept money from Nazi Germany on the bogus pretext that they suffered from ongoing famine-like conditions. As a result, hundreds of Mennonites regularly received cash payments from a German regime that used those gifts to drive a wedge between Mennonites and the Soviet state. Such ongoing German contacts also encouraged the persistence of "emigration fever" among Mennonites and weakened their ties to the new kolkhozes and the Soviet state. In an equally alarming development, former Mennonite ministers, kulaks, and merchant capitalists had all infiltrated kolkhozes and transformed these Soviet bodies into sinister anti-Soviet organizations. Mennonite insistence on German-language discourse had further alienated them from loyal Soviet elements, as did the ongoing influence of those whose fathers had fought for the White Army or been banished as kulaks. Similar charges surfaced in Soviet Ukraine. In the case of Jacob A. Neufeld, the courts charged him and twenty-six others with participation in a secret counter-revolutionary organization working with Nazi Germany in support of a Hitlerite invasion of the Soviet Union. According to Harvey Dyck, the police linked that purported organization with Neufeld's role in the executive of the banned Verband which had been legally active in the 1920s. Soviet investigators claimed that the Verband still existed, though now illegally and surreptitiously as a leading voice in a broader pan-German anti-Soviet conspiracy. Authorities also re-indicted those already banished, as happened in Karaganda on 4 October 1934 when they charged Petr Vins (Wiens), Abram Vins, IUlius (Julius) Bergman, Ivan Penner, Artur Tevs (Toews), David Frese (Froese), and IAkov (Jakob) Mattis (Mathies) with having formed a counter-revolutionary group which met regularly on evenings to undermine Soviet authority. The indictment alleged that they had spread slanderous information about the "Special Settlements" (Gulag) to correspondents in Germany, America, Switzerland, and Holland.[4]

In some ways, these charges emerged naturally out of those directed against Mennonites from the start of the Stalinist revolution. Once again, the state focused on those identified as former kulaks and capitalists as well as Mennonite ministers and Ältesters, including Wladimir Janzen of the Ohrloff Congregation in Molotschna, and Heinrich Winter of Chortitza, both of whom we encountered in the previous chapter. NKVD agents arrested Winter on 26 April 1935 for alleged counter-revolutionary activity and transported him first to Zaporozhe and later Dnepropetrovsk for trial.[5] One dramatic change stood out after 1934, however, as the state previously had linked prosecuted Mennonites and others as kulaks, for their role as spiritual leaders in opposition to a Soviet cultural revolution grounded in atheism. By 1934 it had escalated to where officials now routinely charged Mennonites and others with anti-Soviet and counter-revolutionary activity, and not as kulaks. Those convicted also faced correspondingly stiffer penalties.

In his comprehensive investigation of arrests in the 1930s, Peter Letkemann concludes that authorities exiled relatively few Mennonites from 1933 to the middle of 1936. They arrested seventy in villages on the right bank Dnieper during these years, for example, and thirty persons in 1933 in the Zentral settlement situated between Voronezh and Saratov in the Russian republic. Of these, twenty-two returned home in 1936 after a three-year term, a pattern evident across the Mennonite settlements in terms of length of term.[6] At the same time, the state executed few Mennonites before 1936 despite the severity of the charges brought against them. But that was about to change.

The Soviet Union initiated a new and more devastating assault on Mennonites in the mid-1930s when it began to deport Germans and Poles en masse from its western borderlands. In what Terry Martin calls the onset of Soviet ethnic cleansing, NKVD agents claimed that anti-Soviet saboteurs had immersed themselves in both nationalities. Moscow, in response, called for local officials to exterminate ringleaders and deport Germans and Poles en masse deep into the Soviet interior. Initially Moscow focused on its western borderlands where police agents identified entire populations of Germans and Poles as extreme security threats to the Soviet state. The only solution, they claimed, was forcibly and immediately to remove these peoples. So, it happened. In the first few months of 1935 the Soviet state deported 35,000 people from western Ukraine, of which Kate Brown identifies 57 per cent as ethnic Poles and Germans, even though both ethnicities comprised a small number of the local population compared to Ukrainians themselves. Soviet ethnic cleansing had begun, even at a pace greater than what Moscow had imposed in its quotas and criteria. In the next three years Martin has identified no fewer than nine nationalities that the Soviets forcibly relocated: Poles, Finns, Latvians, Estonians, Koreans, Chinese, Kurds, Iranians, and Germans.[7]

Mennonites understood, of course, that the Soviet state had already subsumed them under the German ethnos, yet they escaped much harm initially as the NKVD focused on the borderlands. All of that changed with the onset of the so-called Great Terror in the fall of 1936 when Stalin appointed Yezhov, the very person who had overseen the investigation of the Kirov murder, as new commissar of the NKVD. Yezhov instantly intensified the search for purported enemies of the Soviet state, so much so that historian J. Arch Getty has identified the entire period as the *Yezhovshchina*.[8] Yezhov oversaw the arrest, trial, and execution of virtually the entire old Bolshevik guard, many of whom, like Zinoviev and Kamenev, had already pleaded guilty to their involvement in a plot to assassinate Kirov. The party hunted down assumed spies within its own ranks as well as in the larger society, and once again "enemy nations" featured prominently. Moscow set quotas for the number of anticipated spies that security police should execute, and the number who deserved long prison sentences, ideally in both instances after the accused had signed confessions of guilt. Once again local officials worked zealously to over-fulfil these quotas.[9]

By the best estimates state security officials arrested some 1.6 million people during the Great Terror, of which they executed a staggering 700,000. Of those not executed we simply do not know how many were tortured to death. We do know that the Gulag prison system almost tripled from a population of 334,300 in 1933 – the year Hitler came to power – to 1,317,195 at the start of 1939.[10]

How many of these were Mennonites? Peter Letkemann concludes that the state arrested approximately 8–9 per cent of all Mennonites, whereas it arrested an estimated 1.5 per cent of the general populace. One can reasonably conclude that children comprised half of the estimated 90,000–100,000 Mennonites in the Soviet Union at the time, and we know that men comprised the vast majority of those arrested. Upon this basis, Letkemann concludes police arrested up to half of all adult Mennonite men during the Great Terror and executed up to half of those arrested. As with the larger society, arrests increased already in 1936, though primarily in the villages of Einlage (thirty-one arrests) and Khortitsa (twelve) adjacent the new industrial powerhouse of Zaporozhe.[11]

Elite Politburo members Khrushchev, Molotov, and Yezhov signalled the start of an intensified purge cycle in August 1937 when they arrived in Kiev to oversee a purge of party members in Ukraine. In lockstep, police arrested sixty-two Mennonites in Einlage between August and the end of the year. More arrests followed as those already detained confessed and named accomplices, all under torture.

For a country so vast it is striking how standardized the arrests became in 1937. The secret police normally arrived in the dead of night, such that many men kept dried snacks (*gerestet Zweiback*) and clothing at the ready. Often a winter sleigh or large black automobile, known everywhere as the dreaded Black Raven, appeared in the village from which several police officers emerged. They pounded on the doors and demanded entry, occasionally accompanied by village witnesses to lend legitimacy to the process. Officials thoroughly searched the homes of these alleged "enemies of the people" and seized Bibles, all religious literature, and especially foreign correspondence, which many had in their possession. By 1937 most men knew they would not return despite occasional assurances to the contrary. So parting words followed with wives and children, and occasionally security police even permitted brief prayers, then off to a prison where interrogations followed, as did torture. The state deemed confessions as essential and sought them by whatever means. Soon thereafter a specially appointed court (a *Troika*) delivered its judgment, and if it pronounced a death sentence it would be undertaken quickly, normally with a single bullet to the back of the skull. The fortunate received prison sentences, which themselves grew steadily throughout the Great Terror, from an initial limit of five years to ten, fifteen, and even twenty, from which few survived. Perhaps the greatest cruelty occurred when secret police re-arrested those sentenced initially in 1932 and 1933 to five-year terms. No one, it seemed, was above suspicion, including the eleven Mennonite factory workers whom security personnel arrested on 8 April 1937, all of whom had previously received the prestigious Order of Lenin for service to the state. Like hundreds of thousands across the Soviet Union, officials now charged the eleven with treasonous activity under Article 58 of the Soviet Criminal Code.[12]

The Great Terror completed what the Stalinist revolution at the start of the decade had begun. Few men remained in the villages by 1939 save for the elderly and infirm. Women in their grief now faced the burden of increased labour demands in the kolkhozes and factories as the state even called youth into active labour service. Most villages lost their coherence by the end of the 1930s. Rumours of Mennonite informants circulated everywhere, such that once-close villagers exchanged little more than pleasantries when they met. In the words of one correspondent: "Everyone is living in fear. One hears constantly of arrests. Because of some insignificant matter a person disappears. No one is spared. I sit at home and go nowhere, so that no one can say anything about me.... People are afraid of one another, they are afraid of their own shadow." Teachers encouraged children to inform authorities of any suspect behaviour in their homes, or if their parents disapproved of Soviet youth clubs. They lionized the exploits of eleven-year-old Pavel Morozov, who had betrayed his own father. Work became more demanding due to the loss of manpower, though now investigators deemed the slightest mishap on the job as an act of terror. Spilt milk, a tractor suddenly unable to work, a broken window; all now became treasonous. No one told jokes. Few conversed about matters of substance. Meanwhile women stood in all conditions in front of prisons day and night in Dnepropetrovsk, Melitopol, Omsk, Saratov, or wherever they believed officials had detained their husbands.[13]

Religious life all but ceased in the Mennonite heartland after the arrests of 1937–8, as the state targeted believers. This reinforced a trend observed at the start of the decade, as those who remained behind largely comprised women in extended households who kept their own counsel, whereas Gulag camps became meeting points for exiled believers. As the state banned German instruction in Mennonite schools in the Mennonite and German heartland the very teachers banned established a German-language school in the coal-rich Kazakhstan city of Karaganda. The stakes were high, as the state executed 1,495 of the 6,228 arrested for counter-revolutionary activity in Karaganda. Even so, those in exile continued in their diaries and correspondence to recall and record treasured Bible verses and hymns, to gather when possible, and to anticipate Christ's return at the end of time.[14]

The Great Patriotic War and Nazi Occupation, 1939–45

Interlude: 1939–41

The purges ended as abruptly as they began, as their termination coincided with Stalin's removal of Yezhov from effective power late in 1938. Soviet agents only executed him in February 1940, by which time the geostrategic world had changed dramatically. The previously unimaginable Molotov–Ribbentrop Non-aggression Pact, signed in Moscow on 23 August 1939, pledged both Nazi Germany and the Soviet Union not to enter into hostilities with the other for a ten-year period. Hitler's armies launched a blistering attack on Poland barely more than a week later, as the war known in the west as the Second World War began.

The dramatic end of the purges coupled with the non-aggression pact brought a temporary halt to anti-German hostilities within the Soviet Union, as both Stalin and Hitler scrambled to divide a defeated Poland. In the spirit of the non-aggression pact, Moscow even banned the Eisenstein film *Alexander Nevsky* because of its overt anti-German message. Mennonites lived these years in the far-flung Gulag or within their devastated communities in moods that were anything but celebratory. Men dominated in the former; women, children, and old men dominated in the latter. The work seemed endless in either setting, but at least the threat of execution and mass arrest receded. Some sentences even came to end at this time as those imprisoned for shorter terms earlier in the thirties returned, including Heinrich Winter of Chortitza, who thrilled to see Moscow decked out for May Day celebrations on his way home.[15] Jacob A. Neufeld returned to Molotschna in February 1939 and described his homecoming later as a gloomy time, with village streets neglected and fathers missing. It tempered his joy-filled reunion, as did his observation that the 1930s transformed the Mennonite character. The years had numbed consciences and moral character, he wrote, and encouraged a greater passivity in social settings. Even so, he hoped a certain spiritual depth might return if the opportunity presented itself. He would soon find out.[16]

Nazi Invasion and Soviet Deportation

The chair of the Engels collective farm near Tokmak abruptly raced onto the fields on 22 June 1941 and urged all kolkhozniks, most of whom were Mennonites, to run to the loudspeaker for an important declaration. Soviet Foreign Minister Molotov spoke to the entire country that day and announced that Nazi Germany had attacked the Soviet Union.

People listened in stunned silence. Jacob A. Neufeld heard the same news but from a different location. He later recorded that he feared both the invasion and what its impact would be for Mennonites.

At three million personnel, Nazi Germany had formed the largest army ever assembled when it invaded the Soviet Union along its poorly defended and ill-prepared border zone. It decimated the Soviet air force on the first day, with most planes still on the ground, and thereafter little hindered its rapid approach to the largest cities in the Soviet Union. Armies of the Third Reich reached Leningrad oblast by early July as Kiev also faced imminent attack. Further south, the German army moved relentlessly across the Black Sea steppe, such that the Dnieper River lay within its grasp by mid-summer, and with it, significant settlements of Mennonites and Germans along with the vaunted Soviet industrial complex which surrounded the Dnepostroi dam. They soon realized that the Soviets had largely destroyed it as they retreated, leaving little of practical value for the Germans.[17]

Mennonites experienced the war in three distinct ways as the Nazi onslaught neared. First, labour demands increased exponentially in factories, kolkhozes, and construction sites. Women, older men, and youth all worked around the clock to increase production and provide sufficient food and military equipment for the vast army summoned by Moscow, much of it volunteer in the initial stages. Second, Soviet authorities subjected all ethnic Germans, by which they incorporated Mennonites, into a labour army (*trudarmei*), one that included women given the paucity of men in German and Mennonite villages.[18] Already in late July Mennonite men and women joined other labour battalions in right bank Ukraine, where they manually dug defensive fortifications, including trenches up to three metres deep and eight wide. They worked at a frantic pace, always supervised by armed guards, that is, until the guards fled in panic as the German forces approached.[19]

The labour army provided a third way for Mennonites to engage with the war effort, and it happened through group deportation. In some ways this flowed smoothly from the Great Terror, but in this instance the Soviets forcibly sought to remove all Mennonites into the interior. Steven Barnes concludes that Soviet Germans comprised "the first and largest" of the Soviet wartime deportations.[20] Though Moscow anticipated the need to deport "socially dangerous" minorities from the start of the Nazi invasion they failed to act with sufficient speed to accomplish this in right bank Ukraine, which involved most of the Chortitza villages. By the time Nazi forces arrived in mid-August the Soviets had only managed to deport fewer than 3,000 of the estimated 14,000 Mennonites in the former Chortitza colony. Soviet troops slowed down the

German advance in the south when they dynamited the Dnepostroi dam and accompanying bridges on 18 August 1941, which made it much more difficult for German troops to move eastward. That single act also ended the forced deportation of Chortitza Mennonites and others, though it did give officials added time to effect Mennonite deportation elsewhere, starting with those who lived on the Crimean Peninsula.

Soviet troops evacuated all 50,000 Germans, Mennonites among them, from Crimea in a single week, from 15 to 22 August 1941, as they herded villagers onto trains destined for the Kazakh Republic. Among Mennonites the army next turned its attention to the Molotschna villages as it forcibly drafted all males between the ages of sixteen and sixty-five into the labour army. They feared that German soldiers in the Soviet army might turn their weapons on their own officers rather than the invading fascists, consistent with rumours of German villagers in the western borderlands who had fired on Soviet troops moving through their region. Fierce fighting delayed the Nazi conquest of the left bank powerhouse of Zaporozhe, though they finally succeeded on 4 October 1941. Two days earlier the Soviets frantically ordered all remaining Mennonites in the Molotschna settlement to prepare for immediate evacuation. They managed successfully to deport the southern villages in their entirety via the Mennonite-built Stulnevo train station in early October. The remaining villagers now congregated at the Stulnevo station only to find that the Soviets had no rail cars at the ready to remove them. So up to six thousand mainly women and children waited on site for days, such that the German troops reached the train station before the final Molotschna deportation began. Instead it was the Soviet troops who fled after several days of fierce combat with the Nazis as soldiers and warplanes fought in a deadly combat. When it had ended, Mennonites returned home to the villages which had begun part of the German occupation zone. Georg Schmidt, whose war road would end in Rochegda, was one of those who now returned to his home village of Margenau, along with his sister Anna and mother Katharina.[21]

Soviet deportation of Mennonites in the Russian republic proved equally haphazard as the army deported the Am Trakt and Alt-Samara settlements eastward and out of the Trans-Volga region. Those in Orenburg and Neu-Samara stayed behind, though all faced horrific conditions as Soviet demands for the war effort increased exponentially. By some estimates half of all those deported died in transit or soon thereafter in the harsh conditions that met them, consistent with mortality rates experienced by other deported nationalities. In sum, Peter Letkemann estimates that Soviet authorities deported 28,000 Mennonites by the end of 1941, itself a relatively small drop in the 894,000 Germans deported in this same period.[22]

Mennonites and the Nazi Occupation, 1941–3

Mennonites in Soviet Ukraine joined the republic's German, Ukrainian, and Russian peasants and countless others when they welcomed the arriving German armies in 1941. As Johannes Due Enstad concludes in his investigation of peasants during the occupation in the Russian north-west, we simply cannot say whether this behaviour "was motivated by a traditional obligation to receive strangers, sincere gratitude, or an impulse to submit to the new masters of the land."[23] That caveat aside, one can reasonably conclude that Mennonites joined countless others who hoped the war would bring a permanent release from Soviet and Stalinist oppression. Few understood anything in detail about what the Nazis intended to accomplish in their newly acquired lands. Instead, they welcomed the chance to return to some semblance of normalcy after the withering 1930s, even though the elderly among them would have been only cautiously hopeful as they recalled how fleeting the German occupation of 1918 had been and the terrible events which followed. Those who had died in the 1930s did not return with the German occupation, of course, nor did the banished make their way home from internal exile. That aside, Mennonites did gather again to worship, and they re-established a German-language and church-based education. Georg Schmidt's mother Katharina formed a youth choir in her modest home in Margenau and taught choristers Christian hymnody, Georg and his sister Anna among them. Katharina taught them one particular hymn which they sang over and over again. Entitled "This Blessed Day" ("*Das selige Heute'*"), it had a particularly compelling call to faithfulness in the second verse: "God's Word calls you today: 'come, take what Jesus bids you! Everything, everything', can't you hear it? 'Has been prepared for you.'" Kolkhozniks had dismantled the Margenau village church in the 1930s, so an inchoate worshipping community met instead in the kolkhoz community centre. In lieu of preachers the village women chose one of their own to sit weekly on the dais and read from the Bible. Prayer followed, as did hymns led by Katharina's youth choir.

In some communities, such as the Grünfeld village of the former Schlachtin daughter colony, Mennonites restored the church from its temporary use as a grain storage shed. That congregation ordained Peter Sawatzky and Abram Rempel as new pastors, and on Pentecost Sunday of 1942 conducted its first baptismal service in years.[24] Heinrich Winter, the recently released Mennonite minister in Chortitza, convened the first worship service in the Chortitza village of Neuenburg at the end of August 1941 as congregants gathered in an available barn. The text for his first public sermon in years included a verse from I Samuel 7: "thus far has the Lord helped us." Other congregations moved to elect ministers and to have them conduct services and catechism classes. The latter were particularly important, as even many ostensibly baptized adherents had largely acculturated to a Soviet system grounded in atheism and materialist sensitivities. People responded to the call to spiritual renewal, as at least fourteen villages in Chortitza elected new ministers, and in the spring of 1943 congregants elected Heinrich Winter as Ältester. The newly installed ministers soon reaped a rich harvest as they brought ninety-nine forward for baptism in Chortitza in 1942 and over a hundred the following year. A gathering of over three hundred delegates considered, but ultimately failed to overcome, the divide between the Mennonite Brethren and the Kirchengemeinde, though they did agree to share in Christian fellowship as the need arose.[25]

Berlin distinguished between Chortitza and Molotschna when it came to governance as it subsumed the former under the *Reichsministerium für die besetzten Ostgebiete* (Imperial Ministry for the Occupied Eastern Region) directed by Alfred Rosenberg. Mennonites found more latitude within this framework, unlike Molotschna, which Berlin placed directly under the control of the infamous *Schutzstaffel* (SS). This elite Nazi organization initially functioned as a police unit, though it later morphed into a deadly para-military unit (the Waffen SS) under Heinrich Himmler as it became an increasingly autonomous entity, almost a state within a state. The SS aggressively drafted Molotschna Mennonites into service as translators for the units (*Einsatzgruppen*) formed to hunt down and kill Jews and other racial groups and later formed those same Mennonites into military anti-partisan units. It discouraged the re-establishment of Christian worship in Molotschna, something which Nazi propagandists opposed, as its officials moved to reshape the region's Mennonites and Germans into solid citizens of the Reich. Not surprisingly, this caused some tension early in the occupation as Nazi administrators wrestled to seize control of the educational system from Molotschna Mennonites, who soon realized that the Nazis resembled the Soviets in how they threatened faith formation among children and youth.

As in Soviet times Mennonites actively participated in the civil administration of their settlements again, as did Ukrainians and Russians in the occupied zone. A Mennonite, Heinrich Wiebe, served as civil head of the Dnieper industrial giant of Zaporozhe, albeit a giant the Soviets had stripped bare and largely destroyed in their hasty retreat.[26] With some exceptions and administrative inconsistencies, the German troops dismantled the kolkhoz structure when they divided up lands and livestock among villagers. In Grünfeld, for example, each family received a parcel of land. Couples received twenty-one hectares and widows fourteen. The army gave each household a horse when possible, though villagers often shared agricultural implements given their paucity. Mennonites also gained permission to divide the kolkhozes into larger collectives of eight to ten households, and thereby also to combine their inventories. In making these changes it soon became apparent that the occupying troops desperately needed grain and other provisions for their own survival, especially after retreating Soviet troops had torched entire fields ripe for harvest.[27]

German and allied troops billeted in Mennonite homes during the occupation and included the Romanian troops who stayed in Margenau in Georg Schmidt's home. Soldiers bedded down in the one room, whereas Georg slept in the other with his mother and sister. The army set up their mess kitchen in the open yard in the village centre and shared bread when they had it in excess, though they also stole chickens and produce on occasion. Many soldiers attended the worship services, especially the Christmas and Easter services where they sang hymns with Mennonites, and they occasionally appeared in group photos, as in the Easter photo of widow Maria Friesen of Rosental, taken on Easter of 1943.[28]

Of course, the occupation troops had more in mind than photo opportunities, as they expected Mennonites to help secure a permanent German presence in a region that Berlin would incorporate into a Greater Germany as Reichskommissariat Ukraine.[29] From the start Nazi officials included Mennonites in their lists of ethnic Germans. They encouraged Mennonites to claim German citizenship and, as incentive, offered German citizens in occupied Ukraine higher salaries and food rations. Not surprisingly, many Mennonites signed on, as did Russians, Ukrainians, and others who suddenly claimed to be German. In line with their racial ideology, Reich officials encouraged Mennonites to distance themselves from the non-German populations found in their midst, including Russians and Ukrainians. They also expected them to participate in the extermination of Ukraine's Jews, who numbered 1.5 million at the start of the war, and likewise the Roma and thousands of Slavs who exceeded projected post-war German needs for slave labour. Others suffered a similar fate, including the region's disabled. Of these Nazi death squads aided by local regiments summarily executed more than one million during the occupation.[30]

Historians have asked: did Mennonites participate in the mass murder of Ukraine's Jews and others, especially given that the Black Sea steppe had long been a place of Jewish settlement? We know that Mennonites interacted freely with Jews before the war, especially given that many lived among Mennonites in the Chortitza villages and in the nearby industrial powerhouse of Zaporozhe. Nazi officials ordered Jews to wear yellow stars soon after they occupied Soviet Ukraine. Nazi death squads and local collaborators began their mass killings in September 1941 and ceased operations the following spring, by which time they had largely destroyed all Jewish life in the occupied lands, including in the Mennonite heartland. In an article published in 2010 historian Gerhard Rempel brought renewed attention to this topic when he suggested that Mennonites in Ukraine actively collaborated with Nazi troops in the mass extermination of Jews. Ben Goossen, James Urry, and Aileen Friesen have added their voices to the discussion of Mennonite complicity and collaboration in these atrocities.[31]

No adult Mennonite could have remained unaware of the Nazis' systematic campaign to exterminate Jews in what later became known as the Holocaust. But there remains little clarity on how Mennonites reacted to this gruesome undertaking at the time or how many may have sympathized with Nazi actions. In terms of direct Mennonite involvement in the killings, however, Viktor Klets, the foremost Ukrainian historian on this topic, concludes that the figure is probably very small. Aileen Friesen suggests that "some Soviet Mennonites participated directly in the Holocaust."[32] There is no reason to disagree. Similarly, some Mennonites voluntarily joined the German army. Many others entered when drafted. Within occupied Ukraine Mennonites greeted visiting dignitaries with apparent enthusiasm, of which the most dramatic was SS head Heinrich Himmler's visit to Molotschna in October 1942.

Some Mennonites from the 1920s emigration in Paraguay, Canada, and Germany welcomed Hitler's rise to power as they hoped he would obliterate the Soviet Union. Horst Gerlach concludes that Mennonites participated in Ukraine's civil administration under the Nazis, just as they had done under the Soviets, but they almost universally avoided combat assignments. Despite obvious signs of support for the Nazi regime by some, Klets concludes that most Mennonites in occupied Ukraine assumed a passive posture towards the occupation regime. Recall that Mennonites during the occupation largely comprised children and young adults who lived with their mothers and elderly grandparents. Many now watched as Nazi troops marched defenceless Jews out of their villages. Many celebrated visiting dignitaries because to do otherwise was fatal, and they clearly welcomed the opportunity to

Figure 9. Parade of ethnic German youth in front of Heinrich Himmler in Halbstadt/Molotschna, 31 October 1942. Bundesarchiv, Bild 146-1878-117-14A/Fotograf(in): o.Ang.

gather for Christian worship again. Yet despite impressive displays of Nazi power, Mennonites could not be certain that the Soviets would not return triumphant and settle scores later. They had already experienced how Moscow had treated perceived enemies of the Soviet state and did not want to face it again. Mennonites and others would have been tempted to hedge their bets soon after the occupation began as German troops failed to conquer Leningrad and Moscow in the fall of 1941, and especially after the stunning defeat of Hitler's massive Sixth Army at the gates of Stalingrad in early February 1943. Few thereafter could confidently anticipate a German victory over Stalin. There is also Karel Berkhoff's observation that most people in a war zone focus on staying alive, which leaves them uninterested in "grand sociopolitical developments."[33]

Evidence suggests that some within the Third Reich became disillusioned with Mennonites over time. Karl Stumpp, the Nazi ethnographer assigned to study Black Sea Germans, reported the following in August 1942: "The Germans, having been exposed for twenty years to the Bolshevik propaganda, are unable to think like Germans of the Fatherland."[34] Despite their best efforts and some limited success, there is little to suggest that Mennonite children joined the newly established Hitler Youth clubs for boys (*Hitlerjugend*) and the League of German Girls (*Bund Deutscher Mädel*). German soldiers sang in Mennonite churches at Christmas, but there is no evidence that these same churches or their ministry councils acted as agents of the Third Reich, nor did Mennonites as a whole appear to turn against their non-Mennonite neighbours. For example, Ukrainian Mikhail Kosa, born in 1929, grew up in the village of Rosental, where his family shared a two-room home with a Mennonite family. He spoke of his childhood friendship with Mennonites in the village, how children played together regardless of ethnicity, directly counter to what Nazi ideologues demanded.

Valentina Dymenko recalled how Mennonites and Ukrainians continued to work side by side during the fascist occupation in Nieder Chortitza. Still others recalled decades later how German occupation troops executed Mennonites deemed to have been loyal to the Soviet state. Mennonites may have had prejudices against their Slavic and even German neighbours before the war, though few of the older Mennonites would have confused what German had come to mean under the Nazis with the German *Kultur* of Goethe, Schiller, and German religious *Pietismus* (piety) that they had long admired. It is reasonable to conclude that many turned away from Nazi ideology and its manifestation as they learned more about it during the occupation. The religious revival in Chortitza and Molotschna, and the reclamation of a Mennonite pacifist theology, further distanced them from a world view grounded in *Mein Kampf* and the militaristic ramblings of Nazi newspapers and pamphlets which flooded the region.

Waldemar Janzen acknowledges that Mennonite preoccupation with their own tortured past likely overshadowed their response to the Holocaust even after they learned of it. He also recalled how Mennonite support for the German occupation weakened as the fascist policy against their Ukrainian neighbours became clear and as the occupying army drafted Mennonite youth to serve in the armies of the Third Reich or in its depleted factories back in Germany. Urry points to Nazi officials who came to identify Mennonites variously as "White Jews" and as a Christian sect, both damning designations for a regime entirely premised on race and hostile to religion.[35] In short, the picture of Mennonite–Nazi relations was as mixed as it was dynamic. It was as confusing as it was complex. It was, after all, a time of total war, with no end in sight.

The Great Trek, 1943–5

Georg Schmidt's village of Margenau emptied out early on 11 September 1943 as all households formed a convoy of horse-drawn wagons headed west. Several days before, Nazi officials had issued an evacuation order to all German settlers east of the Dnieper, Mennonites among them. With a Soviet takeover imminent, Germany now wanted to resettle them in conquered lands it intended to secure closer to the German heartland after they had expelled Poles en masse from their ancestral homes. Without knowing it, Georg's village joined a movement of approximately 35,000 Mennonites heading west, itself part of a movement of Soviet Germans ten times larger.[36] Mennonites across Molotschna found it a difficult parting on that final day. Some pondered how the Mennonite story in the Russian lands had come to such a tragic end; for others the German retreat dashed all hopes that a Nazi victory might lead to the release of their loved ones in the Soviet Gulag. Others scrambled to pack what they could for the trek. They had already harvested some of their summer crops to bring with them but left unripened potatoes, beets, and sunflowers behind. Others loaded bureaus and sewing machines only to discard them on the second day as heavy rains turned the dirt roads into deep mud.[37]

Women largely took charge of their evacuation. In Georg's case, he rode in a wagon that his mother Katharina commandeered for his Aunts Anna and Maria, his sister Anna, and three of his cousins. Their cow trailed behind. Initially the Margenau caravan passed through already abandoned Mennonite villages, including Alexanderwohl, Gnadenheim, and Fürstenwerder, though they caught up with the large two-thousand-wagon Molotschna convoy on the third day. Only German order prevented total chaos at the Dnieper River's pontoon bridge, where Mennonite and German refugees jostled for position with retreating German troops and tanks. Still they found their way and on a sunny day crossed over the constantly moving bridge. It felt as if they were walking on pudding. A few days later they arrived at the Zagradovka settlement, where Georg and his extended family received a home from a suddenly dispossessed Ukrainian family. German soldiers told them to expect a long stay here, as the armies of the Third Reich intended to hold the line at the Dnieper. Such hopes soon vanished, however.

By early October the German army began to evacuate the Chortitza villages as Soviet advances threatened the security of settlement on

Figure 10. The Great Trek. NP128-01-21, Centre for Mennonite Brethren Studies, Winnipeg, Mennonite Archival Information Database.

right bank Ukraine. Mennonites in these villages travelled by train, however, as up to fifty persons crowded with their baggage onto the individual freight cars. Chortitza-Rosental, Einlage, Nieder Chortitza, Blumengart, Neuhorst, Osterwick and so on, all had a date assigned for departure, which gave them added time to put their affairs in order, prepare foods, hold final worship services, and bid neighbours farewell. By November the Molotschna Mennonites in Zagradovka also began to travel westward, again by wagon, as German troops lost their final stronghold in southern Ukraine. The orderly formed caravan of carts travelled through the winter months until it reached Kamenets-Podolsk in March, a distance of approximately 800 kilometres. Occasionally they commandeered entire villages for the night, though many times they simply slept under their wagons in freezing conditions. Countless numbers died en route. Soviet partisans killed others or seized their best horses. But in Kamenets-Podolsk German soldiers finally placed the remaining contingent on freight cars for their final destination in Germany's Reichsgau Wartheland. Most disembarked in Łódź – renamed

Litzmannstadt during the German occupation of Poland – where German officials assigned the eastern arrivals to their new homes. Other Mennonites dispersed to the German administrative unit of Danzig-West Prussia or the Silesian region, which officials had incorporated directly into the German Reich.[38] In so doing, Mennonites and Germans found themselves in a front row seat on Nazi Germany's most horrific wartime policies.

The Reichsgau Wartheland, known more informally as the Warthegau, was representative of the murky moral setting into which officials settled Mennonites and other Germans. The region had been part of an independent interwar Poland until the Nazi invasion of 1939, whereupon Berlin moved quickly to incorporate it into a greater Germany. Demographics combined with racial theory to create a significant obstacle here, as only 325,000 of more than 4 million inhabitants in the new Reichsgau were German, and even those numbers had dropped in 1939 as Poles murdered or evacuated thousands of Germans as fascist forces advanced.[39] There followed the unfolding of the Final Solution[40] as Berlin ordered the removal, if not outright extermination, of Jews, Roma, and hundreds of thousands of Poles from the Warthegau. In their place, Hitler initially demanded the forced relocation of Germans from the east to the newly annexed Reichsgauen on Germany's erstwhile border. Nazi officials even coordinated an agreement with the Soviet Union in 1940 for the forced relocation of Baltic Germans to the Warthegau. However, the pool of available Germans for resettlement had gone dry by 1944, which explains why Nazi Germany so prized Mennonites and Soviet Germans as its troops retreated from the Black Sea steppe.

Though timelines vary, Mennonites generally arrived in Warthegau and adjoining districts from late 1943 to the spring of 1944. Those in rural settings generally moved into homes previously owned by Poles, whereas former Jewish residences dominated in the cities. Others lived in dormitories and makeshift residences. Officials assigned Georg Schmidt, his sister Anna, and mother Katharina to a farmstead near the village of Liubnitsa, one that a refugee Volhynian German had recently obtained. They shared an apartment with a family from Bessarabia for the first few months before they received their own one-room flat. After only a few days local officials drafted all able-bodied Mennonite and German men in their late teens and older into the German army, as appeals for a religious exemption fell quickly flat. Georg, at seventeen years of age, managed to evade the draft, which allowed him to work on the farm, as did many Mennonites. Others drove transport, worked in machine shops, communal kitchens, and factories, including those which produced military equipment. Officials naturalized almost all these East European refugees as German citizens, though few governments later recognized them as such. The few Mennonite ministers who made it to Warthegau, Danzig-West Prussia and Upper Silesia began to organize Christian worship and perform the first baptisms. Then the end came, by their telling at least.

The Mad Dash and Separation: Anna to Canada, Georg to Rochegda

Everything about the Mennonite resettlement plan in a post-war and expanded German Reich depended on Berlin's ability to end the war on favourable terms. Yet by the spring of 1945 that seemed highly unlikely as Soviet troops continued their relentless drive eastward and as their allies closed in on Germany from the west. Given a choice, almost all refugees preferred to take their chances with any western alternative to a return to the Soviet east.

For that reason, chaos erupted on 17 January 1945 when reports reached the Warthegau of a broad Soviet breakthrough in their immediate vicinity. Soviet vengeance suddenly seemed imminent as their tanks drove into and over crowds of west-moving refugees and as Soviet troops continued to sexually assault German women at will.[41] Almost all of the 35,000 Soviet Mennonites fled eastward the very next day, joined by Prussian Mennonites, German Mennonites, and hundreds of thousands of other refugees, along with German soldiers, tanks, trucks, and motorcycles, all in disarray, all crammed onto the same wintry routes. Ten days later Georg Schmidt lost contact with his mother and sister as Soviet troops descended on the Polish–German city of Schrimm (Śrem) and thousands of refugees scattered in all directions. In time those same troops captured him, whereas Katharina and Anna made it to Canada. They sailed into Halifax and cleared immigration on 20 December 1947, bound for Katharina's brother Hans Schoenke (of the 1920s Soviet emigration) and his family in Hespeler, Ontario, where they arrived two days later.[42] For his part, Georg Schmidt arrived in the Rochegda camp on 8 October 1945 along with his Aunt Maria, two cousins, a stepbrother, and many other villagers from Margenau, Mariawohl, and countless other Mennonite and non-Mennonite villages. As a family torn asunder, they represented a larger Mennonite family torn asunder, as only 12,000 of the 35,000 who left southern Ukraine in 1943 made it to the west. Six thousand joined Anna and Katharina Schmidt in Canada, whereas the other half settled initially in Argentina, Paraguay, and Uruguay, though many of these relocated to Canada when circumstances permitted.[43]

Of the remaining 23,000 who had survived the Great Trek, Soviet officials worked in concert with their American and British counterparts to send the rest back to the Soviet Union; that is, if Soviet soldiers did not execute them first as traitors. In this, Mennonites comprised a miniscule portion of the 5.5 million individuals repatriated to the USSR.[44] As regards Mennonites, none returned to southern Ukraine as their substantive presence dating back to 1789 came to an end. Most received sentences of from ten to twenty-five years in hard labour, which they served in far-flung places across the Russian north, Siberia, Uzbekistan, and Kazakhstan. In some ways, their fate overlapped with other Soviet Germans and Mennonites whom Soviet authorities had convicted of treason before the war and whom they had already banished to the Gulag or the labour army. Once again, the process of mass Soviet deportation resulted in multiple casualties, including Soviet Chechens, Tatars, and other nationalities.[45]

Conditions in the Gulag during the war and immediately after were among the deadliest in its entire tragic history, not a surprise given that widespread famine raged across the Soviet Union after the war. Once again, forced labour crews of women, youth, and old men faced demanding daily work schedules in unbearable conditions as they hewed wood, mined coal and gold, dug canals, built railroads and carved out roads through the taiga. They initially found shelter where they could, often in hastily constructed earthen dwellings. Poorly clothed, they confronted metre-deep snowfields and permafrost soils armed with pickaxes and handsaws. For their labours they received no more than 600 grams daily of a bread-like substance often filled with sawdust. Many depended on the kindness of previously exiled co-religionists just to survive.[46] Officials denied religious funerals to the thousands who perished.

Historian Walter Sawatsky points out that initially Moscow did not bother formally to charge or convict the repatriated of any crime. However, that changed in 1948 when the state confirmed it had sentenced repatriated Mennonites and Germans in perpetuity. They would never again enjoy civil rights, the right to internal travel, or placement in educational institutions. As a mark of this permanent designation, all formerly repatriated Mennonites lost their internal passports and received instead "special deported-nationality identity" cards which required them to acknowledge their sentence and report regularly to the "NKVD Deportation Main Directorate." Anyone who attempted escape faced a twenty-year sentence of hard labour.[47]

Those Mennonites in Siberia and Kazakhstan whom Soviets had not relocated also faced dramatically increased demands during and after the war. Moscow invoked the same stringent requirements on them after 1941 as it did with those in the Gulag, along with the half million or so Soviet Germans in that vast domain. It created a Spetskommandatura (Special Command) to administer all Soviet Germans and which lasted from 1941 to 1955. Their punishing work regime and search for daily sustenance after the war also left little space for worship. The same applied to Mennonites in Kazakhstan, where the decision to liquidate the labour army in 1946 brought little relief. In particular, the rise of the Cold War in the 1940s resulted in a new round of Mennonite arrests from within the vast Karaganda camp, including twelve Mennonites in 1948 and six the following year.[48]

On the surface the end of the war had brought little relief. Then again, another dramatic change lay on the horizon, one sparked by an administrative change introduced back in 1943 along with Stalin's death near Moscow at his *blizhnaia dacha* in March 1953. It is to that dramatic change, and how it played itself out in succeeding decades, that we next turn.

Chapter Thirteen

Detour to Dzhetisai: The Soviet Mennonite Renaissance in Stalin's Shadow, 1953–1991

Georg Schmidt left Rochegda in Russia's far north for Dzhetisai, Kazakhstan, in the fall of 1962. His wife, Maria, had departed earlier with their two children, Tina and Leini, along with Maria's cousin and her children. Georg, now thirty-five, stayed behind to close up their home and put their belongings in a container, which he shipped separately. Georg then departed Rochegda by boat, the very means by which he had arrived at this northern outpost on 8 October 1945, though now he travelled up the Northern Dvina River as a free citizen of the socialist state and not as its prisoner. He boarded a long-distance train in Kotlas, which brought him to the Kursk railway station in Moscow. He then transferred to the city's Paveletsky station and boarded another long-distance train, which took him to Tashkent, the capital of the Soviet republic of Uzbekistan. In a journey that covered only a small portion of this immense socialist state, even as it took almost a week, Georg travelled the final 120 kilometres to Dzhetisai by bus where he reunited with his wife and children. Here they undertook a new beginning.

The Schmidt family lived that first winter in a two-room home they shared with Georg's Tante Mariechen and cousin Jakob. The following spring, Georg and Maria acquired their own simple home, which at the time had a dirt floor, no doors, and no windows. They finished the home at their own expense and time. Meanwhile Georg found employment in a firm that constructed sewers and water mains, whereas Maria worked in the local hospital as a midwife and nurse practitioner (*feldsher*), though she did take some time off when their third child, Liesel, was born in 1966. Cotton was king in the region Khrushchev had featured in his Virgin Lands Campaign, and employment was plentiful. No wonder it had attracted hundreds of Mennonites, thousands of Germans, along with Kazakhs, Ukrainians, Russians, Tatars, and a grand total of thirty-nine distinct nationalities. This was their new community and they settled in quickly. Russian united them all in language, as did Soviet in culture.[1] Though they did not know it at the time, Maria, Georg, and their daughters would live in Dzhetisai for less than a decade before they relocated to the Estonian republic in 1969. Thus, even on the face of it, Georg and Maria Schmidt lived lives of constantly new beginnings after 1945, with even more to come.

Starting in the 1970s they and their three daughters joined what became from 1987 to 1993 a massive migration as 100,000 left the Soviet Union and its successor states for Germany, such that few remained behind. In some ways, Georg and Maria's generation represented the most remarkable of all as they carried the Mennonite story to the end of the Soviet era and beyond, even as they were only one generation removed from Soviet beginnings in 1917. There is considerable drama inherent in this post-Stalinist generation, a drama which starred tens of thousands of Mennonites like Georg and Maria who rebuilt lives devastated by Stalinist terror and torn apart by war and the great, futile trek westward. Yet for all that drama, Mennonite historian and theologian Walter Sawatsky has observed that the post-Stalinist Mennonite story is the least appreciated and most weakly investigated of all. For reasons beyond the scope of this chapter, Mennonites of the 1920s migration to Canada generally claimed historical pride of place. They formulated their narrative first, and those who followed from the 1940s into the late twentieth century had little opportunity to present alternate narratives. In some ways, North American Mennonites reflected the dominant American hegemonic and global discourse which emerged after 1945, by which American and Canadian Mennonites assumed that their vision, and their past, comprised the whole story. With a confidence reflective of their larger culture, they trained their own professionals and constructed their own churchly, social, and educational bureaucracies. Soviet Mennonites, by contrast, seemed to disappear, clouded in the opaqueness with which the west generally viewed Soviet society during the Cold War. Few western scholars bothered to investigate the post-Stalinist generation of Mennonites. Fewer still had the linguistic skillset to try. Emblematic is the entry for "Omsk Russia" in the Global Anabaptist Mennonite online encyclopedia. In an article composed decades ago in 1959, it makes only passing reference to the thousands of Mennonites who lived there in the 1950s, with no reference to their experience in the 1960s and beyond. In another instance, the flagship American journal *Mennonite Quarterly Review*'s cumulative index from 1926 to 2000 contains no entry for "Soviet" under title or subject.[2] Only recently have historians of this very post-Stalinist Mennonite generation joined Sawatsky to address this lacuna, including Petr Epp, historian

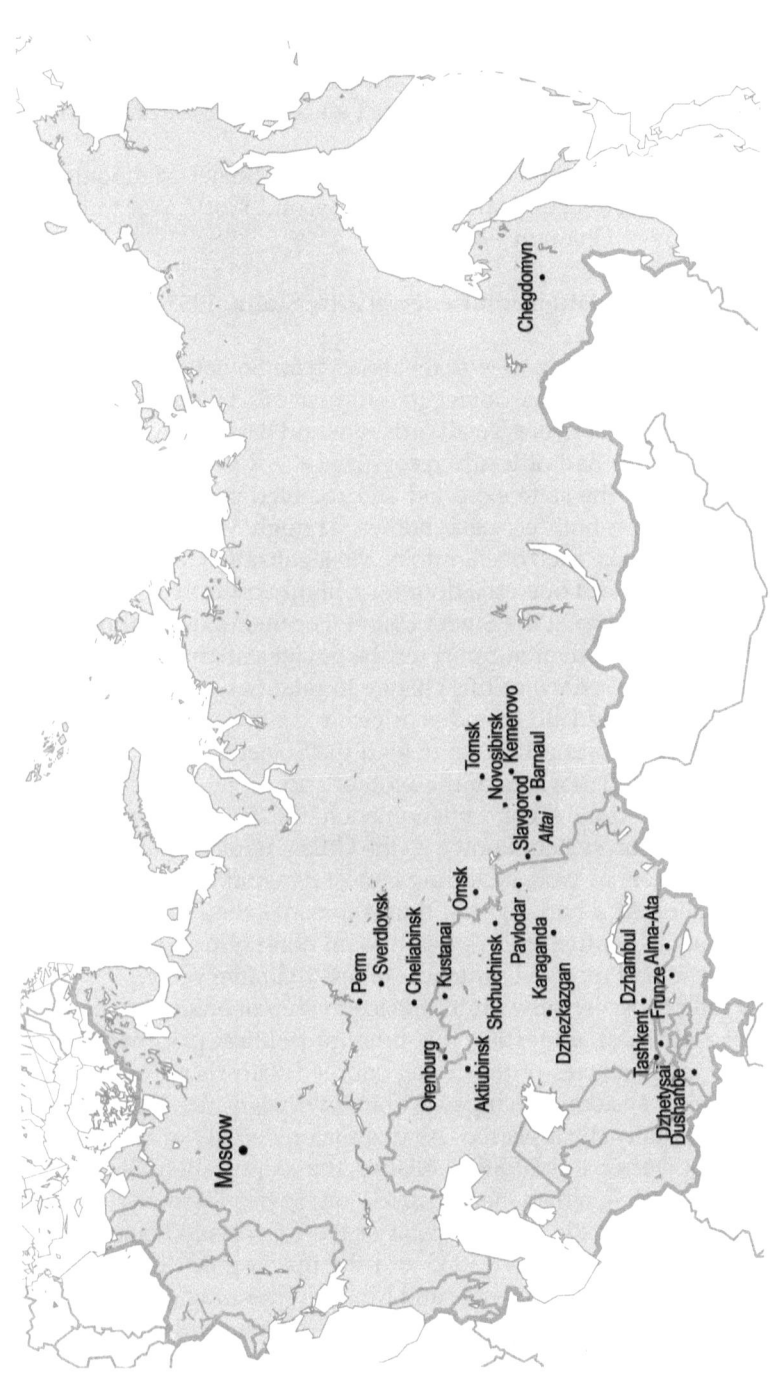

Map 3. Mennonite and other German congregations in the Soviet Union, 1980. S. Solbergj J. (cartographic basis), J. Dyck (Mennonite and German Congregations), CC-BY-SA 3.0.

254   Mennonites in the Soviet Era

of the Soviet Mennonite and Evangelical Baptist community in Omsk. Even as the Soviet Union collapsed in the 1980s knowledge of post-Stalinist Mennonites remained rudimentary, such that we barely knew where they lived, much less how.[3]

This chapter lays out the main contours of the Soviet Mennonite experience in four distinct episodes from the Second World War to the collapse of the Soviet Union in 1991.

Episode One: Consolidation and Renewal after Stalin, 1953–8

Two phenomena sparked a post-war renaissance for Soviet-era Mennonites. The first began when the Soviet government officially recognized the All-Union Council of Evangelical Christians and Baptists (AUCECB) in 1944, a year after it had officially recognized the Russian Orthodox Church. In exchange the state expected and received profuse declarations of support from both ecclesial bodies. Though Mennonites formally hesitated to make such declarations, the legalization of these two religious associations did open the door for a highly controlled form of public Christian worship in the Soviet Union. For their part, Orthodox churches had professed their support for the Soviet state from the first days of the war. Emblematic of this change in relations, the Orthodox Metropolitan Sergii urged all Orthodox priests and believers on the very first day of the war, 22 June 1941, to defend the Soviet state, suddenly referred to as "the holy borders of the Motherland."[4] Stalin's death on 5 March 1953 initiated the second phenomenon, the dismantling of the state's complex prison system known as the Gulag, home to more than two million prisoners in 1950, including almost five hundred thousand political prisoners. As a harbinger of things to come, the state granted amnesty immediately after Stalin's death to all non-political prisoners and to those who had received sentences of less than five years.

One year later Moscow, now under the leadership of Nikita Khrushchev, issued a series of amnesties, this time for political prisoners, as the economic inefficiencies of the Gulag coupled with rising political revolt demanded systemic change. Within five years the infamous Gulag had essentially disappeared. As one major step along the way, the Supreme Soviet of the USSR abolished the Deportation Regime (*Spetskommandatura*) – which had focused on Soviet Germans – in December 1955 to coincide with the visit of West German Chancellor Konrad Adenauer in September 1955 and the opening of diplomatic relations between his fledgling state and Moscow. In Karaganda alone this involved 46,790 prisoners, and hundreds of thousands beyond, all of whom authorities had only recently condemned in perpetuity.

Those previously detained received passes which permitted them to settle anywhere in the Soviet Union where they could obtain housing and employment, though Moscow barred them from any return to their former domiciles in southern Ukraine.[5]

Almost immediately Mennonites joined Germans and others as they re-established their lives as freed Soviet citizens. To that end, they spontaneously initiated a mass internal migration by which they abandoned remote locales such as Rochegda and Chelyabinsk and shifted to a number of rapidly expanding settlements concentrated near the Siberian cities of Omsk, Novosibirsk, and Slavgorod, as well as in Uzbekistan, Kazakhstan (especially Karaganda and Dzhetisai), Tadzhikistan (Dushanbe), and the Kyrgyzstan capital of Frunze as well as in the Chu and Talas valleys. In the process they created what Johannes Dyck called a new Mennonite and German geography in the Soviet Union.[6] How did it happen that scattered Mennonites initially found each other and became reconnected?

Soviet Mennonites began to establish contacts and connections with distant relations almost as soon as officials deposited them in the camps, aided by a surprisingly lax surveillance system which permitted widespread correspondence. Often pre-existing Mennonite settlements such as Orenburg served as central information depots for Mennonites, though Mennonites also chose to follow Soviet Germans engaged in the same process of internal relocation. Ministers played a vital role, in part because they had maintained ties with other ministers whom authorities had imprisoned before the war. For example, Johann Friesen and Johannes Fast re-established a pre-war correspondence in 1950 even though they remained in camps thirty-five kilometres apart in the distant Amur. They, in turn, corresponded far and wide as they begin to knit communities of believers together, whether in Krykyzstan's Grünfeld and Bergtal; Karaganda, Balchasch, and Schortany in Kasakhstan; and Omsk and Chelyabinsk in Siberia. After the December 1955 legislation permitted freedom of movement these same pastors travelled back and forth between settlements which allowed them to carry news and correspondences.

Mennonite Central Committee (MCC) sprang into action when it established an office in post-war Germany to assist in family reunification among Mennonites. In 1948 it began to publish *Der Mennonit* (The Mennonite), a regular publication which sought to link scattered Soviet Mennonites with other Mennonites in South and North America as well as Europe. Initially published on a bi-monthly basis, the demand was such that editors began to publish *Der Mennonit* on a monthly basis in 1950.[7]

Two German-language Mennonite newspapers published in North America, *Der Bote* and *Die Mennonitische Rundschau*, played an equally vital role, as they filled their pages in the 1950s with correspondences from Mennonites across the globe as Soviet Mennonites strove to reconnect with their loved ones. For example, the 18 July 1956 edition of the *Rundschau* declared that a Mrs. Lena Dűck, born a Hűbner, sought her brothers Jacob and Peter. A Mrs. Klein sought her son Jakob, whom officials of the Reich had drafted into the German army. Mothers sought their husbands or husbands their wives. Parents sought their children and children their parents, and the newspapers included such requests in every issue. *Der Bote* contained a regular "Letters from Russia" column and placed it alongside news and letters from across Canada, the United States, Mexico, Paraguay, and so on. The *Rundschau* called this large regular section "In search of Friends and Relations," and they always included information to identify someone, such as date of birth and originating settlement, and usually a name and address in North America whom someone could contact for more information. By this means, Georg Schmidt's sister Anna, who lived in the Niagara region of Ontario at the time, read the following in the 14 March 1956 issue of the *Rundschau*: "Georg Schmidt seeks his mother Katharina Penner (Schmidt) from Margenau village in Molotschna" for which a C.J. Eitzen in Winnipeg could be contacted for more information.[8] Thus by the time Georg and his family joined relatives found in Dzhetisai, he had already located his mother and sister in Canada by means of a newspaper published in Winnipeg Manitoba, though read by Mennonites everywhere. Such points of reconnection reinforced a sense of Mennonite identity among an increasingly Sovietized populace. As a case in point, many of the Soviet Mennonite correspondents apologized that they needed to write their appeals to these German-language Canadian newspapers in Russian but trusted that enough Mennonite readers retained sufficient Russian to translate them for publication.

Soviet Mennonites in the late 1940s and early 1950s did not focus exclusively on family reunification, as they also experienced a significant religious awakening, the term most commonly used in the literature.[9] Scholars have stressed the spontaneous aspects of this awakening across the Soviet Union. Although Moscow's legal recognition of the AUCECB in 1944 opened the door to this movement from the top, the decision to permit only a single Baptist church in Karaganda and other dense settlements necessarily drove thousands into smaller and more informal settings. Those who experienced this awakening had to overcome a host of challenges. Key Mennonite ecclesial leaders had emigrated in the 1920s when the opportunity arose, and public religious life itself ceased in the early 1930s thanks to repressive government measures. In a few short years the state imprisoned those ministers and Ältesters who had not emigrated, closed churches, and confiscated all religious materials. Then came the war and the *Spetskommandatura* when countless more perished. Those who survived did so under harrowing conditions. By 1950 few Mennonites remained with any theological training as no opportunities for such had arisen for over a generation. Few survivors even possessed Bibles, yet somehow a religious revival unfolded. No wonder many who experienced that arrival from within later attributed its very existence to the power of the Holy Spirit.

As with the 1930s women again played a key role in this awakening. They gathered children together for religious instruction and taught them hymns they recalled from earlier days. As more believers began to gather women occasionally took the lead as they read scripture to the assembled and preached at makeshift services. Those who assembled as early as 1944 under the banner of religion's ostensible legalization cared little for theological nuance, and this opened the door for broadly interevangelical worship services as Mennonites joined Orthodox Christians, Baptists, Evangelicals, Catholics, and others. Walter Sawatsky argues that denominationalism became a casualty of the "boiling cauldron" that had typified the period from 1930 to 1953 and opened the door for Orthodox hymnody, spirituality, and rituals to influence Mennonite forms for decades. Often post-war believers gathered and gave emotional testimonies at birthday parties, weddings, and funerals. Those with Bibles read from them, whereas others recalled Bible passages or hymns they had once sung. Communities of believers painstakingly wrote out entire hymnals or New Testaments and distributed them to communities which had nothing. The religious awakening unfolded with heavy participation from the youth, including those in active service in the Red Army. In a representative instance, only fifteen to twenty people gathered initially in Omsk, but within a few months it had risen to several groups with up to fifty people in each, often scattered in a ring of relatively isolated villages around this major Siberian city. Here the persistence of Plautdietsch among Mennonites helped to knit communities together. Though the late Stalinist state continued to arrest leaders in the late 1940s and early 1950s it seemed to do little more than accelerate the growth of these de-centralized and non-denominational gatherings.[10]

In a seminal article Sawatsky maintains that a "post-Gulag" theology took shape among Soviet Mennonites and other Christians as they gathered. Few after all relied on a legacy of theological training which slotted people into denominations in the North American model. Instead,

Figure 11. Thanksgiving celebration in a church, Dzhambul, Kazakhstan. A.A. Martens Collection, Mennonite Historical Society of Saskatchewan.

those who gathered, primarily young men and women along with older women, proclaimed a faith rooted in more broadly shared orthodox tenets, ones that stressed the Lordship of Christ, and the authority of scripture more than any one tradition. It taught Christians to live their faith out in broad faith-based communities, and it forewarned that true Christians would suffer for their faith at a time when the society around them remained resolutely atheistic. Russian scholar Vera Klyueva suggests that Mennonite Brethren ministers in Tyumen' Oblast urged adherents to maintain a distance from that larger society. They should not attend the cinema, read Soviet fiction or newspapers, or visit officially sanctioned clubs. Only Christ could save believers from the persecution that was sure to come. Only Christ could forgive sinners their sins and grant them the assurance of eternal life with Him.[11]

The shape of this religious awakening changed by the mid-1950s as the threat of Stalinist reprisals receded and as the end of the Spetskommandatura and the Gulag allowed hundreds of thousands of prisoners to reclaim their lives. Among them, previously imprisoned ministers and Ältesters now returned to the settlements and took charge in the religious revival. Women stepped back in relative importance as church formation led by all-male ministry councils accelerated. For example, an exiled Mennonite minister named Dyck came to Sverdlovsk Oblast in 1955 upon his release and immediately initiated a revival. Soon small groups of believers had formed in several of the region's kolkhozes led by Mennonites, including I.J. Froese, Dmitri Rempel, and J.P. Krahn. Baptisms followed, something that required male Mennonite Ältesters to administer, such that 140 Mennonite believers resided there by 1958. The Mennonite Brethren began to meet separately from the Baptist congregations in Orenburg in 1954. Their numbers grew so rapidly from mass public baptisms that they had already elected Abram Dyck as Ältester the following year. The form by which Ältesters baptized new converts proved particularly stressful for Kirchliche Mennonites who rejected the immersion baptism demanded by Baptists and practised by Mennonite Brethren.

Mennonites reintroduced German-language sermons in Karaganda congregations by Christmas 1955, in the immediate aftermath of Adenauer's visit to Moscow that year. Harold Bender, a prominent American Mennonite and president of the Mennonite World Conference, visited the Soviet Union the following year as part of a larger American Baptist delegation. A.V. Karev, the general secretary of the AUCECB, had informed Bender at a World Congress in 1955 that some 20,000 Mennonites lived in the USSR, scattered over five republics. Bender – unknown to Soviet Mennonites – now sought to visit their scattered settlements and invite their leaders to a Mennonite World Conference planned for the following year in West Germany. Accompanied by renowned Mennonite radio evangelist D.B. Wiens, Bender sought to reconnect those Mennonites to their relations overseas and encourage the re-formation of Soviet Mennonite churches and conferences lest they compromise their identity as Mennonites. They arrived in Moscow on 26 October 1956, only to be told that their access would be restricted to that city and the Kazakhstan capital of Alma Ata. With their schedule revamped, Bender and Wiens met under state supervision with several Soviet Mennonites in both settings, including former leaders of the long-banned ARMAA and Verband. The delegation did not encourage emigration, nor did it see its role as giving specific advice to Soviet Mennonites as much as to assure them of their fraternal and prayerful support. Despite the delegation's encouragement that Soviet Mennonites seek official recognition as a distinct religious organization, however, Mennonites continued to worship within AUCECB congregations, especially as the state refused to grant Mennonites autonomous recognition in the 1950s, nor did it permit Soviet Mennonites to attend the Mennonite World Conference the following year, a sign of darker clouds on the religious horizon.[12]

Episode Two: Khrushchev's War on Religion, 1958–64

In 1958 Khrushchev attempted to transform the Soviet Union from a socialist to a communist state, by his reckoning at least, though he had powerful allies in the attempt. Key Soviet ideologues within the Communist Party, foremost among them Mikhail Suslov, along with leading Komsomol officials, academics, the security police, and those agencies charged with atheistic propaganda, sought to eliminate religious faith through a series of measures which officials identified as the maintenance of "Leninist legality" (*Leninskaia zakonnost'*). Taken together, they hearkened back to legislation introduced as the Law on Cults in 1929, now made even more stringent. Mistakenly viewed in the west as a moderate, Khrushchev's attempt to root out religious faith dated back to the 1930s when he oversaw the widespread destruction of Orthodox churches in Moscow as part of the Stalinist cultural revolution. By the second half of the 1950s key Soviet officials had become alarmed at the post-war resurgence in religious belief across the Soviet Union. Even church bodies – among them Mennonite – which the state had not legally registered had constructed meeting houses in defiance of local authorities and begun to worship openly in ever-increasing numbers.[13]

In response Khrushchev oversaw a regime that increased antireligious propaganda and removed teachers who refused to declare atheist convictions as he now declared that all Soviet children belonged to the Soviet state. It also broadened the target of its attention to include not only organized religion but also what Victoria Smolkin calls "popular religiosity and folk practices."[14] Moscow ordered the closure of thousands of unregistered churches as authorities even shuttered most that they had previously registered and officially recognized. Among Orthodox Christians, for example, the number of registered churches plummeted from 22,000, itself a miniscule number for the demand in the mid-1950s, to 7,500 by 1966. Registered Baptist churches of the AUCECB suffered the same steep decline. Officials arrested and imprisoned clergy of all faiths to five-year prison terms if the courts determined that they had acted contrary to Leninist legality, including if they had advised parents not to enrol their children as Lenin Pioneers or Octobrists. Heinrich P. Voth, one of a handful of Mennonite leaders whom Harold Bender and D.B. Wiens had seen in 1956, typified those arrested. First elected to the Kirchliche Mennonite ministry in 1921, authorities sentenced Voth to a five-year term in 1931, and arrested him again in 1938, this time for a ten-year term of hard labour. In 1957 Voth worked with other Mennonite church leaders to form an independent Kirchliche Church union as the AUCECB had rejected both their position on baptism and their intention to claim pacifism as a foundational tenet of faith. Later reflections suggest that Voth lacked the administrative acumen needed to move through the Soviet system, whereas senior AUCECB leaders Zhidkov and Karev hesitated to challenge the system, having been cowed by their personal experience in the Gulag. Thus, the initiative died, and shortly thereafter police arrested Voth again. Freed some three years later, he ended his days in Tokmak, Kyrgyzstan, several years after that, by which time his life of sacrificial faithfulness had become an inspiration to a new generation of church leaders.[15]

At first glance Khrushchev's campaign proved a success as church buildings closed in the thousands, ministers disappeared once again, and atheistic propaganda in education increased. Public baptisms (*Tauffesten*) ceased and access to biblical materials curtailed, including numerous German-language publications which had flooded in after the West German–Soviet rapprochement of 1955. Soviet officials withdrew employment from lay congregational leaders and expelled others from their districts.

Yet religious life did not diminish. Once again worshipping congregations broke into smaller groups and shifted to distant villages with limited police presence, as happened in the Alt Samara settlement.

Theologically Mennonites understood the suffering associated with the Khrushchev campaign as God's will, even if it was a will beyond their ability to grasp. Ironically the campaign proved counterproductive as it strengthened churchly admonitions for believers to remove themselves from a fallen world even as they appeared to integrate into the world of state schools, factories, and kolkhozes. Baptisms continued though at night, as did worship services, even if security officials occasionally broke them up and arrested officiants. In some ways believers refused to remain completely hidden. All local police had to do in some villages was stand outside in the dead of night and listen for the quiet sound of singing. Augustina and Jakob Penner arrived in Karaganda in April 1960 from their Siberian exile and settled into their earthen hut with their children. Their home became a magnet for neighbourhood children who gathered there to sing hymns and hear Bible stories. They even performed a Christmas program that year, complete with a children's choir and spoken poetry. Afterwards the children received a candied treat and a Christmas card. Soon others joined in to host other children's programs in defiance of state decrees and local officials. Believers also continued to hold Christian burials, as happened on 2 February 1964 for Otto Wiebe, a minister of the unregistered Karaganda Mennonite Brethren congregation. In defiance of state legislation, the entire congregation gathered for his funeral, where they heard minister Johannes Fast proclaim words of comfort based on a New Testament reading from Romans 12: "Rejoice with those who rejoice; weep with those who weep."[16]

The defiance exemplified by Otto Wiebe's funeral contrasted sharply with the position taken by the AUCECB both before and during the Khrushchev campaign. Critics had long argued that the Union paid too much attention to the whims of the atheistic state, though all Soviet citizens negotiated their way between opposition, accommodation, and acquiescence to the state and its policies. Opposition from less accommodating believers peaked in 1960 when the AUCECB released a new statute which effectively discouraged church growth and mission work of any kind. For example, the new churchly statute strongly discouraged the baptism of any young adults under thirty years of age and did not support mission work among Soviet unbelievers. Believers also needed to undergo a probationary period of up to three years before baptism into the registered churches. In addition, the statute encouraged Christians to abandon their hostility to Soviet media, from television to radio to the cinema, and to embrace Soviet culture in all its forms. Lastly, the AUCECB confirmed that it had supported the recent Khrushchevian process by which registered churches had sharply declined in number. With no vehicle for renewal it seemed plausible that the AUCECB would soon disappear as increasingly elderly congregants found their churches cut off from all possibility of evangelical renewal among their own young or the unbelievers in their midst. Subsequent investigations make plain that the AUCECB reached every one of these decisions through an anguished process as officials sought out the balance point between "Discretion and Valour" in their search for a faith-filled working relationship with the Soviet state.[17]

Opposition to the AUCECB's acquiescence to the Soviet state took shape in the 1950s as those who had served long prison terms for their faith began to return from exile. Many now demanded that churches eschew state control in a movement known as the *Initsiativniki*, or "Initiative Group," often associated in the west with the unregistered or underground church.[18] In an open declaration to the AUCECB's leadership on 13 August 1961, followed by a similar declaration to Khrushchev ten days later, Gennady Kriuchkov, a church leader of an unregistered church in Tula Oblast, and Alexei Prokoviev of Soviet Ukraine announced the formation of a separate union that would soon be known as the Council of Churches of Evangelical Christian Baptists (CCECB). Unlike the AUCECB, the newly formed council called for a strict separation between the church and Soviet society, though it understood that Christians necessarily lived in both entities. The key was always to know what belonged to Caesar and what belonged to God. The CCECB demanded subservience to the gospel, not the Soviet state, and declared that believers should expect to suffer for their faith. It insisted on the right to proselytize among unbelievers and to raise their own children in the faith without state interference. It claimed the right to baptize when congregations alone – not the state or the AUCECB – deemed appropriate. Lastly, the new movement demanded that its adherents live lives of self-discipline and moral purity worthy of Christ's calling. Already by the fall of 1961, and true to their name, the Initsiativniki printed and distributed some two thousand pamphlets to Leningrad youth who claimed to be unbelievers. Authorities quickly detained twenty-four-year-old Liudmila Shcherbakova and other organizers, but by then it was clear that the Soviet state had a significant problem on its hands. Within months they had arrested almost eighty of the Initsiativniki's leaders, including Prokoviev, one of the movement's original spokesmen, whom they sentenced to five years in prison.[19]

How involved were Mennonites in this new movement? The question is difficult to answer as Mennonite identities became increasingly difficult to determine during the Soviet era. For example, the CCECB replaced Prokoviev with Georgii Petrovich Vins, who soon became one of the most recognizable of the Initsiativniki. Was Vins (Wiens) a Mennonite given that his surname suggested he was? His grandfather Jakob certainly had been, having emigrated from the Russian empire to the United States in 1911 and served as a Mennonite Brethren minister in Saskatchewan before he returned to the States. Georgii's father Petr felt called by God to serve as a missionary in the Soviet Union, which he did in 1926 when he settled in Siberia. Petr married Liidia Zharikova in 1927, and Georgii was born the following year. Neither Petr nor his son Georgii ever identified as Mennonites, however. In the 1920s the Soviet government revoked Petr's American citizenship and arrested him in 1930. Released in 1933 they rearrested him two years later and he died in the Gulag in 1943. Georgii eventually moved with his family to Kiev, where he studied engineering and became a passionate Baptist. As the Baptist movement split Vins joined and soon played a leading role in the Initsiativniki. All very compelling, but was Vins truly "Mennonite"? Some concluded that he was not, at least in the narrowest sense of the word. However, the Center for Mennonite Brethren Studies in Fresno, California, does curate the Vins papers, and his biography regularly appears in MB publications. Similarly, Johannes Dyck, whose work has informed much of this chapter, was a Mennonite by background; yet he actively worshipped at an ECB church in Karaganda in the 1970s where both ministers also came from Mennonite backgrounds.[20]

Beyond Vins and Johannes Dyck a search of Initsiativniki leaders reveals that many of them had names which suggested a Mennonite connection, and other key leaders in the movement from Siberia to the Baltic republics identified themselves as Mennonite and Baptist simultaneously and without any sense of contradiction. Soviet scholar A.N. Ipatov, writing in the 1970s, tied the growth of the Mennonite Brethren church in the 1960s to its close association with the CCECB, which he dated back to 1963. One year later the CCECB opened the door to fraternal connections with Kirchliche Mennonites, though relations continued to stumble over the acceptable form of baptism and the CCECB's judgment that the Kirchliche displayed a noticeable lack of religious conviction. Sawatsky agrees that many Mennonites, Mennonite Brethren among them, scorned the seemingly lax position taken by the AUCECB against a state which had imprisoned so many of their spiritual leaders in the Gulag. They found it much easier to identify with the CCECB on that basis, though much also depended on which organization in which region had best access to religious materials and other forms of support. In addition, the Khrushchevian campaign encouraged believers as much as possible not to declare themselves to avoid a return to the camps. Thus, as Mennonite congregations emerged again in the

1950s and early 1960s, they walked a fine line in their attempt to draw minimal attention to themselves at a time when neither association formally recognized them, even as Mennonites themselves worshipped in a variety of settings, especially among German-speaking Baptists who shared the same language of worship. It was not unusual for very different congregations with very different legal statuses to share the same building, maintained by two separate Congregational Councils. Even where unregistered Mennonite churches had formed, as in Omsk, their leaders sought good fraternal relations with both the AUCECB and CCECB. Unbeknownst to all, however, yet another dramatic shift lay on the horizon.[21]

Episode Three: Mennonites and Brezhnevite Dynamism, 1964–85

Elite Communist Party officials had never been overly fond of Nikita Khrushchev, whose erratic ruling style, anti-Stalinist rhetoric, and tendency to disregard them at key moments alienated the very allies his power depended upon. Eventually the chickens came home to roost. In October 1964 a Party coup organized by Leonid Brezhnev and others removed Khrushchev from power, as Brezhnev became the new general secretary and ostensible head of state. Gorbachev famously described the Brezhnev years as a time of stagnation during which state and society ignored a series of mounting crises facing the USSR. Though not all historians accept the stagnation thesis,[22] there is a broad consensus that Brezhnev's time in power was, ironically, extraordinarily dynamic for Soviet Mennonites. For starters, the sudden emergence of the CCECB and its sharp growth in members raised state concerns that the AUCECB would not survive. In response, the Kremlin moved after Khrushchev's ouster to end his failed war on religion. It remained resolute against the CCECB and continued to arrest and jail its leaders, but the state also raised the possibility of legal recognition to Protestant churches that it had previously sought to crush. After 1964 it chose instead to encourage them to register under the AUCECB umbrella and thereby rob the appeal of the CCECB for thousands of previously unregistered Christians, Mennonites among them. Though the numbers are necessarily imprecise Johannes Dyck estimates that up to three-quarters of all Germans chose to join the AUCECB when given the opportunity to do so under Brezhnev.[23]

Already in 1964 the AUCECB encouraged its members to develop fraternal relations with Mennonite congregations. Two years later seventeen delegates identified as Mennonite successfully requested formal, autonomous recognition for the Mennonite Brethren church within the

AUCECB during its conference on 4–6 August 1966. The large eight-hundred-member Mennonite Brethren congregation in Karaganda immediately sent three delegates to the next Congress in October of that year where they formally requested permission to enter the AUCECB as a Mennonite congregation. Delegates approved the motion, which made the Karaganda MB Congregation the first legally recognized Mennonite church in the Soviet Union. One year later, the Karaganda Kirchliche congregation with its three hundred members made a similar request, which the larger association also approved. Other Mennonite congregations followed, among them the Kirchliche congregations in the Russian city of Novosibirsk and Tokmak in Kyrkyzstan. By 1968 the AUCECB claimed that almost 19,000 Mennonites had entered their association in officially recognized congregations, though such statistics belied the tensions that existed for the Kirchliche Mennonites over mode of baptism especially. Not surprisingly, several of their congregations adopted baptism by immersion in the 1970s and thereby entered more fully into fellowship with the larger association. Even then challenges for Mennonite congregations did not end as those newly recognized immediately undertook difficult negotiations with local officials for the right to construct new church buildings. Once again, the Karaganda MB church proved among the first to be successful. It purchased land, received permission, constructed the building, and on 15 December 1968 jubilant parishioners participated in the new structure's dedication, led by Ältester Heinrich Woelk. By the 1970s the Kirchliche also experienced a revival as their officially recognized congregations added new buildings and members. Mennonites, as part of this new strategy of engagement, began to serve in a variety of leadership roles within the AUCECB from the mid-1960s onward, and included Viktor Kriger, who occupied a staff position in the Moscow office.[24]

Not all Mennonites joined the legally recognized Mennonite congregations, however, and not all Mennonite congregations joined the AUCECB. From the rebirth of the post-Stalinist church many had remained in non-registered churches and regarded compromise with an atheist state to be apostasy. Alexander Weiss reports that many Mennonites in the region around Slavgorod, north of Kazakhstan, melded into the Baptist Initsiativniki, and we see similar patterns in Omsk. Security police in Omsk arrested Mennonite Initsiativniki in all but one year from 1967 to 1986. For example, in 1967 they arrested sisters Agatha and Lisa Harms of the Omsk non-registered congregation and sentenced them to three years in prison after police found an illegal printing press in their possession, utilized to produce religious materials. Police arrested two brothers in the following year: Jakob Wiens for having evaded the official registration of his congregation and his brother Petr, who had been caught indoctrinating minors in the Christian faith. Others faced lesser sentences, as when authorities charged two youths in the Omsk raion village of Solntsevka, A.IA. Klassen and G.G. Vibe (Wiebe) with hooliganism after they sang Christian hymns as they walked down the village street following a wedding among unregistered Mennonites. Police also fined believers who continued to teach children in Sunday School settings, a contravention of Soviet law.[25]

The dynamism evident within the early years of Brezhnev's rule took on an entirely different form in the 1970s thanks to a marked easing of tensions between east and west in the Cold War. It began on 19 March 1970 when West German chancellor and former West Berlin mayor Willy Brandt met his East German counterpart in Erfurt of the DDR. Both sides agreed to recognize each other's borders, a process enshrined in the Treaty of Moscow, which they signed on 12 August of that same year. Two years later American President Richard Nixon did the previously unthinkable when he travelled to Moscow for one week of meetings with Soviet leader Brezhnev. Suddenly the era of détente burst forth in a series of treaties which eased nuclear tensions and created a broad range of cultural initiatives designed to further deescalate tensions. As part of it, in 1976 Hedrick Smith, *New York Times* bureau chief in Moscow from 1971 to 1974 published *The Russians*, a bestseller which humanized Soviet citizens, challenged totalitarian conceptions of its state, and opened the country for increased tourism from the west.[26]

MCC utilized the opportunity provided by détente to increase its presence among Mennonites, and Evangelicals more broadly, in the USSR. In some ways this was not new, as MCC began to engage the AUCECB in 1956 with a series of exchanges dedicated to peacemaking, information sharing, and relationship building. Such efforts intensified in 1973 when Walter Sawatsky, a Canadian descendant of the 1874 emigration with German, Plautdietsch, and Russian fluency, made himself available. Sawatsky soon became the MCC ambassador to the AUCECB and a bridge to Soviet Mennonites, even as he completed his doctorate in Russian history from the University of Minnesota. His academic credentials, linguistic competencies, and engaging personality allowed him to integrate into diverse communities and added credibility to MCC's involvements.[27]

It also yielded numerous practical benefits for Soviet evangelical Christians. By the mid-1970s Sawatsky concluded that Evangelical Christians had obtained increased access to Bibles through a variety of means, including limited official runs, self-published (Samizdat) materials, through official agreements reached with foreign Bible societies and, finally, millions of Bibles brought in surreptitiously by tourists.[28] Ministers now clamoured for theological training and, in lieu of that, theological resources such as Bible commentaries, especially given the state's steadfast refusal to permit Evangelicals a seminary of their own in the country. Over the next seven years Sawatsky successfully oversaw an international effort with Baptist World Alliance and the AUCECB to translate and publish a Russian version of the Barclay Bible commentaries; a landmark achievement for Soviet Protestant Christians.

Walter and his wife Margaret Sawatsky began their second three-year term with MCC in 1977, but now they shifted to Neuwied, Germany, which placed them in the middle of a Soviet Mennonite emigration movement that began in the early 1970s as Moscow partially opened the door to emigration. Here Sawatsky interviewed Mennonite Umsiedler (resettlers) to better understand the life of the church in the Soviet Union. Neuwied became a focal point of Mennonite immigration to West Germany, with many Soviet Mennonites having relocated first to the three Baltic republics, where authorities tended to grant permission to emigrate more quickly. By 1984 some 12,500 Mennonite Umsiedler had arrived in Germany, while hundreds more relocated as far away as Canada, often through a process of family reunification. Among those were Georg and Maria Schmidt, who left Dzhetisai, Kazakhstan, for the Baltic with their three daughters in November 1969. They settled in the town of Valga in the Estonian republic, where Georg again found employment in construction. There they waited for permission to immigrate to Canada based on family reunification. They left soon after officials granted them their request four years later, and arrived in Toronto, Canada, on 9 October 1973 where Georg reunited with his mother and sister after a separation of almost thirty years. Dzhetisai, it turned out, had been but a detour on a journey that had taken him from Margenau in Soviet Ukraine to war-torn Berlin to post-war Arkhangelsk Oblast of the Spetskommandatura to post-Stalinist Dzhetisai to Valga to Niagara.[29]

The arrival of the Schmidt family to Niagara and the Sawatsky family to Neuwied coincided with the onset of a new round of emigration fever among Soviet Mennonites. For that reason alone, it is worth pondering that those same Mennonites had never been more Soviet and Russian than they had become by the late Brezhnev era. Several reasons present themselves, including the cultural impact of compulsory state education and mandatory military service for all males, even though Mennonites claimed that officials often placed them in non-combatant roles. Most Soviet Mennonites also lived in cities in Siberia and the Central Asian Republics, which were off-limits to western tourists and which severely constrained their contact with relatives and friends living abroad. Even fleeting family reunions required Soviet Mennonites to travel long distances to Moscow or Leningrad, where family members on formally organized tours could spend brief moments together in heavily supervised Intourist hotels. For example, in 1972, Georg and Maria Schmidt travelled with their children to Leningrad, where they met Georg's cousins Helen and Erna in the Intourist hotel where they had arrived as part of a tourist trip to selected cities of the Soviet Union. Those who travelled to the Russian heartland from the Mennonite heartland in Central Asia faced journeys of more than twenty hours, one way, by train.[30]

No wonder Soviet acculturation had begun to realize significant gains among Mennonites who were often scattered in distant republics. Visitors to Mennonite settlements in Karaganda and elsewhere by the 1980s observed that only the elderly continued to use German in daily discourse. Mennonites in their twenties and younger, by contrast, conversed almost exclusively in Russian, whereas those in between spoke a hybrid language which combined Russian and German, often within the same sentence. Many Mennonites had incorporated Russian words directly into their Plautdietsch dialect. Anthropologist Ipatov observed that Mennonites who maintained a religious affiliation in registered Mennonite congregations tended to maintain German proficiency the longest, though even here congregants increasingly heard Russian spoken during times of communal prayer or in congregational hymns, partly in response to the rise in ethnic Russian congregational members through marriage and informal evangelism. The thousands of Mennonites who worshipped in Baptist congregations within the AUCECB did so overwhelmingly in Russian, and the increasing numbers of Mennonites who had secularized maintained only a rudimentary understanding of German. Even in Germany and Canada transplanted Soviet Mennonites subscribed to Russian-language Soviet journals and magazines years after they had emigrated.[31]

Contrary to the popular stereotype of Mennonite isolationism, Walter Sawatsky maintains that Russian Orthodox theology directly influenced their theological development in the post-Stalinist era. He cites Konstantin Prokhorov of Omsk, who highlights the attention given in Soviet Mennonite churches to the ecclesial working of the Holy Spirit – a bedrock Orthodox tenet – as opposed to more individualized approaches in the west. Orthodox martyrologies also provide a template for how post-Stalinist Evangelicals, Mennonites among them, embraced their own martyrs from the Stalinist era. Taken together, Soviet Mennonite theological development by the 1970s united Mennonite, Evangelical, and Orthodox strands and would later stymy attempts by Umsiedler to create a unified Conference in Germany, where some twenty Umsiedler Mennonite associations had formed by 2004. Umsiedler struggled to establish unified institutions, such as denominational unions, given the fractured legacy and multiple identities formed during the Soviet era. Even the twenty Mennonite congregational associations had been only loosely structured, which allowed key ministers maximum autonomy to program, raise funds, set budgets, and formulate publishing and mission ventures as they saw fit. Those Umsiedler brought together in this manner met annually or semi-annually for large worship events, though leaders consulted perhaps quarterly and more often by phone. Pre-existing German Mennonite Conferences initially gained few of the Umsiedler, although that gradually changed as those of the 1970s migration acclimated to German culture and religious expression.[32]

Johannes Dyck, a representative of this post-Stalinist generation, saw this post-Gulag Mennonite theology work itself out in three circles which mirrored Sawatsky's earlier iteration: a first in which believers evinced a "living personal faith" rooted in a heavenly Father who had forgiven the sins of the repentant believer; a second circle which stressed the corporate life of believers who had forsaken the ways of the world and together sought strength in the battle against alcoholism, divorce, moral laxness, and a variety of other social ills; and a third circle where followers of Jesus proclaimed their faith and non-worldly lifestyle as witnesses to the larger world.[33]

We see all of these themes manifested in a series of recorded sermons delivered by Johannes Fast between 1973 and 1978. Fast's life was itself a remarkable pilgrimage. Born in 1886 in the Mennonite colony of Alexandertal on the left bank of the Volga River, Fast studied theology in Switzerland from 1911 to 1913 and returned to seven devastating years of war, revolution, and civil war in his homeland. In 1931 officials sent Fast, by then a minister, and his young family into the Gulag where they remained for more than twenty years. Freed in 1954, he spent several years seeking a home in Soviet Central Asia; that is, until December 1967 when he made his own detour to Dzhetisai, where he lived until his death in April 1981.[34] In scores of sermons later recorded Fast made plain a post-Gulag theology rooted in the acceptance of Christ as Lord and Saviour, the centrality of the church congregation to a lived faith, and the call for regenerate Christians to live regenerate lives. At no point did he enter into polemics against the Soviet state, a *sine qua non* for all congregations that wished to function with a minimum of police interference.[35] Who could have anticipated as Fast delivered those sermons that it would be the Brezhnevite state itself that soon would come crashing down?

Episode Four: Gorbachev, Collapse, and Mass Emigration, 1985–93

Brezhnev did not immediately give way to Gorbachev, as first Yuri Andropov and then Konstantin Chernenko succeeded the long-infirm General Secretary when he died on 10 November 1982. Both of them died after a few short months in power, the last gasp of a dying generation. Mikhail Gorbachev represented a remarkable shift when he came to power in March 1985. Convinced that the Soviet Union required radical change, he launched a powerful revolution intent on transforming the state while preserving it, along with the hegemony of the CPSU. Within six years it all lay in ruins.[36]

In its sharp downward spiral, however, Gorbachev evoked an approach guided by such exotic terms as *perestroika* and *glasnost'* as he promised a brave new world for all, one that would be honest about the past and hopeful about the future. Much of this appealed to Mennonites, and all peoples initially. In 1987, for example, Gorbachev established a special commission to rehabilitate those whom the Soviet state had repressed in the 1930s. It coincided with a remarkable moment when the general secretary denounced Stalin in his speech to mark the seventieth anniversary of the Great October Socialist Revolution. Two years later, in November 1989 the Supreme Soviet of the Soviet Union condemned the politics of forced relocation of minorities under Stalin, a condemnation that spoke directly to Mennonites.[37]

As if that was not enough, Gorbachev introduced virtually unhindered religious freedom after 1985. Soviet journals such as *Nauka i Religiia* (Science and Religion) markedly changed their approach to religious faith as articles now proclaimed Soviet believers (and Evangelical Christians, especially) as model citizens. Why? They did not drink alcohol, they worked diligently, and they stayed married, with few divorces. The Soviets finally released the Tengiz Aduladze's previously banned film *Repentance*, which immediately became a sensation across the country and internationally with its explicitly Christian motifs. Lastly, Leningrad's Museum of Religion and Atheism, housed in the city's once magnificent Kazan Cathedral, revamped its exhibits to portray a more benign view of clergy, believers, and churches.

As exclamation point, Gorbachev met with Patriarch Pimen, the primate of the Russian Orthodox Church, on 29 April 1988 as the church openly celebrated the millennium of Christianization of Kievan Rus. In a shift that would have been unthinkable even months earlier

Communist officials and Orthodox hierarchs shared the stage to celebrate an explicitly Christian event: the baptism of the Rus. In its honour, Moscow permitted the mass publication of Bibles for the first time in decades, as state officials appeared alongside priests at public celebrations across the USSR. Victoria Smolkin argues that these changes came about because the Soviet state realized by the late 1970s that atheistic inculcation had failed to irradicate religion in Soviet society. Quite the contrary, the election of Karol Józef Wojtyła, the Polish cardinal, as pope of the Roman Catholic Church in 1978 highlighted the degree to which religion had begun to flourish again on the public stage. Nor had it disappeared on the home front within the Soviet Union, where up to half of all infants born in the most populous cities in the country – including Moscow, Kharkov, and Kursk – had been baptized. Rural rates were said to be even higher. Gorbachev's change in approach, then, reflected the degree to which a broad religious revival was underway. All of this was without precedent, and Mennonites responded in two distinct ways.[38]

First, Mennonites joined Baptists and Evangelicals when they claimed a piece of the Millennium as pan-Christian celebrations irrupted across the Soviet Union in the fall of 1988, including in Mennonite strongholds. For example, leader Daniel Janzen of the independent Mennonite Brethren planned an event that fall for the town of Donskoy in Orenburg Oblast. Officials approved the use of the Palace of Culture for the main service, and congregants agreed to stay home as they anticipated unbelievers might attend given the news that a special choir would perform. Even so, church officials closed the doors an hour before the scheduled start as numbers had already well exceeded space. The Donskoy event was replicated elsewhere across the Soviet Union, and the appeal was such that organizers often turned a single commemorative service into a week-long series of evangelistic services, an unimaginable development before Gorbachev.[39]

Petr Epp deemed the unhindered ability to worship as the first sign of true freedom. Previously unidentified guests to a service had always threatened to be state agents. Now those very guests indicated the health of the church as doors opened wide onto the streets. In 1988 two sisters in Solntsevka village of Omsk raion donated their home for church officials to repurpose as a new church building (known in Russian as a "House of Prayer"). The construction continued even after local officials ordered it to stop and had blocked the delivery of building materials. Workers completed the rebuild within months, in time for the official dedication on 4 September 1988. Soon Mennonites had joined other Evangelicals to construct new church buildings in other villages, including Petrovka, Marianovka, and Isil'kul. Choirs sang in these settlements as they walked up and down village streets, and accompanying preachers invited all to attend the weekly gatherings. In total, believers constructed eleven new church buildings in Omsk raion between 1988 and 1990 and repurposed six others.[40] A religious revival had burst forth on ostensibly socialist and atheist soil, and believers seemed ready for the challenge.

That being the case, it is paradoxical that Mennonites undertook a second response to Gorbachev's policies of Perestroika and Glasnost when they emigrated from the USSR to Germany in the largest Mennonite migration in their history. Approximately thirteen thousand Soviet Mennonites had emigrated from the Soviet Union between 1951 and Brezhnev's death in 1982, alongside several hundred thousand Soviet Germans. However, Gorbachev's commitment to freedom of speech and mobility robbed Moscow of any argument to block Soviet Germans, Mennonites included, from emigrating. Two years later, the collapse of the Berlin Wall stimulated an even greater push despite Soviet pleas that they remain and help transform their socialist homeland. Almost one million Soviet Germans emigrated between 1987 and 1997, of which Mennonites comprised 100,000. Almost no self-identified Mennonites remained in the Soviet Union by the time of its collapse in 1991, and the emigration fever continued for several years after that. Nor were they alone, as well over three million Russians and Ukrainians also emigrated at this time, overwhelmingly bound for North America.

They left behind a radically transformed landscape, one largely bereft of its leaders. For example, in the Orenburg raion village of Stepanovka only 30–40 Mennonites stayed behind as some 1,300 had emigrated. One hundred Mennonite Brethren members left the village of Petrovka in those years, whereas fifteen had stayed. Some had clear reasons for their decision to emigrate; others later said they left because everyone else had done so. In Germany these so-called Russian German Umsiedler settled overwhelmingly in the Rhineland, as a new chapter in their storied history had begun.[41]

Chapter Fourteen

Coda: Zaporozhe 1989. One Story Ends and Another Begins

"Through much tribulation you must enter the kingdom of God. Christ himself so suffered and entered into his glory."[1] Mennonites who remained in the Soviet Union as it collapsed could easily have imagined that Menno Simons, the renegade Roman Catholic priest, had composed these words with their experience in mind. One can make a case that no period in the almost five hundred years of Anabaptist and Mennonite history was more wracked with tribulation than the one experienced by Soviet Mennonites from 1917 to 1991.

Of course, Menno Simons wrote "The Foundation of Christian Doctrine," from which this excerpt appears, in 1539 and not 1919, 1929, or 1959. In this, his most beloved and popular work, Menno argued for the creation of a true church of faithful believers. He took this radical stance because, after much prayer and reflection, he had concluded that the existing (Roman Catholic) Church had fallen away from the living Word of God as manifested both in the Bible and in Christ himself. As a result, the Roman church had fallen under the full influence of the Antichrist, such that its vaunted Eucharistic table had become the table of the devil.[2] Menno urged his readers to "to arise with Christ in a new, righteous and penitent existence," and there was no time to lose. Christ's return was imminent, the Kingdom of God was at hand.[3] We have already considered in this study how many of these ideas for radical reform emerged, ironically, out of the Roman Catholic Church itself before and during Menno's time, but what interests us here is Menno's commitment to the full and undivided Christianization of society, a commitment he shared with other Reformers.

What role would the civil magistrate play in this necessary rebirth of the universal church? Contrary to the call made in the Schleitheim Confession among Swiss Mennonites in 1527 to separate themselves out from a fallen world, Menno in 1539 saw a vital role for magistrates in a reconstituted Christendom that would be true to God's desire.[4] They could start by stopping, at least when it came to their wilful persecution of the one true Church, for that is what Menno had begun to create. These words carried special weight in the aftermath of the Münster debacle when magistrates ferociously turned on the re-baptizer movement in Flanders, Netherlands, and the north German states. Though the various magistrates eventually ended the era of the Anabaptist martyrs, they did not convert to Menno's understanding of the one true faith. In response, his followers increasingly portrayed themselves as a faithful remnant at the margins of society, what Scott Hendrix evocatively calls "A New Monasticism." And the magistrates? As I indicated in my introduction, the states formed by these magistrates only became stronger as a result of the Reformation. Meanwhile Christendom fragmented and disappeared as a unifying force. This shift to a post-Christendom state emerged first, ironically, in Menno's backyard, the Dutch Republic over the course of the seventeenth century, and it did not take long for all Reformation faiths to come to terms with that shifting political reality. Henceforth all reformers, even the Roman Catholic Church, needed to find their place in new polities which no longer felt beholden to them. What made the followers of Menno somewhat unique in this transformation is that they refused to align themselves with any single state, unlike, Calvinists, Lutherans, and most dramatically, Anglicans. Although we normally see this post-Reformation story of increased secularization through a West European lens, it is worth noting that Muscovy – the predecessor to Imperial Russia – wrestled with the same issues at the very same time. There also the state won, the independent church lost.[5]

In a sense, this study has comprised a long reflection on the strategies by which Mennonites engaged secularism and the emergence of the nation state in all its variations from its origins in the Dutch Republic to the modernizing Russian empire in the 1860s to the collapse of the Soviet Union in 1991. I have been most interested in the strategies adopted by which their religiosity persisted, and the shape that it took along the way, and have argued that Mennonites who emerged in northern Europe experienced this emergent secularism on two levels. On the one hand, they experienced it as something that happened to them from outside, starting with the birth of the modern state in sixteenth-century Netherlands. Eventually the Dutch Republic tolerated religious minorities with the proviso that they not challenge the hegemonic political power of the nominally Calvinist state and its corresponding power over economic and societal matters. Of course, that seemingly tolerant society emerged from the ashes of hundreds of immolated Christian sectarian martyrs, many of whom were Anabaptists, the forerunner of the Mennonites. From there the path led eastward to Royal Prussia – part of Kingdom Poland – where other complexities in modern state formation presented themselves, most especially in the imperial city of Danzig. Then the Russian empire arose and in the eighteenth century dramatically expanded its borders eastward, westward, and to the south.

Historians of Imperial Russian history disagree on whether St. Petersburg adopted a highly centralist approach to the conquest and settlement of its southern borderlands north of the Black and Azov seas, or whether it governed newly conquered regions and incoming colonists with a more flexible "politics of difference" approach.[6] A consideration of Mennonite history suggests that St. Petersburg did both over time. From the outset, and in lieu of its own ability to mount an adequate bureaucratic infrastructure, imperial bureaucrats relied on Mennonites and other immigrants to govern themselves at the local level with their own civil administration, one that remained fully accountable to the state. St. Petersburg also and always reserved the right to disregard such bodies and administer affairs with its own appointees. This it did with Mennonites, but this situation was not unique to Mennonites. Nancy Shields Kollmann, building on Karen Barkey, concludes that the Russian empire was one of many which governed vertically in this manner, like spokes on a wheel attached to the centre when the outer rim of the wheel is missing. In even this single instance we can see how perceived notions of Mennonite exceptionality within the empire fall away when scrutinized in context.[7]

Alexander II and a cadre of dedicated enlightened bureaucrats reshaped the empire after its humiliating defeat of the Crimean War. Even then it vacillated between rational notions of universal secular state reforms and more parochial and distinctive formations leaning towards a modernized version of Nicholas I's Official Russian nationalism linked to Orthodoxy. Nicholas I's incongruous policies had done neither him nor the empire much service. Alexander's reforms remained unfinished due to his assassination and his successors failed to build on his policies. By doing so they failed to resolve the tension between radical, secularized calls for reform and the equally radical forces of Russian nationalism and Pan-Slavism. Two wars at the dawn of the twentieth century revealed the weakness of the state, its rulers, officialdom, and relative economic backwardness where it mattered most. This led to the collapse of Imperial Russia.

The newly formed Soviet Union set out on a very different path as it waited for a world revolution. We know that the Soviet Union alternated wildly between measured and brutalized attempts to reshape society, and how negatively it viewed religious belief in the process. We know that any one decade contained wild shifts in policy and implementation, though historians generally agree that leading Bolsheviks believed socialism would be in reach if they solved the peasant problem of societal backwardness through agricultural collectivization and the creation of a truly industrial society; the most modern on the planet and the shape of the world to come. To give but one example, Eric Lohr concludes that the regime moved quickly to enshrine citizenship rights after the October Revolution, though it reserved the right to deprive individuals and groups of their citizenship depending on where they fit over time on a mixture of class, ethnic, or cultural or social criteria.[8] Even so it was a modernizing and secularizing society by any measure.

Over more than two centuries, then, the Mennonites found themselves at the epicentre of states caught up in secularization, and that includes the Nazi occupation of the Mennonite heartland in Soviet Ukraine during the Second World War. In this I have accepted Konrad Jarausch's recent formulation that the modernization associated with secularization took three distinct forms in twentieth-century Europe: communism, fascism, and a liberalism deeply embedded with state-protected capitalism.[9] Even such a brief overview indicates how complex and intertwined these historical processes were. Nor did these three forms proceed in a linear manner, as becomes evident when we consider Soviet policies towards religion. Moscow banned all religious services in the late 1920s, legalized religious associations in the early 1940s, launched a war on religion in the early 1960s, and softened its stance again in the 1970s.

At a second level Mennonites were much more than passive victims in this process of modernization and secularization. They engaged it directly and occasionally maintained their congregational life at their own peril. Both women and men acted in this process, starting with the Dutch Republic, where Mennonites and Melchiorites actively participated in the European economic revolution based in Amsterdam. Those who subsequently migrated to Danzig and Kingdom Poland integrated into the society around them, most clearly seen in their acquisition of Plautdietsch, and later, German. Many entered artisinal guilds, others flourished in the arts, and all eventually received permission to construct their own meetinghouses in the sundry jurisdictions even though they needed to comply with regulations designed to limit their visibility. Officials enforced other restrictions when they forbade Mennonites to proselytize, and they regularized these arrangements through a series of negotiated contracts, or privilegia. Each one involved a measure of compromise, as when Mennonites agreed not to proselytize as a condition of settlement. They agreed to pay a special tax in lieu of military service in the local militia and later, in the imperial army after Hohenzollern Prussia introduced conscription. New converts joined the Mennonites during these years, but they needed to do so surreptitiously.

Mennonite engagement with secularization accelerated when they settled in the Russian empire as the state expected the new settlers essentially to govern themselves. This should not surprise in an empire that was as under-governed as this one, but it did result in points of tension between Mennonite ministry councils and Mennonite mayors and other state servitors, of whom Johann Cornies proved the most significant. Once again, Mennonites and the state negotiated their relationship through a privilegium or contract, but what other option did either party have at a time when no notion of citizenship existed? Of even greater significance, "Mennonite" became the legal designation St. Petersburg applied to all who entered the empire as, well, Mennonites. In time a significant number of these Mennonites ceased to engage in any meaningful way with congregational life even though their legal status as Mennonites did not change.

Mennonites engaged the empire in the post-Crimean era when they confronted the twin challenges of imperial modernization and Russian nationalism. By the one Mennonites defended their right to a military exemption after an emerging notion of citizenship and a revamped militarization strategy blurred the distinction between them and peasants. By the other Mennonites struggled against a state that increasingly regarded them by the new category of nationality, by which Russian nationalists classified them as German and a threat to the empire. Of course significant numbers of Mennonites responded to these new challenges when they migrated to North America after 1874, and more migrations would follow. Yet despite these obstacles and departures the Mennonite commonwealth appeared alive and well as late as 1914 as the guns of August boomed out, and the disintegration of Europe began.

Mennonites remained actively engaged as the empire collapsed and the Soviet state emerged from the rubble of the civil war. They alternately sent delegations abroad in search of material aid and assistance with emigration. Others dug deep into the wellsprings of their faith or armed themselves against perceived threats, often to their peril. They formed pan-Mennonite associations in both the Russian and Ukrainian republics after 1921 and persistently lobbied senior officials up to the Politburo itself for the right to re-establish themselves economically, educate their young as they alone saw fit and to worship freely. Others chose a different path as they actively served in the Soviet bureaucracy even as officialdom began to turn against Mennonites for any number of reasons. Even so, countless women continued to worship in the privacy of their homes and instruct their children in story and song, long after Moscow had banned such activity. Mennonite men agreed to serve as ministers and Ältesters, even as the state arrested existing church leaders and sent them off into the Gulag, and many of those sentenced formed worshipping communities in the very locales where officials banished them. We saw the same range of responses during the short-lived Nazi occupation when some, often younger Mennonites, collaborated with the deadly forces of the Nazi regime, whereas many more gathered to worship again and baptize their youth under open skies. In the late Soviet era, long after the Mennonite commonwealth had disintegrated, Mennonites still negotiated their space in a Soviet state intent on modernizing socialist-style. Once again both women and men played vital roles as communities of faith attempted to rejuvenate. That said, many simply abandoned their faith in the face of persistent Soviet acculturation, others found a legal and registered path to maintain it and still others entered fully into the so-called underground church. There is widespread evidence to conclude that Mennonites had culturally Sovietized and Russified by the 1970s, though those who had left the church by then experienced these trends most acutely. Many who remained believers no longer did so from within a formally Mennonite congregation, having joined the Baptists or Evangelicals. Every step of the way, then, Mennonites actively engaged the modernizing and secularizing trajectories of the various states they entered. They were never fully disengaged, never entirely a distinct people who were somehow closeted away from state and society.

Nor did emigration solve all problems when it came to the challenge that modernization and secularization presented, and that becomes clear when one considers the fate of these emigre "Russian" Mennonites and their descendants in South and North America. Survey after survey launched in the first decades of the new millennium warned that the Mennonite church in North America had declined dramatically, "Russian" Mennonites among them. Churches had begun to close as part of a larger pattern across the continent of which Mennonites comprised but a small portion. Attendance at Mennonite churches waned dramatically after the 1970s, while the median age of attendees rose. In other words, fewer Mennonites worshipped, and fewer younger ones especially. As part of the increased marginalization of faith, a growing number of Canadians and Americans, including millions of ostensible believers, now maintained that religion was a matter of personal belief

Figure 12. A baptism service held on the Dnieper River at Zaporozhe (old Chortitza), Soviet Ukraine. Photograph by Neil Janzen. *Mennonite Historian*, vol. 15, no. 3 (September 1989), 5.

and did not deserve a voice in the public square. Believers agreed that religion, if anything, played a negative and divisive role within society, and in any event accepted that it should have no voice in the major society discussions underway, from abortion to gay rights to end-of-life discussions. Meanwhile their numbers continued to drop. Mennonite Church USA, the country's largest conference, declined from 133,000 members in 1998 to below 92,000 in 2016, a figure which included the Lancaster Mennonite Conference, which counted in 1998 but had left by 2015. The decline in Canada followed a similar trajectory. Because many worshipped within congregations identified as formed through historically "Swiss" or "Russian" Mennonite migrations they have also tended not to proselytize in their communities. This meant that churches largely accomplished renewal through generational replacement, which had become unlikely given the disinclination of younger

Mennonites to attend church. Many, especially in urban centres, concluded that life in a multifaith and no-faith society required them to set aside age-old tenets of faith that proclaimed Christ as the only path to salvation. Few regarded ancient creedal formulations and ancient formulations of morality to be authoritative.[10]

On this point, Charles Taylor has suggested that even those in our secular age who deem themselves to be believers cannot overcome their own misgivings and doubts about the veracity of their faith amid this mass liberal and secularized acculturation. Even believers come to believe that their lives unfold solely in profane time, cut off from what Taylor calls "higher time."[11] Meanwhile donations to churches and church agencies steadily declined, which further weakened the evangelical and social work of the whole. Churches shuttered or merged to save on costs and Mennonite schools faced increased challenges to stay afloat as "brand loyalty" waned. After the great era of post-war Mennonite institution building, Mennonites in the new millennium rebranded as they removed the name "Mennonite" itself from churches, insurance companies, and credit unions in favour of more generic appellations.

In his study of Mennonites and politics, James Urry concludes that Mennonites faced debilitating threats to their identity in Canada, even if they did not take the shape of legal prejudice, mass arrest, imprisonment, execution, or group expulsion. Instead, in Urry's words, "the new political forces desired to integrate Mennonites into their increasingly secular nation-states as useful citizens through the promise of freedom and legal equality with others. But this meant that Mennonite religious identities were to be subordinated and subsumed by a secular definition of being and belonging based upon nationalist allegiances. As a consequence, Mennonite separate and separated communities were to be homogenized into a mass society based on principles of common citizenship, associated with a common legal code." Not surprisingly, the end result of this acculturation has led to religious beliefs that stress the personal and emotional, with no offence offered to others, that is, if they survive at all.[12]

All of this is remarkable given the recent critical assessments of the liberal society to which North American Mennonites have become so acculturated. As our introduction suggested, there is a growing literature on what Charles Taylor has evocatively described as the "Malaise of Modernity" for our time. We have not found an adequate substitution for religious belief in the public square or as a means of determining absolute Truth, and this has left us entirely self-referential, adrift in a subjective sea. We have substituted absolute values or meanings for Zygmount Bauman's liquid modernity, one that leaves us with little guidance as we confront what Brad Gregory has called "Life Questions." In his study on the "Disenchantment of Secular Discourse," Stephen Smith posits that we no longer trust the efficacy of reason. Public discourse has become shallow. The solution? He suggests that we find a way to bring other absolute faiths into the public square again beyond, of course, the absolute faith that many have placed in liberalism. If that is to happen we will need to look for other voices with other absolute claims. Sadly at a time when religion of whatever stripe might enrich our public discourse we find Mennonites among those faiths that struggle to survive in North America. We are a long way from Menno Simons and 1539.[13]

Not so in the former Soviet Union, at least not yet, so I want to conclude this study by outlining briefly the emergence of a new Mennonite history and a new Mennonite identity in that part of the world since 1991, one that hearkens back to Menno's original vision. To that end, we need to return to Zaporozhe and Gorbachev's appointment as general secretary in March 1985. It should not surprise that Mennonites left en masse when the opportunity presented itself. By all accounts, this should have marked the end of the Mennonite story in Soviet lands. Yet against all odds, what appeared to be an ending in Gorbachev's time actually marked a fresh start. If Mennonites experience such a revival in the lands of the former Soviet Union it may be that five days in August 1989 will serve as its inaugural event. The year itself marked the bi-centennial of the first Mennonite settlement in the Russian empire when 228 families formed a string of villages along the Dnieper River. As readers will know, those first Mennonite immigrants named their settlement Chortitza, and a great deal followed from it, even as they founded a larger Molotschna settlement fifteen years later on the steppe lands east of Chortitza. Not surprisingly, "Russian" Mennonites around the world marked this bi-centennial with commemorative events focused on the past. They organized tours to the Mennonite homeland, and historian Harvey Dyck began to plan for an academic conference and a broad memorialization of the Mennonite experience across Soviet Ukraine.[14]

Ironically, events that unfolded in the former Chortitza settlement that year marked a dramatic exception to this pattern of nostalgia-based travel and commemoration. Initially it appeared doubtful that any events would happen on site as few Mennonites remained in Chortitza, which the aging industrial powerhouse of Zaporozhe had largely subsumed over many decades. In addition, the Soviet Union remained firmly opposed to the public display of religion in the years leading up to 1989, which blocked any sort of public religious commemoration. But times changed rapidly, as we have discussed. Most dramatically, Soviet officials opened the door for such a Mennonite commemoration when they endorsed the state-wide millennial commemoration in 1988 of Christianity's arrival in ancient Kievan Rus.[15]

The lack of a Mennonite congregational sponsor for such a bi-centennial celebration in Chortitza further hindered any celebration, even though some Mennonites still called that area home. Though few in number, they had managed to return to Chortitza after the Great Patriotic War (1941–44) and in contravention to state decrees. In most instances, this involved Mennonite women or men who married Ukrainians and took on the Ukrainian name and identity. For example, Mennonite Henrikh Dik (Dyck), born in the village of Schönhorst (Ruchaevka today) in 1920 married a Ukrainian woman whom he met while studying in Dneprodzerzhinsk after the war. He then assumed her family name so as to be able to return to the region after his period of wartime service in the Trudarmei ended. After the Trudarmei disbanded in 1956 this suddenly Ukrainian family returned from the Irkutsk region to Dnepropetrovsk, where they set up their home in a squatter settlement amid the deep ravines of Dnepropetrovsk. Other such exceptions included Boris Letkemann, whose family returned to Nieder Chortitza, and countless Mennonite women who married Ukrainian men, which allowed them to live peaceful hidden lives in their home villages or nearby. So there remained scattered Mennonites in the Zaporozhe region in 1989 but insufficient to host a large commemorative gathering.[16]

Viktor Fast, a leader in the Karaganda (Kazakhstan) Mennonite Brethren Church, stepped into the breach along with representatives from the Karaganda Kirchliche Gemeinde and Mennonites who attended registered Evangelical and Baptist congregations. Together they found two registered Baptist congregations in Zaporozhe prepared to sponsor such an event. After a month of intense negotiations with Soviet officials Fast gained permission to organize a five-day celebration planned from 10 to 15 August 1989. It brought together some twenty Mennonite ministers and Ältesters from Soviet Central Asia, West Germany, and North America, along with hundreds of Mennonites who had made the long train journey from across the Central Asian republics. Over one hundred Mennonite congregants came from Karaganda alone. The celebrations coincided with the visit of a fact-finding delegation from Mennonite Economic Development Associates (MEDA), and a tour of North American Mennonites, arranged by a Mennonite tour company in Winnipeg and led by a young Mennonite and Russian historian from Waterloo, Canada.[17] Those who attended from Germany, almost all recent Umsiedler, brought along up to eight thousand New Testaments and other religious materials, almost all of it in Russian and all of it paid for by a consortium of Dutch, German, and North American Mennonites; the later involvement thanks to the intervention of Walter Sawatsky.

In preparation for the occasion members of local Baptist churches distributed promotional leaflets to every single household in Zaporozhe, a city of some 700,000, as well as to neighbouring villages in the region. The two Baptist churches hosted the first gatherings in the evening of Thursday, 10 August 1989, for which the congregational choir of the Karaganda Mennonite Brethren Congregation in Karaganda sang a mixture of Russian- and German-language hymns. Preachers at these and all other events for the week preached in Russian, or in German with Russian translation, and they focused on themes of praise and gratitude to God. A special text on this first day was from 1 Peter 1:3–6 and included an unmistakable allusion to the era of tribulation which was now over. It reads: "Blessed be the God and Father of our Lord Jesus Christ! By his great mercy he has given us a new birth into a living hope through the resurrection of Jesus Christ from the dead, and into an inheritance that is imperishable, undefiled, and unfading, kept in heaven for you, who are being protected by the power of God through faith for a salvation ready to be revealed in the last time. In this you rejoice, even if now for a little while you have had to suffer various trials." No one needed to be told what those "various trials" had been.

The next morning participants gathered outside the ancient oak that marked the focal point of the first Chortitza settlement, even as it had been the lodestone of Zaporozhian Cossacks before that. Here preachers focused on the two-hundred-year history of the Mennonites and how God had faithfully led them throughout their sojourn. At the close of the service Soviet Intourist guides took the participants on a bus tour of Zaporozhe. That evening numerous choirs sang at a large youth gathering open to the city, for which an offering raised rubles for children's support services across Zaporozhe. Here also Viktor Fast addressed the youth on Mennonite history, starting with its origins in the Swiss Anabaptist awakening of the early sixteenth century.

The most remarkable events still lay ahead, starting with a gathering on the banks of the Dnieper River. On Saturday, 12 August, Ältesters baptized fifty-three individuals as some three thousand looked on. The worship service did not stop after the baptism as western observers expected, but instead carried on while participants read Bible passages, sang hymns, prayed aloud, and wept at the sheer joy of public worship. As reported by John Klassen and Hans von Niessen, some in attendance came forward, so moved by the testimonies they had heard. In front of all assembled the penitents declared their sinfulness and beseeched God to forgive their sins for Jesus's sake.

At a service that evening, this time held at the city's large Baptist church building, participants again received spiritual instruction as ministers spoke for two hours in German and another in Russian. The theme? It was "What does the faith of our fathers have to offer today's generation?" Choirs sang intermittently, and international visitors brought greetings, including Art Defehr from MEDA. The capstone event the next day, after Sunday morning services throughout the city, involved an open-air service in Zaporozhe's Avangard Statium. No one knew how many would attend this event given the wide publicity generated across Zaporozhe. Beyond all expectations, the stadium filled up quickly after officials opened the gates, such that it quickly reached its maximum capacity of 10,000. Those unable to enter milled around in the parking lots and listened to the service broadcast on loudspeakers. Choirs sang, preachers preached, and even the head of the Zaporozhe Communist Party delivered greetings, all of it astonishing. Everything unfolded in Russian on this day, including the invitation delivered repeatedly to turn to Jesus Christ. Those who preached made almost no mention of Mennonites in their sermons. It was an evangelistic moment, start to finish. Unexpectedly hundreds towards the end of the service came forward to declare themselves ready to repent and live lives transformed as Christians. At the end of the service more than 8,000 New Testaments and other religious materials, all insufficient to meet demand as crowds surged to the distribution points.

The next day organizers travelled with select participants for a tour of the Molotschna settlement, several hours distant from Zaporozhe on less-than-ideal roadways. Once again a choir sang hymns and preachers preached at key stops, including at Molochansk, the former Halbstadt. With their return to Zaporozhe's Intourist hotel that evening the week's events came to an end. Some returned to their homes in Siberia and Central Area where localized celebrations followed, with the largest in Omsk, Orenburg, and Karaganda. In all settings the focus remained on winning new converts to the faith. International travel on pre-arranged tours carried on, whether to Soviet Central Asia or Moscow and Leningrad, while local Baptist and Evangelical leaders began to engage those for whom those five unprecedented days in Zaporozhe had turned their lives upside down. Correspondent John N. Klassen ended his report as he enthusiastically proclaimed that the Lord had opened the door to a new mission field in the Soviet Union. He challenged Mennonites in the west to become co-workers in this process. They should all take heart, knowing that the body of Christ was alive and well in Russia because the Lord Himself was alive and well.

As dramatic as the Zaporozhe days were in August 1989 they were by no means isolated in space and time. Even in that same year noted Mennonite evangelist Viktor Hamm – soon to become an executive with the Billy Graham crusade – preached before tens of thousands in Riga, Vilnius, Kiev, Moscow, Zarech'e, Novosibirsk, Kemerovo, and Briansk. Authorities cooperated at every turn and hundreds committed themselves to the Christian message at these events. At every turn evangelists encouraged all converts to find a church home to nurture their newfound faith.[18]

The religious awakening experienced in Omsk at the end of the 1980s also continued into the 1990s and beyond. Those "traditional" Mennonites who had not emigrated threw themselves into evangelical outreach. As described in the previous chapter Mennonites initially joined other believers in spontaneous efforts to evangelize their communities and often focused their activity on their own members who had fallen away. But by the 1990s the various Mennonite and evangelical congregations in the region decided that they needed to coordinate their evangelistic efforts among unbelievers, so they formed a leadership council (literally a "soviet") comprised of I.I. Neufeld, P.K. Reger, A.P. Reger, A.F. Flaming, N.N. Dikman, and B.V. Gamm (Hamm). By this plan they developed a new coordinated plan to evangelize, starting in 1990. Among other initiatives they formed an ecumenical travelling library of Christian resources to reach far-flung villages. They arranged to canvas homes of unbelievers more systematically, visited inmates in prison, and arranged for regular presentations in village schools as they shifted away from their initial focus on large-scale tent meetings. They also distributed thousands of publications produced by recent Soviet Mennonite immigrants (Umsiedler) in Germany.[19]

The Umsiedler became a key link in the new evangelism underway from the 1990s to the present day, perhaps motivated by a sense that they should not have emigrated when the opportunity presented itself. One of the church leaders behind Zaporozhe 1989 who subsequently immigrated to Germany, Viktor Fast – formerly of Karaganda – said this at a workshop in 2000: "we have realized that we have sinned, because we did not do enough to carry out the missionary commission of Jesus Christ, afraid to try new strategies. So we are returning with a deep mission commitment."[20] It was a bold confession, but true to his word Fast and many others did indeed pour their energies into ministries of evangelism and mission in their former homeland.

Almost immediately they formed mission agencies dedicated to the former Soviet Union (after its collapse in 1991), of which the Aquila Mission and the Logos Mission are the most important. Both have raised significant funds that have gone to a wide range of needs, including the publication and distribution of Bibles, periodicals, and church histories, the construction of church buildings, as well as the outfitting of summer camps for children and the provision of medical supplies and foodstuffs.

A representative issue of *Aquila* magazine from January 2020 made plain that it supported mission work among congregations in Siberia, Kazakhstan, Kyrgyzstan, Moldavia, Ukraine, and Uzbekistan. It boldly declared a verse from the New Testament book of Acts as its mission statement: "For we cannot keep from speaking about what we have seen and heard." The issue contained a map which demonstrated the geographic breadth of its involvement in the former Soviet Union as well as devotional materials meant to nurture Christian faith. Photos and articles suggested the range of Aquila Mission's activity, from the distribution of food packages to evangelist efforts among all ages and backgrounds.[21] It was clearly ecumenical in approach and committed to the whole of any society where it operated, though the January 2020 issue included a long writing from Menno Simons and a biography of Herman Enns and his father, both evangelists and both of whom suffered for their faith in the early Soviet and Stalinist periods. Mennonitism and ecumenicity intermingled. Interestingly, Viktor Fast, the lead organizer of the 1989 celebrations in Zaporozhe, is a regular author, as he combines historical reflections with evangelical outreach. Several articles appealed for increased child evangelization and the need to win souls among the Kazakh population of Kazakhstan.

Walter Sawatsky and Johannes Dyck have summarized the elements of this latest iteration of an engaged Mennonite faith and find that it follows closely from the late Soviet era. Here we see again a stress on the Lordship of Christ and the centrality of the scriptures to ground a believer's life. Evangelists urge believers of all backgrounds to make a personal decision for Christ because the time is short before He returns. They urge new converts to join a community of faith. They must also do so knowing that a vast sea of occasionally hostile unbelievers surrounds them. They must love those unbelievers, even amid a persecution that is sure to come, for this discipleship comes at a cost. Evangelism is key, and for that reason the distinctions among Christians matters far less than that which places a unified Christianity against the devastation of our present secularized age.

Denominationalism, the very identity marker of "Mennonite" congregations, is not the goal nor the purpose; a redeemed creation is, and the hope of a globally unified Christianity. Nor does ethnicity have any bearing on religious or ecclesial identity, especially at a time when German names like Franz or Jakob have started to give way to new Mennonite names, Kazakh among them, including Abdul and Mohammed. Echoes of Menno Simons in 1539 are everywhere. In that new start and remarkable call lies the future of the Mennonite church in the former Soviet Union, if not worldwide, and an ongoing challenge to unfettered secularizations in the West.[22]

Notes

Acknowledgments

1 See my "Acknowledgments" in *Minority Report: Mennonite Identities in Imperial Russia and Soviet Ukraine Reconsidered, 1789–1945*, edited by Leonard G. Friesen (Toronto: University of Toronto Press, 2018), ix–x.

Introduction

1 John J. Friesen, ed., *Mennonites in Russia, 1788–1988: Essays in Honour of Gerhard Lohrenz* (Winnipeg: CMBC Publications, 1989).
2 Aleksander A. Klaus, *Nashi kolonii. Opyty i materialy po istorii isstatistiki inostrannoi kolonizatsii v Rossii* (St. Petersburg, 1869); David H. Epp, *Die Chortitzer Mennoniten: Versuch einer Darstellung des Entwicklungsgagnes derselben* (Odessa: A. Schulze, 1889); James Urry, *None but Saints: The Transformation of Mennonite Life in Russia, 1789–1889* (Winnipeg: Hyperion, 1989); Walter Sawatsky, "My Pilgrimage to the East" (unpub., dated 20 January 2011), in possession of author; and Walter Sawatsky, *Going Global with God as Mennonites for the 21st Century* (North Newton, KS: Bethel College, 2017). For two dated, but still relevant, overviews of early historiography on this subject, see David G. Rempel, "An Introduction to Russian Mennonite Historiography," *MQR* 48 (1974), 409–46; and Cornelius Krahn, "Historiography: Russia." *GAMEO*, 1956, https://gameo.org/index.php?title=Historiography:_Russia&oldid=134954.
3 Franz Isaak, *Die Molotschnaer Mennoniten: Ein Beitrag zur Geschichte derselben, aus Akten älterer und eneuerer Zeit, wie auch auf Grund eigener Erlebnisse und Erfahrungen dargestellt* (Halbstadt, 1908); and Peter M. Friesen, *The Mennonite Brotherhood in Russia (1789–1910)*, trans. J. B. Toews and others (Fresno, CA: Board of Christian Literature [M.B.], 1978, rev. ed. 1980).

4 On this school, see Leonard G. Friesen, "Dnipropetrovsk State University, Khortitsa '99, and the Renaissance of Public (Mennonite) History in Ukraine," in *Minority Report: Mennonite Identities in Imperial Russia and Soviet Ukraine Reconsidered, 1789–1945*, ed. Leonard G. Friesen (Toronto: University of Toronto Press, 2018), 319–32; and John R. Staples, "The Mennonite Commonwealth Paradigm and the Dnepropetrovsk School Ukrainian Mennonite Historiography," in *Voprosy germanskoi istorii* (Dnepropetrovsk, Ukraine: Porogi, 2007), 58–68.

5 The literature covered here is vast and will be discussed in this study. Citations are available in the bibliography for highlighted works. By way of context, see James Urry, "The Transformation of Scholarship on the Russian Mennonites in a New Age of Transition: A Second Introduction," in *None but Saints: The Transformation of Mennonite Life in Russia, 1789–1989*, 2nd printing with a new Introduction (Kitchener, ON: Pandora Press, 2007); A.I. Savin, *Ethno-Confession in the Soviet State, 1920–1989*, ed. Paul Toews (Fresno, CA: Center for Mennonite Brethren Studies, 2008); Harvey L. Dyck and Ingrid Epp, *The Peter J. Braun Russian Mennonite Archive: A Research Guide* (Toronto: University of Toronto Press, 1996); and *Transformation on the Southern Ukraine Steppe: Letters and Papers of Johann Cornies*, ed. Harvey L. Dyck, Ingrid I. Epp, and John R. Staples, Volume I: *1812–1835* (Toronto: University of Toronto Press, 2015); and Volume II: *1836–1842* (Toronto: University of Toronto Press, 2020).

6 Leonard G. Friesen, "Introduction," in *Minority Report: Mennonite Identities in Imperial Russia and Soviet Ukraine Reconsidered, 1789–1945*, ed. Leonard G. Friesen (Toronto: University of Toronto Press, 2018). "Hungry Village" comes from Geroid Tanquary Robinson, *Rural Russia under the Old Régime: A History of the Landlord-Peasant World and a Prologue to the Peasant Revolution of 1917* (New York: Longmans, Green and Co., 1932), ch. VI. For an example of the more recent periodization, see Mark Edele, *The Soviet Union: A Short History* (Hoboken: Wiley Blackwell, 2019), Part I.

7 As representative of this larger literature, see Lynne Viola, *Peasant Rebels under Stalin: Collectivization and the Culture of Peasant Resistance* (Oxford: Oxford University Press, 1996); Wayne Dowler, *Russia in 1913* (DeKalb: Northern Illinois University Press, 2012); Stephen Kotkin, *Magnetic Mountain: Stalinism as Civilization* (Berkeley: University of California Press, 1995); Moshe Lewin, *The Gorbachev Phenomenon: A Historical Interpretation* (Berkeley: University of California Press, 1991); and Yuri Slezkine, *The House of Government: A Saga of the Russian Revolution* (Princeton, NJ: Princeton University Press, 2017).

8 For example, James Urry, *None but Saints: The Transformation of Mennonite Life in Russia, 1789–1889* (Winnipeg: Hyperion, 1989); and James Urry, *Mennonites, Politics, and Peoplehood: Europe, Russia, Canada, 1525–1980* (Winnipeg: University of Manitoba Press, 2006).

9 Scott H. Hendrix, *Recultivating the Vineyard: The Reformation Agendas of Christianization* (Louisville: Westminster John Knox Press, 2004), ch. 1; and Charles Taylor, *A Secular Age* (Cambridge, MA: Harvard University Press, 2007).
10 Immanuel Wallerstein, *World-Systems Analysis: An Introduction* (Durham, NC: Duke University Press, 2004).
11 Taylor, *A Secular Age*, 25–6; and Max Weber, "Science as a Vocation," in *Max Weber: Essays in Sociology*, ed. Hans H. Gerth and C. Wright Mills (London: Routledge, 1948 [1919]), 129–56.
12 Hannah Arendt, *The Human Condition* (Chicago: University of Chicago Press, 1998), 328.
13 Talal Asad, *Formations of the Secular* (Stanford, CA: Stanford University Press, 2003); Talal Asad, *Genealogies of Religion: Discipline and Reasons of Power in Christianity and Islam* (Baltimore: Johns Hopkins University Press, 1993); Brad S. Gregory, *Rebel in the Ranks: Martin Luther, the Reformation, and the Conflicts That Continue to Shape Our World* (New York: HarperOne, 2017), 4; Marshall Sahlins, "Cosmologies of Capitalism: The Trans-Pacific Sector of "The 'World System,'" *Proceedings of the British Academy*, LXXIV (1988), 1–51; Steven D. Smith, *The Disenchantment of Secular Discourse* (Cambridge, MA: Harvard University Press, 2010); Kathleen Davis, *Periodization and Sovereignty: How Ideas of Feudalism and Secularization Govern the Politics of Time* (Philadelphia: University of Pennsylvania Press, 2008); and Joseph Cardinal Ratzinger and Jürgen Habermas, *The Dialectics of Secularization: On Reason and Religion* (San Francisco: Ignatius Press, 2006). I thank Isaac Friesen for bringing the works of Talal Asad to my attention.
14 Harold S. Bender, Samuel J. Steiner, and Richard D. Thiessen, "World Mennonite Membership Distribution. *GAMEO*, January 2013, https://gameo.org/index.php?title=World_Mennonite_Membership_Distribution&oldid=167818; and Cornelius Krahn and Walter W. Sawatsky, "Russia," *GAMEO*, February 2011, https://gameo.org/index.php?title=Russia&oldid=167837. For a reflection on the various denominations that these numbers conceal, see John D. Roth, "'Blest Be the Ties That Bind': In Search of the Global Anabaptist Church," *CGR* 31 (2013): 5–43.
15 Benjamin Goossen, *Chosen Nation: Mennonites and Germany in a Global Era* (Princeton, NJ: Princeton University Press, 2017), 7–8; and John P.R. Eicher, *Exiled among Nations: German and Mennonite Mythologies in a Transnational Age* (Cambridge: Cambridge University Press, 2020), 11.
16 Brad S. Gregory, *The Unintended Reformation: How a Religious Revolution Secularized Society* (Cambridge, MA: Harvard University Press, 2012); Zygmunt Bauman, *Liquid Modernity* (Cambridge, UK: Polity Press, 2000), Immanuel Wallerstein, "The Construction of Peoplehood:

Racism, Nationalism, Ethnicity," in *Race, Nation, Class: Ambiguous Identities*, ed. Etienne Balibar and Immanuel Wallerstein (London: Verso Books, 1991), 85; Walter Sawatsky, "What Makes Russian Mennonites Mennonite?" *MQR* 53 (1979), 5–20; Johannes Reimer, *Aussiedler sind anders; Russlanddeutsche sind anders* (Wuppertal and Kasse, Germany: Oncken Verlag, 1990); and Johannes Reimer, *Auf der Suche nach Identität: Russlanddeutsche zwischen Baptisten und Mennoniten nach dem Zweiten Weltkrieg* (Lage, Germany: Logos Publishing, 1996).

17 Conrad Hackett and David McClendon, "Christians Remain World's Largest Religious Group, but They Are Declining in Europe," Pew Research Center, April 5, 2017, https://www.pewresearch.org/fact-tank/2017/04/05/christians-remain-worlds-largest-religious-group-but-they-are-declining-in-europe/; and "Status of Global Christianity, 2015, in the Context of 1900–2050," *International Bulletin of Missionary Research* 39, no. 1 (January 2015), 28–9, http://www.internationalbulletin.org/issues/2015-01/2015-01-029-table.html.

18 J.C. Wenger, ed., *The Complete Writings of Menno Simons, c. 1496–1561*, translated from the Dutch by Leonard Verduin (Scottdale, PA: Herald Press, 1956), 190–1, 198.

19 Works of modernization and the Russian empire include Marc Raeff, *Understanding Imperial Russia: State and Society in the Old Regime*, trans. Arthur Goldhammer (New York: Columbia University Press, 1984); Richard Wortman, *Scenarios of Power: Myth and Ceremony in Russian Monarchy*, 2 vols. (Princeton, NJ: Princeton University Press, 1995–2000); David Hoffmann and Yanni Kotsonis, eds., *Russian Modernity: Politics, Knowledge and Practices, 1800–1950* (London: Palgrave Macmillan, 2000); and Michael David-Fox, *Crossing Borders: Modernity, Ideology, and Culture in Russia and the Soviet Union* (Pittsburgh: University of Pittsburgh Press, 2015).

20 David G. Rempel, "The Mennonite Commonwealth in Russia: A Sketch of Its Founding and Endurance, 1789–1919," *MQR* 47 (1973), 259–308; and 48 (1974), 5–54. Rempel adopted the term from the Austrian/American sociologist E.K. Francis. On the origins, usage, and usefulness of the term, see James Urry, "The Mennonite Commonwealth in Imperial Russia Revisited," *MQR* 84 (April 2010), 229–47.

21 N.V. Venger, *Mennonitskoe predprinimatel'stvo v usloviiakh modernizatstsii iuga Rossii: Mezhdu kongregatsiei klanom i Rossiiskim obshchestvom 1789–1920* (Dnepropetrovsk: Dnepropetrovsk National University, 2009); and Abraham Friesen, *In Defense of Privilege: Russian Mennonites and the State before and during World War I* (Winnipeg: Kindred Productions, 2006).

22 Wenger, ed., *Complete Writings*, 225.

23 Igal Halfin, *From Darkness to Light: Class, Conscience, and Salvation in Revolutionary Russia* (Pittsburgh: University of Pittsburgh Press, 2000);

Nina Turmarkin, *Lenin Lives! The Lenin Cult in Soviet Russia* (Cambridge, MA: Harvard University Press, 1993); and Kotkin, *Magnetic Mountain*.
24 Gregory, *Unintended Reformation*, 12–14.
25 V.F. Krest'ianinov, *Mennonity* (Moscow, 1967), 214–16; and A.N. Ipatov, *Mennonity: Voprosy formirovaniia i evoliutsii etnokovfessional'noi obshchnosti* (Moscow: Mysl', 1978), ch. 3.
26 Walter Sawatsky, *Going Global with God as Mennonites for the 21st Century* (North Newton, KS: Bethel College, 2017), 36–7.

1 Foundations: An Ancient Faith, a Swiss Reformation, and Anabaptist Renewal

1 Peter M. Friesen, *Die Alt-Evangelische Mennonitische Brüderschaft in Russland (1789–1910), im Rahmen der Mennonitischen Gesamtgeschichte* (Halbstadt, 1911). John B. Toews and others have translated this work as P.M. Friesen, *The Mennonite Brotherhood in Russia, 1789–1910* (Fresno, CA: Board of Christian Literature. General Conference of the Mennonite Brethren Conference of Mennonite Brethren Churches, 1978).
2 Peter G. Wallace, *The Long European Reformation: Religion, Political Conflict and the Search for Community, 1350–1750*, 2nd ed. (New York: Palgrave Macmillan, 2012), Introduction.
3 Charles Taylor, *A Secular Age* (Cambridge MA: Harvard University Press, 2007), 68–72; Gabriel Audisio, *The Waldensian Dissent Persecution and Survival, c.1170–c.1570*, trans. Claire Davison (Cambridge: Cambridge University Press, 1999); Anne Hudson, *The Premature Reformation: Wycliffite Texts and Lollard History* (Oxford: Clarendon Press, 1988); and Phillip N. Haberkern, *Patron Saint and Prophet: Jan Hus in the Bohemian and German Reformations* (Oxford: Oxford University Press, 2016), 218–19.
4 R.N. Swanson, "The Pre-Reformation Church," in *The Reformation World*, ed. Andrew Pettegree (London: Routledge, 2000), 9.
5 Swanson, "Pre-Reformation," 13–14.
6 Swanson "Pre-Reformation," 15.
7 Swanson "Pre-Reformation," 16.
8 John Vidmar, *The Catholic Church through the Ages*, 2nd ed. (New York: Paulist Press 2014), 187.
9 Jonathan I. Israel, *The Dutch Republic" Its Rise, Greatness and Fall, 1477–1806* (Oxford: Oxford University Press, 1995), 78.
10 Kari A. Duffield, "Hieronymus Bosch in Context: A Re-Evaluation of the Artist through the Enlightened Thinking of Desiderius Erasmus," unpublished MA thesis, California State University, 2014, 27–9.
11 John Van Engen, ed. and trans., *Devotio Moderna: Basic Writings* (New York: Paulist Press, 1988), 25–35, 70–1; and R.R. Post, *The Modern Devotion*

(Leiden, 1968); and Roland H. Bainton, *Erasmus of Christendom* (New York: Scribner, 1969).
12. Thomas à Kempis, *The Imitation of Christ*, Book One, The First Chapter, http://www.ccel.org/ccel/kempis/imitation.all.html.
13. Israel, *Dutch Republic*, 44.
14. Michael Massing, *Fatal Discord: Erasmus, Luther and the Fight for the Western Mind* (New York: HarperCollins Publishers, 2018), 16.
15. Wallace, *Long European Reformation*, 68.
16. Andrew Pettegree, *Reformation and the Culture of Persuasion* (Cambridge: Cambridge University Press, 2005), 130–3.
17. Frédéric Barbier, *Gutenberg's Europe: The Book and the Invention of Western Modernity* (Cambridge, UK: Polity Press, 2017), 66.
18. Massing, *Fatal Discord*, 11.
19. Massing, *Fatal Discord*, 8–9.
20. Raymond Himelick, ed., *The Enchiridion of Erasmus* (Bloomington: Indiana University Press, 1963), 94–5.
21. Himelick, ed., *Enchiridion*, 131.
22. Christine Christ-von Wedel, *Erasmus of Rotterdam: Advocate of a New Christianity* (Toronto: University of Toronto Press, 2013), 6, and ch. 12.
23. Cornelis Augustijn, *Erasmus: His Life, Works, and Influence* (Toronto: University of Toronto Press, 1991), 90–1; and Keith D. Stanglin, ed., *The Reformation of the Modern Church: A Reader in Christian Theology* (Minneapolis: Fortress Press, 2014), 47.
24. Augustijn, *Erasmus*, 92.
25. Abraham Friesen, *Menno Simons: Dutch Reformer between Luther, Erasmus and the Holy Spirit* (Bloomington, IN: Xlibris, 2015), 150–7.
26. Carlos M.N. Eire, *Reformations. The Early Modern World, 1450–1650* (New Haven, CT: Yale University Press, 2016), 223–4; and Christ-von Wedel, *Erasmus*, 90–2.
27. G.R. Potter, *Zwingli* (Cambridge: Cambridge University Press, 1976), 42–6.
28. Emidio Campi, "The Reformation in Zurich," in *A Companion to the Swiss Reformation*, eds. Amy Nelson Burnett and Emidio Campi (Leiden: Brill, 2016), 65–6.
29. On the long-term significance of these actions for western secularization, see Taylor, *A Secular Age*, 77–88; and Brad S. Gregory, "The One or the Many? Narrating and Evaluating Western Secularization," *Intellectual History Review* 27 (January 2017), 31–46.
30. Eire, *Reformations*, 234; Potter, *Zwingli*, ch. 12.
31. Ulrich Zwingli, *Commentary on True and False Religion*, ed. Samuel Macauley Jackson and Clarence Nevin Heller (Eugene, OR: Wipf & Stock, 2015), 93.
32. Wallace *Long European Reformation*, 92–3.

33 C. Arnold Snyder, "Swiss Anabaptism: The Beginnings," in *A Companion to Anabaptism and Spiritualism, 1521–1700*, ed. John D. Roth and James M. Stayer (Leiden: Brill, 2007), 48–9.
34 Snyder "Swiss Anabaptism," 51–3.
35 The "Twelve Articles" can be found in "Grievances and Demands – The Twelve Articles of the Swabian Peasants (February 27–March 1, 1525)," GHDI, http://germanhistorydocs.ghi-dc.org/sub_document.cfm?document_id=4323.
36 James Stayer, "The German Peasants' War and the Rural Reformation"" in *The Reformation World*, ed. Andrew Pettegree (London: Routledge, 2000), 137–8, n. 15.
37 Snyder "Swiss Anabaptism," 54.
38 Snyder "Swiss Anabaptism," 55–9.
39 Snyder "Swiss Anabapitsm," 63–4.
40 John D. Rempel, *The Lord's Supper in Anabaptism: A Study of the Christology of Balthasar Hubmaier, Pilgram Marpeck and Dirk Philips* (Waterloo, ON: Herald Press, 1993), 47.

2 Melchoir, Münster, and Menno: From Early Dutch (Melchiorite) Anabaptists to Mennonites

1 On Strasbourg and the iconoclastic movements of the 1520s, see Lee Palmer Wandel, *Voracious Idols and Violent Hands: Iconoclasm in Reformation Zurich, Strasbourg, and Basel* (Cambridge: Cambridge University Press, 1995), ch. 3.
2 Klaus Deppermann, *Melchior Hoffman: Social Unrest and Apocalyptic Visions in the Age of Reformation*, trans. Malcolm Wren (Edinburgh: T. & T. Clark, 1987), 178–81.
3 Christina Moss, "An Examination of the Visions of Ursula Jost in the Context of Early Anabaptism and Late Medieval Christianity," MA thesis, University of Waterloo, 2013, 62–3; Christina Moss, "Jost, Ursula (d. 1532/39)." *GAMEO*, May 2016, https://gameo.org/index.php?title=Jost,_Ursula_(d._1532/39)&oldid=143139; and Christina Moss, "Marriage as Spiritual Partnership in Sixteenth-Century Strasbourg: The Case of Lienhard and Ursula Jost," in *Newberry Essays in Medieval and Early Modern Studies*, Volume 9: *Selected Proceedings of the Newberry Center for Renaissance Studies 2015 Multidisciplinary Graduate Student Conference*, ed. Karen Christianson and Andrew K. Epps (Chicago: The Newberry Library, 2015), 90, http://www.newberry.org/sites/default/files/textpage-attachments/2015Proceedings.pdf.
4 On the organization of trade in the Netherlands at this time, see Oscar Gelderblom, "The Organization of Long-Distance Trade in England and

the Dutch Republic, 1550–1650," in *The Political Economy of the Dutch Republic*, ed. Oscar Gelderblom (Abingdon: Routledge, 2016), 223–54.

5 Jan de Vries and Ad Van Der Woude, *The First Modern Economy: Success, Failure and Perseverance of the Dutch Economy, 1500–1815* (Cambridge: Cambridge University Press, 1997), 350–76.

6 On the appeal of political integration, see James Tracy, *The Founding of the Dutch Republic: War, Finance, and Politics in Holland, 1572–1588* (Oxford: Oxford University Press, 2008), 60–6 and Jan Glete, *War and the State in Early Modern Europe: Spain, the Dutch Republic and Sweden as Fiscal-Military States* (London: Routledge, 2001), ch. 4.

7 Abraham Friesen, *Menno Simons: Dutch Reformer between Luther, Erasmus, and the Holy Spirit* (Bloomington, IN: Xlibris, 2015), 49–50, n. 161.

8 Recent overviews of Dutch Anabaptism and the emergence of the Mennonites include Samme Zijstlra, *Om de Ware Gemeente en de Oude Gronden: Geschiedenis van de Dopersen in de Nederlanden, 1531–1675* (Leeuwarden: Fryske Academy, 2000); and Piet Visser, "Mennonites and Doopsgezinden in the Netherlands, 1535–1700," in *A Companion to Anabaptism and Spiritualism, 1521–1700*, ed. James Stayer and John Roth (Leiden: Brill, 2007), 299–345.

9 Ralf Klötzer, "The Melchoirites and Münster," in *A Companion to Anabaptism and Spiritualism, 1521–1700*, ed. James Stayer and John Roth (Leiden: Brill, 2007), 221; Karel Vos, "Sicke Freerks (d. 1531)." *GAMEO*, 1959, https://gameo.org/index.php?title=Sicke_Freerks_(d._1531)&oldid=146722; and Friesen *Menno Simons*, 111.

10 Gary K. Waite, *David Joris and Dutch Anabaptism, 1524–1543* (Waterloo, ON: Wilfrid Laurier University, 1990), 29–30.

11 Alistair Hamilton, "The Development of Dutch Anabaptism in the Light of the European Magisterial and Radical Reformation," in *From Martyr to Muppy: A Historical Introduction to Cultural Assimilation Processes of a Religious Minority in the Netherlands: the Mennonites*, ed. Alastair Hamilton, Sjouke Voolstra, and Piet Visser (Amsterdam: Amsterdam University Press, 1994), 9–10.

12 Carlos M.N. Eire, *Reformations: The Early Modern World, 1450–1650* (New Haven, CT: Yale University Press, 2016), 272, n. 23.

13 For a recent, thoughtful reconsideration of the Münster rebellion, see Michael Driedger, "Münster, Monster, Modernity: Tracing and Challenging the Meme of Anabaptist Madness," in *European Mennonites and the Challenge of Modernity over Five Centuries: Contributors, Detractors, and Adapters*, ed. Mark Jantzen, Mary S. Sprunger, and John D. Thiesen (North Newton, KS: Bethel College, 2016), 27–50.

14 Gary K. Waite, "Writing in the Heavenly Language: A Guide to the Works of David Joris," *Renaissance and Reformation / Renaissance et Réforme*

26 (January 1990), 299; Gary K. Waite, "David Joris (ca. 1501–1556)." *GAMEO*, February 2020, https://gameo.org/index.php?title=David_Joris_(ca._1501-1556)&oldid=166692; Gary K. Waite, ed., *The Anabaptist Writings of David Joris, 1535–1543* (Scottdale, PA: Herald Press, 1994), ch. 1; and Geoffrey Dipple, "Anabaptism Spiritualists," in *A Companion to Anabaptism and Spiritualism, 1521–1700*, ed. James Stayer and John Roth (Leiden: Brill, 2007), 283–8.

15 Menno Simons, "The Blasphemy of John of Leiden, 1535," in *The Complete Writings of Menno Simons, c. 1496–1561*, ed. John C. Wenger and trans. Leonard Verduin (Scottdale, PA: Herald Press, 1956), 34.

16 Abraham Friesen, "Menno and Münster: The Man and the Movement," in *Menno Simons: A Reappraisal. Essays in Honour of Irvin B. Horst on the 450th Anniversary of the Fundamentboek*, ed. Gerald R. Brunk (Harrisonburg, VA: Eastern Mennonite College, 1992), 136.

17 Friesen *Menno Simons*, 164.

18 Menno Simons, "Reply to Gellius Faber, 1554" in *The Complete Writings of Menno Simons, c. 1496–1561*, ed. John C. Wenger and trans. Leonard Verduin (Scottdale, PA: Herald Press, 1956), 668; and Sjouke Voolstra, "Themes in the Early Theology of Menno Simons," in *Menno Simons: A Reappraisal. Essays in Honour of Irvin B. Horst on the 450th Anniversary of the Fundamentboek*, ed. Gerald R. Brunk (Harrisonburg, VA: Eastern Mennonite College, 1992), 39.

19 Sjouke Voolstra, *Menno Simons: His Image and Message* (North Newton, KS: Bethel College, 1997), 56.

20 Menno Simons, "Why I Do Not Cease Teaching and Writing, 1539" in *The Complete Writings of Menno Simons, c. 1496–1561*, ed. John C. Wenger and trans. Leonard Verduin (Scottdale, PA: Herald Press, 1956), 299; and Helmut Isaak, "Menno's Vision of the Anticipation of the Kingdom of God in His Early Writings," in *Menno Simons: A Reappraisal. Essays in Honour of Irvin B. Horst on the 450th Anniversary of the Fundamentboek*, ed. Gerald R. Brunk (Harrisonburg, VA: Eastern Mennonite College, 1992), 57.

21 It needs to be said that, though written in 1535, "The Blasphemy of Jan van Leiden" was never published in Menno's lifetime. For an interesting discussion on this, see Friesen *Menno Simons*, ch. 12.

22 Walter Klaassen, "The Relevance of Menno Simons; Past and Present," in *Menno Simons: A Reappraisal. Essays in Honour of Irvin B. Horst on the 450th Anniversary of the Fundamentboek*, ed. Gerald R. Brunk (Harrisonburg, VA: Eastern Mennonite College, 1992), 21.

23 Menno Simons, "Foundation of Christian Doctrine, 1539," in *The Complete Writings of Menno Simons, c. 1496–1561*, ed. John C. Wenger and trans. Leonard Verduin (Scottdale, PA: Herald Press, 1956), 105.

24 Menno Simons, "Foundation," 158.

25 Sjouke Voolstra, "'The Colony of Heaven': The Anabaptist Aspiration to Be the Church without Spot or Wrinkle in the Sixteenth and Seventeenth Centuries," in *From Martyr to Muppy: A Historical Introduction to Cultural Assimilation Processes of a Religious Minority in the Netherlands: The Mennonites*, ed. Alastair Hamilton, Sjouke Voolstra, and Piet Visser (Amsterdam: Amsterdam University Press, 1994), ch. 2.
26 Menno Simons, "Foundation," 169.
27 Menno Simons, "Foundations," 191.
28 Menno Simons, "Foundations," 193.
29 Menno Simons, "Foundations," 193.
30 Menno Simons, "Foundations," 197–8.
31 Menno Simons, "Foundations," 200. Helmut Isaak goes so far as to suggest that Menno will also recognize the right magistrates to torture and execute those who have been justly condemned. See Isaak "Menno's Vision," 70.
32 Piet Visser, "Menno Simons: Printed, Read and Debated," in *Menno Simons: A Reappraisal. Essays in Honour of Irvin B. Horst on the 450th Anniversary of the Fundamentboek*, ed. Gerald R. Brunk (Harrisonburg, VA: Eastern Mennonite College, 1992), 89; and Gary Waite, *Eradicating the Devil's Minions: Anabaptists and Witches in Reformation Europe* (Toronto: University of Toronto Press, 2007), 20.
33 Christian Neff and Richard D. Thiessen, "Anna von Oldenburg-Delmenhorst, Countess of East Friesland (1501–1575)," *GAMEO*, February 2007, https://gameo.org/index.php?title=Anna_von_Oldenburg-Delmenhorst,_Countess_of_East_Friesland_(1501-1575)&oldid=144716.
34 Menno Simons, "Brief Confession on the Incarnation (1544)," in *The Complete Writings of Menno Simons, c. 1496–1561*, ed. John C. Wenger and trans. Leonard Verduin (Scottdale, PA: Herald Press, 1956), 424.
35 Loosjes, Jacob. "Batenburg, Jan van (1495–1538)," *GAMEO*, 1953, https://gameo.org/index.php?title=Batenburg,_Jan_van_(1495-1538)&oldid=144785. For a nuanced understanding of the early Dutch Mennonites and violence, see Troy Osborne, "Mennonites and Violence in Early Modern Amsterdam," *Church History and Religious Culture* 95 (2015), 477–94.
36 Keith Sprunger, "Dutch Anabaptists and the Telling of the Martyr Stories," *MQR* 80 (2006), 153; and Brad S. Gregory, *Salvation at Stake: Christian Martyrdom in Early Modern Europe* (Cambridge, MA: Harvard University Press, 1999), 219–21.
37 Friesen, *Menno Simons*, 188.
38 Menno Simons, "Foundation," 138; The quotation is from Menno Simons, "Christian Baptism," 248; Menno Simons, "Confession of the Distressed Christians, 1522," 520–1, all from Wenger (1956); and Friesen, *Menno Simons*, 188.

39 Voolstra, *Menno Simons*, 44–5.
40 Charles Taylor, *The Secular Age* (Cambridge MA: Harvard University Press, 2007), 25–6.
41 Voolstra, "Colony of Heaven," 20; and Waite, *Eradicating*, 30. On Protestants and the abandonment of churchly tradition, see José Granados, "From Flesh to Flesh: On the Sacramental Meaning of Tradition," *Communio. International Catholic Review* 44 (Winter 2017), 644. On Menno's Christology, see Egil Grislis, "The Doctrine of Incarnation According to Menno Simons," *JMS* 8 (1990), 16–33.

3 A Faith Community on the Move: Mennonites, Poland, and Prussia, 1536–1800

1 Cf. Rudy P. Friesen with Edith Elisabeth Friesen, *Building on the Past: Mennonite Architecture, Landscape and Settlements in Russia/Ukraine* (n.p.: Raduga Publications, 2004).
2 Alastair Duke, *Reformation and Revolt in the Low Countries* (London: The Hambledon Press, 1990), 88.
3 Gary K. Waite, *Eradicating the Devil's Minions: Anabaptists and Witches in Reformation Europe, 1525–1600* (Toronto: University of Toronto Press, 2007), 85, cf. 77–8 on the perceived link between witches and Anabaptism.
4 On the context, see Jonathan Israel, *Radical Enlightenment: Philosophy and the Making of Modernity, 1650–1750* (Oxford: Oxford University Press, 2001), ch. 2.
5 A.L.E. Verheyden, *Anabaptism in Flanders, 1530–1650* (Scottdale, PA: Herald Press, 1961), 15.
6 Waite, *Eradicating*, 105.
7 Thieleman van Braght, *Martyrs Mirror: The Story of Seventeen Centuries of Christian Martyrdom, from the Time of Christ to A.D. 1660*, trans. Joseph F. Sohm (Scottdale, PA: Herald Press, 1950), 723.
8 Piet Visser, "Mennonites and Doopsgezinden in the Netherlands, 1535–1700," in *A Companion to Anabaptism and Spiritualism, 1521–1700*, ed. John D. Roth and James M. Stayer (Leiden: Brill, 2007), 316.
9 Brad S. Gregory, *Salvation at Stake: Christian Martyrdom in Early Modern Europe* (Cambridge, MA: Harvard University Press, 1999), 201; and Verheyden, *Anabaptism*, 23, 35–68.
10 Karin Friedrich, *The Other Prussia: Royal Prussia, Poland and Liberty, 1569–1772* (Cambridge: Cambridge University Press, 2000), 20–4.
11 J. Schildhauer, "Handelsbeziehungen Bedeutender Ostseestädte zu den Niederlanden: Ein Beitrag zur Verlagerung des See- and Handelsverkehrs im Ost- und Nordseeraum während des 16. Jahrhunderts," in *The Interactions of Amsterdam and Antwerp with the Baltic Region, 1400–1800*, ed.

Wiert Jan Wieringa (Leiden: Martinus Nijhoff, 1983), 23–9; R.W. Unger, "Integration of Baltic and Low Countries Grain Markets, 1400–1800," in *The Interactions of Amsterdam and Antwerp with the Baltic Region, 1400–1800*, ed. Wiert Jan Wieringa (Leiden: Martinus Nijhoff, 1983), 1–10; and Maria Bogucka, *Das alte Danzig: Alltagsleben vom 15. bis 17. Jahrhundert* (Leipzig: Koehler & Amelang, 1980), 13–16.

12 Michael North, *The Baltic: A History*, trans. Kenneth Kronenberg (Cambridge, MA: Harvard University Press, 2015), 99; Jan Glete, *War and the State in Early Modern Europe: Spain, the Dutch Republic and Sweden as Fiscal-Military States, 1500–1660* (London: Routledge 2002), 168–71; and Jonathan I. Israel, *The Dutch Republic: Its Rise, Greatness, and Fall 1477–1806* (Oxford: Clarendon Press, 1995), 315–27.

13 H.G. Mannhardt, *The Danzig Mennonite Church: Its Origin and History from 1569–1919*, trans. Victor G. Doerksen (North Newton, KS: Bethel College, 2007), 37.

14 Norman Davies, *God's Playground: A History of Poland in Two Volumes. Volume 1: The Origins to 1795*, revised edition (New York: Columbia University Press, 2005), 203–4.

15 Peter J. Klassen, *Mennonites in Early Modern Poland & Prussia* (Baltimore: The Johns Hopkins University Press, 2009), 29, n. 6.

16 Klassen, *Mennonites*, 32.

17 Karl Koop, *Anabaptist-Mennonite Confessions of Faith: The Development of a Tradition* (Kitchener, ON: Pandora Press, 2004), 37; Michael D. Driedger, *Obedient Heretics: Mennonite Identities in Lutheran Hamburg and Altona during the Confessional Age* (Aldershot: Ashgate Publishing, 2002), 24–6; and Klaasen, *Mennonites*, 49–52. On the importance of the herring fishery for Dutch trade, see Jan de Vries and Ad Van Der Woude, *The First Modern Economy: Success, Failure and Perseverance of the Dutch Economy, 1500–1815* (Cambridge: Cambridge University Press, 1997), 243–54.

18 Edward Kizik, "Religious Freedom and the Limits of Social Assimilation: The History of the Mennonites in Gdansk and the Vistula Delta until Their Tragic End after World War II," in *From Martyr to Muppy: A Historical Introduction to Cultural Assimilation Processes of a Religious Minority in the Netherlands: The Mennonites*, ed. Alastair Hamilton, Sjouke Voolstra, and Piet Visser (Amsterdam: Amsterdam University Press, 1994), 53–5; and Erich Wernicke, *Kreis Marienwerder. Aus der Geschichte des Landkreises bis zum 19. Jahrhundert* (Hamburg, 1979), 210.

19 Driedger, *Obedient Heretics*, 16, n. 28.

20 James Urry, *Mennonites, Politics, and Peoplehood: Europe, Russia, Canada, 1525–1980* (Winnipeg: University of Manitoba Press, 2006), ch. 2.

21 Klassen, *Mennonites*, 65.

22 Driedger, *Obedient Heretics*, 18–20; and Klassen, *Mennonites*, 34–5, 64–5.

23 Edward Carstenn, *Geschichte der Hansestadt Elbing* (Elbing, 1937), 272–4.
24 George Cuny, *Danzigs Kunst und Kultur im 16 und 17 Jahrhundert* (Frankfurt am Main: Heinrich Keller, 1910), 75–9; and Klassen, *Mennonites*, 104; and Rainer Kobe, "Isaac von den Blocke, Painter and Mennonite at Gdansk in the Early Seventh Century: Is There Anything Mennonite in His Paintings *Before the Flood* and *The Narrow and the Broad Way*," in *European Mennonites and the Challenge of Modernity over Five Centuries: Contributors, Detractors, and Adapters*, ed. Mark Jantzen, Mary S. Sprunger, and John D. Thiesen (North Newton, KS: Bethel College, 2016), 217–21. On the context, see Badeloch Noldus, *Trade in Good Taste: Relations in Architecture and Culture between the Dutch Republic and the Baltic World in the Seventeenth Century*, trans. Titus Verheijen (Turnhout: Brepolis Publishers, 2004).
25 Driedger, *Obedient Heretics*, 3–5.
26 Mannhardt, *Danzig*, 50; Klassen, *Mennonites*, 107; and Driedger, *Obedient Heretics*, 48.
27 James Stayer, "The Passing of the Radical Moment in the Radical Reformation," *MQR* 71 (1997), 151. Cf. Troy Osborne, "New Directions in Anabaptist Studies," *MQR* 81 (2007), 46. The classic portrayal of the Radical Reformation remains George Hunston Williams, *The Radical Reformation* (Philadelphia: The Westminster Press, 1962).
28 Karl Koop, "At the Margins and at the Center of Modern Expression: Reconsidering Anabaptist and Mennonite Confessions of Faith," in *European Mennonites and the Challenge of Modernity over Five Centuries: Contributors, Detractors, and Adapters*, ed. Mark Jantzen, Mary S. Sprunger, and John D. Thiesen (North Newton, KS: Bethel College, 2016), 285–300.
29 R. Po-Chia Hsia, *Social Discipline in the Reformation: Central Europe, 1550–1750* (London: Routledge, 1989), 4–5.
30 Troy Osborne, "Saints into Citizens: Mennonite Discipline, Social Control, and Religious Toleration in the Dutch Golden Age," PhD diss., University of Minnesota, 2007, 186; and Klassen, *Mennonites*, 122.
31 Mannhardt, *Danzig*, 40; and Urry, *Mennonites*, 36.
32 Osborne, "Saints into Citizens," 155.
33 Urry, *Mennonites*, 32.
34 Kizik, "Religious Freedom," 57; and Cornelius J. Dyck, *An Introduction to Mennonite History: A Popular History of the Anabaptists and the Mennonites*, 3rd ed. (Scottdale, PA: Herald Press, 1993), 126–7; "External Customs" is from Mannhardt, *Danzig*, 49.
35 Klassen, *Mennonites*, 227, n. 3. For a fascinating discussion on church discipline and the ban among Mennonites, see Troy Osborne, "Honor and Charity in the Church: Mennonites and the 'Disciplinary Revolution' of the Dutch Republic," in *European Mennonites and the Challenge of Modernity over Five Centuries: Contributors, Detractors, and Adapters*, ed. Mark Jantzen,

Mary S. Sprunger, and John D. Thiesen (North Newton, KS: Bethel College, 2016), 265–83.
36 John D. Thiesen, "Danzig," MennLex V, https://www.mennlex.de/doku.php?id=loc:danzig; and Klassen, *Mennonites*, 113–15.
37 James Urry, The Ältesters: Role and Responsibilities," *Preservings: Being the Magazine/Journal of the Hanover Steinbach Historical Society Inc.* 21 (December 2002), 3; Cornelius Krahn, "Lehrdienst," *GAMEO*, 1957, https://gameo.org/index.php?title=Lehrdienst&oldid=88985; and Cornelius Krahn, "Ministry (Prusso-Russian Background Mennonites)," *GAMEO*, 1957, https://gameo.org/index.php?title=Ministry_(Prusso-Russian_Background_Mennonites)&oldid=143670; see Klassen, *Mennonites*, ch. 6 on Mennonite worship practices generally in Royal Prussia.
38 Osborne, "Saints into Citizens," 164.
39 Cornelius Krahn, "Sawatgsky," MennLex, IV, 39; A. Janzen, "Ladekopp," MennLex, II, 604; Klassen, *Mennonites*, 148–9; and Driedger, *Obedient Heretics*, 159–68.
40 For the Dutch Mennonites, see Mary S. Sprunger, "A Mennonite Capitalist Ethic in the Dutch Golden Age: Weber Revisited," in *European Mennonites and the Challenge of Modernity over Five Centuries: Contributors, Detractors, and Adapters*, ed. Mark Jantzen, Mary S. Sprunger, and John D. Thiesen (North Newton, KS: Bethel College, 2016), 51–70.
41 Waite, *Eradicating*, 31.
42 Keith Sprunger, "Dutch Anabaptists and the Telling of the Martyr Stories." *MQR* 80 (April 2006), 156–7; and Robert Friedman, "Devotional Literature of the Mennonites in Danzig and Prussia to 1800," *MQR* 18 (1944): 162–73.

4 A New Homeland in New Russia: Mennonite Settlement in the Russian Empire, 1789–1830

1 Lawrence Klippenstein, "Four Letters to Susanna from Johann Bartsch, a Danzig Mennonite Land Scout, 1786–1787," *Polish Review* 54, no. 1 (2009), 31–59; Lawrence Klippenstein, "The Bartsch-Hoeppner Mennonite Privilegium of 1787," *Preservings* 41 (2020), 37–42; and Viktor Peters, ed., *Zwei Dokumente: Quellen zum Geschichtsstudium der Mennoniten in Russland* (Winnipeg: Echo Verlag, 1965).
2 Norman Davies, *God's Playground: A History of Poland*. Volume 1: *The Origins to 1795* (New York: Columbia University Press, 2005), ch. 18.
3 H.G. Mannhardt, *The Danzig Mennonite Church: Its Origins and History from 1569–1919* (North Newton, KS: Bethel College, 2007), 139.
4 Mark Jantzen, *Mennonite German Soldiers: Nation, Religion, and Family in the Prussian East, 1772–1880* (Notre Dame, IN: University of Notre Dame Press, 2010), 24. See Mannhardt, *Danzig*, 140.

5 Peter J. Klassen, *Mennonites in Early Modern Poland & Prussia* (Baltimore: The Johns Hopkins University Pres, 2009), 176–7.
6 Serhii Plokhy, *The Cossacks and Religion in Early Modern Ukraine* (Oxford: Oxford University Press, 2001).
7 Kelly O'Neill, *Claiming Crimea: A History of Catherine the Great's Southern Empire* (New Haven, CT: Yale University Press, 2017).
8 Roger Bartlett, "Her Imperial Majesty's Director and Curator of the Mennonite Colonies in Russia: Three Letters of Georg Trappe," *JMS* 12 (1994), 48.
9 Leonard G. Friesen, *Rural Revolutions in Southern Ukraine: Peasants, Nobles, and Colonists, 1774–1905* (Cambridge, MA: Harvard Ukrainian Research Institute, 2008), ch. 2.
10 The Guardianship Committee's title was formally changed in 1799 to the "New Russia Guardianship Office" and yet another change in 1818. But its role with respect to the Mennonites remained essentially unchanged.
11 Roger P. Bartlett, *Human Capital: The Settlement of Foreigners in Russia, 1762–1804* (Cambridge: Cambridge University Press, 1979), ch. 2.
12 On Catherine's ambivalent relationship to religious toleration during the settlement period, see Gary M. Hamburg, "Religious Toleration in Russian Thought, 1520–1825," in *Religious Freedom in Modern Russia*, ed. Randall A. Poole and Paul W. Werth (Pittsburgh: University of Pittsburgh Press, 2018), 63–71.
13 David G. Rempel, "The Mennonite Commonwealth in Russia: A Sketch of Its Founding and Endurance, 1789–1919," reprinted from *MQR* (October 1973 and January 1974), 23.
14 Mannhardt, *Danzig*, 143–5.
15 David G. Rempel, "The Mennonite Colonies in New Russia: A Study of Their Settlement and Econmic Development from 1789–1914," unpublished PhD diss., Stanford University, 1933, 66. On Mennonites and the privilegia in the Russian empire, see Nataliya Venger, "Mennonite Privileges and the Russian Modernization: Communities on a Path Leading from Separateness to Legal and Social Integration (1789–1900)," in *European Mennonites and the Challenge of Modernity over Five Centuries: Contributors, Detractors, and Adapters*, ed. Mark Jantzen, Mary S. Sprunger, and John D. Thiesen (North Newton, KS: Bethel College, 2016), 143–59.
16 See the discussion of the numbers involved in Rempel, "Mennonite Commonwealth," 35–6. For a firsthand account of this process, see Peter Hildebrand, *From Danzig to Russia: The First Emigration of Mennonites from the Danzig Region to Southern Russia*, trans. Walter E. Toews with Adolf Ens (Winnipeg: CMBC Publications, 2000).
17 On Mennonite settlements, see the *GAMEO* (https://gameo.org/index.php?title=Welcome_to_GAMEO); Rudy P. Friesen with Edith Elisabeth Friesen, *Building on the Past: Mennonite Architecture, Landscape and Settlements in Russia/Ukraine* (Winnipeg: Raduga Publications, 2004); and

William Schroeder and Helmut T. Huebert, *Mennonite Historical Atlas*, 2nd edition (Winnipeg: Springfield Publishers, 1996).
18 Rempel, "Mennonite Colonies," 80–1, n. 25.
19 Bartlett, *Human Capital*, ch. 6. On the complex history of Mennonites and privilegium in the imperial era, see James Urry, "A History of the Mennonites' Russian Privilegium: 1800-1919," *JMS* 37 (2019), 325–52.
20 For the broader context, see David Christian, *Living Water: Vodka and Russian Society on the Eve of Emancipation* (Oxford: Oxford University Press, 1990).
21 John R. Staples, *Cross-cultural Encounters on the Ukrainian Steppe: Settling the Molochna Basin, 1783–1861* (Toronto: University of Toronto Press, 2003), ch. 2; Sergei Zhuk, *Russia's Lost Reformation: Peasants, Millennialism, and Radical Sects in Southern Russia and Ukraine, 1830–1917* (Washington, DC: Woodrow Wilson Center Press, 2004); and Oksana Beznosova, *Ekaterinoslavskaia guberniia: terra incognita evangel'skogo dvizheniia v Rossiiskoi imperii (seredina xviii v. – 1917 g.)* (Steinhagen, Germany: Samenkorn, 2014), Pts. 1 and 2. For the significance of this Black Sea settlement pattern on Ukrainian history, see Serhii Plokhy, *Ukraine and Russia: Representations of the Past* (Toronto: University of Toronto Press, 2008); and Serhii Plokhy, *The Origins of Slavic Nations: Premodern Identities in Russia, Ukraine and Belarus* (Cambridge: Cambridge University Press, 2006).
22 Rempel, "Mennonite Colonies," 91. For a slightly different accounting, see James Urry, *None but Saints: The Transformation of Mennonite Life in Russia, 1789–1889* (Winnipeg: Hyperion Press, 1989), 57.
23 Friesen, *Rural Revolutions*, 56.
24 Bartlett, *Human Capital*, 179, 230, Appendix 6.
25 James Urry, "The Closed and the Open: Social and Religious Change amongst the Mennonites in Russia (1789–1889)," unpublished PhD diss., Oxford University, 1978),115, n. 1.
26 On the *Kleine Gemeinde*, see Delbert F. Plett, *Saints and Sinners: The Kleine Gemeinde in Imperial Russia, 1812–1875* (Steinbach, MB: Crossway Publications 1999).
27 Oksana Beznosova, "A Foreign Faith, but of What Sort? The Mennonite Church and the Russian Empire, 1789–1917," in *Minority Report: Mennonite Identities in Imperial Russia and Soviet Ukraine Reconsidered*, ed. Leonard G. Friesen (Toronto: University of Toronto Press, 2018), 113.
28 Friesen with Friesen, *Building on the Past*, 39–41; and D.H. Epp, *Die Chortitzeer Mennoniten. Versuch einer Darstellung des Entwicklunganges derselben* (1889, reprinted in Winnipeg, 1984), 54–8.
29 Plautdietsch, a Germanic language related to Dutch and Frisian, spoken in Siberia, https://www.mercator-research.eu/projekten/endangered-languages-and-archives/plautdietsch-a-germanic-language-related-to-dutch-and-frisian-spoken-in-siberia.

30 Rempel, "Mennonite Commonwealth," 4.
31 Clifford Geertz, "Thick Description: Toward an Interpretive Theory of Culture," in *The Interpretation of Cultures: Selected Essays* (New York: Basic Books, 1973), 3–30.
32 On Russia's "undergoverned" empire, see S. Frederick Starr, *Decentralization and Self-Government in Russia, 1830–1870* (Princeton, NJ: Princeton University Press, 1972).
33 Rempel, "Mennonite Colonies," 113–16.
34 Frank H. Epp, *Mennonites in Canada, 1786–1920: The History of a Separate People* (Toronto: Macmillan of Canada, 1974); and Richard K. MacMaster, *Land, Piety, Peoplehood: The Establishment of Mennonite Communities in America, 1683–1790* (Scottdale, PA: Herald Press, 1985).
35 Johannes Dyck, *Am Trakt: A Mennonite Settlement in the Central Volga Region*, based on a text by W.E. Surikikin (Winnipeg: CMBC Publications, 1995); and Mark Jantzen, "Changing Definitions of Treason and Religious Freedom for Mennonites in Prussia, 1780–1880," in *European Mennonites and the Challenge of Modernity over Five Centuries: Contributors, Detractors, and Adapters*, ed. Mark Jantzen, Mary S. Sprunger, and John D. Thiesen (North Newton, KS: Bethel College, 2016), 244.
36 Viktor Fast, ed., *Vorübergehende Heimat: 150 Jahre Beten und Arbeiten in Alt-Samara (Alexandertal und Konstantinow)* (Steinhagen, Germany: Samenkorn, 2009), 74–81.

5 Pietistic Progressivism: Johann Cornies and the Transformation of Russian Mennonitism, 1800–1848

1 "Johann Cornies to Traugott Blueher, 15 February 1826" in *Transformation of the Southern Ukrainian Steppe. Letters and Papers of Johann Cornies*, Volume 1: *1812–1815*, ed. Harvey L. Dyck, Ingrid I. Epp, and John R. Staples (Toronto: University of Toronto Press, 2015), 72.
2 "Johann Cornies to Daniel Schlatter. 6 November 1826," in Dyck et al., 97. For a biography of Daniel Schlatter, see James Urry, "A Critical Gaze: Daniel Schlatter and Mennonite-Nogai Relations," *Preservings* 42 (2021), 2–8.
3 John R. Staples, "Johann Cornies' Aesthetics of Civilization," in *Minority Report: Mennonite Identities in Imperial Russia and Soviet Ukraine Reconsidered, 1789–1945*, ed. Leonard G. Friesen (Toronto: University of Toronto Press, 2017); and James Urry, *None but Saints: The Transformation of Mennonite Life in Russia, 1789–1889* (Winnipeg: Hyperion (1989), ch. 6.
4 On the historiographical debate, see Harvey L. Dyck, "Russian Servitor and Mennonite Hero: Light and Shadow in Images of Johann Cornies," *Journal of Mennonite Studies* 2 (1984), 9–28.

5 Charles Taylor, *The Secular Age* (Cambridge, MA: The Belknap Press of Harvard University Press, 2007), 1–3.
6 H.G. Mannhardt, "Bärwalde," *ML* 1, 129.
7 Staples, "Aesthetics of Civilization," 63.
8 Fred van Lieburg, "The Dutch Factor in German Pietism," in *A Companion to German Pietism, 1660–1800*, ed. Douglas Shantz (Leiden: Brill, 2015), ch. 2; Kelly Joan Whitmer, *The Halle Orphanage as Scientific Community: Observation, Eclecticism, and Pietism in the Early Enlightenment* (Chicago: University of Chicago Press, 2015); Patricia A. Ward, "Continental Spirituality and British Protestant Readers," in *Heart Religion: Evangelical Piety in England & Ireland, 1690–1850*, ed. John Coffey (Oxford: Oxford University Press, 2016), 50–71; Ted A. Campbell, *The Religion of the Heart: A Study of European Religious Life in the Seventeenth and Eighteenth Centuries* (Columbia: University of South Carolina Press, 1991), 42–69; Douglas Shantz, ed., *An Introduction to German Pietism: Protestant Renewal at the Dawn of Modern Europe* (Baltimore: Johns Hopkins University Press, 2013), 6–7; W.R. Ward, *The Protestant Evangelical Awakening* (Cambridge: Cambridge University Press, 1992), 46–51; and Charles Taylor, *Sources of the Self: The Making of the Modern Identity* (Cambridge, MA: Harvard University Press, 1989), 302.
9 This shift has not been without controversy in the historiography. For a measured overview, see Astrid von Schlachta, "Anabaptists and Pietists Influences, Contacts, and Relations," in *A Companion to German Pietism, 1660–1800*, ed. Douglas H. Shantz (Leiden: Brill, 2015), ch. 4.
10 Harvey L. Dyck, Ingrid I. Epp, and John R. Staples, eds., *Transformation of the Southern Ukrainian Steppe. Letters and Papers of Johann Cornies* (Toronto: University of Toronto Press, 2015), 76–8; Oksana Beznosova, *Ekaterinoslavskaia guberniia: Terra incognita evangel'skogo dvizheniia v Rossiiskoi imperii (seredina xviiii v. – 1917 g.* (Steinhagen, Germany: Samenkorn, 2014), 98–9; and Martin Gierl, "Pietism, Enlightenment and Modernity," in *A Companion to German Pietism, 1660–1800*, ed. Douglas H. Shantz (Leiden: Brill, 2014), 361.
11 Ich bete an die Macht der Liebe,
die sich in Jesus offenbart;
ich geb mich hin dem freien Triebe,
wodurch ich Wurm geliebet ward;
ich will, anstatt an mich zu denken,
ins Meer der Liebe mich versenken.
In diesem teuren Jesusnamen
das Vaterherze öfnet sich;
ein Brunn der Liebe, Fried' und Freude
quillt uns so nah, so mildiglich.
Mein Gott, wenn's doch der Sünder wüßte –
sein Herz wohl bald dich lieben müßte.

12 James Urry, "'Servants from Far': Mennonites and the Pan-evangelical Impulse in Early Nineteenth-Century Russia," *MQR* 61 (1987), 213–27; William Allen, *Life of William Allen with Selections from His Correspondence* (London, 1846); and Walter Sawatsky, "Prince Alexander N. Golistyn (1773–1844): Tsarist Minister of Piety," PhD diss., University of Minnesota, 1976, 214–29.
13 Dyck, Epp, and Staples, eds., *Transformation*, 43.
14 P. Ghosh, "Max Weber in the Netherlands 1903–1907. A Neglected Episode in the Early History of 'The Protestant Ethic,'" in *Low Countries Historical Review* 119 (2014), 358–77.
15 Walter Klaassen, *Anabaptism: Neither Catholic nor Protestant* (Waterloo, ON: Conrad Press, 1973).
16 Delbert F. Plett, *Saints and Sinners: The Kleine Gemeinde in Imperial Russia, 1812 to 1875* (Steinbach, MB: Crossway Publications, 1999), 55.
17 Taylor, *A Secular Age*; and Taylor, *Sources of the Self*.
18 The development of individualism is at the heart of Taylor's *Sources of the Self* (2007). For a concise summary of his impact on Lutheran Pietism, see Shantz, ed., *German Pietism*, 276–9.
19 John R. Staples, "Religion, Politics, and the Mennonite Privilegium in Early Nineteenth Century Russia: Reconsidering the Warkentin Affair," *JMS* (2003), 71–88.
20 See P.M. Friesen, *The Mennonite Brotherhood in Russia (1789–1910)*, 2nd edition, translated by J.B. Toews and others (Winnipeg and Fresno, CA: Board of Christian Literature, 1978), for the generally accepted biography of Voth. On the educational revolution underway within Mennonite circles, see James Urry, "'The Snares of Reason': Changing Mennonite Attitudes to 'Knowledge' in Nineteenth Century Russia," *Comparative Studies in Society and History* 25 (April 1983), 306–22.
21 Thomas Howard, *Protestant Theology and the Making of the Modern German University* (Oxford: Oxford University Press, 2006), ch. 4.
22 Irina (Janzen) Cherkazianova, "Mennonite Schools and the Russian Empire: The Transformation of Church-State Relations in Education, 1789–1917," in *Minority Report: Mennonite Identities in Imperial Russia and Soviet Ukraine Reconsidered, 1789–1945*, ed. Leonard G. Friesen (Toronto: University of Toronto Press, 2018); Ben Eklof, *Russian Peasant Schools: Officialdom, Village Culture, and Popular Pedagogy, 1861–1914* (Berkeley: University of California Press, 1990), ch. 1; and Paul W. Werth, *The Tsar's Foreign Faiths, Toleration and the Fate of Religious Freedom in Imperial Russia* (Oxford: Oxford University Press, 2014).
23 Werth, *Tsar's Foreign Faiths*, 53–77.
24 Dyck, Epp, and Staples, eds., *Transformation*, 8–9, 22, 89.
25 Werth, *Tsar's Foreign Faiths*, 48.

26 See classic works by Nicholas V. Riasanovsky, *A Parting of the Ways: Government and the Educated Public in Russia, 1801–1855* (Oxford: Clarendon Press, 1976); and W. Bruce Lincoln, *In the Vanguard of Reform: Russia's Enlightened Bureaucrats, 1825–1861* (DeKalb: Northern Illinois University Press, 1982).
27 Staples, "Aesthetics of Civilization," 64.
28 Staples, "Aesthetics of Civilization," 74–6.
29 J. Arch Getty, *Practicing Stalinism: Bolsheviks, Boyars, and the Persistence of Tradition* (New Haven, CT: Yale University Press, 2013; and Robert Crews, "Empire and the Confessional State: Islam and Religious Politics in Nineteenth-Century Russia," *American Historical Review* 108 (2003), 83.
30 Dyck, Epp, and Staples, eds., *Transformation*, xl–xli, and 67, doc. 58.
31 Cornies claimed that Voth resigned as no one fired him. See Cornies' letter to David Epp dated 1 May 1829 in Dyck, Epp, and Staples, eds., *Transformation*, 174–5, doc. 171.
32 Franz Isaak, *Die Molotschnaer Mennoniten* (Halbstadt, 1908), 276; and Urry, "The Closed and the Open," 306–42.
33 August von Haxthausen, *The Russian Empire, Its People, Institutions, and Resources*, Volume 1 (London, 1856), 423.
34 Max Weber, *The Protestant Ethic and the Spirit of Capitalism with Other Writings on the Rise of the West*, 4th edition, trans. and ed. Stephen Kalberg (Oxford: Oxford University Press 2008), 67; see Kalberg's discussion of "social carriers" in 40–1.
35 Leonard G. Friesen, *Rural Revolutions in Southern Ukraine: Peasants, Nobles, and Colonists, 1774–1905* (Cambridge, MA: Harvard Ukrainian Reasearch Institute, 2008), 60–6. For an overview of population growth in New Russia during this period, see E.I. Druzhinina, *IUzhnaia Ukraina v period krizisa feodalizma, 1835–1860 gg.* (Moscow: Nauka, 1981), ch. 1.
36 Friesen, *Rural Revolutions*, 82–3.
37 Dyck, Epp, and Staples, eds., *Transformation*, 13, doc. 10; 17, doc. 14, and 21, doc. 19.
38 Ibid., 29, doc. 24.
39 Staples, "Religion," 55–7.
40 David H. Epp, *Johann Cornies*, Winnipeg: CMBC Publications, 1995), 17; and Friesen, *Rural Revolutions*, 83–4.
41 Rempel, "Mennonite Colonies," 159–60; and Urry, *None but Saints*, 112–15.
42 Rudy P. Friesen with Edith Elisabeth Friesen, *Building on the Past: Mennonite Architecture, Landscape and Settlements in Russia/Ukraine* (Winnipeg: Raduga Publishers, 2004), 46.
43 Dyck, Epp, and Staples, eds., *Transformation*, part 2.
44 Dyck, Epp, and Staples, eds., *Transformation*, 6–7, doc. 5, and 159–60, doc. 152; Urry, *None but Saints*, 113, 143; Harvey L. Dyck, Ingrid I. Epp, and

John R. Staples, eds., *Transformation of the Southern Ukrainian Steppe: Letters and Papers of Johann Cornies*, Volume 2: *1836–1842* (Toronto: University of Toronto Press, 2020), 19–20, docs. 25–6; and James Urry, "Through the Eye of a Needle: Wealth and the Mennonite Experience in Imperial Russia," *Journal of Mennonite Studies* 3 (1985), 15.
45 Dyck, "Russian Servitor," 9–28.
46 Dyck, "Russian Servitor," 14; and Friesen, *Mennonite Brotherhood*, 199.

6 A Community in Crisis: A Divided Faith, the Revolt of the Landless, and Threatened Military Service, 1860–1874

1 Oksana Beznosova, *Ekaterinoslavskaya guberniia: Terra incognita. Evangel'skogo dvizheniia v Rossiiskoi imperii (seredina xviii v. – 1917 g.)* (Steinhagen, Germany: Samenkorn, 2014), 152.
2 On the Great Reforms, see Ben Eklof, John Bushnell, and Larissa Zakharova, eds., *Russia's Great Reforms, 1855–1881* (Bloomington, IN: Indiana University Press, 1994); and W. Bruce Lincoln, *The Great Reforms: Autocracy, Bureaucracy, and the Politics of Change in Imperial Russia* (DeKalb: Northern Illinois University Press, 1990).
3 On the influence of these developments on the region's peasants, see Sergei Zhuk, "In Search of the Millennium: Convergence of Jews and Ukrainian Evangelical Peasants in Late Imperial Russia," in *Holy Dissent: Jewish and Christian Mysticism in Eastern Europe*, ed. Glenn Dynner (Detroit: Wayne State University Press, 2011), 334–58; and Sergei Zhuk, "'A Separate Nation' of 'Those Who Imitate Germans': Ukrainian Evangelical Peasants and Problems of Cultural Identification in the Ukrainian Provinces of Late Imperial Russia," *Ab Imperio* (2006), 139–60.
4 A full translation of this document is found in P.M. Friesen, *The Mennonite Brotherhood in Russia, 1789–1910*, trans. John B. Toews and others (Fresno, CA: Board of Christian Literature. General Conference of the Mennonite Brethren Conference of Mennonite Brethren Churches, 1978), 230–2. All quotations are taken from this translation.
5 H. Görz, *Die Molotschnaer Ansiedlung: Entstehung, Entwicklung, und Untergang* (Steinbach, MB: Echo Verlag, 1950), 66.
6 Jacob P. Bekker, *Origin of the Mennonite Brethren Church: Previously Unpublished Manuscript by One of the Eighteen Founders* (Hillsboro, KS: Mennonite Brethren Publishing House, 1973), 23.
7 John B. Toews, ed., *The Story of the Early Mennonite Brethren (1860–1869). Reflections of a Lutheran Churchman* (Winnipeg: Kindred Productions, 2002), 22.
8 Friesen, *Mennonite Brotherhood*, 211
9 P.M. Peucker, "Herrnhut and Russia: Archival Records on Moravian Activity in Russia from the Unity Archives in Herrnhut, Germany," in

Foreign Churches in St. Petersburg and Their Archives, 1703–1917, ed. Pieter Holtrop and Henk Slechte (Lieden: Brill, 2007), 129040; and Friesen, *Mennonite Brotherhood*, 105–7.

10 Delbert Plett, ed., *The Golden Years: The Mennonite Kleine Gemeinde in Russia (1812–1849)* (Steinbach, MB: D.F.P. Publications, 1985), 176; Abe J. Dueck, "Mennonite Churches and Religious Developments in Russia, 1850–1914," in *Mennonites in Russia, 1788–1988: Essays in Honour of Gerhard Lohrenz*, ed. John Friesen (Winnipeg: CMBC Publications, 1989), 150; and John Friesen, "Mennonite Churches and Religious Developments in Russia, 1789–1850," in *Mennonites in Russia, 1788–1988: Essays in Honour of Gerhard Lohrenz*, ed. John Friesen (Winnipeg: CMBC Publications, 1989), 45.

11 James Urry and Lawrence Klippenstein, "Mennonites and the Crimean War, 1854–1856," *JMS* 7 (1989), 15.

12 Friesen, *Mennonite Brotherhood*, 102–3; and Bekker, *Origin*, 110.

13 James Urry, "The Closed and the Open: Social and Religious Change amongst the Mennonites in Russia (1789–1889)," unpublished PhD diss., Oxford University, 1978, Volume 2, 499–500; and James Urry, "The Social Background to the Emergence of the Mennonite Brethren in Nineteenth Century Russia," *JMS* 6 (1988): 8–35.

14 Rudy P. Friesen with Edith Elizabeth Friesen, *Building on the Past: Mennonite Architecture, Landscape and Settlements in Russia/Ukraine* (Winnipeg: Raduga Publications, 2004), 129, 146; and John B. Toews, "Early Mennonite Brethren Membership Lists Found in St. Petersburg Archives," *California Mennonite Historical Society Bulletin* 33 (March 1996), 10–14.

15 Friesen, *Mennonite Brotherhood*, 281. I thank James Urry in his correspondence to me dated 5 March 2020 for his comment on the centrality of Oncken to the emerging stress on conversion stories among Chortitza Mennonites. Cf. John B. Toews, "Mennonite Brethren Founders Relate Their Conversion," *Direction: A Mennonite Brethren Forum* 23 (Fall 1994), 31–7.

16 Cf. John B. Toews, ed. and trans., *The Diaries of David Epp, 1837–1843* (Vancouver: Regent College Publishing, 2000), 71, 101, 102, 106, 134, and 147; and Harvey L. Dyck, ed. and trans., *A Mennonite in Russia: The Diaries of Jacob D. Epp, 1851–1880* (Toronto: University of Toronto Press, 1991), 127–8, 170, 196, and 255.

17 Friesen, *Mennonite Brotherhood*, 228–9.

18 John B. Toews, "Early Mennonite Brethren and Evangelism in Russia," *Direction: A Mennonite Brethren Forum* 28 (Fall 1999), 187–200; and Toews, ed., *Story*, 23–4. The report named Mennonites Johannes Claassen and Jacob Reimer as two of the culprits.

19 Aileen Friesen, "Religious Policy in the Russian Borderlands: The 1860s Mennonite Schism," unpublished MA thesis, University of Alberta, 2007, 63–4. Further on the Brune investigation, see Toews, ed., *Story*.

20 For the entire petition, dated November 1863, see Franz Isaak, *Die Molotschnaer Mennoniten. Dein Beitrag zur Geschichte derselben* (Halbstadt, 1908), 28–9. The earlier petition has not survived.
21 David G. Rempel, "The Mennonite Colonies in New Rusisa: A Study of Their Settlement and Economic Development from 1789 to 1914," unpublished PhD diss., Stanford University, 1933) 102–9.
22 Isaak, *Die Molotschnaer*, 18–19, 26.
23 A.A. Klaus, *Nashi Kolonii. Opyty I materialy po istorii I statistike inostrannoi kolonizatsii v Rossii* (St. Petersburg, 1869), 151, 185; and Nataliya V. Venger, *Mennonitskoe predprinimatel'stvo v usloviiakh modernizatsii iuga Rossii: Mezhdu kongregatsiei, klanom I Rossiiskim obshchestvom (1789–1920)* (Dnepropetrovsk, Ukraine: Dnepropetrovskogo natsional'nogo universiteta, 2009), 168–88.
24 David H. Epp, *Sketches from the Pioneer Years of the Industry in the Mennonite Settlements of South Russia*, trans. J.P. Penner from articles in *DB*, 13 July 1938 to 18 January 1939 (n.p., March 1972), 9–37; and N.J. Kroeker, *First Mennonite Villages in Russia, 1789–1943* (Vancouver: N.J. Kroeker, 1981), 104.
25 Urry and Klippenstein, "Mennonites," 21, 24.
26 Rempel, "Mennonite Colonies," 183.
27 Klaus, *Nashi Kolonii*, 169–70; James Urry, *None but Saints: The Transformation of Mennonite Life in Russia, 1789–1889* (Winnipeg: Hyperion Press, 1989), 141.
28 D.H. Epp, *Die Chortitzer Mennoniten. Versuch einer Darstellung des Entwicklungsganges derselben* (Steinbach, MB: Die Mennonitische Post, 1984, originally published by the author in Odessa, Selbstverlag: 1889), 89; Harvey L. Dyck, "Introduction and Analysis," in *A Mennonite in Russia: The Diaries of Jacob D. Epp, 1851–1880* (Toronto: University of Toronto Press, 1991), 32–3; and Friesen with Friesen, *Building on the Past*, 387–8.
29 Isaak, *Die Molotschnaer*, 31, n. 1; and Rempel, "Mennonite Colonies," 186.
30 D.H. Epp, *Die Chortitzer*, 94.
31 John L.H. Keep, *Soldiers of the Tsar: Army and Society in Russia, 1462–1874* (Oxford: Clarendon Press, 1985), 352–6.
32 Elise Kimerling Wirtschafter, *Social Identity in Imperial Russia* (DeKalb: Northern Illinois University Press, 1997), 170; Paul W. Werth, *The Tsar's Foreign Faiths: Toleration and the Fate of Religious Freedom in Imperial Russia* (Oxford: Oxford University Press, 2014), 191; and David L. Hoffmann and Yanni Kotsonis, eds., *Russian Modernity: Politics, Knowledge, Practices* (New York: St. Martin's Press, 2000), especially, in this context, ch. 1, 3, and 4.
33 Gregory L. Freeze, "The Soslovie (Estate) Paradigm in Russian Social History," *AHR* 91 (1986), 11–36, citation is from p. 14; and Alison K. Smith, *For the Common Good and Their Own Well-Being: Social Estates in Imperial Russia* (Oxford: Oxford University Press, 2014), 126–7.
34 On the 1871 legislation in general, see Detlef Brandes, *Von Den Zaren Adoptiert. Die Deutschen Kolonisten und Die Balkansiedler in Neurussland und*

Bessarabien, 1751–1914 (Munich: R. Oldenbourg Verlag, 1993), 348–60; and Julia Malitska, "Negotiating Imperial Rule Colonists and Marriage in the Nineteenth-Century Black Sea Steppe," unpublished PhD diss., Södertörn University, 2017, 355–6. I thank James Urry for steering me to the Malitska dissertation.

35 Robert F. Baumann, "Universal Service Reform: Conception to Implementation, 1873–1883," in *Reforming the Tsar's Army: Military Innovation in mperial Russia from Peter the Great to the Revolution*, ed. David Schimmelpenninck van der Oye and Bruce W. Menning (Cambridge: Cambridge University Press, 2004), 11–33.
36 Dyck, "Introduction and Analysis," 199.
37 Willard Sunderland, *Taming the Wild Field: Colonization and Empire on the Russian Steppe* (Ithaca, NY: Cornell University Press, 2006), 196.
38 On the multiple interactions between these seemingly disparate groups, see Sergei I. Zhuk, *Russia's Lost Reformation: Peasants, Millennialism, and Radical Sects in Southern Russia and Ukraine, 1830–1917* (Baltimore: The Johns Hopkins Press, 2004), 155–88.

7 From Crisis to Consolidation: The Flourishing of Russian Mennonitism, 1865–1883

1 "Baratow," in *MLex* (Frankfurt am Main, 1913), Volume 1, 124.
2 Harvey L. Dyck, trans. and ed., *A Mennonite in Russia: The Diaries of Jacob D. Epp 1851–1880* (Toronto: University of Toronto Press, 1991), 53, 329–31; and Rudy P. Friesen with Edith Elisabeth Friesen, *Building on the Past: Mennonite Architecture Landscape and Settlements in Russia/Ukraine* (Winnipeg: Raduga Publications, 2004), 523–4.
3 Dyck, trans. and ed., *Mennonite in Russia*, 62.
4 "Mennonite Brethren Church," *GAMEO*, https://gameo.org/index.php?title=Mennonite_Brethren_Church#The_Beginning_of_the_Mennonite_Brethren_Church.
5 See Albert W. Wardin Jr., *On the Edge: Baptists and Other Free Church Evangelicals in Tsarist Russia, 1855–1917* (Eugene, OR: Wipf & Stock, 2013), 61; Oksana Beznosova, *Ekaterinoslavskaia Guberniia: Terra incognita evangel'skogo dvizheniia v Rossiiskoi imperii (seredina xviii v. – 1917)* (Steinhagen, Germany: Samenkorn, 2014), 200–21, and 153; and Abe J. Dueck, "Mennonite Churches and Religious Developments in Russia, 1850–1914," in *Mennonites in Russia, 1788–1988. Essays in Honour of Gerhard Lohrenz*, ed. John Friesen (Winnipeg: CMBC Publications), 153.
6 Jacob Bekker, *Origin of the Mennonite Brethren Church: Previously Unpublished Manuscript by One of the Eighteen Founders*, trans. D.E. Pauls and A.E. Janzen (Hillsboro, KS: The Mennonite Brethren Historical Society,

1973), 79; and P.M. Friesen, *The Mennonite Brotherhood in Russia, 1789–1910*, trans. John B. Toews and others (Fresno, CA: Board of Christian Literature. General Conference of the Mennonite Brethren Conference of Mennonite Brethren Churches, 1978), 244.
7 For the June Protocols, see Friesen, *Mennonite Brotherhood*, 436–41.
8 Delbert F. Plett, *Saints and Sinners: The Kleine Gemeinde in Imperial Russia 1812 to 1875* (Steinbach, MB: Crossway Publications, 1999), 94.
9 James Urry, "The Mennonite Brethren Church and Russia's Great Reform in the 1870s," *Direction: A Mennonite Brethren Forum* 46 (Spring 2017), 10–25. https://directionjournal.org/46/1/mennonite-brethren-church-and-russias.html.
10 Although Alt and Neu Danzig were not Mennonite settlements, they did have a Prussian connection and spoke a similar Low German dialect. They appear to have ties with the Frisian Mennonite village of Kronsweide. I thank James Urry for having brought this connection to my attention.
11 A.H. Unruh, *Die Geschichte der Mennoniten-Bruedergemeinde 1860–1954* (Hillsboro, KS: Mennonite Brethren Church of North America, 1955), 144. It was Liebig's second visit to Chortitza. He first came in 1866. For an account of both visits, see Friesen, *Mennonite Brotherhood*, 464–6. See also Urry, "Mennonite Brethren Church."
12 John B. Toews, *Perilous Journey: The Mennonite Brethren in Russia, 1860–1910* (Winnipeg: Kindred Press, 1988), 57. For a translation of the document, see Abe J. Dueck, *Moving beyond Secession: Defining Russian Mennonite Brethren Vision and Identity 1872–1922* (Winnipeg: Kindred Press, 1997), 105–7.
13 Friesen, *Mennonite Brotherhood*, 480.
14 See Urry, "Mennonite Brethren Church," for a more extensive exploration of this transition. On the official recognition of the Brethren as a Mennonite movement by 1880, see Friesen, *Mennonite Brotherhood*, 480.
15 *Mennonitisches Lexicon* (Frankfurt am Main, 1913), Volume 1, 356–7.
16 Bekker, *Origin*, 134–5.
17 C.P. Toews, Heinrich Friesen, and Arnold Dyck, *The Kuban Settlement*, trans. from the German by Herbert Giesbrecht (Winnipeg: Echo Historical Series, 1989), 10, 18.
18 Toews, Friesen, and Dyck, *Kuban Settlement*, ch. 6–8.
19 Recall that the first true daughter colony was Bergthal, established by Chortitza in 1836 to address its mounting landless problem. But unlike the Daughter Colonies established from the 1860s onward, St. Petersburg granted land outright for the Bergthal settlement.
20 John B. Toews, *Perilous Journey*, 52–7. Officials also puzzled over the Mennonite Brethren identity because of the MB association with Russian sectarian Stundists in New Russia. See Sergei Zhuk, *Russia's Lost Reformation: Peasants, Millennialism, and Radical Sects in Southern Russia*

and Ukraine, 1830–1917 (Washington, DC: Woodrow Wilson Center Press, 2004).
21 Dyck, trans. and ed., *Mennonite in Russia*, 134, 168.
22 Friesen, *Mennonite Brotherhood*, 945–58; and "Bernhard Harder (1832–1884)," *GAMEO*, https://gameo.org/index.php?title=Harder,_Bernhard_(1832-1884)&oldid=145404.
23 P.M. Friesen, *Mennonite Brotherhood*, 948.
24 On Mennonite music after 1860, see Peter Letkemann, "The Hymnody and Choral Music of Mennonites in Russia 1789–1915," unpublished PhD diss., University of Toronto, 1985, ch. viii.
25 Franz Isaak, *Die Molotschnaer Mennoniten. Ein Beitrag zur Geschichte derserben* (Halbstadt: H.J. Braun, 1908).
26 Isaak, 33–5. David Rempel also declares that Wiebe also contacted the governor-general of New Russia on behalf of the landless. Cf. Rempel, "Mennonite Colonies," 188.
27 James Urry, *None but Saints: The Transformation of Mennonite Life in Russia, 1789–1889* (Winnipeg: Hyperion Press, 1989), 145.
28 William Schroeder, *The Bergthal Colony* (Winnipeg: CMBC Publications, 1974).
29 Mark Jantzen, *Mennonite German Soldiers: Nation, Religion, and Family in the Prussian East, 1772–1880* (Notre Dame, IN: University of Notre Dame Press, 2010), 153–5.
30 Johannes Dyck, *Am Trakt: A Mennonite Settlement in the Central Volga Region*. Based on a text by W.E. Surukin (Winnipeg: Manitoba Mennonite Historical Society, 1995); and Bernhard J. Harder, *Alexandertal: Die Geschichte der letzten deutschen Stammsiedlung in Russland* (1959?). Cf. https://gameo.org/index.php?title=Am_Trakt_Mennonite_Settlement_(Samara_Oblast,_Russia); and https://gameo.org/index.php?title=Alexandertal_Mennonite_Settlement_(Samara_Oblast,_Russia).
31 Leonard G. Friesen, *Rural Revolutions in Southern Ukraine: Peasants, Nobles, and Colonists, 1774–1905* (Cambridge, MA: Harvard Ukrainian Research Institute, 2008), 199. Former colonists comprised the remaining 10 per cent of New Russia's peasant population after 1870.
32 Friesen, *Rural Revolutions*, 126–8.
33 For an overview of these settlements, see Friesen with Friesen, *Building on the Past*, ch. 7–10. The literature on the daughter colonies is vast. For a representative sampling, see H. Goerz, *Mennonite Settlements in Crimea* (Winnipeg: CMBC Publications, 1992); Svetlana Bobyleva, "'Land of Opportunity, Sites of Devastation': Notes on the History of the Borozenko Colony," in *Minority Report: Mennonite Identities in Imperial Russia and Soviet Ukraine Reconsidered, 1789–1945*, ed. Leonard G. Friesen (Toronto: University of Toronto Press, 2018), ch. 1; Delbert Plett, *Saints and Sinners:*

The Kleine Gemeinde in Imperial Russia, 1812–1875 (Steinbach, MB: Crossway Publications, 1999), ch. 7; Gerhard Lohrenz and Victor G. Doerksen, *Zagradovka: History of a Mennonite Settlement in Southern Russia* (Winnipeg: CMBC Publications, 2000); and also numerous entries in the *GAMEO* and *MennLex*.

34 James Urry, "The Closed and the Open: Social and Religious Change amongst the Mennonites in Russia (1789–1889), unpublished PhD diss., Oxford University, 1978, Volume 2, 731b.
35 https://gameo.org/index.php?title=Bergmann,_Hermann_A._(1850-1919); and Friesen with Friesen, *Building on the Past*, 600.
36 The Schönfeld congregations maintained direct congregational affiliation with Molotschna.
37 Gerhard Töws, *Schönfeld. Werde- und Opfergang einer deutscher Siedlung in der Ukraine* (Winnipeg, 1939). On estates more generally, see Helmut Huebert, *Mennonite Estates in Imperial Russia* (Winnipeg: Kindred Press, 2005).
38 James Urry, "Wealth and Poverty in the Mennonite Experience: Dilemmas and Challenges," *JMS* (2009), 22.
39 On Mennonite photo albums with numerous estates, see Walter Quiring, *In the Fullness of Time: 150 Years of Mennonite Sojourn in Russia* (Waterloo, 1974); and Gerhard Lohrenz, *Heritage Remembered: A Pictorial Survey of Mennonites in Prussia and Russia* (Winnipeg: CMBC Publications, 1974).
40 For a copy of the initial Mennonite appeal, see D.H. Epp, *Die Chortitzer Mennoniten. Versuch einder Darstellung des Entwicklungsganges derserben* (Odessa, 1889; reprinted Steinbach, MB, 1984), 96–9. See also Paul Toews, "Mennonites and the Search for Military Exemption: State Concessions and Conflicts in the 1870s," in *Voprosy germanskoi istorii. Sobrnik nauchnykh trudov* (Dnipropetrovsk, Ukraine: Porogi, 2007), 81–106.
41 Irina (Janzen) Cherkazianova, "Mennonite Schools and the Russian Empire: The Transformation of Church-State Relations in Education, 1789–1917," in *Minority Report: Mennonite Identities in Imperial Russia and Soviet Ukraine Reconsidered, 1789–1945*, edited by Leonard G. Friesen (Toronto: University of Toronto Press, 2018), 93–4.
42 Friesen, *Mennonite Brotherhood*, 586–7.
43 On this latter point, see Harry Loewen, "A House Divided: Russian Mennonite Nonresistance and Emigration in the 1870s," in *Mennonites in Russia, 1788–1988. Essay in Honour of Gerhard Lohrenz*, ed. John J. Friesen (Winnipeg: CMBC Publications, 1989), 127–43.
44 Friesen, *Mennonite Brotherhood*, 596.
45 The upper-end estimate is found in a number of sources, including "Mennonites," Government of Canada, Library and Archives Canada, https://www.bac-lac.gc.ca/eng/discover/immigration/history-ethnic

-cultural/Pages/mennonites.aspx. For a general overview of these migrations, see Frank H. Epp, *Mennonites in Canada, the History of a Separate People, 1786–1920* (Toronto, 1974); and Theron Schlabach, *Peace, Faith, Nation: Mennonites and Amish in Nineteenth-Century America* (Scottdale, PA: Herald Press, 1988). For a detailed study of the Canadian migration, see Royden Loewen, *Family, Church, and Market: A Mennonite Community in the Old and the New Worlds, 1850–1930* (Toronto: University of Toronto Press, 1993).

46 Gustav R. Gaeddert, "Jansen, Cornelius (1822–1894)," *GAMEO*, 1957, https://gameo.org/index.php?title=Jansen,_Cornelius_(1822-1894).

47 Plett (1999), 314–17; and Samuel J. Steiner, *Vicarious Pioneer: The Life of Jacob Y. Shantz* (Winnipeg: Hyperion Press, 1988). For a first-hand account of the delegates' journey to North America, see Delbert Plett, ed., *Storm and Triumph: The Mennonite Kleine Gemeinde, 1850–1875* (Steinbach, MB: D.F.B. Publications, 1986), 293–305. On the numbers, see John P.R. Eicher, *Exiled among the Nations: German and Mennonite Mythologies in a Transnational Age* (Cambridge: Cambridge University Press, 2020), 39–40.

48 Adolf Ehrt, *Das Mennonitentum in Russland von seiner Einwanderung bis zur Gegenwart* (Berlin: Julius Beltz, 1932), 67; and Lawrence Klippenstein, *Mennonite Conscientious Objectors in Tsarist Russia and the Soviet Union before World War II, and Other Cos in Eastern Europe* (Winnipeg: Mennonite Heritage Centre, 2016), 66.

49 Klippenstein, *Mennonite Conscientious Objectors*, 81. For the broader context, see Lawrence Klippenstein, "Mennonite Pacifism and State Service in Russia: A Case Study in Church-State Relations, 1789–1936," unpublished PhD diss., University of Minnesota, 1984, 85–117.

50 N.V. Venger, *Mennonitskoe predprinimatel'stvo v usloviiakh modernizatstsii iuga Rossii: Mezhdu kongregatsiei klanom i Rossiiskim obshchestvom 1789–1920* (Dnepropetrovsk, Ukraine: Porogi, 2009), 295–6.

51 Oksana Beznosova, "A Foreign Faith but of What Sort? The Mennonite Church and the Russian Empire, 1789–1917," in *Minority Report: Mennonite Identities in Imperial Russia and Soviet Ukraine Reconsidered, 1789–1945*, ed. Leonard G. Friesen (Toronto: University of Toronto Press, 2018), 121.

52 For an extensive overview of the multiple reasons why Mennonites chose to leave in the 1870s, see Urry, "The Closed and the Open," 672–86.

53 Leonard G. Friesen, ed., *Lifting the Veil: Mennonite Life in Russia before the Revolution*, by Jacob H. Janzen (Kitchener, ON: Pandora Press, 1998), 76–7. For a biography of Jacob H. Janzen, see Walter Klaassen, "Jacob H. Janzen (1878–1950)," in *Shepherds, Servants and Prophets: Leadership among the Russian Mennonites (ca. 1880–1960)*, ed. Harry Loewen (Kitchener, ON: Pandora Press, 2003), 177–92.

8 Glory Days: The Apogee of Russian Mennonitism, 1883–1904

1. David G. Rempel with Cornelia Rempel Carlson, *A Mennonite Family in Tsarist Russia and the Soviet Union, 1789–1923* (Toronto: University of Toronto Press, 2002), 88–9, 102.
2. David G. Rempel, "The Mennonite Commonwealth in Russia: A Sketch of Its Founding and Endurance, 1789–1919," reprinted from *The Mennonite Quarterly Review* xlvii (October 1973) and xlviii (January 1974).
3. Rempel, "Mennonite Commonwealth," 3.
4. E.K. Francis, "The Russian Mennonites: From Religious to Ethnic Group," *American Journal of Sociology* 54, no. 2 (September 1948), 101–7; John Staples, "The Mennonite Commonwealth Paradigm and the Dnepropetrovsk School; Ukrainian Mennonite Historiography," in *Voprosy germanskoi istorii* (Dnipropetrovsk, Ukraine: Porogi, 2007), 58–69; and James Urry, "The Mennonite Commonwealth in Imperial Russia revisited," *The Mennonite Quarterly Review* 84 (April 2010), 229–47.
5. Rempel with Rempel Carlson, *A Mennonite Family*, 30–1.
6. Adolf Ehrt, *Das Mennonitentum in Russland von seiner Einwanderung bis zur Gegenwart* (Leipzig: Julius Beltz, 1932), 53–4; David G. Rempel, "The Mennonite Colonies in New Russia: A Study of Their Settlement and Economic Development from 1789–1914," unpublished PhD diss., Stanford University, 1933, 212–13; and Rempel with Rempel Carlson, *A Mennonite Family*, 120, and Appendix VI.
7. Aileen Friesen, *Colonizing Russia's Promised Land: Orthodoxy and Community on the Siberian Steppe* (Toronto: University of Toronto Press, 2020), 22.
8. Tena Wiebe, ed., *Neu-Samara: A Mennonite Settlement East of the Volga (A Translation of Neu Samara am Tock)* (Edmonton: Jackpine House, 2002), 22. See also Petr P. Wiebe, "The Mennonite Colonies of Siberia: From the Late Nineteenth to the Early Twentieth Century," *JMS* 30 (2012), 23–35; Petr P. Wiebe, *Nemetskie kolonii v Sibiri: sotsial'no-ekonomicheskii aspect* (Omsk, Russia, 2007); C.P. Toews, *Die Tereker Ansiedlung.* (Steinbach, MB, 1945); and Karl Fast, *Orenburg: die letzte Mennonische Ansiedlung in Osteuropa* (Winnipeg: Das Bunte Fenster, 1995).
9. Ehrt, *Das Mennonitentum*, 81–2. On the larger context, see Detlef Brandes, *Von Den Zaren Adoptiert. Die Deutschen Kolonisten und die Balkansiedler in Neurussland und Bessarbien, 1751–1914* (Munich: R. Oldenbourg, 1993), 372–439.
10. Overviews on this topic are found in James Urry, "Growing up with Cities: The Mennonite Experience in Imperial Russia and the Early Soviet Union," *JMS* 20 (2002), 123–54; George K. Epp, "Urban Mennonites in Russia," in *Mennonites in Russia, 1788–1989. Essays in Honour of Gerhard Lohrenz* (Winnipeg: CMBC Publications, 1989), 239–60; and one strong case study

by Natalia Venger, "The Mennonite Industrial Dynasties in Alexandrovsk," *JMS* 21 (2003), 89–110.
11 Ehrt, *Das Mennonitentum*, 82.
12 Ehrt, *Das Mennonitentum*, 88.
13 Terry Martin, *The Mennonites and the State Duma, 1905–1914*, The Donald W. Treadgold Papers in Russian, East European and Central Asian Studies. Paper No. 4 (Seattle: The Henry M. Jackson School of International Affairs, 1996), 10.
14 A.A Klaus, *Nashi kolonii. Opyty I materialy po istorii I statistike inostannoi kolonizatsii v Rossii* (St. Petersburg, 1869), 161–2; V.E. Postnikov, *Iuzhno-Russkoe krest'ianskoe khoziaistvo* (Moscow, 1891), 168–70; and David G. Rempel, "Mennonite Colonies," 243–7.
15 Gerhard Lohrenz, *Storm Tossed: The Personal Story of a Canadian Mennonite from Russia* (Winnipeg: Christian Press, 1976), 28. Not surprisingly, the Russians also adopted *arbuz* and *bashtan* from the Turkish.
16 On the development of the New Russian infrastructure generally, see Leonard G. Friesen, *Rural Revolutions in Southern Ukraine: Peasants, Nobles, and Colonists, 1774–1905* (Cambridge, MA: Harvard Ukrainian Research Institute, 2008), ch. 5–6; David Moon, *The Plough that Broke the Steppes: Agriculture and Environment on Russia's Grasslands, 1700–1914* (Oxford: Oxford University Press, 2013), Part III; and David Moon, *The American Steppes: The Unexpected Russian Roots of Great Plains Agriculture, 1870s–1930s* (Cambridge: Cambridge University Press, 2020).
17 For a contrast of an excellent overview on demographic change before 1914, see James Urry, "Prolegomena to the Study of Mennonite Society in Russia, 1880–1914," *Journal of Mennonite Studies* 8 (1990), 67–8; and Rempel with Rempel Carlson, *A Mennonite Family*, 68. For the general overview, see Jeffrey Burds, *Peasant Dreams and Market Politics: Labor Migration and the Russian Village, 1861–1905* (Pittsburgh: University of Pittsburgh Press, 1998).
18 Leonard G. Friesen, "Mennonites and their Peasant Neighbours in Ukraine before 1900," *Journal of Mennonite Studies* 10 (1992), 56–69; and Leonard G. Friesen, "Bukkers, Plows and Lobogreikas: Peasant Acquisition of Agricultural Implements in New Russia before 1900," *Russian Review* 53 (1994), 399m–418.
19 Friesen, *Rural Revolutions*, 145–9; Venger, "Mennonite Industrial Dynasties," 92–4; and Theodore H. Friedgut, *Iuzovka and Revolution*, Volume 1: *Life and Work in Russia's Donbass, 1869–1924*; and Volume 2: *Politics and Revolution in Russia's Donbass* (Princeton, NJ: Princeton University Press, 1989 and 1994).
20 David G. Rempel, "Mennonite Colonies," 276, though Rempel bases this on a summary from P.M. Friesen, *Mennonite Brotherhood*, 866–9.

21 Natalia Venger, *Mennonitskoe predprinimatel'stvo v usloviikh modernizatsii iuga Rossii: mezhdu kongregatsiei, klanom I rossiiskim obshchestvom (1789–1920)* (Dnepropetrovsk, Ukraine: 2009), 320–33; and Ehrt, *Das Mennonitentum*, 92.
22 For explanations on these implements, see Leonard G. Friesen, "Bukkers, Plows and Lobogreikas: Peasant Acquisition of Agricultural Implements in New Russia before 1900," *RR* 53 (1994), 399–418.
23 Cornelius Krahn and Ervin Beck, "Clocks," *GAMEO*, 1989, https://gameo.org/index.php?title=Clocks&oldid=139672.
24 Rempel, "Mennonite Colonies," 56. See also Fred V. Carstensen, *American Enterprise in Foreign Markets: Studies of Singer and International Harvester in Imperial Russia* (Chapel Hill: University of North Carolina Press, 1984).
25 Urry gets this date from Ehrt, *Das Mennonitentum*, 96. See the interesting discussion of Mennonite social structure in: Venger, *Mennonitskoe*, 378–404; James Urry, "Through the Eye of the Needle: Wealth and the Mennonite Experience in Imperial Russia," *Journal of Mennonite Studies* 3 (1985), 13, 18–21; and Urry, "Prolegomena," 62–8.
26 Venger, *Mennonitskoe*, 97.
27 In addition to sources on Mennonite estate holding cited in the previous chapter, see also Jacob C. Toews, "Das mennonitische Gutsbesitzertum in Russland," *DB* (30 June–24 November 1954); Al Reimer, "Peasant Aristocracy: The Mennonite *Gutsbesitzertum* in Russia," *Journal of Mennonite Studies* 8 (1990), 76–88; and Anne Konrad, ed., *A Mennonite Estate Family in Southern Ukraine, 1904–1924* (Kitchener, ON: Pandora Press, 2013).
28 Harvey L. Dyck, ed., *A Mennonite in Russia: The Diaries of Jacob D. Epp, 1851–1880* (Toronto: University of Toronto Press, 1991), 62.
29 Rempel with Rempel Carlson, *A Mennonite Family*, ch. 15; and interview with Anna Friesen, who grew up in Margenau. Interview from 1 May 2020.
30 "Thick Culture" as per Clifford Geertz, "Thick Description: Toward an Interpretive Theory of Culture," in *The Interpretation of Cultures: Selected Essay* (New York: Basic Books, 1976), 3–30.
31 John B. Toews, "The Mennonite Brethren in Russia during the 1890s," *Direction: A Mennonite Brethren Forum* 30 (Fall 2001), 144–5. On the role of the MBs in Baptist ecclesial formation in the Russian empire, see Johannes Dyck, "Mennonites as Catalytic Agents in Free Church History in Russia and the Soviet Union," in *European Mennonites and the Challenge of Modernity over Five Centuries: Contributors, Detractors, and Adapters*, ed. by Mark Jantzen, Mary S. Sprunger, and John D. Thiesen (North Newton: Bethel College, 2016). 249–61.
32 Cornelius Krahn, Victor G. Doerksen, and Victor Wiebe, "Temple Society," *GAMEO*, 2010, https://gameo.org/index.php?title=Temple_Society&oldid=146288.

33 Alan M. Guenther, "Selling Bibles: The Bartsch Brothers in Central Asia," *Preservings* 42 (2021), 9–16; Abe J. Dueck, "Claas Epp and the Great Trek Reconsidered," *JMS* 3 (1985), 138–47; and Fred Belk, *The Great Trek of the Russian Mennonites to Central Asia, 1880–1884* (Scottdale, PA: Herald Press, 1976). On the Mennonite settlement in Khiva, see Walter Ratliff, "The Mennonites of Khiva: A Modernizing Community," in *European Mennonites and the Challenge of Modernity over Five Centuries: Contributors, Detractors, and Adapters*, ed. Mark Jantzen, Mary S. Sprunger, and John D. Thiesen (North Newton, KS: Bethel College, 2016), 179–93.

34 For overviews on this topic, see John B. Toews, "Brethren and Old Church Relations in Pre-World War I Russia: Setting the Stage for Canada," *JMS* 2 (1984), 42–59; and Abe J. Dueck, "Mennonite Churches and Religious Developments in Russia, 1850–1914," in *Mennonites in Russia, 1789–1988: Essays in Honour of Gerhard Lohrenz*, ed. John J. Friesen (Winnipeg: CMBC Publications, 1989), 149–82. For more contextual works, see Oksana Beznosova, "A Foreign Faith but of What Sort? The Mennonite Church and the Russian Empire, 1789–1917," in *Minority Report: Mennonite Identities in Imperial Russia and Soviet Ukraine Reconsidered, 1789–1945*, ed. Leonard G. Friesen (Toronto: University of Toronto Press, 2018), 126–35.

35 Dueck, "Mennonite Churches," 167.

36 P.M. Friesen, *The Mennonite Brotherhood in Russia, 1789–1910*, translated by John B. Toews et al., 2nd ed. (Fresno: Board of Christian Literature. General Conference of the Mennonite Brethren Conference of Mennonite Brethren Churches, 1980), 918; John B. Toews, "Russian Mennonites and Allianz," *JMS* 14 (1996), 45–64; and Abe Dueck, "The Quest for a Mennonite Seminary in Russia, 1883–1926: Signs of a Changing Mennonite World," *MQR* 74 (2000), 448–55.

37 Leonard G. Friesen, ed., *Lifting the Veil: Mennonite Life in Russia before the Revolution*, by Jacob H. Janzen (Kitchener, ON: Pandora Press, 1998), 32–71; and N.N. Driedger and Richard D. Thiessen, "Janzen, Jacob H. (1878–1950)." *GAMEO*, March 2009, https://gameo.org/index.php?title=Janzen,_Jacob_H._(1878-1950)&oldid=140933.

38 Irina (Janzen) Cherkazianova, "Mennonite Schools and the Russian Empire: The Transformation of Church-State Relations in Education, 1789–1917," in *Minority Report: Mennonite Identities in Imperial Russia and Soviet Ukraine Reconsidered, 1789–1945*, ed. Leonard G. Friesen (Toronto: University of Toronto Press, 2018), 94; and Paul W. Werth, *The Tsar's Foreign Faiths: Toleration and the Fate of Religious Freedom in Imperial Russia* (Oxford: Oxford University Press, 2014), ch. 6. The classic work on the formation of a Russian national education strategy is Ben Eklof, *Russian Peasant Schools: Officialdom, Village Culture, and Popular Pedagogy, 1861–1914* (Berkeley: University of California Press, 1986).

39 Cherkazianova, "Mennonite Schools," 95 and 97; and Faith Hillis, *Children of Rus': Right-Bank Ukraine and the Invention of a Russian Nation* (Ithaca, NY: Cornell University Press, 2013). For a listing of Mennonite secondary and girls' schools in the empire, see Adolf Ens, "Mennonite Education in Russia," in *Mennonites in Russia, 1788–1989: Essays in Honour of Gerhard Lohrenz*, ed. John J. Friesen (Winnipeg; CMBC Publications, 1989), 86–7. For a case study of a single school, see Ted D. Regehr, with the assistance of J.I. Regehr, *For Everything a Season: A History of the Alexanderkrone Zentralschule* (Winnipeg: CMBC Publications, 1988).
40 Rempel, "Mennonite Commonwealth," 88; and Harry Loewen, "Intellectual Developments among the Mennonites of Russia: 1880–1917," *JMS* 8 (1990), 97. Loewen's article is very useful for its overview of intellectual movements more generally in the period before 1905.
41 James Urry, "The Cost of Community: The Funding and Economic Management of the Russian Mennonite Commonwealth before 1914," in *JMS* 10 (1992), 22–55. The budgets are on p. 25. Cf. Rempel, "Mennonite Commonwealth," 82–5.
42 Rempel, "Mennonite Commonwealth," 84.
43 Rudy P. Friesen with Edith Elisabeth Friesen, *Building on the Past: Mennonite Architecture, Landscape and Settlements in Russia/Ukraine* (Winnipeg: Raduga Publications, 2004), 148–50, 373–4.
44 Tena Wiebe, ed., *Neu-Samara*, 49.
45 Dilaram M. Inoyatova, "Mennonites in Central Asia and Their Role in the Modernization of Economics and Culture in the Region," in *European Mennonites and the Challenge of Modernity over Five Centuries: Contributors, Detractors, and Adapters*, ed. Mark Jantzen, Mary S. Sprunger, and John D. Thiesen (North Newton, KS: Bethel College, 2016), 169; Dilaram M. Inoyatova, "Iz istorii Mennnonitov Turkestana," in *Etnodemograficheskie Protsessy v Turkestane* (Tashkent, 2005), 43–7. and Serhii Plokhy, *Ukraine and Russia: Representations of the Past* (Toronto: University of Toronto Press, 2008), 138–42.
46 Eric Lohr, *Russian Citizenship: From Empire to Soviet Union* (Cambridge, MA: Harvard University Press, 2012), 28–33. On the significance of the under-governed empire, see S. Frederick Starr, *Decentralization and Self-Government in Russia, 1830–1870* (Princeton, NJ: Princeton University Press, 1972). For the roots of Russia's approach to minority rule through self-governance, see Michael Khodarkovsky, "The Non-Christian Peoples on the Muscovite Frontiers," in *The Cambridge History of Russia*, Volume 1: *From Early Rus' to 1689*, ed. *Neu-Samara* (Cambridge: Cambridge University Press, 2006), 317–37.
47 Rempel with Rempel Carlson, *A Mennonite Family*, 73.

9 Confession or Sect? German or German-Speaking? Mennonite Identity Politics on the Edge of the Abyss, 1881–1917

1 Richard Wortman, *Scenarios of Power: Myth and Ceremony in Russian Monarchy*, Volume 2 (Princeton, NJ: Princeton University Press, 2000), 29 and 35. My thanks to James Urry for information about the sole Mennonite representative at the coronation.
2 The classic formulation of this question remains Nicholas Riasanovsky, "'Nationality' in the State Ideology during the Reign of Nicholas I," *RR* 19 (January 1960), 38–46.
3 Cited in Nicholas Riasanovsky, *Nicholas I and Official Nationality in Russia* (Berkeley: University of California Press, 1959), 139.
4 James Urry, "Mennonites, Nationalism and the State in Imperial Russia," *JMS* 12 (1994), 68.
5 On early Russian ethnography, see Nathaniel Knight, "Constructing the Science of Nationality: Ethnography in Mid-nineteenth Century Russia," unpublished PhD diss., Columbia University, 1994, 68–86; and Harvey L. Dyck, Ingrid I. Epp, and John R. Staples, eds., *Transformation of the Southern Ukrainian Steppe: Letters and Papers of Johann Cornies*, Volume II: *1836–1842* (Toronto: University of Toronto Press, 2020), 502. On German ethnographers, see Han F. Vermeulen, *Before Boas: The Genesis of Ethnography in the German Enlightenment* (Lincoln: University of Nebraska Press, 2015). On the "discovery" of Johann Cornies by German ethnographer Haxthausen, see August von Haxthausen, *Studies on the Interior of Russia*, trans. Eleanore L.M. Schmidt and ed. S. Frederick Starr (Chicago: University of Chicago Press, 1972).
6 Eric Lohr, *Russian Citizenship from Empire to Soviet Union* (Cambridge, MA: Harvard University Press, 2012), 34 and 56–7.57.
7 Paul W. Werth, *The Tsar's Foreign Faiths: Toleration and the Fate of Religious Freedom in Imperial Russia* (Oxford: Oxford University Press, 2014), 159.
8 Nataly Venger, *Mennonitskoe predprinimatelstvo v usloviiakh modernizatsii iuga Rossii: mezhdy kongregatsiei klanom i rossiiskim obshchestvom (1789–1920)* (Dnepropetrovsk, Ukraine: DNU, 2009), 410–12.
9 See excerpts from Paltov's articles along with analysis in Harvey L. Dyck, ed. and trans., "Russian Mennonitism and the Challenge of Russian Nationalism," *MQR* 56 (1982), 306–41.
10 On Russian sectarians in the region, see Oksana Beznosova, *Ekaterinoslavskaia guberniia: terra incognita evangel'skogo dvishzhenii v Rosiiskoi imperii (seredina xviii v. – 1917 g.)* (Steinhagen, Germany: Samenkorn, 2014), part 2, ch. 1–3; and Sergei Zhuk, *Russia's Lost Reformation: Peasants, Millennialism, and Radical Sects in Southern Russia and Ukraine, 1830–1917* (Washington: Woodrow Wilson Center, 2004). On

Orthodox concern for growing sectarianism, see Heather J. Coleman, "Theology on the Ground: Dmitrii Bogoliubov, the Orthodox Anti-Sectarian Mission, and the Russian Soul," in *Thinking Orthodox in Modern Russia: Culture, History, Context*, ed. Patrick Lally Michelson and Judith Deutsch Korn (Madison: University of Wisconsin Press, 2014), 64–84.

11 D.H. Epp, *Die Chortitzer Mennoniten. Versuch einer Darstellung des Entwicklungsganges derselben* (Odessa, 1889, reprinted Steinbach, MB, 1984), 119.

12 Cited in James Urry, *Mennonites, Politics, and Peoplehood: Europe – Russia – Canada, 1525–1980* (Winnipeg: University of Manitoba Press, 2006), 107–8.

13 Cited in Nataliya Venger, "Mennonite Entrepreneurs and Russian Nationalists in the Russian Empire, 1830–1917," in *Minority Report: Mennonite Identities in Imperial Russia and Soviet Ukraine Reconsidered, 1789–1945*, edited by Leonard G. Friesen (Toronto: University of Toronto Press, 2018), 151, n. 39.

14 Venger, *Mennonitskoe*, 414. For a study that arrives at this conclusion, see O.V. Beznosova, "Prichiny vozniknoveniia antigermanskoi kampanii v Rossiiskoi imperii nakanune Pervoi mirovoi voiny (na premere Ekaterinoslavskoi gubernii)," in *Voprosy germanskoi istorii* (Dnepropetrovsk, Ukraine: DNY, 2010), 50–8.

15 Venger, *Mennonitskoe*, 414.

16 Roberta Thompson Manning, *The Crisis of the Old Order in Russia: Gentry and Government* (Princeton, NJ: Princeton University Press, 1982), 194. See also N.N. Leshchenko, "Itogi statisticheskogo izucheniia krest'ianskogo dvizhenie na Ukraine v period revoliutsii 1905–1907," in *Sovetskaia istoriografiia agrarnoi istorii SSSR (do 1917 g.)* (Kishenev, Russia, 1978).

17 Leonard G. Friesen, *Rural Revolutions in Southern Ukraine: Peasants, Nobles, and Colonists, 1774–1905* (Cambridge, MA: Harvard Ukrainian Research Institute, 2008), 238; and "Agrarnoe dvizhenie v Rossii v 1905–1906 gg.," in *Trudy Imperatorskogo vol'nogo ekonomicheskogo obshchestva* (July–October 1908), 399.

18 Helena Goossen Friesen, *Daydreams and Nightmares: Life on the Wintergruen Estate* (Winnipeg, 1990), 21–2. See also Oscar H. Hamm, *Erinnerungen aus Igantjewo* (Saskatoon: Author, 1980), 229; MJ, 1905–1906, 11; and A. Shestakov, *Krest'ianskaia revoliutsiia 1905–1907 g.g. v Rossii* (Leningrad, 1926), 24–31.

19 David D. Rempel, *Osterwick (1812–1943)* (Alfert Press, 1973), 128–9; Franz C. Thiessen, *P.M. Friesen, 1849–1914* (Winnipeg: Christian Press, 1974), 18–20; Oscar H. Hamm, *Memoirs of Ignatyevo in the Light of Historical Change* (Saskatoon: Mrs. Ruth F. Hamm, 1984), 188–90; David G. Rempel with Cornelia Rempel Carlson, *A Mennonite Family in Tsarist Russia and the Soviet Union, 1789–1923* (Toronto: University of Toronto Press, 2002), 92 and 117;

Terry Martin, *The Mennonites and the Russian State Duma, 1905–1914*, The Donald W. Treadgold Papers in Russian, East European and Central Asian Studies Paper No. 4 (Seattle: The Henry M. Jackson School of International Studies, 1996), 37; Harvey L. Dyck, "Introduction and Analysis," in Jacob A. Neufeld, *Path of Thorns: Soviet Mennonite Life under Communist and Nazi Rule*, ed. Harvey L. Dyck (Toronto: University of Toronto Press, 2014), 12; and Leonard G. Friesen, "Mennonites in Russia and the Revolution of 1905: Experiences, Perceptions and Responses," *MQR* 62 (1988), 48.

20 Robert Weinberg, *The Revolution of 1905 in Odessa: Blood on the Steps* (Bloomington: Indiana University Press, 1993).

21 Andrey Ivanov, "Stolypin and the Mennonites," *Direction: A Mennonite Brethren Forum* 46 (Spring 2017), 72.

22 Al Reimer, "The Print Culture of the Russian Mennonites 1870–1930," in *Mennonites in Russia, 1788–1988: Essays in Honour of Gerhard Lohrenz*, ed. John J. Friesen (Winnipeg: CMBC Publications, 1989), 227–30; and P.M. Friesen, *The Mennonite Brotherhood in Russia (1789–1910)*, translated, 2nd revised edition, 1980 (Halbstadt: Raduga Publishers, 1911), 831–41.

23 Leonard G. Friesen, "Mennonites in Russia," 46–7.

24 Charles Steinwedel, *Threads of Empire: Loyalty and Tsarist Authority in Bashkiria, 1552–1917* (Bloomington: Indiana University Press, 2016), 206ff for the complexity of these positions and its impact on Bashkiria as a case in point.

25 Martin, *The Mennonites*, 41–5.

26 Martin, *The Mennonites*, 27.

27 Urry, *Mennonites, Politics, and Peoplehood*, 116 and 120–1; and Adolf Ens, "Mennonite Education in Russia," in *Mennonites in Russia, 1788–1988: Essays in Honour of Gerhard Lohrenz*, ed. John J. Friesen (Winnipeg: CMBC Publications, 1989), 87–8.

28 Martin, *The Mennonites*, 17–18; and Lawrence Klippenstein, "Mennonite Pacifism and State Service in Russia: A Case Study in Church-State Relations, 1789–1936," unpublished PhD diss., University of Minnesota, 1984, 135–51.

29 Abraham Friesen, *In Defence of Privilege: Russian Mennonites and the State before and during World War I* (Winnipeg: Kindred Productions 2006), 122–9.

30 Werth, *Tsar's Foreign Faiths*, 208–13 and 224; and Aileen Friesen, *Colonizing Russia's Promised Land: Orthodoxy and Community on the Siberian Steppe* (Toronto: University of Toronto Press, 2020), 136–43.

31 David McDonald, *United Government and Foreign Policy in Russia, 1900–1914* (Cambridge, MA: Harvard University Press, 1992).

32 Rempel with Rempel Carlson, *A Mennonite Family*, 127–30.

33 Urry, *Mennonites, Politics, and Peoplehood*, 117; and Irina (Janzen) Cherkazianova, "Church-State Relations in Education, 1780–1917," in

Minority Report: Mennonite Identities in Imperial Russia and Soviet Ukraine Reconsidered, 1789–1945, ed. Leonard G. Friesen (Toronto: University of Toronto Press, 2018), 98–100. Baptists also suffered from this Germanophobia. See Heather Coleman, *Russian Baptists and Spiritual Revolution, 1905–1929* (Bloomington: Indiana University Press, 2005), 27.

34 Venger, "Mennonite Entrepreneurs," 152–3.
35 Martin, *The Mennonites*, 46; Urry, *Mennonites, Politics, and Peoplehood*, 129–30; and Beznosova, "A Foreign Faith," 132.
36 On the Moscow riots of May 1914, see Eric Lohr, *Nationalizing the Russian Empire: The Campaign against Enemy Aliens during World War I.* (Cambridge, MA: Harvard University Press, 2003), 31–54.
37 Cited in Lawrence Klippenstein, *Peace and War*, Volume 1: *Mennonite Conscientious Objectors in Tsarist Russia and the Soviet Union before World War II, and Other COs in Eastern Europe* (Winnipeg: Mennonite Heritage Centre, 2017), 86.
38 Venger, "Mennonite Entrepreneurs," 164; and C.P. Toews, Heinrich Friesen, and Arnold Dyck, *The Kuban Settlement* (Winnipeg: CMBC Publications, 1989), ch. 11. On the Moscow Mennonite Service Centre, see Klippenstein, *Peace and War*, 91–2.
39 Beznosova, *Ekaterinoslavskaia guberniia*, 367–8; and Lohr, *Russian Citizenship*, 118–19.
40 Glenn Penner, "Weapons Confiscated from Russian Mennonites in 1914, St. Petersburg Archives: Fond 821 Opis 133 Delo 322," unpublished, n.d. I thank James Urry for bringing this document to my attention and for the observation on why Mennonites might have owned handguns.
41 David G. Rempel, "The Expropriation of the German Colonists in South Russia during the Great War," *Journal of Modern History* 4 (1932), 54. See also Lohr, *Russian Citizenship*, 125; Rempel with Rempel Carlson, *A Mennonite Family*, 160–1; and Venger, *Mennonitskoe*, 418–42.
42 P.P. Wiebe (Vibe), *Nemetskie kolonii v Sibiri: Sotsial'no-ekonomicheskii aspect* (Omsk, Russia, 2007), 99–122.
43 On the Peter Braun archive, see Harvey L. Dyck, "Recovering an Inheritance," in *The Peter J. Braun Russian Mennonite Archive: A Research Guide*, ed. Harvey L. Dyck and Ingrid I. Epp (Toronto: University of Toronto Press, 1996), xi–xxiv.
44 It helped that the Netherlands remained neutral in the First World War. Quotation is cited in Friesen, *In Defence of Privilege*, 234.
45 Jacob H. Janzen, *Lifting the Veil: Mennonite Life in Russia before the Revolution*, ed. Leonard G. Friesen (Kitchener, ON: Pandora Press, 1998), 82; and N.V. Ostasheva (Venger) *Na perelome epoch … Mennonitskoe soobshchestvo Ukrainy v 1914–1931 gg.* (Moscow: Gotika, 1998), 47–50.
46 Rempel with Rempel Carlson, *A Mennonite Family*, 169.

47 Jacob H. Brucks, "World War, Revolution and Famine," in *Neu-Samara: A Mennonite Settlement East of the Volga*, compiled by Jacob H. Brucks and Henry P. Hooge, trans. John Isaak (Edmonton: Jackpine House Ltd., 2002), 123. See also David G. Rempel, "Mennonite Revolutionaries in the Khortitza Settlement under the Tsarist Regime as Recollected by Johann G. Rempel," *JMS* 10 (1992), 70–86.

10 After Eichenfeld: Soviet-Era Mennonites between Reconstruction and Emigration, 1917–1927

1 Studies on this episode include Sean Patterson, *Makhno and Memory: Anarchist and Mennonite Narratives of Ukraine's Civil War, 1917–1921* (Winnipeg: University of Manitoba Press, 2020), ch. 3; and Harvey L. Dyck, John R. Staples, and John B. Toews, eds., *Nestor Makhno and the Eichenfeld Massacre: A Civil War Tragedy in a Ukrainian Mennonite Village* (Kitchener, ON: Pandora Press, 2004).
2 Patterson, *Makhno and Memory*, 129–31.
3 Dietrich Neufeld, *A Russian Dance of Death: Revolution and Civil War in the Ukraine*, trans. and ed. Al Reimer (Winnipeg: Hyperion Press, 1977), 43–4.
4 On two radically different responses to the unveiling of the Eichenfeld memorial, see Anne Konrad, "Massacre Memorial Dedicated in Ukraine [Eichenfeld and Nikolaipole regions between 1918 and 1920]," *Canadian Mennonite* 5 (10 September 2001), 12; and James Urry, "Time and Memory: Secular and Sacred Aspects of the World of the Russian Mennonites and Their Descendants," *Conrad Grebel Review* 25 (Winter 2007), 49–52. For the larger context of the changing historiography, see Leonard G. Friesen, "Introduction," in *Minority Report: Mennonite Identities in Imperial Russia and Soviet Ukraine Reconsidered, 1789–1945*, ed. Leonard G. Friesen (Toronto: University of Toronto Press, 2018). On the general context of the Eichenfeld memorial project, see Leonard G. Friesen, "Dnipropetrovsk State University, Khortitsa '99, and the Renaissance of Public (Mennonite) History in Ukraine," in *Minority Report: Mennonite Identities in Imperial Russia and Soviet Ukraine Reconsidered, 1789–1945*, ed. Leonard G. Friesen (Toronto: University of Toronto Press, 2018), 319–32.
5 N.V. Ostasheva (Venger), *Na perelome epoch ... Mennonitskoe soobshchestvo Ukrainy v 1914–1931 g.g.* (Moskva: Gotika, 1998), 49; and P.P. Wiebe (Vibe), *Nemetskie kolonii v Siberi: Sotsioal'no-ekonomichiskii aspect* (Omsk, Russia: 2007), 123–4.
6 Gerald Peters, ed. and trans., *Diary of Anna Baerg* (Winnipeg: CMBC Publications, 1985), 4.
7 Gerhard Lohrenz, *Storm Tossed: The Personal Story of a Canadian Mennonite from Russia* (Winnipeg: The Christian Press, 1976), 83.

8 Cornelius Krahn, "Terek Mennonite Settlement (Republic of Dagestan, Russia)," *GAMEO*, 1959, https://gameo.org/index.php?title=Terek_Mennonite_Settlement_(Republic_of_Dagestan,_Russia)&oldid=135015. Such raids dated back to 1910 at least. See Andrey Ivanov, "Stolypin and the Mennonites," *Direction: A Mennonite Brethren Forum* 46 (Spring 2017), 69–80.
9 David G. Rempel cites a diary entry from Abram Dyck in David G. Rempel with Cornelia Rempel Carlson, *A Mennonite Family in Tsarist Russia and the Soviet Union, 1789–1923* (Toronto: University of Toronto Press, 2002), 170.
10 Gerhard P. Schroeder, *Miracles of Grace and Judgement* (Lodi, CA: 1974), 11–12; and David G. Rempel, "Mennonite Revolutionaries in the Khortitza Settlement under the Tsarist Regime as Recollected by Johann G. Rempel," *JMS* 10 (1992), 76.
11 James Urry, "A Mennonite Witness to Revolution: Johann G. Rempel's Memoir of Moscow, March–June 1917," trans. David G. Rempel, *MQR* 91 (2017): 511–40.
12 John B. Toews, ed., *The Mennonites in Russia, 1917–1930: Selected Documents* (Winnipeg: The Christian Press 1975), 449–80; and Cornelius Krahn, "Mennozentrum (Bureau der Molotschnaer Mennonitischen Vereinigung)," *GAMEO*, 1959, https://gameo.org/index.php?title=Mennozentrum_(Bureau_der_Molotschnaer_Mennonitischen_Vereinigung)&oldid=83518. For a good overview of these Conferences, see Rempel with Rempel Carlson, *A Mennonite Family*, 171–6; and James Urry, *Mennonites, Politics, and Peoplehood: Europe – Russia – Canada, 1525–1980* (Winnipeg: University of Manitoba Press, 2006, 134–6.
13 Wiebe (Vibe), *Nemetskie kolonii*, 132 and 33. For an example of an historian who suggests a much more coordinated Bolshevik takeover, see John B. Toews, *Lost Fatherland: The Story of the Mennonite Emigration from Soviet Russia, 1921–1927* (Vancouver: Regent College Publishing, 1967), 24–6. For a solid overview on the complexity of Dnieper bend, Ukraine, in this period and the low formal support for the Bolsheviks in the region, see Paul R. Magocsi, *A History of Ukraine: The Land and its Peoples* (Toronto: University of Toronto Press, 2010), ch. 37. On the slow Bolshevization of Petrograd, see Mary McAuley, *Bread and Justice: State and Society in Petrograd 1917–1922* (Oxford: Clarendon Press, 1989).
14 John B. Toews, "The Halbstadt Volost, 1918–1922: A Case Study of the Mennonite Encounter with Early Bolshevism," *MQR* 48 (October 1974), 491.
15 Peters, ed. and trans., *Diary*, 6–7; and Helena Goossen Friesen, *Daydreams & Nightmares: Life on the Wintergruen Estate* (Winnipeg: CMBC Publications, 1990), 36. See also Gerhard Tōws, *Schönfeld: Werde- und Opfergang einer deutschen Siedlung in der Ukraine* (Winnipeg: Rundschau, 1939); and Terry

Martin, "The Terekers' Dilemma: A Prelude to the Selbstschutz," *MH* 17 (December 1991), 1–2.
16 C.P. Toews, *Die Tereker Ansiedlung* (Winnipeg: Echo Verlag, 1945); and Cornelius Krahn, "Terek Mennonite Settlement (Republic of Dagestan, Russia)," *GAMEO*, 1959, https://gameo.org/index.php?title=Terek_Mennonite_Settlement_(Republic_of_Dagestan,_Russia)&oldid=135015.
17 Magocsi, *A History*, 513–17.
18 Toews, "The Halbstadt Volost," 492; and Rempel with Rempel Carlson, *A Mennonite Family*, ch. 21.
19 For the minutes of the Lichtenau Conference, see Toews, ed., *Mennonites in Russia*, 202–427. The resolutions are located on p. 416. On the role that German Baptist seminaries may have played in shaping Mennonite theology on pacifism, see John B. Toews, *Pilgrimage of Faith: The Mennonite Brethren Church, 1860–1990* (Winnipeg: Kindred Press, 1993), 141–2.
20 On the prehistory of this, see James Urry and Harry Loewen, "Protecting Mammon. Some Dilemmas of Mennonite Non-resistance in Late Imperial Russia and the Origins of the Selbstschutz," *JMS* 9 (1991): 34–53.
21 Lawrence Klippenstein, "The Selbstschutz: A Mennonite Army in Ukraine, 1918–1919," in *History and Mission in Europe: Continuing the Conversation*, ed. Mary Raber and Peter F. Penner (Schwarzenfeld, Germany, 2011), 49–82. See also John P. Dyck, ed., *Troubles and Triumphs 1914–1924: Excerpts from the Diary of Peter J. Dyck, Ladekopp, Molotschna Colony, Ukraine* (Springstein, MB: n.p., 1981), esp. 47 for executions that took place on 20 April 1918. On the activity of the Selbstschutz among Mennonite estates acting alongside German and Russian estate owners in Schönfeld, see Gerhard Tőws, *Schönfeld: Werde und Opfergang einer deutschen Siedlung in der Ukraine* (Winnipeg: Rundschau Publishing House, 1939), 90f.
22 Schroeder, *Miracles*, 113; and Rempel with Rempel Carlson, *A Mennonite Family*, 208.
23 Patterson, *Makhno and Memory*, 43.
24 Patterson's recent study provides a helpful introduction into the competing narratives of Makhno, as anarchist freedom fighter and as bloodthirsty tyrant. See also, for example, Gerhard Lohrenz, *Zagradovka: History of a Mennonite Settlement in Southern Russia* (Winnipeg: CMBC Publications, 2000); Dyck, Staples, and Toews, eds., *Nestor Makhno*; and Neufeld, *A Russian Dance*. For a broader perspective of Ukrainian history at this time, see Svetlana Bobyleva, "'Land of Opportunity, Sites of Devastation': Notes on the History of the Borozenko Daughter Colony," in *Minority Report: Mennonite Identities in Imperial Russia and Soviet Ukraine Reconsidered, 1789–1945*, ed. Leonard G. Friesen (2018), 25–60, esp. 37–46.
25 Petr P. Wiebe (Vibe), "The Mennonite Colonies of Siberia: From the Late Nineteenth to the Early Twentieth Century," *JMS* 30 (2012), 30–1.

26 For the larger context, see Peter Gatrell, *A Whole Empire Walking: Refugees in Russia During World War I* (Bloomington: Indiana University Press, 1999); and Alan Ball, *And Now My Soul Is Hardened: Abandoned Children in Soviet Russia, 1918–1930* (Berkeley: University of California Press, 1994).
27 Peters, ed. and trans., *Diary*, 77. See also Ostasheva (Venger), *Na perelome epoch*, 60–1; and Toews, "The Halbstadt Volost," 497.
28 C.P. Toews, Heinrich Friesen, and Arnold Dyck, *The Kuban Settlement* (Winnipeg: Echo Historical Series, 1989), 74.
29 Ostasheva (Venger), *Na perelome epoch*, 68; Adolf Ehrt, *Das Mennonitentum in Russland von seiner Einwanderung bis zur Gegenwart* (Berlin: Julius Beltz, 1932), 106–16; Jacob A. Neufeld, *Path of Thorns: Soviet Mennonite Life under Communist and Nazi Rule*, ed. Harvey L. Dyck (Toronto: University of Toronto Press, 2014), 381; and Cornelius Bergmann and Cornelius Krahn, "Chortitza Mennonite Settlement (Zaporizhia Oblast, Ukraine)," *GAMEO*, 1955, https://gameo.org/index.php?title=Chortitza_Mennonite_Settlement_(Zaporizhia_Oblast,_Ukraine)&oldid=156357; and see *Zhivi i pomni … Istoriia Mennonitskikh kolonii Ekaterinoslavshchiny* (Dnepropetrovsk, Ukraine: Dnepropetrovsk National University, 2006), 151.
30 Rempel with Rempel Carlson, *A Mennonite Family*, 241–7.
31 P.C. Hiebert and Orie O. Miller, eds., *Feeding the Hungry: Russia Famine 1919–1925: American Mennonite Relief Operations under the Auspices of Mennonite Central Committee* (Scottdale, PA: Mennonite Central Committee, 1929), 227–36; Wiebe (Vibe), *Nemetskie kolonii*, 191–3; and P.P. Wiebe (Vibe), ed., *Materialy po istorii nemetskikh i Mennonitskikh kolonii v Omskom priirtysh'e, 1895–1930* (Omsk, Russia, 2002), 178–9. For its impact on just one Mennonite village, that of Blumengart, see *Zhivi i pomni*, 123. For the larger context, see Robert Conquest, *Harvest of Sorrow: Soviet Collectivization and the Terror-Famine* (Oxford: Oxford University Press, 1986), 53–4.
32 Harold S. Bender and Richard D. Thiessen, "Klassen, Cornelius Franz 'C. F.' (1894–1954)," *GAMEO*, May 2013, https://gameo.org/index.php?title=Klassen,_Cornelius_Franz_%22C._F.%22_(1894-1954)&oldid=168316; and John B. Toews, "Mennonite Identities in a New Land: Abraham A. Friesen and the Russian Mennonite Migration of the 1920s," in *Minority Report: Mennonite Identities in Imperial Russia and Soviet Ukraine Reconsidered, 1789–1945*, ed. Leonard G. Friesen (Toronto: University of Toronto Press, 2018), 181–208. J.J. Esau served somewhat later on this committee.
33 Jakob Warkentin, "Benjamin Heinrich Unruh: Teacher, Scholar, Statesman, 1881–1959," in *Shepherds, Servants and Prophets: Leadership among the Russian Mennonites (ca. 1880–1960)*, ed. Harry Loewen (Kitchener, ON: Pandora Press, 2003), 405.

34 Frank H. Epp, *Mennonite Exodus: The Rescue and Resettlement of the Russian Mennonites since the Communist Revolution* (Altona, Germany: D.W. Friesen & Sons Ltd., 1962), 47, 53, 59.
35 Toews, "Mennonite Identities," 183.
36 Epp, *Mennonite Exodus*, 55.
37 Hiebert and Miller, eds., *Feeding the Hungry*, 165–70, 332–4; Ivan J. and Della Miller, "Reflections on the Life and Passing of Alvin J. Miller," *The Historian* 12 (July 2000), 2; Epp, *Mennonite Exodus*, 41; and James C. Juhnke, *Vision, Doctrine, War: Mennonite Identity and Organization in America, 1890–1930* (Scottdale, PA: Herald Press, 1989), ch. 9. The Dutch also provided valuable aid to Mennonites. The Dutch neutrality in the war made such assistance more palatable to Moscow. See Ad van de Staaij, "Rein Willink's Rescue Expedition to the Molochna between Reconstruction and Emigration: Dutch Aid to Ukraine, 1922–1929," *MQR* (2019), 473–505. For a copy of the agreement signed by Alvin J. Miller with the Soviet government, see Tatiana P Nazarova, *Blagotvoritel'naia Deiatel'nost' Zarubezhnyikh Mennonitskikh Organizatsii v Sovetskom Gosudarstve (1920–1930gg)* (Volgograd 2010), 306–7.
38 A.W. Slagel, "Organizing Feeding Operations," in *Feeding the Hungry. Russia Famine 1919–1925: American Mennonite Relief Operations under the Auspices of Mennonite Central Committee*, ed. P.C. Hiebert and Orie O. Miller (Scottdale, PA: Mennonite Central Committee, 1929), 204–21; Paul Schrag, "'In God's Name, Bread!' MCC Celebrates and Serves Where Its Work Began," MCC https://mcccanada.ca/stories/gods-name-bread; and Mary Raber, *Ministries of Compassion among Russian Evangelicals, 1905–1929* (Eugene, OR: Pickwick Publications, 2016), 164. For the emergence of MCC in Canada, see Esther Epp-Tiessen, *Mennonite Central Committee in Canada: A History* (Winnipeg: CMU Press, 2013). On the broader context of the famine and American relief, see Bertrand M. Patenaude, *The Big Show in Bololand: The American Relief Expedition to Soviet Russia in the Famine of 1921* (Stanford, CA: Stanford University Press, 2002), esp. part 2.
39 James Urry, "After the Rooster Crowed: Some Issues Concerning the Interpretation of Mennonite/Bolshevik Relations during the Early Soviet Period," *JMS* 13 (1995), 26–50. For examples of the historiographical reconsideration of Soviet society in the 1920s, see Richard Stites, *Revolutionary Dreams: Utopian Vision and Experimental Life in the Russian Revolution* (Oxford: Oxford University Press, 1988).
40 Tracy McDonald, *Face to the Village: The Riazan Countryside under Soviet Rule, 1921–1930* (Toronto: University of Toronto Press, 2011).
41 Schroeder, *Miracles*, 161.
42 Lohrenz, *Storm Tossed*, 110–39 and 212–14.
43 Schroeder, *Miracles*, 161–3; and Lohrenz, *Storm Tossed*, 118.

44 Glennys Young, *Power and the Sacred in Revolutionary Russia: Religious Activists in the Village* (University Park: The Pennsylvania State University Press, 1997), ch. 7–8.
45 Gregory L. Freeze, "Subversive Atheism: Soviet Antireligious Campaigns and the Religious Revival in Ukraine in the 1920s," in *State Secularism and Lived Religion in Soviet Russia and Ukraine*, ed. Catherine Wanner (Oxford: Oxford University Press, 2012), 37. On the persistence of Orthodox faith in the 1920s, see Robert H. Greene, *Bodies Like Bright Stars: Saints and Relics in Orthodox Russia* (DeKalb: Northern Illinois University Press, 2009). On Pentecostal growth in the 1920s, see Heather Coleman, *Russian Baptists and Spiritual Revolution, 1905–1929* (Bloomington: Indiana University Press, 2005), ch. 8.
46 John B. Toews, "Revival and Mission in Early Communist Russia (1917–1927)," *Direction: A Mennonite Brethren Forum* 31 (Fall 2002), 211–12. Cf. Anna Baerg's diary entry for 22 May 1922 in Peters, *Diary*, 100. Also A.I. Savin, *Sovetskoe gosudarstvo I evangel'skie tserkvi Sibiri v 1920–1941 gg. Dokumenty i materialy* (Novosibirsk: Posokh, 2004), doc. 141, pp. 222–3; Urry, "After the Rooster," 41.
47 Savin, *Sovetskoe*, doc. 74, pp. 13–33, regarding sectarianism in Siberia as of 15 July 1923. Cf. Central State Archives of Public Organizations of Ukraine, f. 1, o. 6, s. 68, p. 187–8 as recorded in John B. Toews and Paul Toews., eds., *Union of Citizens of Dutch Lineage in Ukraine (1922–1927): Mennonite and Soviet Documents* (Fresno, CA: Center for Mennonite Brethren Studies, 2011), 269–71; and State Archives of Zaporizhzhya Oblast, f. PR-1, op. 1, d. 399, 100–5, in Toews and Toews, eds., *Union*, 322; and *Zhivi i pomni*, 107.
48 Oksana Beznosova and Aleksandr Beznosov, "'Religioznaia zhizn' Mennonitov v seredine 20-x gg. XX ct. glazami sovetskoi politicheskoi politsii na premere poseleniia Fiurstenland," in *History and Mission in Europe: Continuing the Conversation*, ed. Mary Raber and Peter F. Penner (Schwarzenfeld, Germany: Neufeld Verlag, 2011), 42–6. For the minutes of the Moscow conference with the eight-point memorandum, see John B. Toews, ed., *Mennonites in Russia*, 430–1. On the Soviet state's association of Mennonites with militarism in the civil war period, see Walter Sawatsky, "Patsifisty-protestanti v Sovetskoi Rossii mezhdy dvymia mirovymi voinami," in *Dolgii put' Rossiiskogo Patsifizma: Ideal mezhdynarodnogo i vnyutrennego mira v religiozno-filosofskoi I obshchestvenno-politicheskoi mysli Rossii*, ed. Tatiana A. Pavlova (Moscow, 1997), 262–84.
49 Terry Martin, "The Russian Mennonite Encounter with the Soviet State, 1917–1955," *Conrad Grebel Review* 20 (2002), 15–19. Cf. Walter Sawatsky, "Russian Mennonite Organizational Collapse and the Failed Attempts to Form an Independent Organization, 1917–1989," *MQR* 89, no. 4 (2015), 539. Gale Literature Resource Center, https://link-gale-com.libproxy.wlu

.ca/apps/doc/A434142179/LitRC?u=wate18005&sid=LitRC&xid=9a068 8c5.

50 Tatiana Pavlovna Navarova, "Agrotekhnicheskaia pomoshch Mennonite Central Committee v Rossii v period NEPa," *Vestnik* 15 (February 2010), 36; Patenaude, *The Big Show*, ch. 2; and Urry, "After the Rooster," 30.

51 Olga IU. Red'kina, *Sel'skhokhoziaistvennye religioznie trudovye kollektivy v 1917-m – 1930-e gody: na materialakh evropeiskoi chasti RSFSR* (Volgograd: Volgograadovo gosudarstvennovo universiteta, 2004), ch. 4; Peter F. Froese, "Allrussischer Mennonitischer Landwirtschaftlicher Verein," *GAMEO*, 1955, https://gameo.org/index.php?title=Allrussischer _Mennonitischer_Landwirtschaftlicher_Verein&oldid=132606.; Toews, ed., *Mennonites in Russia*, 87–294; Peter Letkemann, *A Book of Remembrance: Mennonites in Arkadak and Zentral, 1908–1941* (Winnipeg: Old Oak Publishing, 2016), 142; and Toews and Toews, eds., *Union*, for detailed minutes and Soviet assessments of these unions.

52 There are numerous examples of Mennonite economic engagement in the 1920s, village by village, in Chortitza settlement. See *Zhivi i pomni*. For Siberian Mennonites, see Wiebe (Vibe), "Mennonite Colonies of Siberia," 31–3, and the listing of relevant archival documents in *Ethno-Confession in the Soviet State. Mennonites in Siberia, 1920–1989: Annotated List of Archival Documents*, ed. A.I. Savin, translated by Olga Shmakina with assistance from Ludymilla Kariaka (Fresno, CA: Center for Mennonite Brethren Studies, 2008), 11–68.

53 N.J. Kroeker, *First Mennonite Villages in Russia, 1789–1989: Khortitsa – Rosental* (Vancouver: N.J. Kroeker, 1981), 221–2; and Martin, "Russian Mennonite Encounter," 19–21. For a case study of Mennonite reconstruction efforts, see Bobyleva, "Land of Opportunity," 44–51.

54 Oksana Beznosova, "The Ukrainian Evangelicals under Pressure from the NKVD, 1928–1939," in *Ethnic and Religious Minorities in Stalin's Soviet Union: New Dimensions of Research*, ed. Andrej Kotljarchuk and Olle Sundström (Huddinge: Södertörn University, 2017), 179; and Toews and Toews, eds., *Mennonites in Russia*, 201–2.

55 Rempel with Rempel Carlson, *A Mennonite Family*, 259. There is some dispute, as Frank H. Epp records the date as 21 July 1923. See Epp, *Mennonite Exodus*, 145.

56 Epp, *Mennonite Exodus*, 145–6.

57 Frank H. Epp, *Mennonites in Canada, 1920–1940: A People's Struggle for Survival* (Toronto: Macmillan of Canada, 1982), 150 and 154; and Epp, *Mennonite Exodus*, 60–1.

58 Epp, *Mennonite Exodus*, 105; John G. Rempel and Richard D. Thiessen, "Toews, David (1870–1947)," *GAMEO*, April 2012, https://gameo .org/index.php?title=Toews,_David_(1870-1947)&oldid=148320. Jacob

Gerbrandt, "Canadian Mennonite Board of Colonization," *GAMEO*, September 2011, https://gameo.org/index.php?title=Canadian_Mennonite_Board_of_Colonization&oldid=167400; John B. Toews, "Mennonite Identities in a New Land: Abraham A. Friesen and the Russian Mennonite Migration of the 1920s," in *Minority Report: Mennonite Identities in Imperial Russia and Soviet Ukraine Reconsidered*, ed. Leonard G. Friesen (Toronto: University of Toronto Press, 2018), 186–7. The reference of "Mennonite Bishop of Canada" comes from Epp, *Mennonites in Canada, 1920–1940*, 151.
59 John B. Toews, *With Courage to Spare: The Life of B. B. Janz, 1877–1964* (Winnipeg: General Conference Mennonite Brethren Churches, 1978).
60 For a photograph taken at the departure of the Chortitza Mennonite emigrants in 1923, see Kroeker, *First Mennonite Village*, 226.
61 Toews, *Lost Fatherland*, ch. 9–14; Toews, ed., *Mennonites in Russia*, 295–372; Epp, *Mennonite Exodus*; Toews and Toews, eds., *Union*, esp. 365–510; and Peter Letkemann, "Mennonite Refugee Camps in Germany, 1921–1951: Part I – Lager Lechfeld," *MH* 38 (September 2012), 1–2.
62 Epp, *Mennonites in Canada, 1920–1940*, 169–79. On the unique contributions of this immigration cohort, see Urry, *Mennonites, Politics, and Peoplehood*, 185–204.
63 Toews and Toews, eds., *Union*, 401. The letter is dated 12 March 1922 and is part of the A.A. Friesen Collection.
64 On the Soviet state's complex relationship with official atheism, see Victoria Smolkin, *A Sacred Space Is Never Empty: A History of Soviet Atheism* (Princeton, NJ: Princeton University Press, 2018).
65 Ehrt, *Das Mennonitentum*, 121.
66 Red'kina, *Sel'skhokhoziaistvennye*; A.P. Sokolov, *Krasnyi nemetskii skot v Omskoi gubernii* (Omsk, Russia, 1926); and Wiebe (Vibe), "Mennonite Colonies of Siberia," 31–2. In a private correspondence, James Urry writes: "This interest in co-operatives in Siberia (and to a lesser extent) goes back to pre 1914; there was a competition between private enterprise shopkeepers and co-operative enterprises (shops/production/distribution). It is not surprising that the 'new' settlements such as Orenburg and those in Siberia had a stronger commitment to co-ops and this was carried over to Canada. But in Canada, due to the immigration of 'richer' Mennonites co-ops failed to make much headway."
67 Ehrt, *Das Mennonitentum*, 122; Wiebe (Vibe), *Materialy*, 226–28; Wiebe (Vibe), "Mennonite Colonies of Siberia," 32–3; Venger, *Na perelome epoch*, 110–19; Red'kina, *Sel'skhokhoziaistvennye*, 436; and Urry, *Mennonites, Politics, and Peoplehood*, 148–9.
68 Terry Martin, *The Affirmative Action Empire: Nations and Nationalism in the Soviet Union, 1923–1939* (Ithaca, NY: Cornell University Press, 2001), 9–15.

11 When God Leads You into the Wilderness: Mennonites in the Stalinist Crucible, 1927–1934

1 Lynne Viola et al., eds., *The War against the Peasantry, 1927–1930: The Tragedy of the Soviet Countryside*, Volume 1, trans. Steven Shabad (New Haven, CT: Yale University Press, 2005), 118. Information on Anna Ivanovna comes from interview conducted by the author on 27 August 2020; Anni Schmidt, "My Life on the Road," unpublished (Waterloo, 2006); and Georg Schmidt, "And Now I Shall Write from My Memories," unpublished (Vineland, 1995).
2 Helmut T. Huebert, *Molotschna Historical Atlas* (Winnipeg: Springfield Publishers, 2003), 157.
3 Terry Martin, *The Affirmative Action Empire: Nations and Nationalism in the Soviet Union, 1923–1939* (Ithaca, NY: Cornell University Press, 2001), 211–12.
4 Important sources for this include Terry Martin, "The Russian Encounter with the Soviet State, 1917–1955," *CGR* 20 (2002): 3–59. The reference to the secretariat of the Central Committee comes from Martin, p. 25. Cf. Colin Neufeldt, "The Fate of Mennonites in Ukraine and the Crimea during Soviet Collectivization and the Famine (1930–1933)," PhD diss., University of Alberta, 1999; Colin P. Neufeldt, "Collectivizing the Mutter Ansiedlungen: The Role of Mennonites in Organizing Kolkhozy in the Khortytsia and Molochansk German National Districts in Ukraine in the Late 1920s and Early 1930s," in *Minority Report: Mennonite Identities in Imperial Russia and Soviet Ukraine Reconsidered, 1789–1945*, ed. Leonard G. Friesen (Toronto: University of Toronto Press, 2018), 219–26; and Harvey L. Dyck, "Introduction," in *Path of Thorns. Soviet Mennonite Life under Communist and Nazi Rule*, by Jacob A. Neufeld (Toronto: University of Toronto Press, 2014), 3–50; P.P. Wiebe (Vibe), *Materialy po Istorii Nemetskikh i Mennonitskikh kolonii v Omskom priirtysh'e, 1895–1930* (Omsk, Russia, 2002); and John B. Toews and Paul Toews, eds., *Union of Citizens of Dutch Lineage in Ukraine (1922–1927): Mennonite and Soviet Documents* (Fresno, CA: Center for Mennonite Brethren Studies, 2011), 257–330.
5 Martin, "The Russian Encounter," 23–4; and Toews and Toews, eds., *Union*, 272–3.
6 P.P. Wiebe (Vibe), *Nemetskie kolonii v Sibiri: sotial'no-ekonomicheskii aspect* (Omsk, Russia, 2007), 195–9.
7 Toews and Toews, eds., *Union*, 301, 321–3.
8 Alan M. Ball, *Russia's Last Capitalists: The Nepmen, 1921–1929* (Berkeley: University of California Press, 1987).
9 James Hughes, *Stalinism in a Russian Province: Collectivization and Dekulakization in Siberia* (London: Palgrave, 1996); Wiebe (Vibe), *Nemetskie kolonii v Sibiri*, 218–19; Viola et al., eds., *War against Peasantry*, 61–9.

10 Beatrice Rosenthal, *New Myth, New World: From Nietzsche to Stalinism* (University Park, PA: Penn State University Press, 2002), 237; and Valerie A. Kivelson and Ronald Grigor Suny, *Russia's Empires* (Oxford: Oxford University Press, 2017), 295.
11 There is much to consider here, but it starts with Sheila Fitzpatrick, ed., *Cultural Revolution in Russia, 1928–1931* (Bloomington: Indiana University Press, 1984). For a recent example, see Yuri Slezkine, *The House of Government: A Sage of the Russian Revolution* (Princeton, NJ: Princeton University Press, 2017).
12 Gregory L. Freeze, "The Stalinist Assault on the Parish, 1929–1941," in *Stalinismus vor dem Zweiten Weltkrieg: Neue Wege der Forschung*, ed. Manfred Hildermeier (Munich: Oldenburg Verlag, 1998), 213; Martin, *Affirmative Action Empire*, 211; and Kivelson and Suny, *Russia's Empires*, 297.
13 *Ia s vami vo vse dni do skonchaniia veka*, Volume 1: *Tiazhelye vremena gonenii i repressii 1931–1946* (Karaganda, Kazakhstan: Shtainkhagen, 2001), 35.
14 GARF f. 1235, op. 73, d. 1651 in A.I. Savin, ed., *Etnokonfessiia v Sovetskom gosudarstve. Mennonity Sibiri v 1920–1930-e gody: emigratsiia i repressii. Dokumenty i materialy* (Novosibirsk: Posokh, 2009), 215–16.
15 Colin P. Neufeldt, "The Fate of Mennonites in Soviet Ukraine and the Crimea on the Eve of the 'Second Revolution' (1927–1929)," unpublished MA thesis, University of Alberta, 1989, 23.
16 Oksana Beznosova and Aleksandr Beznosov, "'Religioznaia zhizn' Mennonitov v seredine 20-x gg. XX ct. glazami sovetskoi politicheskoi politsii na premere poseleniia Fiurstenland," in *History and Mission in Europe: Continuing the Conversation*, ed. Mary Raber and Peter F. Penner (Schwarzenfeld, Germany: Neufeld Verlag, 2011), 33–48; and Sheila Fitzpatrick, *Stalin's Peasants: Resistance and Survival in the Russian Village after Collectivization* (Oxford: Oxford University Press, 1994), 33–7.
17 Freeze, "Stalinist Approach," 214–19. The quotation is from 214. Cf. Victoria Smolkin, *A Sacred Space Is Never Empty: A History of Soviet Atheism* (Princeton, NJ: Princeton University Press, 2018), 45–7; and Daniel Peris, *Storming the Heavens: The Soviet League of the Militant Godless* (Ithaca, NY: Cornell University Press, 1998), 164–73. For the broader context see Gregory Freeze, "Subversive Atheism: Soviet Antireligious Campaigns and the Religious Revival in Ukraine in the 1920s," in *State Secularism and Lived Religion in Soviet Russia and Ukraine*, ed. Catherine Wanner (Oxford: Oxford University Press, 2012), 27–62.
18 Martin, "The Russian Encounter," 32; and Henry H. Winter, *A Shepherd of the Oppressed: Heinrich Winter, Last Ältester of Chortitza* (Wheatley, ON: Author, 1990), 19.
19 RGASPI, f. 17, op. 3, d. 627, l. 10–11, in Savin, ed., *Etnokonfessiia*, 210–11; A.I. Savin, *Sovetskoe gosudarstvo i evangel'skie tserkvi Sibiri v 1920–1941 gg.*

Dokumenty i materialy (Novosibirsk, 2004), 61–3. For an overview of this process, see Colin P. Neufeldt, "The Fate of Mennonites in Soviet Ukraine and the Crimea on the Eve of the 'Second Revolution' (1927–1929)," unpublished MA thesis, University of Alberta, 1989, 63–9.

20 Winter, *Shepherd*, 8–17.
21 Neufeldt, "The Fate of Mennonites in Ukraine," 90–1. Orthodox priests also saw their status equated with that of kulaks at this time. See Glennys Young, *Power and the Sacred in Revolutionary Russia: Religious Activists in the Village* (University Park: The Pennsylvania State University Press, 1997), 259–65.
22 Neufeldt, "The Fate of Mennonites in Soviet Ukraine," 67; Peter Epp, "The Advent of Atheism," in *The Silence Echoes: Memoirs of Trauma and Tears*, ed. Sarah Dyck (Kitchener, ON: Pandora Press, 1997), 73–4; and Jacob H. Brucks, "World War, Revolution, and Famine," in *Neu-Samara: A Mennonite Settlement East of the Volga*, ed. Tina Wiebe (Calgary: Jackpine House, 2002), 131.
23 Mariechen Peters, "Dearly Beloved," in *The Silence Echoes: Memoirs of Trauma and Tears*, ed. Sarah Dyck (Kitchener, ON: Pandora Press, 1997), 57–8; and Marlene Epp, *Women without Men: Mennonite Refugees of the Second World War* (Toronto: University of Toronto Press, 2000).
24 John B. Toews, ed. and trans., *Letters from Susan: A Woman's View of the Russian Mennonite Experience (1928–1941)* (North Newton, KS: Bethel College, 1988), 85.
25 Peter J. Rahn, ed. and trans., *Among the Ashes: In the Stalinkova Kolkhoz (Kontinusfeld), 1930–1935* (Kitchener, ON: Pandora Press, 2011), 71–2, 83.
26 Ruth Derksen Siemens, *Remember Us: Letters from Stalin's Gulag (1930–1937)*, Volume 1: *The Regehr Family* (Kitchener, ON: Pandora Press, 2008), letter sent in June 1931, 64–5.
27 There is a rich literature on this, which includes Viola et al., eds., *War against Peasantry*, 2006; Lynne Viola, *Best Sons of the Fatherland: Workers in the Vanguard of Soviet Collectivization* (Oxford: Oxford University Press, 1987); and Robert Conquest, *The Harvest of Sorrow: Soviet Collectivization and the Terror-Famine* (Edmonton: University of Alberta Press, 1986).
28 Colin Neufeldt, "Separating the Sheep from the Goats: The Role of Mennonites and Non-Mennonites in the Dekulakization of Khortitsa, Ukraine (1928–1930)," *MQR* 83, no. 2 (April 2009), 221–91; and Colin Neufeldt, "Through the Fires of Hell: The Dekulakization and Collectivization of the Soviet Mennonite Community (1928–1933)," *JMS* 16 (1998), 9–32.
29 Peter Letkemann, "The Fate of Mennonites in the Volga-Ural Region, 1929–1941," *JMS* 26 (2008), 185–6; Neufeldt, "The Fate of Mennonites in Ukraine," 91–2; and Martin, "The Russian Encounter," 33; and Anne

Konrad, *Red Quarter Moon: A Search for Family in the Shadow of Stalin* (Toronto: University of Toronto Press, 2012), 38.
30 Neufeldt, "The Fate of Mennonites in Ukraine," 95–6. Important studies on the Gulag include Steven A. Barnes, *Death and Redemption: The Gulag and the Shaping of Soviet Society* (Princeton, NJ: Princeton University Press, 2011); Lynne Viola, *The Unknown Gulag: The Lost World of Stalin's Special Settlements* (Oxford: Oxford University Press, 2007); Nicolas Werth, *Cannibal Island: Death in a Siberian Gulag* (Princeton, NJ: Princeton University Press, 2007); and Alan Barenberg, *Gulag Town, Company Town: Forced Labor and Its Legacy in Vorkuta* (New Haven, CT: Yale University Press, 2014).
31 Viktor Fast and Jakob Penner, *Wasserströme in der Einöde. Die Anfangsgeschichte der Mennoniten-Brüdergemeinde Karaganda 1956–1968* (Steinhagen, Germany: Samenkorn, 2007), 40; and *Ia s vami vo vse dni* (2001), 51–4, 67, 95.
32 Viktor Dik, *Svet Evangeliia v Kazakhstane: Evangel'skie techeniia v pervoi polovine XX veka* (Steinhagen, Germany: Samenkorn, 2003); John B. Toews, ed. and trans., *Journeys: Mennonite Stories of Faith and Survival in Stalin's Russia* (Winnipeg: Kindred Publications, 1998), 149. On the role played by the Gulag in Soviet acculturation, see Barnes, *Death and Redemption*.
33 David R. Shearer, "Stalinism, 1928–1940," in *The Cambridge History of Russia*, Volume 3: *The Twentieth Century*, ed. Ronald G. Suny (Cambridge: Cambridge University Press, 2006), 195; and Neufeldt, "Collectivizing," 239.
34 *Zhivi i pomni ... Istoriia mennonitskikh kolonii Ekaterinslavshchiny* (Dneproeptrovsk, Ukraine: 2006), 79, 86.
35 Jacob A. Neufeld, *Tiefenwege. Erfahrungen und Erlebnisse von Russland-Mennoniten in zwei Jahrzehnten bis 1949* (Virgil, ON: Niagara Press, 1958), 21.
36 Colin P. Neufeldt, "The Public and Private Lives of Mennonite Kolkhoz Chairmen in the Khortytsia and Molochansk German National Raĭony in Ukraine (1928–1934)," *The Carl Beck Papers in Russian and East European Studies* no. 2305 (January 2015), 1–87; and Neufeldt, "Collectivizing," 240.
37 Toews, ed. and trans., *Letters from Susan*, 106, 116; Rahn, ed. and trans., *Among the Ashes*, 225 and 228–9; David D. Rempel, *Osterwick, 1812–1943* (Alfert Press, 1973), 163–4; and *Zhivi i pomni*, 86.
38 Alexander I. Beznosov, "Mennonity Iuga Ukrainy v gody 'velikogo pereloma' (1928–1933 gg.) in *Voprosy germanskoi istorii. Sbornik nauchnykh trudov* (Dnepropetrovsk, Ukraine, 2001), 83. For the larger context, see Conquest, *Harvest*; Sarah Cameron, *The Hungry Steppe: Famine, Violence, and the Making of Soviet Kazakhstan* (Ithaca, NY: Cornell University Press, 2018); R.W. Davies and Stephen G. Wheatcroft, *The Years of Hunger: Soviet Agriculture, 1931–1933* (London: Palgrave MacMillan, 2003); and David R. Marples, Eduard Baidaus, and Mariya Melentyeva, "Causes of the

1932 Famine in Soviet Ukraine: Debates at the Third All-Ukrainian Party Conference," in *Canadian Slavonic Papers* 56 (2014), 291–312.
39 Barnes, *Death and Redemption*, 41–3. Cf. diary entries and correspondence in Rahn, ed. and trans., *Among the Ashes*, 182 and 192; and Derksen Siemens, *Remember Us*, 186 and 210.
40 Peter Letkemann, *A Book of Remembrance: Mennonites in Arkadak and Zentral, 1908–1941* (Winnipeg: Old Oak Publishing, 2016), 257.
41 Colin Neufeldt, "Reforging Mennonite Spetspereselentsy: The Experience of Mennonite Exiles at Siberian Special Settlements in the Omsk, Tomsk, Novosibirsk and Narym Regions, 1930–1933," *JMS* 30 (2012), 299–300. On famine refugees in Karaganda, see Robert Kindler, *Stalin's Nomads: Power & Famine in Kazakhstan*, trans. Cynthia Klohr (Pittsburgh: University of Pittsburgh Press, 2018), 172–4.
42 GANO, f. 1027, op. 2, l. 144, doc. 341, in Savin, ed., *Etnokonfessiia*, 616–17.
43 *Ia s vami*, 82; Serhii Plokhy, *The Gates of Europe: A History of Ukraine* (New York: Basic Books, 2015); and Alexander Beznosov, "Kulak, Christian, and German: Ukrainian Mennonite Identities in a Time of Famine," in *Minority Report: Mennonite Identities in Imperial Russia and Soviet Ukraine Reconsidered, 1789–1945*, ed. Leonard G. Friesen (Toronto: University of Toronto Press, 2018), 268, n. 26. Beznosov accepts Colin Neufeldt's statistical rendering. Cf. R.W. Davies and Stephen Wheatcroft, *The Years of Hunger: Soviet Agriculture, 1931–1933* (Basingstoke: Palgrave Macmillan, 2004).
44 See, for example, document #321 in Savin, ed., *Etnokonfessiia*, 579–81. Cf. Abraham Kroeker, *Unsere Brüder in Not! Bilder vom Leidensweg der deutschen Kolonisten in Russland* (Striegau, Poland: Theodor Urban, 1930). For a detailed discussion with respect to international assistance to Soviet Ukraine, see Beznosov, "Kulak." Aid packages from Germany continued to flow to Karaganda Mennonites until 1935, though by then recipients faced a potentially fatal response from Soviet authorities. See *Ia s vami*, 82; and Gábor T. Rittersporn, *Anguish, Anger and Folkways in Soviet Russia* (Pittsburgh: University of Pittsburgh Press, 2014), 43.
45 Leonard G. Friesen, "More than Sheep to Slaughter: Reflections on Mennonites and the Stalinist Terror," *CGR* 18 (Spring 2000), 69–73. For a similar conclusion framed in a broader approach, see James Urry, "Mennonites, Anthropology, and History: A Complicated Intellectual Relationship," *JMS* 39 (2021), 31.
46 Derksen Siemens, *Remember Us*, 304–6. Cf. Walter Sawatsky, "Historical Roots of a Post-Gulag Theology for Russian Mennonites," *MQR* 76 (April 2002), 149–80.
47 Lynne Viola, *Peasant Rebels under Stalin: Collectivization and the Culture of Peasant Resistance* (Oxford: Oxford University Press, 1996), 61–6.

48 Rahn, ed. and trans., *Among the Ashes*, 143, 210, 237, and 239.
49 Harry Loewen, "'Can the Son Answer for the Father?' Reflections on the Stalinist Terror (On the 60th Anniversary of My Father's Arrest, 1937–1997)," *JMS* 16 (1998), 88.
50 Waldemar Janzen, *Reminiscences of My Father Vladimir Janzen: Teacher, Minister, Gulag Survivor, July 26, 1900–May 15, 1957* (Winnipeg, 2017), 13; Toews, ed., *Journeys*, memoir of Justina Martens, 55; N.J. Kroeker, *First Mennonite Villages in Russia, 1789–1943: Khortitsa – Rosental* (Vancouver: N.J. Kroeker, 1981), 58; Heinrich Woelk and Gerhard Woelk, *A Wilderness Journey: Glimpses of the Mennonite Brethren Church in Russia, 1925–1980* (Fresno, CA: Center for Mennonite Brethren Studies, 1982), memoir by Maria Riesen, 40–1; *Siberian Diary of Aron P. Toews: With a Biography by Olga Rempel*, ed. Lawrence Klippenstein and trans. Esther Klassen Bergen (Winnipeg: CMBC Publications, 1984), 118–19; *IA c vami*, 87; Hans Rempel, *Waffen der Wehrlosen. Ersatzdienst der Mennoniten in der UdSSR* (Winnipeg: CMBC Publications, 1980), 93, 106–7, and 111; and Aron A. Töws (Toews), *Mennonitishche Märtyrer der jüngsten Vergangenheit und der Gegenwart* (Winnipeg: The Christian Press, 1949), 187.
51 *Ia s vami vovse dni*, 79–81, 87, and 127; and Winter, *Shepherd*, 31.
52 The report is found in Wiebe (Vibe), *Nemetskie kolonii v Sibiri*, 307–9. On the international context for the 1929 movement, see Harvey L. Dyck, *Weimar German and Soviet Russia 1926–1933: A Study in Diplomatic Instability* (London: Chatto and Windus, 1966). For contemporary accounts by Mennonites, see Harold Janz, ed., *Flight: Mennonites Facing the Soviet Empire in 1929–30, from the Pages of the Mennonitische Rundschau* (Winnipeg: Eden Echoes Publishing, 2018). On the emigration of several hundred Mennonites to China, see Robert L. Klassen, "Harbin (Heilongjiang, China) Refugees," *GAMEO*, July 2009, https://gameo.org/index.php?title=Harbin_(Heilongjiang,_China)_Refugees&oldid=131881; H.P. Isaak, *Escape from Russia! A Flight from Death* (Grand Rapids, MI: Bert Block Ministries, 2017); Martin Durksen, *Die Krim war Unsere Heimat* (Winnipeg: Martin Durksen, 1980); and Abram J. Friesen, Victor G. Doerksen, and Abram J. Loewen, *Escape across the Amur River: A Mennonite Village Flees (1930) from Soviet Siberia to Chinese Manchuria* (Winnipeg: CMBC Publications, 2001).
53 Konrad, *Red Quarter Moon*, 39–40; John P.R. Eicher, *Exiled among Nations: German and Mennonite Mythologies in a Transnational Age* (Cambridge: Cambridge University Press, 2020), 85; and Frank H. Epp, *Mennonite Exodus: The Rescue and Resettlement of the Russian Mennonites since the Communist Revolution* (Altona, Germany: D.W. Friesen & Sons, 1962), 231.
54 Document located in Savin, ed., *Etnokonfessiia*, 545–7.

340   Notes to pages 224–8

55 Stephen Kotkin, *Magnetic Mountain: Stalinism as Civilization* (Berkeley: University of California Press, 1995), ch. 5; Sheila Fitzpatrick, *Tear Off the Masks! Identity and Imposture in Twentieth-Century Russia* (Princeton, NJ: Princeton University Press, 2005); and Fitzpatrick, *Stalin's Peasants*, 313–14.
56 Toews, ed., *Journeys*, memoir of Abram Berg, 116; and Neufeldt, "Public and Private."
57 TsDNIOO, f. 415, op. `, d. 311, l. 7, doc. 336, in Savin, ed., *Etnokonfessiia*, 607. Cf. A.I. Savin, *Etnokonfessiia v Sovetskom gosudarstve Mennonity Sibiri v 1920–1980 gody: Annotirovannyi perechen arkhivnykh dokumentov i materialov.*, TsLNIOO, f. 415, op. 1, d. 311, l. 9, 16–17, doc. 67 (Novosibirsk: Posokh, 2006), 409.
58 *Novoe Zaporozh'e: khornika razvitiia bol'shogo goroda. 1921–2006* (Dnepropetrovsk, Ukraine, 2006), 37–53; Cornelius Krahn, "Einlage (Chortitza Mennonite Settlement, Zaporizhia Oblast, Ukraine)," *GAMEO*, 1956, https://gameo.org/index.php?title=Einlage_(Chortitza _Mennonite_Settlement,_Zaporizhia_Oblast,_Ukraine)&oldid=169287; Rempel, *Waffen der Wehrlosen*, 100, 112; and Letkemann, "The Fate of Mennonites," 191.
59 Hans Werner, *The Constructed Mennonite: History, Memory and the Second World War* (Winnipeg: University of Manitoba Press, 2013), 41; *Zhivi i pomni*, 84 and 88; and Letkemann, *Book of Remembrance*, 292.
60 Jochen Hellbeck, *Revolution on My Mind: Writing a Diary under Stalin* (Cambridge, MA: Harvard University Press, 2006).
61 Toews, trans. and ed., *Letters from Susan*, 51; Neufeldt, "Collectivizing," 225; Harry Loewen, "Anti-Menno: Introduction to Early Soviet-Mennonite Literature (1920–1940)," *JMS* 11 (1993), 23–42; A. Reinmarus (Penner), *Anti-Menno: Beiträge zur Geschichte der Mennoniten in Russland* (Moscow, 1930); and Peter Letkemann, "David Johann Penner [A. Reinmarus]: A Mennonite Anti-Menno (1904–1993)," in *Shepherds, Servants and Prophets: Leadership among the Russian Mennonites (ca. 1880–1960)*, ed. Harry Loewen (Kitchener, ON, 2003), 297–311.
62 Moshe Lewin, *The Making of the Soviet System: Essays in the Social System of Interwar Russia* (New York: The New Press, 1994), esp. 209–23.
63 Toews, trans. and ed., *Letters from Susan*, 38, 40, 56, 58, 86, 88, 101, 103, 106, and 111.
64 Neufeldt, "Collectivizing," 221–8.

12 The Road to Rochegda: Soviet Terror, Nazi Occupation, and Stalinist Repatriation, 1934–1953

1 Information taken from Georg Schmidt's and Anni Schmidt's unpublished memoirs, in possession of author.

2 For a recent investigation of the Kirov murder and Stalin's role within it, see Matthew Lenoe, *The Kirov Murder and Soviet History* (New Haven, CT: Yale University Press, 2010).
3 Cited in Terry Martin, "The Russian Mennonite Encounter with the Soviet State, 1917–1955," *CGR* 20 (Winter 2002), 39.
4 Selected archival documents recorded in A.I. Savin, ed., *Etnokonfessiia v sovetskom gosudarstve. Mennonity Sibiri v 1920–1930-e gody: emigratsiia i repressii. Dokumenty i materialy* (Novosibirsk: Posokh, 2009), 608–30; *IA s vami vo vse dni do skonchaniiia Veka Kniga I: Tiazhelye vremena gonenii I repressii 1931–1946 gg.* (Karaganda – Steinhagen, 2001), 91; and Jacob A. Neufeld, *Path of Thorns: Soviet Mennonite Life under Communist and Nazi Rule*, ed. and trans. Harvey L. Dyck (Toronto: University of Toronto Press, 2014), 39–45 and 60.
5 Henry H. Winter, *A Shepherd of the Oppressed: Heinrich Winter, the Last Ältester of Chortitza* (Wheatley, ON: Author, 1990), 17–25; and Waldemar Janzen, *Reminiscences of My Father Wladimir Janzen: Teacher, Minister, Gulag Survivor, July 26, 1900–May 15, 1957* (Winnipeg: Waldemar Janzen, 2017).
6 Peter Letkemann, *A Book of Remembrance: Mennonites in Arkadak and Zentral, 1908–1941* (Winnipeg, 2016), 295 and 311.
7 Terry Martin, "The Origins of Ethnic Cleansing," *JMH* 70 (December 1998), 86; and Kate Brown, *A Biography of No Place: From Ethnic Borderland to Soviet Heartland* (Cambridge, MA: Harvard University Press, 2005), 132–3. For a comprehensive overview, see Terry Martin, *The Affirmative Action Empire: Nations and Nationalism in the Soviet Union, 1923–1939* (Ithaca, NY: Cornell University Press, 2001), Part III. The listing of nations is from Martin, *Affirmative Action Empire*, 311. For a comparable listing, see O.V. Khlevniuk and Nora Seligman Favorov, *Stalin: New Biography of a Dictator* (New Haven, CT: Yale University Press, 2015), 151.
8 J. Arch Getty and Oleg V. Naumov, *Yezhov: The Rise of Stalin's "Iron Fist"* (New Haven, CT: Yale University Press, 2008).
9 For three very different examples of local initiative in the purges, see Lynne Viola, *Stalinist Perpetrators on Trial Scenes from the Great Terror in Soviet Ukraine* (Oxford: Oxford University Press, 2017) ch. 6; Stephen Kotkin, *Magnetic Mountain: Stalinism as Civilization* (Berkeley: University of California Press, 1995), 316–54; and Igal Halfin, *Stalinist Confessions: Messianism and Terror at the Leningrad Communist University* (Pittsburgh: University of Pittsburgh Press, 2009).
10 Oleg V. Khlevniuk, *The History of the Gulag: From Collectivization to the Great Terror* (New Haven, CT: Yale University Press, 2004), 165–70 and 289–90; and Stephen A. Barnes, *Death and Redemption: The Gulag and the Shaping of Soviet Society* (Princeton, NJ: Princeton University Press, 2011), 34.

11 Peter Letkemann, "Mennonite Victims of the 'Great Terror' 1936–1938," *JMS* 16 (1998), 37. On Mennonite and German children in the Gulag, see Irina Tscherkazjanowa, "die Kinder der Russlanddeutschen unter den Verhältnissen von Deportation, Trudarmee und Sondersiedlung," in *Von der Autonomiegründung zur Verbannung und Entrechtung. Die Jahre 1918 und 1941 bis 1948 in der Geschichte der Deutschen in Russland*, ed. Alfred Eisfeld (Stuttgart, 2008), 180–203.

12 Aron A. Toews, *Mennonitische Märtyrer der jüngsten Vergangenheit under der Gegenwart*, 2 vols. (Winnipeg: The Christian Press, 1941 and 1949); Helmut T. Huebert, *1937: Stalin's Year of Terror* (Winnipeg: Springfield Publishers, 2009), 29–30, 216; "Memoirs of Justina Martens," in *Journeys: Mennonite Stories of Faith and Survival in Stalin's Russia*, ed. John B. Toews (Winnipeg: Kindred Press, 1998), 60–1; Franz Thiessen, "A Most Unusual Year: 1937," in *The Silence Echoes: Memoirs of Trauma and Tears*, ed. and trans. Sarah Dyck (Kitchener, ON: Pandora Press, 1997), 103–10; Anne Konrad, *Red Quarter Moon: A Search for Family in the Shadow of Stalin* (Toronto: University of Toronto Press, 2012), 95 and 109; John Friesen, *Against the Wind: The Story of Four Mennonite Villages (Gnadental, Gruenfeld, Neu-Chortitza and Steinfeld) in the Southern Ukraine, 1872–1943* (Winnipeg: Henderson Books, 1994), 95; and Peter Epp, *Ob tausent fallen … Mein Leben im Archipel Gulag* (Weichs: Memra-Verlag, 1988), 23.

13 The quotation is from Letkemann, "Mennonite Victims," 42, n. 63. Cf. Konrad, *Red Quarter Moon*, 108, 110, and 134; Julius Loewen, *Jasykowo: Mennonite Colony on the Dnieper*, trans. Jakob B. Klassen (Beausejour: The Standard Press, 1995), 140–1; Jacob Sawatzky, "Never a Pioneer," in *The Silence Echoes: Memoirs of Trauma and Tears*, ed. Sarah Dyck (Kitchener, ON: Pandora Press, 1997), 117; and Karl Fast, *Gebt der Wahrheit de Ehre! Ein Schicksalbericht*, 2nd edition (Winnipeg: Canzona Publications, 1989), 27.

14 *IA s vami*, 96–102 and 124–8; Olga Rempel, *Einer von Vielen. Die Lebensgeschichte von Prediger Aaron P. Toews* (Winnipeg: CMBC Publications, 1979), 169–75; John B. Toews, *Letters from Susan: A Woman's View of the Russian Mennonite Experience (1928–1941)* (North Newton, KS: Bethel College, 1988), 141–8.

15 Winter, *Shepherd*, 48–54; and Neufeld, *Path of Thorns*, 144–8.

16 Jacob A. Neufeld, *Tiefenwege. Erfahrungen und Erlebnisse von Russland-Mennoniten in zwei Jahrzehnten bis 1949* (Virgil, ON: Niagara Press, 1958), 46–50. In translation, see Neufeld, *Path of Thorns*, 184–7.

17 James Urry, "Mennonites in Ukraine during World War II: Thoughts and Questions," *MQR* 93 (2019), 91–3.

18 Alfred Eisfeld and Viktor Herdt, eds., *Deportation, Sondersiedlung, Arbeitsarmee: Deutsche in der Sowjetunion 1941 bis 1956* (Köln: Verlag Wissenschaft und Politik, 1996); Steven A. Barnes, "'All for the Front,

Notes to pages 237–9   343

All for Victory!' The Mobilization of Forced Labor in the Soviet Union during World War Two," *International Labor and Working-Class History* 58 (Fall 2000), 242–6; Wilson T. Bell, *Stalin's Gulag at War: Forced Labour, Mass Death, and Soviet Victory in the Second World War* (Toronto: University of Toronto Press, 2019), ch. 20–3; and Irina Mukhina, "Reshaping Lives, Reconstructing Identities: Ethnic Germans of the Soviet Union, 1941–1956," unpublished PhD diss., Boston University, 2006, ch. 3.

19 Neufeld, *Path of Thorns*, 198; and Konrad, *Red Quarter Moon*, 143. For the context, see Irina Mukhina, "Gendered Division of Labor among Special Settlers in the Soviet Union, 1941–1956," *Women's History Review* 23 (January 2014), 99–119.

20 Barnes, *Death and Redemption*, 145; Rempel, *Osterwick*, 178–9; Pavel Polian, *Ne po svoei vole ... Istoriia I geografiia prinuditel'nykh migratsii v SSSR* (Moscow, 2001); and Viktor Krieger, "Deportationen der Russlanddeutschen 1941–1945 und die Folgen," in *Von der Autonomiegründung zur Verbannung und Entrechtung. Die Jahre 1918 und 1941 bis 1948 in der Geschichte der Deutschen in Russland*, ed. Alfred Eisfeld (Stuttgart, 2008), 106–22; and Denis Kozlov and Eleaonory Gilburd, "The Thaw as an Event in Russian History," in *The Thaw: Soviet Society and Culture During the 1950s and 1960s*, ed. Denis Kozlov and Eleonory Gilburd (Toronto: University of Toronto Press, 2013), 33. Much of the material that follows specific to Mennonite deportations is found in Viktor K. Klets, "Caught between Two Poles: Ukrainian Mennonites and the Trauma of the Second World War," in *Minority Report: Mennonite Identities in Imperial Russia and Soviet Ukraine Reconsidered, 1789–1945*, ed. Leonard G. Friesen (Toronto: University of Toronto Press, 2018), 287–317.

21 *Novoe Zaporozh'e: khronika razvitiia bol'shovo goroda, 1921–2006* (Dnepropetrovsk, Ukraine, 2006), 63; Klets, "Caught," 287–8 and 292; and Agatha Loewen Schmidt, *Gnadenfeld, Molotschna, 1835–1943* (Kitchener, ON: Author, 1997), 32–3; and George K. Epp, "World War (1939–1945) – Soviet Union," *GAMEO*, 1989, https://gameo.org/index.php?title=World_War_(1939-1945)_-_Soviet_Union&oldid=163501.

22 Letkemann, *Book of Remembrance*, 349–75.

23 Johannes Due Enstadt, *Soviet Russians under Nazi Occupation: Fragile Loyalties in World War II* (Cambridge: Cambridge University Press, 2018), 51. Cf. Serhii Plokhy, *The Gates of Europe: A History of Ukraine* (New York: Basic Books, 2015); 265; Karel C. Berkhoff, *Harvest of Despair: Life and Death in Ukraine under Soviet Rule* (Cambridge, MA: The Belknap Press of Harvard University Press, 2004), 28–9; and Rempel, *Osterwick*, 175.

24 Notes from interview with Georg Schmidt in possession of author; Fast, *Gebt der Wahrheit*, 70; and Heinrich Löwen and Cornelius Krahn, "Grünfeld (Schlachtin Mennonite Settlement, Dnipropetrovsk Oblast, Ukraine),"

GAMEO, 1956, https://gameo.org/index.php?title=Gr%C3%BCnfeld
_(Schlachtin_Mennonite_Settlement,_Dnipropetrovsk_Oblast,
_Ukraine)&oldid=145353. For a listing of churches that opened in the
Chortitza villages alone, see Horst Gerlach, *Die Russlandmennoniten: Ein
Volk Unterwegs*, 3rd edition (Weierhof, 1998), 86–7.

25 Winter, *Shepherd*, 68 and 80, which includes group baptismal photos on 66–71.
26 James Urry, "Mennonites in Ukraine during World War II: Thoughts and Questions," *Mennonite Quarterly Review* 93 (2019), 94–6. Gorbachev himself recalled how Germans drafted an elderly villager, "Grandpa Stavka," in Gorbachev's village of Privolnoe during the occupation to serve as "village elder." Gorbachev later recalled that Savka had only agreed to do so in the hopes that it would save the villagers from harm. Tragically, for Gorbachev, Soviet troops arrested and imprisoned Savka for "betrayal of the Motherland" after the occupation had ended. See William Taubman, *Gorbachev: His Life and Times* (New York: W.W. Norton and Company, 2017), 23. On the Nazi world view, see Claudia Koontz, *The Nazi Conscience* (Cambridge, MA: Harvard University Press, 2003).
27 Friesen, *Against the Wind*, 99; and Neufeld, *Path of Thorns*, 224.
28 N.J. Kroeker, *First Mennonite Villages in Russia, 1789–1943* (Vancouver: N.J. Kroeker, 1981), 233.
29 Eric C. Steinhart, *The Holocaust and the Germanization of Ukraine* (Cambridge: Cambridge University Press, 2015); and Paul R. Magocsi, *A History of Ukraine: The Land and Its Peoples* (Toronto: University of Toronto Press, 2010), 669f.
30 Tanja Penter, "Vergessene Opfer von Mord und Missbrauch: Behindertenmorde unter deutscher Besatzungsherrschaft in der Ukraine (1941–1943) und ihre juristische Aufarbeitung in der Sowjetunion," *Journal of Modern European History* 17 (2019), 353–76; and Wendy Lower, *Nazi Empire-Building and the Holocaust in Ukraine* (Chapel Hill: University of North Carolina Press, 2005), ch. 4; and Magocsi (2010), 674–8.
31 Gerhard Rempel, "Mennonites and the Holocaust: From Collaboration to Perpetuation," *MQR* 84, no. 4 (2010): 507–49; Urry, "Mennonites in Ukraine"; Benjamin W. Goossen, *Chosen Nation: Mennonites and Germany in the Global Era* (Princeton, NJ: Princeton University Press, 2017), ch. 6; and Aileen Friesen, "A Portrait of Khortytsya/Zaporizhzhia under Occupation," in *European Mennonites and the Holocaust*, ed. Mark Jantzen and John D. Thiesen (Toronto: University of Toronto Press, 2020), ch. 8. Cf. John D. Thiesen, "Menno in the KZ or Münster Resurrected: Mennonites and National Socialism – Historiography and Open Questions," in *European Mennonites and the Challenge of Modernity over Five Centuries:*

Contributors, Detractors, and Adapters, ed. Mark Jantzen, Mary S. Sprunger, and John D. Thiesen (North Newton, KS: Bethel College, 2016), 322–3.

32 Klets, "Caught," 309; Urry, "Mennonites in Ukraine," 92; Friesen, "Portrait"; and Aileen Friesen, "Soviet Mennonites, the Holocaust & Nazism," *Anabaptist Historians* (25 April 2017), n.p.

33 Berkhoff, *Harvest*, 5. Cf. Stathis N. Kalyvas, *The Logic of Violence in Civil War* (Cambridge: Cambridge University Press, 2006), ch. 5.

34 Quoted in Klets, "Caught," n. 114; and John P.R. Eicher, *Exiled among Nations: German and Mennonite Mythologies in a Transnational Age* (Cambridge: Cambridge University Press, 2020), ch. 5–6.

35 *Zhivi i pomni ... Istoriia Mennonitskikh koloonii Ekaterinoslavshchiny* (Dneptropetrovsk, Ukraine, 2006), 88, 113, 156, and 183; Urry, "Mennonites in Ukraine," 98–109; James Urry, private correspondence with the author on 14 November 2020; Waldemar Janzen, *Growing Up in Turbulent Times: Memoirs of Soviet Oppression, Refugee Life in Germany, and Immigrant Adjustment to Canada* (Winnipeg: CMU Press, 2007), 46; Klets, "Caught," 289–90 and 303–4. Klets engages with Horst Gerlach, "Mennonites, the Molotschna, and the Volksdeutsche Mittelstelle in the Second World War," *ML* 41, no. 3 (1986), 4–9; and Berkhoff, *Harvest*, 5.

36 Marlene Epp, *Women without Men: Mennonite Refugees of the Second World War* (Toronto: University of Toronto Press, 2000), 42–3.

37 Georg Schmidt, "And Now I Shall Write from My Memories," unpublished, Vineland, 1995; Katharina Ediger and Elizabeth Schulz, *Under His Wings: Events in the Lives of Elder Alexander Ediger and His Family* (Kitchener, ON, 1994); Winter, *Shepherd*, 81; and Schmidt, *Gnadenfeld*, 48.

38 Gerhard Fast, *Das Ende von Chortitza* (Winnipeg: Selbstverlag, 1973), 99–115; and Pamela E. Klassen, *Going by the Moon and the Stars: Stories of Two Russian Mennonite Women* (Waterloo: Wilfrid Laurier University Press, 1994), ch. 1.

39 On Wartheland, see Catherine Epstein, *Model Nazi: Arthur Greiser and the Occupation of Western Poland* (Oxford: Oxford University Press, 2010) ch. 4–5; and Ian Kershaw, *Hitler, the Germans, and the Final Solution* (New Haven, CT: Yale University Press, 2008), ch. 3.

40 Adolf Eichmann apparently coined this term. See Hans Mommsen, "Die Realisierung des Utopischen: Die 'Endlösung der Judenfrage' im 'Dritten Reich,'" *Geschichte und Gesellschaft* 9, no. 3 (1983), 381–420.

41 In addition to sources mentioned above, see Neufeld, *Path of Thorns*, ch. 12; Anna Klassen, nee Thiessen, "Exiled Again: 1943," in *The Silence Echoes: Memoirs of Trauma and Tears*, ed. Sarah Dyck (Kitchener, ON: Pandora Press, 1997), 148–57; Norman Naimark, *The Russians in Germany: A History of the Soviet Zone of Occupation, 1945–1949* (Cambridge, MA: Harvard University Press), ch. 2; Peter and Elfrieda Dyck, *Up from the Rubble* (Scottdale, PA: Herald Press, 1991): 87–99. For the record of German troops

and sexual assault in the east, see Soenke Neitzel and Harald Welzer, *Soldaten: On Fighting, Killing, and Dying: The Secret World War II Tapes of German POWs* (London: Simon & Schuster, 2012), chapter on "Sex."
42 Anni Schmidt, *My Life on the Road*, unpublished, n.d., in possession of author, 15.
43 On the larger immigration, see Ted Regehr, "Of Dutch or German Ancestry? Mennonite Refugees, MCC, and the International Refugee Organization," *JMS* 13 (1995), 7–25; and Ted Regehr, *Mennonites in Canada, 1939–1970*, Volume 3: *A People Transformed* (Toronto: University of Toronto Press, 1996), ch. 4.
44 Serhii Plokhy, *Yalta: The Price for Peace* (New York: Penguin Books, 2010); Nikolai Tolstoi, *Victims of Yalta: The Secret Betrayal of the Allies, 1944–1947* (London: Hodder and Stoughton, 1977); Mark Elliott, *Pawns of Yalta: Soviet Refugees and America's Role in Their Repatriation* (Champaign: University of Illinois Press, 1982); and Helmut T. Huebert, "Great Trek, 1943–1945," *GAMEO*, April 2009, https://gameo.org/index.php?title=Great_Trek,_1943-1945&oldid=155816.
45 Walter Sawatsky, "Journey of the Unwanted: Soviet Mennonite Deportation, Special Settlement, Exile and Exodus," unpublished paper in possession of author, 10–11; and Martin, "Russian Mennonite Encounter," 49.
46 Viktor Bruhl, "Deutsche Frauen in der Sondersiedlung und in den Arbeitskolonnen in den Jahren 1941–48," in *Von der Autonomiegründung zur Verbannung und Entrechtung. Die Jahre 1918 und 1941 bis 1948 in der Geschichte der Deutschen in Russland*, ed. Alfred Eisfeld (Stuttgart, 2008), 162–79; Konrad, *Red Quarter Moon*, ch. 6–7; Barnes, *Death and Redemption*, ch. 4–5;Peter Epp, *Ob tausent fallen...Mein Leben im Archipel Gulag* (Weichs: Memra-Verlag, 1988); and selected memoirs in Toews, *Letters from Susan*, and Dyck, ed., *Silence*.
47 Walter Sawatsky, "From Russian to Soviet Mennonites, 1941–1988," in John Friesen ed., *Mennonites in Russia, 1788–1988: Essays in Honour of Gerhard Lohrenz* (Winnipeg: CMBC Publications, 1989), 302–3.
48 Viktor Fast and Jakob Penner, *Wasserströme in der Einöde: Die Anfangsgeschichte der Mennonite-Brüdergemeinde Karaganda 1956–1968* (Steinhagen, Germany: Samenkorn, 2007), 49–66; Walter Sawatsky, "Russian Mennonite Organizational Collapse and the Failed Attempts to Form an Independent Organization, 1917–1989," *MQR* (2015), 27–9; Sawatsky, "From Russian to Soviet," 303–5; and *IA s vami*, 144–5 and 151.

13 Detour to Dzhetisai: The Soviet Mennonite Renaissance in Stalin's Shadow, 1953–1991

1 Notes taken from Georg Schmidt's unpublished memoir and from an interview undertaken with him by the author on 16 October 2020. For

the location of Dzhetsai, see William Schroeder and Helmut T. Huebert, *Mennonite Historical Atlas*, 2nd edition (Winnipeg: Springfield Publishers, 1996), 104. For more on the larger context, see Michaela Pohl, "From White Grave to Tselinograd to Astana: The Virgin Lands Opening, Khrushchev's Forgotten First Reform," in *The Thaw: Soviet Society and Culture During the 1950s and 1960s*, ed. Denis Kozlov and Eleonory Gilburd (Toronto: University of Toronto Press, 2013), 269–307.

2 https://www.goshen.edu/mqr/search.php. I thank James Urry for this observation.

3 Walter Sawatsky, "Historical Roots of a Post-Gulag Theology for Russian Mennonites," *MQR* (April 2002), 152; Walter Sawatsky, "Mennonite Congregations in the Soviet Union Today," *ML* (March 1978), 13; Walter Sawatsky, "Changing Mentalities: Inter-Relationships between Mennonites and Slavic Evangelicals in Siberia and Central Asia," *JMS* 30 (2012), 326; Cornelius Krahn, "Omsk (Siberia, Russia)," *GAMEO*, 1959, https://gameo.org/index.php?title=Omsk_(Siberia,_Russia)&oldid=135148; and Petr Epp, *100 let pod krovom Vsyvyshnego: Istorria Omskikh obshchin EkkB ikh ob'edineniia, 1907–2007* (Omsk, Russia: Samenkorn, 2007), parts 3 and 4.

4 Tatiana A. Chumachenko, *Church and State in Soviet Russia: Russian Orthodoxy From World War II to the Khrushchev Years* (New York: Routledge, 2015), 4; Walter Sawatsky, *Soviet Evangelicals since World War II* (Scottdale, PA: Herald Press, 1981), ch. 1; and Felix Corley, *Religion in the Soviet Union: An Archival Reader* (New York: New York University Press. 1996), 156–83.

5 Ivan Shnaider, *Sto let pervoi obshchine baptistov v Aktiubinskie: Evangel'skie obshchiny v Aktiubinskoi stepi* (Steinhagen, Germany: Samenkorn, 2006), 74; Heinrich Bergen, ed., *Verbannung. Unschuldig nach Sibirien ins Verderben, 1935–1955* (Regina, SK, 2006), 109; Steven Anthony Barnes, *Death and Redemption: The Gulag and the Shaping of Soviet Society* (Princeton, NJ: Princeton University Press, 2011); ch. 6; Walter Sawatsky, "Protestantism," in *Protestantism and Politics in Eastern Europe and Russia: The Communist and Postcommunist Eras*, ed. Sabrina P. Ramet (Durham, NC: Duke University Press, 1992), 252; and Alan Barenberg, *Gulag Town, Company Town: Forced Labor and Its Legacy in Vorkuta* (New Haven, CT: Yale University Press, 2014), ch. 4–6.

6 Sawatsky, "Mennonite Congregations"; and Johannes Dyck, "Revival as Church Restoration: Patterns of a Revival among Ethnic Germans in Central Asia after World War II," in *Mission in the Former Soviet Union*, ed. Walter W. Sawatsky and Peter F. Penner (Schwarzenfeld, Germany: Neufeld Verlag, 2005), 83–4.

7 Walter Sawatsky, "Journey of the Unwanted: Soviet Mennonite Deportation, Special Settlement, Exile and Exodus," unpublished paper in possession of the author, 12; and Harold S. Bender, "*Der Mennonit* (Periodical)," *GAMEO*, 1957, https://gameo.org/index

.php?title=Mennonit,_Der_(Periodical)&oldid=134661; and https://cmbs.mennonitebrethren.ca/publications/mennonite-der/.
8 See various issues of *Der Bote* and *Die Mennonitische Rundschau* for the 1950s. The reference to Georg Schmidt is found in *Mennonitsche Rundschau* (14 March 1956), 2.
9 "Probuzhdenie" in Russian, "Erweckung" in German. The literature on this is rich. See Petr Epp, *100 let pod*, part III, ch. 1–2; Viktor Fast and Jacob Penner, *Wasserströme in der Einöde. Die Anfangsgeschichte der Mennoniten-Brüdergemeinde Karaganda 1956–1968* (Steinhagen, Germany: Samenkorn, 2007), pt. 1, ch. 3, and pt. 2; and Walter Sawatsky, *Soviet Evangelicals since World War II* (Kitchener, ON: Herald Press, 1981), ch. 2.
10 Sawatsky, "Changing Mentalities," 324. Also on this, see Epp, *100 let pod*, 300; Johannes Dyck, "A Root out of Dry Ground: Revival Patterns in the German Free Churches in the USSR after World War II," *JMS* 30 (2012), 97–112; Johannes Dyck, "Frauen als Säulen der Erweckung," in *History and Mission in Europe: Continuing the Conversation*, ed. Mary Raber and Peter F. Penner (Schwarzenfeld, Germany: Neufeld Verlag, 2011), 179–96; Fast and Penner, eds., *Wasserströme*; Heinrich Woelk and Gerhard Woelk, *A Wilderness Journey: Glimpses of the Mennonite Brethren Church in Russia, 1925–1980* (Fresno, CA: Center for Mennonite Brethren Studies, 1982), 80ff.
11 Sawatsky, "Historical Roots"; and Vera P. Klyueva, "The Mennonite Community of the Tyumen Oblast: A Short History from the 1940s to the 1980s," *JMS* (2012), 91. Cf. Johannes Dyck, "Elements of Post-Gulag Mennonite Theology: View of an Eyewitness," in *History and Mission in Europe: Continuing the Conversation*, ed. Mary Raber and Peter F. Penner (Schwarzenfeld, Germany: Neufeld Verlag, 2011), 199–211; Abram Hamm and Maria Hamm, *Die Wege des Herrn sind lauter Güte* (Gummersbach, Germany: Verlag Friedensstimme, 1985); Viktor Fast, ed., *Vorübergehende Heimat: 150 Jahre Beten und Arbeiten in Alt-Samara (Alexandertal und Konstantinow)* (Steinhagen, Germany: Samenkorn, 2009), 570–85.
12 Johannes Dyck, Mennonity Severnoi Ameriki i SSSR v seredine 1950e godov: malen'kie liudi I vol'shaia politika," *Gosudarstvo, Religiia, Tserkov* 35 (2017), 138–9; Karl Fast, *Orenburg: die letze Mennonitische Ansiedlung in Osteuropa* (Winnipeg: Das Bunte Fenster, 1995), 101; Klyueva, "The Mennonite Community,", 90; Fast and Penner, eds., *Wasserströme*, 91; and Walter Sawatsky, "Russian Mennonite Organizational Collapse and the Failed Attempts to Form an Independent Organization, 1917–1989," *MQR* 89 (October 2015), 557.
13 The best overviews on Khrushchev's war on religion from a Mennonite perspective are found in Sawatsky, *Soviet Evangelicals*, ch. 5–6; Fast and Penner, eds., *Wasserströme*, part III; Epp, *100 let pod*, part III, ch. 5; Walter Sawatsky, "Secret Soviet Lawbook on Religion," *Religion in Communist*

Lands (1980), 24–34; and Corley, *Religion*, 184–243. For the larger context, see Victoria Smolkin, *A Sacred Space Is Never Empty: A History of Soviet Atheism* (Princeton, NJ: Princeton University Press, 2018), ch. 2.

14 Smolkin, *Sacred*, 75.
15 Abram Hamm and Maria Hamm, *Die Wege*, 122. The biography of Heinrich P. Voth is located in Sawatsky, "Historical Roots," 157; and comments by an anonymous reviewer.
16 Fast and Penner, eds., *Wasserströme*, 193–227; Epp, *100 let pod*, 360–1; Iraida V. Nam, "The Mennonite Congregations in the Tomsk Oblast during 'Thaw' and 'Stagnation,'" *JMS* 30 (2012), 74–5; Fast ed., *Vorübergehende*, 579–87; Dyck, "Revival," 84–5.
17 Years later the AUCECB acknowledged that it had failed in its search for the proper balance. See Sawatsky, *Soviet Evangelicals*, 177–9; and the comments of an anonymous reviewer. "Discretion and Valor" hearkens to Trevor Beeson, *Discretion and Valour: Religious Conditions in Russia and Eastern Europe* (Glasgow: Collins Publishers, 1974).
18 For overviews of the movement, see Tatiana Nikol'skaia, "Istoriia dvizheniia baptistov-initsiativnikov," in *History and Mission in Europe: Continuing the Conversation*, ed. Mary Raber and Peter F. Penner (Schwarzenfeld, Germany: Neufeld Verlag, 2011), 111–39; Sawatsky, *Soviet Evangelicals*, ch. 6; Fast and Penner, eds., *Wasserströme*, part IV; and Epp, *100 let pod*, pt. 3, ch. 6.
19 Nikol'skaia, "Istoriia," 121; and Epp, *100 let pod*, 364–5.
20 Andrew Brown, "Peter Wiens and Georgi Vins: Faith Strengthened by Trial," *Profiles of Mennonite Faith* (Fall 2016), 1–2; and https://cmbs.mennonitebrethren.ca/personal_papers/vins-wiensgeorgi-1928-1998/; and the comments by an anonymous reviewer.
21 Private correspondence with Walter Sawatsky dated 9 November 2020; A.N. Ipatov, *Mennonity: Voprosy formirovaniia I evoliutsii etnokonfessional'noi obshchnosti* (Moscow, 1978), 162–3; and Walter W. Sawatsky, "Council of Churches of Evangelical Christians-Baptists," *GAMEO*, 1987, https://gameo.org/index.php?title=Council_of_Churches_of_Evangelical_Christians-Baptists&oldid=86947.
22 Stephen Kotkin, *Armageddon Averted: The Soviet Collapse, 1970–2000*, updated edition (Oxford: Oxford University Press, 2008).
23 Dyck, "Elements," 210; Corley, *Religion*, 244–88; and Sawatsky, *Soviet Evangelicals*, ch. 10.
24 Johannes Reimer, *Auf der Suche nach Identität: Russlanddeutsche zwischen Baptisten und Mennoniten nach dem Zweiten Weltkrieg* (Lage, Germany: Logos, 1996), 93–6; Fast and Penner, eds., *Wasserströme*, 305–13; the comments of an anonymous reviewer; and Woelk and, *Wilderness Journey*, 98–121. Cf. Konstantin A. Morgunov, "Test of

Faith: Religious Mennonite Organizations of Orenburg Region, 1945–1991," *JMS* (2012), 83.
25 Petr Epp, "A Brief History of the Omsk Brotherhood," *JMS* (2012), 126–31; and Epp, *100 let pod*, 370–2 and 389–90.
26 Hedrick Smith, *The Russians* (New York, 1976).
27 Unpublished notes in possession of author dated 11 October 2020, and personal correspondence from Walter Sawatsky dated 27 July 2021. Walter Sawatsky received his doctorate in 1976. On his contributions, see John A. Lapp, "Taking Contextual Influences Seriously: The Contributions of Walter W. Sawatsky," in *History and Mission in Europe: Continuing the Conversation*, ed. Mary Raber and Peter F. Penner (Schwarzenfeld, Germany: Neufeld Verlag, 2011), 11–24; and Walter W. Sawatsky, "My Pilgrimage to the East," unpublished paper in possession of the author dated 20 January 2011.
28 Mary Raber, "Remembering the Russian Bible Commentary: A Memoir in Context," in *History and Mission in Europe: Continuing the Conversation*, ed. Mary Raber and Peter F. Penner (Schwarzenfeld, Germany: Neufeld Verlag, 2011), 307; and Walter Sawatsky, *Going Global with God as Mennonites for the 21st Century* (North Newton, KS: Bethel College, 2017), 29–30.
29 Regina Lőneke, *Die "Hiesigen" und die "Unsrigen": Werteverständnis MennonitischerAussiedlerfamilien aud Dörfern der RegionOrenburg/Ural* (Marburg, Germany: N.G. Ewert, 2000), 62–3; Fast, ed., *Vorübergehende*, 591; Schmidt, "And Now I Shall Write"; Walter W. Sawatsky, e-mail correspondence to the author, 1 November 2020; and notes by author on research trip to Karaganda, May 1988.
30 Schmidt, "And Now I Shall Write,", 36.
31 Alexander Weiss, "The Transition of Siberian Mennonites to Baptists: Causes and Results," *JMS* (2012), 133–8; Sergey V. Sokolovsky, "The Mennonites of Altai: Marriage Structures and Cultural Transmission," *JMS* (2012), 57–66; Lőneke, *Die "Hiesigen,"* 60, 193–5; Ipatov, *Mennonity*, 190–4; and Reimer, *Auf der Suche*, 107.
32 Sawatsky, "Changing Mentalities," 326.
33 Dyck, "Elements," 205–11; and Johannes Dyck, "Revival as Church Restoration: Patterns of a Revival among Ethnic Germans in Central Asia after World War II," *Transformation: An International Journal of Holistic Mission Studies* (2004), 174–80. For Sawatsky's earlier iteration, see Sawatsky, "Historical Roots," 149–80.
34 Johannes Dyck, "Johannes – Gott is gnädig," in *Er gibt dem Müden Kraft: 63 Predigten aus 1973–78*, by Johannes Fast (Steinhagen, Germany: Samenkorn, 2004), 9–22.
35 Fast, *Er gibt dem Müden*.

36 Moshe Lewin, *The Gorbachev Phenomenon: A Historical Interpretation* (Berkeley: University of California Press, 1988); William Taubman, *Gorbachev, His Life and Times* (New York: W.W. Norton, 2017); and Kotkin, *Armageddon Averted*; and Stephen F. Cohen, *Rethinking the Soviet Experience: Politics and History Since 1917* (Oxford: Oxford University Press, 1985).
37 Epp, *100 let pod*, 575–6.
38 Smolkin, *Sacred*, 215–27; "Gorbachev Confronts the Challenge of Christianity," https://www.cia.gov/library/readingroom/docs/DOC_0000498825.pdf; and author's notes from his time living in Leningrad in 1987 and 1988.
39 Walter W. Sawatsky, "Return of Mission and Evangelization in the CIS (1980s – Present)," in *Mission in the Former Soviet Union*, ed. Walter W. Sawatsky and Peter F. Penner (Schwarzenfeld, Germany: Neufeld Verlag, 2005), 96–7.
40 Epp, *100 let pod*, 579–81.
41 John N. Klassen, *Russlanddeutsche Freikirchen in der Bundesrepublik Deutschland: Grlundlinien ihrer Geschichte, ihrer Entwicklung und Theologie* (Nűrnberg, Germany: Verlag fűr Theologie und Religionswissenschaft, 2007), 63–6; Sawatsky, "Journey of the Unwanted," 24–5; Epp, *100 let pod*, 588–9; and Lőneke, *Die "Hiesigen*," 96–8.

14 Coda: Zaporozhe 1989. One Story Ends and Another Begins

1 Menno Simons, "Foundation of Christian Doctrine, 1539" in *The Complete Writings of Menno Simons c. 1496–1561*, ed. J.C. Wenger and trans. Leonard Verduin (Scottdale, PA: Herald Press, 1956), 225.
2 Wenger, ed., *Complete Writings*, 148 and 98; Abraham Friesen, *Menno Simons: Dutch Reformer between Luther, Erasmus and the Holy Spirit: A Study in the Problem Areas of Menno Scholarship* (Bloomington, IN: Xlibris, 2015), 241–51; and Helmut Isaak, *Menno Simons and the New Jerusalem* (Kitchener, ON: Pandora Press, 2006), 104–11.
3 Wenger, ed., *Complete Writings*, 108.
4 John C. Wenger and C. Arnold Snyder, "Schleitheim Confession," *GAMEO*, 1990, https://gameo.org/index.php?title=Schleitheim_Confession&oldid=143737. I thank Walter Sawatsky for making this comparative observation in his e-mail to me dated 27 November 2020.
5 Valerie A. Kivelson, "The Devil Stole His Mind: The Tsar and the 1648 Moscow Uprising," *AHR* 98 (June 1993), 733–56. Scott H. Hendrix, *Recultivating the Vineyard: The Reformation Agendas of Christian Martyrdom in Early Modern Europe* (Cambridge, MA: Harvard University Press, 1999), ch. 6; and Brad S. Gregory, *The Unintended Reformation: How a Religious Revolution Secularized Society* (Cambridge, MA: The Belknap Press of Harvard University Press, 2012), 373–4.

6 Contrast here Nancy Shields Kollman, *The Russian Empire, 1450–1801* (Oxford: Oxford University Press, 2017); and John LeDonne, *Forging a Unitary State: Russia's Management of the Eurasian Space, 1650–1850* (Toronto: University of Toronto Press, 2020).
7 Kollmann, *Russian Empire*, 160; S. Frederick Starr, *Decentralization and Self-Government in Russia, 1830–1870* (Princeton, NJ: Princeton University Press, 1972); J. Arch Getty, *Practicing Stalinism: Bolsheviks, Boyars, and the Persistence of Tradition* (New Haven, CT: Yale University Press, 2013); and David L. Hoffmann and Yanni Kotsonis, eds., *Russian Modernity Politics, Knowledge and Practices, 1800–1950* (London: Palgrave MacMillan, 2000).
8 Eric Lohr, *Russian Citizenship: From Empire to Soviet Union* (Cambridge, MA: Harvard University Press, 2012), 151–2.
9 Konrad Jarausch, *Out of Ashes: A New History of Europe in the Twentieth Century* (Princeton, NJ: Princeton University Press, 2015), 1–18.
10 Charles Taylor, *The Secular Age* (Cambridge, MA: Harvard University Press, 2007); Joel Thiessen, *The Meaning of Sunday: The Practice of Belief in a Secular Age* (Montreal, ON: McGill-Queen's University Press, 2015); Joel Thiessen and Sarah Wilkins-Laflamme, *None of the Above: Nonreligious Identity in the US and Canada* (Regina, SK: University of Regina Press, 2020); Reginald W. Bibby, Joel Thiessen, and Monetta Bailey, *The Millennial Mosaic: How Pluralism and Choice Are Shaping Canadian Youth and the Future of Canada* (Toronto: Dundurn Press, 2019); personal e-mail correspondence from Walter Sawatsky dated 27 November 2020 on trends in South America; and Will Braun, "A Picture of Gradual Decline: Giving to Nationwide and Regional Churches is Trending Downwards," *CM* 22 (30 May 2018), https://canadianmennonite.org/stories/picture-gradual-decline.
11 Charles Taylor, *Modern Social Imaginaries* (Durham, NC: Duke University Press, 2005), 186.
12 James Urry, *Mennonites, Politics, Peoplehood: Europe, Russia, Canada, 1525–1980* (Winnipeg: University of Manitoba Press, 2006), 257–9.
13 Steven D. Smith, *The Disenchantment of Secular Discourse* (Cambridge, MA: Harvard University Press, 2010); Gregory, *Unintended Reformation*; Zygmunt Bauman, *Liquid Life* (Cambridge, UK: Polity Press, 2005); and Charles Taylor, *The Malaise of Modernity* (Toronto: House of Anansi Press, 1991). For a similar argument to Steven Smith's, see Leonard G. Friesen, *Transcendent Love: Dostoevsky and the Search for a Global Ethic* (Notre Dame, IN: University of Notre Dame Press, 2016), 171–88.
14 See reports of commemorative events from around the world in *Mennonite Weekly Review*, *Der Bote*, and *Mennonitisches Rundschau*. On the context for the academic conference, see Leonard G. Friesen, "Dnipropetrovsk State University, Khortitsa '99, and the Renaissance of Public (Mennonite)

History in Ukraine," in *Minority Report: Mennonite Identities in Imperial Russia and Soviet Ukraine Reconsidered, 1789–1945*, ed. Leonard G. Friesen (Toronto: University of Toronto Press, 2018), 319–32.
15 Both modern Ukraine and Russia claim this much earlier state, which stretched along the Dnieper River and north through the Russian city of Novgorod to the Baltic.
16 For overviews of these days, see Walter Sawatsky, "Mennonites and Mission in Eurasia," *Mission in Focus: Annual Review* 13 (2005), 131–2; Helen Wiens, "200jährige Feier under der Eiche in Chortitza," *DB* (4 October 1989), 3; Hans von Niessen and John N. Klassen, "Gottes Führung – 200 Jahre Mennoniten in Russland. Jubilämsfeier in Chortitza, Schönwiese und Saporoshje," *DB* (1 November 1989), 3–5 and 11; Peter Dyck and Elfrieda Dyck, "Mennoniten feiern 200jähriges Jubiläum ihres Daseins in der Sowjetunion: neue Möglichkeiten für Evangelisation," *MR* (11 October 1989), 18–19; John N. Klassen, "Christen in Russland feiern und danken Gott für Seine Führung. Eine Jubiläumsfeier under der Eiche in Saporoshje: 200 Jahre Mennoniten in Russland," *MR* (25 October 1989), 18–21; and Neil Janzen, "USSR – Trip Report #1," http://artdefehr.com/wp-content/uploads/2013/05/Bl056-USSR-Trip-1-1989-08.pdf.
17 I was that young historian. Some of the information in this section comes from my notes from that visit to Zaporozhe.
18 *MR* (8 November 1989), 18.
19 Petr Epp, *100 let pod krovom Vsevyshnego: Istoriia Omskikh obshchina EKhB i ix ob'edineniia* (Omsk-Steinhagen: Samenkorn, 2007), 592–9.
20 Personal correspondence from Walter Sawatsky, June 2021.
21 *AQ* 115 (January–March 2020); and Sawatsky, "Mennonites and Mission," 131–4.
22 Walter Sawatsky, "Ripe unto Harvest (Karaganda, Kazakhstan, May 1998)," *Mennonite Life* 55 (June 2000), https://mla.bethelks.edu/ml-archive/2000june/sawatsky_ripe_harvest.html; Johannes P. Dyck, "War, Revolution & Cold War Upheavals in Eastern and Western Europe," *MF: Annual Review* 19 (2011), 140–8; and Walter Sawatsky, *Going Global with God as Mennonites for the 21st Century* (North Newton, KS: Bethel College, 2017), 36–8. In an e-mail written to me on 27 November 2020 Walter Sawatsky recalled a time he encountered six members of the Ethiopian Mennonite Church (Meserete Kristos Church) in the Tashkent (Uzbekistan) airport who had come because their church believed that it had much to learn from the Mennonite encounter with hostile regimes in the USSR. This gets at what I have in mind.

Bibliography

Unpublished

Duffield, Kari A. "Hieronymus Bosch in Context: A Re-Evaluation of the Artist through the Enlightened Thinking of Desiderius Erasmus." MA thesis. California State University, 2014.
Friesen, Aileen. "Religious Policy in the Russian Borderlands: The 1860s Mennonite Schism." MA Thesis. University of Alberta, 2007.
Klippenstein, Lawrence. "Mennonite Pacifism and State Service in Russia: A Case Study in Church-State Relations, 1789–1936." PhD diss. University of Minnesota, 1984.
Knight, Nathaniel. "Constructing the Science of Nationality: Ethnography in Mid-nineteenth Century Russia." PhD diss. Columbia University, 1994.
Letkemann, Peter. "The Hymnody and Choral Music of Mennonites in Russia 1789–1915." PhD diss. University of Toronto, 1985.
Malitska, Julia. "Negotiating Imperial Rule Colonists and Marriage in the Nineteenth-Century Black Sea Steppe." PhD diss. Södertörn University, 2017.
Moss, Christina. "An Examination of the Visions of Ursula Jost in the Context of Early Anabaptism and Late Medieval Christianity." MA Thesis. University of Waterloo, 2013.
Mukhina, Irina. "Reshaping Lives, Reconstructing Identities: Ethnic Germans of the Soviet Union, 1941–1956." PhD diss. Boston University, 2006.
Neufeldt, Colin. "The Fate of Mennonites in Soviet Ukraine and the Crimea on the Eve of the 'Second Revolution' (1927–1929)." MA thesis. University of Alberta, 1989.
– "The Fate of Mennonites in Ukraine and the Crimea during Soviet Collectivization and the Famine (1930–1933)." PhD diss. University of Alberta, 1999.

Osborne, Troy. "Saints into Citizens: Mennonite Discipline, Social Control, and Religious Toleration in the Dutch Golden Age." PhD diss. University of Minnesota, 2007.

Penner, Glenn. "Weapons Confiscated from Russian Mennonites in 1914, St. Petersburg Archives: Fond 821 Opis 133 Delo 322" (unpublished, n.d.).

Rempel, David G. "The Mennonite Colonies in New Russia: A Study of Their Settlement and Economic Development from 1789–1914." PhD diss. Stanford University, 1933.

Sawatsky, Walter. "Prince Alexander N. Golistyn (1773–1844): Tsarist Minister of Piety." PhD diss. University of Minnesota, 1976.

– "Journey of the Unwanted: Soviet Mennonite Deportation, Special Settlement, Exile and Exodus." n.d.

– "My Pilgrimage to the East." 20 January 2011.

Schmidt, Anni. "My Life on the Road." Waterloo, 2006.

Schmidt, Georg. "And Now I Shall Write from My Memories." Vineland, 1995.

Urry, James. "The Closed and the Open: Social and Religious Change amongst the Mennonites in Russia (1789–1889)." PhD diss. Oxford University, 1978.

Published

"Agrarnoe dvizhenie v Rossii v 1905–1906 gg." In *Trudy Imperatorskogo vol'nogo ekonomicheskogo obshchestva*, July–October 1908: 394–539.

Allen, William. *Life of William Allen with Selections from His Correspondence*. London, 1846.

Arendt, Hannah. *The Human Condition*. Chicago: University of Chicago Press, 1998.

Asad, Talal. *Genealogies of Religion: Discipline and Reasons of Power in Christianity and Islam*. Baltimore: Johns Hopkins University Press, 1993.

– *Formations of the Secular*. Stanford, CA: Stanford University Press, 2003.

Audisio, Gabriel. *The Waldensian Dissent Persecution and Survival, c.1170–c.1570*. Translated by Claire Davison. Cambridge: Cambridge University Press, 1999.

Augustijn, Cornelis. *Erasmus: His Life, Works, and Influence*. Toronto: University of Toronto Press, 1991.

Bainton, Roland H. *Erasmus of Christendom*. New York: Scribner, 1969.

Ball, Alan M. *Russia's Last Capitalists: The Nepmen, 1921–1929*. Berkeley: University of California Press, 1987.

– *And Now My Soul Is Hardened: Abandoned Children in Soviet Russia, 1918–1930*. Berkeley: University of California Press, 1994.

Barbier, Frédéric. *Gutenberg's Europe. The Book and the Invention of Western Modernity*. Cambridge, UK: Polity Press, 2017.

Barenberg, Alan. *Gulag Town, Company Town: Forced Labor and Its Legacy in Vorkuta*. New Haven, CT: Yale University Press, 2014.

Barnes, Steven A. "'All for the Front, All for Victory!' The Mobilization of Forced Labor in the Soviet Union during World War Two." In *International Labor and Working-Class History* 58 (Fall 2000): 239–60.
– *Death and Redemption. The Gulag and the Shaping of Soviet Society*. Princeton, NJ: Princeton University Press, 2011.
Bartlett, Roger. *Human Capital: The Settlement of Foreigners in Russia, 1762–1804*. Cambridge: Cambridge University Press, 1979.
– "Colonists, *Gastarbeiter*, and the Problems of Agriculture in Post-emancipation Russia." *Slavonic and East European Review* 60, no. 4 (1982): 547–71.
– "Her Imperial Majesty's Director and Curator of the Mennonite Colonies in Russia: Three Letters of Georg Trappe." *JMS* 12 (1994): 45–64.
Bauman, Zygmunt. *Liquid Modernity*. Cambridge, UK: Polity Press, 2000.
Baumann, Robert F. "Universal Service Reform and Russia's Imperial Dilemma." *War and Society* 4, no. 2 (1986): 31–49.
– "Universal Service Reform: Conception to Implementation, 1873–1883." In *Reforming the Tsar's Army: Military Innovation in Imperial Russia from Peter the Great to the Revolution*, edited by David Schimmelpenninck van der Oye and Bruce W. Menning. Cambridge: Cambridge University Press, 2004.
Beeson, Trevor. *Discretion and Valour: Religious Conditions in Russia and Eastern Europe*. Glasgow: Collins Publishers, 1974.
Bekker, Jacob P. *Origin of the Mennonite Brethren Church. Previously Unpublished Manuscript by One of the Eighteen Founders*. Translated by D.E. Pauls and A.E. Janzen. Hillsboro, KS: Mennonite Brethren Publishing House, 1973.
Belk, Fred R. *The Great Trek of the Russian Mennonites to Central Asia, 1880–1884*. Scottdale, PA: Herald Press, 1976.
Bell, Wilson T. *Stalin's Gulag at War: Forced Labour, Mass Death, and Soviet Victory in the Second World War*. Toronto: University of Toronto Press, 2019.
Bender, Harold S. "Der Mennonit (Periodical)." *GAMEO*, 1957, https://gameo.org/index.php?title=Mennonit,_Der_(Periodical)&oldid=134661.
Bender, Harold S., Samuel J. Steiner, and Richard D. Thiessen. "World Mennonite Membership Distribution." *GAMEO*, January 2013, https://gameo.org/index.php?title=World_Mennonite_Membership_Distribution.
Bender, Harold S., and Richard D. Thiessen. "Klassen, Cornelius Franz 'C. F.' (1894–1954)." *GAMEO*, May 2013, https://gameo.org/index.php?title=Klassen,_Cornelius_Franz_%22C._F.%22_(1894–1954)&oldid=168316.
Berg, Abram. *Dietrich Heinrich Epp. Aus seinem Leben, Wirken und selbstaufgezeichneten Erinnerungen*. Saskatoon: Heese House of Printing, 1973.
Berg, Wesley. *From Russia with Music: A Study of the Mennonite Choral Singing Tradition in Canada*. Winnipeg: Hyperion Press, 1985.
Bergen, Heinrich, ed. *Verbannung. Unschuldig nach Sibirien ins Verderben, 1935–1955*. Regina, SK: n.p., 2006.

Bergmann, Cornelius, and Cornelius Krahn. "Chortitza Mennonite Settlement (Zaporizhia Oblast, Ukraine)." GAMEO, 1955, https://gameo.org/index.php?title=Chortitza_Mennonite_Settlement_(Zaporizhia_Oblast,_Ukraine)&oldid=156357.

Berkhoff, Karel C. *Harvest of Despair: Life and Death in Ukraine under Soviet Rule.* Cambridge, MA: The Belknap Press of Harvard University Press, 2004.

Beznosov, Alexander I. "Mennonity Iuga Ukrainy v gody 'velikogo pereloma' (1928–1933 gg.)." In *Voprosy germanskoi istorii. Sbornik nauchnykh trudov.* Dnepropetrovsk, Ukraine: n.p., 2001.

– "Kulak, Christian, and German: Ukrainian Mennonite Identities in a Time of Famine." In *Minority Report: Mennonite Identities in Imperial Russia and Soviet Ukraine Reconsidered, 1789–1945*, edited by Leonard G. Friesen, 260–86. Toronto: University of Toronto Press, 2018.

Beznosova, Oksana. "Prichiny vozniknoveniia antigermanskoi kampanii v Rossiiskoi imperii nakanune Pervoi mirovoi voiny (na premere Ekaterinoslavskoi gubernii)." In *Voprosy germanskoi istorii*, 50–8. Dnepropetrovsk, Ukraine: DNY, 2010.

– *Ekaterinoslavskaia guberniia: terra incognita evangel'skogo dvizheniia v Rossiiskoi imperii (seredina xviii v. – 1917 g.).* Steinhagen, Germany: Samenkorn, 2014.

– "The Ukrainian Evangelicals under Pressure from the NKVD, 1928–1939." In *Ethnic and Religious Minorities in Stalin's Soviet Union: New Dimensions of Research*, edited by Andrej Kotljarchuk and Olle Sundström, 175–98. Huddinge, Sweden: Södertörn University, 2017.

– "A Foreign Faith, but of What Sort? The Mennonite Church and the Russian Empire, 1789–1917." In *Minority Report: Mennonite Identities in Imperial Russia and Soviet Ukraine Reconsidered*, edited by Leonard G. Friesen, 110–41. Toronto: University of Toronto Press, 2018.

Beznosova, Oksana, and Aleksandr Beznosov. "'Religioznaia zhizn' Mennonitov v seredine 20-x gg. XX ct. glazami sovetskoi politicheskoi politsii na premere poseleniia Fiurstenland." In *History and Mission in Europe: Continuing the Conversation*, edited by Mary Raber and Peter F. Penner, 33–48. Schwarzenfeld, Germany: Neufeld Verlag, 2011.

Bibby, Reginald W., Joel Thiessen, and Monetta Bailey. *The Millennial Mosaic: How Pluralism and Choice Are Shaping Canadian Youth and the Future of Canada.* Toronto: Dundurn Press, 2019.

Bobyleva, Svetlana. "'Land of Opportunity, Sites of Devastation': Notes on the History of the Borozenko Colony." In *Minority Report. Mennonite Identities in Imperial Russia and Soviet Ukraine Reconsidered, 1789–1945*, edited by Leonard G. Friesen, 25–60. Toronto: University of Toronto Press, 2018.

Bogucka, Maria. *Das alte Danzig. Alltagsleben vom 15. bis 17. Jahrhundert.* Leipzig: Koehler & Amelang, 1980.

Bondar, S.D. *Sekta mennonitov Rossii, v sviazi s istoriei nemetskoi kolonizatsii na iuge Rossii*. Petrograd: 1916.
Braght, Thieleman van. *Martyrs Mirror: The Story of Seventeen Centuries of Christian Martyrdom from the Time of Christ to A.D. 1660*. Translated by Joseph F. Sohm. Scottdale, PA: Herald Press, 1950.
Brandes, Detlef. *Von Den Zaren Adoptiert. Die Deutschen Kolonisten und Die Balkansiedler in Neurussland und Bessarabien, 1751–1914*. Munich: R. Oldenbourg Verlag, 1993.
Brandes, Detlef, and Andrej Savin. *Die Sibieriendeutschen im Sowjetstaadt 1989–1938*. Essen: Klartext Verlag, 2001.
Braun, Peter. *Kto Takie Mennonity? Kratkii istoricheskii ocherk*. Halbstadt: Raduga, 1914.
– "The Educational System of the Mennonite Colonies in South Russia." *MQR* 3 (1929): 175–8.
Braun, Will. "A Picture of Gradual Decline: Giving to Nationwide and Regional Churches Is Trending Downwards." *CM* 22 (30 May 2018), https://canadianmennonite.org/stories/picture-gradual-decline.
Brown, Andrew. "Peter Wiens and Georgi Vins: Faith Strengthened by Trial." In *Profiles of Mennonite Faith*. (Fall 2016): 1–2.
Brown, Kate. *A Biography of No Place from Ethnic Borderland to Soviet Heartland*. Cambridge, MA: Harvard University Press, 2005.
Brucks, Jacob H. "World War, Revolution and Famine." In *Neu-Samara. A Mennonite Settlement East of the Volga*, edited by Tina Wiebe, compiled by Jacob H. Brucks and Henry P. Hooge, translated by John Isaak, 119–51. Edmonton, AB: Jackpine House Ltd., 2002.
Bruhl, Viktor. "Deutsche Frauen in der Sondersiedlung und in den Arbeitskolonnen in den Jahren 1941–48." In *Von der Autonomiegründung zur Verbannung und Entrechtung. Die Jahre 1918 und 1941 bis 1948 in der Geschichte der Deutschen in Russland*, edited by Alfred Eisfeld, 162–79. Stuffgart, 2008.
Brunk, Gerald R., ed. *Menno Simons: A Reappraisal. Essays in Honour of Irvin B. Horst on the 450th Anniversary of the Fundamentboek*. Harrisonburg, VA: Eastern Mennonite College, 1992.
Burds, Jeffrey. *Peasant Dreams and Market Politics: Labor Migration and the Russian Village, 1861–1905*. Pittsburgh: University of Pittsburgh Press, 1998.
Cameron, Sarah. *The Hungry Steppe: Famine, Violence, and the Making of Soviet Kazakhstan*. Ithaca, NY: Cornell University Press, 2018.
Campbell, Ted A. *The Religion of the Heart: A Study of European Religious Life in the Seventeenth and Eighteenth Centuries*. Columbia: University of South Carolina Press, 1991.
Campi, Emidio. "The Reformation in Zurich." In *A Companion to the Swiss Reformation*, edited by Amy Nelson Burnett and Emidio Campi, 59–125. Leiden: Brill, 2016.

Carstensen, Fred V. *American Enterprise in Foreign Markets: Studies of Singer and International Harvester in Imperial Russia*. Chapel Hill: University of North Carolina Press, 1984.

Cherkazianova (Tscherkazjanowa), Irina (Janzen). "Die Kinder der Russlanddeutschen under den Verhältnissen von Deportation, Trudarmee und Sondersiedlung." In *Von der Autonomiegründung zur Verbannung und Entrechtung. Die Jahre 1918 und 1941 bis 1948 in der Geschichte der Deutschen in Russland*, edited by Alfred Eisfeld, 180–203. Stuttgart: Heimatbücher der Landsmannschaft der Deutschen aus Russland e.V, 2008.

– "Mennonite Schools and the Russian Empire: The Transformation of Church-State Relations in Education, 1789–1917." In *Minority Report: Mennonite Identities in Imperial Russia and Soviet Ukraine Reconsidered, 1789–1945*, edited by Leonard G. Friesen, 85–109. Toronto: University of Toronto Press, 2018.

Christian, David. *Living Water: Vodka and Russian Society on the Eve of Emancipation*. Oxford: Oxford University Press, 1990.

Christ-von Wedel, Christine. *Erasmus of Rotterdam. Advocate of a New Christianity*. Toronto: University of Toronto Press, 2013.

Chumachenko, Tatiana A. *Church and State in Soviet Russia: Russian Orthodoxy from World War II to the Khrushchev Years*. New York: Routledge, 2015.

Clasen, Claus-Peter. *Anabaptism: A Social History, 1525–1618. Switzerland, Austria, Moravia, South and Central Germany*. Ithaca, NY: Cornell University Press, 1972.

Coffey, John, ed. *Heart Religion: Evangelical Piety in England & Ireland, 1690–1850*. Oxford: Oxford University Press, 2016.

Cohen, Stephen F. *Rethinking the Soviet Experience: Politics and History Since 1917*. Oxford: Oxford University Press, 1985.

Coleman, Heather. *Russian Baptists and Spiritual Revolution, 1905–1929*. Bloomington: Indiana University Press, 2005.

– "Theology on the Ground: Dmitrii Bogoliubov, the Orthodox Anti-Sectarian Mission, and the Russian Soul." In *Thinking Orthodox in Modern Russia: Culture, History, Context*, edited by Patrick Lally Michelson, and Judith Deutsch Korn, 64–84. Madison: University of Wisconsin Press, 2014.

Conquest, Robert. *The Harvest of Sorrow: Soviet Collectivization and the Terror-Famine*. Edmonton: University of Alberta Press, 1986.

Corley, Felix. *Religion in the Soviet Union: An Archival Reader*. New York: New York University Press, 1996.

Crews, Robert. "Empire and the Confessional State: Islam and Religious Politics in Nineteenth-Century Russia." *AHR* 108, no. 1 (2003): 50–83.

Cuny, George. *Danzigs Kunst und Kultur im 16 und 17 Jahrhundert*. Frankfurt am Main: Heinrich Keller, 1910.

David-Fox, Michael. *Crossing Borders: Modernity, Ideology, and Culture in Russia and the Soviet Union*. Pittsburgh: University of Pittsburgh Press, 2015.
Davies, Norman. *God's Playground: A History of Poland*. Volume 1: *The Origins to 1795*. Revised edition. New York: Columbia University Press, 2005.
Davies, R.W., and Stephen Wheatcroft. *The Years of Hunger: Soviet Agriculture, 1931–1933*. Basingstoke, UK: Palgrave Macmillan, 2004.
Deppermann, Klaus. *Melchior Hoffman: Social Unrest and Apocalyptic Visions in the Age of Reformation*. Translated by Malcolm Wren. Edinburgh: T. & T. Clark, 1987.
Dik, Viktor. *Svet Evangeliia v Kazakhstane: Evangel'skie techeniia v pervoi polovine XX veka*. Steinhagen, Germany: Samenkorn, 2003.
Dipple, Geoffrey. "Anabaptism Spiritualists." In *A Companion to Anabaptism and Spiritualism, 1521–1700*, edited by James M. Stayer and John D. Roth, 257–97. Leiden: Brill Publishers, 2007.
Dowler, Wayne. *Russia in 1913*. DeKalb: Northern Illinois University Press, 2012.
Driedger, Leo. "From Martyrs to Muppies: The Mennonite Urban Professional Revolution." *MQR* 67, no. 3 (1993): 304–22.
Driedger, Michael D. *Obedient Heretics: Mennonite Identities in Lutheran Hamburg and Altona during the Confessional Age*. Aldershot: Ashgate, 2002.
– "Münster, Monster, Modernity: Tracing and Challenging the Meme of Anabaptist Madness." In *European Mennonites and the Challenge of Modernity over Five Centuries: Contributors, Detractors, and Adapters*, edited by Mark Jantzen, Mary S. Springer, and John D. Thiesen, 27–50. North Newton, KS: Bethel College, 2016.
Driedger, N.N., and Richard D. Thiessen. "Janzen, Jacob H. (1878–1950)." *GAMEO*, March 2009, https://gameo.org/index.php?title=Janzen,_Jacob_H._(1878–1950)&oldid=140933.
Druzhinina, E.I. *Severnoe prichernomore v 1775–1880 gg.* Moscow: n.p., 1959.
– *IUzhnaia Ukraina v 1800–1825 gg.* Moscow: n.p., 1970.
– *IUzhnaia Ukraina v periode krizisa feodalizma, 1825–1860 gg.* Moscow: n.p., 1981.
Dueck, Abe. "Class Epp and the Great Trek Reconsidered." *JMS* 3 (1985): 138–47.
– "Mennonite Churches and Religious Developments in Russia, 1850–1914." In *Mennonites in Russia, 1788–1988: Essays in Honour of Gerhard Lohrenz*, edited by John Friesen, 149–82. Winnipeg: CMBC Publications, 1989.
– "Mennonites, the Russian State, and the Crisis of Brethren and Old Church Relations in Russia, 1900–1918." *MQR* 69 (1995): 453–85.
– *Moving beyond Secession: Defining Russian Mennonite Brethren Mission and Identity 1872–1922*. Winnipeg: Kindred Press, 1997.
– "The Quest for a Mennonite Seminary in Russia, 1883–1926: Signs of a Changing Mennonite World." *MQR* 74 (2000): 448–55.

- "Peter Martinovitch Friesen (1849–1914)." In *Shepherds, Servants and Prophets: Leadership among the Russian Mennonites (ca. 1880–1960)*, edited by Harry Loewen. 131-48. Kitchener, ON: Pandora Press, 2003.
Duke, Alastair. *Reformation and Revolt in The Low Countries*. London: The Hambledon Press, 1990.
Durksen, Martin. *Die Krim war Unsere Heimat*. Winnipeg: Martin Durksen, 1980.
Dyck, Cornelius J. *An Introduction to Mennonite History: A Popular History of the Anabaptists and the Mennonites*. Third edition. Scottdale, PA: Herald Press, 1993.
Dyck, Harvey L. *Weimar German and Soviet Russia 1926–1933: A Study in Diplomatic Instability*. London: Chatto and Windus, 1966.
–, trans. and ed. "Russian Mennonitism and the Challenge of Russian Nationalism." *MQR* 56 (1982): 306–41.
- "Russian Servitor and Mennonite Hero: Light and Shadow in Images of Johann Cornies." *JMS* 2 (1984): 9–28.
Dyck, Harvey L., and Ingrid I. Epp. *The Peter J. Braun Russian Mennonite Archive: A Research Guide*. Toronto: University of Toronto Press, 1996.
Dyck, Harvey L., Ingrid I. Epp, and John R. Staples, eds. *Transformation on the Southern Ukraine Steppe: Letters and Papers of Johann Cornies*. Volume I: *1812–1835*. Toronto: University of Toronto Press, 2015; and Volume II: *1836–1842*. Toronto: University of Toronto Press, 2020.
Dyck, Harvey L., John R. Staples, and John B. Toews, eds. *Nestor Makhno and the Eichenfeld Massacre: A Civil War Tragedy in a Ukrainian Mennonite Village*. Kitchener: Pandora Press, 2004.
Dyck, Johannes J. *Am Trakt: A Mennonite Settlement in the Central Volga Region*. Based on a text by W.E, Surukin. Winnipeg: CMBC Publications, 1995.
Dyck, Johannes P. "Johannes – Gott is gnädig." In Johannes Fast, *Er gibt dem Müden Kraft: 63 Predigten aus 1973–78*, 9–22. Steinhagen, Germany: Samenkorn, 2004.
- "Revival as Church Restoration: Patterns of a Revival among Ethnic Germans in Central Asia after World War II." *Transformation: An International Journal of Holistic Mission Studies* (2004): 174–80.
- "Revival as Church Restoration: Patterns of a Revival among Ethnic Germans in Central Asia after World War II." In *Mission in the Former Soviet Union*, edited by Walter W. Sawatsky and Peter F. Penner, 74–93. Schwarzenfeld, Germany: Neufeld Verlag, 2005.
- "Elements of Post-Gulag Mennonite Theology: View of an Eyewitness." In *History and Mission in Europe: Continuing the Conversation*, edited by Mary Raber and Peter F. Penner, 199–212. Schwarzenfeld, Germany: Neufeld Verlag, 2011.
- "Frauen als Säulen der Erweckung." In *History and Mission in Europe: Continuing the Conversation*, edited by Mary Raber and Peter F. Penner, 179–96. Schwarzenfeld, Germany: Neufeld Verlag, 2011.

- "War, Revolution & Cold War Upheavals in Eastern and Western Europe." *MF: Annual Review* 19 (2011): 140–8.
- "A Root out of Dry Ground: Revival Patterns in the German Free Churches in the USSR after World War II." *JMS* 30 (2012): 97–112.
- "Mennonites as Catalytic Agents in Free Church History in Russia and the Soviet Union." In *European Mennonites and the Challenge of Modernity over Five Centuries: Contributors, Detractors, and Adapters*, edited by Mark Jantzen, Mary S. Sprunger, and John D. Thiesen, 249–61. North Newton, KS: Bethel College, 2016.
- "Mennonity Severnoi Ameriki I SSSR v seredine 1950e godov: malen'kie liudi I vol'shaia politika." *Gosudarstvo, Religiia, Tserkov* 35 (2017): 123–46.

Dyck, John P., ed. *Troubles and Triumphs 1914–1924: Excerpts from the Diary of Peter J. Dyck, Ladekopp, Molotschna Colony, Ukraine*. Springstein, MB: n.p., 1981.

Dyck, Peter P. *Orenburg am Ural: die Geshichte einer mennonitischen Ansiedlung in Russland*. Clearbrook, BC: The Christian Book Store, 1951.

Dyck, Peter P., and Elfrieda Dyck. "Mennoniten feiern 200jähriges Jubiläum ihres Daseins in der Sowjetunion: neue Möglichkeiten für Evangelisation." *MR* (11 October 1989): 18–19.

- *Up from the Rubble*. Scottdale, PA: Herald Press, 1991.

Dyck, Sarah, ed. and trans. *The Silence Echoes: Memoirs of Trauma and Tears*. Kitchener, ON: Pandora Press, 1997.

Edele, Mark. *The Soviet Union: A Short History*. Hoboken: Wiley Blackwell, 2019.

Ediger, Katharina, and Elizabeth Schulz. *Under His Wings: Events in the Lives of Elder Alexander Ediger and His Family*. Kitchener: 1994.

Ehrt, Adolf. *Das Mennonitentum in Russland vom seiner Einwanderung bis zur Gegenwart*. Langensalza, Germany: Julious Belz, 1932.

Eicher, John P.R. *Exiled among Nations: German and Mennonite Mythologies in a Transnational Age*. Cambridge: Cambridge University Press, 2020.

Eire, Carlos M.N. *Reformations. The Early Modern World, 1450–1650*. New Haven, CT: Yale University Press, 2016.

Eisfeld, Alfred, and Viktor Herdt, eds. *Deportation, Sondersiedlung, Arbeitsarmee: Deutsche in der Sowjetunion 1941 bis 1956*. Köln, Germany: Verlag Wissenschaft und Politik, 1996.

–, eds. *Von der Autonomiegründung zur Verbannung und Entrechtung. Die Jahre 1918 und 1941 bis 1948 in der Geschichte der Deutschen in Russland*. Stuttgart, Germany: n.p., 2008

Eklof, Ben. *Russian Peasant Schools: Officialdom, Village Schools and Popular Pedagogy 1861–1914*. Bloomington: Indiana University Press, 1986.

Eklof, Ben, John Bushnell, and Larissa Zakharova, eds. *Russia's Great Reforms, 1855–1881*. Bloomington: Indiana University Press, 1994.

Elliott, Mark. *Pawns of Yalta: Soviet Refugees and America's Role in Their Repatriation*. Champaign: University of Illinois Press, 1982.

Ens, Adolf. "Mennonite Education in Russia." In *Mennonites in Russia, 1788–1988: Essays in Honour of Gerhard Lohrenz*, edited by John Friesen, 75–98. Winnipeg: CMBC Publications, 1989.

Enstad, Johannes Due. *Soviet Russians under Nazi Occupation: Fragile Loyalties in World War II*. Cambridge: Cambridge University Press, 2018.

Epp, David H. *Die Chortitzer Mennoniten: Versuch einer Darstellung des Entwicklungsganges derselben*. Odessa: A. Schulze, 1889.

– *Kurze Erklärungen und Erläuterungen zum "Katechismus der christlichen, taufgesinnten Gemeinden, so Mennoniten genannt werden"* Odessa: A. Schultze, 1896. Second edition. Ekaterinoslav: D.H. Epp, 1899 [Reprinted Rosthern: Dietrich Epp Verlag, 1941].

– *Sketches from the Pioneer Years of the Industry in the Mennonite Settlements of South Russia*. Translated by J.P. Penner from articles in *DB*, 13 July 1938 to 18 January 1939. N.P., March 1972.

– "The Emergence of German Industry in the South Russian Colonies." Translated and edited by John B. Toews. *MQR* 55 (1981): 289–371.

– *Johann Cornies*. Winnipeg: CMBC Publications, 1995.

Epp, Frank H. *Mennonite Exodus: The Rescue and Resettlement of the Russian Mennonites since the Communist Revolution*. Altona: D.W. Friesen, 1962.

– *Mennonites in Canada, 1786–1920: The History of a Separate People*. Toronto: Macmillan, 1974.

– *Mennonites in Canada, 1920–1940. A People's Struggle for Survival*. Toronto: Macmillan, 1982.

Epp, George K. "Urban Mennonites in Russia." In *Mennonites in Russia 1788–1988. Essays in Honour of Gerhard Lohrenz*, edited by John Friesen, 239–60. Winnipeg: CMBC Publications, 1989.

– "World War (1939–1945) – Soviet Union." *GAMEO*, 1989, https://gameo.org/index.php?title=World_War_(1939–1945)_-_Soviet_Union&oldid=163501.

Epp, Ingrid H., and Harvey L. Dyck, eds. *The Peter J. Braun Archive 1803–1920*. Toronto: University of Toronto Press, 1996.

Epp, Jacob D. *A Mennonite in Russia: The Diaries of Jacob D. Epp 1851–1880*. Translated and edited by Harvey L. Dyck. Toronto: University of Toronto Press, 1991.

Epp, Marlene. *Women without Men: Mennonite Refugees of the Second World War*. Toronto: University of Toronto Press, 2000.

Epp, Peter. *Ob tausent fallen ... Mein Leben im Archipel Gulag*. Weichs, Germany: Memra-Verlag, 1988.

– "The Advent of Atheism." In *The Silence Echoes. Memoirs of Trauma and Tears*, edited and translated by Sarah Dyck, 73–6. Kitchener, ON: Pandora Press, 1997.

- *100 let pod krovom Vsyvyshnego: Istorria Omskikh obshchin EkkB ikh ob'edineniia, 1907–2007*. Omsk, Russia: Samenkorn, 2007.
- "A Brief History of the Omsk Brotherhood." *JMS* (2012): 114–32.

Epp-Tiessen, Esther. *Mennonite Central Committee in Canada: A History*. Winnipeg: CMU Press, 2013.

Epstein, Catherine. *Model Nazi: Arthur Greiser and the Occupation of Western Poland*. Oxford: Oxford University Press, 2010.

Fast, Gerhard. *Das Ende von Chortitza*. Winnipeg: Selbstverlag, 1973.

Fast, Johannes. *Er gibt dem Müden Kraft: 63 Predigten aus 1973–78*. Steinhagen, Germany: Samenkorn, 2004.

Fast, Karl. *Gebt der Wahrheit de Ehre! Ein Schicksalbericht*. Second edition. Winnipeg: Canzona Publications, 1989.
- *Orenburg: die letzte Mennonische Ansiedlung in Osteuropa*. Winnipeg: Das Bunte Fenster, 1995.

Fast, Viktor, ed. *IA s vami vo vse dni do skonchaniia veka. Volume 1. Tiazhelye vremena gonenii i repressii 1931–1946*. Karaganda: Shtainkhagen, 2001.

Fast, Viktor, and Jakob Penner, eds. *Wasserströme in der Einöde. Die Anfangsgeschichte der Mennoniten-Brüdergemeinde Karaganda 1956–1968*. Steinhagen, Germany: Samenkorn, 2007.
- *Vorübergehende Heimat: 150 Jahre Beten und Arbeiten in Alt-Samara (Alexandertal und Konstantinow)*. Steinhagen, Germany: Samenkorn, 2009.

Fitzpatrick, Sheila, ed. *Cultural Revolution in Russia, 1928–1931*. Bloomington: Indiana University Press, 1984.
- *Stalin's Peasants: Resistance and Survival in the Russian Village after Collectivization*. Oxford: Oxford University Press, 1994.
- *Tear Off the Masks! Identity and Imposture in Twentieth-Century Russia*. Princeton, NJ: Princeton University Press, 2005.

Fleischhauer, Ingeborg. *Das Dritte Reich und die Deutschen in der Sowjetunion*. Stuttgart, Germany: Deutsche Verlags-Anstalt, 1983.

Francis, E.K. "The Russian Mennonites: From Religious Group to Ethnic Group." *American Journal of Sociology* 54 (1948): 101–7.
- *In Search of Utopia: The Mennonites in Manitoba*. Altona, Germany: D.W. Friesen, 1955.

Freeze, Gregory. "The *Soslovie* (Estate) Paradigm and Russian Social History." *AHR* 91 (1986): 11–36.
- "The Stalinist Assault on the Parish, 1929–1941." In *Stalinismus vor dem Zweiten Weltkrieg: Neue Wege der Forschung*, edited by Manfred Hildermeier, 209–32. Munich: Oldenburg Verlag, 1998.
- "Subversive Atheism: Soviet Antireligious Campaigns and the Religious Revival in Ukraine in the 1920s." In *State Secularism and Lived Religion in Soviet Russia and Ukraine*, edited by Catherine Wanner, 27–62. Oxford: Oxford University Press, 2012.

Friedgut, Theodore H. *Iuzovka and Revolution*. 2 vols. Princeton, NJ: Princeton University Press, 1989–94.
Friedmann, Robert. "Devotional Literature of the Mennonites in Danzig and Prussia to 1800." *MQR* 18 (1944): 162–73.
– *Mennonite Piety through the Centuries: Its Genius and Its Literature*. Goshen, IN: Mennonite Historical Society. 1949.
Friedrich, Karin. *The Other Prussia: Royal Prussia, Poland and Liberty, 1569–1772*. Cambridge: Cambridge University Press, 2000.
Friesen, Abraham. "Menno and Münster: The Man and the Movement." In *Menno Simons: A Reappraisal. Essays in Honour of Irvin B. Horst on the 450th Anniversary of the Fundamentboek*, edited by Gerald R. Brunk, 131–62. Harrisonburg, VA: Eastern Mennonite College, 1992.
– *History and Renewal in the Anabaptist/Mennonite Tradition*. North Newton, KS: Bethel College, 1994.
– "Peter J. Braun: Educator, Archivist, Scholar 1880–1933." In *Shepherds, Servants and Prophets: Leadership among the Russian Mennonites (ca. 1880–1960)*, edited by Harry Loewen, 47–68. Kitchener, ON: Pandora Press, 2003.
– *In Defence of Privilege: Russian Mennonites and the State before and during World War I*. Winnipeg: Kindred Publications, 2006.
– *Menno Simons: Dutch Reformer between Luther, Erasmus, and the Holy Spirit: A Study in the Problem Areas of Menno Scholarship*. Bloomington, IN: Xlibris, 2015.
Friesen, Abram J., Victor G. Doerksen, and Abram J. Loewen. *Escape across the Amur River: a Mennonite Village Flees (1930) from Soviet Siberia to Chinese Manchuria*. Winnipeg: CMBC Publications, 2001.
Friesen, Aileen. "Soviet Mennonites, the Holocaust & Nazism." *Anabaptist Historians* (25 April 2017).
– *Colonizing Russia's Promised Land: Orthodoxy and Community on the Siberian Steppe*. Toronto: University of Toronto Press, 2020.
– "A Portrait of Khortytsya/Zaporizhzhia under Occupation." In *European Mennonites and the Holocaust*, edited by Mark Jantzen and John D. Thiesen, 229–49. Toronto: University of Toronto Press, 2020.
Friesen, Helena Goossen. *Daydreams and Nightmares: Life on the Wintergruen Estate*. Winnipeg: CMBC Publications, 1990.
Friesen, John J. "The Relationship of Prussian Mennonites to German Nationalism." In *Mennonite Images: Historical, Cultural, and Literary Essays Dealing with Mennonite Issues*, edited by Harry Loewen, 61–72. Winnipeg: Hyperion Press, 1980.
– "Mennonite Churches and Religious Developments in Russia, 1789–1850." In *Mennonites in Russia, 1788–1988: Essays in Honour of Gerhard Lohrenz*, edited by John J. Friesen, 43–74. Winnipeg: CMBC Publications, 1989.

–, ed. *Mennonites in Russia, 1788–1988: Essays in Honour of Gerhard Lohrenz*. Winnipeg: CMBC Publications, 1989.
– *Against the Wind: The Story of Four Mennonite Villages*. Winnipeg: Kindred Publications, 1994.
Friesen, Leonard G. "Mennonites in the Russian Revolution of 1905: Experiences, Perceptions and Responses." *MQR* 62 (1988): 42–55.
– "Mennonites and Their Peasant Neighbours in Ukraine before 1900." *JMS* 10 (1992): 56–69.
– "Bukkers, Plows and Lobogreikas: Peasant Acquisition of Agricultural Implements in New Russia before 1900." *RR* 53 (1994): 399–418.
–, ed. *Lifting the Veil: Mennonite Life in Russia before the Revolution*, by Jacob H. Janzen. Kitchener, ON: Pandora Press, 1998.
– "More than Sheep to Slaughter: Reflections on Mennonites and the Stalinist Terror." *CGR* 18, no. 2 (Spring 2000): 69–73.
– *Rural Revolutions in Southern Ukraine: Peasants, Nobles, and Colonists, 1774–1905*. Cambridge, MA: Harvard Ukrainian Research Institute, 2008.
– *Transcendent Love: Dostoevsky and the Search for a Global Ethic*. Notre Dame, IN: University of Notre Dame Press, 2016.
– "Acknowledgements." In *Minority Report: Mennonite Identities in Imperial Russia and Soviet Ukraine Reconsidered, 1789–1945*, edited by Leonard G. Friesen, ix–x. Toronto: University of Toronto Press, 2018.
– "Dnipropetrovsk State University, Khortitsa '99, and the Renaissance of Public (Mennonite) History in Ukraine." In *Minority Report: Mennonite Identities in Imperial Russia and Soviet Ukraine Reconsidered, 1789–1945*, edited by Leonard G. Friesen, 319–32. Toronto: University of Toronto Press, 2018.
– "Introduction." In *Minority Report: Mennonite Identities in Imperial Russia and Soviet Ukraine Reconsidered, 1789–1945*, edited by Leonard G. Friesen, 3–24. Toronto: University of Toronto Press, 2018.
–, ed. *Minority Report: Mennonite Identities in Imperial Russia and Soviet Ukraine Reconsidered, 1789–1945*. Toronto: University of Toronto Press, 2018.
Friesen, Peter M. *Die Alt-Evangelische Mennonitische Brüderschaft in Russland (1789–1910), im Rahmen der Mennonitischen Gesamtgeschichte*. Halbstadt: n.p., 1911.
– *The Mennonite Brotherhood in Russia, 1789–1910*. Translated by John B. Toews et al. Fresno: Board of Christian Literature. General Conference of the Mennonite Brethren Conference of Mennonite Brethren Churches, 1978.
– *The Mennonite Brotherhood in Russia, 1789–1910*. 2nd ed. Translated by John B. Toews et al. Fresno: Board of Christian Literature. General Conference of the Mennonite Brethren Conference of Mennonite Brethren Churches, 1980.
Friesen, Rudy P., with Edith Elisabeth Friesen. *Building on the Past. Mennonite Architecture, Landscape and Settlements in Russia/Ukraine*. Moscow: Raduga Publications, 2004.

Froese, Peter F. "Allrussischer Mennonitischer Landwirtschaftlicher Verein." *GAMEO*, 1955, https://gameo.org/index.php?title=Allrussischer_Mennonitischer_Landwirtschaftlicher_Verein&oldid=132606.

Gatrell, Peter. *A Whole Empire Walking: Refugees in Russia during World War I*. Bloomington: Indiana University Press, 1999.

Geertz, Clifford. *The Interpretation of Cultures: Selected Essays*. New York: Basic Books, 1973.

Gelderblom, Oscar. "The Organization of Long-Distance Trade in England and the Dutch Republic, 1550–1650." In *The Political Economy of the Dutch Republic*, edited by Oscar Gelderblom, 223–54. Abingdon: Routledge, 2016.

Gerbrandt, Jacob. "Canadian Mennonite Board of Colonization." *GAMEO*, September 2011, https://gameo.org/index.php?title=Canadian_Mennonite_Board_of_Colonization&oldid=167400.

Gerlach, Horst. "Mennonites, the Molotschna, and the Volksdeutsche Mittelstelle in the Second World War." *ML* 41, no. 3 (1986): 4–9.

– *Die Russlandmennoniten: Ein Volk Unterwegs*. Third edition. Weierhof, Germany: n.p., 1998.

Getty, J. Arch, and Oleg V. Naumov. *Yezhov: The Rise of Stalin's "Iron Fist."* New Haven, CT: Yale University Press, 2008.

– *Practicing Stalinism: Bolsheviks, Boyars, and the Persistence of Tradition*. New Haven, CT: Yale University Press, 2013.

Ghosh, P. "Max Weber in the Netherlands 1903–1907: A Neglected Episode in the Early History of 'The Protestant Ethic.'" *Low Countries Historical Review* 119 (2014): 358–77.

Gierl, Martin. "Pietism, Enlightenment and Modernity." In *A Companion to German Pietism, 1660–1800*, edited by Douglas H. Shantz, 348–92. Leiden: Brill, 2014.

Glete, Jan. *War and the State in Early Modern Europe: Spain, the Dutch Republic and Sweden as Fiscal-Military States*. London: Routledge, 2001.

Goossen, Benjamin. *Chosen Nation: Mennonites and Germany in a Global Era*. Princeton, NJ: Princeton University Press, 2017.

"Gorbachev Confronts the Challenge of Christianity." Central Intelligence Agency Freedom of Information Act Electronic Reading Room, https://www.cia.gov/readingroom/docs/DOC_0000498825.pdf.

Görz (Goerz), H. *Die Molotschnaer Ansiedlung: Entstehung, Entwicklung, und Untergang*. Steinbach, MB: Echo Verlag, 1950.

– *Mennonite Settlements in Crimea*. Winnipeg: CMBC Publications, 1992.

Granados, José. "From Flesh to Flesh: On the Sacramental Meaning of Tradition." *Communio: International Catholic Review* 44 (Winter 2017): 643–66.

Greene, Robert H. *Bodies Like Bright Stars: Saints and Relics in Orthodox Russia*. DeKalb: Northern Illinois University Press, 2009.

Gregory, Brad S. *Salvation at Stake: Christian Martyrdom in Early Modern Europe*. Cambridge: Cambridge University Press, 1999.
– *The Unintended Reformation: How a Religious Revolution Secularized Society*. Cambridge, MA: Harvard University Press, 2012.
– "The One or the Many? Narrating and Evaluating Western Secularization." *Intellectual History Review* 27 (January 2017): 31–46.
– *Rebel in the Ranks: Martin Luther, the Reformation, and the Conflicts That Continue to Shape Our World*. New York: HarperOne, 2017.
"Grievances and Demands – The Twelve Articles of the Swabian Peasants (February 27–March 1, 1525)." GHDI, http://germanhistorydocs.ghi-dc.org/sub_document.cfm?document_id=4323.
Grislis, Egil. "The Doctrine of Incarnation According to Menno Simons." *JMS* 8 (1990): 16–33.
Guenther, Alan M. "Selling Bibles: The Bartsch Brothers in Central Asia." *Preservings* 42 (2021): 9–16.
Haberkern, Phillip N. *Patron Saint and Prophet: Jan Hus in the Bohemian and German Reformations*. Oxford: Oxford University Press, 2016.
Hackett, Conrad, and David McClendon. "Christians Remain World's Largest Religious Group, but They Are Declining in Europe." Pew Research Center, 5 April 2017, https://www.pewresearch.org/fact-tank/2017/04/05/christians-remain-worlds-largest-religious-group-but-they-are-declining-in-europe/#:~:text=Christians%20remained%20the%20largest%20religious,Pew%20Research%20Center%20demographic%20analysis.
Halfin, Igal. *From Darkness to Light: Class, Conscience, and Salvation in Revolutionary Russia*. Pittsburgh: University of Pittsburgh Press, 2000.
– *Stalinist Confessions: Messianism and Terror at the Leningrad Communist University*. Pittsburgh: University of Pittsburgh Press, 2009.
Hamburg, Gary M. "Religious Toleration in Russian Thought, 1520–1825." In *Religious Freedom in Modern Russia*, edited by Randall A. Poole and Paul W. Werth, 44–80. Pittsburgh: University of Pittsburgh Press, 2018.
Hamilton, Alistair. "The Development of Dutch Anabaptism in the Light of the European Magisterial and Radical Reformation." In *From Martyr to Muppy: A Historical Introduction to Cultural Assimilation Processes of a Religious Minority in the Netherlands: The Mennonites*, edited by Alastair Hamilton, Sjouke Voolstra, and Piet Visser, 3–14. Amsterdam: Amsterdam University Press, 1994.
Hamilton, Alistair, Sjouke Voolstra, and Piet Visser, eds. *From Martyr to Muppy: A Historical Introduction to Cultural Assimilation Processes of a Religious Minority in the Netherlands: The Mennonites*. Amsterdam: Amsterdam University Press, 1994.
Hamm, Abram, and Maria Hamm. *Die Wege des Herrn sind lauter Güte*. Gummersbach, Germany: Verlag Friedensstimme, 1985.

Hamm, Oscar H. *Erinnerungen aus Igantjewo*. Saskatoon: Author, 1980.
– *Memoirs of Ignatyevo in the Light of Historical Change*. Saskatoon: Mrs. Ruth F. Hamm, 1984.
Harder, Bernhard J. *Alexandertal: Die Geschichte der letzten deutschen Stammsiedlung in Russland*. c. 1959.
Harms, J.F. *Geschichte der Mennoniten Brüdergemeinde*. Hillsboro, KS: Mennonite Brethren Publishing House, 1925.
Haxthausen, August von. *The Russian Empire, Its People, Institutions, and Resources*. 2 vols. London, 1856.
– *Studies on the Interior of Russia*. Translated by Eleanore L.M. Schmidt and edited by S. Frederick Starr. Chicago: University of Chicago Press, 1972.
Hellbeck, Jochen. *Revolution on My Mind: Writing a Diary under Stalin*. Cambridge, MA: Harvard University Press, 2006.
Hendrix, Scott H. *Recultivating the Vineyard: The Reformation Agendas of Christianization*. Louisville: Westminster John Knox Press, 2004.
Hiebert, P.C., and Orie O. Miller, eds. *Feeding the Hungry: Russia Famine 1919–1925: American Mennonite Relief Operations under the Auspices of Mennonite Central Committee*. Scottdale, PA: Mennonite Central Committee, 1929.
Hildebrand, Peter. *From Danzig to Russia: The First Emigration of Mennonites from the Danzig Region to Southern Russia*. Translated by Walter E. Toews with Adolf Ens. Winnipeg: CMBC Publications, 2000.
Hillis, Faith. *Children of Rus': Right-Bank Ukraine and the Invention of a Russian Nation*. Ithaca, NY: Cornell University Press, 2013.
Himelick, Raymond, ed. *The Enchiridion of Erasmus*. Bloomington: Indiana University Press, 1963.
Howard, Thomas. *Protestant Theology and the Making of the Modern German University*. Oxford: Oxford University Press, 2006.
Hsia, R. Po-Chia. *Social Discipline in the Reformation: Central Europe, 1550–1750*. London: Routledge, 1989.
Hudson, Anne. *The Premature Reformation: Wycliffite Texts and Lollard History*. Oxford: Clarendon Press, 1988.
Huebert, Helmut. *Molotschna Historical Atlas*. Winnipeg: Springfield Publishers, 2003.
– *Mennonite Estates in Imperial Russia*. Winnipeg: Kindred Press, 2005.
– "Great Trek, 1943–1945." *GAMEO*, April 2009, https://gameo.org/index.php?title=Great_Trek,_1943-1945&oldid=155816.
– *Stalin's Year of Terror*. Winnipeg: Springfield Publishers, 2009.
Hughes, James. *Stalinism in a Russian Province: Collectivization and Dekulakization in Siberia*. London: Palgrave, 1996.
IA s vami vo vse dni do skonchaniia veka. Volume 1: *Tiazhelye vremena gonenii i repressii 1931–1946*. Edited by Viktor Fast. Karaganda, Kazakhstan: Shtainkhagen, 2001.

Inoyatova, Dilaram M. "Iz istorii Mennnonitov Turkestana." In *Etnodemograficheskie Protsessy v Turkestane*, 43–7. Tashkent, Uzbekistan: n.p., 2005.
– "Mennonites in Central Asia and Their Role in the Modernization of Economics and Culture in the Region." In *European Mennonites and the Challenge of Modernity over Five Centuries: Contributors, Detractors, and Adapters*, edited by Mark Jantzen, Mary S. Sprunger, and John D. Thiesen, 161–7. North Newton, KS: Bethel College, 2016.
Ipatov, A.I. *Mennonity: Voprosy formirovaniia i evoliutsii etnokovfessional'noi obshchnosti*. Moscow: Mysl', 1978.
Isaak, Franz. *Die Molotschnaer Mennoniten. Ein Beitrag zur Geshichte derselben*. Halbstadt: H.J. Braun, 1908.
Isaak, Helmut. "Menno's Vision of the Anticipation of the Kingdom of God in His Early Writings." In *Menno Simons: A Reappraisal. Essays in Honour of Irvin B. Horst on the 450th Anniversary of the Fundamentboek*, edited by Gerald R. Brunk, 57–80. Harrisonburg, VA: Eastern Mennonite College, 1992.
– *Menno Simons and the New Jerusalem*. Kitchener, ON: Pandora Press, 2006.
Israel, Jonathan I. *The Dutch Republic: Its Rise, Greatness, and Fall 1477–1806*. Oxford: Clarendon Press, 1995.
– "The Intellectual Debate about Toleration in the Dutch Republic." In *The Emergence of Tolerance in the Dutch Republic*, edited by C. Berkvens-Stevelinck, J. Israel, and G.H.M. Posthumus Meryjes, 3–36. Leiden: Brill, 1997.
– *Radical Enlightenment: Philosophy and the Making of Modernity 1650–1720*. Oxford: Oxford University Press, 2001.
Ivanov, Andrey. "Stolypin and the Mennonites." *Direction* 46 (Spring 2017): 69–80.
Jantzen, Mark. *Mennonite German Soldiers: Nation, Religion, and Family in the Prussian East, 1772–1880*. Notre Dame, IN: University of Notre Dame Press, 2010.
Jantzen, Mark, Mary S. Sprunger, and John D. Thiesen, eds. *European Mennonites and the Challenge of Modernity over Five Centuries: Contributors, Detractors, and Adapters*. North Newton, KS: Bethel College, 2016.
– "Changing Definitions of Treason and Religious Freedom for Mennonites in Prussia, 1780–1880." In *European Mennonites and the Challenge of Modernity over Five Centuries: Contributors, Detractors, and Adapters*, edited by Mark Jantzen, Mary S. Sprunger, and John D. Thiesen, 233–48. North Newton, KS: Bethel College, 2016.
–, eds. *European Mennonites and the Holocaust*. Toronto: University of Toronto Press, 2020.
Janz, Harold, ed. *Flight: Mennonites Facing the Soviet Empire in 1929–30, from the Pages of the Mennonitische Rundschau*. Winnipeg: Eden Echoes Publishing, 2018.

Janzen, Neil. "USSR – Trip Report #1." http://artdefehr.com/wp-content/uploads/2013/05/Bl056-USSR-Trip-1-1989-08.pdf.

Janzen, Waldemar. *Growing Up in Turbulent Times: Memoirs of Soviet Oppression, Refugee Life in Germany, and Immigrant Adjustment to Canada.* Winnipeg: CMU Press, 2007.

– *Reminiscences of My Father Vladimir Janzen: Teacher, Minister, Gulag Survivor, July 26, 1900–May 15, 1957.* Winnipeg: Author, 2017.

Jarausch, Konrad. *Out of Ashes: A New History of Europe in the Twentieth Century.* Princeton, NJ: Princeton University Press, 2015.

Juhnke, James C. *Vision, Doctrine, War: Mennonite Identity and Organization in America, 1890–1930.* Scottdale, PA: Herald Press, 1989.

Kalyvas, Stathis N. *The Logic of Violence in Civil War.* Cambridge: Cambridge University Press, 2006.

Keep, John L.H. *Soldiers of the Tsar: Army and Society in Russia, 1462–1874.* Oxford: Clarendon Press, 1985.

Kempis, Thomas à. *The Imitation of Christ.* Book One: *The First Chapter.* Milwaukee: The Bruce Publishing Company, 1940. http://www.ccel.org/ccel/kempis/imitation.all.html.

Kershaw, Ian. *Hitler, the Germans, and the Final Solution.* New Haven, CT: Yale University Press, 2008.

Khlevniūk, O.V. *The History of the Gulag: From Collectivization to the Great Terror.* New Haven, CT: Yale University Press, 2004.

Khlevniūk, O.V., and Nora Seligman Favorov. *Stalin: New Biography of a Dictator.* New Haven, CT: Yale University Press, 2015.

Khodarkovsky, Michael. "The Non-Christian Peoples on the Muscovite Frontiers." In *The Cambridge History of Russia,* edited by Maureen Perrie. Volume 1: *From Early Rus' to 1689,* 317–37. Cambridge: Cambridge University Press, 2006.

Kindler, Robert. *Stalin's Nomads: Power & Famine in Kazakhstan.* Translated by Cynthia Klohr. Pittsburgh: University of Pittsburgh Press, 2018.

Kivelson, Valerie A. "The Devil Stole His Mind: The Tsar and the 1648 Moscow Uprising." *AHR* 98 (June 1993): 733–56.

Kivelson, Valerie A., and Ronald Grigor Suny. *Russia's Empires.* Oxford: Oxford University Press, 2017.

Kizik, Edmund. "A Radical Attempt to Resolve the Mennonite Question in Danzig in the Mid-Eighteenth Century: The Decline of the Relations between the City of Danzig and the Mennonites." *MQR* 66, no. 2 (1982): 127–54.

– "Religious Freedom and the Limits of Social Assimilation: The History of the Mennonites in Danzig and the Vistula Delta until Their Tragic End after World War II." In *From Martyr to Muppy: A Historical Introduction to Cultural Assimilation Processes of a Religious Minority in the Netherlands: The*

Mennonites, edited by Alastair Hamilton, Sjouke Voolstra, and Piet Visser, 48–64. Amsterdam: Amsterdam University Press, 1994.

Klaassen, Walter. *Anabaptism: Neither Catholic nor Protestant.* Waterloo: Conrad Press, 1973.

– "The Relevance of Menno Simons; Past and Present." In *Menno Simons: A Reappraisal. Essays in Honour of Irvin B. Horst on the 450th Anniversary of the Fundamentboek*, edited by Gerald R. Brunk, 17–36. Harrisonburg, VA: Eastern Mennonite College, 1992.

– "Jacob H. Janzen (1878–1950)." In *Shepherds, Servants and Prophets: Leadership among the Russian Mennonites (ca. 1880–1960)*, edited by Harry Loewen, 177–92. Kitchener, ON: Pandora Press, 2003.

Klassen, Anna, nee Thiessen. "Exiled Again: 1943." In *The Silence Echoes: Memoirs of Trauma and Tears*, edited by Sarah Dyck, 148–57. Kitchener, ON: Pandora Press, 1997.

Klassen, C.F. "The Mennonites of Russia, 1917–1928." *MQR* 55 (1981): 218–30.

Klassen, Herbert, and Maureen Klassen. *Ambassador to His People: C.F. Klassen and the Russian Mennonite Refugees.* Winnipeg: Kindred Press, 1990.

Klassen, John N. "Christen in Russland feiern und danken Gott für Seine Führung. Eine Jubiläumsfeier unter der Eiche in Saporoshje: 200 Jahre Mennoniten in Russland." *MR* (25 October 1989): 18–21.

– *Russlanddeutsche Freikirchen in der Bundesrepublik Deutschland: Grundlinien ihrer Geschichte, ihrer Entwicklung und Theologie.* Nürnberg, Germany: Verlag für Theologie und Religionswissenschaft, 2007.

Klassen, Pamela E. *Going by the Moon and the Stars: Stories of Two Russian Mennonite Women.* Waterloo: Wilfrid Laurier University Press, 1994.

Klassen, Robert L. "Harbin (Heilongjiang, China) Refugees." *GAMEO*, July 2009, https://gameo.org/index.php?title=Harbin_(Heilongjiang,_China)_Refugees&oldid=131881.

Klaus, Aleksander A. *Nashi kolonii. Opyty i materialy po istorii isstatistiki inostrannoi kolonizatsii v Rossii.* St. Petersburg: n.p., 1869.

Klets, Viktor K. "Caught between Two Poles: Ukrainian Mennonites and the Trauma of the Second World War." In *Minority Report: Mennonite Identities in Imperial Russia and Soviet Ukraine Reconsidered, 1789–1945*, edited by Leonard G. Friesen, 287–317. Toronto: University of Toronto Press, 2018.

Klibanov, A.I. *Istoriiā religioznogo sektantstva v Rossii, 60-e gody XIX v. – 1917 g.* Moscow: Nauka, 1965.

Klippenstein, Lawrence, ed. *Siberian Diary of Aron P. Toews: With a Biography by Olga Rempel*, translated by Esther Klassen Bergen. Winnipeg: CMBC Publications, 1984.

– "Four Letters to Susanna from Johann Bartsch, a Danzig Mennonite Land Scout, 1786–1787." *Polish Review* 54, no. 1 (2009): 31–59.

- "The Selbstschutz: A Mennonite Army in Ukraine, 1918–1919." In *History and Mission in Europe: Continuing the Conversation*, edited by Mary Raber and Peter F. Penner, 49–82. Schwarzenfeld, Germany: Neufeld Verlag, 2011.
- *Mennonite Conscientious Objectors in Tsarist Russia and the Soviet Union before World War II, and Other Cos in Eastern Europe*. Winnipeg: Mennonite Heritage Centre, 2016.
- "The Bartsch-Hoeppner Mennonite Privilegium of 1787." *Preservings* 41 (2020): 37–42.
Klötzer, Ralf. "The Melchoirites and Münster." In *A Companion to Anabaptism and Spiritualism, 1521–1700*, edited by James Stayer and John Roth, 217–56. Leiden: Brill Publishers, 2007.
Klyueva, Vera P. "The Mennonite Community of the Tyumen Oblast: A Short History from the 1940s to the 1980s." *JMS* (2012): 89–96.
Kobe, Rainer. "Isaac von den Blocke, Painter and Mennonite at Gdansk in the Early Seventh Century: Is There Anything Mennonite in His Paintings *Before the Flood* and *The Narrow and the Broad Way*?" In *European Mennonites and the Challenge of Modernity over Five Centuries: Contributors, Detractors, and Adapters*, edited by Mark Jantzen, Mary S. Sprunger, and John D. Thiesen, 233–49. North Newton, KS: Bethel College, 2016.
Kollman, Nancy Shields. *The Russian Empire, 1450–1801*. Oxford: Oxford University Press, 2017.
Konrad, Anne, ed. "Massacre Memorial Dedicated in Ukraine [Eichenfeld and Nikolaipole Regions between 1918 and 1920]." *CM* 5 (10 September 2001): 12.
- *Red Quarter Moon: A Search for Family in the Shadow of Stalin*. Toronto: University of Toronto Press, 2012.
-, ed. *A Mennonite Estate Family in Southern Ukraine, 1904–1924*. Kitchener, ON: Pandora Press, 2013.
Koontz, Claudia. *The Nazi Conscience*. Cambridge, MA: Harvard University Press, 2003.
Koop, Karl. *Anabaptist-Mennonite Confessions of Faith*. Kitchener, ON: Pandora Press, 2004.
- "At the Margins and at the Center of Modern Expression: Reconsidering Anabaptist and Mennonite Confessions of Faith." In *European Mennonites and the Challenge of Modernity over Five Centuries: Contributors, Detractors, and Adapters*, edited by Mark Jantzen, Mary S. Sprunger, and John D. Thiesen, 285–300. North Newton, KS: Bethel College, 2016.
Kotkin, Stephen. *Magnetic Mountain: Stalinism as Civilization*. Berkley: University of California Press, 1995.
- *Armageddon Averted: The Soviet Collapse, 1970–2000*. Updated edition. Oxford: Oxford University Press, 2008.
Kozlov, Denis, and Eleaonory Gilburd. "The Thaw as an Event in Russian History." In *The Thaw: Soviet Society and Culture during the 1950s and 1960s*,

edited by Denis Kozlov and Eleonory Gilburd, 18–81. Toronto: University of Toronto Press, 2013.
–, eds. *The Thaw: Soviet Society and Culture during the 1950s and 1960s*. Toronto: University of Toronto Press, 2013.
Krahn, Cornelius. "Einlage (Chortitza Mennonite Settlement, Zaporizhia Oblast, Ukraine)." *GAMEO*, 1956, https://gameo.org/index.php?title =Einlage_(Chortitza_Mennonite_Settlement,_Zaporizhia_Oblast ,_Ukraine)&oldid=169287.
– "Historiography: Russia." *GAMEO*, 1956, https://gameo.org/index .php?title=Historiography:_Russia&oldid=134954.
– "Lehrdienst." *GAMEO*, 1957, https://gameo.org/index.php?title=Lehrdienst &oldid=88985.
– "Ministry (Prusso-Russian Background Mennonites)." *GAMEO*, 1957, https://gameo.org/index.php?title=Ministry_(Prusso-Russian _Background_Mennonites)&oldid=143670.
– "Mennozentrum (Bureau der Molotschnaer Mennonitischen Vereinigung)." *GAMEO*, 1959, https://gameo.org/index.php?title=Mennozentrum _(Bureau_der_Molotschnaer_Mennonitischen_Vereinigung)&oldid=83518.
– "Omsk (Siberia, Russia)." *GAMEO*, 1959, https://gameo.org/index .php?title=Omsk_(Siberia,_Russia)&oldid=135148.
– "Terek Mennonite Settlement (Republic of Dagestan, Russia)." *GAMEO*, 1959, https://gameo.org/index.php?title=Terek_Mennonite_Settlement _(Republic_of_Dagestan,_Russia)&oldid=135015.
Krahn, Cornelius, and Ervin Beck. "Clocks." *GAMEO*, 1989, https://gameo .org/index.php?title=Clocks&oldid=139672.
Krahn, Cornelius, Victor G. Doerksen, and Victor Wiebe. "Temple Society." *GAMEO*, 2010, https://gameo.org/index.php?title=Temple _Society&oldid=146288.
Krahn, Cornelius, and Walter W. Sawatsky. "Russia." *GAMEO*, February 2011, https://gameo.org/index.php?title=Russia&oldid=167837.
Krest'ianinov, V.F. *Mennonity*. Moscow: n.p., 1967.
Krieger, Viktor. "Deportationen der Russlanddeutschen 1941–1945 und die Folgen." In *Von der Autonomiegründung zur Verbannung und Entrechtung. Die Jahre 1918 und 1941 bis 1948 in der Geschichte der Deutschen in Russland*, edited by Alfred Eisfeld, 106–22. Stuttgart, Germany: n.p., 2008.
Kroeker, Abraham. *Unsere Brüder in Not! Bilder vom Leidensweg der deutschen Kolonisten in Russland*. Striegau: Theodor Urban, 1930.
Kroeker, Nikolai. "Mennonite Intelligentsia in Russia." *ML* 24 (1969): 51–60.
–, ed. *First Mennonite Villages in Russia 1789–1943: Khortitsa-Rosental*. Vancouver: N.J. Kroeker, 1981.
Lapp, John A. "Taking Contextual Influences Seriously: The Contributions of Walter W. Sawatsky." In *History and Mission in Europe: Continuing*

the Conversation, edited by Mary Raber and Peter F. Penner, 11–24. Schwarzenfeld, Germany: Neufeld Verlag, 2011.
LeDonne, John. *Forging a Unitary State: Russia's Management of the Eurasian Space, 1650–1850*. Toronto: University of Toronto Press, 2020.
Lenoe, Matthew. *The Kirov Murder and Soviet History*. New Haven, CT: Yale University Press, 2010.
Leshchenko, N.N. "Itogi statisticheskogo izucheniia krest'ianskogo dvizhenie na Ukraine v period revoliutsii 1905–1907." In *Sovetskaia istoriografiia agrarnoi istorii SSSR (do 1917 g.)*. Kishenev, Russia: n.p., 1978.
Letkemann, Peter. "Mennonite Victims of the 'Great Terror' 1936–1938." *JMS* 16 (1998): 33–58.
– "David Johann Penner [A. Reinmarus]: A Mennonite Anti-Menno (1904–1993)." In *Shepherds, Servants and Prophets: Leadership among the Russian Mennonites (ca. 1880–1960)*, edited by Harry Loewen, 297–312. Kitchener, ON: Pandora Press, 2003.
– "The Fate of Mennonites in the Volga-Ural Region, 1929–1941." *JMS* 26 (2008): 181–200.
– "Mennonite Refugee Camps in Germany, 1921–1951: Part I – Lager Lechfeld." *MH* 38 (September 2012): 1–2.
– *A Book of Remembrance: Mennonites in Arkadak and Zentral, 1908–1941*. Winnipeg: Old Oak Publishing, 2016.
Lewin, Moshe. *The Gorbachev Phenomenon: A Historical Interpretation*. Berkeley: University of California Press, 1988.
– *The Making of the Soviet System: Essays in the Social System of Interwar Russia*. New York: The New Press, 1994.
Lincoln, W. Bruce. *In the Vanguard of Reform: Russia's Enlightened Bureaucrats, 1825–1861*. DeKalb: Northern Illinois University Press, 1982.
– *The Great Reforms: Autocracy, Bureaucracy, and the Politics of Change in Imperial Russia*. DeKalb: Northern Illinois University Press, 1990.
Littell, Franklin Hamlin. *The Anabaptist View of the Church: A Study on the Origins of Sectarian Protestantism*. Boston: Starr King Press, 1958.
Loewen, Harry. "A House Divided: Russian Mennonite Non-resistance and Emigration in the 1870s." In *Mennonites in Russia, 1788–1988: Essays in Honour of Gerhard Lohrenz*, edited by John Friesen: 127–46. Winnipeg: CMBC Publications, 1989.
– "Intellectual Developments among the Mennonites of Russia: 1880–1917." *JMS* 8 (1990): 89–107.
– "Anti-Menno: Introduction to Early Soviet-Mennonite Literature." *JMS* 11 (1993): 23–42.
– "'Can the Son Answer for the Father?' Reflections on the Stalinist Terror (On the 60th Anniversary of My Father's Arrest, 1937–1997)." *JMS* 16 (1998): 76–90.

Loewen, Helmut-Harry, and James Urry. "Protecting Mammon: Some Dilemmas of Mennonite Non-resistance in Late Imperial Russia and the Origins of the Selbstschutz." *JMS* 9 (1991): 34–53.
Loewen, Julius. *Jasykowo: Mennonite Colony on the Dnieper*. Translated by Jakob B. Klassen. Beausejour, MB: The Standard Press, 1995.
Loewen, Royden K. *Family, Church, and Market: A Mennonite Community in the Old and the New Worlds, 1850–1930*. Toronto: University of Toronto Press, 1993.
Lohr, Eric. *Nationalizing the Russian Empire: The Campaign against Enemy Aliens during World War I*. Cambridge, MA: Harvard University Press, 1993.
– *Russian Citizenship: From Empire to Soviet Union*. Cambridge, MA: Harvard University Press, 2012.
Lohrenz, Gerhard. *Heritage Remembered: A Pictorial Survey of Mennonites in Prussia and Russia*. Winnipeg: CMBC Publications, 1974.
– *Storm Tossed: The Personal Story of a Canadian Mennonite from Russia*. Winnipeg: Christian Press, 1976.
Lohrenz, Gerhard, and Victor G. Doerksen. *Zagradovka: History of a Mennonite Settlement in Southern Russia*. Winnipeg: CMBC Publications, 2000.
Lőneke, Regina. *Die "Hiesigen" und die "Unsrigen": Werteverständnis MennonitischerAussiedlerfamilien aud Dörfern der RegionOrenburg/Ural*. Marburg, Germany: N.G. Ewert, 2000.
Long, James W. *From Privileged to Dispossessed: The Volga Germans, 1860–1917*. Lincoln: University of Nebraska Press, 1988.
Loosjes, Jacob. "Batenburg, Jan van (1495–1538)." *GAMEO*, 1953, https://gameo.org/index.php?title=Batenburg,_Jan_van_(1495–1538)&oldid=144785.
Lőwe (Loewe), Heinz-Dietrich. "Russian Nationalism and Tsarist Nationalities Policies in Semi-constitutional Russia, 1905–1914." In *New Perspectives in Modern Russian History*, edited by Robert B. McKean, 250–77. New York: St. Martin's Press, 1992.
Löwen (Loewen), Heinrich, and Cornelius Krahn. "Grünfeld (Schlachtin Mennonite Settlement, Dnipropetrovsk Oblast, Ukraine)." *GAMEO*, 1956, https://gameo.org/index.php?title=Gr%C3%BCnfeld_(Schlachtin_Mennonite_Settlement,_Dnipropetrovsk_Oblast,_Ukraine)&oldid=145353.
MacMaster, Richard K. *Land, Piety, Peoplehood: The Establishment of Mennonite Communities in America, 1683–1790*. Scottdale, PA: Herald Press, 1985.
Magocsi, Paul R. *A History of Ukraine: The Land and Its Peoples*. Toronto: University of Toronto Press, 2010.
Mannhardt, Wilhelm. *Die Danziger Mennonitengemeinde. Ihre Entstehung und ihre Geschichte von 1509–1919*. Danzig: Danziger Mennonitengemeinde, 1919.
– *The Danzig Mennonite Church: Its Origin and History from 1569–1919*. Translated by Victor G. Doerksen. North Newton, KS: Bethel College, 2007.

Manning, Roberta Thompson. *The Crisis of the Old Order in Russia: Gentry and Government.* Princeton, NJ: Princeton University Press, 1982.

Martin, Terry. "The German Question in Russia, 1848–96." *RH* 18 (1991): 371–432.

– "The Terekers' Dilemma: A Prelude to the Selbstschutz." *MH* 17 (December 1991): 1–2.

– *The Mennonites and the Russian State Duma, 1905–1914.* The Donald W. Treadgold Papers in Russian, East European and Central Asian Studies Paper No. 4. Seattle: The Henry M. Jackson School of International Affairs, 1996.

– "The Origins of Ethnic Cleansing." *JMH* 70 (December 1998): 813–61.

– *The Affirmative Action Empire: Nations and Nationalism in the Soviet Union, 1923–1939.* Ithaca, NY: Cornell University Press, 2001.

– "The Russian Mennonite Encounter with the Soviet State, 1917–1955." The 2001 Bechtel Lectures in Anabaptist Mennonite Studies. *CGR* 20 (2002): 3–59.

Massing, Michael. *Fatal Discord: Erasmus, Luther and the Fight for the Western Mind.* New York: HarperCollins Publishers, 2018.

McAuley, Mary. *Bread and Justice: State and Society in Petrograd 1917–1922.* Oxford: Clarendon Press, 1989.

McDonald, David. *United Government and Foreign Policy in Russia, 1900–1914.* Cambridge, MA: Harvard University Press, 1992.

McDonald, Tracy. *Face to the Village: The Riazan Countryside under Soviet Rule, 1921–1930.* Toronto: University of Toronto Press, 2011.

"Mennonites." Library and Archives Canada, 9 November 2020, https://www.bac-lac.gc.ca/eng/discover/immigration/history-ethnic-cultural/Pages/mennonites.aspx.

Miller, Ivan J., and Della Miller. "Reflections on the Life and Passing of Alvin J. Miller." *The Historian* 12 (July 2000): 2.

Mommsen, Hans. "Die Realisierung des Utopischen: Die "Endlösung der Judenfrage" im "Dritten Reich." *Geschichte und Gesellschaft*. 9, no. 3 (1983): 381–420.

Moon, David. *The Plough That Broke the Steppes: Agriculture and Environment on Russia's Grasslands, 1700–1914.* Oxford: Oxford University Press, 2013.

– *The American Steppes: The Unexpected Russian Roots of Great Plains Agriculture, 1870s-1930s.* Cambridge: Cambridge University Press, 2020.

Morgunov, Konstantin A. "Test of Faith: Religious Mennonite Organizations of Orenburg Region, 1945–1991." *JMS* (2012): 79–88.

Moss, Christina. "Marriage as Spiritual Partnership in Sixteenth-Century Strasbourg: The Case of Lienhard and Ursula Jost." In *Newberry Essays in Medieval and Early Modern Studies*, Volume 9: *Selected Proceedings of the Newberry Center for Renaissance Studies 2015 Multidisciplinary Graduate*

Student Conference, edited by Karen Christianson and Andrew K. Epps, 83–94. Chicago: The Newberry Library, 2015. http://www.newberry.org/sites/default/files/textpage-attachments/2015Proceedings.pdf.
- "Jost, Ursula (d. 1532/39)." *GAMEO*, May 2016, https://gameo.org/index.php?title=Jost,_Ursula_(d._1532/39)&oldid=143139.

Mukhina, Irina. "Gendered Division of Labor among Special Settlers in the Soviet Union, 1941–1956." *Women's History Review* 23 (January 2014): 99–119.

Naimark, Norman. *The Russians in Germany: A History of the Soviet Zone of Occupation, 1945–1949*. Cambridge, MA: Harvard University Press, 1997.

Nam, Iraida V. "The Mennonite Congregations in the Tomsk Oblast during 'Thaw' and 'Stagnation.'" *JMS* 30 (2012): 73–8.

Nazarova, Tatiana Pavlovna. "Agrotekhnicheskaia pomoshch Mennonite Central Committee v Rossii v period NEPa." *Vestnik* 15 (February 2010): 35–43.
- *Blagotvoritel'naia Deiatel'nost' Zarubezhnyikh Mennonitskikh Organizatsii v Sovetskom Gosudarstve (1920–1930gg)*. Volgograd, Russia: n.p., 2010.

Neff, Christian, and Richard D. Thiessen. "Anna von Oldenburg-Delmenhorst, Countess of East Friesland (1501–1575)." *GAMEO*, February 2007, https://gameo.org/index.php?title=Anna_von_Oldenburg-Delmenhorst,_Countess_of_East_Friesland_(1501–1575)&oldid=144716.

Neitzel, Soenke, and Harald Welzer. *Soldaten: On Fighting, Killing, and Dying. The Secret World War II Tapes of German POWs*. London: Simon & Schuster, 2012.

Neufeld, Dietrich. *A Russian Dance of Death: Revolution and Civil War in the Ukraine*. Translated and edited by Al Reimer. Winnipeg: Hyperion Press, 1977.

Neufeld, Jacob A. *Tiefenwege. Erfahrungen und Erlebnisse von Russland-Mennoniten in zwei Jahrzehnten bis 1949*. Virgil, ON: Niagara Press, 1958.
- *Path of Thorns: Soviet Mennonite Life under Communist and Nazi Rule*. Edited by Harvey L. Dyck and translated by Harvey L. Dyck and Sarah Dyck. Toronto: University of Toronto Press, 2014.

Neufeldt, Colin P. "Through the Fires of Hell: The Dekulakization and Collectivization of the Soviet Mennonite Community (1928–1933)." *JMS* 16 (1998): 9–32.
- "Separating the Sheep from the Goats: The Role of Mennonites and Non-Mennonites in the Dekulakization of Khortitsa, Ukraine (1928–1930)." *MQR* 83, no. 2 (April 2009): 221–91.
- Reforging Mennonite Spetspereselentsy: The Experience of Mennonite Exiles at Siberian Special Settlements in the Omsk, Tomsk, Novosibirsk and Narym Regions, 1930–1933." *JMS* 30 (2012): 269–314.
- "The Public and Private Lives of Mennonite Kolkhoz Chairmen in the Khortytsia and Molochansk German National Raĭony in Ukraine (1928–

1934)." *The Carl Beck Papers in Russian and East European Studies* No. 2305 (January 2015): 1–87.
– "Collectivizing the Mutter Ansiedlungen: The Role of Mennonites in Organizing Kolkhozy in the Khortytsia and Molochansk German National Districts in Ukraine in the Late 1920s and Early 1930s." In *Minority Report: Mennonite Identities in Imperial Russia and Soviet Ukraine Reconsidered, 1789–1945*, edited by Leonard G. Friesen, 211–59. Toronto: University of Toronto Press, 2018.
Niessen, Hans von, and John N Klassen. "Gottes Fűhrung – 200 Jahre Mennoniten in Russland. Jubilämsfeier in Chortitza, Schönwiese und Saporoshje." *DB* (1 November 1989): 3–5, 11.
Nikol'skaia, Tatiana. "Istoriia dvizheniia baptistov-initsiativnikov." In *History and Mission in Europe: Continuing the Conversation*, edited by Mary Raber and Peter F. Penner, 107–41. Schwarzenfeld, Germany: Neufeld Verlag, 2011.
Noldus, Badeloch. *Trade in Good Taste: Relations in Architecture and Culture between the Dutch Republic and the Baltic World in the Seventeenth Century*. Translated by Titus Verheijen. Turnhout, Belgium: Brepolis Publishers, 2004.
North, Michael. *The Baltic: A History*. Translated by Kenneth Kronenberg. Cambridge, MA: Harvard University Press, 2015.
Novoe Zaporozh'e: khornika razvitiia bol'shogo goroda, 1921–2006gg. Dnepropetrovsk, Ukraine: n.p., 2006.
O'Neill, Kelly. *Claiming Crimea; A History of Catherine the Great's Southern Empire*. New Haven, CT: Yale University Press, 2017.
Osborne, Troy. "New Directions in Anabaptist Studies." *MQR* 81 (2007): 43–8.
– "Mennonites and Violence in Early Modern Amsterdam." *Church History and Religious Culture* 95 (2015): 477–94.
– "Honor and Charity in the Church: Mennonites and the 'Disciplinary Revolution' of the Dutch Republic." In *European Mennonites and the Challenge of Modernity over Five Centuries: Contributors, Detractors, and Adapters*, edited by Mark Jantzen, Mary S. Sprunger, and John D. Thiesen, 265–83. North Newton, KS: Bethel College, 2016.
Patenaude, Bertrand M. *The Big Show in Bololand: The American Relief Expedition to Soviet Russia in the Famine of 1921*. Stanford, CA: Stanford University Press, 2002.
Patterson, Sean. *Makhno and Memory: Anarchist and Mennonite Narratives of Ukraine's Civil War, 1917–1921*. Winnipeg: University of Manitoba Press, 2020.
Pavlova, Tatiana A., ed. *Dolgii put' Rossiiskogo Patsifizma: Ideal mezhdynarodnogo i vnyutrennego mira v religiozno-filosofskoi I obshchestvenno-politicheskoi mysli Rossii*. Moscow: n.p., 1997.
Penter, Tanja. "Vergessene Opfer von Mord und Missbrauch: Behindertenmorde unter deutscher Besatzungsherrschaft in der Ukraine (1941–1943) und ihre

juristische Aufarbeitung in der Sowjetunion." *Journal of Modern European History* 17 (2019): 353–76.
Peters, Gerald, ed. and trans. *Diary of Anna Baerg*. Winnipeg: CMBC Publications, 1985.
Peters, Mariechen. "Dearly Beloved." In *The Silence Echoes: Memoirs of Trauma and Tears*, edited by Sarah Dyck, 57–60. Kitchener, ON: Pandora Press, 1997.
Peters, Viktor, ed. *Zwei Dokumente: Quellen zum Geschichtsstudium der Mennoniten in Russland*. Winnipeg: Echo Verlag, 1965.
Pettegree, Andrew. *Reformation and the Culture of Persuasion*. Cambridge: Cambridge University Press, 2005.
Peucker, P.M. "Herrnhut and Russia: Archival Records on Moravian Activity in Russia from the Unity Archives in Herrnhut, Germany." In *Foreign Churches in St. Petersburg and Their Archives, 1703–1917*, edited by Pieter Holtrop and Henk Slechte, 129–39 Lieden: Brill, 2007.
"Plautdietsch, a Germanic Language Related to Dutch and Frisian, Spoken in Siberia." Mercator, European Research Centre on Multilingualism and Language Learning, https://www.mercator-research.eu/projekten/endangered-languages-and-archives/plautdietsch-a-germanic-language-related-to-dutch-and-frisian-spoken-in-siberia.
Plett, Delbert F., ed. *History and Events: Writings and Maps Pertaining to the History of the Mennonite Kleine Gemeinde from 1866–1876*. Steinbach, MB: D.F.P. Publications, 1982.
–, ed. *The Golden Years: The Mennonite Kleine Gemeinde in Russia (1812–1849)*. Steinbach, MB: D.F.P. Publications, 1985.
–, ed. *Storm and Triumph: The Mennonite Kleine Gemeinde, 1850–1875*. Steinbach,MB: D.F.B. Publications, 1986.
– *Saints and Sinners: The Kleine Gemeinde in Imperial Russia, 1812–1875*. Steinbach, MB: Crossway Publications 1999.
Plokhy, Serhii. *The Cossacks and Religion in Early Modern Ukraine*. Oxford: Oxford University Press, 2001.
– *The Origins of Slavic Nations: Premodern Identities in Russia, Ukraine and Belarus*. Cambridge: Cambridge University Press, 2006.
– *Ukraine and Russia: Representations of the Past*. Toronto: University of Toronto Press, 2008.
– *Yalta: The Price for Peace*. New York: Penguin Books, 2010.
– *The Gates of Europe: A History of Ukraine*. New York: Basic Books, 2015.
Pohl, Michaela. "From White Grave to Tselinograd to Astana: The Virgin Lands Opening, Khrushchev's Forgotten First Reform." In *The Thaw: Soviet Society and Culture During the 1950s and 1960s*, edited by Denis Kozlov and Eleonory Gilburd, 269–307. Toronto: University of Toronto Press, 2013.
Polian, Pavel. *Ne po svoei vole ... Istoriia I geografiia prinuditel'nykh migratsii v SSSR*. Moscow: n.p., 2001.

Poole, Randall A., and Paul W. Werth, eds. *Religious Freedom in Modern Russia*. Pittsburgh: University of Pittsburgh Press, 2018.
Post, R.R. *The Modern Devotion: Confrontation with Reformation and Humanism*. Leiden: Brill, 1968.
Postnikov, V.E. *Iuzhno-Russkoe krest'ianskoe khoziaistvo*. Moscow: n.p., 1891.
Potter, G.R. *Zwingli*. Cambridge: Cambridge University Press, 1976.
Quiring, Walter. *In the Fullness of Time: 150 Years of Mennonite Sojourn in Russia*. Waterloo: A. Klassen, 1974.
Raber, Mary, and Peter F. Penner, eds. *History and Mission in Europe: Continuing the Conversation*. Schwarzenfeld, Germany: Neufeld Verlag, 2011.
– "Remembering the Russian Bible Commentary: A Memoir in Context." In *History and Mission in Europe: Continuing the Conversation*, edited by Mary Raber and Peter F. Penner, 303–26. Schwarzenfeld, Germany: Neufeld Verlag, 2011.
– *Ministries of Compassion among Russian Evangelicals, 1905–1929*. Eugene, OR: Pickwick Publications, 2016.
Raeff, Marc. *Understanding Imperial Russia: State and Society in the Old Regime*. Translated by Arthur Goldhammer. New York: Columbia University Press, 1984.
Rahn, Peter J., ed. and trans. *Among the Ashes: In the Stalinkova Kolkhoz (Kontinusfeld), 1930–1935*. Kitchener, ON: Pandora Press, 2011.
Ratliff, Walter. "The Mennonites of Khiva: A Modernizing Community." In *European Mennonites and the Challenge of Modernity over Five Centuries: Contributors, Detractors, and Adapters*, edited by Mark Jantzen, Mary S. Sprunger, and John D. Thiesen, 179–93. North Newton, KS: Bethel College, 2016.
Red'kina, Olga IU. *Sel'skhokhoziaistvennye religioznie trudovye kollektivy v 1917–1930-e gg.: na materialakh evropeiskoi chasti RSFSR*. Volgograd, Russia: Volgograadovo gosudarstvennovo universiteta, 2004.
Regehr, Ted D., with the assistance of J.I. Regehr. *For Everything a Season: A History of the Alexanderkrone Zentralschule*. Winnipeg: CMBC Publications, 1988.
– "Of Dutch or German Ancestry? Mennonite Refugees, MCC, and the International Refugee Organization." *JMS* 13 (1995): 7–25.
– *Mennonites in Canada, 1939–1970*. Volume 3: *A People Transformed*. Toronto: University of Toronto Press, 1996.
Reimer, Al. "The Print Culture of the Russian Mennonites 1870–1930." In *Mennonites in Russia, 1788–1988. Essays in Honour of Gerhard Lohrenz*, edited by John Friesen, 221–38. Winnipeg: CMBC Publications, 1989.
– "Peasant Aristocracy: The Mennonite *Gutsbesitzertum* in Russia." *JMS* 8 (1990): 76–88.
Reimer, Johannes. *Aussiedler sind anders. Russlanddeutsche sind anders*. Wuppertal and Kassel, Germany: Oncken Verlag, 1990.

– *Auf der Suche nach Identität: Russlanddeutsche zwischen Baptisten und Mennoniten nach dem Zweiten Weltkrieg*. Lage, Germany: Logos Publishing, 1996.
Reinmarus (Penner), A. *Anti-Menno: Beiträge zur Geshichte der Mennoniten in Russland*. Moscow: n.p., 1930.
Rempel, David D. *Osterwick (1812–1943)*. A. Olfert Press, n.p., 1973.
Rempel, David G. "The Expropriation of the German Colonists in South Russia during the Great War." *Journal of Modern History* 4 (1932): 49–67.
– "An Introduction to Russian Mennonite Historiography." *MQR* 48 (1974): 409–46.
– "The Mennonite Commonwealth in Russia: A Sketch of Its Founding and Endurance, 1789–1919." *MQR* 47 (1973): 259–308; and *MQR* 48 (1974): 5–54. Also reprinted as a separate document.
– "Mennonite Revolutionaries in the Khortitza Settlement under the Tsarist Regime as Recollected by Johann G. Rempel." *JMS*, 10 (1992): 70–86.
Rempel, David G., with Cornelia Rempel Carlson. *A Mennonite Family in Tsarist Russia and the Soviet Union, 1789–1923*. Toronto: University of Toronto Press, 2002.
Rempel, Gerhard. "Mennonites and the Holocaust: From Collaboration to Perpetuation." *MQR* 84, no. 4 (2010): 507–49.
Rempel, Hans. *Waffen der Wehrlosen: Ersatzdienst der Mennoniten in der UdSSR*. Winnipeg: CMBC Publications, 1980.
Rempel, John D. *The Lord's Supper in Anabaptism: A Study of the Christology of Balthasar Hubmaier, Pilgram Marpeck and Dirk Philips*. Scottdale, PA: Herald Press, 1993.
Rempel, John G., and Richard D. Thiessen. "Toews, David (1870–1947)." *GAMEO*, April 2012, https://gameo.org/index.php?title=Toews,_David_(1870–1947)&oldid=148320.
Rempel, Olga. *Einer von Vielen: Die Lebensgeschichte von Prediger Aaron P. Toews*. Winnipeg: CMBC Publications, 1979.
Riasanovsky, Nicholas V. *Nicholas I and Official Nationality in Russia*. Berkley: University of California Press, 1959.
– "'Nationality' in the State Ideology during the Reign of Nicholas I." *RR* 19 (January 1960): 38–46.
– *A Parting of the Ways: Government and the Educated Public in Russia, 1801–1855*. Oxford: Clarendon Press, 1976.
Rittersporn, Gábor T. *Anguish, Anger and Folkways in Soviet Russia*. Pittsburgh: University of Pittsburgh Press, 2014.
Robinson, Geroid Tanquary. *Rural Russia under the Old Régime: A History of the Landlord-Peasant World and a Prologue to the Peasant Revolution of 1917*. New York: Longmans, Green and Co., 1932.
Rosenthal, Beatrice. *New Myth, New World: From Nietzsche to Stalinism*. University Park: Penn State University Press, 2002.

Roth, John D., and James M. Stayer, eds. *A Companion to Anabaptism and Spiritualism, 1521–1700*. Leiden: Brill, 2007.
– "'Blest Be the Ties That Bind': In Search of the Global Anabaptist Church." *CGR* 31 (2013): 5–43.
Sahlins, Marshall. "Cosmologies of Capitalism: The Trans-Pacific Sector of "The 'World System.'" *Proceedings of the British Academy* LXXIV (1988): 1–51.
Savin, A.I., ed. *Sovetskoe gosudarstvo i evangel'skie tserkvi Sibiri v 1920–1941 gg. Dokumenty i materialy*. Novosibirsk, Russia: Posokh, 2004.
–, ed. *Etnokonfessiia v Sovetskom gosudarstve Mennonity Sibiri v 1920–1980 gody: Annotirovannyi perechen arkhivnykh dokumentov i materialov*. Novosibirsk, Russia: Posokh, 2006.
– *Ethno-Confession in the Soviet State, 1920–1989*. Edited by Paul Toews and ranslated by Olga Shmakina. Fresno, CA: Center for Mennonite Brethren Studies, 2008.
–, ed. *Etnokonfessiia v sovetskom gosudarstve. Mennonity Sibiri v 1920–1930-e gody: emigratsiia i repressii. Dokumenty i materialy*. Novosibirsk, Russia: Posokh, 2009.
Sawatsky, Walter. "Mennonite Congregations in the Soviet Union Today." *ML* (March 1978): 12–26.
– "What Makes Russian Mennonites Mennonite?" *MQR* 53 (1979): 5–20.
– *Soviet Evangelicals since World War II*. Scottdale, PA: Herald Press, 1981.
– "Council of Churches of Evangelical Christians-Baptists." *GAMEO*, 1987, https://gameo.org/index.php?title=Council_of_Churches_of_Evangelical_Christians-Baptists&oldid=86947.
– "From Russian to Soviet Mennonites, 1941–1988." In *Mennonites in Russia, 1788–1988: Essays in Honour of Gerhard Lohrenz*, edited by John Friesen, 299–338. Winnipeg: CMBC Publications, 1989.
– "Protestantism." In *Protestantism and Politics in Eastern Europe and Russia: The Communist and Postcommunist Eras*, edited by Sabrina P. Ramet, 237–75. Durham, NC: Duke University Press, 1992.
– "Patsifisty-protestanti v Sovetskoi Rossii mezhdy dvymia mirovymi voinami." In *Dolgii put' Rossiiskogo Patsifizma: Ideal mezhdynarodnogo i vnyutrennego mira v religiozno-filosofskoi i obshchestvenno-politicheskoi mysli Rossii*, edited by Tatiana A. Pavlova, 262–84. Moscow: n.p., 1997.
– "Ripe unto Harvest (Karaganda, Kazakhstan, May 1998)." *ML* 55 (June 2000), https://mla.bethelks.edu/ml-archive/2000june/sawatsky_ripe_harvest.html.
– "Historical Roots of a Post-Gulag Theology for Russian Mennonites." *MQR* 76 (April 2002): 149–80.
Sawatsky, Walter, and Peter F. Penner. "Mennonites and Mission in Eurasia." *Mission in Focus: Annual Review* 13 (2005): 131–2.

–, eds. *Mission in the Former Soviet Union*. Schwarzenfeld, Germany: Neufeld Verlag, 2005.
– "Return of Mission and Evangelization in the CIS (1980s–Present)." In *Mission in the Former Soviet Union*, edited by Walter W. Sawatsky and Peter F. Penner, 94–119. Schwarzenfeld, Germany: Neufeld Verlag, 2005.
– "Changing Mentalities: Inter-Relationships between Mennonites and Slavic Evangelicals in Siberia and Central Asia." *JMS* 30 (2012): 315–37.
– "Russian Mennonite Organizational Collapse and the Failed Attempts to Form an Independent Organization, 1917–1989." *MQR* 89, no. 4 (2015), https://link-gale-com.libproxy.wlu.ca/apps/doc/A434142179/LitRC?u=wate18005&sid=LitRC&xid=9a0688c5.
– *Going Global with God as Mennonites for the 21st Century*. North Newton, KS: Bethel College, 2017.
Sawatzky, Jacob. "Never a Pioneer." In *The Silence Echoes: Memoirs of Trauma and Tears*, edited and translated by Sarah Dyck, 111–18. Kitchener, ON: Pandora Press, 1997.
Schildhauer, J. "Handelsbeziehungen Bedeutender Ostseestädte zu den Niederlanden: Ein Beitrag zur Verlagerung des See- and Handelsverkehrs im Ost- und Nordseeraum während des 16. Jahrhunderts." In *The Interactions of Amsterdam and Antwerp with the Baltic Region, 1400–1800*, edited by Wiert Jan Wieringa, 23–9. Leiden: Martinus Nijhoff, 1983.
Schlabach, Theron. *Peace, Faith, Nation: Mennonites and Amish in Nineteenth-Century America*. Scottdale, PA: Herald Press, 1988.
Schmidt, Agatha Loewen. *Gnadenfeld, Molotschna, 1835–1943*. Kitchener, ON: A.L. Schmidt, 1997.
Schrag, Paul. "'In God's Name, Bread!' MCC Celebrates and Serves Where Its Work Began." MCC, 19 July 2019, https://mcccanada.ca/stories/gods-name-bread.
Schroeder, Gerhard P. *Miracles of Grace and Judgement*. Lodi, CA: Author, 1974.
Schroeder, William. *The Bergthal Colony*. Winnipeg: CMBC Publications, 1974.
Schroeder, William, and Helmut T. Huebert. *Mennonite Historical Atlas*. Second edition. Winnipeg: Springfield Publishers, 1996.
Shantz, Douglas. *An Introduction to German Pietism: Protestant Renewal at the Dawn of Modern Europe*. Baltimore: Johns Hopkins University Press, 2013.
–, ed. *A Companion to German Pietism, 1660–1800*. Leiden: Brill, 2015.
Shearer, David R. "Stalinism, 1928–1940." In *The Cambridge History of Russia*. Volume 3: *The Twentieth Century*, edited by Ronald G. Suny, 192–216. Cambridge: Cambridge University Press, 2006.
Shestakov, A. *Krest'ianskaia revoliutsiia 1905–1907 g.g. v Rossii*. Leningrad: n.p., 1926.
Shnaider, Ivan. *Sto let pervoi obshchine baptistov v Aktiubinskie: Evangel'skie obshchiny v Aktiubinskoi stepi*. Steinhagen, Germany: Samenkorn, 2006.

Siberian Diary of Aron P. Toews: With a Biography by Olga Rempel, edited by Lawrence Klippenstein and translated by Esther Klassen Bergen. Winnipeg: CMBC Publications, 1984.

Siemens, Ruth Derksen. *Remember Us: Letters from Stalin's Gulag (1930–1937)*. Volume 1: *The Regehr Family*. Kitchener, ON: Pandora Press, 2008.

Simons, Menno. "The Blasphemy of John of Leiden, 1535." In *The Complete Writings of Menno Simons, c. 1496–1561*, edited by John C. Wenger and translated by Leonard Verduin, 31–50. Scottdale, PA: Herald Press, 1956.

– "Brief Confession on the Incarnation." In *The Complete Writings of Menno Simons, c. 1496–1561*, edited by John C. Wenger and translated by Leonard Verduin, 419–54. Scottdale, PA: Herald Press, 1956.

– "Christian Baptism." In *The Complete Writings of Menno Simons, c. 1496–1561*, edited by John C. Wenger and translated by Leonard Verduin, 227–88. Scottdale, PA: Herald Press, 1956.

– "Confession of the Distressed Christians, 1552." In *The Complete Writings of Menno Simons, c. 1496–1561*, edited by John C. Wenger and translated by Leonard Verduin, 499–522 Scottdale, PA: Herald Press, 1956.

– "Foundation of Christian Doctrine, 1539." In *The Complete Writings of Menno Simons, c. 1496–1561*, edited by John C. Wenger and translated by Leonard Verduin, 103–226. Scottdale, PA: Herald Press, 1956.

– "Reply to Gellius Faber, 1554." In *The Complete Writings of Menno Simons, c. 1496–1561*, edited by John C. Wenger and translated by Leonard Verduin, 623–782. Scottdale, PA: Herald Press, 1956.

– "Why I Do Not Cease Teaching and Writing, 1539." In *The Complete Writings of Menno Simons, c. 1496–1561*, edited by John C. Wenger and translated by Leonard Verduin, 289–320. Scottdale, PA: Herald Press, 1956.

Slagel, A.W. "Organizing Feeding Operations." In *Feeding the Hungry. Russia Famine 1919–1925: American Mennonite Relief Operations under the Auspices of Mennonite Central Committee*, edited by P.C. Hiebert and Orie O. Miller, 204–21. Scottdale, PA: Mennonite Central Committee, 1929.

Slezkine, Yuri. *The House of Government: A Saga of the Russian Revolution*. Princeton, NJ: Princeton University Press, 2017.

Smith, Alison K. *For the Common Good and Their Own Well-Being: Social Estates in Imperial Russia*. Oxford: Oxford University Press, 2014.

Smith, Hedrick. *The Russians*. New York: Quadrangle, 1976.

Smolkin, Victoria. *A Sacred Space Is Never Empty: A History of Soviet Atheism*. Princeton, NJ: Princeton University Press, 2018.

Snyder, C. Arnold. "Swiss Anabaptism: The Beginnings." In *A Companion to Anabaptism and Spiritualism, 1521–1700*, edited by John D. Roth and James M. Stayer, 45–81. Leiden: Brill, 2007.

Sokolov, A.P. *Krasnyi nemetskii skot v Omskoi gubernii*. Omsk, Russia: n.p., 1926.

Sokolovsky, Sergey V. "The Mennonites of Altai: Marriage Structures and Cultural Transmission." *JMS* (2012): 57–66.
Sprunger, Keith. "Dutch Anabaptists and the Telling of the Martyr Stories." *MQR* 80 (2006): 149–83.
Sprunger, Mary S. "A Mennonite Capitalist Ethic in the Dutch Golden Age: Weber Revisited." In *European Mennonites and the Challenge of Modernity over Five Centuries: Contributors, Detractors, and Adapters*, edited by Mark Jantzen, Mary S. Sprunger, and John D. Thiesen, 51–70. North Newton, KS: Bethel College, 2016.
Staaij, Ad van de. "Rein Willink's Rescue Expedition to the Molochna between Reconstruction and Emigration: Dutch Aid to Ukraine, 1922–1929." *MQR* 93, no. 4 (2019): 473–505.
Stanglin, Keith D., ed. *The Reformation of the Modern Church: A Reader in Christian Theology*. Minneapolis: Fortress Press, 2014.
Staples, John R. *Cross-cultural Encounters on the Ukrainian Steppe: Settling the Molochna Basin, 1783–1861*. Toronto: University of Toronto Press, 2003.
– "Religion, Politics, and the Mennonite Privilegium in Early Nineteenth Century Russia: Reconsidering the Warkentin Affair." *JMS* (2003): 71–88.
– "The Mennonite Commonwealth Paradigm and the Dnepropetrovsk School Ukrainian Mennonite Historiography." In *Voprosy germanskoi istorii*, edited by Svetlana Bobyleva, 58–68. Dnepropetrovsk, Ukraine: Porogi, 2007.
– "Johann Cornies' Aethetics of Civilization." In *Minority Report: Mennonite Identities in Imperial Russia and Soviet Ukraine Reconsidered, 1789–1945*, edited by Leonard G. Friesen, 61–84. Toronto: University of Toronto Press, 2018.
Starr, S. Frederick. *Decentralization and Self-Government in Russia, 1830–1870*. Princeton, NJ: Princeton University Press, 1972.
"Status of Global Christianity, 2015, in the Context of 1900–2050." *International Bulletin of Missionary Research* 39, no. 1 (January 2015): 28–9. http://www.internationalbulletin.org/issues/2015-01/2015-01-029-table.html.
Stayer, James. "The Passing of the Radical Moment in the Radical Reformation." *MQR* 71 (1997): 147–52.
– "The German Peasants' War and the Rural Reformation." In *The Reformation World*, edited by Andrew Pettegree, 127–45. London: Routledge, 2000.
Steiner, Samuel J. *Vicarious Pioneer: The Life of Jacob Y. Shantz*. Winnipeg: Hyperion Press, 1988.
Steinhart, Eric C. *The Holocaust and the Germanization of Ukraine*. Cambridge: Cambridge University Press, 2015.
Steinwedel, Charles. *Threads of Empire: Loyalty and Tsarist Authority in Bashkiria, 1552–1917*. Bloomington, IN: Indiana University Press, 2016.
Stites, Richard. *Revolutionary Dreams: Utopian Vision and Experimental Life in the Russian Revolution*. Oxford: Oxford University Press, 1988.

Sunderland, Willard. *Taming the Wild Field: Colonization and Empire on the Russian Steppe*. Ithaca, NY: Cornell University Press, 2006.

Swanson, R.N. "The Pre-Reformation Church." In *The Reformation World*, edited by Andrew Pettegree, 9–30. London: Routledge, 2000.

Taubman, William. *Gorbachev: His Life and Times*. New York: W.W. Norton, 2017.

Taylor, Charles. *Sources of the Self: The Making of the Modern Identity*. Cambridge, MA: Harvard University Press, 1989.

– *A Secular Age*. Cambridge, MA: Harvard University Press, 2007.

Thiesen, John D. "Menno in the KZ or Münster Resurrected: Mennonites and National Socialism – Historiography and Open Questions." In *European Mennonites and the Challenge of Modernity over Five Centuries: Contributors, Detractors, and Adapters*, edited by Mark Jantzen, Mary S. Sprunger, and John D. Thiesen, 313–28. North Newton, KS: Bethel College, 2016.

– "Danzig." MennLex V, https://www.mennlex.de/doku.php?id=loc:danzig.

Thiessen, Franz C. *P.M. Friesen, 1849–1914*. Winnipeg: Christian Press, 1974.

Thiessen, Joel. *The Meaning of Sunday: The Practice of Belief in a Secular Age*. Montreal, QC: McGill–Queen's University Press, 2015.

Thiessen, Joel, and Sarah Wilkins-Laflamme. *None of the Above: Nonreligious Identity in the US and Canada*. Regina, SK: University of Regina Press, 2020

Toews, C.P. *Die Tereker Ansiedlung*. Winnipeg: Echo Historical Series, 1945.

Toews, C.P., Heinrich Friesen, and Arnold Dyck. *The Kuban Settlement*. Translated from the German by Herbert Giesbrecht. Winnipeg: Echo Historical Series, 1989.

Toews, J.B. *Pilgrimage of Faith: The Mennonite Brethren Church, 1860–1990*. Winnipeg: Kindred Press, 1993.

Toews, Jacob C. "Das mennonitische Gutsbesitzertum in Russland." *DB* 30 June–24 November 1954).

Toews, John B. *Lost Fatherland: The Story of the Mennonite Emigration from Soviet Russia, 1921–1927*. Vancouver: Regent College Publishing, 1967.

– "The Halbstadt Volost, 1918–1922: A Case Study of the Mennonite Encounter with Early Bolshevism." *MQR* 48 (October 1974): 8–22.

–, ed. *The Mennonites in Russia, 1917–1930: Selected Documents*. Winnipeg: The Christian Press, 1975.

– *With Courage to Spare: The Life of B. B. Janz, 1877–1964*. Winnipeg: General Conference Mennonite Brethren Churches, 1978.

– *Czars, Soviets and Mennonites*. Newton, KS: Faith & Life Press, 1982.

– "Brethren and Old Church Relations in Pre–World War I Russia: Setting the Stage for Canada." *JMS* 2 (1984): 42–59.

–, ed. and trans. *Letters from Susan: A Woman's View of the Russian Mennonite Experience (1928–1941)*. North Newton, KS: Bethel College, 1988.

- *Perilous Journey: The Mennonite Brethren in Russia, 1860–1910*. Winnipeg: Kindred Press, 1988.
- "Mennonite Brethren Founders Relate Their Conversion." *Direction* 23 (Fall 1994): 31–7.
- "Early Mennonite Brethren Membership Lists Found in St. Petersburg Archives." *California Mennonite Historical Society Bulletin* 33 (March 1996): 10–14.
- "Russian Mennonites and Allianz." *JMS* 14 (1996): 45–64.
–, ed. and trans. *Journeys: Mennonite Stories of Faith and Survival in Stalin's Russia*. Winnipeg: Kindred Publications, 1998.
- "Early Mennonite Brethren and Evangelism in Russia." *Direction* 28 (Fall 1999): 187–200.
–, ed. and trans. *The Diaries of David Epp, 1837–1843*. Vancouver: Regent College Publishing, 2000.
- "The Mennonite Brethren in Russia during the 1890s." *Direction* 30 (Fall 2001): 139–52.
- "Revival and Mission in Early Communist Russia (1917–1927)." *Direction* 31 (Fall 2002): 206–19.
–, ed. *The Story of the Early Mennonite Brethren (1860–1869): Reflections of a Lutheran Churchman*. Winnipeg: Kindred Productions, 2002.

Toews, John B., and Paul Toews, eds. *Union of Citizens of Dutch Lineage in Ukraine (1922–1927): Mennonite and Soviet Documents*. Translated by John B. Toews, Walter Regehr, and Olga Shmakina. Fresno, CA: Center for Mennonite Brethren Studies, 2011.
- "Mennonite Identities in a New Land: Abraham A. Friesen and the Russian Mennonite Migration of the 1920s." In *Minority Report: Mennonite Identities in Imperial Russia and Soviet Ukraine Reconsidered, 1789–1945*, edited by Leonard G. Friesen, 181–210. Toronto: University of Toronto Press, 2018.

Toews, Paul. "Mennonites and the Search for Military Exemption: State Concessions and Conflicts in the 1870s." In *Voprosy germanskoi istorii: Sobrnik nauchnykh trudov*, edited by Svetlana Bobyleva, 81–106. (Dnipropetrovsk, Ukraine: Porogi, 2007.
–, ed. *Ethno-Confession in the Soviet State, 1920–1989*, by A.I. Savin. Fresno, CA: Center for Mennonite Brethren Studies, 2008.

Tolstoi, Nikolai. *Victims of Yalta: The Secret Betrayal of the Allies, 1944–1947*. London: Hodder and Stoughton, 1977.

Tōws (Toews), Aron A. *Mennonitishche Märtyrer der jüngsten Vergangenheit und der Gegenwart*. Winnipeg: The Christian Press, 1949.

Tōws (Toews), Gerhard. *Schönfeld. Werde- und Opfergang einer deutscher Siedlung in der Ukraine*. Winnipeg: n.p., 1939.

Tracy, James. *The Founding of the Dutch Republic: War, Finance, and Politics in Holland, 1572–1588*. Oxford: Oxford University Press, 2008.

Turmarkin, Nina. *Lenin Lives! The Lenin Cult in Soviet Russia*. Cambridge, MA: Harvard University Press, 1993.

Unger, R.W. "Integration of Baltic and Low Countries Grain Markets, 1400–1800." In *The Interactions of Amsterdam and Antwerp with the Baltic Region, 1400–1800*, edited by Wiert Jan Wieringa, 1–10 Leiden: Martinus Nijhoff, 1983.

Unruh, A.H. *Die Geschichte der Mennoniten-Bruedergemeinde 1860–1954*. Hillsboro, KS: Mennonite Brethren Church of North America, 1955.

Urry, James. "'The Snares of Reason': Changing Mennonite Attitudes to 'Knowledge' in Nineteenth Century Russia." *Comparative Studies in Society and History* 25 (April 1983): 306–22.

– "Through the Eye of a Needle: Wealth and the Mennonite Experience in Imperial Russia." *JMS* 3 (1985): 7–35.

– "'Servants from Far': Mennonites and the Pan-evangelical Impulse in Early Nineteenth Century Russia." *MQR* 61 (1987): 213–27.

– "The Social Background to the Emergence of the Mennonite Brethren in Nineteenth Century Russia." *JMS* 6 (1988): 8–35.

– Mennonite Economic Development in the Russian Mirror." In *Mennonites in Russia, 1788–1988: Essays in Honour of Gerhard Lohrenz*, edited by John Friesen, 99–126. Winnipeg: CMBC Publications, 1989.

– *None but Saints: The Transformation of Mennonite Life in Russia, 1789–1989*. Winnipeg: Hyperion Press, 1989.

– "Prolegomena to the Study of Mennonite Society in Russia 1880–1914." *JMS* 8 (1990): 52–75.

– "The Russian State, the Mennonite World and the Migration from Russia to North American in the 1870s." *ML* 46 (1991): 11–16.

– "The Cost of Community: The Funding and Economic Management of the Russian Mennonite Commonwealth before 1914." *JMS* 10 (1992): 22–55.

– "Mennonites, Nationalism and the State in Imperial Russia." *JMS* 12 (1994): 65–88.

– "Russian Mennonites and the Boers of South Africa: A Forgotten Connection." *MH* 20, no. 3 (1994): 1–2, 12.

– "The Russian Mennonites, Nationalism and the State 1789–1917." In *Canadian Mennonites and the Challenge of Nationalism*, edited by Abe J. Dueck, 21–67. Winnipeg: Mennonite Historical Society, 1994.

– "After the Rooster Crowed: Some Issues Concerning the Interpretation of Mennonite/Bolshevik Relations during the Early Soviet Period." *JMS* 13 (1995): 26–50.

– "Of Borders and Boundaries: Reflections on Mennonite Unity and Separation in the Modern World." *MQR* 73 (1999): 503–24.

– "The Ältesters: Role and Responsibilities." *Preservings: Being the Magazine/Journal of the Hanover Steinbach Historical Society Inc.* 21 (December 2002): 3–5.

- "Growing Up with Cities: the Mennonite Experience in Imperial Russia and the Early Soviet Union." *JMS* 20 (2002): 123–54.
- "David H. Epp: Intellectual, Spiritual, Cultural Leader 1861–1934." In *Shepherds, Servants and Prophets: Leadership among the Russian Mennonites (ca. 1880–1960)*, edited by Harry Loewen, 85–102. Kitchener, ON: Pandora Press, 2003.
- *Mennonites, Politics, and Peoplehood: Europe, Russia, Canada, 1525–1980.* Winnipeg; University of Manitoba Press, 2006.
- "Time and Memory: Secular and Sacred Aspects of the World of the Russian Mennonites and Their Descendants." *CGR* 25 (Winter 2007): 4–62.
- "The Transformation of Scholarship on the Russian Mennonites in a New Age of Transition: A Second Introduction." In *None but Saints: The Transformation of Mennonite Life in Russia, 1789–1989*, 2nd printing with a new Introduction. Kitchener, ON: Pandora Press, 2007.
- "Wealth and Poverty in the Mennonite Experience: Dilemmas and Challenges." *JMS* 27 (2009): 11–40.
- "The Mennonite Commonwealth in Imperial Russia Revisited." *MQR* 84 (April 2010): 229–47.
- "The Mennonite Brethren Church and Russia's Great Reform in the 1870s." *Direction* 46 (Spring 2017): 10–25. https://directionjournal.org/46/1/mennonite-brethren-church-and-russias.html.
- "A Mennonite Witness to Revolution: Johann G. Rempel's Memoir of Moscow, March–June 1917." Translated by David G. Rempel. *MQR* 91 (2017): 511–40.
- "A History of the Mennonites' Russian Privilegium: 1800–1919." *JMS* 37 (2019): 325–52.
- "Mennonites in Ukraine during World War II: Thoughts and Questions." *MQR* 93, no. 1 (2019): 81–111.
- "A Critical Gaze: Daniel Schlatter and Mennonite-Nogai Relations." *Preservings* 42 (2021): 2–8.
- "Mennonites, Anthropology, and History: A Complicated Intellectual Relationship." *JMS* 39 (2021): 11–37.

Urry, James, and Lawrence Klippenstein. "Mennonites and the Crimean War, 1854–1856." *JMS* 7 (1989): 9–32.

Van Engen, John, ed. and trans. *Devotio Moderna: Basic Writings*. New York: Paulist Press, 1988.

Van Lieburg, Fred. "The Dutch Factor in German Pietism." In *A Companion to German Pietism, 1660–1800*, edited by Douglas Shantz, 50–80. Leiden: Brill, 2015.

Venger, Nataliya V. (Ostasheva). *Na perelome ėpokh: mennonitskoe soobshchestvo Ukrainy v 1914–1931 gg*. Moscow: Gotika, 1998.

- "The Mennonite Industrial Dynasties in Alexandrovsk." *JMS* 21 (2003): 89–110.
- *Mennonitskoe predprinimatel'stvo v usloviiakh modernizatstsii iuga Rossii: Mezhdu kongregatsiei klanom i Rossiiskim obshchestvom 1789–1920.* Dnepropetrovsk, Ukraine: n.p., 2009.
- "Mennonite Privileges and the Russian Modernization: Communities on a Path Leading from Separateness to Legal and Social Integration (1789–1900)." In *European Mennonites and the Challenge of Modernity over Five Centuries: Contributors, Detractors, and Adapters*, edited by Mark Jantzen, Mary S. Sprunger, and John D. Thiesen, 143–59. North Newton, KS: Bethel College, 2016.
- "Mennonite Entrepreneurs and Russian Nationalists in the Russian Empire, 1830–1917." In *Minority Report: Mennonite Identities in Imperial Russia and Soviet Ukraine Reconsidered, 1789–1945*, edited by Leonard G. Friesen, 142–80. Toronto: University of Toronto Press, 2018.

Verheyden, A.L.E. *Anabaptism in Flanders, 1530–1650.* Scottdale, PA: Herald Press, 1961.

Vermeulen, Han F. *Before Boas: The Genesis of Ethnography in the German Enlightenment.* Lincoln: University of Nebraska Press, 2015.

Vidmar, John. *The Catholic Church through the Ages.* Second edition. New York: Paulist Press, 2014.

Viola, Lynne. *Best Sons of the Fatherland: Workers in the Vanguard of Soviet Collectivization.* Oxford: Oxford University Press, 1987.
- *Peasant Rebels under Stalin: Collectivization and the Culture of Peasant Resistance.* Oxford: Oxford University Press, 1996.
- *The Unknown Gulag: The Lost World of Stalin's Special Settlements.* Oxford: Oxford University Press, 2007.
- *Stalinist Perpetrators on Trial Scenes from the Great Terror in Soviet Ukraine.* Oxford: Oxford University Press, 2017.

Viola, Lynne, V.P. Danilov, N.A. Ivnitski, and Denis Kozlov, eds. *The War Against the Peasantry, 1927–1930: The Tragedy of the Soviet Countryside.* Volume 1. Translated by Steven Shabad. New Haven, CT: Yale University Press, 2005.

Visser, Piet. "Menno Simons: Printed, Read and Debated." In *Menno Simons: A Reappraisal. Essays in Honour of Irvin B. Horst on the 450th Anniversary of the Fundamentboek*, edited by Gerald R. Brunk, 83–104. Harrisonburg, VA: Eastern Mennonite College, 1992.
- "Mennonites and Doopsgezinden in the Netherlands, 1535–1700." In *A Companion to Anabaptism and Spiritualism, 1521–1700*, edited by John D. Roth and James M. Stayer, 299–345. Leiden: Brill, 2007.

Von Schlachta, Astrid. "Anabaptists and Pietists: Influences, Contacts, and Relations." In *A Companion to German Pietism, 1660–1800*, edited by Douglas H. Shantz, 116–38. Leiden: Brill, 2015.

Voolstra, Sjouke. "Themes in the Early Theology of Menno Simons." In *Menno Simons: A Reappraisal. Essays in Honour of Irvin B. Horst on the 450th Anniversary of the Fundamentboek*, edited by Gerald R. Brunk, 37–56. Harrisonburg, VA: Eastern Mennonite College, 1992.
– "'The Colony of Heaven': The Anabaptist Aspiration to Be the Church without Spot or Wrinkle in the Sixteenth and Seventeenth Centuries." In *From Martyr to Muppy: A Historical Introduction to Cultural Assimilaton Processes of a Religious Minority in the Netherlands: the Mennonites*, edited by Alastair Hamilton, Sjouke Voolstra, and Piet Visser, 15–29. Amsterdam: Amsterdam University Press, 1994.
– *Menno Simons: His Image and Message*. North Newton, KS: Bethel College, 1997.
Vos, Karel. "Sicke Freerks (d. 1531)." *GAMEO*, 1959, https://gameo.org/index.php?title=Sicke_Freerks_(d._1531)&oldid=146722.
Vries, Jan de, and Ad Van Der Woude. *The First Modern Economy: Success, Failure and Perseverance of the Dutch Economy, 1500–1815*. Cambridge: Cambridge University Press, 1997.
Waite, Gary K. *David Joris and Dutch Anabaptism, 1524–1543*. Waterloo: Wilfrid Laurier University, 1990.
– "Writing in the Heavenly Language: A Guide to the Works of David Joris." *Renaissance and Reformation / Renaissance et Réforme* 26 (January 1990): 297–319.
–, ed. *The Anabaptist Writings of David Joris, 1535–1543*. Scottdale, PA: Herald Press, 1994.
– *Eradicating the Devil's Minions: Anabaptists and Witches in Reformation Europe*. Toronto: University of Toronto Press, 2007.
– "David Joris (ca. 1501–1556)." *GAMEO*, February 2020, https://gameo.org/index.php?title=David_Joris_(ca._1501–1556)&oldid=166692.
Wallace, Peter G. *The Long European Reformation: Religion, Political Conflict and the Search for Community, 1350–1750*. Second edition. New York: Palgrave Macmillan, 2012.
Wallerstein, Immanuel. "The Construction of Peoplehood: Racism, Nationalism, Ethnicity." In *Race, Nation, Class: Ambiguous Identities*, edited by Etienne Balibar and Immanuel Wallerstein, 71–85. London: Verso Books, 1991.
– *World-Systems Analysis: An Introduction*. Durham, NC: Duke University Press, 2004.
Wandel, Lee Palmer. *Voracious Idols and Violent Hands: Iconoclasm in Reformation Zurich, Strasbourg, and Basel*. Cambridge: Cambridge University Press, 1995.
Ward, Patricia A. "Continental Spirituality and British Protestant Readers." In *Heart Religion: Evangelical Piety in England & Ireland, 1690–1850*, edited by John Coffey, 50–71.. Oxford: Oxford University Press, 2016.

Ward, W.R. *The Protestant Evangelical Awakening*. Cambridge: Cambridge University Press, 1992.
Wardin, Albert W., Jr. *On the Edge: Baptists and Other Free Church Evangelicals in Tsarist Russia, 1855–1917*. Eugene, OR: Wipf & Stock, 2013.
Warkentin, Jakob. "Benjamin Heinrich Unruh: Teacher, Scholar, Statesman, 1881–1959." In *Shepherds, Servants and Prophets: Leadership among the Russian Mennonites (ca. 1880–1960)*, edited by Harry Loewen, 401–26. Kitchener, ON: Pandora Press, 2003.
Weber, Max. "Science as a Vocation." In *Max Weber: Essays in Sociology*, edited by Hans H. Gerth and C. Wright Mills, 129–56. London: Routledge, 1948 [1919].
– *The Protestant Ethic and the Spirit of Capitalism with Other Writings on the Rise of the West*. Fourth edition. Translated and edited by Stephen Kalberg. Oxford: Oxford University Press, 2008.
Weinberg, Robert. *The Revolution of 1905 in Odessa: Blood on the Steps*. Bloomington: Indiana University Press, 1993.
Weiss, Alexander. "The Transition of Siberian Mennonites to Baptists: Causes and Results." *JMS* 30 (2012): 133–8.
Wenger, John C., ed. *The Complete Writings of Menno Simons, c. 1496–1561*. Translated from the Dutch by Leonard Verduin. Scottdale, PA: Herald Press, 1956.
Wenger, John C., and C. Arnold Snyder. "Schleitheim Confession." *GAMEO*, 1990, https://gameo.org/index.php?title=Schleitheim_Confession&oldid=143737.
Werner, Hans. *The Constructed Mennonite: History, Memory and the Second World War*. Winnipeg: University of Manitoba Press, 2013.
Wernicke, Erich. *Kreis Marienwerder. Aus der Geschichte des Landkreises bis zum 19. Jahrhundert*. Hamburg, Germany: n.p., 1979.
Werth, Nicolas. *Cannibal Island: Death in a Siberian Gulag*. Princeton, NJ: Princeton University Press, 2007.
Werth, Paul W. *The Tsar's Foreign Faiths, Toleration and the Fate of Religious Freedom in Imperial Russia*. Oxford: Oxford University Press, 2014.
Whitmer, Kelly Joan. *The Halle Orphanage as Scientific Community: Observation, Eclecticism, and Pietism in the Early Enlightenment*. Chicago: University of Chicago Press, 2015.
Wiebe, Petr P., ed. *Materialy po istorii nemetskikh i Mennonitskikh kolonii v Omskom priirtysh'e, 1895–1930*. Omsk, Russia: n.p., 2002.
–, ed. *Nemetskie kolonii v Sibiri: sotsial'no-ekonomicheskii aspect*. Omsk, Russia: Omskiigos, 2007.
– "The Mennonite Colonies of Siberia: From the Late Nineteenth to the Early Twentieth Century." *JMS* 30 (2012): 23–35.
Wiebe, Tena, ed. *Neu-Samara: A Mennonite Settlement East of the Volga (A Translation of Neu Samara am Tock)*. Edmonton: Jackpine House, 2002.

Wiens, Helen. "200jährige Feier unter der Eiche in Chortitza." *DB* (4 October 1989): 3.
Williams, George Hunston. *The Radical Reformation*. Philadelphia: The Westminster Press, 1962.
Winter, Henry H. *A Shepherd of the Oppressed: Heinrich Winter, Last Ältester of Chortitza*. Wheatley, ON: Author, 1990.
Wirtschafter, Elise Kimerling. *Social Identity in Imperial Russia*. DeKalb: Northern Illinois University Press, 1997.
Woelk, Heinrich, and Gerhard Woelk. *A Wilderness Journey: Glimpses of the Mennonite Brethren Church in Russia, 1925–1980*. Fresno, CA: Center for Mennonite Brethren Studies, 1982.
Wortman, Richard. *Scenarios of Power: Myth and Ceremony in Russian Monarchy*. 2 vols. Princeton, NJ: Princeton University Press, 1995–2000.
Young, Glennys. *Power and the Sacred in Revolutionary Russia: Religious Activists in the Village*. University Park: The Pennsylvania State University Press, 1997.
Zhivi i pomni ... Istoriia Mennonitskikh kolonii Ekaterinoslavshchiny. Dnepropetrovsk, Ukraine: Dnepropetrovsk National University, 2006.
Zhuk, Sergei. *Russia's Lost Reformation: Peasants, Millennialism, and Radical Sects in Southern Russia and Ukraine, 1830–1917*. Washington, DC: Woodrow Wilson Center Press, 2004.
– "'A Separate Nation' of 'Those Who Imitate Germans': Ukrainian Evangelical Peasants and Problems of Cultural Identification in the Ukrainian Provinces of Late Imperial Russia." *Ab Imperio* (2006): 139–60.
– "In Search of the Millennium: Convergence of Jews and Ukrainian Evangelical Peasants in Late Imperial Russia." In *Holy Dissent: Jewish and Christian Mysticism in Eastern Europe*, edited by Glenn Dynner, 334–58. Detroit: Wayne State University Press, 2011.
Zijstlra, Samme. *Om de Ware Gemeente en de Oude Gronden: Geschiedenis van de Dopersen in de Nederlanden, 1531–1675*. Leeuwarden: Fryske Academy, 2000.
Zwingli, Ulrich. *Commentary on True and False Religion*. Edited by Samuel Macauley Jackson and Clarence Nevin Heller. Eugene, OR: Wipf & Stock, 2015.

Index

Agricultural Union, 95, 108
Alexander I, 78, 91, 94
Alexander II, 10, 105, 120, 128, 134, 161–3, 276
Alexander III, 144, 161–2, 166–7
Alexandertal (Alt Samara), 84, 133, 216, 223, 238, 261, 270
Alexandertal (Molotschna), 108, 110, 186, 245
All-Russian Mennonite Agricultural Association, 199–200, 202, 208–9, 211, 216, 252, 260
All-Union Council of Evangelical Christians-Baptists, 254, 256, 259–69
Alt Samara settlement. *See* Alexandertal (Alt Samara)
Am Trakt, 84–5, 133, 238
Arendt, Hannah, 6, 12
ARMAA. *See* All-Russian Mennonite Agricultural Association
atheism, 198, 203, 209, 214, 232, 240, 271, 333n64
AUCECB. *See* All-Union Council of Evangelical Christians-Baptists

Baerg, Anna, v, 185, 188, 192
Baltic, 36, 54, 60, 70–2, 76, 79, 165; Soviet era, 192, 247, 264, 268
Bartsch, Johann, 69, 75–7

Berdiansk, 99–100, 109, 111, 138, 145, 150, 157
Bergmann, Hermann, 173–4
Bergthal settlement, 119, 133
Brezhnev, Leonid, 265–8

Catherine II, 69, 73–5, 78, 96, 112, 167, 178
CCECB. *See* All-Union Council of Evangelical Christians-Baptists
Central Asia, 3–4, 11, 154, 159, 166, 170, 174, 188, 198, 268–70, 283, 285
Chortitza (village), 43, 78, 81, 91, 103, 117–18, 121, 150–1, 169, 175, 177; Soviet era, 193, 196–7, 213, 217, 222, 226, 232, 236, 240, 246
Claassen, Johannes, 114, 126–9, 310n18
collectivization, 206, 211–12, 215, 217–18, 221, 224–7, 277
Commonwealth (Mennonite), 10, 121, 143–4, 158–60, 164; Soviet era, 184, 212, 278–9
Contenius, Samuel, 78, 95, 101
Conteniusfeld (Molotschna), 214
Cossacks, 72–3, 76, 162, 169, 284
Crimean Peninsula, 69, 73, 88, 119, 128, 138, 139, 169, 174, 177; Soviet era, 194, 223, 238

Crimean War, 105–6, 110, 117, 119, 122, 128, 137, 139, 151, 159, 162; Soviet era, 276, 278

daughter colony (colonies), 129–31, 133–6, 141, 143, 145, 149, 153, 155–6, 166, 179; Soviet era, 186, 188, 190–1, 193, 197, 215–17, 240

dekulakization, 206, 21, 214–15, 217–18, 225–6

Der Botschafter, 170, 172–3, 176–7

Dnepropetrovsk (Dnipro), 4, 167, 232, 235, 283

Dnieper River, 69, 73, 76–8, 142, 147–50, 153, 168; Soviet era, 183, 187, 189, 201, 204, 225, 232, 237, 240, 245, 280, 282, 284

Donbas, 149–50, 168

Dukhobors, 74, 79, 88, 95, 102, 167

Duma, 169–70, 172–4, 176

Dyck, Harvey L., 4, 103, 124, 171, 153, 231, 282

Dyck, Johannes, 255, 264–5, 270, 287

Eichenfeld, 183–5, 188–9, 191, 213

Einlage (Chortitza), 77, 112, 117, 126–8, 130, 158; Soviet era, 225, 234, 246

Ekaterinoslav, 74, 77, 100–1, 119, 135, 145, 147–8, 157, 167–9; Soviet era, 186–7

Epp, David H., 3, 90, 103, 167, 176–7, 222

Epp, Jacob, 121, 123, 129–30

Epp, Petr, 3, 4, 252, 272

Erasmus of Rotterdam, 18, 21–5, 27, 30, 37, 47–8

Evangelicals, 198, 211, 216, 257, 267–9, 272, 279

Fast, Johannes, 255, 262, 270

Fast, Viktor, 3, 4, 283–4, 286–7

Fitzpatrick, Sheila, 211, 224

Flemish/Frisian Mennonites, 50, 62, 65, 75, 77, 80–1, 83, 88, 90, 93, 97–8, 108, 110, 112, 155

Flight to Moscow, 222–4

Foresteidienst, 136, 140, 150, 155, 157, 159, 173

Foundation of Christian Doctrine, 44–6, 275

Friesen, A.A., 194–5, 201–2

Friesen, Abraham, v, 42, 46, 48

Friesen, Aileen, 3, 4, 174, 242

Friesen, Peter M., 4, 17–18, 103, 109, 130, 173, 176

Frisian/Flemish Mennonites. *See* Flemish/Frisian Mennonites

Gnadenfeld (Gnadenfelders), 108, 110–13, 116, 126, 156–7, 217

Gorbachev, Mikhail S., 5, 265, 271–3, 282

Great Reforms (1860s), 105, 159, 161, 164

Gregory, Brad, 6–7, 12, 54, 282

Guardians Committee, 74, 78, 83, 95–9, 101–2, 106, 108, 108, 113–14, 121, 131–2, 134

Halbstadt, 95, 118, 130, 151, 157, 170, 187–8, 243, 285

Hamm, Viktor, 286

Harder, Bernhard, 130

Haxthausen, August von, 98, 164

Hierschau, 116, 226

Hitler, Adolf, 225, 229–31, 233, 236, 242–4, 247

Höppner (Hoeppner), Jakob, 69, 75–7

Initsiativniki, 263–4, 266

Ipatov, A.I., 13, 264, 269

Isaak, Franz, 4, 131

Janz, B.B., 200, 202–3
Jews/Jewish, 12, 50, 58–9, 102, 119, 142, 169; Soviet era, 186, 191, 229–30, 240–2, 244, 247

Karaganda, 216, 219–20, 222, 225, 232, 235, 250, 254–6, 259, 262, 264, 266, 269, 283–6
Karlag (Karaganda Corrective Labour Camp), 217, 219, 225
Kazakhstan, 216, 218–19, 235, 249–51, 255, 258, 266, 268, 283, 287
Kempis, Thomas à, 19–21
Kherson, 69, 74, 76, 99, 142, 145, 168, 186
Khrushchev, Nikita S., (Khrushchevian), 234, 251, 254, 260–5
Khrushchev's War on Religion, 260–5
Kiev (Kyiv), 157, 189, 202, 219, 234, 237, 264, 286
Kievan Rus, 271, 283
Kirchengemeinde, 154–6, 167, 170, 176, 240
Kirov, Sergei, 229–30, 233
Klassen, C.F., 196, 199, 202–3
Klaus, Alexander, 3, 147
Kleefeld, 116, 222
Kleine Gemeinde, 81, 83, 108, 130, 134, 141, 155
Klets, Viktor, 242
korenizatsiia, 204, 206, 209, 211, 217
Krivoi Rog, 149–50
Kronsweide, 77, 81, 112, 158, 213
Kuban, 129, 133, 188, 193, 223

Lenin, Vladimir I., 11, 187–9, 192, 199–200, 208, 223, 226, 229, 235, 261
Leningrad, 4, 192, 229, 237, 243, 263, 269, 271, 285
Lepp (& Wallman) factory, Chortitza, 117–18, 150, 177
Letkemann, Peter, 3, 216, 219, 232–3, 238
Lichtenau, 49, 189, 222, 328n19

Lohrenz, Gerhard, 125, 186, 190–1, 197, 207
Luther, Martin, 22, 25–6, 27, 29, 31–3, 38, 42, 47

Makhno, Nestor, 183, 191–4
Margenau, 91, 153, 205–6, 214, 217, 219, 222, 228, 238–9, 241, 245, 248, 256, 268
Marienwerder (Kingdom Poland), 57, 72
Martin, Terry, 199, 206, 212, 232
Martyrs (martyrdom, martyrologies), 30–1, 39, 50–2, 54–5, 64–5, 110, 269, 275–6
Martyr's Mirror, 64, 110
MCC. *See* Mennonite Central Committee
Melitopol, 115, 156, 235
Memrik, 214, 223
Mennonite Central Committee, 195–6, 199, 202, 204, 255, 267–8
Mennozentrum, 18
merchants (Anabaptist/Mennontie), 28, 51, 111–12, 114, 127, 137–8, 142, 145, 150, 231
millers (Mennonite), 117, 142, 150, 160
Molokans, 79, 88, 95, 102

Napoleon, 91, 93, 164
Napoleonic wars, 80–1, 120, 137
Neufeld, Jacob A., 217, 231, 236–7
Neufeldt, Colin, 3, 213, 215, 217, 225, 227
Neu Samara settlement, 145–79, 216, 238
Nicholas I, 103, 163, 166, 276
Nicholas II, 161–2, 169–70, 172, 174, 179
Nieder Chortitza, 78, 142, 153, 174–5, 187, 193, 201, 244, 246, 283
Nikolaev, 99, 197

NKVD. *See* People's Commissariat of Internal Affairs
Nogai Tatars, 73, 79, 86–8, 90, 97, 100, 102, 117, 122, 128, 188
Novosibirst, 255, 266, 286

Octobrist Party, 172, 174, 176, 261
Odessa, 17, 74, 99–100, 106, 121, 132, 142, 145, 157, 168, 186, 187
Odessaer Zeitung, 156, 170
Ohrloff (Molotschna), 81, 88, 90, 93–4, 108, 130–1, 156; Soviet era, 214, 222, 227, 232
Omsk, 147, 185–6, 188, 194–5, 204, 208, 219, 223, 235, 252–5, 257, 265–7, 269, 272–3, 285–6
Oncken, Johann, 112, 127
Osterwick, 169, 214, 246

Paltov, A.A. (Velitsyn), 166
Paraguay, 201–2, 224, 242, 248, 256
Paul I, 78, 82
People's Commissariat of Internal Affairs, 213, 230, 231–3, 249
Petershagen, 81, 82, 91
Petrograd, 179, 186–8
Plautdietsch, 75, 82, 85, 108, 142, 153, 156, 160; Soviet era, 257, 267, 269, 277
Plokhii, Serhii, 159
Potemkin, Grigory, 73, 75–6
privileges, 72, 78, 83, 96, 107, 166, 173–4
Privilegia/Privilegium, 50, 57–9, 62–3, 75, 78, 96, 119, 173, 277–8
Provisional Government, 119, 185–7, 222
purges, 234–6

Rahn, Peter, 214–15, 221
rail/railroads, 135, 145, 148, 150, 192, 216, 238, 249

Rempel, David G., 4, 10, 79, 82, 101–2, 114, 118, 142–3, 149, 151, 158, 160, 174, 179, 193, 201–2
Rempel, Johann G., 187, 197
Rosental, 77, 197

Samara, 84–5, 133, 173
Saratov, 173, 232, 235
Savin, Andrei, 3, 4, 213, 231
Sawatsky, Walter, 3, 8, 13, 249, 252, 257, 267, 269, 284, 287, 353
Schlatter, Daniel, 86–7, 90
Schmidt, Anna, 205–6, 213, 217, 219, 222, 225–6, 228, 238–9, 245, 248
Schmidt, Georg, 229, 238–9, 241, 245, 248, 251, 256
Schönfeld Colony, 135–6, 187, 191, 197
Schönwiese, 77, 142, 147–50, 152–3, 169, 213, 225
Schroeder, Gerhard, 186–7, 197, 204
Selbstschutz, 183, 189–91, 198, 328n21
sheep, 86–7, 95, 99–103, 116–18, 122
Slavgorod, 215, 223, 255, 266
Staples, John, 3, 4, 87, 88, 144
Strasbourg, 31–5, 38, 40
Stolypin, Petr, 162, 170, 172–4
Study Commission, 194–5, 201

Tavrida, 74, 79, 99, 113, 147, 157
Taylor, Charles, 5, 6, 18, 48, 92, 281
Terek settlement, 145, 186, 188
Tiege (Molotschna), 158, 203, 222
Toews, John B., 3, 4, 198
Toews, Susan, 214, 226–7
Trappe, Georg, 69, 75–6, 80–1

Umsiedler, 268, 270, 273, 283, 286
Unger, Abraham, 112–13, 127
Unruh, B.H., 187, 194, 202
Ural, 194, 211, 215, 223

Urry, James, 3, 5, 57, 111, 124, 133, 144, 150, 157, 175, 196, 242, 281
Uzbekistan, 249, 251, 255, 287

Volga River, 69, 84–5, 122, 133, 145, 179, 270; Soviet era, 194–6, 198, 206, 216, 218, 238
Venger, Nataly (Nataliya), 3, 152, 165–7, 203
Vins, Georgi, 263–4

Warkentin, Jakob, 93, 97
Warthegau, 246–8
Weber, Max, 5–6, 92, 98, 227
Werth, Paul, 96, 120, 165, 174

White Army, 183, 192, 194, 223, 231
Wiebe, Philipp, 131–2
Wieler, Gerhard, 113, 126
Winter, Heinrich, 213, 232, 236, 239–40
Württemberg, 33, 95, 109–11
Wüst, Edward (and Wüst Brethren), 109–13, 127

Yushanlee estate, 103, 116, 132

Zagradovka, 134, 186, 190–1, 197, 215, 245–6
Zaporozhe, 225–6, 234, 238, 240, 242, 274, 280, 282–7
Zwingli, Ulrich, 24–5, 27–31, 38

TSARIST AND SOVIET MENNONITE STUDIES

General Editor: Harvey L. Dyck, Department of History, University of Toronto

A Mennonite in Russia: The Diaries of Jacob D. Epp, 1851–1880. Edited and translated by Harvey L. Dyck

Ingrid I. Epp and Harvey L. Dyck, *The Peter J. Braun Russian Mennonite Archive, 1803–1920: A Research Guide*

David G. Rempel with Cornelia Rempel Carlson, *A Mennonite Family in Tsarist Russia and the Soviet Union, 1789–1923*

John R. Staples, *Cross-Cultural Encounters on the Ukrainian Steppe: Settling the Molochna Basin, 1783–1861*

Anne Konrad, *Red Quarter Moon: A Search for Family in the Shadow of Stalin*

Jacob A. Neufeld, *Path of Thorns: Soviet Mennonite Life under Communist and Nazi Rule*. Edited, with an introduction and analysis, by Harvey L. Dyck. Translated from the German by Harvey L. Dyck and Sarah Dyck

Transformation on the Southern Ukrainian Steppe: The Letters and Papers of Johann Cornies, Volume 1: 1812–1835. Translated by Ingrid I. Epp and edited by Harvey L. Dyck, Ingrid I. Epp, and John R. Staples

Leonard G. Friesen, ed., *Minority Report: Mennonite Identities in Imperial Russia and Soviet Ukraine Reconsidered, 1789–1945*

Transformation on the Southern Ukrainian Steppe: The Letters and Papers of Johann Cornies, Volume 2: 1836–1842. Translated by Ingrid I. Epp and edited by Harvey L. Dyck, Ingrid I. Epp, and John R. Staples

Leonard G. Friesen, *Mennonites in the Russian Empire and the Soviet Union: Through Much Tribulation*

www.ingramcontent.com/pod-product-compliance
Lightning Source LLC
Chambersburg PA
CBHW030259080526
44584CB00012B/372